Techniques and Guidelines for Social Work Practice

Techniques and Guidelines for Social Work Practice

F I F T H   E D I T I O N

Bradford W. Sheafor
Colorado State University

Charles R. Horejsi
The University of Montana

Gloria A. Horejsi
Community Medical Center
Missoula, Montana

A L L Y N   A N D   B A C O N

Boston   London   Toronto   Sydney   Tokyo   Singapore

Series Editor, Social Work and Family Therapy: *Judy Fifer*
Vice President, Editor in Chief, Social Sciences: *Karen Hanson*
Editorial Assistant: *Julianna Cancio*
Marketing Manager: *Jackie Aaron*
Executive Marketing Manager: *Lisa Kimball*
Editorial-Production Administrator: *Annette Joseph*
Editorial-Production Coordinator: *Susan Freese*
Editorial-Production Service: *TKM Productions*
Design and Electronic Composition: *Denise Hoffman*
Composition Buyer: *Linda Cox*
Manufacturing Buyer: *Julie McNeill*
Cover Administrator: *Linda Knowles*

A Pearson Education Company
160 Gould Street
Needham Heights, MA 02494
Internet: www.abacon.com

Between the time website information is gathered and then published, it is not unusual for some sites to have closed. Also, the transcription of URLs can result in unintended typographical errors. The publisher would appreciate being notified of any problems with URLs so that they may be corrected in subsequent editions. Thank you.

Library of Congress Cataloging-in-Publication Data

Sheafor, Bradford W.
Techniques and guidelines for social work practice / Bradford W. Sheafor, Charles R. Horejsi, Gloria A. Horejsi. — 5th ed.
p. cm.
Includes bibliographical references and index.
ISBN 0-205-29555-X
1. Social service—United States. I. Horejsi, Charles R. II. Horejsi, Gloria A. III. Title.
HV91.S48 1999
361.3'2—dc21 98-43814
CIP

Printed in the United States of America

10 9 8 7 6 5 4 3 2 04 03 02 01 00

To the next generation of social workers
who have chosen to devote their time and talents to
the service of others and the struggle for social justice

and

To our families
Nadine, Laura, Brandon, Perry, Christopher,
Angela, Martin, and Katherine
for their love and support

CONTENTS

CHAPTER 14
Intervention and Monitoring 437

PREFACE

An increasing number of people are influenced, directly and indirectly, by the decisions and actions of social workers. Working in courts, clinics, hospitals, schools, businesses, private practice, and a myriad of social agencies, social workers deliver a wide variety of services directly to clients while they also work toward positive community and social changes. The whole society benefits from social workers' activities because improving the quality of life for an individual, a family, or the people of a community will ultimately have an impact on the general society and elevate the health, happiness, safety, and productivity of all its members.

This book is about what social workers actually do when helping their clients solve problems and/or enhance functioning. Although many excellent books describe the general principles and theories used by social workers, *Techniques and Guidelines for Social Work Practice,* Fifth Edition, focuses on a more concrete level. It describes many of the basic techniques and guidelines that social workers use in everyday practice.

Recognizing that this emphasis on techniques and specific guidelines is unusual in a social work book, we offer the reader an explanation of why we believe this collection of practice tools is needed. It is our perception that most social workers have been exposed to a wide variety of practice theories and conceptual frameworks reported in the literature and taught in social work education programs.* Although that knowledge base is essential, practice is much more than a set of ideas. In reality, practice is a set of actions and behaviors by the social worker. Clients are not directly affected by theory; rather, they are influenced by what the worker actually does—by the specific actions taken by the social worker. In the Foreword to the first edition of this book (1988), Barbara Solomon clearly articulated this point and placed techniques and guidelines into perspective:

> It is the utilization of theory to determine practice that distinguishes the professional from the technician. However, our theoretical framework may provide insights as to how a problem develops and even in general terms what we ought to do to resolve it, but rarely will it specify our actions. An ecological systems frame of reference, for example, might dictate that a particular client should be referred to a community resource. It will not, however, specify *how* that referral should be made. Furthermore, no theoretical orientation goes so far as to point out the most effective ways for the social worker to utilize the telephone, testify in court, write a report, use supervision, or engage in many of the activities often considered essential to the social work change process and, therefore, included in this handbook. (p. xi)

* A short synopsis of many of these basic frameworks is included in Chapter 6, "Practice Frameworks for Social Work."

Our emphasis is not intended to suggest that attention to the techniques can or should replace attention to theoretical frameworks. Rather, techniques and specific guidelines complete the package of knowledge and skills that the social worker needs.

Plan and Structure

This book has four major parts. Parts I and II describe basic concepts and principles of practice that lay the foundation for understanding the 160 specific techniques and guidelines found in Parts III and IV.

Part I, "Social Work and the Social Worker," reviews background knowledge and characteristics we believe a social worker must possess, including the following:

- A clear conception of the domain of social work and the competencies the social worker is expected to bring to the change process (Chapter 1)
- An understanding of the challenges a social worker faces in merging his or her personal life with professional roles and responsibilities (Chapter 2)
- The native talents or artistic abilities necessary for perceptively creating and entering into the interpersonal relations that are at the heart of practice (Chapter 3)
- A commitment to draw on and apply the science of social work, the profession's knowledge base, and its ethical principles (Chapter 3)

Part II, "The Building Blocks of Social Work Practice," stresses the need for the social worker to understand the roles, principles, theories, and change and decision-making processes that are the central features of effective helping. To serve clients ranging from individuals to communities, a social worker must have:

- An understanding of the varied roles performed by social workers in delivering human services and the specific functions associated with these roles (Chapter 4)
- The ability to apply the fundamental practice principles of social work (Chapter 5)
- A basic knowledge of the various perspectives, theories, and models that have proven useful in practice (Chapter 6)
- Skill in guiding clients through the change process and helping them make sound decisions about how to improve their lives (Chapter 7)

From this point to the end of the book, we present specific techniques and guidelines. Each presentation follows the same format or structure. It begins with a technique or guideline ***Number*** and ***Name*** (e.g., 11.3: Making a Referral). In this example, 11.3 signifies the third technique or guideline in Chapter 11. This system of numbering is used to refer the reader to related information in other parts of the book. These numbers are also keys to using the *Cross-Reference Guide,* which is intended to help the reader locate techniques useful when working with specific client groups.

Following each number and name is a one-sentence description of ***Purpose.*** This very brief statement is intended to help the reader quickly determine if the technique or guideline is relevant to his or her concern or interest.

Under the heading labeled ***Discussion,*** anywhere from a few to many paragraphs are used to describe the technique or guideline and its application. After the discussion is completed, we present a ***Selected Bibliography,*** which usually lists three to five books or articles that we consider particularly useful for obtaining additional information. We have made an effort to identify sources that are current and available in most university libraries.

In Part III of the book, "Techniques Common to All Social Work Practice," we have included techniques that strengthen the social worker's performance regardless of agency setting and independent of whether the client is an individual, family, group, organization, or community. Underlying our selection was the belief that the social worker must:

- Have the interpersonal competence to carry out effective communication and engage in a set of basic helping activities (Chapter 8)
- Be skilled at organizing the details of service delivery and effectively managing his or her own workload (Chapter 9)
- Be able to maintain a pattern of personal and professional growth and development that keeps him or her current, enriched, and energized (Chapter 10)

Part IV, "Techniques and Guidelines for Phases of the Planned Change Process," lists techniques and guidelines for both direct and indirect practice in chapters organized around the five phases of the change process. Although various authors use differing descriptions of this process, we have elected to use the following:

- Intake and Engagement (Chapter 11)
- Data Collection and Assessment (Chapter 12)
- Planning and Contracting (Chapter 13)
- Intervention and Monitoring (Chapter 14)
- Evaluation and Termination (Chapter 15)

In this edition, we have expanded our descriptions of what should be accomplished in these phases in the introduction to each chapter. We then refined the general concepts to more clearly describe the direct practice applications (Section A) and the indirect practice applications (Section B) of those chapters. A worker can readily examine several suggested techniques or guidelines by identifying the phase of the change process, determining if the activity is a direct or indirect intervention, and then locating the appropriate chapter and section.

Although 160 different techniques and guidelines are described in Parts III and IV of this book, many more exist. We have selected a sufficient range with the intent that one or more will be useful in most practice situations. If not, the ***Suggested Readings*** will lead the worker to other approaches. Most of these techniques need not be applied rigidly. They should be approached with the idea of both *adopting* and *adapting* them for practice.

Definition of Terms

Writing about social work practice inherently presents some language problems. One has to read only a few social work texts or articles to become at least a little confused with the terminology used to describe practice. Perhaps that is to be expected in a profession that focuses on complex and dynamic human and social interactions. This book cannot overcome these long-standing problems of terminology, nor can it present definitions that will be acceptable to every reader. Yet the ideas presented here will be more readily understood if we make the meanings of three terms more explicit.

The reader should be alert to the term ***client.*** Common usage implies a narrow view of an individual who is the consumer of services. As used in this book, the term has a broader connotation. The client of the social worker may be an individual, a family or another form of household, or even a small group, committee, organization, neighborhood, community, or larger social system. Throughout the book, the term *client* is occasionally expanded to mention *clientele, clients, client groups,* or *client systems,* reminding the reader that the narrow definition of client is not intended.

A ***technique*** is viewed as a circumscribed, goal-oriented behavior performed in a practice situation by the social worker. It is a planned action deliberately taken by the practitioner. The application of a simple technique (e.g., using an "I-message") may take only a few seconds, whereas more complex techniques (e.g., family sculpting) may require an hour or more.

Guidelines, by comparison, are a set of directions intended to influence the social worker's behavior and decisions. Guidelines are essentially lists of do's and don'ts. They might be used when working with a specific type of client (e.g., a child, a client with a mental illness) or when carrying out workload management tasks (e.g., recording or writing reports).

Supplements for Instructors

For instructors using this book in their classes, two supportive resources are available. First, we have placed a document entitled "Ideas for Teaching from *Techniques and Guidelines for Social Work Practice*" on Allyn and Bacon's website (see http://www.abacon.com/sheafor). In that material, we describe ways we have used the materials in this book to help beginning-level students learn to serve clients using social work's knowledge, ethical prescriptions, as well as specific techniques and guidelines that will enhance their practice effectiveness. Second, this Fifth Edition of *Techniques and Guidelines* is the first to have an Instructor's Manual. This manual can be obtained from your regional Allyn and Bacon representative or by writing Allyn and Bacon (160 Gould Street, Needham Heights, MA 02494).

Acknowledgments

We would like to recognize a number of people who have contributed to the techniques and guidelines we present in this book, including current and former students and professional colleagues who have graciously given their time and expertise to offer constructive criticisms on selected sections of this book. A special thank-you is extended to each of the following individuals:

- Leslie Adler, M.S.W.; Allison Campbell, M.S.W.; Terri Gorman, M.S.W.; Jan Overmyer, M.S.W.; Christine Stevens, M.S.W.; and Jennifer York, M.S.W. (direct practice evaluation)
- Angeline Barretta-Herman, Ph.D. (staff meetings)
- Barbara Benjamin, M.S.W.; Bob Jackson, Ph.D.; Lowell Jenkins, M.S.W.; and Randy Wood, M.S.W. (practice frameworks)
- Mary Birch, M.S.W. (small groups)
- Jo Ann Blake, M.A.; Lance Eller, B.S.W.; and Mark Long (chemical dependency)
- Charlotte Booth, M.S.W. (hard-to-reach clients)
- Vicky Buchan, Ph.D., and Charles Neidt, Ph.D. (understanding quantitative data)
- Robert Deaton, Ed.D. (suicide)
- Jerry Finn, Ph.D. (using electronic technology)
- Kathleen Gallacher, M.A., and Kristin Dahl Horejsi, M.S. (child development)
- Cindy Garthwait, M.S.W. (working with the elderly)
- Sr. Anne Hogan, M.S.W.; Ryan Tolleson-Knee, M.S.W.; and Shaen McElravy, M.S.W. (merging person and profession)
- Helen Holmquist, B.A. (eating disorders)
- Ken Hoole, M.S.W. and Suzanne Grubaugh, B.S.W. (gay and lesbian issues)
- Mike Jakupcak, Ed.D.; Bill LaForest, M.S.W.; and George Camp, Ph.D. (mental retardation)
- Dan Morgan, M.S.W., and Cindy Bartling, M.S.W. (children and adolescents)
- Kevin Oltjenbruns, Ph.D. (grief and loss)
- Peter Pecora, Ph.D. (evaluation)
- Jeannette Sale, B.S.W., Kelly Slattery-Robinson, B.S.W., and Frank Clark, Ph.D. (battered women)
- Mona Schatz, D.S.W. (social work roles and functions)
- Barbara W. Shank, Ph.D. (sexual misconduct)

- Michael Silverglat, M.D., and Mel Mason, M.S.W. (psychotropic medication and mental illness)
- John Spores, Ph.D.; Iris Heavy Runner, M.S.W.; Rodney Brod, Ph.D.; Victor A. Baez, Ph.D.; and Janet Finn, Ph.D. (cross-cultural interaction)
- Elizabeth Tracy, Ph.D., and James Whittaker, Ph.D. (social support assessment)
- Sue Wilkins, B.S.W. (involuntary and manipulative clients)

We also express our appreciation to Sue Polich (The University of Montana), who typed several portions of this book, and to Joyce Takacs, Linda Tippett, Karen Scott, Dawn Carlson, and Karla Burleson (Colorado State University), who helped create a work environment that facilitated the completion of this manuscript.

Finally, we would like to acknowledge the following individuals, who reviewed previous editions of this book: Mary Boes, University of Northern Iowa; Joan Dworkin, California State University–Sacramento; Patricia Ann Guillory, Southern University at New Orleans; Larry Lister, University of Hawaii at Manoa; Santos Torres, Jr., University of Pittsburg; and Kay van Buskirk, Mankato State University.

Techniques and Guidelines for Social Work Practice

Part I Social Work and the Social Worker

Social work is an indispensable profession in our increasingly complex and ever-changing society. But it is an often misunderstood profession, as well, in part because it cannot be easily described or explained. It is a profession characterized by diversity. Social workers engage in a broad range of activities within many types of settings and with many different people. Some work intensely with individuals and families, while others work with small groups, organizations, or whole communities. Some deal primarily with children, others with elderly persons. Some are counselors and psychotherapists, while others are supervisors, administrators, program planners, or fund-raisers. Some focus on family violence, others on how to provide housing or medical care to the poor. This variety is what makes social work so challenging and stimulating. But it is because of this diversity of both clients and activities that it is so difficult to answer the simple question: What is social work?

The task of concisely defining *social work* in a manner that encompasses all of the activities in which social workers engage has challenged the profession throughout its first century of development. At a very fundamental level, ***social work*** is a profession devoted to helping people function as well as they can within their social environments and to changing their environments to make that possible. This theme of *person-in-environment* is clarified and illustrated throughout this book.

The authors' perspective of social work is made explicit in the following three-part definition of a social worker. A ***social worker***

1. has recognized professional preparation (i.e., education in the requisite knowledge, ethics, and competencies);
2. is sanctioned by society to provide specific services targeted primarily at helping vulnerable populations (e.g., children, the aged, the poor, minorities, women, families) engage in efforts to change themselves, the people around them, or social institutions; and
3. has the purpose of helping others meet social needs or eliminate difficulties so that they might make maximum use of their abilities to lead full and satisfying lives and contribute fully to society.

Most of this book is devoted to a presentation of techniques and guidelines commonly used by social workers. Parts I and II, however, lay the groundwork for that presentation. In Part I, the essential mix of personal attributes and professional competencies in social workers is examined.

In order to be a responsible professional, the social worker must understand and function within the profession's accepted areas of expertise. Chapter 1, "The Domain of the Social Work Profession," elaborates on the authors' definition of social work and presents its central mission as helping people change so they fit and function more comfortably within their environments, and also helping to modify those environments to be more supportive of the people. This help is provided through social programs that include making tangible social provisions available to people in need, offering intangible social services such as counseling or treatment, and engaging in organizational and community change activities.

The primary resource the social worker brings to the helping process is his or her own capacity to develop positive helping relationships and assist clients to take actions that will improve the quality of their lives. A social worker must have the ability to understand client issues, creatively select ways to address those issues (i.e., apply the appropriate techniques and guidelines), and assist clients in changing those factors that are negatively affecting their lives. To do this, the social worker must keep physically, intellectually, and emotionally "in shape" for this rigorous personal interaction with clients or client groups. At the same time, the social worker must avoid having one's personal life consumed by the events that arise in his or her work environment. Chapter 2, "Merging Person with Profession," identifies many of the factors a social worker should be prepared to address in keeping personally and professionally fit for practice.

Throughout its history, social work has been portrayed as both an art and a science. Chapter 3, "Merging the Person's Art with the Profession's Science," builds on the material introduced in Chapters 1 and 2 and provides a more detailed description of the personal characteristics (i.e., the art) that contribute to effective practice. The chapter also identifies the knowledge base (i.e., the science) required of beginning-level social workers. During the last half-century of the profession's growth and development, scant attention has been given to the unique artistic personal traits that are prerequisite to effective practice. Chapter 3 renews the consideration of these features of the social worker by recognizing the central place that such factors as compassion, empathy, genuineness, creativity, hopefulness, energy, values, and professional style play in the helping process. However, the chapter also reflects the view that the professional social worker is obligated to bring the best scientific knowledge to the helping process.

Part I, then, addresses the most fundamental elements of social work practice—the blending of the person and the profession—in order to most effectively assist individuals, families or other households, small groups, organizations, and communities as they work to prevent or resolve the complex social problems that arise in their daily lives.

1 The Domain of the Social Work Profession

When a person sets out to help others, especially those most vulnerable to social problems, he or she assumes a serious responsibility. The responsible professional must practice within his or her ***professional domain*** (i.e., the profession's area of expertise or its "professional turf") if clients are to receive the services that the profession is sanctioned to provide. Indeed, professional helpers can harm clients if the helpers' activities extend beyond their professional boundaries because it is these boundaries that establish the content of the profession's formal education and identify the services its members are prepared to deliver.

This book is concerned with the profession of social work and how social workers assist people in addressing a variety of different issues that confront them. Social work is, indeed, a curious name for a profession. In times that emphasize image over substance, it is clearly a title that lacks pizzazz. In fact, the use of the word *work* makes it sound dreary. It is a title that many social workers have wished they could change, possibly without understanding where it came from in the first place.

The title is attributed to Jeffrey Brackett (1860–1949). Brackett, initially an influential volunteer in the Baltimore Charity Organization Society, served for nearly 30 years on the Massachusetts Board of Charities and later became the first director of what is now the Simmons College School of Social Work. In the early 1900s, Brackett argued that the word *social* should be part of this developing profession's title because it depicts the focus on people's interactions with important forces that shape their lives, such as family members, friends, or a myriad of other factors, including their relevant cultural or ethnic group, school, job, neighborhood, community, and so on. He added the word *work* to differentiate professional practice from what he considered to be the often misguided and self-serving philanthropic activity of wealthy volunteers. He believed including *work* in the profession's title emphasized that its activities were to be orderly, responsible, and disciplined—not something to be engaged in by the unprepared, curious, or whimsical.

Although Brackett did not select a name that a modern public relations firm would suggest, *social work* is an accurate title for a profession that applies helping techniques in a disciplined manner to address social problems. During the years since Brackett convinced early helping services providers to accept this title, the domain of social work has expanded and its approach has been reshaped by the increasing knowledge generated by the social and behavioral sciences. It is understandably a dynamic profession.

The Social Work Domain

It is important for the social worker to examine periodically the ***domain*** of social work (i.e., to review its purpose, focus, scope, and sanction). This is especially important for the student or new social worker because educational programs divide the study of social work into units, or courses, and this can lead to a familiarity with the parts without necessarily understanding the whole. Reexamination of the domain is also important for the experienced practitioner, especially one whose vision of the profession may have been constricted by years of practice in only one type of agency or possibly by the narrowing of vision that often follows the necessity to generate income from client fees. Taking time to stand back from one's daily routine to view the profession as a whole may help the practitioner truly appreciate the depth and breadth of the profession's concerns and the varied and creative approaches used by its practitioners.

A periodic examination of the social work domain is also important to guard against ***professional drift*** (i.e., the neglect of the profession's traditional purpose and functions in favor of activities associated with another profession or discipline). Shulman (1991, 10) alludes to the problem of professional drift when he observes that social workers who align themselves too closely with models and theories borrowed from medicine, psychology, and other disciplines that ignore social policy and social justice issues "can lead to social workers who adopt a view of themselves as therapists first and social workers second, or not even social workers at all." When this occurs, it is a disservice to both clients and one's employing agency, for it diminishes the commitment, perspective, and competencies unique to social work.

A precise and generally agreed upon understanding of the boundaries that mark the several helping professions does not exist. Different disciplines (e.g., social work, clinical psychology, school counseling, and marriage and family therapy) have claimed their domains without collaboration or mutual agreement about where one profession ends and another begins, or where they appropriately overlap. This problem is even further complicated by the fact that each state that chooses to license the practice of these professions is free to establish its own descriptions of professional boundaries. For this reason, a person who is licensed to practice social work in one state may not be eligible to be licensed in a neighboring state. It is important, therefore, to approach learning about social work's domain with a recognition that the boundaries between professions are blurred. However, being knowledgeable about social work's purpose, focus, scope, and sanction provides a reasonably clear picture of its domain.

Social Work's Purpose

The *Social Work Dictionary* (Barker 1995, s.v. "social work") defines ***social work*** as "the professional activity of helping individuals, families, groups, or communities enhance or restore their capacity for social functioning and for creating societal conditions favorable to that goal." Thus, the two separate, but interrelated, objectives of social work are (1) to help individuals and social systems improve their social functioning and (2) to change social conditions to prevent those individuals and systems from experiencing difficulties in their functioning.

In its Curriculum Policy Statement (CPS), the Council on Social Work Education (CSWE) elaborates on the two fundamental purposes of social work practice. The CPS (Council on Social Work Education 1994) indicates that professional social work practice services the four following ***purposes:***

1. The promotion, restoration, maintenance, and enhancement of the social functioning of individuals, families, groups, organizations, and communities by helping them to accomplish tasks, prevent and alleviate distress, and use resources.
2. The planning, formulation, and implementation of social policies, services, resources, and programs needed to meet basic human needs and support the development of human capacities.
3. The pursuit of policies, services, resources, and programs through organizational and administrative advocacy and social or political action, so as to empower groups at risk and promote social and economic justice.
4. The development and testing of professional knowledge and skills related to these purposes. (pp. 97 and 135)

The first of these purposes is concerned with enhancing social functioning and preventing impediments to good social functioning. The final three relate to creating conditions that assure that clients receive appropriate human services when needed and, where possible, preventing social problems from occurring in the first place.

Social Functioning. An understanding of social work begins with a deep appreciation for humans as social beings. People need other people. Human growth, development, and learning require guidance, nurturing, and protection from others. An individual's concept of self—and even one's very survival, both physically and psychologically—is tied to the decisions and actions of other people. It is this interdependence among people and each person's need for interaction with family, friends, and community that has called forth a profession devoted to helping people improve those interactions (i.e., to enhance their social functioning).

The concept of social functioning is pivotal to understanding the unique focus of social work and to distinguishing social work from the other helping professions. According to Longres (1995, 546), ***social functioning*** is "social well-being, especially with regard to the ability of an individual to meet the role expectations associated with a particular status or role." The major social roles that social workers are most likely to help clients perform more effectively are those of parent, child, spouse, student, employee, friend, neighbor, citizen, and patient. Often, as the expectations of clients change through their life cycles, the social worker helps them learn new roles or make adjustments in the way they have been performing their roles.

Karls and Wandrei (1988, 1) describe *social functioning* as "the ability to accomplish the activities necessary for daily living . . . and to fulfill major social roles as required by a particular subculture or community." In this definition, the phrase *activities necessary for daily living* refers to the decisions and behaviors required to meet basic human needs such as obtaining food, shelter, medical care, and transportation, as well as those necessary to protect oneself from harm, to develop social supports, to find meaning and purpose in life, and so on. Karls and Wandrei also remind us that social roles are culturally determined. The social worker, too, must be sensitive to differing role expectations that are associated with a person's gender, ethnicity, culture, religion, occupation, and community in order to effectively serve clients. In sum, the concept of social functioning draws attention to the match or fit between an individual's motivation and abilities and the demands, requirements, and opportunities in his or her social environment.

Although social work is concerned with the social functioning of all people, it has traditionally given priority to addressing the needs of the most vulnerable members of the society. Typically, these vulnerable populations have been victims of neglect, social injustices, discrimination, and oppression. Included in this category are children and youth, older people, women, individuals living in poverty, individuals with physical limitations, people with mental or emotional illness, gays and lesbians, and people of minority ethnic, racial, and national backgrounds.

To carry out their commitment to improving people's social functioning, social workers are involved in providing *social care* to those individuals with few capacities and opportunities to function satisfactorily. Also, when people's poor judgment or inappropriate actions seriously limit or interfere with their own functioning or the functioning of others, *social treatment* services may be the most helpful response. Finally, because people may want to improve their social functioning even though they may not be experiencing a defined "problem," social workers also offer *enhancement services.*

Social care includes actions and efforts designed to provide people in need with access to the basics of life (e.g., food, shelter, protection from harm, etc.) and opportunities to meet their psychosocial needs such as belonging, acceptance, and comfort in times of distress. In situations of social care, the focus is on providing needed resources and/or helping the client be as comfortable as possible in difficult, but more or less unchangeable, circumstances. Examples of social care include efforts to address the problems of people who are homeless or living in poverty, highly dependent people such as children who do not have families, the frail elderly, and individuals with serious and chronic physical or mental illnesses or disabilities.

Social treatment involves actions designed to modify or correct an individual's or family's dysfunctional patterns of thought, feeling, and behavior. In social treatment, the focus is primarily on facilitating individual or family change through training, counseling, or discreet forms of therapy. Of course, in many cases (e.g., work with children in foster care), the social worker may provide both social care and social treatment to the same client.

A third form of intervention to enhance clients' social functioning is social enhancement services. Rather than beginning practice by finding and documenting "the problem" an individual or family experiences, ***social enhancement services*** emphasize "the growth and development of clients in a particular area of functioning without a 'problem' having necessarily been identified" (Morales and Sheafor 1998, 18). Some examples of enhancement-oriented services are youth or senior citizen recreation programs, well-baby clinics, marriage enrichment sessions, and parent effectiveness training.

Social Conditions. Social work's second area of emphasis is on creating an environment for people that is supportive of their development and functioning. The social worker's intervention at the environment level consists of a set of actions intended to modify those conditions or situations that will contribute to people's problems in social functioning. This includes efforts to influence organizations, neighborhoods, communities, or even larger social structures. These efforts might be designed to prevent problems from occurring in the first place or to modify organizations, programs, social policies, and so on.

Prevention consists of those actions taken to eliminate social, economic, psychological, and other conditions known to cause or contribute to the formation of human problems. To be effective in prevention, social workers must be able to identify the specific factors, conditions, and situations that contribute to the development of social problems and then select actions and activities that will reduce or eliminate their impact. Borrowing from the public health model, three distinct levels of prevention can be identified:

1. *Primary prevention* (Level 1) reflects actions intended to prevent the problem from developing.
2. *Secondary prevention* (Level 2) describes actions intended to detect a problem in its early stages and address it while it is still relatively easy to change or treat.
3. *Tertiary prevention* (Level 3) requires actions intended to address an already serious problem in ways that prevent it from spreading to others, expanding the damage, and growing even worse.

As society grows more complex, people must look to specialized organizations and social programs for the resources and opportunities they require. Prevention efforts by social workers are especially concerned about how people relate to and utilize resources provided by the organizations that make up the complex, legalistic, and highly bureaucratic social welfare system. Such efforts include those intended to develop and improve laws, social policies, social institutions, and social systems in ways that will promote social and economic justice, expand opportunities, or improve the conditions and circumstances in which people live (i.e., bring about *social change*). Examples of social change goals include expanding the availability of safe and affordable housing, creating incentives for businesses to hire those with little work experience, amending laws so they better prevent discrimination, and empowering neighborhood and community organizations to become politically active in addressing issues they face. Social change efforts, then, are focused on correcting problems in agency services delivery or creating new community structures to prevent or reduce societal problems.

Social Work's Focus

Several professions are concerned with individual and family functioning—their physical functioning, emotional functioning, psychological functioning, and, to some extent, social functioning. Other professions are concerned about social conditions and engage in the planning and evaluation of organizations, communities, and so on. Social work, however, is simultaneously concerned with both social functioning and social conditions. Social work focuses on the interactions or transactions between and among people, as well as the multitude of social policies, agencies, and programs that comprise the social welfare system. These interactions include those of person to person, person to community, person to social agency, and agency to agency. This ***person-in-environment*** focus is the most distinguishing characteristic that sets social work apart from other professions.

The focus on person-in-environment requires that the social worker attend to several interrelated dimensions of the person: biological, intellectual, emotional, social, familial, spiritual, economic, communal, and so on. This concern for the ***whole person*** contributes to the breadth of concern by the social work profession—for example, the individual's capacity to meet basic physical needs (food, housing, health care, etc.), the person's levels of knowledge and skills needed to cope with life's demands and to earn a living, the person's thoughts about others and his or her own life, the individual's goals and aspirations, and the like. It is important to note the person-in-environment construct uses the word *person,* not *personality.* Personality is but one component of the whole person. A focus only on personality would be incongruous with the domain of social work and slant it toward the domain of psychology.

The term ***environment*** refers to one's surroundings—that multitude of physical and social structures, forces, and processes that affect humans and all other life forms. Of particular interest to social workers are those systems, structures, and other factors that most frequently and most directly affect a person's day-to-day social functioning (i.e., the person's ***immediate environment***). One's immediate environment includes the person's family, close friends, neighborhood, workplace, and the services and programs he or she uses.

Based on their empirical analysis of social work practice tasks, Teare and Sheafor (1995) state that social workers devote a major part of their attention to clients' efforts to improve interactions with their immediate environment. Social workers focus to a lesser extent on the broader environment, possibly because the impact of problems in the more ***distant environment*** is less evident and more difficult to change. In order to grow, develop, and survive, humans need clean air, drinkable water, shelter, and good soil to produce food. And because biological well-being is a prerequisite to positive social functioning, social workers must also be concerned with problems such as prevention of disease and pollution. In addition, they seek to change damaging societal values, correct human rights violations, and address unjust political and economic structures that may affect their clients. Concern over factors in both the immediate and distant environments is central to fulfilling social work's mission.

Social Work's Scope

A profession's ***scope*** can be thought of as the range of activities and involvements appropriate to its mission. Because the scope of social work is broad, social workers often have a difficult time giving a concise answer to the question: What do social workers do? Coming up with a simple answer is complicated by the fact that the social work client may be an individual or a whole social system, including a family, group, organization, or community.

One useful way of describing social work practice involves classifying the intervention by the size of the client system being addressed (i.e., micro-, mezzo-, or macro-level practice). Practice at the ***micro level*** focuses on a person's most intimate interactions, such as exchanges between husband and wife, parent and child, close friends, and family members. The terms *interpersonal helping, direct practice,* and *clinical practice* are often used interchangeably with micro-level practice.

At the other extreme, ***macro-level*** practice may involve work with an organization, community, or even society as a whole. Obviously, macro-level practice also deals with interpersonal relations, but these are the interactions between people who represent organizations or who are members of a work group such as an agency committee or interagency task force. When engaged in macro-level practice, the social worker is frequently involved in activities such as administration, fund-raising, testifying on proposed legislation, policy analysis, class advocacy, and social resource development.

Between the micro and macro levels is ***mezzo-level*** (midlevel) practice. Practice at this level is concerned with interpersonal relations that are somewhat less intimate than those associated with family life but more personally meaningful than those that occur among organizational and institutional representatives. Included would be relationships among individuals in a self-help or therapy group, among peers at school or work, and among neighbors.

Some practice approaches address more than one intervention level. For example, social treatment, as defined by Whittaker and Tracy (1989), includes the micro and mezzo levels, and the generalist perspective (Schatz, Jenkins, and Sheafor 1990) requires the social worker to be capable of practice at the micro, mezzo, and macro levels.

Social Work's Sanction

Sanction refers to the authorization, approval, or permission needed to perform certain professional tasks and activities. Sanction has the effect of defining the profession's domain. Four major sources of sanction for social work activities are (1) legal codes and government regulation, (2) legally incorporated human services agencies, (3) the collective body of social work professionals, and (4) the clients or consumers of social work services.

Federal, state, and city governments authorize the actions of social workers through legislation that creates social programs, through the allocation of funds for social work activities, through the licensing of organizations (e.g., licensed child-placing agencies) that employ social workers, and through the licensing and regulation of individual social work practitioners.

Many government and private human services organizations (both nonprofit and profit-making agencies) sanction social work by recruiting and hiring social workers to provide services or by purchasing services from those who are in private practice or employed by other agencies. Indirectly, then, the community sanctions and pays social workers to provide specific services. In return for this sanction to practice, social workers are obliged to provide high-quality services and to protect clients from possible abuse those professionals who might be unethical or incompetent.

The profession, acting through the National Association of Social Workers (NASW), sets standards for appropriate and ethical practice. By requiring adherence to its *Code of Ethics,* offering certification (e.g., the Academy of Certified Social Workers, Diplomat in Clinical Social Work, etc.), and providing education to its membership through publications and conferences, the NASW serves as a vehicle for protecting the public trust.

The true test of public sanction for practice, however, is the willingness of clients to seek out and use services offered by social workers. In order to win the trust of clients, social workers must demonstrate on a daily basis that they are capable of providing effective services and are committed to conducting their practice in a responsible and ethical manner.

An Overview of Social Work Practice

Figure 1.1 presents a model of the key factors that influence social work practice. It shows the client (or client system) and the social worker joining together in a process of change while both are being influenced by the social agency (e.g., its policies and programs) and by the wider social environment.

The reason clients and social workers come together is to engage in a ***planned change process.*** That process involves several phases of activity during which the client and social worker move from their decision to initiate a course of action, through the change activity, to an evaluation of its success and a decision to terminate the helping activity (see Chapter 7). Although the social worker is expected to guide this process, the client must ultimately make decisions about whether to make changes or utilize resources made available by the worker.

The Client side of Figure 1.1 indicates that the problem or situation the client seeks to change is the product of a combination of personal and environmental factors. Each client has *personal characteristics* that contributed to the situation being addressed and/or that might be used to help change that situation. Regardless of whether the client is an individual, family, or some larger system, every situation is unique due to the client's special needs, wants, capacities, knowledge, beliefs, physical characteristics, and life experiences.

Clients do not exist in isolation. They have an *immediate environment* that also influences the situation (sometimes called a *near environment*). This environment might include friends, family, school personnel, employers, natural helpers, neighborhood or community groups, or even other professional helpers, to mention just a few. Because environmental influences have contributed to the problem or concern creating a need for change, they must also be a part of the solution; people in the client's immediate environment must be kept in the foreground as possible targets and resources for the change activity.

The Social Worker side of Figure 1.1 suggests that the worker brings unique personal characteristics and a professional background to the change process. These are experienced by the client through what the social worker actually does with the client (i.e., the worker's activities and application of skills and techniques). What

FIGURE 1.1 An Integrative View of Social Work Practice

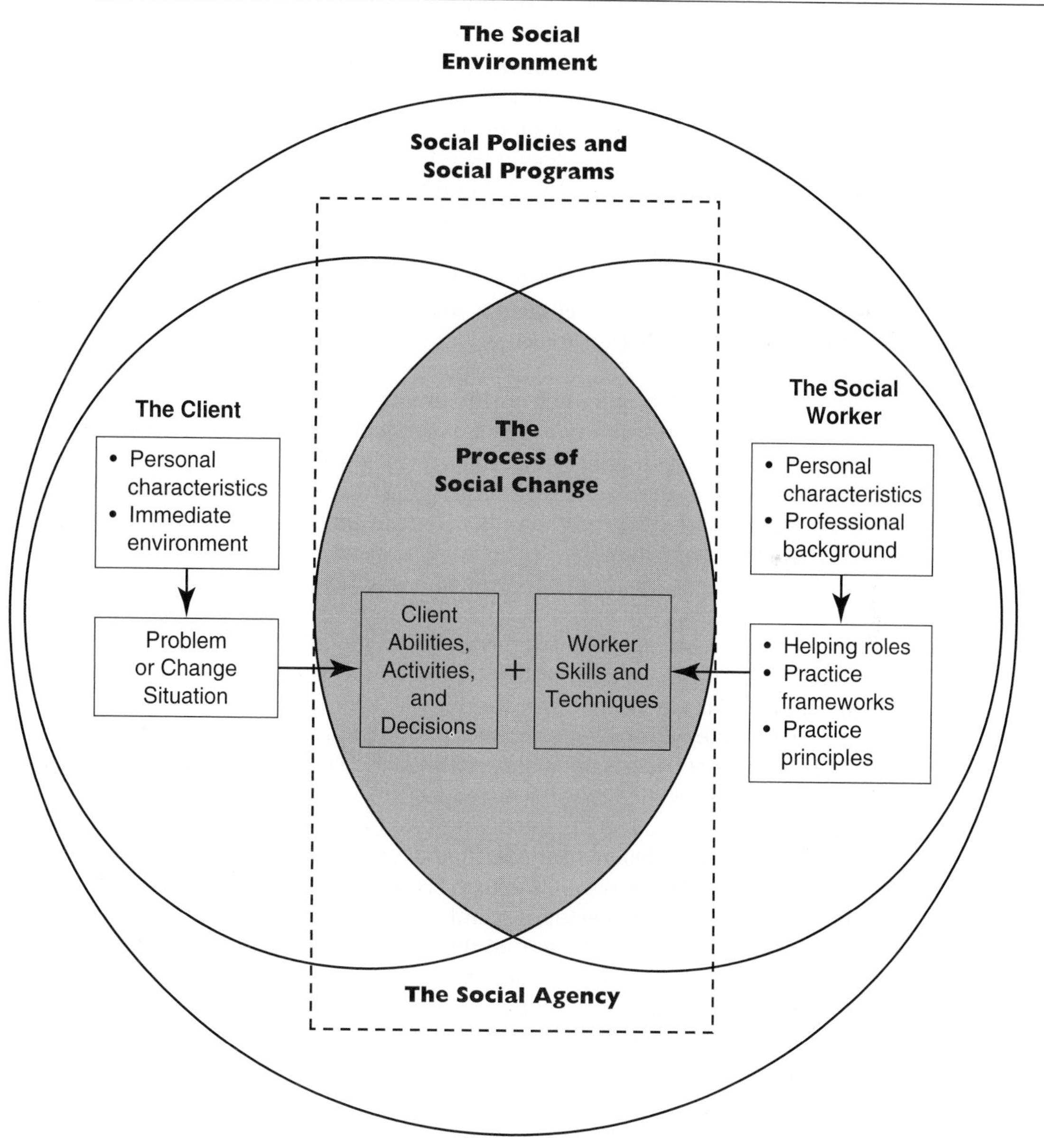

the worker does is a function of the specific professional role he or she has assumed and the conceptual frameworks selected to guide practice. The worker's *personal characteristics* encompass such factors as life experience and especially one's artistic talents or natural abilities in providing services. The social worker's unique perspectives on the human condition, as well as his or her particular values, are inevitably introduced into the change process. The worker's view on life and human problems is shaped by his or her racial or cultural background, socioeconomic status, gender, age, sexual orientation, and the like. All affect the social worker–client relationship.

At the same time, the practitioner brings the special contribution of a *professional background* to social work, which differentiates the social worker from the client's friends, family, natural helpers, and the professionals representing other disciplines who may also be working with the client or who attempted to help in the past. What is this professional background? First and foremost, the social worker brings the belief system, values, ethical principles, and focus on social functioning that are common to the domain of social work. Through education and experience, the social worker develops a practice wisdom and an ability to use his or her personal characteristics, special talents, and unique style to help clients. In addition, the social worker brings a knowledge base, much of it derived from the social and behavioral sciences. Chapter 3 presents an overview of the necessary artistic abilities, knowledge base, and value positions relevant to practice.

As social workers carry out their responsibilities, they perform various *helping roles.* As Chapter 4 describes more fully, social workers must be prepared to perform a wide variety of roles and functions, ranging from linking clients to appropriate resources, to assessing case situations and providing direct services, to planning and conducting social action.

An important element of professional background is that portion of the social worker's knowledge base consisting of various *practice frameworks* that guide practice (e.g., practice perspectives, theories, and models) and provide direction to the change process. The ways in which these frameworks might be selected and utilized are discussed in Chapter 6.

The profession has informally tested the applicability of its approach to providing human services, largely through trial and error. Some of these tried-and-true guidelines for practice have been reduced to *practice principles* that serve as the most fundamental directives to practice (see Chapter 5).

Finally, the social worker's *skills* and mastery of *techniques* are his or her most evident and tangible contribution to the change process. The skills or techniques selected by the social worker will depend, of course, on the nature of the client's problem or concern, the expectations of the practice setting, and the worker's own competence in using them. A wide variety of techniques and guidelines are described in Parts III and IV of this book.

Returning again to Figure 1.1, it is important to recognize that social work practice takes place within a ***social environment*** and, more specifically, usually within the context of a social agency. Typically, the agency has been shaped by local, state, and/or national social policies, and its programs are a reflection of society's values and beliefs. Commitment to the social welfare of its members varies among societies; within the United States, it even varies among regions, states, and communities. We know that having sound social programs supports quality living for all people—the more secure as well as the most vulnerable members of that society. Yet every social worker knows that our social policies and programs leave much to be desired. Moreover, U.S. society has demonstrated an ambivalent and transient commitment to people whose needs are not adequately met through their employment or help provided by family and friends. Therefore, social workers, who might be viewed as agents of the society, must frequently work with fewer than the desired tools for assisting their clients.

Through its legislative and other decision-making bodies, society creates ***social programs*** intended to help certain people. These programs take three forms. *Social provisions* involve giving tangible goods (e.g., money, food, clothing, and housing) to persons in need. *Social services* include intangible services (e.g., counseling, therapy, and learning experiences) intended to help people resolve and/or prevent problems. Finally, *social action* programs are concerned with changing aspects of the social environment to make it more responsive to people's needs and wants.

The particular philosophy on which social programs are built has a significant bearing on how they operate, how effective they are, and how they affect both the client and the social worker. The dominant social welfare philosophy in the United States contends that social programs should be of a residual nature; they should be a safety net that is available only to people who can demonstrate "real need." In other words, social programs should exist only to help people solve already serious problems and be available only to those who are deemed eligible. A second philosophy, the institutional conception, considers social programs to be first-line functions of society (similar to education and law enforcement). This approach places greater emphasis on prevention and avoids forcing the client to identify a problem or admit to some personal failure in order to benefit from human services.

The benefits and services associated with a particular social program are typically offered through a ***social agency.*** Thus, for the most part, social work is an agency-based profession and most social workers are agency employees. A social agency might be a public welfare department, mental health center, school, hospital, neighborhood center, or any of a number of differing organizational structures. It may be a public agency supported by tax funds and governed by elected officials or a private agency operating under the auspices of a volunteer board and supported primarily by fees, voluntary donations, or purchase of service contracts. The basic functions of the agency are to administer social programs and to monitor the quality of the helping process. To perform these functions, the agency must secure money, staff, and other resources; determine which people in the community are eligible for its services; and maintain an administrative structure that will meet targeted social needs in an efficient and effective manner.

The most important ingredient of a social agency is its people. Receptionists, custodians, administrators, and service providers all must work together to deliver successful programs. Often, several helping professions are employed by the same agency. In such interdisciplinary programs, each profession brings its own perspective on helping—as well as the special competencies appropriate to the domain of that profession.

Conclusion

Social work is one of several human services professions that have been sanctioned by society to help improve the quality of life for all people. Other such helping professions include clinical psychology, drug and alcohol counseling, marriage and family counseling, school psychology, medicine, rehabilitation counseling, nursing, and so on. The uniqueness of social work among these professions is its focus on the social functioning of people and helping people interact more effectively with their environments—both their near and distant environments. Social workers perform this role by assisting people to address issues in their social functioning and working to prevent social problems from emerging or, if they already exist, from getting worse.

Increasingly, conflict and competition arise among the various human services professions over issues of the domain (or turf) of each. These conflicts tend to center around competition for jobs, salary, status, and control, as well as disagreements over which profession is most qualified to perform certain tasks. To minimize the effect of these problems on clients, it is important for the members of these professions to engage in *interprofessional collaboration* as they provide their services. However, each discipline must avoid letting its practice activities drift into the areas of expertise of the other professions.

Social workers have historically claimed they represent the profession best prepared to help people resolve problems in social functioning and to guide social change efforts to prevent problems from occurring or becoming worse. It is important that social workers maintain their focus on these central features of their domain.

SELECTED BIBLIOGRAPHY

Barker, Robert L. *The Social Work Dictionary,* 3rd ed. Washington, DC: NASW Press, 1995.

Council on Social Work Education. *Handbook of Accreditation Standards and Procedures,* rev. ed. Alexandria, VA: CSWE, 1994.

Karls, James, and Karin Wandrei. *Person in Environment: A System for Describing, Classifying and Coding Problems of Social Functioning.* Silver Spring, MD: NASW, 1988.

Longres, John. *Human Behavior and the Social Environment,* 2nd ed. Itasca, IL: F. E. Peacock, 1995.

Morales, Armando T., and Bradford W. Sheafor. *Social Work: A Profession of Many Faces,* 8th ed. Boston: Allyn and Bacon, 1998.

Schatz, Mona S., Lowell E. Jenkins, and Bradford W. Sheafor. "Milford Redefined: A Model of Initial and Advanced Generalist Social Work," *Journal of Social Work Education* 26 (Fall 1990): 217–231.

Shulman, Lawrence. *Interactional Social Work Practice.* Itasca, IL: F. E. Peacock, 1991.

Teare, Robert J., and Bradford W. Sheafor. *Practice-Sensitive Social Work Education: An Empirical Analysis of Social Work Practice and Practitioners.* Alexandria, VA: CSWE, 1995.

Whittaker, James, and Elizabeth Tracy. *Social Treatment,* 2nd ed. New York: Aldine, 1989.

2 Merging Person with Profession

A social worker's professional responsibilities and his or her personal life are in constant interaction. Most social workers cannot simply go to work, do their job, and then leave their thoughts and feelings about work at the office when returning home. They try to keep professional concerns separate from their other roles and responsibilities but the nature of the work makes this difficult.

As explained in Chapter 1, social work professionals view the client, when an individual, as a *whole person* with various dimensions, including the physical, spiritual, emotional, psychological, social, and intellectual. They also view the client within a situational and ecological context. These same concepts apply to the individual who takes on the role and responsibilities of a social worker within a human services organization. The social worker responds to the challenges of practice with his or her whole being; therefore, the worker's beliefs, values, physical and emotional well-being, spirituality, family relationships, friendships, and all other facets of living will both influence and be influenced by the day-to-day experiences of social work practice.

The worker has many roles, responsibilities, and interests besides those that are related to the job. For example, he or she is usually part of a family or household, often a spouse or partner, sometimes a parent, part of friendship and social networks, and a resident in a particular neighborhood and community. Moreover, he or she may be a member of a particular ethnic group, affiliated with a religious denomination or faith community, a member of a special-interest group or political party, and a member of service and recreational groups. Given this multitude of roles, every social worker is challenged to resolve the inevitable tensions that arise between personal and professional obligations.

Although this book is primarily devoted to activities that occur during the hours that the social worker devotes to his or her job, this chapter focuses on how the realities of practice may impinge on the worker's private life. The observations presented here are intended to assist social workers to strike a healthy balance between their personal needs and responsibilities and the demands and responsibilities of practice.

Selecting Social Work as a Career

Our lives are shaped by the choices we make. Because choosing social work as a career has some unique implications for self and family, those attracted to this profession must consider (and periodically reconsider) if social work should be their life's work. There must be a good fit between the person and his or her occupation and job. A mismatch can be destructive to one's health and emotional well-being. A person who feels trapped in the profession or in a particular social work job cannot bring the desired energy and commitment to the helping process, and consequently, clients will be poorly served.

Social Work as a Life Companion

Life is a journey that we take only one time. As a social worker makes that one journey through life, it is important that he or she is truly comfortable with social work as a traveling companion. An individual considering a social work career must be satisfied with his or her answers to the following questions:

- Is being a social worker a meaningful and worthwhile way for me to live my life?
- Is there a good fit between my personal beliefs, values, and needs and the values and demands of the social work profession?
- Is the practice of social work an appropriate and satisfying use of my unique gifts, abilities, and skills?
- What impact will being a social worker have on my own physical and mental health, my intellectual development, my religious beliefs and practices, and my economic situation?
- What impact will my career in social work have on my family and friends?
- How will being a social worker affect where I live and work and the overall quality of my life?

Each person needs to identify his or her core values and decide what is really important in life. The work and rewards that accrue from being a social worker should be consistent with those beliefs and goals.

The School-to-Job Transition

Many students do not fully realize that their program of social work education, including the practicum, takes place within a protected environment. Once they enter the world of full-time practice as a paid professional, they may experience reality shock. Many are surprised by the sheer difficulty of their jobs. For example, in describing her new job, a very capable recent graduate told one of the authors: "I simply had no idea that my clients would be so troubled, my job so difficult and frustrating, and my agency setting would be so overwhelmingly complex."

Those beginning their first social work job quickly discover that there is seldom enough time to do what needs to be done. Many are angered when they recognize that in far too many agencies, social work values and principles and a concern for clients have taken a backseat to the forces of political pressure, administrative fiat, budget limitations, the fear of lawsuits, and the day-by-day struggle to cope with an overwhelming caseload. Many are disillusioned by the discovery that some colleagues have lost their enthusiasm and are too fatigued and demoralized to be effective. Within such an environment, it can be a challenge to maintain one's professional ideals and standards.

Every new social worker is somewhat surprised and frustrated by the slowness of change, whether that change is by individual clients, organizations, or communities. They also discover that identifying what needs to change is relatively easy compared to achieving the change. Programs of social work education teach about the process of change and describe techniques for facilitating change but they cannot teach the personal qualities of patience, perseverance, tenacity, and tolerance that are so necessary to moving good ideas into reality.

Some new social workers who were high academic achievers face a special challenge when they move into an agency-based practice. Simply put, they are accustomed to doing grade A academic work and expect to do A-quality work on the job, but discover that there is only enough time and resources to do average work. Those unable to modify their expectations will surely experience much frustration on the job.

Some agencies provide a superb work environment, but far too many offer an environment that is noisy, crowded, unattractive, and sometimes even dangerous. Dissatisfaction with an agency-based practice has led many experienced social workers to seek a practice setting that offers a more pleasant place to work and more control over what they do and how they do it. Specht and Courtney (1993), for example, document a trend by social workers to shift from agency-based to private practice. Although this may be an understandable response to frustrations associated with bureaucratic settings, it has the effect of drawing social workers away from the profession's traditional commitment to the poor and oppressed. Throughout their careers, conscientious social workers will struggle to reconcile their desire for adequate income and a decent work environment with their concern for the poor and their commitment to social and economic justice.

Many new social workers become disenchanted when they discover that politics plays a significant role in the decisions and functioning of their practice settings. This issue needs to be put in perspective. Within every group and organization—whether a business, a social agency, a religious body, or a professional organization—people use power and authority to move the organization in directions they see as desirable. Thus, all organizations are inherently political; this is a reality that must be acknowledged rather than ignored. On the other hand, politics is certainly not the most important thing about an organization or a work setting. Social workers must guard against becoming so preoccupied with workplace politics that they lose sight of what their agency can achieve or forget about the people it is to serve.

Earning a Living as a Social Worker

The social worker and his or her dependents are directly affected by the worker's earning capacity. Social work has never been a high-paying profession. In contrast to some occupations, the earning power of social workers does not go up rapidly or continually as they gain skill and experience. Social workers earn a modest income and have limited opportunity to climb the economic ladder. However, the satisfaction of doing something truly worthwhile and making a difference in the lives of people is often viewed by social workers as an offsetting form of compensation.

Most entry-level jobs are ones involving the provision of services directly to clients. After a few years in direct services, many social workers apply for higher-paying jobs in supervision and administration as a way of increasing their income and prestige. This may be a good job change for those attracted to management tasks such as budgeting, policy development, public relations, personnel selection, and staff training. It may be an unwise decision for those whose job satisfaction comes primarily from direct contact with clients.

As an individual thinks about or plans a career in social work, he or she should consider the following questions:

- Given my current personal and family responsibilities, can I manage on a social worker's salary?
- Given probable changes in my personal and family life over the next 5, 10, and 20 years, will my salary keep up with my income requirements?
- How will my earning capacity affect my family? How will it affect decisions on where I live and work?
- Will I be content and at peace with a modest income or will I become distressed and bitter?

Those entering social work should expect to change jobs from 5 to 10 times during their working years. Sometimes a job change is prompted by poor performance or an agency's staff reductions, but most often it is a matter of personal choice. Among the personal and professional reasons why social workers change jobs are the following:

- Desire for higher salary, better benefits, or job security
- Desire to learn a new field of practice or test one's ability to perform certain tasks and activities
- Desire to have more discretion and control over practice decisions and methods
- Desire to work in a setting that is more accepting of new ideas and new approaches to practice
- Desire to work with clients having a different set of problems, concerns, or situations
- Desire for a less stressful work environment
- Opportunity to receive better supervision and in-service training
- Desire to remove self from conflicts with a supervisor or agency administrator

- Need to adjust work to changes in personal or family life (e.g., marriage, divorce, birth of child, illness, etc.)
- Desire to live and work in another city or state

Those preparing to enter social work are advised to identify their personal and career goals and formulate a plan for reaching those goals. Examples of goals include obtaining a particular type of job, having the opportunity to design an innovative program, becoming an administrator of a certain type of agency, becoming skilled in work with certain client populations, conducting research on a particular topic, and so on. The plan should cover the next 5, 10, and 20 years. In these times of rapid change, it can be difficult to develop such a plan and even more difficult to follow it. However, career planning provides direction and a framework for making decisions about what special training and work experiences to pursue as preparation.

Establishing Oneself as a Social Worker

It is not enough for the new social worker to carry his or her credentials into a job and assume that everything is now in place for a satisfying and effective practice. The worker must first demonstrate to clients, colleagues, and other agencies in the community that he or she is competent and trustworthy. In addition, the worker will be challenged to reconcile his or her personal and professional standards with the everyday operations of human services systems. The new worker is beginning a lifelong struggle to have some impact on large-scale social problems and to promote social justice in a society that seeks simple answers to complex problems and is politically divided on how to respond to human needs and growing levels of poverty and violence.

Acquiring a Reputation

Every social worker acquires a reputation within his or her agency, within the local human services network, and among the clients he or she serves. That reputation, whether good or bad, has an impact on his or her effectiveness with clients, interagency and interprofessional communication and cooperation, and whether he or she is considered for promotion or offered other social work jobs.

One need only sit in on a few support group meetings or spend just an hour in an agency waiting room to realize that many clients talk freely about the social workers, doctors, teachers, and other professionals they know. They tell friends, neighbors, and other clients about how they have been treated and who does a good job and who to avoid. Clients are especially sensitive to whether social workers are willing to listen, available when needed, and fair in the decisions they make.

Within an agency, each social worker acquires a reputation as an employee. Over time, the other agency employees form an opinion about the worker's competence and whether he or she is dependable and carries a fair share of the workload.

That reputation will affect the willingness of the other employees to offer their support, assistance, and cooperation.

Reputation is a determining factor in whether a private practice or fee-for-service program will succeed. If they have a choice, clients will avoid agencies and professionals who have bad reputations. In addition, the professionals of a community who are in a position to refer clients to a particular social worker will do so only if that worker has a reputation for being competent and ethical.

Social workers should regularly review how their statements, actions, and associations are shaping their reputations. Socrates observed that "the way to gain a good reputation is to endeavor to be what you desire to appear." A good reputation is difficult to build but easy for others to destroy. For this reason, many cultures consider slander and the spreading of gossip that could ruin a person's reputation to be among the most reprehensible of moral transgressions.

One of the most painful situations social workers can experience is to find themselves employed by an organization that does not respect clients or value professional competence and ethical conduct. Such situations can arise when an organization's administration and policy board is more concerned about politics, cost cutting, or profit than providing needed and appropriate services.

All organizations develop a culture consisting of its values, expectations, and group norms. Employees are rewarded when they accept this culture and ostracized when they do not. Once established, an organization's culture tends to perpetuate itself while exerting a pervasive effect on employees and their job performance. Social workers employed by organizations with destructive cultures will need to work hard to change that culture or look for another job.

Conflict over Agency Policy

Every social worker comes to the profession and to his or her practice setting with a set of personal beliefs, values, standards, and expectations. It is inevitable that he or she will, from time to time, disagree with agency decisions and methods of operation. There may also be times when the worker disagrees with official positions taken by the National Association of Social Workers (NASW) or other professional organizations to which he or she belongs. How is a worker to respond to such situations? In the final analysis, the social worker must follow his or her conscience. However, the worker's decision about what to do must be based on a thoughtful examination of the issue. One might begin this examination by seeking answers to the following questions:

- Why has my agency or professional organization taken this position at this particular time? What is the history and rationale behind this position? What are the arguments for and against this position? What data support this viewpoint? What political, economic, and social forces gave rise to this position? Was it prompted by political and administrative expediency or was it rooted in principles of social justice and efforts to allocate scarce resources in a fair and responsible manner? If it was driven by a lack of fiscal resources, what actions were take to secure additional resources?

- Why do I disagree with my agency or professional organization? Which of my beliefs, values, or standards is being threatened or violated? Are my concerns based on identifiable principles or possibly arising from personal bias or differences in personal, professional, and/or administrative style?
- Does the action or position in question recognize that every individual has worth and dignity, regardless of his or her strengths and limitations, successes and failings? Does it recognize that each person is unique and precious?
- Does the action or position recognize and respect the rights and responsibilities of each person? Does the position honor the principle that every mentally competent individual has a right to self-determination, as long as his or her actions do not harm others? Does the position recognize that every competent person is also responsible for his or her own actions and must accept the consequences for violating legitimate laws and rules?
- Does the action or position in question promote the common good? Does the position enhance and strengthen the functioning of individuals, families, and the community? Does it recognize the obligation of individuals, communities, and society to expand social and economic opportunities and, where necessary, to provide direct assistance to persons who are at risk of harm, deeply troubled, adversely affected by a physical or mental limitations, or socially or economically oppressed?

Once the social worker understands why the agency or professional organization has taken the action or position in question and is also clear about why he or she disagrees, the worker must decide on a course of action. Each possible option needs to be examined in terms of its immediate and long-term consequences and in regard to what might be gained and lost. The following suggestions may prove useful:

- If the worker concludes that this is indeed a matter that demands a response, he or she might begin by seeking further advice and direction from trusted peers and/or the agency supervisor.
- If the worker is expected by his or her agency to take some action that would violate his or her professional or moral standards, the worker should voice these concerns, document them in a letter to the administrator, and formally request to be excused from having to participate in the questionable activity.
- If the social worker objects to actions or positions taken by a professional organization to which he or she belongs, the worker should write to the organization's leaders and describe his or her concerns and objections. The worker might also volunteer to join the committee that recommended the position in hopes of having the issue and position reexamined in the future.
- In extreme cases and when there is no acceptable alternative, the worker will need to seek employment in a different agency. Similarly, in extreme cases, he or she may need to withdraw from a professional organization that has taken positions that are personally or professionally offensive.

When issues are complex, knowing what is right is never easy and doing what is right is always difficult.

Promoting Social Justice

Most individuals attracted to social work are somewhat idealistic. They want to make the world a better place. They possess a vision of a just and humane society. They believe that every individual has certain basic rights, such as those identified in the Declaration of Independence, the Bill of Rights, and the Universal Declaration of Human Rights issued by the United Nations. In short, they seek ***social justice,*** which Barker (1995, 354) describes as "an ideal condition in which all members of a society have the same rights, protection, opportunities, obligations and social benefits."

All considerations of social justice rest on a core belief: Every human being is intrinsically valuable. This worth is not something that must be earned or proved, nor is it a function of one's skin color, nationality, gender, social status, health, education, political affiliation, occupation, or other external characteristics or life circumstances. Simply by virtue of being human, every person has a right to be treated with fairness and respect, protected from abuse and exploitation, and granted opportunities to have a family, a basic education, meaningful work, and access to essential health care and social services. The Universal Declaration of Human Rights (United Nations, 1948, 1) observes that the "recognition of the inherent dignity and of the equal and inalienable rights of all members of the human family is the foundation of freedom, justice and peace in the world."

A multitude of complex and interrelated economic, political, historical, and social forces give rise to and perpetuate injustice. The term *social injustice* refers to various forms of exploitation, oppression, and discrimination that are embedded in societal beliefs and attitudes and reinforced by laws, policies, and social norms. Because the fundamental causes of social injustice tend to be woven into dominant belief systems and social and economic structures, an injustice and its effects may go unnoticed by all but those directly harmed. Social workers must be always open to the possibility that they or their agencies may unknowingly contribute to social injustice.

Social justice is a complex ideal, and even among people of goodwill and compassion, there will be different perspectives on what is truly fair and what specific actions will move us toward a more just and humane society. Social workers must work for social and economic justice and needed reforms in ways that recognize differences of opinion and maintain respect for those who may disagree with their ideas about how best to achieve a just society.

All too often, we do not feel personally responsible for the existence of social injustice. When an injustice is brought to our attention, we are likely to conclude that it is the fault of society and beyond our control. When we seriously examine a situation of injustice, we often end up feeling helpless and concluding that we are too small a force to make any difference. Social injustice is indeed a community or societal problem, but the responsibility to oppose injustice rests with the individual. Martin Luther King reminded us that "whoever accepts evil without protesting against it, is really cooperating with it."

In order to correct an injustice, people must become politically involved, speak out, and propose practical solutions. However, those who seek social reform must understand that they will pay a price for challenging powerful individuals and groups that stand to lose money, power, or position if the status quo is altered. Those who speak out may be ridiculed, lose their jobs, or, in extreme cases, subjected to physical threats and injury.

Political Involvement

Efforts to work for social and economic justice require participation in the political process. Basically, politics is the art of gaining, exercising, and retaining power. Some social workers are fascinated by politics; others find it distasteful. How and to what degree one involves himself or herself in political activity is a matter of choice, reflecting such factors as interest, available time, energy level, and personal style. Being an informed and conscientious voter is an essential first step, but more is required of social workers who wish to remain true to the "soul" of their profession.

A social worker's participation in the political process will usually involve one or more of the following activities:

- Evaluating how existing and proposed public policy affects people in need, the common good of society, and the profession
- Educating the public regarding the social dimensions and ramifications of law and public policy
- Entering into the debate on matters of public policy and advocating for desirable changes
- Participating with other concerned parties in the formulation of public policy
- Working for the election of those who represent the worker's beliefs and values

As social workers become involved in the political process, they must make hard decisions about where they stand on complex issues. Politically speaking, most social workers tend to be on the liberal side of the conservative-to-liberal continuum. However, it is mistake for social workers to assume that they must choose between being either a liberal or a conservative. Rather, they should be something of both. Everyone who is intellectually and spiritually alive is liberal in the sense of being open to the truth, regardless of its source, and desirous of change and even governmental action if those changes will improve the lives of people and their society. Similarly, every thoughtful and responsible person is conservative in the sense of wanting to preserve those values and approaches that have been beneficial to people and because he or she knows that the newest idea is not necessarily the best one and that there is usually a negative side to government intervention. Thus, depending on the issue, a social worker might line up on either the liberal or conservative side of the debate. The merits and wisdom of a proposal, and not political ideology, should dictate one's stance on an issue.

Some, like Wallis (1995, xvi), a long-time advocate for the poor and social justice activist, concludes that both ideological options—liberal and conservative—fail to address the complexity of the nation's social crisis and neither provides the vision needed to create a more just society. He explains that those on the liberal side seem unable to articulate or demonstrate the moral values that must undergird a genuine social transformation. The critically important link between personal responsibility and positive societal change is missing on the left. On the other hand, those on the conservative side seem unable to recognize the existence of social oppression and structural injustice within the country's economic system. For the right to call for individual self-improvement and a return to traditional family values while ignoring the effects of poverty, racism, and sexism is to deny reality and simply blame the victim.

The political health of a nation, state, or city depends on informed citizens debating the issues and the best ways of achieving justice and the common good. Such a debate requires not only mutual trust and goodwill among all involved but also a common language, respect for diversity, and agreement on a core of basic beliefs about people, society, and government. Debate, discussion, and decision making can be constructive only within a context of such fundamental agreement. Destructive to this process are those who replace dialogue with monologue, civility with coercion, and reason with slogans and rhetoric.

Political involvement can be tiring and frustrating. Some social workers begin to lose heart when confronted with setbacks. Some who are frustrated by the slowness of change become belligerent toward those who resist their ideas and actions. Such hostility becomes an obstacle to real change. In order to continue working for desirable social and community change, year after year, social workers must strive to develop personal qualities of hopefulness, patience, perseverance, and tolerance. It is important to adhere to the following guidelines:

- Hold to your principles without being ideological.
- Be political without being partisan.
- Be respectful of those with whom you disagree without being soft or compromising.
- Be active and engaged without being used and manipulated.

Many social workers are in a position to identify responsible leaders and support their election to public office or seek office themselves. They are also able to observe the actual impact of social policies and programs on the lives of people. These direct observations are rarely available to the politicians who consider legislation and the administrators who develop policy and design programs. Thus, the social worker has both the opportunity and the obligation to document and communicate the effects of social legislation and administrative decisions, as well as to offer ideas on how policies and programs can be made more humane, effective, and efficient. Social workers with special abilities to speak and write can make valuable contributions to the education of decision makers and the citizenry.

The Interplay of One's Personal and Professional Lives

Social workers often receive intangible gifts from their clients. For example, workers often meet people who have overcome great obstacles and who care deeply about their families and communities. Getting to know such people can be an inspiring and life-changing experience. On the other hand, social work is often stressful and requires a heavy commitment of time and energy. Those factors also affect social workers and sometimes their families and friends.

Being Changed by Clients

In every type of agency setting, social workers will meet clients who are truly remarkable because of their courage, wisdom, compassion, and generosity. Some have survived and overcome great hardships and trauma. Such encounters are memorable and uplifting. One of the great privileges of social work practice is the opportunity to meet these individuals and learn from them. Social workers open themselves to learning when they set aside their desire to learn about their clients and, instead, seek to learn from their clients. In a real sense, the professional relationship is an exchange of gifts, and both the social worker and client stand to be changed by what they give and receive.

One cannot begin to really know a client without coming to understand how that individual thinks and feels about life. In many cases, the client's perspectives, beliefs, and values will be significantly different from those of the social worker. This may challenge the worker to rethink his or her own life experiences and values. Whenever one begins to understand things in a new way or look at the familiar from a different angle, one begins to change.

The social worker may also be changed by clients who are critical of his or her work. Clients may accuse workers of being uncaring and prejudiced or claim that their decisions are unfair. The worker must always remain open to the possibility that these clients are accurate in their assessments and, if that is the case, strive to modify the attitudes and behaviors that have offended clients.

The clients that cause the social worker great anguish are a particularly painful source of personal change. Not infrequently, the worker's skills and the available resources are insufficient to encourage or help clients make needed changes. When this is the case, the worker must watch helplessly as clients make decisions that get them into trouble with the law, ruin their health, or cause further disruptions in their lives. These humbling experiences teach that even the greatest knowledge and best skills are often inadequate and that a social worker is but one small influence in a client's life.

Personal Responses to the Client in Need

Many of the clients served by social workers live in poverty or suffer other deprivations. They may, for example, experience constant stress because they cannot pay for even the basics such as food and shelter. By comparison, the social worker with only a modest income seems quite well off. This situation confronts the worker with hard questions of individual responsibility. Once a social worker has done all he or she can do as a professional and as an agency's representative, what, if anything, remains as a personal responsibility? Should a social worker use his or her own money to deal with a client's emergency?

Some would answer that meeting basic needs is a community and governmental responsibility and that the employees who work in human services agencies should not attempt to make up for system deficiencies. To even try would be an unfair and unreasonable drain on the employees' fiscal and emotional resources. It might also make it too easy for the community to avoid its responsibility to correct inadequacies in the system.

Others might answer that even when our social welfare systems fail to meet basic needs, the individual social worker still has a moral and ethical responsibility to respond personally in certain cases. They might further argue that a social worker, because of his or her knowledge, has a unique obligation that is above and beyond that of the ordinary citizen.

Ultimately, one's answer is a matter of conscience and a judgment call concerning what action would be helpful to the client and reasonable and proper for the social worker. The social worker might consider the following questions in formulating his or her response:

- After all possible sources of assistance have been explored but are unable to address the client's needs, does the social worker, as an individual, have an obligation to do something more?
- What situations, if any, require some extraordinary and personal response? What if the situation involves a person who is especially vulnerable, such as a young child or a person who is sick or at risk of being injured?
- Is a personal response realistic for a social worker who encounters truly desperate situations on a daily basis? If a personal response is not reasonable, is some type of political or community action required?
- Is it appropriate for a social worker to make a personal contribution to a client (e.g., buy food, pay for a night's lodging, pay cab fare, etc.)? If yes, under what conditions and how is this to be done? If one decides to make a personal contribution, should it be done in a way that keeps the donor's identity confidential so as to maintain a proper boundary between worker and client and so the client is not placed in a position of feeling obligated to a particular worker?
- What personal, ethical, and legal pitfalls await the social worker who makes a donation directly to a client? What are the advantages and disadvantages of an agency having a policy on whether, when, and how a personal contribution is to occur? Is it appropriate for the workers of an agency to create and donate to a special, nonagency emergency fund?

The Social Worker's Family

It is difficult to keep work-related concerns from adversely affecting one's personal life and family relationships. It is also difficult to keep one's personal and family problems from affecting professional performance. Nevertheless, social workers must strive to maintain a healthy separation.

Social workers, like everyone, experience personal and family problems. Sometimes the problems are serious and create much stress, anxiety, or depression.

When worry associated with personal concerns is added to the stress of practice, the social worker may become overwhelmed. During these times, the social worker needs the support of colleagues and friends and must be open to guidance provided by those able to see more objectively what is happening.

The social worker must protect his or her personal and family relationships from being adversely affected by work-related responsibilities. The daily transitions between one's family relationships and the often harsh realities and tension-filled relationships encountered at work can be difficult. The norms and expectations of these two environments are quite different.

Those who provide direct services to seriously troubled and highly dysfunctional clients will observe behaviors and situations that can only be described as bizarre, cruel, and/or depraved. Long-term exposure to such behavior and circumstances can distort one's moral compass and beliefs concerning what is socially acceptable and right and wrong. In an adult correctional setting, for example, the daily exposure to intimidation, violence, and manipulation can dull one's sensitivity and gradually increase one's tolerance for abuse and inhumane treatment. Skewed views on what is usual and normal, if brought home to one's family or into one's friendships, can strain those relationships.

A Fitness Program for the Social Worker

To be of maximum assistance to clients, a social worker must be able to maintain a proper boundary in professional relationships. The worker's need for meaningful relationships and friendships must be met outside of professional relationships with clients. In addition, effective practice requires that the worker be intellectually alert and physically, emotionally, and spiritually healthy.

Friendships and Community

Good friends provide us with support and encouragement and help us to examine our assumptions, test reality, and maintain perspective. Good friends also provide constructive criticism when we behave inappropriately. Because people tend to choose friends who are similar to themselves in age, interests, and socioeconomic status, many friendships develop in the workplace.

All too often, social workers come to believe that no one, except another social worker, is capable of understanding their concerns and frustrations. This role-centeredness in the selection of friends limits exposure to differing points of view and constricts opportunity for personal growth. In some cases, it leads to an "us against them" type of thinking. In addition to friendships with colleagues, the social worker needs to cultivate friendships with people who are from outside the work setting and the profession.

The sense of belonging to a community is increasingly missing in urban society. Many who deliberately seek this feeling are disappointed; too often they assumed that a lasting sense of community could be acquired from a flurry of organizational activity or during a weekend workshop. A genuine sense of community develops slowly. It begins to grow when the members of a group realize that they share the same concerns and interests and that each member is making sacrifices of time, energy, or money to reach a shared goal. Long-term associations, trust, mutual respect, and loyalty to the group are the building blocks of community; there are no shortcuts to achieving it.

Many social workers find a spirit of community in professional associations such as the National Association of Social Workers. This is fortuitous because it helps to advance the profession. However, social workers should also participate in neighborhood activities and local community projects so they meet people who have perspectives different from their own.

Self-Worth and Self-Image

Social work is not an esteemed profession. To a large extent, this is because social work is inherently controversial; it calls attention to problems and deplorable conditions that most people want to ignore. Many of those served by social workers (e.g., the poor, parents who abuse their children, people who are mentally ill, individuals addicted to drugs, the homeless, etc.) are devalued and avoided by the respected and powerful elements of society. In 1973, Richan and Mendelsohn described social work as the "unloved profession." Its status and image has improved since then, but not much.

Given the concerns they address, it is not surprising that social agencies and social workers are targeted for criticism from politicians and the media as well as from clients. These critics discount the profession, its purpose, its values, and its methods. Not infrequently, social workers are blamed for situations that are beyond the control and influence of any one person, profession, or agency. Even when the workers recognize that this criticism is unreasonable or misdirected, it is still painful. Social workers, like all people, want to be understood, valued, and respected.

The social worker must possess a sense of personal worth and dignity that will counter the discomfort of being devalued. That sense of worth can arise only from the worker's own firmly held beliefs concerning the value of the services provided by social work professionals. If the social worker doubts his or her own value or the importance of the profession, he or she is vulnerable to demoralization. No one needs to feel apologetic for being a social worker; the profession's mission, values, and history reflect that which is most noble about humankind.

Physical and Emotional Well-Being

When selecting a practice field and a specific job, a social worker needs to consider his or her physical limitations, disabilities, and health problems, as well as anticipate the normal developmental changes that will occur over the years of work. There must be a suitable match between the worker's physical and emotional stamina and the demands of the job. Physical abilities change over time. As people grow older, their level of energy decreases and they experience some degree of loss in vision and hearing. Even such ordinary changes can affect the performance of specific social work tasks. Family and group therapy, for example, require excellent hearing. Also, one's age can make it either easier or more difficult to build relationships with clients in certain age categories.

For the most part, social work is a sedentary occupation. Inactivity can place the worker at greater risk of heart disease and other health problems. In order to counter this risk, it is important for workers to adhere to a program of regular exercise.

One of the more challenging aspects of this professional role has to do with handling the stress and strong emotions (e.g., sadness, anger, fear) experienced during work with certain clients such as children who suffer great losses, those who inflict injury on other people, or those who verbally abuse or threaten the worker with physical harm. Other common sources of frustration on the job are the limitations of agency resources, the difficulty of adhering to complex agency policies, and the crazy quilt of laws, rules, and regulations. Because of these and other emotional and intellectual demands, along with the typically heavy workload, social work is a stressful occupation. (See Item 10.7 in Chapter 10 for information on stress management.)

Those providing direct services must care deeply about their clients, but this can be a painful experience. Key elements of practice such as empathy and compassion describe the worker's efforts to "be with" and "feel with" the client. In an attempt to cope with the pain and distress they experience when "feeling with" their clients, some workers suppress their own emotions. The frequent and long-term exposure to the pain of others can have a numbing effect on the worker's own feelings. This is damaging, both professionally and personally.

Many clients are so overwhelmed by their problems that they develop *learned helplessness*—a pervasive feeling of hopelessness and a belief that no matter what they do, the pain will continue. Social workers who meet these clients on a daily basis or who work in inflexible organizations are vulnerable to developing this same sense of helplessness. The gallows humor observed in some agencies suggests that the workers are struggling to maintain perspective in the face of human conditions that defy acceptance, but have neither the time nor the resources needed to respond in a truly humane manner.

A social worker must be able to endure the emotional pain and conflict of practice while keeping it from adversely affecting his or her own mental health and relationships with family and friends. Social workers who have not satisfactorily resolved issues in their own family relationships or who carry emotional baggage related to traumatic life experiences are prone to distort and mishandle a professional relationship when their clients are struggling with issues similar to their own. In extreme cases, vulnerable workers have been so knocked off balance emotionally that they could no longer function as professionals. It is critically important that social workers be able to acknowledge their emotional weak spots and, if needed, obtain professional help. If that is not possible or successful, they should arrange for work assignments that help them avoid handling the types of cases that might threaten their emotional well-being. (See Item 10.11 on worker self-awareness.)

Intellectual Growth

Ideas are powerful. One's thoughts can bring joy and comfort and also cause fear and anguish. What people know about themselves and the world around them has a profound effect on the kind of people they become, on what they value, and how they behave toward others.

The United States, and the world as a whole, is changing at a fast pace. Social work practice and agency programs are also changing rapidly. This is due, in part, to the explosion of new information. Social workers are challenged to identify the information that is relevant to their practice and continue their learning while guarding against being exhausted from information overload.

In order to learn, people must allow themselves to feel unsure about what they "know" and open themselves to new and sometimes disturbing ideas. Learning begins with a question and an inner dissatisfaction with one's level of skill or understanding. It continues as the individual searches for answers, either alone or with others. Learning requires a willingness to give up familiar ideas and experience the uncertainty of moving in new directions.

It is hard to imagine a type of work that can evoke as many truly significant and challenging questions as does the practice of social work. The situations social workers encounter each day touch the very heart of questions about social justice; human rights and responsibilities; ethical behavior; the causes of individual, family, and organizational problems; and the nature of personal and social change. However, those who seek to become a social worker must recognize that social work is not an academic discipline nor a pure science wherein the search for knowledge is driven by the excitement of ideas and the joy of discovery. Those who want most of all to acquire a theoretical understanding of behavior and social problems and to build new knowledge are usually not content in the role of a social work practitioner. Social workers spend most of their time trying to patch together practical solutions to very serious but quite common and ordinary human problems, dilemmas, and crises.

Learning and intellectual growth should continue throughout one's life. Unfortunately, many people experience periods of stagnation. Some type of deliberate planning is needed to maintain motivation and momentum. People can put themselves in touch with new ideas and clarify their thinking by engaging in reading and writing, listening to presentations by experts, and participating in thoughtful discussions with family, friends, and colleagues. It is helpful to occasionally place oneself in situations that will generate pressure to study and think. Examples include teaching a class, making a presentation, or writing an article. (See Items 10.4 and 10.5.) Ideally, every new social worker will find a mentor within his or her field of practice who will provide encouragement and direction as the worker seeks to learn a new job or develop his or her knowledge and skills.

It is important to strike a balance between personal and professional learning. Too much attention to professional interests can narrow one's vision. On the other hand, if attention is devoted mostly to topics of purely personal interest, one's professional knowledge will soon be outdated.

Religion and Spirituality

Throughout history, people have sought answers to enduring questions such as these: What is the meaning and purpose of life? How should I live my life? How am I to decide what is right and wrong? Why is there evil and suffering? Why is there goodness and love? How am I to relate to God? Is there a God? These are not questions that the scientific method nor professional knowledge can answer. Rather, they are matters of religious faith, spirituality, and choice. The major religions of the world offer perspectives that have been meaningful to millions of people over thousands of years, but ultimately, each individual must choose his or her own spiritual path.

Although the concepts and experiences of religion and spirituality are intertwined and overlapping, it is helpful to make a somewhat arbitrary distinction. ***Religion*** is a set of beliefs, stories, traditions, and practices that are passed from generation to generation and that nurture and support particular approaches to spiritual growth. A religion provides a language and a conceptual framework for describing and understanding the spiritual life. It is passed from one generation to another by some form of leadership and institutional structure. The elements of a religion typically include public prayer and worship by the community of believers, various rituals that mark transitions in the life cycle, a moral code, and usually a reverence for certain sacred writings and sacred places.

As compared to a religion, which is public and institutional in nature, a ***spirituality*** is more a quality of the inner self or soul—that deepest and most private dimension of our being. Both involve a sense of the sacred and the recognition that there exists some power, life force, or divine being that transcends the material world.

Although most people of the world cannot separate their spirituality from their religion, this distinction is helpful because some individuals appear to possess a deep and active spiritual life but engage in few public and observable religious practices. On the other hand, some participate in many religious activities without seeming to possess much in the way of a deep inner faith or spirituality. Still others attempt to develop a spirituality that is separate from all religion, often because they have been somehow hurt by formal religion.

To a considerable extent, a person's spirituality is his or her unique way of interpreting and assigning meaning to life and living. Our spirituality is our way of life that becomes visible to others in how we respond to other people, what we do with our money, how we react to success and setbacks, and the value and meaning we place on very ordinary aspects and events of living.

Given the fact that a social worker's clients come from diverse backgrounds in terms of culture, religion, and spirituality, a worker must understand and be accepting of how different individuals and groups formulate different answers to questions about meaning and purpose of life and how best to live one's life. Equally as important, the social worker must have grappled with these same questions. In other words, the social worker must be accepting of the beliefs and the spiritual paths chosen by others as well as understand and be comfortable with his or her own beliefs and choices.

As people struggle to make sense of their experiences, especially those that bring great joy or cause great distress, they often gain new insights and their beliefs slowly change. Thus, spirituality is dynamic and an ongoing journey. The deeply religious and spiritual people who describe their spiritual struggles and growth emphasize the importance of occasional solitude for reflecting on life experiences, striving to achieve self-knowledge and self-discipline, providing service to others, developing a sense of humility, and having patience with themselves and compassion for others. They also identify common barriers to spiritual growth such as a desire for control, power, prestige, and possessions, and the fear of change.

One's spirituality must be durable in the sense that it provides meaning, purpose, and direction throughout the life cycle, during both good times and difficult times and especially as the person faces hardship, suffering, and death. A genuine and lasting spirituality is difficult to develop outside of a supportive community made up of like-minded people. Moore (1992) explains:

> Religions around the world demonstrate that spiritual life requires constant attention. . . . For good reason we go to church, temple, or mosque regularly and at appointed times: it's easy for consciousness to become lodged in the material world and forget the spiritual. Sacred technology [e.g., prayer, meditation, solitude, ritual, study, fasting, etc.] is largely aimed at helping us remain conscious of spiritual ideals and values. (p. 204)

As people grow spiritually, they see more clearly that they are capable of great love and generosity as well as hate and selfishness. An important task in one's spiritual journey is to recognize and come to terms with one's own potential to be cruel, dishonest, and destructive as well as one's capacity for self-deception. Kelsey (1981) describes this potential as our "inner murderer": "I have come to trust only those people who are aware of their inner rage, or the murderers within them capable of murdering me. Only those who know their capacity to destroy can keep it in check. . . . If we are to love others it appears that we must know and love ourselves, even the destructive and idiotic parts of us" (p. 18).

Social workers appreciate the complexity of human behavior and the uncertainties and fragility of life. Every day, social workers meet people who have been hurt by acts of ignorance, injustice, discrimination, and violence. In order to cope with the pain and harshness encountered on a daily basis, the social worker must strive to develop a hopeful spirituality—one that views all people, including those that hurt others, as having inherent worth and dignity and capable of positive change. In order to maintain a healthy and positive perspective, the social worker must seek opportunities to observe and to celebrate the basic goodness of people.

Artistic Expression

Another piece of the social worker's fitness program should be to develop and/or maintain his or her own capacities for artistic expression. There is evidence that creative people are effective social workers (see Chapter 3); it is not uncommon to meet social workers who are talented in various forms of artistic expression such as music, painting, acting, creative writing, sewing, photography, dance, woodworking, and so on.

At meetings of the Council of Social Work Education, for example, opportunities for participants to demonstrate their special creativity (i.e., in addition to their creative expression through teaching and practice activities) have become a regular part of annual conferences. In recent years, these programs have included a scene from a play acted by social workers that depicted social problems experienced by the aged, a social worker's photo exhibit that captured the essence of rural poverty, and music (see *Hull House Revival* 1992 and *Concerned in Concert* 1995) and dance performances that not only entertained but also provided expressions of social concern.

It is important for social workers to cultivate and share their artistic talents. Such activities can be a diversion from the stress of practice and a gift that enhances the quality of life of other people.

Having Fun in Social Work

Human beings need to play and have fun. Adults often satisfy this need by introducing various forms of humor (e.g., jokes, kidding, playful pranks, and silly antics) into their work environment. How is a social worker to reconcile his or her need for fun with the serious business of social work? In many ways, the practice of social work is a rather grim and emotionally heavy endeavor. Clients are often in truly desperate and tragic situations, and the helping resources at a social worker's disposal are woefully inadequate. Although human distress is not a laughing matter, humor can be a counterbalance to the frustrations and despair experienced in practice.

Humor is rarely mentioned in the social work literature. This probably reflects a concern that expressions of humor by a professional are easily misunderstood and misinterpreted as insensitivity. For example, Shulman (1991) observes that

> macabre humor is often noted in high stress situations. Workers can joke about events in a way that would shock the public. This humor is often a defense against the pain of the client's problems. It also provides a release for many stresses in the peer system. Unfortunately, when humor becomes a substitute for facing client pain and self-pain, . . . it can be a maladaptive form of coping. (p. 145)

Despite the risks associated with inappropriate expressions of humor, without an active sense of humor, social work practice can be unbearable and social workers can be very boring. Social workers must take their work seriously yet acknowledge and appreciate those things that are genuinely funny about themselves, their jobs, the situations they encounter, and especially their social work professors.

Finding the humor in work requires that social workers not take themselves too seriously. They need to feel secure about who they are and what they do so they can, on occasion, poke fun at themselves, their profession, and their agencies. Humor is a willingness to accept life and ourselves with a lightheartedness. Social workers must allow themselves to laugh at the absurdities of life and temporarily to slip out from under societal demands for conformity and the many restrictions they place on themselves. However, it is important to remember that real humor is an occasional and temporary state.

The use of humor with clients is always somewhat risky, but given proper precautions, it has a place in helping relationships. Often, it is the clients who teach the workers the importance of finding the humor in the clients' situations. It is always wrong to laugh at clients, but it may be appropriate and even helpful to laugh with them as they describe the humorous aspects of their experiences. Humor is an essential coping mechanism that should be affirmed and supported. Many individuals who live with harsh realities come to deeply appreciate the importance of humor as a way of achieving self-detachment from painful situations. For example, Viktor Frankl (1963), a psychiatrist who survived three years in the Auschwitz and Dachau death camps, describes joking and laughable situations in the midst of unrelenting starvation, brutality, and murder.

Humor is an antidote to adversity, stress, and frustration. Social workers, who work with clients facing some of the most difficult issues people can experience, need to cultivate an appropriate use of humor in working with their clients and with their colleagues. (See Item 10.8 for more information on humor.)

Conclusion

Social work practice involves the blending or merging of a unique human being with a set of professional responsibilities. The social worker, like the client and all other people, has many dimensions, such as the physical, emotional, intellectual, spiritual, and social. The social worker responds to his or her professional role and responsibilities as a whole person, and all these dimensions affect and are affected by the moment-by-moment activities of practice.

The social worker may be closely identified with his or her professional role but is not in that role 24 hours a day. He or she has a life, relationships, and responsibilities apart from those of a social worker. Each worker must achieve a proper and healthy balance between his or her personal and professional lives.

SELECTED BIBLIOGRAPHY

Barker, Robert. *The Social Work Dictionary,* 3rd ed. Washington, DC: NASW Press, 1995.

Doelling, Carol. *Career Development: A Handbook for Job Hunting and Career Planning.* Washington, DC: NASW, 1997.

Frankl, Viktor. *Man's Search for Meaning.* Boston: Beacon, 1963.

Hull House Revival and *Concerned in Concert.* Compact disks and audiotapes of performances by social work educators. *Hull House Revival,* 1992, features Kathy Bentley, Fred Seidel, and Dean Santos. It is available from Local Folkel Records, P.O. Box 17196, Rochester, NY 14617. *Concerned in Concert*, 1995, features Phil Brown, Mari Ann Graham, Tom Lawson, Susan Martin Robbins, Dean Santos, and Fred Seidel. It is available from HRI Records, 2503 Cherokee Parkway, Louisville, KY 40204.

Kelly, Anthony, and Sandra Sewell. *With Head, Heart and Hand: Dimensions of Community Building*, 3rd ed. Brisbane, Australia: Boolarong Publications, 1988.

Kelsey, Morton. *Caring: How Can We Love One Another?* New York: Paulist Press, 1991.

Moore, Thomas. *Care of the Soul*. New York: HarperCollins, 1992.

Reid, P. Nelson, and Philip Popple, eds. *The Moral Purposes of Social Work*. Chicago: Nelson-Hall, 1992.

Richan, Willard, and Allan Mendelsohn. *Social Work: The Unloved Profession*. New York: New Viewpoints, 1973.

Shulman, Lawrence. *Interactional Social Work Practice*. Itasca, IL: F. E. Peacock, 1991.

Specht, Harry, and Mark Courtney. *Unfaithful Angels: How Social Work Has Abandoned Its Mission*. New York: Macmillan, 1993.

United Nations General Assembly. *Universal Declaration of Human Rights*. New York: United Nations, December 1948.

Wallis, Jim. *The Soul of Politics*. New York: The New Press, 1995.

Whitmyer, Claude. *In the Company of Others: Making Community in the Modern World*. New York: Jeremy Tarcher/Perigee Books, 1993.

3 Merging the Person's Art with the Profession's Science

In addition to achieving a proper blending of one's personal and professional lives, the social worker must combine his or her personal qualities, creative abilities, and social concern with the profession's knowledge in order to help clients enhance their social functioning or prevent social problems from developing. Each person has unique personal qualities that represent the artistic component of social work practice. Professional education cannot teach these artistic features, although it can help the learner identify such strengths and develop the ability to focus and apply them in work with clients. Professional education can also assist the learner in developing a beginning understanding of the knowledge (or science) that is necessary for effective practice. This merging and blending of one's art and the profession's science is initiated in social work education programs, but it is a lifelong activity, as social work knowledge is constantly expanding and the worker is being continually changed by life experiences.

The Social Worker as Artist

Art is defined as "a specific skill in adept performance, conceived as requiring the exercise of intuitive faculties that cannot be learned solely by study" (*American Heritage Dictionary* 1978, s.v. "art"). One need not look far to observe successful helpers who rely entirely on their artistic or intuitive abilities. For example, natural helpers, volunteers, and untrained human services providers demonstrate daily that even without formal education, they can be helpful in many situations. Similarly, it is not uncommon to see well-educated and knowledgeable people fail in their efforts to serve clients because they lack artistic elements required for their practice.

What factors comprise the art of social work? There are numerous components: the compassion and courage to confront human suffering; the capacity to build a meaningful and productive helping relationship; the creativity to overcome barriers to change; the ability to infuse the change process with hopefulness and energy; the exercise of sound judgment; the appropriate personal values; and the formation of an effective professional style.

Compassion and Courage

A prerequisite to effective social work practice is the social worker's ***compassion.*** The word *compassion* means to suffer with others; it refers to a willingness to join with and enter into the pain of those who are distressed or troubled. Although most people see themselves as compassionate, it is important to recognize that a high level of compassion is not typical of most people. In fact, it is natural to want to avoid involvement in the pain of others. A social worker who lacks compassion is likely to distance himself or herself from client concerns.

Social work also demands personal ***courage,*** not in the sense of being bold or daring but rather in being able to confront on a daily basis human suffering and turmoil and, not infrequently, the negative and destructive behaviors of the human species. Aspects of human behavior that come to the social worker's attention are often ones that are unimaginable and unthinkable to most people in our society.

Day after day, case by case, the social worker must be able to respond constructively to people who are directly affected by disease, disability, violence, neglect, sexual abuse, addiction, criminal exploitation, poverty, bizarre and chaotic family life, separation from a loved one, loneliness, abandonment, and other types of human suffering. Moreover, the social worker must be able to respond constructively to people who have, by their acts of commission or omission, directly or indirectly inflicted suffering on others. They must be able to deal with sometimes appalling human problems without becoming distracted or immobilized by their emotional reactions.

Over time, an individual can develop this fortitude or courage but it is not something that can be learned from books or in a classroom. If it can be learned at all, it is learned from being with those who model an inner strength and a capacity to accept human suffering as part of the human condition and thereby avoid being consumed by anger or frustration. Those who have this courage are able to value and treat with dignity even those who have hurt others.

Professional Relationship

A bond of trust must exist before people are willing to risk that difficult human experience—change. Thus, the most fundamental tool of the trade is the use of a ***professional relationship*** to help people become open to the possibility of change and actively engage in the change process. A positive relationship is a precondition for effective work with individuals, families, or groups of clients, but it is also important in work with the people who make up organizations and communities.

The qualities of a helping relationship are elusive—almost mysterious. For example, what makes it possible for a social worker to somehow enter the life experience of a troubled individual and establish a bond that allows them to work together on making a needed change? Why are clients willing to reveal private information to a stranger? What is it about the presence of a social worker that enables a group of people to take action when they failed to mobilize their resources on previous tries?

The answers are that in all these situations the social worker was able to build and use the power of relationship.

What are the essential qualities of successful helping? Within many Native American tribes there is a saying: "If you want to understand another person you must first walk a mile in his [or her] moccasins." In other words, one must get inside that person's thoughts, beliefs, and life experiences. But before that is possible, one must first set aside his or her own values, attitudes, and judgments. This ability to take on another's perspective is known as having ***empathy.***

Although no one can ever fully appreciate the viewpoint of another person, the social worker needs to get as close as possible to that level of understanding. Empathy is needed, for example, to understand the fear and anger of a battered wife and her possible love and concern for the man who hurt her; to be sensitive to the anger and guilt of an abusive parent; to appreciate the difficulty of a teenager risking criticism by peers for speaking up in a group; or even to hear out the frustrations of an overworked staff member. A capacity for empathy is critical to all social workers, from caseworker to administrator.

Empathy requires an investment of energy; it is difficult to live vicariously—even temporarily—in another person's world. Moreover, it is easier to have empathy for some people than for others. For these reasons, a social worker cannot maintain the same level of empathy for all clients or for the same client at all times. Fatigue and stress, for example, can diminish one's capacity for empathy.

Nonpossessive warmth is a quality of relationship that communicates respect, acceptance, and interest in the well-being of others. However, warmth is much more than just saying "I care," although at times, that is important. Warmth is transmitted in many forms of communication, from a reassuring smile to an offer of concrete and tangible assistance. Warmth is a highly individual quality that is expressed differently by each person, but inherent in all expressions of warmth is acceptance and a nonjudgmental attitude.

Linked to warmth and empathy is the quality of ***genuineness.*** Trite as it may sound, the social worker must behave like a "real" person and must truly like people and care about their well-being. The social worker may know the correct words to say or the proper action to recommend, but the client will assign them little value if the worker appears phony or does not seem to genuinely care.

Creativity

Creative thinking is characterized by the integration of diverse facts and information and the formation of original ideas. Parnes, Noller, and Biondi (1967, 14) describe ***creative thinking*** as "the association of thoughts, facts, ideas, etc., into a new and relevant configuration, one that has meaning beyond the sum of the parts." Creativity is important because each client's situation is unique and constantly changing. So-called textbook answers to human problems are always strained by this uniqueness. Overspecialization can result in a narrowing of vision and the loss of creativity.

A social worker with ***imagination*** can identify a variety of ways to approach and solve a problem, whereas the unimaginative one sees only one or two options—or perhaps none at all. For example, an agency board attempting to improve the accessibility of people with physical disabilities to public facilities might think only of encouraging local merchants or the city parking control office to create more "handicapped parking" spaces. On the other hand, the imaginative social worker might help the board identify additional ways to address the problem. The number of existing spaces may be adequate; perhaps more effective enforcement of parking restrictions is a better solution. Still another option might be to deputize people with disabilities to ticket an auto illegally parked in a restricted parking space. The imaginative social worker might also encourage the board to examine the possibility of increased public information programs, or expanded public transportation, or any of a dozen other strategies.

Another area in which the social worker must be imaginative is in interpreting and implementing agency policies. Policies are created to serve the typical client, yet people are characterized by infinite variety. Although the social worker cannot ethically (or legally) ignore or subvert agency policy, he or she must find ways to adapt or bend a policy to meet unique client needs. The social worker who is bound by a literal interpretation of "The Manual" is simply not able to make the system work for many clients.

Flexibility is also a dimension of creativity. Helping others change requires an ability to understand the situation from the perspective of all those affected and to continually modify and adapt prior plans and decisions. The social worker making a foster home placement, for example, must have the flexibility to appreciate the often diverse perspectives of biological parents, foster parents, the child, the court, the agency, and even the neighborhood. To align oneself rigidly with any of the affected parties limits the social worker's ability to resolve problems and conflicts.

Practice requires that the social worker be flexible in how he or she relates to clients. At times, one needs to be supportive; at other times, it is necessary to challenge the client; and at still other times, the social worker must be hard nosed, be directive, or exercise legitimate legal or professional authority. The effective social worker must be able to shift from one approach to another and correctly decide when a shift is appropriate.

In addition, the creative social worker must possess the trait of ***persistence***—the capacity to continue on a course of action, despite difficulties and setbacks. Self-discipline and goal directness are needed to translate creative ideas into action. The term *flexible persistence* emphasizes the need for both flexibility and persistence in the problem-solving process.

Hopefulness and Energy

The willingness and motivation of a client to work for change, when the prospect of change is often anxiety producing or painful, is often a reflection of the social worker's ability to communicate the perspective that together the two of them can improve the client's situation. Two characteristics of the social worker that are central to increasing client motivation are hopefulness and energy.

Hopefulness refers to a firm belief and a trust in the basic goodness of people, in their capacity to change in positive ways, and in their willingness to work cooperatively with others for the common good. Clients have typically been unsuccessful when attempting other avenues to address their issues or they would not be seeking professional help. Consequently, they often approach professional services with a carryover of skepticism and despair. Given the serious and intractable nature of many of the situations encountered in practice, the social worker, too, is vulnerable to feelings of discouragement. The worker's hopefulness makes it possible for him or her to approach each practice situation with a genuine sense that this helping effort can make a difference.

Energy may be defined as the capacity to move things along, get results, and bounce back from mistakes and failures. The social worker's energy is needed to activate the client or client group and counteract the client's hesitation. One need not assume the posture of an effervescent cheerleader to communicate energy nor should the worker offer a false sense of optimism. To simply reflect one's willingness to commit time and effort to the change process can encourage clients to also invest themselves in that activity.

Judgment

The nature of the helping process and the uniqueness of every client's situation require that social workers make difficult ***judgments,*** including assessing client situations, providing alternative solutions, helping plan and conduct change activities, and deciding when to terminate services. Helping also involves making judgments about when the services needed by the client are beyond the capacities of the social worker. Ultimately, professional judgments depend on clear and critical thinking by the social worker.

The qualifier *mature* is often used to describe the type of judgments expected of a social worker. Two definitions of maturity often become mixed in our thinking. One definition relates to having reached an advanced stage of growth. The second relates to the use of careful and wise consideration to arrive at judgments. Sometimes, we assume that chronologically mature people are better at making sound judgments. This is not so. Certainly, life experience presents opportunities to gain insight, and if one learns from those experiences, then age and wisdom are surely associated. However, some of us are apparently slow learners and the lessons of life have contributed little to our ability to make wise judgments.

Similarly, providing human services over many years affords opportunities to test and refine one's ability to make wise practice decisions. However, the repetition of an experience by itself does not assure that the social worker will gain insight. To grow in practice wisdom, the social worker must be analytical, reflective, and open to learning from successes as well as failures.

Personal Values

The reasons one might enter social work are varied, but the motive is almost always a concern for others and a desire to make the world a better place. No one should have to apologize for such a motive, since most would agree that living a life that makes a difference is what really matters. However, it is important to remember that when a person becomes an instrument for change, there is in that person's mind some notion about what constitutes a desirable and good life for people. In other words, social workers—like all people—possess personal values. A ***value*** is a consistent preference that affects one's decisions and actions and is based on that person's deepest beliefs and commitments. Values are our fundamental beliefs about how things ought to be and what is right and worthwhile.

The dilemma arises when there is a difference of opinion over what is "right." The social worker's view of the "right" outcome or the best course of action may be different from the client's, and both may differ from those who fund and sanction the agency that employs the social worker. Is it "right," for example, to encourage a single mother to find employment if having a job necessitates placing her children in day care? Is it "right" to refer a woman to an abortion clinic? Is it "right" to withhold further financial assistance from a client who has violated an agency rule by not reporting income from a part-time job? Is it "right" to force homeless people to reside in shelters against their will? Whose "right" is right? Whose values are to be followed?

Given that one person's values and conscience cannot serve as absolute guides for all others to follow, is it appropriate to expect the client to conform to what the social worker or his or her agency considers desirable or the right thing to do? Logic would answer no, but there is reason for believing that many clients feel pressured to go along with what they think the agency or social worker expects. If a social worker accepts the principle of maximizing clients' self-determination, he or she must allow clients to make the decisions and to move toward outcomes they believe are most desirable. And apart from those values codified in law and universally recognized moral principles, the social worker should hold his or her personal beliefs and values in abeyance in favor of client self-determination.

This is not to suggest that the social worker is always to remain neutral with regard to client behaviors or decisions that are socially irresponsible, self-destructive, or harmful to others. A social worker is of little help to a client if he or she sidesteps or avoids discussing moral and ethical issues directly related to a client's concerns. Laws, basic moral principles, and even the rules of civility do matter. They are an essential part of our social fabric and of life in a community and they are an important aspect of the client's social functioning. However, when such issues are discussed, it must be done in ways that are nonjudgmental and respectful of the client.

Prerequisite to developing a ***nonjudgmental attitude*** is a knowledge of one's own belief system. As new value conflicts arise, it is important for the social worker to consider what he or she believes about the situation and why. It is useful to discuss values and various moral dilemmas with family, friends, and colleagues to obtain alternate views that might contribute to refinements in one's thinking.

The social worker's personal values should be compatible with the values of the social work profession. If these two value systems are in conflict, one of two things is likely to happen: (1) the worker goes through the motions of being a professional social worker but because his or her heart is not in it, the lack of genuineness is apparent to both clients and colleagues; or (2) the worker rejects the profession's values and principles as a guiding force and responds to clients entirely on the basis of personal beliefs and values. In both instances, the client and the employing agency lose the benefit of the social work perspective.

What are the values that characterize professional social work? The *NASW Code of Ethics* (NASW 1996) is predicated on six core values that drive this profession:

1. *Service.* The primary purpose of social work is to help clients deal with issues of social functioning. The obligation to serve clients takes precedence over the workers' self-interests.
2. *Social justice.* As social workers engage in efforts to change unjust societal conditions, they are particularly sensitive to the most vulnerable members of the population (i.e., those individuals and groups who have experienced poverty, discrimination, and other forms of injustice). In doing this, social workers are committed to promoting public understanding of the effects of such oppression and encouraging an appreciation of the richness to be gained from human diversity.
3. *Dignity and worth of the person (and the society).* Social workers are committed to considering each client a person of value, and therefore treating the client with respect—even when his or her behavior may have been harmful to self or others. At the same time, social workers are committed to improving societal conditions and resolving conflicts between clients and the broader society.
4. *Importance of human relationships.* Social workers understand that relationships are central to human development as well as to a successful helping process, whether serving individuals, families, groups, organizations, or communities. Further, clients are hesitant to risk change unless they are true partners in the helping process, feel supported by a meaningful relationship with the social worker, and maintain as much control as possible over the decisions about how to achieve change.
5. *Integrity.* A helping relationship cannot be sustained unless clients can trust social workers to be honest and to respect the clients' rights to privacy. Moreover, workers are obligated to assure that any human services agency with which they are affiliated treats clients and client information in an appropriate and professional manner.
6. *Competence.* Social workers are committed to bringing the best knowledge and skill possible to the helping process. They are obligated to practice within their areas of expertise (i.e., the social work domain), to search for the best knowledge and skills related to the practice situation, and to contribute to the profession's knowledge base.

None of these values is unique to social work, but the effect of the combined set of values differentiates social work from other professions. Using a different, but similar, list of core social work values (i.e., respect for basic rights, a sense of social responsibility, commitment to individual freedom, and support for client self-determination), Abbott (1988) compares a sample of social workers with members of other professions. Her research indicates that social workers' values are most similar to that of psychologists; are somewhat different from that of teachers, physicians, and nurses; and are quite different from that of people employed in business and industry.

Professional Style

In the final analysis, it is the social worker himself or herself who is the instrument of change and, as such, each social worker has an unique style of practice. According to Siporin (1993, 257), "The social worker's personality, craftsmanship, and artistry in the application of knowledge and skill are articulated through professional and personal styles." One's style can open up and facilitate the helping process or close it down.

Style is expressed in how social workers relate to clients—their energy, creativity, wisdom, and judgment, as well as their passion and commitment to particular social issues. In addition, their uniqueness is expressed in their clothing, hairstyle, posture, speech, and in a hundred other choices and behaviors that send out messages about who they are and what they believe about themselves and others.

One's professional style must be appropriate to the situation, the clients served, and the agency setting. For example, a social worker dressed in a three-piece suit will surely have difficulty establishing rapport with a group of street people, yet may be highly effective in persuading a city council to create needed services for people living on the street. Similarly, a worker might dress casually when working with children and families but should dress more formally when making a court appearance in their behalf.

Know thyself is an important admonition for the social worker. Continuing introspection helps the social worker monitor the impact of his or her style. Knowing oneself is never easy, however. It is helpful for the social worker to step back periodically and examine how others perceive his or her style. Clues from clients, family, friends, colleagues, and supervisors are helpful in making these assessments.

A social worker's practice style emerges as he or she balances individuality with the behaviors required for practice. Inherent in professional socialization is pressure to conform. The need to balance expectations of profession, agency, and clients with one's individuality is an issue for every social worker. The social worker must ask: How far am I willing to compromise my individuality and personal preferences in order to serve my clients and meet agency expectations? So long as clients are properly served and not alienated or harmed, one has considerable latitude. In fact, the profession is enriched by the varied styles of its members.

The Social Worker as Scientist

Social workers must use both heart and head when interacting with clients and providing services. With artistic abilities as a foundation, the social worker builds professional capacity by drawing from the available knowledge about his or her clients and the most effective methods of helping. One form of knowledge, ***practice wisdom,*** is derived from the worker's personal observations and the collective experiences for several generations of social workers who informally share their observations with colleagues. It is expected that professionals will also use tested knowledge (i.e., science). One dictionary (*Webster's New World Dictionary* 1980, s.v. "science") defines ***science*** as "systematized knowledge derived from observation, study, and experimentation carried on in order to determine the nature or principles of what is being studied." Like other professions, social work strives to increase the amount of scientific knowledge available to its practitioners.

The ***scientific method*** is the most accepted approach in Western societies to the study of phenomena and the building of knowledge. In its most rigorous applications, the scientific method involves carefully defining and isolating the problem under study, precisely defining all concepts and terminology used, formulating hypotheses to be tested, following appropriate sampling procedures and an established protocol for gathering data, using control and experimental groups for comparison, using valid and reliable tools of measurement, and, finally, submitting the research findings to scrutiny by professional peers so they can replicate the study and either confirm or repudiate the findings. Although the use of the scientific method is not the only source of knowledge, it is one that helps to minimize errors of judgment caused by bias and subjectivity.

The application of the scientific method is difficult within social work because many of the problems that concern social workers cannot be easily quantified, client confidentiality prohibits some studies, and identical client situations seldom exist for rigorous comparison and testing. Also, for ethical reasons, social workers and agencies cannot assign vulnerable, at-risk clients (e.g., an abused child) to a no-treatment or control group. Single-subject designs may be used or the relative effectiveness of two or more interventions may be studied, but seldom can the effectiveness of an intervention be directly compared to doing nothing at all. Further complicating the use of the scientific method is the fact that the various forms of intervention typically share several common characteristics (e.g., a worker-client relationship), and for that reason it is often difficult to determine the true impact of a single factor or variable.

In addition, many variables cannot be easily quantified or clearly separated from others, principles of client confidentiality prohibit some studies, and identical client situations seldom exist for rigorous comparison and testing. For ethical reasons, the profession may never be a completely scientific discipline, nor should it. Practice wisdom, values, and beliefs also are important elements of social work practice. Nevertheless, the social worker must strive to be scientific in his or her thinking. Social work is not a science to the same degree as, for example, physics, botany, or chemistry. However, social work makes use of scientific knowledge from other fields and increasingly uses the scientific method in developing its theoretical frameworks and evaluating its effectiveness. Social work can be said to be scientific in the following ways:

- It gathers, organizes, and analyzes data that describe the social functioning of people.
- It uses its observations, experiences, and formal studies to create new techniques, formulate new practice guidelines, and develop new programs and policies.
- It uses data as the basis for formulating propositions and conceptual frameworks that guide social work interventions.

- It objectively examines its interventions and their impact on the social functioning of people.
- It exchanges and critically evaluates the ideas, studies, and practices described by others in the profession.

Kadushin and Martin (1988) explain that, like many other professionals, the social worker is more of a technologist than a scientist. "The doctor, as technologist, uses the findings of the biologist, the engineer uses the findings of the physicist and the social worker uses the findings of the sociologist. . . . A social scientist seeks only to understand the world of the client. The social worker, as a technologist, seeks to change it" (p. 3).

To assist clients with problems of social functioning, social workers need knowledge of the social phenomena (e.g., individual, family, group, organization, or community) with which they will be working. Because social workers are also concerned with the social environment of people, they must be knowledgeable about the social conditions in communities, agencies, and the human services delivery system. Finally, because they are representing one of several helping professions, social workers need to have knowledge of the social work profession and possess the requisite knowledge to be effective in social work practice.

Knowledge Regarding Social Phenomena

Given their focus on the social functioning of people as an outcome of person-in-environment interaction, social workers are especially concerned with interactions between and among people and interactions between people and the systems that deliver social programs. Thus, they must understand social phenomena and the various levels of person-in-environment interaction. As described in Chapter 1, each level (i.e., micro, mezzo, and macro) varies in interpersonal intensity and closeness.

In addition to understanding the interrelatedness of the various system levels and the kind of situations being addressed in the social worker's practice, the worker must understand the individual person, for which a knowledge of physical and psychological development (including both normal and abnormal functioning) is essential. The social worker must also understand families and other households. The family has long been a dominant point of intervention for social workers, and knowledge of family dynamics is critically important. With the increase of nontraditional family structures, understanding alternate living and intimacy patterns has become especially important. Further, a considerable amount of practice takes place with small groups, including support groups, therapeutic groups, and committees. Thus, the social worker needs to understand small group behaviors and processes.

The social worker must also understand cultural and religious differences and personal and social issues related to ethnic identity, cross-cultural interaction, and the impact of racism and discrimination. Since people are influenced by the neighborhoods and communities in which they live, the social worker must be familiar with, for example, theories of decision making, intergroup conflict, and community change. In addition, he or she needs to understand prevailing community beliefs and attitudes related to ethnicity, race relations, gender roles, aging, sexual orientation, and disabling conditions.

Most social work practice takes place under the auspices of a formal organization such as a social agency, school, hospital, or correctional facility. The social worker must understand how clients and other members of the community view these organizations and how people are affected by the behavior of organizations. To work effectively within an agency or program, a social worker must understand organizational development, structure, methods of operation, and communication patterns. Indeed, the social worker is required to possess substantial knowledge regarding the people and organizations with which he or she works.

Knowledge Regarding Social Conditions and Social Problems

Social workers must understand the problems commonly brought to the attention of social agencies and how human problems cluster together and overlap. In discussing the problems of adolescent crime, school-age childrearing, school dropout, poverty, unemployment, drug abuse, family violence, and so on, Schorr (1989) states the following:

> Each can be studied separately, but in the real world they interact, reinforce one another, and often cluster together in the same individuals. Increasingly, the individuals also cluster [together in families] and the damage that begins in childhood and becomes so visible in adolescence reverberates throughout a neighborhood as part of an intergenerational cycle of social devastation. (p. 15)

The interrelatedness of human problems is an inescapable fact.

As background for dealing with social problems, the social worker should be familiar with factors that contribute to the overall quality of life on this planet. Some of these are clean air and water, a safe and sufficient supply of food and energy, opportunities for employment, worldwide political and economic conditions that support personal freedom and social justice, the wise use of technology to improve human welfare, success in controlling communicable illnesses and promoting wellness, and a world free of racial hatred and war. In short, the thoughtful social worker possesses a world view.

Social work practice and related social programs and services are particularly influenced by decisions at the national level. When practicing in the United States, for example, the social worker must understand the beliefs, values, and organization of U.S. society and its governmental, political, and economic systems.

Although some social conditions and problems are national and international in scope, others are a function of regional and state characteristics. For example, the market success of Japanese automobiles affects most directly the economy of auto-producing states such as Michigan. Drought conditions or low prices for farm products directly affect people in the agricultural states of the midwest or Rocky Mountains.

Finally, some social conditions affect local communities but not whole states or regional areas. The well-publicized crime rate in Washington, DC, and the high incidence of juvenile gang activity in Los Angeles have dramatically affected those cities, whereas towns a few miles away are relatively free of those problems. Rural areas may also experience locality-relevant social and economic problems caused by, for example, a decline in available timber in Montana and Oregon or the closing of a small town's single industry in Kansas.

When social conditions are perceived as either harmful to people or a threat to the community or the society, social policies may be formulated and social programs created to help those in need or to address the threatening problem. Essentially, a ***social policy*** is a set of principles, usually expressed in law and governmental regulation, that guides the assignment of specific benefits and opportunities or the regulation of behavior. Social policies and programs tend to develop around major problems. Thus, we have policy clusters related to areas such as health care, mental illness, crime, child welfare, education, disabilities, old age, poverty, unemployment, and so forth. Social workers must be familiar with the policies that most strongly influence the programs through which they work and understand their effect on the clients served by those programs.

Social programs consist of three major elements: organizational structure, benefits or services, and providers. Social programs must be delivered through some form of *organization* or *agency.* No matter what service or benefit is provided, there must be an organizational and administrative structure that determines who is eligible, how it will be provided, who will provide it, and what costs are acceptable. Thus, social workers must be knowledgeable about the fiscal, administrative, and organizational aspects of service delivery.

The *benefits and services* provided by a social program can take the form of social provisions, social services, and/or social action (these terms were explained in Chapter 1). The social worker must understand the programs offered by his or her own agency and be familiar with those provided by the agencies to which clients might be referred.

Social programs require *providers,* people who are in direct contact with the client, or the consumers of the services and benefits. Providers may be volunteers, but most often they are paid professionals. Social work is only one of the professions that deliver services and benefits. Teachers, psychologists, physicians, nurses, occupational therapists, and others provide a wide array of human services. Each has its own focus but there are areas of overlap. Understanding the competencies of each profession, as well as the dynamics of teamwork and interprofessional cooperation, are important aspects of the social worker's knowledge base.

Knowledge Regarding the Social Work Profession

The social worker must understand the functions that a profession performs in society and the benefits, as well as the responsibilities, that accrue from this status. When society grants professions the authority to provide the specific services that fall within their domain, in essence, a monopoly is given to that profession to determine the qualifications of its members (e.g., educational and experiential prerequisites for membership). In return, the profession is charged with monitoring and policing its members to protect the public against abuses of that monopoly.

A profession is not so much an occupational activity as it is a means or a social mechanism for controlling an occupation. According to Hardcastle (1983):

> A profession exercises authority over an occupation, and the public recognizes the right of the profession to exercise that control. The rationale for this arrangement, instead of relying upon marketplace authority, stems from other attributes of a profession: a definable, systematic body of knowledge and specialized skills; a regulatory code of ethics; a professional culture or community; and most basically, a service ethic or commitment. This last attribute provides the justification for professional authority and peer regulation. (p. 826)

Social workers have been ambivalent about professionalizing their discipline. They have devoted considerable effort to identifying their knowledge base, creating professional organizations, staking out their domain, specifying criteria for identifying qualified social workers, and taking other steps to become a valued profession. At the same time, they have been uncomfortable about the inherent elitism that characterizes any profession, and have struggled with the conflict between assuring quality services to clients and keeping access to the profession open to as many people as possible.

Professional standards, as defined by the NASW, represent an important feature that has emerged from the professionalization of social work. These standards help both the consumers of social work practice (agencies and the general public) and prospective social workers by designating necessary preparation for various practice activities and specifying personnel standards for organizations that employ social workers. This classification system identifies the requisite educational and experiential preparation at four levels:

> 1. *Basic professional.* Requires a baccalaureate degree from a social work program accredited by the Council on Social Work Education (CSWE).
> 2. *Specialized professional.* Requires a master's degree from a social work program accredited by CSWE.
> 3. *Independent professional.* Requires an accredited MSW and at least two years of post-master's experience under appropriate professional supervision.
> 4. *Advanced professional.* Requires special theoretical, practice, administrative or policy proficiency or ability to conduct advanced research or studies in social welfare; usually demonstrated through a doctoral degree in social work or closely related social science discipline. (NASW 1981, 9)

In its complete form, this classification system elaborates the knowledge and skill the social worker at each level should possess, the kind of responsibilities that might appropriately be undertaken, and the variations in the difficulty of practice activities due to the complexity of the situation, vulnerability of the client, and potential consequences of the practice activity.

Another set of standards was developed by the NASW (1971) to guide social agencies in establishing ***personnel practices*** that support good social work practice.

It includes such items as personnel selection, staff development, worker evaluation, promotion, fringe benefits, and termination of employment. An agency that does not follow these guidelines may be the subject of a complaint and, if found to be in violation after an investigation by the local NASW chapter and the National Committee on Inquiry, may be placed on the NASW's published list of agencies that have failed to operate in compliance with these standards. A study by the National Committee on Inquiry indicated that of those cases of violations of personnel standards that were substantiated through a review process between 1983 and 1993, more than half involved unfair performance evaluations, discharge without notice, or the worker being denied a grievance process (NASW 1995).

It is essential that the social worker possess a thorough understanding of a third set of professional standards—the ***ethical principles*** that guide practice. Ethics are concerned with what is morally right or, in a profession, what is the correct course of professional action. Perhaps no single document is more important to the practice of a social worker than the *NASW Code of Ethics* (1996).

When a social worker joins the NASW, he or she pledges to practice within the profession's ethical code. The NASW uses the *Code* as a standard for determining if charges of unethical practice have a basis. If accusations are made that an individual worker has violated the *Code,* the local NASW chapter and NASW's National Committee on Inquiry may review the complaint and possibly apply negative sanctions to that social worker. The most typical violations of the *Code of Ethics* that were substantiated through this monitoring process involved exploitation of a worker's professional relationship with clients for personal gain, with sexual activity the leading violation (NASW 1995).

Knowledge Regarding Social Work Practice

In a profession such as social work, it is not possible to separate theory from practice or concept from action. In fact, practice is the process of using knowledge and applying theory in order to bring about specific types of change. A practice uninformed by theory tends to become repetitive and sterile, whereas theory uninformed by the realities of practice tends to be merely interesting and usually irrelevant.

The many theories, models, and perspectives discussed in the social work literature can all be considered conceptual frameworks. A ***conceptual framework*** is composed of a coherent set of concepts, beliefs, values, propositions, assumptions, hypotheses, and principles. Such a framework can be thought of as an outline of ideas that help one to understand people, how people function, and how people change. These frameworks are important because they have utility. Consider the following:

- They provide a structure for analyzing complex and often highly emotional human problems and situations.
- They organize information, beliefs, and assumptions into a meaningful whole.
- They provide a rationale for action and decision making.
- They promote a systematic, orderly, and predictable approach to work with people.
- They facilitate communication among professionals.

Social workers use a variety of theories, models, and perspectives. Although these terms have somewhat different meanings, they are often lumped together and simply termed *theory*. However, it is helpful to make some distinctions when describing these conceptual frameworks (see Figure 3.1). Howe (1987, 166) explains that there are theories of social work and theories for social work. The ***theories of social work*** focus on the profession and explain its purpose, domain, and character within a society. They describe what the profession is all about and why it functions as it does. By contrast, the ***theories for social work*** focus on clients and helping activities. They explain human behavior, the social environment, how change occurs, and how change can be facilitated by the social worker in order to benefit clients.

In their work, social workers make use of orienting theories and practice frameworks. Mailick (1990) indicates that ***orienting theories*** describe and explain behavior and how and why certain problems develop. They provide important background knowledge and are usually borrowed from other disciplines such as biology, psychology, sociology, economics, cultural anthropology, and the like. Examples include the various theories related to human development, personality, family systems, socialization, organizational functioning, and political power, as well as theories related to specific types of problems such as poverty, family violence, mental illness, teen pregnancy, crime, and racial discrimination. Orienting theories, by themselves, provide little guidance on how to bring about change. For such guidance one must look to ***practice frameworks.*** There are three types: practice perspectives, practice theories, and practice models.

A ***practice perspective*** is a particular way of viewing and thinking about practice. It is a conceptual lens through which one views social functioning and it offers very broad guidance on what may be important considerations in a practice situa-

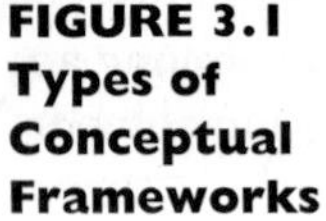

FIGURE 3.1 Types of Conceptual Frameworks

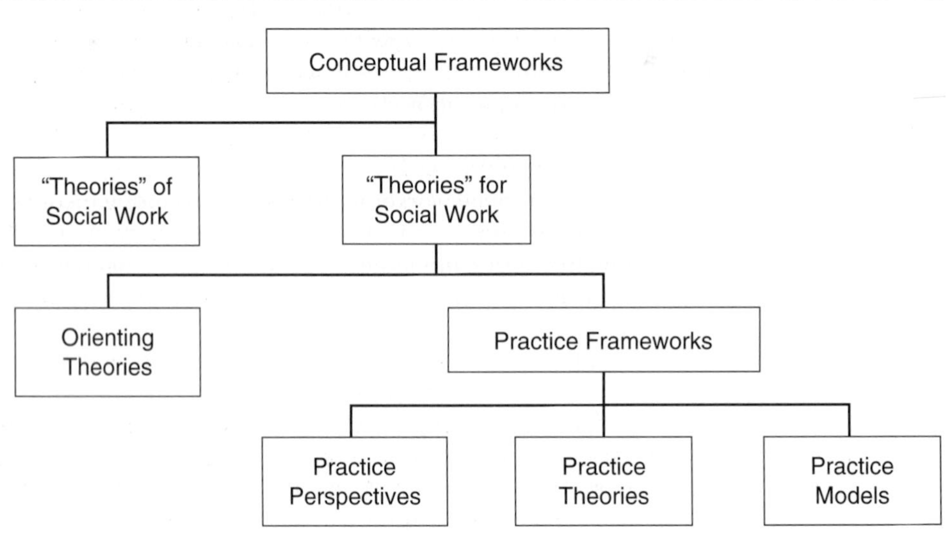

tion. Like a camera lens, a perspective serves to focus on or magnify a particular feature. Two perspectives, the general systems perspective and the ecosystems perspective, are commonly used in assessing relationships between people and their environment. The generalist perspective focuses a worker's attention on the importance of considering several practice roles and various levels of intervention. Others, such as the feminist and the ethnic-sensitive perspectives, remind the worker of special challenges faced by certain groups in society.

A second type of framework, a ***practice theory,*** offers both an explanation of certain behaviors or situations and guidance on how they can be changed. A practice theory serves as a road map for bringing about a certain type of change. Most practice theories are rooted in one or more orienting theories. An example is psychosocial therapy, which is based primarily on psychodynamic theory and ego psychology. Another is behavioral therapy, which derived from the psychology of learning.

A distinction is made here between a practice theory and a practice model. A ***practice model*** is a set of concepts and principles used to guide intervention activities. However, in contrast to a practice theory, a model is not tied to a particular explanation of behavior. For example, crisis intervention is viewed as a practice model rather than a practice theory because it does not rest on a single explanation of crisis situations. For the same reason, task-centered practice is termed a model. Most often, a model develops out of experience and experimentation rather than as a derivation from a theory of human behavior.

The term *model* is also used when referring to a conceptual framework that is borrowed from one field and applied in another. For example, when someone refers to an approach to change based on the medical model, he or she is describing practice activity that mirrors that used in scientific medicine—one that places emphasis on the practitioner as an expert and an authority figure, careful gathering and categorization of data (study), the classification system to properly label the problem (diagnosis), and an intervention (treatment) dictated by the diagnosis. Similarly, social workers may refer to the legal model as a way of describing an approach to social action and client advocacy—one that involves competition and conflict among adversaries. Many innovations in practice are spread from agency to agency by borrowing the essence of a successful program. Thus, we hear such terms as the *Homebuilders Model,* the *self-help model,* the *grass-roots model,* the *12-step model,* the *case-management model,* and so on.

It is rare for a social worker to use a single orienting theory or a single practice framework. Rather, most social workers utilize a variety of orienting theories and a set of compatible and complementary perspectives, theories, and models. Such a combination can be termed one's *theoretical frame of reference* or *theoretical orientation to practice.*

This book presumes that social workers use many of the same techniques and guidelines, regardless of practice perspective, theory, or model. A ***technique*** is a set of actions directed at accomplishing a particular outcome. Although a worker's frame of reference might lead him or her to select particular techniques, they are, for the most part, independent of specific theories. ***Guidelines,*** on the other hand, are typically a mix of prescriptions (do this) and proscriptions (avoid this). (More precise definitions of these two terms appear in the Preface.)

Conclusion

In order to perform effectively, the social worker uses a combination of art and science. It is recognized that a worker brings certain intangibles to the practice situation that affect process and outcome—the art encompassed in building relationships, creative thinking, compassion and courage, hopefulness and energy, using sound judgment, and committing to appropriate values. At the same time, the social worker must combine his or her artistic abilities with the profession's knowledge and scientific base. Without art, the knowledge base is of little value. But without the knowledge, the art is of limited effectiveness.

The social worker merges his or her art and science into a practice framework. Chapter 6 provides descriptions of over two dozen selected practice perspectives, theories, and models that commonly are included in practice frameworks. The intent is not to provide a comprehensive description of any of these frameworks nor is it to provide a complete listing of all those available to the social worker. Rather, the chapter is intended to supply enough information to suggest how practice frameworks differ and what might be required for constructing one's own theoretical orientation to practice.

SELECTED BIBLIOGRAPHY

Abbott, Ann A. *Professional Choices: Values at Work.* Silver Spring, MD: NASW, 1988.

American Heritage Dictionary of the English Language, New College Edition. Boston: Houghton Mifflin, 1978.

Hardcastle, David. "Certification, Licensure and Other Forms of Regulation." In *Handbook of Clinical Social Work,* edited by Aaron Rosenblatt and Diana Waldfogel. San Francisco, CA: Jossey-Bass, 1983.

Howe, David. *An Introduction to Social Work Theory.* Aldershot, Honts, England: Wildwood House, 1987.

Kadushin, Alfred, and Judith Martin. *Child Welfare Services,* 4th ed. New York: Macmillan, 1988.

Mailick, Mildred. "Social Work Practice with Adolescents: Theoretical Saturation." In *Serious Play: Creativity and Innovation in Social Work,* edited by Harold Weissman. Silver Spring, MD: NASW, 1990.

National Association of Social Workers. *NASW Code of Ethics.* Washington, DC: NASW, 1996.

_____. *Overview of a Decade of Adjudication.* Washington, DC: NASW, 1995.

_____. *NASW Standards for the Classification of Social Work Practice.* Washington, DC: NASW, 1981.

_____. *NASW Standards for Social Work Personnel Policies,* Washington, DC: NASW, 1971.

Parnes, S. J., R. Noller, and A. Biondi. *A Guide to Creative Action.* New York: Charles Scribner's Sons, 1967.

Schorr, Lisbeth. *Within Our Reach: Breaking the Cycle of Disadvantage.* New York: Doubleday, 1989.

Siporin, Max. "The Social Worker's Style." *Clinical Social Work Journal* 21 (Fall 1993): 257–270.

Webster's New World Dictionary of the American Language, 2nd ed. New York: Simon and Schuster, 1980.

Part II The Building Blocks of Social Work Practice

Once the social worker is personally prepared to engage in practice, several other factors will shape the nature of that practice. These factors are (1) the roles and functions performed in an agency and with a specific client, (2) the basic principles that should guide each social worker's approach to practice activities, (3) the conceptual frameworks that direct the manner in which clients are served, and (4) the social worker's competence in leading clients through the change process and assisting clients to make decisions that will lead to successful outcomes. An understanding of these four building blocks is prerequisite to the selection and application of the techniques and guidelines described in Parts III and IV of this book.

In Chapter 4, "The Roles and Functions Performed by Social Workers," attention is directed to 10 dominant roles typically performed by social workers. One can readily discern that social work differs from other helping professions simply by examining these roles. Although other disciplines perform some of these roles and associated functions, the collection of roles (e.g., broker, advocate, case manager, social change agent) reflects social work's breadth and its emphasis on helping people interact more effectively with their environments.

Chapter 5, "Guiding Principles for Social Workers," describes 21 fundamental principles that should guide the social worker's practice. These principles provide the "bottom line" for consistently offering appropriate and effective service to clients. To many social workers, the phrases used to communicate these principles have becomes clichés: "Begin where the client is," "Help the client help himself (or herself)," "Guide the process, not the client." The casual use of these phrases too often masks the wisdom of these principles.

A social worker selects and uses specific techniques that have been individualized to the needs and situation of the client or client group being served and to the resources that are applied to help resolve the client's problem or concern. In helping the client formulate a plan, the worker draws on various conceptual frameworks that provide an overall strategy for the change process. Chapter 6, "Practice Frameworks for Social Work," identifies criteria one should consider in selecting practice frameworks. It also highlights the central features of nearly 25 perspectives, theories, or models that are commonly used in social work practice. Although no one social worker is expected to master all of these conceptual frameworks, each should be familiar with these possible approaches to practice in order to help clients connect with social workers who are competent to use the most appropriate frameworks for any practice situation.

Two key elements in successful practice are the social worker's ability to (1) guide clients through the phases of the change process and (2) assist clients in making decisions that will result in enhancement of their social functioning or the improvement of a social condition. In Chapter 7, "Facilitating Change through Decision Making," the five phases of the change process are introduced (to be expanded in the introductions to Chapters 11 through 15) and the importance of critical thinking and good decision making during the change process are reviewed.

By examining these building blocks for social work practice, the foundation is established for the rest of the book. It is within this context that the social worker should select and apply the techniques and guidelines described in Chapters 8 through 15.

4 The Roles and Functions Performed by Social Workers

Every occupational category (e.g., engineer, teacher, farmer, etc.) is expected to perform a set of ***occupational roles.*** For example, when functioning as a physician, an individual is expected to conduct tests to diagnose a patient's condition, prescribe treatment, and monitor the results. Similarly, when functioning as a social worker, an individual is expected to think and behave in a manner consistent with the expectations of a social worker. It is important to note that these work-related expectations are determined by the position, not by the individual who happens to be occupying that position. Although there is individuality in how a person performs an occupational role, there are also boundaries that govern what can and cannot be done.

Associated with the roles are a number of ***job functions*** that can best be described as the tasks or activities one performs within a specific role. This chapter describes 10 roles and nearly 40 distinct functions expected of social workers. In the course of a day, most social workers engage in several practice roles. However, one's personal preferences, talents, or job duties may lead to specialized practice using a more limited number of these roles and functions. To fully appreciate social work, then, it is important to understand the roles and job functions typically performed by social workers.

Defining Professional Roles

The roles and job functions expected of the members of a given profession are defined by social norms and historical traditions, by the legal codes and administrative regulations that sanction the activity, and by agency policy and procedure. In any practice role, the performance of several distinct functions may be required. Similarly, a specific job function may be applied in the performance of more than one role. For example, a social worker might engage in an assessment of a client's situation in the role of a broker of human services, a counselor or clinician, and a case manager. In the following pages, however, each function is described only once.

1. The Social Worker as Broker

Purpose. To link clients to appropriate human services and other resources.

Description. Social work's particular emphasis among the helping professions is to assist people in relating to their social environment. That places the social worker in the position of being the professional person most likely to facilitate linkage between client and community resources (i.e., to bring together a person needing a service and a provider of that service). To carry out the ***broker role,*** the social worker identifies clients' needs, assesses their motivation and capacity to use various resources, and helps them gain access to the most appropriate resources.

As a broker of human services, the social worker must be knowledgeable about the various services and programs available, maintain an up-to-date assessment of each one's strengths and limitations, and understand the procedures for accessing those resources. These resources may include social provisions (e.g., money, food, clothing, and housing) and/or social services (e.g., counseling, therapy, group interaction experiences, and rehabilitative services).

Functions

Client Situation Assessment. The first step in brokering is to understand thoroughly and accurately the needs and abilities of the client or clients. An effective broker should be skilled at assessing such factors as the client's vulnerability, culture, resources, verbal ability, emotional stability, intelligence, and commitment to change.

Resource Assessment. The social worker must assess the various resources available to meet client needs. For his or her own agency, as well as for other community agencies, the social worker must be familiar with what is offered, the quality of staff, the general eligibility requirements, and the costs of those services. Additionally, the social worker must know the best way to help clients gain access to those resources.

Referral. The process of connecting the client to a resource requires that the social worker make a judgment regarding the motivation and ability of the client to follow through and the likelihood that the resource will accept the client for service. Depending on these judgments, the social worker will be more or less active in the referral process. A proper referral also entails a follow-up activity wherein the worker checks to assure the client-resource connection is working to meet the client's needs. If there has been a breakdown, further service may be warranted.

Service System Linkage. Brokering requires that the social worker facilitate continuing interaction between various segments of the service delivery system. To strengthen the linkage among agencies, programs, and professionals, the social worker may engage in networking to establish communication channels, negotiating resource sharing, and/or participating in interagency planning, information exchange, and coordination activities.

Information Giving. Brokering often requires the transmittal of information to clients, community groups, and legislators or other community decision makers. As a repository of knowledge about the service delivery system, the social worker helps others by sharing this knowledge. Also, the social worker may make the general public aware of gaps between available services and needs.

2. The Social Worker as Advocate

Purpose. To assist clients in upholding their rights to receive resources and services or to actively support causes intended to change programs and policies that have a negative effect on individual clients or client groups.

Description. At the heart of social work is advocacy. This role is fundamental to social work's mission and is clearly embodied in the *Code of Ethics* (NASW 1996). For example, Section 3.07 of the *Code* calls for social workers to *advocate* "within and outside their agencies for adequate resources to meet clients' needs" and to assure that the resource allocation procedures are open and fair for all clients (p. 20). At the macro level, Section 6.04 indicates that social workers are expected to "*advocate* for changes in policy and legislation to improve social conditions in order to meet human needs and promote social justice" (p. 27).

Mickelson (1995) defines social work ***advocacy*** as "the act of directly representing, defending, intervening, supporting, or recommending a course of action on behalf of one or more individuals, groups, or communities with the goal of securing or retaining social justice" (p. 95). Social workers must balance their methods of advocacy with the principles of maximizing client self-determination and client participation in the change process (see Chapter 5). To the extent possible, advocacy should take the form of assisting clients to be their own advocates.

Needless to say, advocacy is not usually popular within one's own agency or with the community service system. Nevertheless, advocacy is a necessary function performed by social workers. What is right is not always popular. The social worker should be prepared for negative responses to advocacy activities.

Functions

Client or Case Advocacy. A common goal in this type of advocacy is to assure that the services or resources to which an individual client is entitled are, in fact, received. Such advocacy efforts may be directed toward one's own agency or to others in the human services network. Critical steps include gathering information and determining if the client is, in fact, entitled to the desired service. If so, negotiation, mediation, and, if necessary, more strident and confrontational tactics are used to secure the service. The client is helped to make use of available appeal procedures and, in some instances, to take legal action against the agency or service provider.

Class Advocacy. The social worker must often serve as an advocate for groups of clients or a segment of the population that have a common problem or concern.

Typically, class advocacy entails action intended to remove obstacles or barriers that restrict a class or category of people from realizing their civil rights or receiving entitlements or benefits due them. It usually requires efforts aimed at changing agency regulations, social policies, or laws. Consequently, class advocacy requires activity within the political and legislative arena and building coalitions with organizations that are concerned about the same issue.

3. The Social Worker as Teacher

Purpose. To prepare clients or the general public with knowledge and skills necessary to prevent problems or enhance social functioning.

Description. Much of social work practice involves teaching clients or client groups to deal with troublesome life situations or to anticipate and prevent crises. Some of the knowledge the social worker has gained through education and experience is shared with the client. This is empowering to clients. In the *Social Work Dictionary,* Barker (1995, s.v. "educator role") defines this ***teaching role*** as "the responsibility to teach clients necessary adaptive skills . . . by providing relevant information in a way that is understandable to the client, offering advice and suggestions, identifying alternatives and their probable consequences, modeling behaviors, teaching problem-solving techniques, and clarifying perceptions."

A fundamental purpose of social work practice is to help clients change dysfunctional behavior and learn effective patterns of social interaction. This may require teaching clients to adhere to the various rules or laws and norms of society, modify their immediate environment, develop social skills, learn role functioning, and gain insights into their own behavior. The teaching may occur informally during one-on-one interviews or in more structured educational activities such as presentations and workshops. The teaching method selected is based on an assessment of the readiness and ability of the clients to learn.

The teaching role also has a macro-level application. Social workers should be prepared to engage in activities that educate the public about the availability and quality of needed human services and the adequacy of social policies and programs for meeting client needs. This public education activity lays the foundation for the social worker's efforts as a change agent.

Functions

Teach Social and Daily Living Skills. Teaching skills in conflict resolution, money management, use of public transportation, adjusting to new living arrangements, personal care and hygiene, and effective communication are examples of activities regularly engaged in by some social workers.

Facilitate Behavior Change. The social worker may use intervention approaches such as role modeling, values clarification, and behavior modification in teaching clients more effective interpersonal behaviors. When dealing with larger social systems, the social worker may, for example, educate a board of directors about an emerging social issue or teach a client advocacy group how to redesign a change strategy that is failing.

Primary Prevention. Throughout its history, the social work profession has been mostly concerned with addressing and modifying serious human problems and conditions. In recent years, social workers have given greater attention to primary prevention (i.e., preventing the development of problems). Many such prevention efforts place the social worker in the role of a teacher or even a public educator. Examples include such activities as providing premarital counseling, teaching parenting skills, offering information on family planning, and informing the public of ways to address a social problem or issue (see Item 13.12).

4. The Social Worker as Counselor/Clinician

Purpose. To help clients improve their social functioning by helping them better understand their feelings, modify their behaviors, and learn to cope with problematic situations.

Description. Perhaps the most visible and frequently performed social work role is that of counselor or clinician. According to the National Association of Social Workers (1984):

> ***Clinical social work*** shares with all social work practice the goal of enhancement and maintenance of psychosocial functioning of individuals, families, and small groups. Clinical social work practice is the professional application of social work theory and methods to the treatment and prevention of psychosocial dysfunction, disability, or impairment, including emotional and mental disorders. . . . Clinical social work includes interventions directed to interpersonal interactions, intrapsychic dynamics, and life-support and management issues. (p. 4)

In order to perform this role, the social worker needs a knowledge of human behavior and an understanding of how the social environment impacts on people, an ability to assess client needs and functioning and to make judgments about what interventions can help clients deal with these stresses, skill in applying intervention techniques, and the ability to guide clients through the change process.

Functions

Psychosocial Assessment and Diagnosis. The clients' situations must be thoroughly understood and their motivation, capacities, and opportunities for change assessed. This involves selecting conceptual frameworks to organize the information in ways that promote an understanding of both the client and the social environment in order to produce a workable action plan. The labeling and categorizing process inherent in diagnosis is necessary in some settings for purposes of interprofessional communication, research, program planning, and obtaining payment for services provided.

Ongoing Stabilizing Care. The counselor/clinician role does not always involve efforts to change the client or social situation. Sometimes it consists of providing support or care on an extended basis. For example, counseling people who are severely disabled or terminally ill—or working with their families—may involve efforts to increase their choices and help them to more comfortably deal with difficult but unchangeable situations or conditions.

Social Treatment. This function involves such activities as helping clients understand the relationships among relevant persons and social groups, supporting client efforts to modify social relationships, engaging clients in the problem-solving or interpersonal change efforts, and mediating differences or conflicts between individuals and/or between individuals and social institutions. Whittaker and Tracy (1989, 9) define ***social treatment*** as "interpersonal helping that utilizes direct and indirect strategies to aid individuals, families and small groups in improving social functioning and coping with social problems." Direct strategies might include face-to-face meetings with the client, whereas indirect strategies often involve helping the client negotiate the human services system by using such tools as advocacy, referral, and the provision of concrete services.

Practice Evaluation. At the direct-service level, practice evaluation takes two forms. First, the social worker examines his or her own performance to assess the effectiveness of the interventions utilized. In this way, the social worker can be accountable to clients, the employing agency, the general public, and the profession. Second, the social worker collects data to detect emerging social problems that might need to be addressed by new or revised services and public policies.

5. The Social Worker as Case Manager

Purpose. To achieve continuity of service to individuals and families through the process of connecting clients to appropriate services and coordinating the utilization of those services.

Description. The social work role of case manager is of critical importance for clients who must utilize multiple services provided by several different programs or agencies. This is especially true for vulnerable and highly dependent populations such as children, the seriously disabled, and the frail elderly.

The *NASW Guidelines for the Selection and Use of Social Workers* (1981a, 7) describes the ***case manager role*** as "the activity of developing, implementing, and monitoring a social service plan to meet the needs of an individual or family." There are two basic models of case management. One limits the activities of the case manager exclusively to coordination. In the other model, the case manager, in addition to the coordination function, also serves as the client's primary counselor or therapist. The coordination-focused model is common in fields such as child protection, whereas the coordinator-counselor model is common in mental health settings.

Effective case management requires a social worker who plans ahead and is goal oriented, proactive, and assertive. It requires a professional who can get things done. According to Moxley (1989), activities common to case management include the following:

- Coordinating client-level goals, services, and information.
- Serving as a "fixed point of responsibility" for clients [and for service providers] so they have one specific professional (or team of professionals) to look to for assistance. . . .
- Obtaining access to services for clients who may "fall through the cracks" of a categorical service delivery system, or for clients who may not fit into existing categories because of multiple problems. (p. 16)

Modern case management practice strives to establish for the client *wraparound services*—a package of services selected or created to address the client's unique situation and often paid for with funds drawn from several sources. This is in contrast to an expectation that the client's concerns and situation will fit a preexisting service or funding category. When funds are earmarked for only one type of service, the ability to creatively address the client's concerns is severely limited.

Functions. Drawing on the work of Rothman (1992), Rose (1992), and Moxley (1989), several core functions of case managers can be identified.

Client Identification and Orientation. This involves directly identifying and selecting those individuals for whom service outcomes, quality of life, or the cost of care and service could be positively affected by case management.

Client Assessment. This function refers to gathering information and formulating an assessment of the client's needs, life situation, and resources. It may also involve reaching out to potential clients who have not requested services.

Service/Treatment Planning. In concert with the clients and other relevant actors, the social worker identifies the various services that can be accessed to meet client needs. Bertsche and Horejsi (1980, 96) describe these tasks as the work necessary to "assemble and guide group discussions and decision-making sessions among relevant professionals and program representatives, the client and his or her family, and significant others to formulate goals and design an integrated intervention plan."

Linkage and Service Coordination. As in the broker role, the case manager must connect clients with the appropriate resources. The case manager role differs, however, in that the social worker remains an active participant in the delivery of services to the individual or family. The case manager places emphasis on coordinating the clients' use of resources by becoming a channel and a focal point for interagency communication.

Follow-Up and Monitoring Service Delivery. The case manager makes regular and frequent follow-up contacts with both the client and the service provider to ensure that the needed services are actually received and properly utilized by the client. If not, action is taken to correct the situation or modify the service plan. Typically, it is the case manager that completes the necessary paperwork to document client progress, service delivery, and adherence to the plan.

Client Support. During the time the services are being provided by the various resources, the case manager assists the client and his or her family as they confront the inevitable problems in obtaining the desired services. This activity includes resolving personality conflicts, counseling, providing information, giving emotional support, and, when appropriate, advocating on behalf of clients to assure that they receive the services to which they are entitled.

6. The Social Worker as Workload Manager

Purpose. To manage one's workload to most efficiently provide client services and be responsible to the employing organization.

Description. Social workers must simultaneously provide the services needed by clients and adhere to the ***workload management*** requirements of the employing social agency. In other words, they must balance their obligations to both clients and agency. Although the emphasis on accountability to funding sources has increased in recent years, social workers have always been responsible for maximizing the services provided within an environment of scarcity.

Functions

Work Planning. Social workers must be able to assess their workloads, set priorities according to importance and urgency, and make plans that will accomplish work in the most efficient and effective way possible. They must be effective in managing the typically heavy workloads they carry.

Time Management. If the social worker is to give each client proper attention, priorities for the use of one's time must be set and the working hours carefully allocated. Time management requires that the worker learn to use technology such as word processors and the agency's computer systems.

Quality Assurance Monitoring. The social worker regularly evaluates the effectiveness of his or her own service provision and is also involved in the assessment of services provided by colleagues. These activities might include reviewing agency records, conducting job performance evaluations, and holding performance review conferences with colleagues or volunteers.

Information Processing. Social workers must collect data to document need and service provision, complete reports, maintain case records, and substantiate various expenditures. Further, information about agency regulations and procedures must be understood by all, which requires that workers be skilled at preparing and interpreting memoranda, participating in staff meetings, and engaging in other activities that facilitate communication.

7. The Social Worker as Staff Developer

Purpose. To facilitate the professional development of agency staff through training, supervision, consultation, and personnel management.

Description. Social workers often serve in middle-management positions. In that capacity, they devote a part of their energies to maintaining and improving staff performance. That might involve working with secretaries, receptionists, volunteers, and others, but most often the ***staff developer role*** centers on maximizing the effectiveness of professional helpers.

Staff development requires many of the skills used in the teacher role. In this case, however, the knowledge is transmitted to peers rather than clients or the general public. Staff development is predicated on an accurate assessment of the training needs, with the training taking the form of individualized instruction such as job coaching, supervision and consultation, and/or conducting or participating in training sessions and workshops.

Functions

Employee Orientation and Training. Orientation to the agency and training for specific job assignments are necessary for all new employees and volunteers. Among the tasks required to perform this function are specifying job expectations, orienting workers to the organizational policies and procedures, and teaching helping skills and techniques.

Personnel Management. Personnel management activities may range from the selection of new employees to the termination of employment. Many of these middle-management activities affect the professional development of other workers. For example, the selection of case assignments not only involves judgments about the worker's capacities but also provides opportunity for new and challenging professional experiences. In addition, the staff development role may call for the social worker to allocate funds for attendance at workshops or conferences.

Supervision. This function involves overseeing and directing the activities of other staff members to enhance the quality of services they provide and making sure that agency rules and regulations are followed. It includes such tasks as making and monitoring work assignments, developing performance standards, and negotiating staffing changes to better address the needs of clients.

Consultation. As compared to supervision, which is a part of the agency's administrative hierarchy, consultation is given on a peer level—from one professional to another. The consultee is free to use or not use the advice offered by the consultant. Typically, consultation focuses on how best to handle a particularly challenging practice situation.

8. The Social Worker as Administrator

Purpose. To plan, develop, and implement policies, services, and programs in a human services organization.

Description. In the administrator role, the social worker assumes responsibilities for implementing the agency policies and managing its programs. Skidmore (1983, 5–6) defines ***social work administration*** as "the action of staff members who utilize social processes to transform social policies of agencies into the delivery of social services . . . the basic processes most often used are planning, organizing, staffing, directing and controlling." When performing this role, the social worker might be the chief administrative officer, where administration is one's primary role, or the worker might engage in administrative tasks along with other practice roles.

In the role of administrator, the social worker is responsible for implementing policies, programs, or laws made by others. Agency boards or elected officials typically define agency purposes, establish administrative guidelines, and allocate the funds required to operate the agency. Normally, either the governing board of a volunteer agency or, in a public agency, a body designated by law appoints the chief administrative officer (or executive director) to administer the organization. Depending on the size and complexity of the organization, the agency administrator or a social worker occupying another position in the agency may perform all or some of the following functions.

Functions

Management. The management function calls for the administrator to maintain operational oversight of a program, service unit, and/or the entire organization. It includes such responsibilities as facilitating the work of the agency board, recruiting and selecting staff, directing and coordinating staff activities, developing and setting priorities, analyzing the organizational structure, promoting professional standards within the organization, adjudicating employee conflicts, and obtaining the necessary resources to operate the organization. In addition, management involves budgeting, documenting the use of resources, and arranging for the acquisition and maintenance of buildings and equipment.

Internal and External Coordination. A primary task of the administrator is to coordinate the work of the agency. Internally, this involves developing plans for implementing the agency's programs in an efficient and effective manner. Often, this requires negotiating among several units or programs and working with staff to assure that new programs are understood and integrated into the agency's functioning. The administrator also serves as the primary representative of the agency to external constituencies. These external tasks include serving as a buffer to protect staff from external pressures, negotiating disputes with consumers, and interpreting programs to the community in order to maintain viability. Thus, the administrator is engaged in external work not only with the governing board but is also a key figure in the agency's public relations and communication with consumers, other social agencies, and the general public.

Policy and Program Development. The effective administrator is proactive. Although considerable time and energy must be devoted to maintaining established programs, an administrator should regularly assess the need for new or different services by conducting a needs assessment, being knowledgeable about social trends, generating alternative policy goals for the governing body to consider, and translating new program or policy goals adopted by the governing board into services.

Program Evaluation. Finally, the administrator is responsible for quality control. When overseeing the functioning of an agency, the social worker must monitor and evaluate the agency's programs and collect data that will help document the adequacy of the services and/or suggest actions that might be taken to improve them. Program evaluation, then, is concerned with both program development and program compliance.

9. The Social Worker as Social Change Agent

Purpose. To participate in the identification of community problems and/or areas where the quality of life can be enhanced, and to mobilize interest groups to advocate for change or new resources.

Description. Social work's dual focus on both the person and environment requires that the social worker facilitate needed change in neighborhoods, communities, or larger social systems. The role of ***social change agent*** has been a part of social work since its beginnings. Its inclusion in the social worker's repertoire of practice roles distinguishes social work from the many other helping professions.

When working directly with clients, social workers are in an excellent position to recognize conditions that are contributing to people's distress and the need for human services. The social worker must take responsibility for assuring that resources are available to meet those needs and/or stimulating action by others to address those problems. Social change typically does not occur rapidly or easily, and the authority to make the political decisions to achieve change is rarely held by social workers. Rather, change requires skill in stimulating action by influential groups and decision-making bodies that have the power to address the problems.

Functions

Social Problem or Policy Analysis. A first requirement for social change is to understand the nature of the problem. Trends must be analyzed, data collected and synthesized, and findings reported in ways that are understandable to decision makers. Without this background work, change efforts have little chance of success. The *NASW Standards* (1981b, 16) identify the tasks involved in such analysis as (1) developing criteria for the analysis, (2) ascertaining the impact of the policy on clients and social problems, and (3) analyzing community values and beliefs that affect the issue.

Mobilization of Community Concern. Translating one's understanding of problems into social change efforts requires mobilizing and energizing concerned individuals, groups, and organizations. This might involve encouraging clients, special-interest groups, human services organizations, and/or other citizen groups to address and speak out on the problem. Mobilization for action might involve assembling interested parties and presenting an analysis of the situation, helping expand their understanding of the issues and identify goals they could achieve, aiding in the selection of change strategies, identifying the decision makers who can effect the desired change, and planning and/or carrying out the activities necessary to induce change.

Social Resource Development. The social change agent might also work toward the development of needed programs and services. The *NASW Guidelines* (1981a, 27) describe *resource development* as "the activity of creating new resources where they do not exist, extending or improving existing resources, [and the] planning and allocation of available resources in order to avoid unnecessary duplication of human services [and] . . . increase the effectiveness and efficiency of services offered by a unit, an agency, or a group of agencies." This may involve lobbying and providing expert testimony to legislative committees, or more informal communication with decision makers.

10. The Social Worker as Professional

Purpose. To engage in competent and ethical social work practice and contribute to the development of the social work profession.

Description. Basically, a ***professional*** is a person whose actions are thoughtful, purposeful, appropriate, responsible, and ethical. It is incumbent on the social worker to practice in a manner that reflects the highest professional standards. The social worker must constantly seek to develop his or her knowledge and skills and to examine and increase the quality of his or her practice.

As one who benefits from professional status, the social worker should actively engage in the enhancement and strengthening of the profession. Active participation in professional associations at the local, state, and national levels is an essential component of the professional role.

Functions

Self-Assessment. The autonomy required for professional decision making carries with it the responsibility for ongoing self-assessment. In their national task analysis of social work practice, Teare and Sheafor (1995) found that social workers serving virtually every type of client, working in virtually every type of human services organization (including private practice), and performing virtually every social work role devote a substantial amount of effort to self-assessment and their own professional development based on that assessment.

Personal/Professional Development. The corollary to self-assessment is further developing one's abilities and addressing any performance problems that have been identified. In their job-analysis study, Teare and Sheafor (1995) found that most social workers regularly read articles in professional and scientific journals, newspapers, and magazines related to their job responsibilities; seek critique of their practice from colleagues; and periodically attend workshops, seminars, and other programs intended to improve their job knowledge and skills for practice.

Enhancement of the Social Work Profession. Social workers should contribute to the growth and development of the profession and the expansion of its knowledge base. Maintaining membership in the National Association of Social Workers and contributing time and energy to the efforts of NASW to strengthen the quality of professional practice and support legislative initiatives are obligations of each social worker. In addition, social workers should contribute knowledge gained from their practice or research to colleagues through presentations at conferences and by contributing to the professional literature.

Conclusion

The range of practice roles performed by the social worker is large and varied. The effective social worker must master at least the basic job functions associated with most of these roles. The specialist practitioner might develop more in-depth competence in fewer roles, but the generalist social worker, in particular, must seek to expand his or her competence in each.

SELECTED BIBLIOGRAPHY

Barker, Robert L. *The Social Work Dictionary,* 3rd ed. Washington, DC: NASW Press, 1995.

Bertsche, Anne Vandeberg, and Charles R. Horejsi. "Coordination of Client Services." *Social Work* 25 (March 1980): 94–98.

Mickelson, James. "Advocacy." In *Encyclopedia of Social Work.* Vol. 1, 19th ed., edited by Richard L. Edwards. Washington, DC: NASW Press, 1995, pp. 95–100.

Moxley, David. *The Practice of Case Management.* Newbury Park, CA: Sage, 1989.

National Association of Social Workers. *NASW Code of Ethics.* Washington, DC: NASW, 1996.

———. *NASW Standards for the Practice of Clinical Social Work.* Silver Spring, MD: NASW, 1984.

———. *NASW Guidelines for the Selection and Use of Social Workers.* Silver Spring, MD: NASW, 1981a.

———. *NASW Standards for the Classification of Social Work Practice.* Silver Spring, MD: NASW, 1981b.

Rose, Stephen M. *Case Management and Social Work Practice.* New York: Longman, 1992.

Rothman, Jack. *Guidelines for Case Management.* Itasca, IL: F. E. Peacock, 1992.

Skidmore, Rex. *Social Work Administration.* Englewood Cliffs, NJ: Prentice Hall, 1983.

Teare, Robert J., and Bradford W. Sheafor. *Practice-Sensitive Social Work Education: An Empirical Analysis of Social Work Practice and Practitioners.* Arlington, VA: CSWE, 1995.

Vourlekis, Betsy S., and Robert R. Green, eds. *Social Work Case Management.* New York: Aldine, 1992.

Weinbach, Robert W. *The Social Worker as Manager: Theory and Practice,* 2nd ed. Boston: Allyn and Bacon, 1994.

Whittaker, James, and Elizabeth Tracy. *Social Treatment,* 2nd ed. New York: Aldine, 1989.

5 Guiding Principles for Social Workers

Within each profession there exists a number of fundamental principles that guide practice decisions and actions. These principles apply in all practice situations, regardless of client characteristics, practice setting, or roles assumed by the professional. In addition, they are independent of any specific theories, models, and techniques selected in a specific practice situation. ***Principles*** are basic rules or guides to one's practice behavior, but they are not prescriptions that are to be applied without careful and thoughtful analysis.

Social work's practice principles are grounded in the profession's philosophy, values, ethical prescriptions, and practice wisdom. Most are not supported by empirical verification nor are they compiled in a single document. Yet, there are frequent references in social work literature to *the social work practice principles,* as if there is an agreed upon set of practice guidelines that all social workers follow. To the contrary, social work's practice principles are largely unwritten and typically are passed on informally from seasoned workers to those who are entering the profession. They are often expressed as clichés such as "start where the client is" or "accept the client as he or she is." Many of the principles seem so obvious and self-evident to the experienced worker that they often are not consciously taught in professional education programs or during supervision. However, they are central to effective social work practice.

This chapter presents a synopsis of 21 fundamental principles that should guide social work practice. The first 5 focus on the social worker. The remainder are concerned with the social worker in interaction with a client or client group—whether it be an individual, family, small group, organization, neighborhood, community, or even larger social structure.

Principles Focused on the Social Worker as a Professional Person

1. The Social Worker Should Practice Social Work

This fundamental principle seems so obvious that it appears trite. We expect the teacher to teach, the physician to practice medicine, and the social worker to practice within the boundaries of the social work profession. Yet it is not uncommon to find these and other professionals extending their activities into the domain of another profession. This principle admonishes the social worker to do what he or she is sanctioned and trained to do.

As discussed in Chapter 1, social work is sanctioned to focus on social functioning and help improve the interaction between people and their environment—that is the social work domain. The requisite educational preparation equips the social worker with the knowledge, values, and skills to work at the interface of person and environment, and that, more than anything else, is the unique contribution of social work among the helping professions. The social worker is not sanctioned to be either a cut-rate psychiatrist, at one extreme, or a humanistic environmental planner at the other.

Due to areas of overlap, the "turf" problems among the disciplines are difficult enough when each practices within professional boundaries. Such problems are magnified when a member of one discipline strays into another discipline's area of operation. Ethical practice requires that the social worker function within his or her professional expertise. Although individual social workers may have special talents that exceed the profession's domain, the social worker who drifts from the profession's area of focus and expertise deprives clients of a critically important perspective on human problems and change.

2. The Social Worker Should Engage in Conscious Use of Self

The social worker's primary practice tool is the self (i.e., his or her motivation and capacity to communicate and interact with others in ways that facilitate change). The skilled worker is purposeful in making use of his or her unique manner and style of relating to others. One's ability to build and maintain positive helping relationships with clients is fundamental to social work practice.

In professional relationships, workers reveal—verbally or nonverbally, directly or indirectly—their values, life-styles, morals, attitudes, biases, and prejudices. Workers must be consciously aware of how their own beliefs, perceptions, and behaviors may have an impact on their professional relationships, as these personal attributes will surely affect the ability to be helpful to clients. Part of the "art" that the social worker brings to the helping process (see Chapter 3) is his or her enthusiasm for helping people improve the quality of their lives. This personal commitment to serving others often has a religious or spiritual motivation that makes the work, frustrating as it is sometimes, fulfilling to the worker and facilitates communicating energy and hope to the client. A former welfare recipient (Majors 1996) expressed this viewpoint by noting, "I can't use your pity, but I sure can use your passion."

The social worker must also be comfortable with his or her unique personality and be at peace with whatever problems he or she has experienced in life. For most people, acquiring such self-knowledge and self-acceptance is a lifelong journey that requires a willingness to take risks, for taking a close look at who we are can indeed be disquieting. (See Item 10.11 for more information on developing self-awareness.) But the worker must discover and build on his or her special strengths and minimize the impact of deficiencies, identify the types of clients and situations that respond positively to his or her practice style, and develop a pattern of regular, objective, and nondefensive examination of how one's professional self is functioning.

3. The Social Worker Should Maintain Professional Objectivity

By the time most clients come into contact with a professional helper, they have attempted to resolve their troublesome situation themselves—by either struggling alone or seeking assistance from family, friends, or other helpers. Often, these efforts are thwarted by high levels of emotion and the conflicting advice they receive. This may only add to the person's frustration and preclude clear understanding and response to the situation.

The professional adds a new dimension to the helping process by operating with a degree of personal distance and neutrality. Maintaining this neutrality without appearing unconcerned or uncaring is a delicate balancing act. The worker who becomes too involved and too identified with the client's concerns can lose perspective and objectivity. At the other extreme, the worker who is emotionally detached fails to energize clients or, even worse, discourages clients from investing the energy necessary to achieve change. The social worker can best maintain this balance through a controlled emotional involvement.

Further, this professional objectivity is important to the social worker's own mental health. A degree of emotional detachment is needed, allowing the worker to set aside the troubles of clients and society and separate the professional and personal aspects of one's life. Professional objectivity is, perhaps, the best antidote to worker burnout.

4. The Social Worker Should Respect Human Diversity

The practice of social work involves activity with and in behalf of people from virtually all walks of life, most racial and ethnic backgrounds, a variety of cultures and religions, a range of physical and intellectual abilities, both genders, as well as various sexual orientations and ages. Human diversity is expressed in the behavior of individuals, families, communities, and even societies.

The worker must understand and respect such differences and human uniqueness and recognize that what may appear to be deviance or unusual behavior from one perspective may be quite appropriate given a different set of values and life experiences. To the social worker, diversity brings richness to the quality of life. Failure to accept and appreciate difference creates barriers to helping.

Respect for diversity requires sensitivity to the fact that various population groups have had differing experiences in U.S. society. In addition, individuals within a particular group or class may have had quite different experiences from other persons in that group. The social worker, then, must also appreciate the variations within any group and avoid making assumptions about any one person's cultural identity, beliefs, or values on the basis of that person's external characteristics or membership in a particular population or demographic group. Practitioners who respect diversity are careful to guard against jumping to conclusions or making decisions based on overgeneralizations and stereotypes.

5. The Social Worker Should Seek Personal and Professional Growth

Social work is a contemporary discipline. Its focus is on the here-and-now concerns of ever-changing people living in a dynamic environment. Helping people interact more effectively with their environments requires that the social worker be in tune with the world as it is experienced by others. One cannot be empathic and creative in working with a wide range of clients while holding a narrow and uninformed view of life. The social worker must continuously seek growth and development—both personally and professionally.

The rapid growth and change in the knowledge relevant to social work requires constant updating. New concepts, theories, and intervention techniques regularly appear in the literature or are presented at workshops or conferences. The social worker must be current with the professional information. However, the person who becomes immersed in social work to the exclusion of other activities and experiences actually limits his or her ability to be helpful. To appreciate the infinite variety of the human condition, one must understand life from various orientations. Ideas gathered from history, literature, science, the arts, travel, and interaction with a wide range of people are vital to the continuing development of the social worker.

Principles That Guide Practice Activities

In addition to the principles related to the social worker as an individual and a professional person, a number of other principles are concerned with the social worker's intervention with individual clients and client groups.

6. The Social Worker Should Do No Harm

Social work practice is about the facilitation of desired change. However, there is always an element of risk in any effort to bring about change, no matter how well intended or desirable the goal. Because planned change is a very human process, the responsible professional must assume that some mistakes will be made. The social worker must anticipate such possibilities and have a plan for dealing with the things that can go wrong in an intervention. In the effort to do good and enhance the social functioning of people, the social worker must strive to at least minimize any harm.

A social worker's change goals and intervention activities should not damage appropriate and healthy levels of social functioning by an individual, family, neighborhood, or community. Professional actions and the programs social workers implement should in no way discourage or undermine responsible client behaviors nor erect barriers to appropriate social functioning. Furthermore, social workers engaged in efforts to change an unjust condition or unfair social policies must avoid using methods that inflict harm or create conditions similar to those they seek to change. For example, social workers must fight oppression without oppressing others and should fight injustice without being unjust or unfair to those they seek to influence.

7. The Social Worker Should Engage in Conscious Knowledge-Guided Practice

At the very core of society's trust in professions is the expectation that the professional will bring to the change effort the latest and most appropriate knowledge. A social worker cannot possibly stay abreast of all the knowledge that relates to the many dimensions of social work practice. However, the worker is obligated to be familiar with the most current knowledge that directly relates to his or her practice activities and should know how to retrieve needed knowledge in related areas.

A part of the knowledge of social workers is drawn from their own life experiences and, as they engage in social work practice over time, from practice wisdom. Through regular reading of professional journals and books, attendance at professional conferences, and participation in agency staff development programs, social workers can continuously update and expand the knowledge they bring into their practice.

It is also important that social workers are careful consumers of the knowledge available through electronic technology, presented in the social work literature, and discussed at social work conferences. After all, it is the clients that are most at risk if practice assessments and intervention decisions are based on faulty information. Each social worker should be prepared to engage in critical review of social work's theoretical and intervention knowledge before adopting that as a basis for his or her practice activities (see Items 9.4, 10.13, and 10.14).

8. The Social Worker Should Engage in Conscious Value-Guided and Ethical Practice

It is critical that the social worker recognize and address key value and ethical issues as a part of social work practice. Values are at the center of many practice situations. For example, problems for which many clients seek help involve value differences between individuals or between individuals and relevant groups or organizations in their environment. The social worker must recognize that one's values are powerful forces in human behavior. Helping clients clarify and understand value issues in their lives can be a critical step in bringing about change. However, in many cases, if clients are to change themselves or their situations, they must take some action to adjust or adapt their values to be more congruent with those of others in their lives—or learn to help others adjust or adapt their values to be more congruent with those of the client. When working directly with clients, then, the social worker must be sensitive to the value issues that inevitably arise in the lives of their clients.

Organizations and communities also operate from values about who should be served, who should pay for the services, and how the services should be delivered. When engaged in practice activities that relate to the agencies that employ them, the social conditions that exist in the community, or the social programs that are created at the city, county, state, or federal level, the social worker should attempt to understand the values that have affected that situation. Societal problems are often a result of value differences, and an important step in finding solutions to those problems is to address the value issues.

Social workers must also be sensitive to their own values and beliefs and be prepared to suspend or set aside their own preferences and perspectives to avoid inappropriately imposing their beliefs on their clients. Social work practice, however, is not value free. At times, the social worker must take actions to protect the health and safety of others or achieve a broader social benefit than the interests of a single client. Making those practice decisions ethically requires careful consideration. (See Item 10.9 for guidelines that assist in sorting out ethical dilemmas that arise in social work practice.)

9. The Social Worker Should Be Concerned with the Whole Person

Most professions focus on a single dimension of the person. Physicians are primarily interested in physical well-being, teachers focus on intellectual development, and psychologists are concerned with emotional and cognitive processes. Social work, however, is unique among the professions because of its concern for the whole person—biological, psychological, social, and spiritual. For the social worker, practice activities rarely relate to a single dimension of human life and living.

Concern for the whole person requires attention to the client's past, present, and future. It requires the social worker to look beyond the client's immediate or presenting problem and be alert to the possible existence of other issues, ranging from a lack of food and shelter to a lack of meaning and purpose in life. The social worker must focus attention on both the client's problems and strengths. He or she must attend to the client's presenting problem or concern and to possible underlying causative factors (i.e., the symptoms as well as their causes). In keeping with the person-in-environment construct, the social worker must be concerned with the well-being of the client and also the many other people who may be affected by the client's behavior and by the worker's intervention. Finally, the social worker must be concerned with both the short-term and long-term implications of the change process for both the client and others.

10. The Social Worker Should Treat the Client with Dignity

Philosophically, the social worker must accept the proposition that each person or group deserves to be treated with dignity, respect, and understanding. The phrase "accept the client as he or she is" reminds and encourages the social worker to approach clients as people with dignity who deserve respect, regardless of behavior, appearances, or circumstances. Biestek (1957, 72) describes ***acceptance*** as occurring when the worker "perceives the client as he really is, including his strengths and weaknesses, his congenial and uncongenial qualities, his positive and negative feelings, his constructive and destructive attitudes and behavior, maintaining all the time a sense of the client's innate dignity and personal worth."

Communicating acceptance and respect requires that the social worker avoid making moral judgments concerning clients. The worker's nonjudgmental attitude helps clients overcome the common fear of being judged by others and frees up the helping relationship for positive action. Treating the client with dignity helps guard against the inappropriate intrusion of the social worker's biases into the client's life. Weick, Rapp, Sullivan, and Kisthardt (1989, 353) observe that the importance of acceptance and the nonjudgmental attitude in practice rests on the belief that people have "an inner wisdom about what they need and that ultimately, people make choices based on their own best sense of what will meet that need [and that] it is impossible for even the best trained professional to judge how another person should best live his or her life."

The need to treat each and every client with respect and acceptance does not imply approval of all behavior by a client. One can accept and care for the client as a person of worth and dignity without approving of, for example, illegal, harmful, or socially destructive behavior. The key to adhering to this principle is to remember that the purpose of social work is to help people make changes, and it has been amply demonstrated that acceptance of and respect for the person are prerequisite for change and that condemnation and judgmentalism erect barriers to change.

11. The Social Worker Should Individualize the Client

"Starting where the client is" is frequently the first practice principle to which the social worker is exposed. From the first day in the first social work class, the social worker can expect to be taught that no two people are alike, and therefore the social worker must treat each as being unique. This means that the worker must be in tune with and pay attention to what the client is thinking and feeling and how he or she is behaving from moment to moment and from one session to another. In short, the worker must adapt his or her practice to the unique characteristics of each person, family, group, or community (i.e., individualize the client).

The principle of individualization requires that the social worker be sensitive to each client's unique history, characteristics, and situation. The social worker must also appreciate the differing ability and readiness of clients to participate in a particular intervention strategy. What works with one client may or may not work with others. Individualization asks social workers to be flexible in how they work with clients and what they expect from those with whom they work.

12. The Social Worker Should Lend Vision to the Client

A central feature of professional helping is to bring new ideas, new perspectives, and more effective change strategies to a problem situation. If an individual or group is to invest in the difficult process of changing, they must be convinced that the outcome will be worth the effort. The social worker must introduce and nurture a sense of hopefulness and offer a vision that change is possible and that there are new and better ways to deal with the situation. The client will become more hopeful and more open to change if the worker can display a genuine belief and faith in the client's potential for change, in his or her power to overcome obstacles, and in the capacity to build working alliances with others who can become resources to the client.

While offering new perspectives, encouragement and support, and techniques for change, the social worker must also be realistic and honest about limits and possibilities. Clients are not helped by raising false hopes or by projecting unrealistic outcomes for the helping process. A tempered infusion of energy and vision allows the client or client group to make real progress toward achievable outcomes.

13. The Social Worker Should Build on Client Strengths

All too often, social workers and other human services professionals become preoccupied with client problems and invest considerable effort in identifying all that is wrong with a situation and in describing the specific limitations or deficiencies of a client or client group. Such an essentially negative way of thinking about clients and their situations is reinforced by the diagnostic labels now required for statistical purposes within many service agencies or by insurance companies that pay for social work services. This preoccupation with the negative is so common that it is not unusual, for example, to observe an interdisciplinary staffing in which the client assessment reveals that, when the various disciplines combine their evaluations, the client is more than 100 percent disabled—and that none of the professionals addressed the client's abilities.

For the social worker, it is the clients' abilities and potentials that are most important in helping to bring about change. Since a change in social functioning is largely under the control of the client, it is important to help clients recognize and utilize their strengths. The emphasis on maximizing and building on clients' strengths helps change the tone of the helping relationship from one of gloom over problems and pathology to one of optimism.

14. The Social Worker Should Maximize Client Participation

"Help your clients to help themselves" is a principle based on the belief that if meaningful and lasting change is to occur for an individual, group, community, or other client system, the people who will need to change must be active participants in the change process. It is the responsibility of the social worker in guiding the process to be sure that, as far as possible, all relevant persons participate in identifying the problem, formulating a plan of action, and implementing that plan.

In order to maximize client participation, the social worker should "do *with* the client and not *to* or *for* the client." For example, it does little good for the social worker to construct a sophisticated diagnosis of a client's situation if that client does not understand or accept those conclusions. Meaningful change will occur only when those who must change clearly understand the need for change and are willing and able to take action.

Similarly, an intervention plan is most likely to be followed when it is developed with active client participation. As opposed to the attorney, who single-handedly presents a case for the client, or the physician, who injects the patient with a chemical that can cure an illness with minimal patient involvement, the social worker must assume a very different posture. The social worker must view himself or herself as primarily a collaborator, facilitator, and catalyst. Although situations do arise in which a social worker must act in behalf of clients, the social worker should always seek to maximize client involvement.

15. The Social Worker Should Maximize Client Self-Determination

The instruction to "guide the process—not the client" captures another important principle. This principle maintains that those who must ultimately live with the outcomes of decisions should have the freedom to make those decisions. The job of the social worker is to help clients explore alternatives and the implications of various options but not to prescribe their final choices.

The principle of self-determination must be qualified in its application. It assumes that the client is capable and legally competent to make decisions in relation to self and others. Sometimes that is not a valid assumption. Some clients may not understand the consequences of an action or may lack the mental capacity to make sound judgments and might therefore make choices that are clearly harmful to themselves or others. At times, the social worker must take on a decision-making role for these clients (e.g., children, the person who is mentally ill, etc.). This may involve persuading them to take a particular action, using the authority or power that the social worker's position might command, securing a court order declaring mental incompetence, or, in the most extreme situations, calling for police assistance in order to prevent a tragedy.

The social worker should reluctantly assume the responsibility for making decisions in behalf of clients and then only after careful review of the situation, after consultation with others, and always with the intent of returning that responsibility to the client as soon as possible. In the final analysis, the social worker should attempt to maximize the client's ability to determine his or her own destiny.

16. The Social Worker Should Help the Client Learn Self-Directed Problem-Solving Skills

Most social workers are familiar with the idea of helping people help themselves. Perhaps this should be extended to "helping people help themselves *now and also in the future.*"

Many of us have had the experience of being pleased with our loss of weight only to discover a few months later that we had slipped back into old eating patterns and regained the lost pounds. Similarly, the changes in social functioning made by a client with the assistance of a professional helper can come unraveled unless the client is prepared to sustain that change over time. Ideally, a social work intervention helps prepare clients to cope successfully with future difficulties and to engage in self-directed problem solving when faced with another problem.

Hopefully, what the client learns during his or her interaction with the social worker can be applied to additional concerns in day-to-day living—in the present and in the future. The admonition "Don't do for clients what they can do for themselves" relates to this principle of helping clients learn the skills needed to be independent and self-reliant.

An important aspect of preparing clients for the future is to teach them how to identify and make use of resources that might be found in their immediate environment. Such resources may include family members, relatives, friends, service clubs, and church or synagogue groups.

17. The Social Worker Should Maximize Client Empowerment

Because social workers are committed to serving society's most vulnerable citizens, they regularly work with people who have been victims of various forms of discrimination and oppression. One especially helpful contribution social workers can make to their clients' social functioning is to help them gain increased power over their lives. While some of the principles described here have the effect of giving clients more control over some dimensions of their lives (e.g., maximizing participation, maximizing self-determination, or helping to develop problem-solving skills), a principle that should guide all of a social worker's practice activity is the goal of ***empowerment.***

The goal of helping people, both individually and collectively, to gain power over their lives has been a part of social work's philosophy since its founding. However, use of the term *empowerment* to capture this commitment to working collaboratively with people to attain their goals by increasing their personal and political power to influence their life situations has gained prominence in recent years.

A continuing challenge for social workers is to find ways to empower their clients. This is particularly difficult because many practice models are based on professionals using their expertise to make up for inadequacies experienced by their clients. To empower, a worker must creatively find ways to help individuals and families take control of their lives and assume responsibility for their actions.

18. The Social Worker Should Protect Client Confidentiality

Individuals and families seeking help from a social worker often discuss very private aspects of their lives. In groups, clients may reveal secrets and self-perceptions that could be embarrassing or damaging if made public. The community worker, too, encounters instances when information about individuals, agencies, and organizations must be protected. All social workers must therefore be capable of handling private and sensitive information in a confidential manner.

There are two basic forms of confidentiality: absolute and relative. ***Absolute confidentiality*** refers to a situation when information imparted by the client can never go beyond the social worker. That degree of confidentiality is rare in social work practice. It is only under the protection of some professional licensing statutes that a client can claim a legal right to privileged communication. Most social work practice involves ***relative confidentiality,*** meaning that the most the social worker can promise is to act responsibly within the profession's *Code of Ethics,* adhere to existing laws, and follow agency policy concerning the handling of client information.

The degree of confidentiality that can be provided will, of course, depend on the type of information communicated, the nature of the agency where the practice occurs, the state and federal laws and regulations that govern its operation, and the existence of other legal requirements such as the mandated reporting of child abuse. In correctional programs (e.g., prison, parole, probation), the client can expect little confidentiality. On the other hand, a client who receives social services within a hospital setting will have a much higher level of protection; but even here, a client's records might be reviewed by nonhospital personnel such as insurance companies, Medicaid or Medicare authorities, worker's compensation officials, hospital accreditation teams, and others who have authority to review patient records for purposes of quality control. When it may be an especially important issue for a client, he or she should be advised early in the helping process of the limits of confidentiality the social worker can guarantee.

The social worker must be prudent regarding what information is placed in agency files, and care must be taken in preparing clerical staff to respect the confidential nature of any materials they may type, file, or inadvertently overhear. To protect confidential information, social workers must carefully plan the location of interviews and cautiously select the information to be discussed during professional consultations and in case conferences. Further, clearly separating one's personal life and work life is important in protecting against breaches of confidentiality that might occur when discussing work experiences with family and friends.

19. The Social Worker Should Adhere to the Philosophy of Normalization

Many social work clients have significant mental and physical disabilities. Because of these limitations, they often experience discrimination and social isolation. The philosophy of normalization is a powerful force in efforts to integrate persons with disabilities into the life of the community and ensure that their lives resemble that of the so-called normal person as much as possible. This philosophy originated in the field of mental retardation but has spread to programs serving other groups such as the elderly, the physically disabled, and the seriously mentally ill.

The National Association for Retarded Citizens (NARC) (1973) defines ***normalization*** as follows:

> The concept of helping the developmentally disabled persons to obtain an existence as close to the normal as possible, making available to them patterns and conditions of everyday life that are as close as possible to the norms and patterns of the mainstream of society. Specifically, the use of means that are as culturally normative as possible to elicit and maintain behavior that is as culturally normative as possible. (p. 72)

The term *normative* in this definition can be equated with typical or conventional. This means, for example, that a person with mental retardation should, to the greatest extent possible, live in a typical or conventional home in an ordinary neighborhood. Also, his or her work, recreation, religious participation, clothing, transportation, and daily activities should be as conventional as possible. Likewise, the individual should be able to receive educational, medical, and social services in ways and in an environment that closely resembles how other citizens secure these formal resources.

Horejsi (1979) describes the behavioral rationale for seeking to normalize the life of persons with severe disabilities:

> The principle of normalization rests on the assumption that adaptive or socially acceptable behavior is learned and maintained because the individual has been given an opportunity to behave in conventional ways and that such behavior has been reinforced. Moreover, appropriate behavior is more likely to be emitted and reinforced in a normal environment. (p. 45)

The theoretical underpinnings of the normalization philosophy are rooted in learning theory, especially concepts of modeling and imitation. More importantly, it is a philosophy that recognizes the dignity and worth of all people, regardless of appearance or physical or mental limitation.

20. The Social Worker Should Continuously Evaluate the Progress of the Change Process

The practice of social work is far from an exact science. It involves working with ever-changing people and ever-changing situations. The objectives of helping activities, therefore, must be clearly delineated and regularly reviewed to be certain that they remain relevant to the client's needs. It is not enough to set the course of an intervention strategy and assume that the desired outcome will be achieved. Rather, a continuous monitoring and evaluation of the change process by both the social worker and the client is necessary. To achieve this, both the worker and the client or client group must regularly collect and record data that are indicators of change and these data must be reviewed and carefully analyzed. If the desired change is not occurring, the worker is obligated to try another approach or redesign the intervention.

21. The Social Worker Should Be Accountable to Clients, Agency, Community, and the Social Work Profession

One factor that complicates practice is that the social worker must answer to a number of parties. Practitioners in some disciplines might feel that they are accountable only to the client, but the social worker—working at the interface of person and environment—faces multiple sources of accountability.

Social workers are obligated to give their best service to all clients at all times and therefore must be accountable to those individuals, families, and groups they directly serve. In addition, since virtually all social workers are employed in a social agency or are part of a private practice group, they are also responsible for carrying out the programs and procedures of that organization. Further, for the agency to be accountable to its public, the workers must be accountable to the organization since its reputation, funding, and success ultimately rest with the quality of services provided.

In addition, the existence of a professional monopoly demands that the members of the profession also be accountable to the community. For many social workers, this accountability is formalized through licensing. For others, the accountability is less structured but nevertheless expected.

As clearly stated in the *NASW Code of Ethics,* the social work profession expects accountability to clients, colleagues, employers, the profession, and society. At times, practice situations place the individual worker in a position that makes it impossible to be fully and equally accountable to all audiences. In those situations, the social worker should attempt to maximize the accountability to each.

Conclusion

The new social worker is often inundated with information that reveals, in bits and pieces, the knowledge and values that guide social work practice. Some of this information is formally taught in both baccalaureate and master's degree programs, whereas other information, such as the principles described in this chapter, is typically transmitted in a more subtle and informal manner.

Practice principles reflect that combination of values and knowledge that should underlay all practice activities. If all else fails, the worker cannot go too far wrong if he or she is operating within these principles. They might be viewed as a fail-safe mechanism in social work practice. The 21 principles identified in this chapter represent the authors' efforts to ferret out such principles from the social work literature. With these principles firmly in mind, the social worker is prepared to engage the client in a change process and to identify and select appropriate techniques for addressing the problems or enhancement needs of the client.

SELECTED BIBLIOGRAPHY

Biestek, Felix P. *The Casework Relationship.* Chicago: Loyola University Press, 1957.

Cox, Enid, and Ruth J. Parsons. *Empowerment-Oriented Social Work Practice with the Elderly.* Pacific Grove, CA: Brooks/Cole, 1994.

Horejsi, Charles R. "Applications of the Normalization Principle in the Human Services: Implications for Social Work Education." *Journal of Education for Social Work* 15 (Winter 1979): 44–50.

Lee, Judith A. B. *The Empowerment Approach to Social Work Practice.* New York: Columbia University Press, 1994.

Majors, Barbara. NASW Teleconference. February 9, 1996.

National Association for Retarded Citizens. *The Right to Choose.* Arlington, TX: National Association for Retarded Citizens, 1973.

Saleebey, Dennis. "The Strengths Perspective in Social Work Practice: Extensions and Cautions." *Social Work* 41 (May 1996): 296–305.

Weick, Ann, Charles Rapp, W. Patrick Sullivan, and Walter Kisthardt. "A Strengths Perspective for Social Work Practice." *Social Work* 35 (July 1989): 350–354.

6 Practice Frameworks for Social Work

It is said that there is nothing so practical as a good theory. Some social workers may question that notion when faced with the task of trying to understand and sort out the multitude of conceptual frameworks that are somehow supposed to help them become more knowledgeable, more effective, and more professional. For example, the *Encyclopedia of Social Work* (1995) and books by Brandell (1997), Dorfman (1994, 1998), Payne (1997), Turner (1996), and Greene and Ephross (1991) describe dozens of the frameworks used in both direct and indirect practice. Given the number and complexity of these frameworks, it is understandable why one might get a bit confused. Nevertheless, they are important and their proper application does improve social work practice.

At the end of Chapter 3, under the heading "Knowledge Regarding Social Work Practice," the topic of practice frameworks was introduced and the difference between a practice perspective, a practice theory, and a practice model was explained. The reader may want to review those pages before proceeding. Basically, a ***practice framework*** consists of a set of beliefs and assumptions about how and under what conditions people change and what a social worker can do to facilitate desirable change. Some focus mostly on individual change, whereas others focus on families, small groups, organizations, or communities. This chapter suggests criteria for selection, explains how different frameworks may be more or less useful depending on the phase of the helping process, and provides brief descriptions of commonly used practice perspectives, theories, and models. In each description, an effort has been made to identify the primary reasons social workers use the framework. Key concepts are noted, and a list of suggested readings about each framework is provided.*

Requirements of a Practice Framework

A practice framework should meet the following criteria:

- It should be consistent with the purpose, values, and ethics of the profession.
- It should be capable of being communicated to others (i.e., its concepts, principles, and hypotheses should be clearly described and defined).

*If a reference mentioned or cited does not appear under the relevant list of Suggested Readings, the full citation will be found in the Selected Bibliography at the end of the chapter.

- It should make sense to laypersons (i.e., most clients and volunteers should be able to understand the framework's connection to their concerns and life experiences).
- It should help the worker analyze and understand highly complex and often chaotic situations.
- It should provide guidance and direction during the various phases of the change process.
- It should rest on an empirical foundation (i.e., it should be based on facts and observations).

Because of the wide variety of practice settings, types of clients, and situations addressed by social workers, it is not possible to identify a single social work practice framework that is superior to all others. However, a framework is most likely to yield successful practice outcomes if it encourages the social worker to do the following:

- Focus on those factors, issues, and conditions that can, in fact, be changed and over which the client or the social worker have some influence and control.
- Address both personal and environmental factors in the client situation and make use of both "hard" and "soft" services.
- Display a genuine sense of caring for clients.
- Recognize and build on client strengths and avoid focusing only on limitations, deviance, and psychopathology.
- Be proactive and reach out with offers of relevant and appropriate services.
- Permit the client to make final decisions on the methods to be used in the helping process.
- Offer services and use approaches that are congruent with the client's concerns, values, culture, and religion.
- Offer services for which the costs to the client in time and money are reasonable given the probable benefits or outcome.
- Achieve some immediate success so as to demonstrate the usefulness of intervention and maintain client motivation.
- Facilitate the acquisition of knowledge, skills, and power that will decrease client need for professional and formal resources.
- Encourage and facilitate the use of mutual support and self-help networks and groups in the client's community.

Guidelines for Selecting a Practice Framework

The choice of a practice framework can either enlarge or narrow the social worker's vision and options. Students and new workers especially must guard against becoming locked into a single practice framework and then assuming that it has universal applicability. During their formal education, social workers often become committed to a single theory or modality and remain invested in that approach throughout their professional careers. Such a narrow "have theory—will travel" mentality is both shortsighted and a disservice to clients.

Professionals must also avoid falling into the habit of using practice frameworks in an uncritical manner. The concepts, beliefs, and assumptions that are the foundation of particular frameworks must be continually reexamined and tested against changing times and new research findings. The usefulness and the appropriateness of a practice framework does change over time.

An additional caution is important. Within the human services, the term *theory* is loosely used. For example, some people apply the term to ideas that have no empirical basis or are so vague that they defy verification and testing. Sometimes, the ideas called a "theory" are little more than a description of someone's personal style. The social worker must be able to distinguish between practitioner style and a genuine conceptual framework for practice.

The utility of a given framework depends on the nature of the problems or issues receiving the worker's attention, the characteristics of the clients or consumers, the phase in the helping process, and the setting or organizational context of practice. A framework that is useful under one set of circumstances may be misleading in another. For example, a framework that is helpful in guiding work with voluntary clients may be of little use with involuntary, court-ordered clients. A framework that is useful with teenagers may not be useful with elderly persons, and one that is useful with persons of one ethnic group may prove ineffective when used with clients of another group. When selecting a framework, one must grapple with the question: With what types of clients, with what kinds of problems, in what practice settings, and under what circumstances will a particular conceptual framework provide guidance? In addition, the worker must always ask: Does the framework allow me to address the uniqueness of this particular client or client group? Social workers must beware of frameworks that are either so narrow or so abstract that they no longer describe life's realities as experienced by the clients.

In working with a specific client or client group, social workers may use several practice frameworks together or sequentially. They may shift from one to another as they move through the phases of the helping process (see Chapter 7). For example, the general systems perspective and the ecosystems perspective are most helpful in the beginning phases (e.g., problem definition and assessment), but neither are prescriptive when it comes to the later phases of planning, implementing, or evaluating an intervention. On the other hand, a framework such as behavior modification provides detailed guidance on implementing behavior change, but presumes that a specific behavior will be the focus of the intervention. Questions that a social worker might consider when selecting a practice framework include the following:

1. What is the unit of intervention? Does the framework focus on the individual? Couple? Family unit? Peer group? Organization? Community?
2. What type of client change is expected? For example, changes in values or attitudes? Changes in behavior? Expanded knowledge? Access to new resources? Acquisition of new skills?

3. Does the framework offer an explanation of how and why change occurs?
4. When applying the framework, what is the role of the social worker? For example, is the worker an advisor? Teacher? Counselor? Broker of services? Case manager? Administrator? Planner? Researcher? Advocate?
5. What are the implicit or explicit assumptions concerning the relationship between the professional and the client? For example, consider the following:
   - *Clients as objects.* Professionals are the experts and know what should be done; the clients are expected and encouraged to do what the professionals decide is "best" for them.
   - *Clients as recipients.* Professionals possess and control the services needed by the clients; the clients are expected to utilize the services given to them in a cooperative and appreciative manner.
   - *Clients as resources.* Professionals presume that the clients are in the best position to know what they need and what will and will not work. They actively solicit the clients' ideas on the problems they face and on possible solutions. The clients' thoughts and decisions are respected.
6. What power balance exists in the client-worker relationship? For example, is the worker to be viewed by the client as a friend? Expert? Authority figure? Advisor? Consultant? Companion? Colleague?
7. What is the primary medium of communication? Does the framework rely on verbal exchanges? Expression through art or games? Writing and reading? Precise and planned communication or unplanned and freewheeling exchanges?
8. Does the framework specify when its use is appropriate and effective, as well as when its use would be inappropiate? Are data used to support these beliefs?
9. Does the framework identify types of clients or situations for which use of this approach might be harmful?
10. Does the framework acknowledge the importance and impact of cultural or ethnic differences and religious values and beliefs? Do descriptions of the framework explain how it can be adapted to clients of various backgrounds?
11. Does the framework describe the setting or organizational context required for effective application? Agency-based practice? Private practice? Will the client be seen in an office? In the client's home?
12. Is the framework applicable when the client is involuntary or court ordered? When the client is not cooperative?
13. Does the framework offer an explanation of how it is similar to and different from other commonly used frameworks?
14. Does the framework require the application of a unique set of techniques or are the suggested techniques the same as those used with other frameworks?
15. Does the framework exclude certain clients or situations, either explicitly or implicitly? For example, what about the individual who does not understand the English language? The person who does not read? The individual who cannot or will not attend an office interview? The individual who cannot pay a fee? The individual whose primary concerns are a lack of food, shelter, health care,

protection from harm, and so on? The individual with significant physical, sensory, or intellectual limitations?

16. Does the framework emphasize keeping the client within his or her family and social networks? Or does it emphasize removal of the client from the influence of family, peers, or others in the client's near environment?

It should be recognized that a worker's selection of a practice framework is never a completely objective process. A worker brings subjective factors to the selection process, such as the feeling that a particular approach fits best with his or her practice style or that it works better than other approaches. However, subjective factors alone are not sufficient. By passing the various practice approaches through a screen of questions such as those just described, a greater degree of rationality can be added to the process.

Selected Practice Frameworks

Developing a *practice frame of reference* requires the thoughtful selection of the perspectives, theories, and models that will make up the social worker's repertoire. When first developing one's frame of reference, the worker may adopt only a limited number of frameworks. Gradually, the number can be expanded to fit the needs of one's agency and one's interests and abilities.

To aid in the selection process, a sampling of commonly used frameworks is described next. Each brief description highlights a few key concepts and assumptions that set the framework apart from others. Taken as a whole, these descriptions heighten one's awareness of how different professionals may view the problems of social functioning and how and why they might approach the change process in different ways. These descriptions begin with six perspectives (generalist, general systems, ecosystems, strengths, ethnic-sensitive, and feminist). A sampling of practice theories and models is also provided, beginning with those that are more individually oriented and progressively moving to families, small groups, organizations, and concluding with the identification of a few frameworks used in work with communities. The reader is reminded that no one approach is always best. Most social workers draw ideas and techniques from several theoretical frameworks, and are therefore somewhat *eclectic* in their approaches.

Selected Practice Perspectives

One element of a social worker's practice framework is his or her practice perspective(s). As identified in Chapter 3, a practice perspective directs the worker to focus most attention on certain factors when approaching a practice situation. One or more of the following (or other) perspectives might be selected as part of the worker's frame of reference.

THE GENERALIST PERSPECTIVE

Purpose. To ensure that the social worker will approach every client and situation in a manner open to the use of various models, theories, and techniques and will focus on several levels of intervention, from micro to macro.

Application. This way of thinking about practice is most relevant and most needed during the beginning phases of the helping process, when the problem is being defined and assessed and when decisions are being made concerning what needs to be changed and what approaches might be used. This perspective directs the worker to identify and consider several possible points and levels of intervention and then select the one or ones that are most appropriate and feasible.

Description. Social work practice has been described as inherently generalist (Landon and Feit 1999). According to the *American Heritage Dictionary*, a ***generalist*** is "a person with broad general knowledge and skills in several disciplines, fields, or areas." Thus, the terms *generalist practice* and *generalist social worker* refer to a social work practitioner who has a broad range of knowledge and skills, who draws on several practice theories and models, and who can move with minimal difficulty from one field of practice to another. The opposite of generalist practice is one characterized by specialization, either by type of client served, by method used, by level of intervention, or by primary role assumed by the social worker.

The social worker utilizing the generalist perspective is willing and able to focus on a variety of factors that may contribute to problems in social functioning. These include conflicts among values and beliefs; broken relationships; distortions of thinking; lack of knowledge and information; destructive individual and family patterns; alienation and loneliness; oppression, injustice, and racism; poverty and the lack of basic resources; misuse of power by those in authority; misguided or unworkable programs and policies; and so on.

The generalist social worker is prepared to work with a variety of client systems, such as the following:

- Face to face, one on one, with a single person
- A whole family
- A formed group such as a treatment or support group
- Committees or task groups
- A formal organization such as an agency or a network of agencies
- Legislators and policymakers

Given the wide range of activities, the generalist must be prepared to assume a variety of social work roles. These include, for example, the roles of advocate, case manager, counselor or therapist, group facilitator, broker of service, fund-raiser, program planner, policy analyst, and researcher. The generalist expects to mold and fit his or her approach to the client's unique situation and concerns and to characteristics of the local community, rather than expect the client to conform to the professional's or agency's preferred way of responding.

Based on their study of the generalist conception of practice, Schatz, Jenkins, and Sheafor (1990, 223) identify four elements that most clearly characterize the generalist perspective:

1. *A multidimensional, theoretical orientation that emphasizes an interrelatedness of human problems, life situations, and social conditions.* At the heart of this perspective is the view that both the type and level of intervention should not be decided until after carefully considering the different ways in which the client's concern or problem might be defined and approached. This perspective is especially compatible with both the general systems and ecosystems perspectives as they too assist the social worker in assessing a situation by focusing on system interactions without predisposing that worker toward a specific intervention strategy.

2. *A knowledge, value, and skill base that is transferable between and among diverse contexts, locations, and problems.* The more specialized frameworks may, implicitly or explicitly, prescribe or limit the settings where a worker is prepared to practice or the type of client, problem, or concern the worker is prepared to address. However, the generalist perspective can be applied in any human services organization or geographic context and used with a wide variety of clients and concerns. That transferability has job mobility value to the worker, but is a trade-off for the more in-depth knowledge and skills that are required in specialized settings.

3. *An assessment unconstricted by any particular theoretical or interventive approach.* The generalist perspective requires that the social worker be *eclectic* (i.e., draw ideas and techniques from many sources). It requires that the worker be versatile enough to at least initiate practice activities in a variety of situations. That is not to say that the generalist is expected to be an expert in the application of all theories and models. Rather, the generalist should be knowledgeable enough to know when he or she can responsibly serve the client and when it is necessary to refer elsewhere for more specialized interventions.

4. *Selection of strategies and worker roles are made primarily on the basis of the client's problem, goals, situation, and the size of the systems that are targeted for change.* The generalist perspective calls for the social worker to adapt his or her practice activities to the unique client situation. Sometimes that may require working directly with the client, with key persons in the client's immediate environment, and at other times working to change agency and community factors that affect the clients or the services.

The flexibility offered by this perspective is particularly useful when the social worker's job description demands the performance of multiple roles (see Chapter 4). However, it is recognized that many agencies have missions, job descriptions, and policies that point practitioners in certain directions (e.g., individual change, group services, community development) that may not always make it appropriate to approach practice from a generalist perspective.

Generalist is, perhaps, the most universally held perspective among social workers. The accreditation standards of the Council on Social Work Education (CSWE) require that all baccalaureate programs prepare graduates for generalist practice. Also, master's-level social work education programs are now required to build their more specialized programs on a generalist base and several schools have advanced generalist practice as the primary practice approach for which their graduates are prepared.

SUGGESTED READINGS

Kirst-Ashman, Karen, and Grafton Hull. *Understanding Generalist Practice.* Chicago: Nelson-Hall, 1993.

Landon, Pamela, and Marvin Feit. *Generalist Social Work Practice.* Dubuque: Eddie Bowers Publisher, 1999.

Schatz, Mona S., Lowell E. Jenkins, and Bradford W. Sheafor. "Milford Redefined: A Model of Initial and Advanced Generalist Social Work." *Journal of Social Work Education* 26 (Fall 1990): 217–231.

THE GENERAL SYSTEMS PERSPECTIVE

Purpose. To assist the social worker in maintaining a focus on the dynamic interplay of the many biological and social systems that affect client behavior and functioning.

Application. This way of thinking about clients and their situations is most useful in the beginning stages of the helping process, especially during assessment. Also, given the principle that every part of a system is affected by every other part, this perspective reminds the worker that usually there are several points of intervention and types of intervention that can help client systems to change.

Description. A *system* is an aggregate of interrelated and interconnected elements and activities that forms an identifiable whole. A system has a hierarchic, multilevel structure and displays a particular pattern of behavior. General systems theory seeks to describe the principles by which systems function, grow, develop, and interact with other systems. These principles are used to predict the behavior of biological and social systems and to formulate strategies for changing a system. Systems theory has been attractive to social workers because it provides terminology and metaphors for describing client systems (e.g., individuals, families, organizations) and the process of change.

As just indicated, a system consists of numerous parts. If, for example, a family is the primary system of attention—the *focal system*—it is possible to identify several subsystems: the spouse subsystem (husband-wife relationship), the parental subsystem (parent-child relationship), and the sibling subsystem (child-child relationships). Each system is also part of a larger *suprasystem*. The suprasystem for a social agency, for example, would be the community social welfare system.

A *symbiotic relationship* is assumed to exist among the parts of a system. Each component is, to some degree, affected by all other parts of the system. A change in one part will have an impact on all other parts. Because of this, a social worker's assessment must anticipate how a given intervention will affect others in the client's immediate environment. For example, social workers usually want to work with both the husband and wife when focusing on a marriage problem, recognizing that a change by one will affect the other.

All systems have boundaries. It is a person's skin, for example, that defines the physical boundary of that individual. The boundary of a social system (e.g., family, organization, community) is less distinct. The *boundary* of a social system distinguishes between those individuals who "belong" and those who do not. That determination often requires a judgment call related to the situation being addressed. For instance, regarding a family's plans to purchase an automobile, an emancipated 30-year-old child would probably not be considered part of the system. However, if funeral plans for a grandparent were being made, that same adult-aged child might be an essential component of the family system. All biological and social systems are *open systems,* which means that the boundary is permeable and allows the exchange of matter, energy, and information across the boundary. However, systems vary in degree of openness. Some have such a tight or thick boundary that the system is highly resistant to outside influences. On the other extreme, some have boundaries that are so thin and permeable that the system is so easily influenced by outside forces that it is unstable and is easily destroyed.

Systems are constantly changing and are often more chaotic and unpredictable than it seems. However, systems tend to function in ways that preserve a dynamic equilibrium, or a *steady state,* but these times of relative stability are temporary at best. Although systems naturally seek a certain amount of growth and development, they resist radical change, attempting to maintain a safe degree of sameness. When significant change does occur, the system tends to move rather quickly to a more stable level of functioning, thereby establishing a new steady state. A pattern of ongoing change, then, tends to be one of plateaus rather than progress at a constant pace. It is useful for the social worker to recognize every system's inherent resistance to rapid or extensive change.

The concept of *entropy* refers to the tendency of systems to become disorganized, to disintegrate, or to run down and die. Without a minimum level of organization, a system loses its identity and ability to interact meaningfully with other systems. *Negative entropy* (or negentropy) refers to the forces that preserve the system's organization, promote its development, and keep it alive. All systems need matter (resources), energy, and/or information to counteract entropy and maintain organization. Social work practice often involves helping systems achieve a favorable steady state by preserving or increasing their negentropy.

System functioning includes four interrelated activities: (1) *input* (taking in needed energy, information, etc.); (2) *conversion operations* (activities that process the input and convert it into forms that can be used by the system to sustain functioning); (3) *output* (interactions with other systems); and (4) *feedback* (processes by which the system monitors its own functioning and makes needed adjustments in order to maintain a steady state).

We are reminded by systems theory that cause and effect relationships are complex and not nearly as predictable as we may think. The principle of *equifinality* (same end) tells us that a single effect or outcome may result from several different causes, and the principle of *multifinality* (many ends) helps us understand that a single action (one cause) may produce many different effects or outcomes.

The concept of *interface* refers to the meeting or overlapping of two or more systems. One can visualize, for example, the interface of a family and a school or the interface of a patient and his or her family with a hospital. The social worker works at the interface of these systems (i.e., does "boundary work") in order to improve the interactions between the client system and other relevant systems in that client's environment.

SUGGESTED READINGS

Andreae, Dan. "Systems Theory and Social Work Treatment." In *Social Work Treatment,* 4th ed., edited by Francis Turner. New York: Free Press, 1996.

Greene, Roberta. "General Systems Theory." In *Human Behavior Theory and Social Work Practice,* edited by Roberta Greene and Paul Ephross. New York: Aldine, 1991, pp. 227–259.

Norlin, Julia, and William Chess. *Human Behavior and the Social Environment: A Systems Model,* 3rd ed. Boston: Allyn and Bacon, 1997.

THE ECOSYSTEMS PERSPECTIVE

Purpose. To maintain the social worker's focus on the concept of person-in-environment in a practice situation.

Application. This conceptual lens adds to understanding of the various ways a client system may adapt to a changing environment in order to cope, survive, and compete for needed resources. It is most useful during the phases of assessment and planning because it conceptually places the client system within a situational and environmental context. For example, it reminds the social worker that families must function within and adapt to a certain neighborhood, community, and cultural environment and that the social agencies and social programs designed to serve families must operate and compete for resources within a particular economic and political context.

Description. The ecological perspective draws selected concepts from the science of ecology and uses them as metaphors for describing social interactions and social change. *Ecology* focuses on the relationship between organisms and their biological and physical environment. Smith (1986, 344) defines an *ecosystem,* the unit of study in ecology, as "a partially or completely self-contained mass of organisms . . . [that engages in] energetic interactions and material cycling that link the organisms in a community with one another and their environment." It is this emphasis on concepts of interdependence, exchange, and interrelatedness that has attracted social workers to ecology.

Ecosystems are never static; each species in an ecosystem is slowly but constantly adapting to an ever-changing environment. If the environment changes too rapidly or if the species cannot change fast enough, the species may be overpowered by a competing and more adaptable species. *Competition* among the various species is the major process that shapes ecological communities. As long as commonly used resources are abundant, different species can share them, but since certain resources are usually limited, the species must compete in order to survive.

The concept of *symbiosis* refers to a close and frequent interaction between two species wherein one or both benefit from this interaction. There are three major types of symbiosis. In *mutualism,* both species benefit from the interaction (e.g., bees and flowers). In *commensalism,* one species benefits while the other is neither helped or harmed. However, in *parasitism,* the parasite benefits while its host is harmed. When assessing a case situation, the social worker can use these concepts to understand person-environment interactions and, when planning intervention activities, should attempt to maximize mutualism and commensalism.

In order to become more competitive and cope successfully with a changing environment, a species must be *adaptive.* One form of adaptation is *specialization.* When a species is specialized, it is at an advantage because its specialization has the effect of reducing competition. On the other hand, a highly specialized species is more vulnerable to the effects of a rapidly changing environment. As a general rule, specialization will increase a species' survivability in a relatively stable environment, but decreases survivability in a rapidly changing environment.

The concept of *niche* refers to all the physical, chemical, and biological conditions and circumstances needed by a particular species to survive within its ecosystem. Most plant and animal species are limited to a rather narrow niche but we humans are quite adaptable and can live in a variety of environments, primarily because we use technology to modify our environment and make it more supportive of our goals. Unfortunately, we sometimes modify it in ways that cause long-term damage to our water, air, and land and also destroy the social fabric of communities and cultures.

Related to niche is the concept of *carrying capacity* (i.e., the maximum number of individuals of each species that can live in a particular ecosystem). If the population of a species exceeds the ecosystem's carrying capacity for that species, disease, starvation, and predation naturally diminish the population.

These and other ecological concepts provide new ways of thinking about the functioning of individuals, families, groups, and organizations. The ecological perspective reminds us that people shape their environment and are shaped by it and that problems in social functioning result from people-environment exchanges rather than of only personality characteristics or only environmental factors. Drawing on ideas put forth by Germain and Gitterman (1996), Kemp, Whittaker, and Tracy (1997, 42) explain that from an ecological perspective, social work interventions seek to enhance the growth, development, and adaptive capacities of people; remove environmental obstacles; and increase the responsiveness and nutritive properties of the social and physical environment. Social work seeks to restore the fit or adaptive balance between people and their environment by changing the person, the environment, or both.

SUGGESTED READINGS

Germain, Carel, and Alex Gitterman. *The Life Model of Social Work Practice*, 2nd ed. New York: Columbia University Press, 1996.

Kemp, Susan, James Whittaker, and Elizabeth Tracy. *Person-Environment Practice.* New York: Aldine de Gruyter, 1997.

Meyer, Carol. "The Ecosystems Perspective: Implications for Practice." In *The Foundations of Social Work Practice,* edited by Carol Meyer and Mark Mattaini. Washington, DC: NASW, 1995, pp. 16–27.

THE STRENGTHS PERSPECTIVE

Purpose. To ensure that the social worker is attentive to client strengths during assessment and intervention.

Application. This perspective is necessary in work with all clients and during all phases of the helping process. It is an important counterbalance to the preoccupation with client problems, pathology, and deficits that is so pervasive in the service delivery system and inherent in many of the practice theories and models used by social workers.

Description. The strengths perspective rests on the observation that it is much easier to help a client achieve positive and lasting change by focusing on and building on the client's strengths than by focusing on and trying to eliminate the client's problems or deficiencies. Saleebey (1997, 3) explains that practicing in this way is "a dramatic departure from conventional social work practice. [It means that] everything you do . . . will be predicated, is some way, on helping to discover and embellish, explore, and exploit clients' strengths and resources in the service of assisting them to achieve their goals."

Saleebey (1997, 12–15) has identified the basic assumptions of this practice framework:

1. Every individual, group, family, and community has strengths.
2. Trauma, abuse, illness, and struggle may be injurious but they may also be sources of challenge and opportunity.
3. No one can know the upper limits of a client's capacity to grow and change.
4. Clients are served best by collaborating with them and by taking their stated aspirations and goals seriously.
5. The environment in which the client lives and functions is full of resources.

This approach presumes that all individuals and groups have overlooked untapped reserves of ability, energy, courage, knowledge, experience, fortitude, goodwill, integrity, and other assets. If these strengths are recognized and used in the helping process, they elevate the client's motivation and the possibility for positive change. It also recognizes that in every environment, no matter how harsh, there are individuals and organizations that do care and have something to contribute. Because this perspective views clients as true experts on their situations, the professional's role is mostly that of facilitator or consultant (see Item 12.7).

SUGGESTED READINGS

Cowger, Charles. "Assessing Client Strengths." *Social Work* 39 (3) (1994): 262–268.
Rapp, Charles. *The Strengths Model.* New York: Oxford University Press, 1998.
Saleebey, Dennis, *The Strengths Perspective in Social Work Practice,* 2nd ed. New York: Longman, 1997.

THE ETHNIC-SENSITIVE PERSPECTIVE

Purpose. To ensure that the social worker is attentive to ethnic, cultural, and religious diversity among clients and that the problem and effects of discrimination are addressed in practice.

Application. This perspective is needed whenever the practice involves a client who has a background different from the worker, and especially when there is reason to believe that oppression and discrimination may be related to the client's problem or concern. It is relevant during all phases of the helping process.

Description. The ethnic-sensitive conceptual lens draws attention to the fact that many of the clients served by social agencies are members of an ethnic group; therefore, social work practice and the service delivery system must be attuned to that reality. A client's social class, culture, ethnicity, and religious beliefs have a significant impact on help-seeking behavior and on whether a particular approach—or even a specific type of service—will be perceived as needed, relevant, and useful. It has a bearing on whether and how a client defines a particular situation as a problem, which possible solutions make sense, and how the client expects to be treated by the service system and its service providers.

Norton (1978) observes that every person is simultaneously part of (1) a *sustaining subsystem,* which includes such powerful influences as those of our economic, political, legal, and educational systems; and (2) a *nurturing subsystem,* which consists of a person's more intimate relationships, such as those within one's family, support networks, and neighborhood. Conflict, tension, alienation, and deflated self-esteem can result if there is an incongruence between the values and beliefs represented by a person's nurturing system and those of the sustaining system. Such an incongruence is most likely to occur among minority populations and recent immigrants.

It is increasingly important for social workers to become culturally competent, which Green and Leigh (1989) describe as the ability

> to give aid or assistance to patients or clients in ways that are acceptable and useful to them because they are congruent with the [client's] cultural background and expectations. Ethnic competence also refers to the service provider's ability to learn about the cultural context of a presenting problem and to integrate that knowledge into a professional assessment, diagnosis, and intervention. (p. 8)

If a client's ethnic group is one that has been subjected to oppression and discrimination, the social worker must be alert to client fear and distrust based on prior experiences. (For more information on culture and ethnicity, see Items 8.8 and 12.2.)

SUGGESTED READINGS

Cox, Carole, and Paul Ephross. *Ethnicity and Social Work Practice.* New York: Oxford University Press, 1998.

Devore, Wynetta, and Elfride Schlesinger. *Ethnic Sensitive Social Work Practice,* 4th ed. Boston: Allyn and Bacon, 1996.

Harper, Karen, and Jim Lantz. *Cross-Cultural Practice.* Chicago: Lyceum Books, 1996.

THE FEMINIST PERSPECTIVE

Purpose. To ensure that the effects of societal beliefs and stereotypes concerning gender and sex roles are addressed in social work practice.

Application. This perspective is probably needed whenever the client is a female and always when there is reason to believe that gender discrimination or sex-role stereotyping is related to the concerns brought to the social worker's attention. It is applicable throughout the phases of the helping process but is especially important during problem definition and assessment.

Description. Fundamentally, this perspective seeks to validate the *feminine* dimension of the human person, which finds expression in the value placed on relationships, compassion, cooperation, loyalty, intuition, caring, sharing, and openness. It challenges three assumptions that underpin society's dominant way of interpreting reality and that often give rise to the oppression and exploitation of women: patriarchy, androcentrism, and sexism. *Patriarchy* refers to a way of thinking that places a high value on certain supposedly male characteristics such as rationality, competition, authority, leadership, decisiveness, fortitude, and honor. *Androcentrism* is the belief that the male is inherently more important and worthwhile than the female. *Sexism* refers to an ordering of roles and responsibilities and social and economic structures and opportunities according to gender.

The feminist perspective calls attention to the fact that societal beliefs concerning gender and sex roles and the social policies and programs formulated and designed by male-dominated institutions affect how a client's problem is defined by a professional or agency, the nature of the relationship between helper and client, and the type of assistance or service actually provided. There is a cultural and political dimension to all personal problems, and this is especially true for women. Central to practice based on the feminist perspective is the idea that the helping process cannot be limited to clinical activities; it must also emphasize political action and advocacy to modify social policy and the functioning of organizations and institutions. A feminist therapist, for example, is by definition, also a political and community activist.

Other principles important to this perspective are the following:

- The client–social worker relationship is egalitarian. The helper is viewed as a partner or a colleague to the client, not as an expert or authority figure.
- The client's concerns and problems are assessed within a sociopolitical context. Special attention is given to the assessment of power relationships in the client's life.
- The helper is willing to share relevant personal experiences.
- The helping process emphasizes empowerment and has a strong educational component, including teaching about sexism, sex-role stereotyping, gender discrimination, and social and historical factors that have affected attitudes toward women, including how women view themselves.
- The client is expected to be an active participant in the helping process, and its focus is on client strengths rather than deficits or pathology.
- An emphasis is placed on creating women's social networks and support groups.

The feminist perspective is especially important in work with women, but it has many characteristics—such as its emphasis on empowerment, social justice, and political action—that should be a part of social work practice in all settings and also in work with male clients.

SUGGESTED READINGS

Bricker-Jenkins, Mary, Nancy Hooyman, and Naomi Gottlieb. *Feminist Social Work Practice in Clinical Settings.* Newbury Park, CA: Sage, 1991.

Bricker-Jenkins, Mary, and Patricia Lockett. "Women: Direct Practice." In *Encyclopedia of Social Work,* Vol. 3, 19th ed., edited by Richard Edwards. Washington, DC: NASW, 1995 (pp. 2529–2539).

Van Den Bergh, Nan. *Feminist Practice in the 21st Century.* Washington, DC: NASW, 1995.

Valentich, Mary. "Feminist Theory and Social Work Practice." In *Social Work Treatment,* 4th ed., edited by Francis Turner. New York: Free Press, 1996.

Selected Practice Theories and Models

A practice perspective does not stand alone; it is used in conjunction with various practice theories and models. For example, a social worker operating from the generalist perspective may elect to use behavioral techniques, small group theories, and/or theories of organizational change, depending on the roles being performed and the demands of the practice situation. More specialized practitioners may draw on a smaller number of theories or models, but apply them with more depth of knowledge and skill.

In addition to the reference books mentioned in the opening paragraph of this chapter and those listed as Suggested Readings, there exist a number of general reference books that provide one-chapter overviews of the common theoretical frameworks used in therapeutic work with individuals, families, and small groups. These include, for example, Corsini and Wedding (1995), Prochaska and Norcross (1994), Vondracek and Corneal (1994), and Gilliland and James (1998).

PRACTICE BASED ON PSYCHODYNAMIC THEORY

Purpose. To improve the social functioning of individuals by helping them understand better their thoughts and conflicting feelings.

Application. Prerequisite to the use of this approach is a client who is motivated, verbal, and willing and able to participate actively in a series of regularly scheduled sessions. This approach is seldom useful if the client has limited intellectual ability, is chemically dependent, or is overburdened by problems related to adverse social or economic conditions (e.g., poverty, inadequate housing, etc.).

Description. This frame of reference is rooted in psychoanalytic theory and therapy. Psychodynamic explanations of behavior are built around the concept of unconscious motivation and the belief that much of our behavior serves some underlying and often hidden purpose. It recognizes the power of emotions (e.g., fear, anger, envy, revenge, sexual attraction, etc.) and the inner conflicts that arise in trying to cope with them in a socially acceptable manner. Largely unconscious *ego defense mechanisms* operate to manage our anxiety and intrapsychic conflict (see Item 12.8).

The concept of *ego* refers to various intrapersonal processes that mediate between primitive drives (e.g., fight-flight) and the demands of external reality and social norms. The ego is also the problem-solving part of personality. Thus, a term such as *ego supportive treatment* refers to interventions that maintain and enhance problem solving and adjustment. Many internal psychological conflicts and interpersonal problems are presumed to be rooted in early childhood experiences that disrupt or distort the normal stages of personality development. The concept of *object relations* (people relations) explains how current patterns of thinking, feelings, and behavior reflect, at an unconscious level, one's childhood relations with others, especially parent figures.

Change results from the cathartic expression of inner conflicts and emotion and from gaining insight (understanding) into how prior experiences gave rise to troublesome thoughts, feelings, and behavior. The change process requires a lengthy and in-depth therapeutic relationship wherein the client feels safe to explore and express private thoughts and feelings.

Social workers have adapted psychodynamically based therapeutic methods to the realities of agency-based practice and to the social work profession's emphasis on viewing the client within a situational and environmental context. Examples include those approaches that make heavy use of *ego psychology* (Goldstein 1995), *psychosocial therapy* (Woods and Hollis 1990; Turner 1988) and the *problem-solving approach* (Perlman 1957).

As a general rule, the practice frameworks based on psychodynamic concepts give relatively more attention to the client's thoughts and feelings than to the social and environmental factors. Recent contributions to this literature incorporate concepts from the cognitive-behavioral approach and various theories of family treatment.

SUGGESTED READINGS

Brandell, Jerrold, and Fredric Perlman. "Psychoanalytic Theory." In *Theory and Practice in Clinical Social Work,* edited by Jerrold Brandell. New York: Free Press, 1997.

Goldstein, Eda. *Ego Psychology and Social Work Practice,* 2nd ed. New York: Free Press, 1995.

Polansky, Norman. *Integrated Ego Psychology,* 2nd ed. New York: Aldine, 1991.

Woods, Mary, and Florence Hollis. *Casework: A Psychosocial Therapy,* 4th ed. New York: McGraw-Hill, 1990.

PRACTICE BASED ON BEHAVIORAL THEORY

Purpose. To improve the social functioning of individuals, couples, families, or organizations by helping them learn new behaviors and eliminate troublesome ways of behaving.

Application. In order to use this approach successfully, it must be possible to specify and operationally define a behavior(s) that needs either to increase or decrease in frequency, duration, or intensity. Also, either the client or the professional must be able to control the consequences that follow the behavior targeted for change. This approach can be used with a nonvoluntary client if the professional has the ability to monitor the client's behavior closely and the authority to allocate reinforcement (rewards) to the client. It has less applicability when the client's concerns center primarily on covert mental processes such as decision making, value conflicts, and distorted thinking.

Description. Gambrill (1997, 46) explains that in "behavioral theory, actions, thoughts, and feelings are considered to be largely a function of our learning history." The key premise of behavioral theory is that people repeat behaviors that are rewarded and abandon behaviors that are not rewarded or for which they are punished. In other words, behavior is shaped and patterned by its consequences. By manipulating and changing the availability of *reinforcement,* the worker can help clients eliminate dysfunctional behaviors and learn desirable patterns of functioning.

The change process requires modification of the client's immediate environment so that it elicits and rewards the desired behaviors and no longer reinforces dysfunctional ones. This approach, more than any other, emphasizes observation, data collection, and careful measurement before, during, and after the intervention. Decisions that guide the change process are made on the basis of data, not on the basis of assumptions about why people might behave as they do.

The behavioral approach has been attractive to professionals working in residential treatment and correctional settings where it is possible to observe the behavior of clients and exercise control over the rewards they receive. In many applications, the client is taught how to modify his or her own behavior through the self-administration of reinforcers. (See Item 14.4 for more explanation.)

SUGGESTED READINGS

Gambrill, Eileen. "Behavioral Theory." In *Encyclopedia of Social Work.* 1997 Supplement to the 19th ed., edited by Richard Edwards. Washington, DC: NASW, 1997 (pp. 46–57).
Mattaini, Mark. *Clinical Practice with Individuals.* Washington, DC: NASW Press, 1997.
Thyer, Bruce, and John Wodarski. *Handbook of Empirical Social Work Practice.* New York: Wiley, 1998.

PRACTICE BASED ON COGNITIVE-BEHAVIORAL THEORY

Purpose. To improve social functioning by assisting the client to learn more realistic and positive ways of perceiving, thinking about, and interpreting his or her life experiences.

Application. This approach requires that the client have the requisite intellectual capacity and be willing to invest the time needed to monitor and analyze his or her ways of thinking and to practice techniques designed to change long-standing habits of thought. Cognitive-behavioral theory is especially useful in work on problems of depression, low self-esteem, and self-defeating thoughts and behaviors. It can be used with children (age 10 and older), adolescents who are developing their patterns of thinking, and, of course, adults.

Description. This framework integrates selected concepts from behavioral and learning theory and applied behavioral analysis with ones drawn from the study of cognitive processes (i.e., how people think and process information). It focuses on the interplay among cognitions (thoughts), emotions, and behavior.

How and what people think strongly influence their emotional reactions (feelings) and their behaviors. In a sense, we humans live at the mercy of our beliefs and assumptions. Problem behaviors and personal distress are often rooted in faulty, irrational, and rigid thinking and in unfounded and unrealistic beliefs about the way things ought to be. For example, if people operate on the belief that one must always keep others from getting upset, they face a lifetime of distress because this is an unrealistic expectation.

During a course of cognitive-behavioral therapy, the client is encouraged and helped to identify, monitor, reexamine, and correct patterns of thought and faulty assumptions that give rise to problems. The client is usually taught specific skills and procedures to recognize the content and impact of their cognitions, evaluate the validity of their perceptions and assumptions, and view events and situations with greater objectivity. A variety of techniques are used: cognitive restructuring, logical analysis, role modeling, behavioral rehearsal, paradoxical instruction, desensitization, covert extinction, cognitive flooding, and so on.

Within this general framework there are subdivisions, such as rational emotive therapy and cognitive therapy. Practitioners and theoreticians tend to differ on whether to emphasize the cognitive side or the behavioral side of the cognitive-behavioral construct and the degree to which they work to modify fundamental cognitive process such as perception, memory, information processing, judgment, and decision making (see Items 8.6, 14.8, and 14.12).

SUGGESTED READINGS

Beck, Judith. *Cognitive Therapy.* New York: Guilford, 1995.

Lantz, Jim. "Cognitive Theory and Social Work Treatment." In *Social Work Treatment,* 4th ed., edited by Francis Turner. New York: Free Press, 1996.

Schuyler, Dean. *A Practical Guide to Cognitive Therapy.* New York: W. W. Norton, 1991.

PRACTICE BASED ON PERSON-CENTERED THEORY

Purpose. To improve social functioning by increasing self-understanding and feelings of self-worth through a nondirective helping process that emphasizes intense listening and reflecting on the client's thoughts and feelings.

Application. This approach usually requires that the client be voluntary, highly motivated, articulate, thoughtful, and not overburdened by problems caused by external or environmental factors.

Description. With roots in humanistic and existential philosophic traditions, this approach emphasizes the uniqueness of every person, perceptions of self, and the meanings assigned to personal experience. It is built on a positive and optimistic view—people are fundamentally good, prosocial, striving for self-actualization, and in search of life's meaning.

Change occurs when self-imposed psychological barriers are identified and examined, thereby freeing the client's innate potential for positive personal growth. The social worker strives to demonstrate openness, empathy, warmth, and genuineness and makes frequent use of paraphrase, reflection, and other techniques of active listening (see Item 8.3). The practitioner must be deeply respectful and nonjudgmental, refrain from giving advice, and avoid diagnosing and labeling. The focus is on the here and now rather than on past experience.

SUGGESTED READINGS

Levant, R. F., and J. M. Shileim, eds. *Client-Centered Therapy and the Person-Centered Approach.* New York: Praeger, 1984.

Rowe, William. "Client Centered Theory." In *Social Work Treatment,* 4th ed., edited by Francis Turner. New York: Free Press, 1996.

THE INTERACTIONAL MODEL

Purpose. To improve social functioning by mediating the interactions between people.

Application. This model developed out of practice experience with typical social work clients in a variety of social agencies. It can be used to guide work with individuals, families, groups, and communities. It presumes that many clients are involuntary.

Description. This model of social work practice is associated with the research and writing of Lawrence Shulman. It consists of four major elements: (1) people (i.e., clients); (2) the interactions among and between people; (3) the social systems and people with whom the client interacts; and (4) the element of time or the phases in the helping process. In addition to providing concepts for understanding interactions, this model describes nearly 30 specific skills or techniques that might be applied in the four phases of helping. These phases are the preliminary or preparatory phase, the beginning contracting phase, the middle or work phase, and the ending or transition phase. Each phase has unique dynamics and requires the application of a special set of skills.

Great emphasis is placed on social context. Neither the client's relationships with others nor the client's problem can be understood apart from their social and environmental contexts. And, of course, the social worker is part of that ever-changing context. The model calls on the worker to be very active, responsive, and human—a "third force" who functions as a mediator among people and between people and systems.

This highly process-oriented approach focuses on the client's here-and-now experiences. It is presumed that both the client and those with whom the client interacts are striving toward deeper involvement and connectedness in interpersonal relationships, even though there is often conflict and ambivalence about these relationships.

SUGGESTED READINGS

Shulman, Lawrence. *The Skills of Helping Individuals, Families, Groups, and Communities,* 4th ed. Itasca, IL: F. E. Peacock, 1999.

———. *Interactional Supervision.* Washington, DC: NASW, 1993.

———. *Interactional Social Work Practice: Toward an Empirical Theory.* Itasca, IL: F. E. Peacock, 1991.

THE STRUCTURAL MODEL

Purpose. To ensure that a social work intervention gives adequate and appropriate attention to the client's social environment and to social change.

Application. This model is intended for use in all social work interventions involving direct practice with individuals, couples, and families.

Description. Given the social work profession's focus on the person-in-environment and the inherent difficulty of giving equal attention to both dimensions, social workers have tended to choose either a clinical orientation or a social change orientation. The structural approach addresses this tension by asking practitioners to consider, first, changing the client's environment. Whereas most other orientations to direct practice focus mostly on helping individuals adjust to their situations, the structural approach aims to modify the environment first so it better meets the needs of the individual. Goldberg and Middleman (1989) explain that this approach rests on two assumptions:

> 1) Problems are not viewed as individual pathology, but as a manifestation of inadequate social arrangements. Thus, clients . . . are not . . . seen as impaired or deficient individuals. . . . 2) Social change is the obligation of all social workers wherever they are in the bureaucratic hierarchy. In fact, [social change] begins with how the direct service practitioners conceptualize their response to a specific client. Social change is not . . . relegated to specialists within the social work profession (community organizers, planners, social policy-makers). Rather it is pursued at every level of assignment, every working day by all social workers, and especially by those who must face the clients directly. (p. 16)

The model identifies four social work roles (conferee, broker, mediator, and advocate) and assumes the worker will move from role to role, depending on the needs of the client. It is built on several fundamental principles: Be accountable and responsible to the client; take actions that identify and engage others who have concerns or problems similar to those of the client; maximize the supports that exist in the client's environment; proceed on the basis of "least contest" (e.g., assume the role of broker before mediator and mediator before advocate); and teach and reinforce behaviors and skills that will help the client take control of his or her life. For use with the structural model and other approaches, Middleman and Wood (1990) describe 63 specific interpersonal skills.

SUGGESTED READINGS

Goldberg, Gale, and Ruth Middleman. *The Structural Approach to Direct Practice in Social Work.* New York: Columbia University Press, 1989.

Middleman, Ruth, and Gale Goldberg Wood. *Skills for Direct Practice in Social Work.* New York: Columbia University Press, 1990.

THE CRISIS INTERVENTION MODEL

Purpose. To address the special needs and concerns of a client in an acute, psychological crisis.

Application. The crisis intervention model is applicable whenever the functioning of an individual or family has been suddenly and dramatically affected by some personal loss or tragedy. It is to be used during a four- to six-week period following the event that precipitated the crisis.

Description. This model emphasizes the importance of providing a focused and time-limited intervention to the person who is unable to function because of a personal crisis. Parad and Parad (1990) explain that crisis intervention is a process for

> actively influencing psychosocial functioning during a period of disequilibrium in order to alleviate the immediate impact of disruptive stressful events and to help mobilize the . . . psychological capabilities and social resources of persons directly affected by the crisis. . . . Interventive efforts have two principal aims: (1) to cushion the stressful event by immediate or emergency emotional and environmental first aid and (2) to strengthen the person in his or her coping . . . through immediate therapeutic clarification and guidance during the crisis period. (p. 4)

This approach differs from most others because it calls for (1) quick access to the client and rapid response by the helper; (2) use of time limits (e.g., five sessions over four-week period); (3) focused attention on the crisis configuration (i.e., on the nature of the precipitating event and its subjective meaning to client); (4) emphasis on helping the client make decisions and take action; and (5) mobilization of helping resources within the client's social network. Those using the model may draw on a variety of theories, techniques, and intervention procedures (see Item 14.28).

SUGGESTED READINGS

Ell, Kathleen. "Crisis Theory and Social Work Practice." In *Social Work Treatment,* 4th ed., edited by Francis Turner. New York: Free Press, 1996.

Gilliland, Burl, and Richard James. *Crisis Intervention Strategies.* Pacific Grove, CA: Brooks/Cole, 1997.

Hoff, Lee Ann. *People in Crisis,* 4th ed. San Francisco: Jossey-Bass, 1995.

Parad, Howard, and Libbie Parad, eds. *Crisis Intervention—Book 2.* Milwaukee, WI: Family Service Association of America, 1990.

THE TASK-CENTERED MODEL

Purpose. To improve the social functioning of a client through the use of an intervention structure that emphasizes action steps by the client.

Application. This approach can be used with individuals, couples, families, and small groups and can be adapted to work with the nonvoluntary client. Because of its emphasis on taking action and the completion of agreed upon tasks, it is especially useful with clients who are attempting to manage problems caused by insufficient resources such as a job, housing, day care, transportation, and so on.

Description. After discussing their problem or situation, some clients know what they need to do but are unable to move ahead and take the actions necessary to significantly change their situation. The emphasis of this model is on helping the client take those actions. Specific actions are called *tasks.*

The tasks to be worked on can take many forms: making a decision within a certain time frame, securing a needed resource, learning a skill, expressing concerns to an employer, and so forth. Large tasks are broken down into several smaller ones so the client will experience success and sustain motivation. Priority setting is used to limit the number of tasks to only two or three per week. Such structuring and the time limits help the client stay focused and mobilize inner resources. The model is largely empirical, stressing the monitoring and measurement of task completion.

This model's emphasis on action and the completion of tasks should not be interpreted as a lack of concern about clients' inner thoughts and feelings. However, this approach rests on the belief that people are more likely to change as a result of taking action than as a result of simply discussing their thoughts and feelings. Task-centered practitioners draw on a variety of theories and techniques to help clients accomplish agreed upon tasks (see Items 13.1, 13.2, and 15.3).

SUGGESTED READINGS

Epstein, Laura. *Brief Treatment and a New Look at the Task-Centered Approach,* 3rd ed. New York: Macmillan, 1992.

Reid, William. "Task-Centered Social Work." In *Social Work Treatment,* 4th ed., edited by Francis Turner. New York: Free Press, 1996.

———. *Task Strategies: An Empirical Approach to Clinical Social Work.* New York: Columbia University Press, 1992.

Tolson, Eleanor, William Reid, and Charles Garvin. *Generalist Practice: A Task-Centered Approach.* New York: Columbia University Press, 1994.

THE SOLUTION-FOCUSED MODEL

Purpose. To improve social functioning and facilitate client change within 1 or not more than about 12 sessions.

Application. This approach is used with individuals, couples, and families. It is appropriate when the client and worker are limited in the number of times they can meet together. The model can be adapted for use with the nonvoluntary client.

Description. A variety of influences, some of them economic, are forcing social workers and agencies to place great emphasis on efficiency and to limit the number of times they meet with a client. This has given birth to new models of brief and time-limited counseling and therapy. Solution-focused therapy is one of the better-developed approaches. It is built on several assumptions and principles:

- Rapid change and rapid resolution of problems are possible. (Research has not been able to demonstrate that long-term therapy is more effective that brief therapy.)
- All clients (individuals and families) have within them the ideas, strengths, and resources to begin resolving their problems; these must be identified, mobilized, and supported by the social worker.
- Clients do not resist changes that make sense and provide relief from distress. Problems do not serve a hidden purpose; clients are not invested in maintaining their problems for some unconscious motive.
- It is not necessary to understand the cause of a problem in order to resolve it. Because problems are social constructions, there are many ways of viewing and defining a situation and many ways of solving a problem. There is no one right way to deal with a troublesome situation.
- Because of the ripple effect, only small positive changes are needed because even small changes will, over time, have a positive impact on all other parts of the client system.

This model focuses on the nature of the client's solutions to a problem rather than on the nature of the problem. It emphasizes solution finding by the client rather than problem solving directed by the professional. The professional's task is to help the client identify and implement his or her own solutions. Various questioning techniques are used to help the client recognize that he or she already has some control over the problem and some workable ideas on how best to solve it.

SUGGESTED READINGS

Christensen, Dana, and Jeffrey Todahl. *Solution-Based Casework.* Hawthorne, NY: Aldine de Gruyter, 1999.

Dejong, Peter, and Insoo Kim Berg. *Interviewing for Solutions.* Pacific Grove, CA: Brooks/Cole, 1998.

Miller, Scott, Mark Hubble, and Barry Duncan, eds. *Handbook of Solution Focused Brief Therapy.* Washington, DC: NASW, 1996.

PRACTICE BASED ON THE FAMILY THERAPIES

Purpose. To improve the social functioning of families by working with the family as a system and changing the interactions among family members.

Application. Prerequisite to the use of the various family therapies are family members who have at least a minimum level of concern for each other and want to preserve or strengthen their families. At least some of the members should be voluntary clients, although it is expected that others will have been coerced into participation.

Description. Within this broad framework, there are numerous theories and models that have much in common: The family system is the unit of attention, all or most family members are engaged in the change process, focus is on the interaction of members within the family system, emphasis is on current behavior (here and now), and active techniques are employed (e.g., family sculpture, role-play, homework, etc.). The differences between the approaches are mostly a matter of emphasizing certain concepts and procedures over others. The practitioner of family therapy must be eclectic. In order to illustrate how work with families might differ from one practitioner to another, a few of the key assumptions associated with commonly used approaches are presented.

The ***communications approach*** presumes that family problems are caused mostly by faulty communication. Change occurs when family members learn to really listen to each other and express themselves openly and honestly. The practitioner models forthright communication and uses various experiential exercises to help family members express themselves.

As suggested by its name, the ***structural approach*** focuses primarily on a family's structures. Special attention is given to the delineation and interaction of the spousal, parental, and sibling subsystems and their interaction. Unhealthy alliances and splits among these subsystems and either overly rigid or overly flexible boundaries are major sources of family dysfunction. Change occurs when the roles and responsibilities of the family's members and the subsystems are clarified and agreed to by all.

The ***family systems approach*** focuses on the struggle of family members to simultaneously be a part of a family group and be individuals apart from the family system. Problems arise when an individual either suppresses the self and is overly involved (enmeshed) with his or her family or, at the other extreme, rejects his or her family connection. This approach also recognizes the tendency of a family to repeat patterns established in prior generations (i.e., the intergenerational transmission of dysfunction) and is sensitive to issues related to the family life cycle.

The ***strategic family therapy*** approach gives primary attention to family rules (the often unstated family beliefs about how family members should think and behave) and to the distribution and use of power. The word *strategic* connotes an active and directive role by the therapist in strategically selecting interventions that move the family toward a pattern of behavior deemed desirable by the therapist.

A model termed the ***social learning approach*** draws its concepts and techniques from behavior therapy and behavior modification. It presumes that family conflicts and problems arise because the members have not learned basic skills such as communication, relationship and conflict resolution, and/or that appropriate behavior is not reinforced within the family system. Thus, the practitioner places much emphasis on the teaching skills. *Functional family therapy* resembles the social learning approach but also examines the social context of family problems and the function served by problem behaviors. Problem behaviors are viewed as unsuccessful efforts by family members to cope with issues of dependence versus independence, freedom versus control, and intimacy versus distance.

The ***narrative approach*** derives its name from its focus on personal stories and anecdotes and the stories of a community or culture (e.g., fables, movies, biographies, novels, etc.) that people use as frames of reference to describe their situations and create meaning and purpose. It recognizes the power of language and the patterns of thought embedded in our society to shape the way we think about ourselves, construct our "reality," and define our individual and family problems. Special questioning techniques are used to help family members reexamine the way they think and to construct alternative stories that lead to new patterns of behavior.

As is true of psychotherapy in general, most approaches to family therapy developed out of work with middle-class and upper-class families. They may not work as well with families that are economically poor or members of a minority group. Social workers are challenged to select approaches that can be adapted to agency-based practice and their profession's emphasis on social functioning and the person-in-environmental construct. To help them make that selection, Kilpatrick and Holland (1995) offer a practical ***integrative model*** that ties the use of various approaches or types of family interventions to four possible levels of family functioning. Consequently, the recommended approach for a family that is struggling with meeting basic needs (food, safety, etc.) is different from the approaches recommended for the economically stable family having problems around issues of unclear boundaries or a lack of intimacy in family relationships. (For additional information on work with families, see Items 12.3, 12.11, 12.12, 14.7, 14.13, and 14.14.)

SUGGESTED READINGS

Becvar, Dorothy, and Raphael Becvar. *Family Therapy,* 3rd ed. Boston: Allyn and Bacon, 1996.

Janzen, Curtis, and Oliver Harris. *Family Treatment in Social Work Practice,* 3rd ed. Itasca, IL: F. E. Peacock, 1997.

Kilpatrick, Allie, and Thomas Holland. *Working with Families: An Integrative Model by Level of Functioning.* Boston: Allyn and Bacon, 1995.

Nichols, Michael, and Richard Schwartz. *Family Therapy,* 4th ed. Boston: Allyn and Bacon, 1998.

Worden, Mark. *Family Therapy Basics.* Pacific Grove, CA: Brooks/Cole, 1998.

PRACTICE BASED ON MODELS OF FAMILY PRESERVATION

Purpose. To avoid having to place a child into foster care by focusing on those dysfunctions or circumstances that place the child at risk of placement.

Application. This approach is appropriate whenever a child is at risk of placement and when there is reason to believe that an intense and focused intervention and frequent monitoring will sufficiently reduce the chances that the child will be abused or neglected.

Description. There are several models of family-based or home-based services. All are designed to prevent out-of-home placements and all share a common set of beliefs about what works best with dysfunctional families in which children are at high risk of being removed and placed in foster care because of abuse, neglect, or the parent's inability to deal with a rebellious adolescent. Most of these programs share the following characteristics:

- A primary worker or case manager establishes and maintains a supportive, nurturing relationship with the family.
- One or more associates serve as team members or provide backup with the primary worker.
- Workers (or their backup person) are available 24 hours a day for crisis calls or emergencies.
- The home is the primary setting for service delivery (i.e., heavy to exclusive use of in-home interviews).
- A wide variety of helping options are used (e.g., both concrete and clinical services).
- Emphasis is placed on identifying and building on family strengths.
- Keep the size of caseloads small (two to six families per worker).
- Employ maximum use of informal and natural helping resources, including the extended family, neighbors, churches, support groups, and so on.
- The parents remain in charge of and responsible for their family as primary caregivers.

- To prevent placement, the agency is willing to invest at least as much in a child's own family as society is willing to pay for the foster care of that child.
- Services are goal oriented and time limited, usually lasting from one to four months.

SUGGESTED READINGS

Berg, Insoo Kim. *Family-Based Services.* New York: W. W. Norton, 1994.

Kinney, Jill, David Haapla, and Charlotte Booth. *Keeping Families Together: The Homebuilders Model.* New York: Aldine, 1991.

Whittaker, James, Jill Kinney, Elizabeth Tracy, and Charlotte Booth. *Reaching High-Risk Families.* New York: Aldine, 1990.

PRACTICE BASED ON THE CLUBHOUSE MODEL

Purpose. To improve the social and vocational functioning of adults with serious mental illness by providing a supportive community based on mutual needs, interests, and shared work.

Application. Member and staff experiences in this model are structured and given meaning through work that benefits both the clubhouse and individual members of the community. Each member chooses the character and extent of his or her involvement in the activity of the clubhouse community. For many people with mental illness and their families, the clubhouse model is considered an especially helpful, noncoercive source of continuing support for adaptive community living.

Description. At the heart of the clubhouse model is the recognition that people need to be valued and contributing members of a group. The participants in a clubhouse are viewed as members rather than as clients or patients. Their days are ordered by shared work and by a focus on work-related roles and tasks, rather than by a schedule of treatment or rehabilitation services or sessions with professionals. Three themes characterize social work practice in clubhouses.

First, respect and equality among members and staff are emphasized. Both members and staff are full participants in the daily operation of the clubhouse. Typically, members and staff cook and serve meals, write and produce a newsletter, clean and maintain the club, reach out to isolated members, and serve in other useful, contributing work roles. Members are involved in all aspects of program development, operation, and governance of the clubhouse. By design, member work is essential in the life of the club, yet is not coerced.

Second, attention is given to enhancing many aspects of each member's life, including social relations, recreation, housing, transportation, medical care and medication management, and employment. The value of meaningful work and its regenerative potential is recognized in the "work-ordered day" of the clubhouse and in the array of competitive work opportunities developed by the clubhouse. Through competitive, *transitional employment* placements, members (as they become ready) choose real jobs, as opposed to the sheltered or "make-work" experiences often found in conventional rehabilitation programs.

Third, it is recognized that mental illness often produces complex, idiosyncratic, and disabling social and psychiatric symptoms and that most members utilize psychotropic medications to manage symptoms of illness. Nonetheless, clubhouses are based on the belief that illness should not define the person. Members are viewed as valued human beings with abilities to be discovered and applied. The focus is on developing strengths and competencies and providing a foundation for satisfying and successful social functioning. Members are not trained in daily living skills; rather, they learn such skills through the practical work of building and maintaining the clubhouse and making use of the many learning opportunities it offers.

The central task of social work staff within the clubhouse model, then, is to lead the creation and maintenance of member roles within the club and the larger community. Members and staff collaborate to build and maintain a clubhouse, centered in work-ordered daily life (i.e., clubhouse work units, transitional employment placements, and permanent placements). The staff assists members in developing and carrying out new roles and applying their skills and aptitudes in work, training, and/or education. Generalist practice skills are considered the most relevant preparation for work in this model (Dougherty 1994).

SUGGESTED READINGS

Dougherty, S. J. "The Generalist Role in Clubhouse Organizations." *Psychosocial Rehabilitation Journal* 18 (July 1994): 95–108.

Flannery, Mary, and Mark Glickman. *Fountain House: Portraits and Lives Reclaimed for Mental Illness.* Center City, MN: Hazelden, 1996.

Jackson, Robert L., Dorothy Purnell, Stephen B. Anderson, and Bradford W. Sheafor. "The Clubhouse Model of Community Support for Adults with Mental Illness: An Emerging Opportunity for Social Work Education." *Journal of Social Work Education* 32 (Spring/Summer 1996): 173–180.

Propst, Rudyard. "Standards for Clubhouse Programs: Why and How They Were Developed." *Psychosocial Rehabilitation Journal* 11 (October 1987): 25–30.

PRACTICE BASED ON SMALL GROUP THEORIES

Purpose. To improve the social functioning of individuals or couples through participation in a small group experience under the guidance of a professional.

Application. The client must be willing to participate in discussions and small group activities and behave in ways that do not disrupt the group or harm other members. Group experiences can be designed for a number of purposes (e.g., training, therapy, mutual support, social action, etc.). A skillful group leader will be able to engage clients who are nonvoluntary participants.

Description. Work with groups occurs in a variety of settings for a multitude of purposes. Although there are some differences in approach, these differences are usually a matter of emphasis, rather than in terms of fundamental concepts and skills. The differences are related to the purpose of the group (e.g., a task group vs. a treatment group); the role assumed by the professional (e.g., group leader, therapist, teacher, mediator, or facilitator); and whether attention is focused mostly on the behavior of the individuals that make up the group or mostly on the functioning of the group as a social system. Numerous small group–related orienting theories provide social workers with background knowledge on such dimensions as group leadership, goals, structure and norms, group cohesion, conflict, stages of group development, and intragroup communication. For purposes of illustration, it is useful to identify some of the ways in which work with groups may differ and a few of the frameworks that influence practice.

Task groups are common to practice in the indirect services. These goal-oriented groups tend to be quite structured and formal. Examples include agency boards, committees, staff meetings, and community planning groups. Such groups are characterized by the use of a written agenda, *Robert's Rules of Order,* and clear assignments of leadership roles and member responsibilities.

The ***interactional model,*** or mediating model, places the social worker in the role of a mediator between members of the group and between the group and its environment, including the agency that has sanctioned the group's formation. This approach places a high value on client self-determination.

The ***group treatment approach*** (remedial model) views the group as a therapeutic environment and a behavior-changing influence on its members. The focus is mostly on the members as individuals and on the problems they are having outside the group. However, a client's behavior within the group may be used as a way of assessing and illustrating his or her attitudes and behavioral patterns. In these groups, the social worker assumes the role of a therapist, expert, and group leader. In some groups, such as those used in the treatment of sex offenders and persons addicted to alcohol or drugs, there is heavy use of confrontation and members are required to complete assigned homework and strictly adhere to established rules. In such groups, self-determination is not a priority.

In many agency settings, groups are used to promote normal growth and development and the learning of ordinary skills for living rather than for the purpose of coping with serious problems or correcting dysfunctional behavior. Many of the groups that are part of the YMCA/YWCA programs, summer camps, after-school programs, and senior citizen programs are of this type. These groups make use of the ***developmental approach.*** The worker typically assumes the role of leader, planner, and arranger of group activities and makes heavy use of programming (see Item 14.21).

When groups are used for the purpose of ***teaching and training,*** they are goal oriented and the worker assumes the roles of leader and teacher. Depending on the topic being addressed (e.g., parent training, learning communications skills, learning job skills, learning about a medical condition, etc.) and the number of times the group will meet, there may or may not be a lot of emphasis on member interaction, building trust, and developing a sense of belonging to the group.

A number of theoretical influences from outside the social work profession have had an impact on how social workers approach their practice with groups and, of course, also with individuals and families. These include *Gestalt therapy, transactional analysis, encounter groups, psychodrama, behavior modification,* and *positive peer culture.* Descriptions of these can be found in the *Encyclopedia of Social Work* (1995), Fatout (1992), and Corsini and Wedding (1995). (For additional information on group work, see Items 12.28, 13.8, 14.21, and 14.41.)

SUGGESTED READINGS

Anderson, Joseph. *Social Work with Groups.* New York: Longman, 1997.

Fatout, Marian. *Models for Change in Social Group Work.* New York: Aldine, 1992.

Fatout, Marian, and Steven Rose. *Task Groups in Social Services.* Thousand Oaks, CA: Sage, 1995.

Garvin, Charles. *Contemporary Group Work,* 2nd ed. Boston: Allyn and Bacon, 1997.

Greif, Geoffrey, and Paul Ephross, eds. *Group Work with Populations at Risk.* New York: Oxford University Press, 1997.

Reid, Kenneth. *Social Work Practice with Groups: A Clinical Perspective,* 2nd ed. Pacific Grove, CA: Brooks/Cole, 1997.

Toseland, Ronald, and Robert Rivas. *An Introduction to Group Work Practice,* 3rd ed. Boston: Allyn and Bacon, 1998.

PRACTICE BASED ON THE ADDICTION MODEL

Purpose. To improve the social functioning of individuals by helping them overcome compulsive behavioral patterns.

Application. This model has proven useful in explaining and changing behaviors that have certain common characteristics: They have a mood-altering quality, they have grown more frequent over time, and they are now out of control. Given the nature of addiction, this model presumes that most clients are nonvoluntary. Since a direct confrontation of the client's defenses is a first step in treatment, the structure and control provided by an institutional or hospital setting are often necessary during the beginning stages of the process.

Description. The addiction model recognizes that many people are unable to discontinue patterns that cause them much misery. These patterns often take the form of alcohol, drug, and tobacco abuse; eating disorders; child molestation; dangerous risk taking; and compulsive sexual activities, spending, gambling, or physical exercise. Even the compulsive pursuit of money or power can be viewed as an addiction. It is believed that during the beginning phases of an addiction, the individual uses the substance or activity mostly as a means of feeling better and coping with distress caused by emotional pain or some unmet need. When it works to help the person feel better, usage is further reinforced and, subsequently, it is used again and again. Over time, the substance or activity consumes more and more of the individual's attention and resources and displaces other aspects of living. As the addiction spins out of control, the individual develops a system of denial, rationalizations, and behaviors that ensure access to the substance or activity.

Successful treatment requires the breakdown of the denial and helping the client learn more functional means of meeting his or her needs and coping with life's problems.The process of treatment and recovery from an addiction typically moves through six stages:

1. There is a breakdown of denial and defensiveness; the person recognizes that he or she has a problem.
2. The person with the addiction develops a sense of hope based on an awareness that other people with similar problems have made a successful recovery.
3. The person comes to understand how the addiction developed and why it has continued and gotten worse over time.
4. The person acquires the personal resolve, strength, and social support necessary to change the patterns of thought, behavior, and life-style that reinforce the addiction.
5. The person takes action, one step at a time and over an extended period of time, to abandon old patterns and practice healthy patterns.
6. The person continues to monitor and manage his or her life so as to stay free of the addictive substance or activity.

Both one-on-one counseling and small group experiences (e.g., 12-step programs) help the person move through these stages and achieve sobriety and a healthy life-style. Even after the individual is able to function without the addictive substance or activity, he or she must constantly work to avoid being drawn back into the addiction. (For further information, see Item 11.8 and the journal entitled *Addictive Behaviors.*)

SUGGESTED READINGS

Doweiko, Harold. *Concepts of Chemical Dependency,* 3rd ed. Pacific Grove, CA.: Brooks/Cole, 1996.

Freeman, Edith. *The Addiction Process: Effective Social Work Approaches.* New York: Longman, 1992.

Van Wormer, Katherine. *Alcoholism Treatment: A Social Work Perspective.* Chicago: Nelson-Hall, 1996.

PRACTICE BASED ON MODELS OF SELF-HELP

Purpose. To improve social functioning through a group experience and discussions with others who have or have had similar concerns or problems.

Application. In order for this approach to be effective, the client must be willing and able to attend a series of group meetings, listen to others, and share personal information and concerns. However, some self-help groups include nonvoluntary and even court-ordered participants.

Description. This approach rests on the belief that an individual can be helped by those who have experienced similar problems and that, in the process of helping others, people learn to better cope with their own problems. Alcoholics Anonymous,

Parents Without Partners, and Parents Anonymous are but a few of the many self-help groups.

Self-help groups usually depend on leaders indigenous to the group. Some rotate the leadership role from one member to another. A few look to leadership by professionals or members who have received special training on how to conduct and facilitate meetings. Most self-help groups are designed around five basic assumptions and beliefs:

1. People have a need to tell their story and to be heard by others. They are especially receptive to suggestions from those who have similar concerns and life experiences.
2. All people have strengths that can be mobilized. People are helped as they help others. We all have much to learn from and to teach others.
3. People are attracted to and feel most comfortable in small groups that are informal, noncompetitive, nonbureaucratic, nonintellectual, and nonelitist.
4. People want and can use simple rules and principles that provide practical guidance on how to cope with day-to-day problems (e.g., live one day at a time, walk your talk, follow the 12 steps, etc.).
5. Helping and caring for others is a natural human activity and not a commodity to be bought and sold.

Social workers may relate to self-help groups in a number of ways: (1) refer clients to an appropriate group, (2) provide consultation when asked for assistance, (3) serve on the group's advisory board, (4) serve as a guest speaker when asked, and (5) help create and/or lead a needed self-help group.

SUGGESTED READINGS

Gitterman, Alex, and Lawrence Schulman. *Mutual Aid Groups, Vulnerable Populations and the Life Cycle,* 2nd ed. New York: Columbia University Press, 1994.

Kurtz, Linda. *Self-Help and Support Groups. Thousand* Oaks, CA: Sage, 1997.

Powell, Thomas. *Understanding the Self-Help Organization.* Newbury Park, CA: Sage, 1994.

MODELS FOR CHANGING ORGANIZATIONS

Purpose. To change the functioning of a human services agency in order to increase its ability to address the needs and concerns of its staff and clients.

Application. The various models of organizational development and change can be used with both private and public agencies. However, their application presumes that the social worker has been given sanction by the agency's governing board or administration to plan and facilitate a change process.

Description. The complexity of organizational change becomes evident when one recognizes that organizations are made up of numerous individuals, each with a unique personality and each with numerous roles and tasks to perform; a set of formal and informal structures, procedures, and norms; and a set of power and authority relationships. Moreover, an organization is an legal entity whose purpose and functioning is tied to a charter and bylaws or to certain legislation, in the case of a public or governmental organization. Every organization is shaped by its financial resources and all must function within an ever-changing social, political, and economic environment.

Every social worker employed by an organization, regardless of position, must give some attention to how well it is functioning. A social agency, for example, must operate in an effective and efficient manner if it is to provide appropriate services and continue to receive the funding it needs to achieve its goals. As one moves from line worker to supervisor or middle manager, or to agency administrator, the responsibility to engage in organizational maintenance and change activities increases. The activities at any level, however, may include informing upper-level administrators and/or board members of staff concerns and client needs, proposing specific changes in agency policies and procedures, arranging input from consultants or persons providing training programs, participating on committees to study specific aspects of the organization's performance, designing program evaluation tools, and so on.

The selection of a method or an approach to planned organizational change will depend on one's beliefs about the nature and functioning of a particular organization. Descriptions of organizations are usually drawn from three conceptual models. The ***rational model*** assumes that those who are part of the organization are in agreement about its goals and committed to those goals. Thus, an organization is primarily a way of structuring the work that needs to occur in order to reach a goal. Given that view, proposed changes (e.g., restructuring, personal assignments, adoption of new technologies, reallocation of resources, etc.) will be accepted if it becomes apparent that they would improve the organization's capacity to achieve its goals. Change, therefore, results from such activities as self-study, obtaining the advice of consultants, examining the complaints or suggestions made by clients or consumers, in-service training on new technologies, and so forth.

The ***natural-system model*** views an organization as a system made up of a multitude of individuals, roles, subsystems, and formal and informal processes striving to function and survive in a wider social environment. It recognizes that the personnel and the many subdivisions of an organization can be easily distracted from the organization's official mission by such things as job stress, unclear work assignments, and disagreements over duties and responsibilities. This model views an organization as needing to balance its goal achievement with maintenance functions. Change efforts emphasize the clarification of goals and objectives, improving communication, recognizing and addressing the social and emotional needs of personnel, morale building, and the like.

The ***power-politics model*** assumes that an organization is essentially a political arena in which various individuals, departments, and other units compete for power, resources, and personal advantage (Gummer 1990). The achievement of the organization's official or stated goals may take a backseat to other agendas. To change such an organization, one needs access to persons in positions of influence over the organization and must be able to persuade those within the organization that a specific change is in their self-interest. External forces such as media exposure, investigations by citizen groups, legislative oversight, and lawsuits might be necessary for modifying organizations.

There are five fundamental approaches to planned change in a human services organization. The ***policy approach*** achieves change by developing and adopting new policies that will guide the organization and its operation. Those working for change direct their efforts toward the groups and individuals who are authorized to make policy and allocate resources at either the local, state, or national level. They provide these decision makers with data and new insights concerning a specific condition, problem, need, or issue, and advocate for a specific policy change.

The ***program approach*** seeks to change the organization by designing and introducing new or additional programs and services to better express and implement existing policy. Change efforts are directed primarily at people in administrative and managerial positions (i.e., those who have authority to modify programs and alter the procedures and technology used to carry out the work of the organization).

The ***project approach*** introduces change at the interface between line staff and the clients or consumers of the organization's services. Small-scale projects are used to try out or demonstrate new ways of working with agency clients. Policies and programs remain the same but staff skills and performance are enhanced. Change efforts often take the form of in-service training and increasing sensitivity to clients' needs and behavior.

An approach known as ***client-centered management*** focuses attention on the relationship between managerial behaviors and client outcomes. It is predicated on the belief that an excessive emphasis on powerful decision makers, funding bodies, interagency communication, and personnel issues has diverted the attention of administrators from their primary purpose—assuring that the social agency provides high-quality services that truly respond to client needs. This approach strives to secure client input into agency decision making and planning.

The ***teamwork model*** is primarily concerned with the manner in which workers interact to implement agency programs. It is based on two premises. First, it recognizes that the typical bureaucratic organization places excessive control in the hands of administrators, which, in turn, reduces innovation and consensus among workers about how best to provide services. Second, it recognizes that given the explosion of knowledge and technology, specialization is increasingly required in almost every occupation. But with specialization comes the need for better coordination. The providers of human services must be especially able to coordinate practice activities since services to clients are often provided simultaneously by several disciplines and several different agencies. Unfortunately, the typical department structure used in most agencies may erect barriers to coordination because the lines of communication and decision making are organized by profession, role, and job title, rather than by the need for an integrated approach to service delivery.

The teamwork approach has proven especially useful as a means of retaining the specialized knowledge and competencies of the several helping professions, and at the same time coordinating their practice activities. To make multidisciplinary teams viable working units, they are given the authority to plan and implement programs and to make decisions about the personnel and resources necessary to carry out their assignments. In this process, the teams become powerful forces for innovation and policy and program change.

SUGGESTED READINGS

Brueggemann, William. *The Practice of Macro Social Work.* Chicago: Nelson-Hall, 1996.

Gummer, Burton. *The Politics of Social Administration: Managing Organizational Politics in Social Agencies.* Englewood Cliffs, NJ: Prentice Hall, 1990.

Rapp, Charles A., and John Poertner. *Social Administration: A Client-Centered Approach.* White Plains, NY: Longman, 1992.

MODELS FOR CHANGING COMMUNITIES

Purpose. To improve the functioning of a community and increase its capacity to address the social needs and concerns of its members.

Application. The selection of a particular approach to community change must be based on an assessment of the problem or concern targeted for change and, to a large extent, on political factors. Unless the social worker has the authority, responsibility, and/or support of others to work toward a specific community change, his or her efforts are unlikely to succeed, no matter how noble the cause or how much the change is needed.

Description. Rothman (1995) identifies three models of community organization and planning. Each rests on a different set of assumptions concerning how *community* is defined, the change process, and the role of the professional. The three models are locality development, social planning, and social action.

The ***locality development model*** (or community development) presupposes that the community consists of people who share a sense of belonging to their locality and can therefore reach a consensus on the nature of community problems and what should be done about them. It emphasizes broad citizen participation, sharing of ideas, democratic decision making, cooperative problem solving, and self-help. In the process of working on problems, people learn the practical and leadership skills needed to tackle other concerns of the community. In performing most community-level social work practice (including activities connected to federated fund-raising, coalitions of human services organizations, ad hoc task forces, and neighborhood organizations), the professional assumes the roles of enabler, facilitator, coordinator, and teacher.

The model known as ***social planning*** focuses on specific social problems (i.e., crime, inadequate housing, lack of health care, etc.) and the response of the human services delivery system to these problems. It recognizes the complex legal, economic, and political factors that must be addressed in solving a major community problem. Although involvement by ordinary citizens is welcome, the key to community problem solving and change is involvement by influential persons, government officials, and organizations that have authority, power, and influence. This approach also recognizes the vertical dimension in community dynamics and therefore the need to involve influential persons and organizations from outside the immediate locality such as city, county, state, and federal government agencies, as well as major national corporations that do business in the community. The social worker using this model gives much attention to fact gathering, data analysis, policy analysis, sharing technical information, and program planning.

The third model, ***social action,*** is usually associated with efforts to correct a social injustice or achieve a needed change for a devalued or disadvantaged group (e.g., those living in poverty, those who suffer discrimination, etc.). It views a community as consisting of diverse groups and special interests that are competing for power and limited resources. Thus, in order to bring about a change in human services programs, there must be a shift in the decisions of those who exercise power and influence—or new decision makers must be given authority to take action. Since it is assumed that those in control will not easily relinquish their power, change requires confrontation with those who have power. The roles of the professional within this model include those of organizer, activist, advocate, and negotiator.

SUGGESTED READINGS

Hardcastle, David, Stanley Wenocur, and Patricia Powers. *Community Practice: Theories and Skills for Social Workers.* New York: Oxford University Press, 1997.

Netting, F. Ellen, Peter Kettner, and Steven McMurty. *Social Work Macro Practice,* 2nd ed. New York: Longman, 1998.

Rothman, Jack. "Approaches to Community Intervention." In *Strategies of Community Intervention,* 5th ed., edited by Jack Rothman, John Erlich, and John Tropman. Itasca, IL: F. E. Peacock, 1995, pp. 26–63.

Conclusion

As suggested by this survey of conceptual frameworks, the intervention approaches used by social workers have similarities but may differ in what they emphasize. Some differ in terms of basic assumptions about how and why change occurs (see Chapter 7 for additional ideas about the nature of change) and others differ in the characteristics of the clients they are intended to serve. A lifelong activity of the social worker is to carefully select a configuration of perspectives, theories, and models that matches his or her practice style and best meets the needs of his or her clients.

The reader is reminded that no one approach is always superior to others and that a social worker needs to have a basic understanding of several. One's practice framework might include multiple perspectives and an ever-growing repertoire of practice theories and models. Since all frameworks are concerned with helping people change, the worker must always be cognizant of the whole person—humans are thinking, feeling, and behaving biological beings whose survival, growth, and development depend on constant interaction with others and their environment.

SELECTED BIBLIOGRAPHY

Brandell, Jerrold, ed. *Theory and Practice in Clinical Social Work.* New York: Free Press, 1997.

Brilliant, Eleanor L. "Community Planning and Community Problem Solving: Past, Present, and Future." *Social Service Review* 60 (December 1986): 568–589.

Corsini, Raymond, and Danny Wedding. *Current Psychotherapies,* 5th ed. Itasca, IL: F. E. Peacock, 1995.

Dattilio, Frank, ed. *Case Studies in Couple and Family Therapy.* New York: Guilford, 1998.

Dorfman, Rachelle, ed. *Paradigms of Clinical Social Work,* vol. 1. New York: Brunner/Mazel, 1994.

———, ed. *Paradigms of Clinical Social Work,* vol. 2. New York: Brunner/Mazel, 1998.

Encyclopedia of Social Work, 19th ed., edited by Richard L. Edwards. Washington, DC: NASW, 1995.

Gambrill, Eileen. *Critical Thinking in Clinical Practice.* San Francisco: Jossey-Bass, 1990.

Garner, Howard Glenn. *Helping Others through Teamwork: A Handbook for Professionals.* Washington, DC: Child Welfare League of America, 1988.

Gilliland, Burl, and Richard James. *Theories and Strategies in Counseling and Psychotherapy,* 4th ed. Boston: Allyn and Bacon, 1998.

Green, James, and James Leigh. "Teaching Ethnographic Methods to Social Service Workers." *Practicing Anthropology* 11 (1989): 8–9.

Greene, Roberta, and Paul Ephross, eds. *Human Behavior Theory and Social Work Practice.* New York: Aldine, 1991.

Janzen, Curtis, and Oliver Harris. *Family Treatment in Social Work Practice,* 3rd ed. Itasca, IL: F. E. Peacock, 1997.

Norton, Dolores. *The Dual Perspective.* New York: Council on Social Work Education, 1978.

Payne, Malcolm. *Modern Social Work Theory,* 2nd ed. Chicago: Lyceum Books, 1997.

Perlman, Helen. *Social Casework: A Problem Solving Process.* Chicago: University of Chicago Press, 1957.

Prochaska, James, and John Norcross. *Systems of Psychotherapy,* 3rd. ed. Pacific Grove, CA: Brooks/Cole, 1994.

Reid, William. *Family Problem Solving.* New York: Columbia University Press, 1985.

Smith, Robert. *Elements of Ecology.* New York: Harper & Row, 1986.

Turner, Francis. "Psychosocial Therapy." In *Paradigms of Clinical Social Work,* edited by Rashelle Dorfman. New York: Brunner/Mazel, 1988.

———, ed. *Social Work Treatment: Interlocking Theoretical Approaches,* 4th ed. New York: Free Press, 1996.

Vondracek, Fred, and Sherry Corneal. *Strategies for Resolving Individual and Family Problems.* Pacific Grove, CA: Brooks/Cole, 1994.

7 Facilitating Change through Decision Making

In previous chapters, social work was described as a profession devoted to helping people make changes in their own social functioning and in the functioning of their families, groups, organizations, and communities. "Guide the process, not the client" is an admonition often heard in social work. The fundamental abilities for guiding the process of change involve identifying what needs to change, determining what can be changed, and deciding how change can best be facilitated. Underpinning these abilities, as discussed in this chapter, are the social worker's knowledge of the nature of change (including people's competing desire for and resistance to change), understanding key elements of the planned change, competence in critical thinking about practice situations, and skill in making and in helping clients make informed and prudent decisions.

Elements of the Change Process

Change is inevitable. Humans and all of the social systems created by humans are constantly adjusting and adapting within their ever-changing environments. Most of the changes that people experience in life are unplanned. Some of these are welcomed while others are feared. Many changes in our social functioning—both the positive and the negative—are set in motion by the natural consequences of biological maturation and aging and by personal choices such as selecting a certain occupation, taking a specific job, choosing a particular person as a spouse or partner, raising children, or getting a divorce. These ordinary events and experiences change the way we think, feel, and behave. Still other changes are forced on us by illness, accidents, natural disasters, and even world events such as wars and shifts in the global economy.

Although many of the changes we experience are unplanned, others can be chosen and achieved through individual and group effort. These are termed ***planned changes.*** In social work, the thoughtful and planned efforts to bring about a specific change are called *interventions.* They are designed to alter some specified condition, pattern of behavior, or set of circumstances that affects social functioning.

Change is often described as a *process*. However, the use of the word *process* is not meant to imply that change, once begun, will naturally unfold and proceed on a predictable path toward its goal. Quite the opposite is true. Given the complexity of change, change efforts can easily come apart and movement toward a goal is easily derailed. Change efforts must be painstakingly assembled and built little by little and piece by piece. They must be constantly supported, nurtured, restarted, repaired, and rebuilt.

Making a planned change happen is far from an exact science. Moreover, an intervention will usually have both expected and unexpected outcomes. For instance, after deliberately moving from *A* to *B,* we may discover that *B* is not quite what we had hoped for or perhaps that *B* has an unanticipated adverse effect on ourselves or others. Therefore, change always involves a certain amount of risk taking.

Change—even if wanted and planned—is often difficult and frustrating. Consequently, some degree of conflict, accompanied by emotion, can be expected during periods of change. Change may provoke personal turmoil and discord between the people and groups affected by the change. The social worker who is helping others make a change must be ready to address these conflicts and be comfortable with clients' expressions of fear, frustration, and other intense feelings.

Resistance to change is also a characteristic of humans and their social systems. People tend toward preserving the status quo. They resist change, particularly if it is rapid or especially upsetting to familiar patterns. The social worker must anticipate and be prepared to deal with resistance, even in a case where the client has demonstrated a strong desire to change.

Closely related to resistance is ***ambivalence,*** which is a condition of both wanting and not wanting a particular change. For example, an abused wife may want to leave her abusing husband in order to escape the abuse but at the same time not want to risk the loss of the financial security she has while married. Such a client is pulled in opposite directions and may become immobilized and unable to make decisions or take action to change the situation. The social worker must be alert to the forces of ambivalence and, when necessary, assist the client in working through this common block to decision making and action.

Helping clients sort through their perceptions of the ***risks and rewards*** associated with change is another important social work activity. If the potential rewards far outweigh the risks, most clients will attempt the change. On the other hand, if the change involves high risk or promises few or uncertain rewards, many clients will be reluctant to work toward change.

Success in making change is largely a function of the client's motivation to change, capacity for change, and opportunity to change. ***Motivation,*** which can be viewed as a state of readiness to take action, consists of the pull of hope and the push of discomfort. Clients will work and struggle toward a desired change if they believe this change is truly possible (i.e., the pull of hope) and if they are dissatisfied or distressed with their current situation (i.e., the push of discomfort). Change requires a balance between hope and discomfort. If people have hope but no real discomfort, they tend to give up when they encounter the stress and conflict associated with making change. On the other hand, if they feel discomfort but have no hope, they will see little reason to work at changing the unchangeable.

A client can be highly motivated toward one action while having little or no motivation toward another. Moreover, level of motivation varies over time and from one social context to another. Thus, a meaningful and useful description of a client's motivation must be tied to some specified goal or action rather than being viewed as a personal trait or characteristic.

Change requires a capacity for change. ***Capacity*** can be thought of as the various abilities and resources that clients or other people in the clients' environment bring to the change process. These capacities include time, energy, knowledge, experience, self-discipline, optimism, self-confidence, communication skills, problem-solving skills, money, political power, and so on. Different types of change require different types and combinations of capacity. For example, the capacities needed by a man to obtain and retain a job in road construction may be significantly different from the capacities required to change the way he communicates with his adolescent son or adjusts to the limitations of a chronic illness.

Change further requires ***opportunity,*** which here refers to various conditions and circumstances within the client's immediate environment that invite and support positive change. For example, consider the situation of a young man on probation who wants to find a job and stay out of trouble. His environment consists of his family, peer group, neighborhood, law-enforcement agencies, and so on, that will influence his ability to bring about the desired change. His opportunity for change may also be affected by community attitudes, the availability jobs, discrimination, and other social forces. Some environmental factors encourage change while others are barriers to change.

When a social worker becomes involved in the change process as a facilitator of planned change, he or she brings a fourth element—***professional resources and knowledge***—to the client's motivation, capacities, and opportunities. The role of the social worker in helping people make change can be conceptualized as taking action and applying knowledge and skills designed to increase motivation, expand capacity, and create or uncover opportunities for change. The relationship among these factors in planned change, and their effect on social functioning, can be presented as a formula (Horejsi 1976):

$$SF = \frac{(M \times C \times O)\,R}{P}$$

In this formula, *SF* refers to a level of social functioning resulting from planned change, *M* refers to motivation, *C* to capacity, and *O* to opportunity for change. *R* represents the services or actions provided by the social worker. Finally, *P* refers to the problem or concern that the client and worker are addressing. An examination of this formula reveals several important relationships. For example, as the client's problem *(P)* grows larger or more serious, the need for outside assistance *(R)* becomes more critical. Also, note, for example, that high motivation *(M)* can to a degree compensate for low capacity *(C)* or low opportunity *(O)*, but no amount of motivation can make up for a complete lack of opportunity or capacity. Likewise, no amount of opportunity *(O)* or assistance by a social worker *(R)* can compensate for an absence of client motivation *(M)* or capacity *(C)*.

The Context of Planned Change

Whether the social worker's client is an individual, a family, a group, an organization, or a community, the client's concern or problem always exists within a wider context. A multitude of social, economic, cultural, legal, and political factors are known to affect client functioning in some way and to some degree. However, many of these are beyond the influence of both the client and worker. Reality demands that the client and social worker narrow their focus and zero in on those aspects of the total situation that can be changed, given the client's motivation, capacity, and opportunity, and the resources that the social worker can bring to bear on the situation.

For the purpose of further explaining the process of planned change, the term ***client situation*** is used to describe that segment of the client's total existence, experience, and circumstances that the client can comprehend and actually influence. However, deciding what can and cannot be influenced and changed may be difficult because the client situation is always a mix of the objective and the subjective, the actual and the perceived.

The ***observed situation*** (or objective situation) is the client's situation as observed by people in the client's environment and perhaps described by professionals using commonly understood terminology, categories, and classifications. By contrast, the ***perceived situation*** (or the subjective situation) is the situation as it is felt by and uniquely interpreted and subjectively constructed by the client. It consists of the client's hopes and fears, desires and aspirations, and it usually reflects the client's history and life experiences. The situation as perceived by the client may be significantly different from the client's situation as understood and interpreted by the social worker and others in the client's environment.

The importance of the client's perceived situation to the change process is recognized in the social work axiom, "Start where the client is." It is necessary for the worker to understand the client's concern and situation from the client's point of view. The social worker must continually explore the client's perceptions and subjective interpretations and consider their implications for facilitating change. It is this element of subjectiveness that makes it so difficult to predict how clients will respond to a given intervention.

The concept of the ***social work practice situation*** encompasses both the client situation (as described) and the contextual factors that determine the worker's decision and actions. What the worker does is shaped by agency purpose, policy and procedure, practice frameworks, and the worker's skill, workload, and commitment to social work values and ethics.

An awareness of the contextual and situational aspects of social functioning and planned change yields several fundamental ***guidelines for social work practice:***

- The social worker must give primary attention to the client's problem or concern as it is defined, perceived, and experienced by the client.
- The worker must focus primarily on those aspects of the situation and the client's environment that most immediately and directly affect the client.
- The intervention must address those aspects of the situation over which the client and/or the worker have some control and influence.

- The social worker must recognize the multitude of forces pushing and pulling on the client but understand that the actual impact of those forces is at least partially dependent on the client's subjective interpretation.
- The worker must be prepared to intervene at one or more levels (e.g., individual, family, organization, community, etc.), depending on the nature of the client's concern, the client's interpretation of the situation, what the client wants to do about it, and what the client can reasonably expect to be able to do about it.
- The worker must be prepared to use a variety of techniques, approaches, and services since whatever is done must make sense to the client, given his or her perceptions and interpretations of reality.

Within all client situations—whether the client is an individual, family, group, organization, or community—there are factors and forces pushing and pulling the client toward healthy, positive, and constructive functioning. These are often called ***strengths*** (see Items 12.7 and 12.17). At a fundamental level, most social work approaches to planned change are efforts to encourage, guide, and build on the positive forces already at work in the client's life and, at the same time, to remove or overcome barriers that block change.

Reasons Why Clients May Seek Change

A deeper awareness of the change process can be derived from considering the multitude of factors, forces, and circumstances that may set in motion an effort to change.

Individual Change

Some of the reasons an individual might work with a social worker, either on a voluntary or involuntary basis, in a planned change process are:

- To cope with a crisis (old patterns no longer work and the individual is pushed by circumstances to develop new ways of functioning)
- To better cope with physical or emotional pain or illness or physical limitations
- To adjust to changes that have occurred within family, work, or school environments and in life circumstances (e.g., birth of child, divorce, new job responsibilities, etc.)
- To learn more effective and more socially acceptable ways of behaving and coping with responsibilities and problems
- To resolve uncomfortable dissonance between one's values and one's behavior

Family and Group Change

Families and small groups change for many of the same reasons as individuals. In addition, they may seek change for the following reasons:

- To adapt to the addition or loss of members, which altered patterns of communication, decision making, daily routines, and so on
- To cope with the changes made by other individuals or subgroups within the system
- To adapt to changing social and economic realities (e.g., shortage of housing, increased cost of transportation, fear of crime in neighborhood, etc.)

Organizational Change

Among the factors that might push and pull an organization to seek change are:

- To bring the organization's accomplishments more in line with its mission and goals
- To make better use of personnel (e.g., reassignment of jobs and responsibilities)
- To introduce new technology (i.e., new ways of doing the work)
- To adapt to increases or decreases in fiscal resources
- To respond to powerful external factors (e.g., public opinion, new laws or government regulations, accreditation standards, etc.)

Community Change

If the social worker's client is a neighborhood or community, reasons for seeking change might include:

- To adjust to shifts in demographics (e.g., population growth, aging of a population, increase in single-parent households, infusion of a culturally different population, etc.)
- To adapt to changes in the economic base of the community (e.g., jobs, family incomes, tax base, and investments)
- To cope with shifts in dominant values, political climate, and political power
- To cope with changes in interactional and travel patterns caused by such factors as relocation of highways, zoning changes, new housing developments and industrial tracts, and so on
- To adjust to a crisis (e.g., flood, riot, etc.)

Identifying the Actors in Planned Change

Efforts by a social worker or agency program to facilitate change typically involves numerous individuals, groups, and organizations. In complex situations, and especially in mezzo- and macro-level practice, dozens or even hundreds may be involved. To be effective, the social worker must be clear about the purpose and goal of each intervention and clear as to what is expected of each of the many actors in the change process. Drawing from a conceptualization proposed by Pincus and Minahan (1973, 63), we suggest the following terminology to help make needed distinctions among the various actors:

- ***Change agent system.*** The social worker and the worker's agency
- ***Client system.*** The person, group, or organization who has requested the social worker's or agency's services and expects to benefit from what the worker does (It is the client system that enters into an agreement or contract with the change agent system.)
- ***Target system.*** The person, group, or organization that needs to change and is targeted for change in order for the client to benefit from the intervention (In many situations of direct practice, the client system and the target system are one and the same.)
- ***Action system.*** All of the people, groups, and organizations that the change agent system (e.g., the social worker) works with or through in order to influence the target system and help the client system to achieve the desired outcome

An episode of practice typically begins with the client system and the change agent system coming together and contracting to address a particular client concern. They identify the person(s), group(s), or organization(s) that need to change and then reach out to and involve others to help facilitate the change. For example, a single mother (the client system) may approach and contract with a human services agency to receive counseling from an agency social worker (the change agent) on how to help her 10-year-old son who is withdrawn and socially isolated because he is ridiculed by schoolmates. If both the mother and child need to change, both would be target systems. If the social worker draws the child's teacher, the school principal, and the school psychologist into the helping process, these become part of the action system. If the intervention also attempts to change the behavior of the other children at school, they are also part of the target system.

Phases of the Planned Change Process

An intervention or a planned change typically moves through several sequential phases, with each phase building on previous ones. If the social worker is to guide the change process, he or she must become an expert regarding the tasks that must be accomplished at each phase.

Descriptions of these phases have been a part of the social work literature throughout the history of the profession. In her classic book, *Social Diagnosis* (1917), Mary Richmond described several steps necessary in helping people. Forty years later, Helen Perlman (1957) echoed the same theme when describing helping as a problem-solving process that involved three major phases: (1) beginning with *study* that would ascertain and clarify the facts of the problem, followed by (2) *diagnosis*, where the facts would be analyzed, and concluding with (3) *treatment* that involves making choices and taking actions to resolve the problem. In subsequent years, various authors divided these phases into more discrete units, described them in more detail, and demonstrated their application in a range of helping approaches and in work with client systems of various sizes. The ***phases of planned change*** presented here are typical of such descriptions:

- Identify, define, and describe the client's concern, troublesome situation, or problem.
- Collect additional data needed to better understand the client's concern or situation and its context.
- Assess and analyze the concern and situation and decide what needs to change, what can be changed, and how it might be changed.
- Identify and agree upon the goals and objectives (outcomes) to be achieved by the process of planned change.
- Formulate a relevant and realistic plan for reaching the goals and objectives.
- Take action based on the plan (i.e., implement the plan carry out the intervention).
- Monitor progress of the intervention and determine if it is achieving the desired outcomes and, if not, modify the plan and try again.
- Once goals and objectives have been reached, terminate the intervention and evaluate the change process to inform future practice activities.

The logical progression of these phases makes the process appear to be a linear, step-by-step set of activities. In reality, change rarely proceeds in an orderly fashion; rather, it is more of a spiral, with frequent returns to prior phases for clarification or a reworking of various tasks and activities (see Figure 7.1). During each phase, the worker also anticipates future phases, tasks, and activities and lays the groundwork for their completion.

At any given time, it is helpful to be clear about where the client is in the process of planned change, because the worker draws on somewhat different techniques to accomplish the tasks of each phase. What is helpful in one phase might be ineffective or even counterproductive in another. For example, it would be an error for a worker to discuss with an abusive mother her possible participation in an anger-management group when she has not yet concluded that there is something inappropriate and harmful about how she disciplines her child.

In this book, the change process is divided into five phases, each with two central tasks:

Phase I	Intake and Engagement
Phase II	Data Collection and Assessment
Phase III	Planning and Contracting
Phase IV	Intervention and Monitoring
Phase V	Termination and Evaluation

FIGURE 7.1 Phases of the Planned Change Process

Intake and Engagement	Data Collection and Assessment	Planning and Contracting	Intervention and Monitoring	Final Evaluation and Termination
Begin relationship; identify and define client's concern or problem; determine eligibility for service.	Gather information and "study" problem or situation; decide what needs to change, what can be changed, and how it can be changed.	Formulate objectives; evaluate possible strategies; agree on an intervention plan; determine who shall do what and when it shall be done.	Carry out plan; monitor progress; revise plan if not getting results.	Evaluate overall progress; bring relationship to an end; give feed-back to agency.

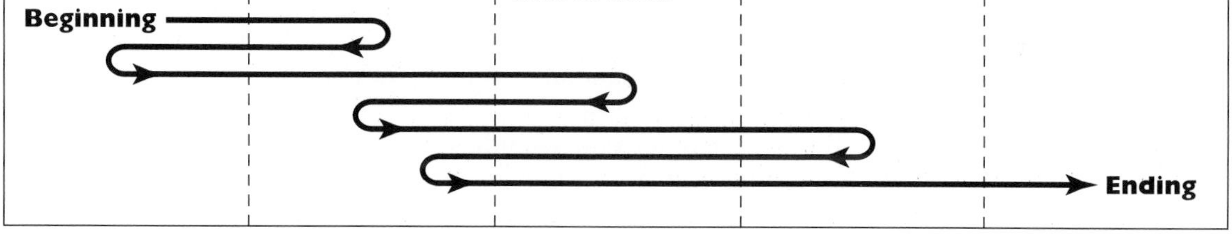

Part IV (Chapters 11 through 15) of this book is organized around this five-phase model. The introduction to each chapter describes tasks and activities associated with a particular phase. The remainder of each chapter presents numerous techniques and guidelines for accomplishing these tasks and activities.

Critical Thinking in Planned Change

The social worker's skills of critical thinking are essential to guiding the process of planned change. Most of us assume that we are careful thinkers and that our beliefs, decisions, and actions are rooted in facts and logic. In reality, many of us are rather careless in how we think and make decisions. When one steps into the role of a social work professional, loose and sloppy thinking is unacceptable and potentially harmful to clients.

Careful and critical thinking is a habit, just as is careless thinking. ***Critical thinking*** involves consciously thinking about how we think while we are thinking. The critical thinker adheres to principles of logic and is alert to the many tendencies and foibles that give rise to erroneous and superficial thinking. The skills of critical thinking include the following:

- Clarifying and defining key terms and concepts and using them in a consistent manner
- Determining the credibility of an information source
- Differentiating relevant from irrelevant information
- Distinguishing between verifiable and unverifiable claims and statements
- Checking the accuracy of a statement or claim
- Recognizing proper and improper use of statistics
- Separating thoughts and logic from emotions and feelings
- Identifying biased, ambiguous, irrelevant, and deceptive arguments
- Recognizing logical fallacies and inconsistencies in an argument or line of reasoning
- Reaching conclusions about the overall strength of an argument or conclusion

Critical thinking requires self-discipline. It requires that one take charge of his or her mental processes. According to Ruggiero (1990, 16–17):

- Critical thinkers are honest with themselves, acknowledge what they do not know, recognize their limitations, and are watchful for errors in their own thinking.
- Critical thinkers strive for understanding, remain patient in the face of complexity, are willing to invest the time needed to get the facts, and carefully analyze an issue in order to achieve clarification and overcome their confusion.
- Critical thinkers set aside personal preferences and base their judgment on evidence, defer judgment whenever evidence is insufficient, and revise their judgments and conclusions when new evidence reveals a need to do so.
- Critical thinkers are genuinely interested in ideas, and they read and listen attentively, even when they disagree with what others are saying.
- Critical thinkers recognize that extreme views (whether conservative or liberal) are seldom correct, and they seek a balanced view.
- Critical thinkers practice self-discipline, control their feelings rather than being controlled by them, and think before acting.

Broadly speaking, unclear and uncritical thinking results in two types of errors: (1) believing something is true when it is false and (2) believing something is false when it is true. Unfortunately, when the matter under consideration is complex, it may be difficult to know for sure what is true. History demonstrates that some of what our best minds now believe to be true will be proven erroneous in the future. Wisdom suggests that it is best to define truth in terms of probability. Thus, a ***truth*** is a statement that has a high probability of being accurate and true and for which there is currently insufficient reason to challenge or doubt.

People develop systems of beliefs or bundles of ideas that they draw upon to interpret new experiences. While such frames of reference or conceptual maps are necessary to human thought, they are also a potential source of bias and distortion. Such a framework is like a computer software program in that it interprets input (ideas and experiences) in only a certain way, and therefore it limits one's ability to accept and understand new ideas or to view facts from a different perspective.

A critical thinker recognizes that all ideas (e.g., concepts, theories, definitions, etc.) are essentially human inventions—that is, they are mental and social constructions that attempt to describe and explain perceptions and understandings at a given point in time. The critical thinker understands that our perceptions and ways of understanding are always incomplete and likely to shift as we have new experiences, acquire information, and experiment with new ways of interpretation.

Critical thinking requires an ability to distinguish between a fact, an assumption, an opinion, and a value. A ***fact*** is a statement of what is or of what happened that can be independently verified by empirical means. A fact is more or less solid, depending on how easily it can be confirmed. An ***assumption*** is an idea that is taken for granted or presumed for the sake of making an argument but is recognized as possibly untrue or inaccurate. An ***opinion*** puts forward one particular interpretation or viewpoint when it is understood that other credible interpretations are also possible. An opinion of worth has some factual basis, is rooted in extensive experience, and is derived from careful judgment. A ***value*** is a strongly held belief concerning what is truly worthwhile, right or wrong, and the way things are supposed to be.

In our efforts to think clearly, it is also useful to distinguish between information, knowledge, and wisdom. The term ***information*** refers to a more or less random collection of concepts, facts, and opinions. ***Knowledge*** refers to an orderly and coherent arrangement of relevant and trustworthy information related to a specific topic. The term ***wisdom*** refers to a higher level of knowledge that has a truly lasting quality. Typically, wisdom is a distillation of key ideas and principles drawn from a broad base of knowledge, a careful and in-depth examination, and many years of practical experience. These distinctions help us realize that a person can possess much information but lack real knowledge. Also, a person can be very knowledgeable on a topic but lack wisdom.

The critical thinker is aware of his or her capacity for self-deception. All too often, we believe what we want to believe and what is convenient and comfortable for us to believe. We tend to ignore facts and ideas that do not fit with our expectations. We often hold tightly to whatever we believe even in the face of evidence to the contrary. Another aspect of our capacity for self-deception is our tendency to find what we are looking for, whether or not it is really there. When we want support for our ideas, positions, and personal agenda, we usually find it. Moreover, we tend to look harder for evidence that supports our views than for evidence that refutes it.

We humans are quite suggestible and we often mistake our feelings and emotions for thoughts and logic. We are rather easily swayed and impressed by arguments presented by people we respect or admire and by those with whom we agree. We are most easily influenced by those who appear sure of themselves, especially when we are uncertain. Because we prefer certainty over uncertainty, we are often willing to relinquish our powers of inquiry in order to achieve it.

An important dynamic giving rise to uncritical thinking is our desire to be right and to have others believe we are right. That is why we so often become defensive when our beliefs are questioned. The more fragile our self-esteem, the more likely we are to be threatened by new ideas; the more likely we are also to uncritically accept ideas proposed by others.

When considering and examining a claim or assertion, the critical thinker will ask himself or herself questions such as the following:

- Why should I believe this claim or assertion?
- Who is making this claim? How reliable and trustworthy are these individuals or sources?
- Why do those making the claim or assertion want me to believe it?
- What motives or circumstances might cause them to make erroneous claims? Do they have something to gain from my acceptance of this claim or assertion?
- Am I attracted to this argument or claim because I want to believe it or perhaps because it meets some emotional need?
- Are the terms used to present the claim clearly defined and explained?
- Is the claim or assertion rooted in facts? Opinion? Values? Ideology?
- Does the claim or assertion recognize the complexity of the matter being considered or is it based on an oversimplification or superficial understanding of the topic?
- Are the facts and figures used to support the argument correct and complete? Have relevant facts been omitted or distorted?
- Are the facts and figures used in the argument drawn from the original (primary) sources or have they been drawn from secondary sources that offer only interpretations of the original data and studies?
- Could the facts and figures be interpreted in other ways or assigned different meanings?
- Have irrelevant and extraneous facts been added to the argument in order to create confusion or divert the focus from the central question?
- Has the claim or assertion been framed or stated in a way that allows it to be subjected to independent verification, objective observation, and scientific study?
- Has the claim been subjected to careful studies? Were the studies as free as possible from bias? Have the studies been replicated? Has the claim been tested in experimental studies?
- What samples were used in the studies? Were the samples representative and of sufficient size to justify generalization?
- Have criticisms of the claim or assertion been effectively refuted?

Decision Making in Planned Change

Critical thinking in social work practice is important because it leads to thoughtful and well-reasoned decisions concerning what needs to be changed, what can be changed, and how it can be changed. ***Decision making*** is the activity of consciously choosing among available options. A social worker must be able to make difficult decisions and do so with a conscious awareness of the logic being used.

To the extent possible, conclusions and decisions should be based on solid evidence. The term ***evidence*** refers to objects or information presented to the human senses for the purpose of supporting or refuting a particular argument. Powerful evidence consists of relevant and reliable facts and figures, unbiased observations, demonstrations and examples, and logical arguments. Examples of weak evidence are opinions (rather than facts), hearsay, and statements offered by people who have an "axe to grind" or something to gain personally from the outcome.

When sorting and weighing evidence for the purpose of arriving at a decision, the social worker must be alert to the following tendencies that can give rise to bad decisions:

- Tendency to pay most attention to information that one finds interesting, dramatic, or exciting
- Tendency to reject or overlook information that conflicts with one's own beliefs, feelings, preconceived notions, and personal values
- Tendency to assign greatest value to that information with which one is most familiar and finds easiest to grasp and understand
- Tendency to assign greatest value to information that was either the first or the most recently heard on the topic
- Tendency to assign greatest value to information that is easiest to obtain and to disregard or devalue information that would be more difficult to obtain

When faced with an especially difficult decision, the social worker should seek consultation and advice from experienced and informed colleagues and recognized experts. There is wisdom in the adage "Many heads are better than one." Securing several different perspectives and insights on a matter greatly increases the chances of making the best possible decision.

However, the social worker must be aware of the phenomena termed *group think*, the tendency to accept or reject a certain choice because of how others in one's group, agency, or profession think about the issue. One should never ignore the logic of one's conclusion or decision simply because it will invite criticism by others. What is common or popular is not always right and what is uncommon or unpopular is not always wrong.

A common error in decision making is to overlook some of the available options. Many people approach decisions as if there can be only two alternatives (e.g., yes-no, win-loose, stop-go, etc.). It is important to consider seriously all possible alternatives before making a decision.

Careful decision makers are alert to the special power of first impressions and first choices. Once a person commits to a particular position or option, he or she is inclined to look for and give undue weight to evidence that supports that position and to disregard evidence that supports other options. To counter this tendency, we must strive to remain open to all evidence, avoid becoming overly committed to a particular position, and give special attention to the arguments with which we disagree.

All too often, decisions are made for the purpose of justifying a past action or prior decision. When making a decision, one should give priority to the present situation and to current arguments and data. One must be cautious of making decisions based only on what was done in the past, on tradition, and on precedent.

When faced with complexity and uncertainty, humans are inclined to oversimplify the question or issue with which they are struggling in order to feel more secure and less anxious. We should be alert to this pitfall, avoiding a simple solution to a truly complex and multidimensional problem.

It is important to guard against being pushed into a premature decision by the pressure of time. Decisions made in haste can result in additional problems and cause harm. Decisions should be delayed, if possible, when one lacks sufficient information and when the various alternatives are unclear or uncertain. If a decision must be made under these conditions, it is best to select the most cautious or conservative option so that the negative effects of a possibly bad decision will be minimized.

Conclusion

The belief that change is possible and that planned change can resolve problems or create better lives for people is embedded in Western culture and especially in U.S. society. Faith in the ability to change social conditions and human interactions is at the very heart of social work practice and a prerequisite characteristic of effective workers.

The social worker's central activity in helping clients is that of guiding them through the several phases of the change process. In doing so, the worker assists them in identifying their goals, their special strengths and capacities, and their opportunities for change. Critical thinking and careful and sound decision making are fundamental to planned change.

SELECTED BIBLIOGRAPHY

Gambrill, Eileen. *Critical Thinking in Clinical Practice.* San Francisco: Jossey-Bass, 1990.

Gibbs, Leonard, and Eileen Gambrill. *Critical Thinking for Social Workers: A Workbook.* Thousand Oaks, CA: Sage, 1996.

Horejsi, Charles. "A Mathematical Presentation of the Motivation, Capacity and Opportunity Construct." *Journal of Social Welfare* 3 (Winter 1976).

Perlman, Helen. *Social Casework: A Problem Solving Process.* Chicago: University of Chicago Press, 1957.

Pincus, Allen, and Anne Minahan. *Social Work Practice: Model and Method.* Itasca, IL: F. E. Peacock, 1973.

Richmond, Mary. *Social Diagnosis.* New York: Russell Sage Foundation, 1917.

Ruggiero, Vincent. *Beyond Feelings: A Guide to Critical Thinking,* 3rd ed. Mountain View, CA: Mayfield,1990.

Part III Techniques Common to All Social Work Practice

The three chapters in Part III focus on techniques and guidelines basic to social work practice, regardless of agency setting or type of client served. In every practice setting, the social worker must be a skillful communicator, be able to develop relationships, know how to manage a workload, cope with job-related pressures, and continue to learn and grow as a professional person.

Chapter 8, "Basic Communication and Helping Skills," presents information on effective communication and relationship building. The chapter lays a foundation for understanding and applying the more specialized practice techniques and guidelines discussed in Part IV. Although many of the examples used to illustrate these skills are drawn from direct service, most can and are applied in administrative, community organization, and social planning activities. It is assumed that those using this book have been exposed to the ideas in this chapter; however, the authors' experiences suggest that readers will appreciate this concise review.

Chapter 9, "Workload and Caseload Management," is especially important to the social worker who is going into a social agency for the first time. Few new workers are adequately prepared to cope with the time pressures and paperwork they encounter. This chapter provides practical guidance on such things as time management, how to write reports, and how to maintain records. The worker's ability to master these tasks often determines whether an individual can make it in social work.

Chapter 10, "Personal and Professional Development," recognizes the importance of the social worker being able to handle job-related pressures and dilemmas while continuing to acquire new knowledge and professional skills. The day-to-day struggles of the practicing social worker are frequently overlooked by agency administrators, program planners, and sometimes even supervisors. Consequently, many workers get little or no guidance on how to survive and grow as professional people.

8 Basic Communication and Helping Skills

INTRODUCTION

This chapter presents what might be called "the basics" of social work communication and relationship. The focus is on generic communication and helping skills—namely, those used with all clients, whether the client is an individual, a family, a small group, an organization, or a community.

The specific purpose of a professional interaction will determine the type of relationship the worker attempts to develop and the messages communicated to the client. In general, the social worker providing direct services attempts to develop a relationship that has attributes known to positively affect the outcome of the helping process. These include empathy, warmth, and genuineness. The worker in the indirect-service area places more emphasis on precision, clarity, and goal directness. This is not to say, however, that the factors of empathy, warmth, and genuineness are not important in the relationships of the indirect-service worker. Rather, it is a matter of emphasis.

Essentially, ***communication*** is a process where one individual conveys information—either intentionally or unintentionally—to another person. It occurs when one person attaches meaning to the verbal or nonverbal behavior of another. Communication is a form of behavior, but not all behavior is communication; it all depends on whether a person perceives a message in the words or behavior of another. Communication is primarily a receiver phenomenon; regardless of what one says in words or intends to communicate, it is the person on the receiving end that assigns meaning to those words and body movements.

It is important to recognize the complexity and limitations inherent in human communication. Because each individual is a unique personality and has had a unique set of life experiences, each person has developed various perceptual filters and patterns of thought that affect how messages are sent and received. Thus, one individual may notice things that others overlook, and messages that are important to one person may seem inconsequential to another.

A word is but a symbol and it may have different meanings to different people, depending on a person's familiarity with the language, ethnicity, belief system, and capacity for abstract thinking. The words and other symbols used in communication have both denotive and connotative aspects. Thus, the meaning of a word or a gesture may change according to who uses it, and when, where, and how it is used.

Communication depends on the proper functioning of the senses (e.g., vision, hearing, touch, etc.) and the cognitive activities of the brain, which include ***attention*** (focusing on certain stimuli while disregarding others); ***perception*** (using attention, pattern recognition, and sensory memory to interpret stimuli picked up by our senses); ***memory*** (retaining information over time); ***language*** (interpreting, expressing, and remembering verbal and written words and symbols); ***conceptualization*** (organizing information and ideas into categories); ***reasoning*** (drawing conclusions from information); and ***decision making*** (making choices based on an anticipation of future events). These cognitive processes are interrelated and overlapping. If the senses are impaired or if the brain has been damaged, the ability to communicate will be limited to some degree. Common causes of brain damage are strokes, trauma, chemical intoxication, tumors, and dementia-type illnesses.

The capacity to send and receive messages accurately can also be distorted by one's emotional state and expectations. In general, we tend to hear what we want to hear, hear what we have learned to expect, and hear what serves our self-interests at the moment. We often distort messages in order to avoid discomfort and to meet our emotional needs. In addition, individuals with certain personality disorders characteristically distort messages in a self-serving fashion. Situational and social-interactional factors also have a powerful influence on how words and gestures are interpreted. How, when, and where a message is sent are usually as important as the literal meaning of the words used.

The lack of clear communication is a common cause of problems within families, organizations, and other social systems. In general, communication problems develop when:

- We speak for others rather than let them speak for themselves.
- We let our prejudices and stereotypes affect what we hear and say.
- We do not take the time to listen to and to understand what the other person is trying to say.
- We keep things to ourselves because we think others will disapprove of what we believe and feel.
- We make no attempt to communicate because we assume others already know, or should know, how we feel and what we think.
- We discourage or suppress communication by ordering, threatening, preaching, judging, blaming, or humoring.
- Negative feelings about ourselves (low self-esteem) cause us to conclude that we have nothing to say and that no one wants to listen to us.

Factors such as a person's ethnicity, gender, religion, and socioeconomic class can have a significant impact, not only on communication but also on help-seeking activity, how problems are defined, and what is expected of a professional relationship.

8.1 Basic Communication Skills

PURPOSE: To improve verbal communication with other professionals and agencies.

DISCUSSION: Communication, especially verbal communication, is at the heart of social work practice. Social workers make frequent use of two broad categories of communication skills: (1) those intended to facilitate interpersonal helping and (2) those intended to facilitate the exchanges of information within an agency, between agencies, and among professionals. The communication skills used in direct practice activities (e.g., face-to-face work with individual clients, families, therapeutic groups) are described in Item 8.3. The other category, basic communication skills, is used frequently when the social worker is communicating with another social worker, another professional (e.g., physician, lawyer, judge, etc.), an agency supervisor or administrator, or members of a committee or other task group. A description of those skills is presented here.

Among the attitudes that lay a foundation for good communication are the following:

- A willingness to understand that every human being is unique; consequently, each person experiences and perceives events and interpersonal exchanges in a unique manner. Thus, you should anticipate some degree of misunderstanding and plan to take steps to minimize problems of miscommunication.
- A willingness to organize your thoughts and present your message in ways that make it easy for others to understand.
- A willingness to lower your defenses so you can hear what others have to say.
- A willingness to listen carefully to the person who is speaking.
- A willingness to take responsibility for your own thoughts, feelings, and behaviors.
- A willingness to take the time needed to communicate—that is, to understand and to be understood.

Communication involves both a message sender and a message receiver. The sender has a responsibility to convey his or her message in a way that is easily received and not likely to be misunderstood. The receiver has a responsibility to make sure that he or she has accurately received the intended message and has not, in some way, distorted or misunderstood the sender's message.

When in the position of listening to or ***receiving a message,*** remember these rules:

- Stop talking. You cannot listen when you are talking.
- Put the message sender at ease. Do what you can to lessen his or her anxiety and remove distractions (e.g., close the door).
- Demonstrate, verbally and nonverbally, that you want to listen. Really pay attention.
- Be patient with the message sender. Do not interrupt.

- Ask questions if it will help you understand or help the sender to clarify his or her message.
- Control your emotions. Do not criticize or argue, for that will erect a barrier to further communication.

When ***sending a message,*** follow these rules:

- Use clear, simple language. Speak distinctly and not too fast.
- Pay attention to your body language; make sure it is congruent with your message. Maintain appropriate eye contact and utilize gestures.
- Do not overwhelm or overload the receiver with information. Break up a lengthy or complex message into several parts so it can be more easily followed and understood.
- Ask for comments, questions, or feedback so you will know whether you are being understood.

A number of specific skills can help the social worker communicate more effectively. The skill of ***planning a message*** refers to the worker thinking about an upcoming episode of communication and planning the message around the answers to several questions or concerns, such as the following:

- How much time is available for this exchange?
- When and where am I most likely to have the full attention of the person who is to receive my message?
- What are the essential points of my message?
- What aspects of my message are most likely to be misunderstood or confusing?
- How can I organize or frame my message so it will be easily understood and accepted by the receiver?
- Do I have the credibility, position, and status to deliver this message or should it be sent by someone else?

It is the middle portion of a message that is most likely to be distorted by the receiver. Thus, the most important points should placed at the beginning and the end of your message.

The skill of ***identifying self*** is an important first step in meaningful communication. It requires a concise description of who you are and how your role and responsibilities relate to the intended message or exchange of information. For example:

> You may remember me from a previous meeting, but let me begin by introducing myself. My name is Mary Jones. I am a social worker with the Evergreen Family Services Center. A client of mine has asked me to speak with you to find out if . . .

The skill of ***explaining the purpose of the communication*** refers to the sender's statements that explain the reason behind the message. This helps the receiver place the message in a proper context. For example, a child welfare social worker speaking to a prosecuting attorney might say:

> As you know, my agency has Jimmy Johnson in one of our foster homes. I need to talk with you and get a clear idea about when you plan to have Jimmy testify in court. This information is important to us because we have to inform his school of a planned absence and also work out his transportation to the courthouse.

Sometimes it is important to respond to a receiver's nonverbal communication if it suggests confusion or disagreement with the message. The skill of ***following up on nonverbal communication*** refers to such efforts. For example:

> John, I noticed that you looked a bit puzzled when I was explaining the new agency procedure. If you have any questions, please feel free to ask me at this time.

Similar follow-up efforts are important when the receiver's nonverbal communication suggests that he or she disagrees with the message. For example:

> When I was explaining the proposed policy change, I could not help but notice that several of you were looking rather distressed. It is important for me to know how you feel about the proposal. I really want to know what you are thinking. Bob, Anna, and Judy—please react to the proposed policy change.

The skill of ***checking for message reception*** refers to various questions and probes intended to verify that your message was completely and accurately received by the other party. For example:

> I am aware that what I have described as needed modifications in the agenda for our meeting might be confusing. I want to make sure you understand. Would you please repeat to me what you heard me say?

When on the receiving end of a message, it is desirable to use the skill of ***checking one's receipt of a message.*** This refers to various probes and questions intended to verify that you have, in fact, received the message and did not misunderstand what was intended by the sender. For example:

> Before we end this conversation, I want to make sure I understand completely what you have said. Let me take a minute and repeat what I heard you say. If it sounds as if I have misunderstood, please correct me.

It is surprisingly difficult to ask questions so that they can be answered in a clear and concise manner. All too often we attach unnecessary words and extraneous topics to our questions that can confuse the point of our query. In order to receive a clear answer, your question needs to be very focused and precise. This calls for the skill termed ***asking a focused question.*** Consider this example of a confusing question directed to an agency administrator:

> I am confused about these new agency policies, especially the ones about foster care and, in some ways, about a lot of the policies. This manual is organized in an unusual way. What is really expected of us? I mean, what are we supposed to do with new cases and how do we handle the court-ordered evaluations?

It would be difficult for the administrator to give a clear answer to this communication because many different questions are being asked at the same time and all of them are rather vague. A much more focused question would be:

> I have a question about policy number 8.6 on page 99 of our agency manual. In order to secure a psychological evaluation on a foster child, do I need my supervisor's written approval?

The skill of ***answering a question*** refers to statements that respond directly to the question asked and answering it in a complete manner. This seems simple; however, people often fail to really listen to the question. In the following example, a supervisor makes this error but then makes a correct response:

Worker: I need some direction on where to send this report. Do I send it to the County Attorney or directly to Judge Smith?

Supervisor: Just remember that Judge Smith is a real stickler for details. Also, he wants the report as concise as possible.

Worker: Well, yes, I know that but what I want to know is where to send the report.

Supervisor: Oh, I'm sorry. I didn't answer your question. Send it directly to Judge Smith.

When responding to a question, do not make assumptions or engage in "mind reading" about what the person meant to ask or should have asked. Listen carefully to the question and answer it without adding extraneous details.

Many communication problems arise because people use words or phrases in different ways. The skill of ***checking for word meaning*** refers to inquiries intended to make sure that all parties in an exchange agree on the meaning of key words. Consider the following example:

Chair of Planning Group: I think we need to shift about 20 percent of our budget into child abuse prevention programs.

Committee Member (checking for meaning of words): Well, I may or may not agree, depending on what you mean by prevention. What level of prevention are you talking about? Primary or secondary?

SELECTED BIBLIOGRAPHY

Burley-Allen, Madelyn. *Listening: The Forgotten Skill.* New York: John Wiley and Sons, 1995.

Gordon, Raymond. *Basic Interviewing Skills.* Itasca, IL: F. E. Peacock, 1992.

Maple, Frank. *Goal Focused Interviewing.* Thousand Oaks, CA: Sage, 1997.

8.2 Creating an Effective Helping Relationship

PURPOSE: To develop a helping relationship with a client.

DISCUSSION: At the very heart of an effective helping relationship is human caring. A social worker must genuinely care about his or her clients. Clients want a social worker to be knowledgeable but they do not pay attention to how much the worker knows until they know how much he or she cares.

Studies of helping and therapeutic relationships conclude that a positive relationship between the helper and client is necessary but not sufficient for client change to occur. The application of appropriate techniques and procedures is also necessary. Without a positive relationship, change is not likely. With a positive relationship, the techniques and procedures designed to promote change are more likely to have their intended effect.

Some type of relationship will develop whenever a social worker and client interact. The relationship may be either a positive or negative one, depending on the worker's behavior and the client's perception or interpretation of that behavior. Thus, the social worker cannot *make* a positive relationship happen. At most, he or she can strive to be the type of person that most clients find helpful and to do those things that increase the chances that a positive relationship will develop.

The content and character of a specific relationship will be shaped by such influences as the treatment plan, the social worker's practice framework, and the agency's purpose and procedures. But fundamentally, a professional relationship is a very human struggle for meaningful communication and interaction. It is important to recognize that a helping relationship is not necessarily pleasant and free of conflict. In fact, a genuinely helpful, positive, and therapeutic relationship can be a stressful experience for both the client and the social worker.

Extensive research has identified the core conditions or key characteristics of a helpful relationship. These are empathy, positive regard, personal warmth, and genuineness. ***Empathy*** refers to the worker's capacity to perceive accurately a client's feelings and subjective experiences and to grasp the meanings they have for the client. Empathy is sometimes described as stepping into the client's shoes and feeling and seeing things as the client does. The truly empathetic social worker is able to sense the meaning of a client's experiences even when the worker has not had a similar life experience. Empathy is conveyed primarily by giving the client undivided attention and by responding sensitively to nonverbal cues. The techniques of active listening such as paraphrasing and reflection are critical to the worker's display of empathy (see Item 8.3).

Essentially, ***positive regard*** means believing that all clients are persons of value and treating them with dignity regardless of appearance, behavior, or life circumstances. This does not mean that the social worker must accept or approve of destructive behaviors but rather that the client is viewed and treated as a person of inherent worth. Our tendency to judge others is a major barrier to effective communication; it is strongest when our feelings and emotions are stirred. When we judge, we are usually looking at a situation from our point of view rather than the client's.

Communication can be improved by maintaining a *nonjudgmental attitude,* which is the willingness and capacity to suspend moral judgment of the client's statements, motives, and actions and to avoid either condoning or criticizing the client's thoughts, feelings, and behavior.

The core condition of ***personal warmth*** exists when the social worker responds to clients in ways that make them feel safe, accepted, and understood. Without the quality of warmth, the worker's words will sound hollow and insincere and will have no therapeutic impact. Warmth is mostly nonverbal communication and is expressed in a smile, a soft and soothing voice, a relaxed but interested posture, eye contact, and gestures that convey acceptance and openness.

Genuineness means being one's self, being real, and "speaking from the heart." People who are genuine are nondefensive and spontaneous, and what they say matches what they do. They lack pretentiousness and any hint of phoniness. What they reveal about their own thoughts and feelings is true and real. They are honest with others, but that does not mean that they strive to be totally honest, for they are sensitive to the needs and feelings of other people. When they have a negative feeling toward a client's behavior, they exercise self-discipline so it does not damage the professional relationship or harm the client.

Those who are new to social work sometimes worry that they cannot simultaneously take on a professional role and be truly genuine in their relationships with clients. Being professional has nothing to do with "playing the role" or trying to imitate some idealized image of a professional person. A true professional is knowledgeable, self-disciplined, responsible, ethical, and, most of all, effective. There is no conflict between those qualities and being genuine.

Much of the research on helping relationships has been conducted outside the field of social work, but those research findings are consistent with ones that have emerged from social work research. Fischer (1981, 204) concludes that the core conditions of empathy, positive regard, warmth, and genuineness are clearly relevant to social work: "They constitute the essential skills involving relationships and therapeutic interviewing that are the heart of practice." Maluccio (1979) uses in-depth interviewing to secure clients' opinions about social workers and his data also underscore the importance of these core conditions. However, three additional worker qualities emerged from his study: ***concreteness*** (ability to communicate thoughts and ideas clearly and specifically), ***competence*** (proficiency in carrying out professional tasks and activities), and ***objectivity*** (being unbiased and able to appreciate differing points of view).

Maluccio (1979, 125) states that, from the client's perspective, an ideal social worker is "warm, accepting, understanding, involved, natural, genuine, competent, objective and able to share of himself or herself with the client." Fischer (1978) concludes that the effective social worker is

> deeply involved, deeply personal, deeply caring. Effective caseworkers are *real* people, unafraid of their own experiences, trusting those experiences, knowing who they are, and offering every client all they are. Effective caseworkers are not afraid of emotions, their own or their client's; they are not afraid to *feel* or express those feelings. And when they express feelings, they do so in a way that is constructive for others. Effective case-

> workers are both secure and competent enough to recognize that one can be deeply involved with the problems of others, yet retain the objectivity necessary for appropriate selection and use procedures that will be facilitative for clients. (p. 213)

The term ***structuring*** refers to the use of various interpersonal arrangements (e.g., worker-client matching) and symbols (e.g., worker dress and office environment) to enhance relationship building. For example, a client is most likely to be influenced by someone to whom he or she is attracted. People are usually attracted to and feel most comfortable with those who have beliefs, backgrounds, and a life-style similar to their own. It follows, therefore, that a social worker who wants to increase his or her attractiveness to a client and decrease a client's uncomfortableness should look for similarities and mention them to the client. For example, the worker might point out that he or she and the client both have children of about the same age or that both grew up on a farm. It should be noted, however, that some studies have found that client-worker matching by age, race, sex, marital status, parenthood, and socioeconomic status had little or no effect on intervention outcome.

Whether particular differences between the client and the worker have a significant impact on the helping relationship is mostly a function of the client's expectations and perceptions. Davis and Proctor (1989) suggest that a client who is different from the social worker in terms of race, gender, or socioeconomic status is likely to have three major concerns:

> 1. Is the helper a person of goodwill? That is, does this person have my best interests at heart? Does he or she dislike . . . people like me? The client's answer to this question determines the extent to which the client will initially trust the helper.
> 2. Does the worker have professional expertise or mastery of skills that can resolve my problems? That is, is this person adequately skilled or trained? The answer to this question will also affect the client's trust in the worker. The central issue, however, is the worker's competence, or capacity to be helpful.
> 3. Does the worker have sufficient understanding of my social reality or my world view? That is, is this person sufficiently familiar with people like me? Will this person understand my life experiences? The answer to this question will determine the extent to which the worker is seen as credible, and the extent to which advice and suggestions can be accepted as valid and meaningful. (p. ix)

How the client answers such questions will obviously have an impact on whether and how the client uses the services of the social worker.

One's waiting room and office can also have a significant impact on clients, either positive or negative. For example, if a client must talk with the social worker in a space that lacks privacy and comfort, respect for the worker is greatly diminished. It is important to make offices and meeting rooms as comfortable and respectful as possible.

Research findings tell us that ***expertness***—or at least the appearance of expertness—can have a positive impact on the initial phases of the helping process. Such things as certificates and diplomas on the wall, a large office, proper use of language, and professional dress can increase the client's respect for the helper and result in the client being more open to influence. Clearly, one must be alert to the importance of such factors, but the social worker should remember that clients, like all people, make deliberate decisions about whose influence they accept and whose they reject.

SELECTED BIBLIOGRAPHY

Davis, Larry, and Enola Proctor. *Race, Gender and Class: Guidelines for Practice with Individuals, Families and Groups.* Englewood Cliffs, NJ: Prentice Hall, 1989.

Fischer, Joel. "The Social Work Revolution." *Social Work* 26 (May 1981): 199–207.

———. *Effective Casework Practice: An Eclectic Approach.* New York: McGraw-Hill, 1978.

Maluccio, Anthony. *Learning from Clients: Interpersonal Helping as Viewed by Clients and Social Workers.* New York: Free Press, 1979.

8.3 Basic Helping Skills

PURPOSE: To use verbal messages that can assist and encourage a client during the intervention process.

DISCUSSION: As used here, the term ***helping skill*** refers to a message that the practitioner conveys to the client because the worker believes it will have a beneficial effect on the client's thinking, feelings, or behavior. The moment-to-moment decisions concerning what message to send should be guided by the purpose of the interview and based on what the social worker knows about the client and his or her situation. Moreover, a specific skill or message will be more or less useful depending on the phase of the change process (i.e., intake, assessment, planning and contracting, intervention, and termination). The appropriateness of a message also depends on whether it is offerred during the beginning, middle, or ending phase of an interview or meeting. Needless to say, all communication has a significant nonverbal component—including the use of eye contact, gestures, and other movements—to help convey the message; information on nonverbal communication appears in Item 8.4.

Writers in the fields of social work, clinical psychology, and counseling have described dozens of helping skills. There is no agreed upon terminology and various authors use different names for what are essentially the same skills. Possible exceptions are the terms associated with the skills of active listening (e.g., paraphrase, reflection, summarization). These are used fairly consistently by most writers. On the following pages brief descriptions of commonly used helping skills are offered. In several instances, terminology is borrowed from Shulman (1981, 1999). The examples that illustrate how a particular skill might be used are drawn from one-on-one interviews, but these same skills can be adapted for use in work with families and therapeutic groups. Many of the more specialized techniques presented in Part IV of this book can be viewed as elaborations and special applications of the basic skills described here.

Getting Ready

In a sense, the social worker's helping actions begin *before* the first face-to-face meeting with the client. Prior to the meeting, the worker should imagine what the client might be thinking and feeling as he or she enters the agency or office expecting to discuss personal matters with a stranger. By trying to anticipate how the client might feel, the worker begins to develop empathy for the client and mentally prepares to address the client's initial feelings (e.g., anger, fear, confusion, etc.) and to identify ways to ease the client into the helping relationship. Shulman (1999, 44) has termed this the *tuning-in phase* of the helping process. (See Items 11.1, 11.2, and 14.1 for more information on how to prepare for an interview.)

Getting Started

During the intake and engagement phase of the change process and also at the beginning of each session with a client, the social worker must give special attention to clarifying the purpose of the meeting and the worker's role. The helping skill of ***explaining purpose*** refers to a simple, nonjargonized statement by the worker about the general purpose of the meeting. It serves to define expectations and reduce client confusion and anxiety. For example:

> *Worker:* I am pleased that you were able to meet with me today. As you know, your wife first came to this agency about three weeks ago. She expressed concern about your marriage. I would like to hear your thoughts and find out if you also believe there are problems in the marriage.

When the first contact is initiated by the client, the worker should encourage the client to begin by describing the reason for requesting the interview. If the client has a hard time explaining his or her purpose, the worker might ask some general questions about the circumstances that led up to the request for an interview and what the client hopes will come from the meeting.

When the social worker initiates the first contact, he or she should begin by explaining the purpose. The explanation should be clear and to the point, such as:

> *Good Explanation:* I need to talk with you about your son Max. He has missed 14 out of the last 20 school days. This is a serious problem.
>
> *Poor Explanation:* Hi there. I know your son Max. I was in the neighborhood so I decided to stop by to chat. How are things going?

The skill of ***encouraging the client's feedback on purpose*** (Shulman 1981) refers to statements that encourage the client to respond to the worker's explanation. This gives the client an opportunity to ask questions or perhaps voice disagreement. Consider these two examples:

> *Worker:* What are your reactions to what I have said about the purpose of this meeting? Do you see things differently?
>
> *or*
>
> *Worker:* It's quite possible you and I have different thoughts about why we are talking today. I want to know if you were expecting something else.

The skill of ***describing the worker's role and method*** refers to statements intended to give the client a beginning idea of how the worker might be able to help and the approaches or methods to be used. For example:

> ***Worker:*** As you get ready to leave this hospital, it is important to anticipate the problems you may face when you get home and to figure out how to deal with them. Basically, that is why I want to meet with you two or three times before you leave. I will ask for your ideas and I will share my ideas, as well. Between the two of us, I hope we can come up with a plan that will minimize the difficulties you will have when you are at home.

Each session with a client has three time phases: (1) getting started, (2) the central work of the session, and (3) drawing the session to a close. At the beginning of each session, the social worker should provide an opportunity for what Shulman (1981, 12) terms *sessional contracting.* Even when there has been a prior agreement on how the session's time will be used, it is important to check once again for consensus. Quite possibly, some change in the client's situation has altered the client's sense of priorities. The skill of ***reaching for between-session data*** (Shulman 1981) is used to initiate sessional contracting. This form of "checking in" involves asking the client to bring the worker up to date and to identify the key topics to be discussed, even if they are different from what was planned during the previous meeting. This can be viewed as an attempt to adhere to the principle of *starting where the client is.* For example:

> ***Worker:*** You will recall that during last week's session we agreed to spend today's session talking about your reluctance to visit your children in foster care. Do you still think that is how we should spend our time today, or do you now have a more pressing concern?

Asking Questions

A social worker uses various types of questions to obtain needed information and assist the client in expressing his or her thoughts and feelings. A question such as "What are the names of your children?" is termed a ***closed-ended question;*** it limits how the client can respond. By contrast, a question such as "Tell me about your children" is called an ***open-ended question*** because it gives the client an opportunity to say whatever he or she thinks is important. However, open-ended questions can vary in the amount of freedom they allow. These three questions are all open ended, but some are more open than others:

> "Tell me about your job."
>
> "What do you like and what do you dislike about your job?"
>
> "What tasks and responsibilities are part of your job?"

During counseling sessions, the worker will use mostly open-ended questions. Close-ended questions are appropriate when the worker needs specific information or when the client is so confused or overwhelmed that structure is needed to maintain focus and direction.

The skill of ***narrowing the focus*** (or *funneling*) refers to a series of questions intended to assist the client in describing his or her concerns or situation with more specificity. For example:

> ***Client:*** Things are really a mess at home.
> ***Worker:*** I'm not sure what you mean by "a mess." What happened?
> ***Client:*** We were eating when Dad came home from work. He was drunk and ended up hitting Mom.
> ***Worker:*** What did you do when all this was happening?
> ***Client:*** First I ran out of the room. Then I came back and yelled at my dad to stop it or I would call the cops.
> ***Worker:*** What were you thinking and feeling at that time you threatened to call the police?

Common errors in questioning technique include the overuse of close-ended questions, stacking questions, asking leading questions, and asking too many "why" questions. *Stacking questions* refers to the undesirable practice of asking several questions all at once. Consider this example:

> ***Worker:*** So, you are interested in adoption. How long have you been thinking about adoption? Have you known others who have adopted? Are you thinking about an infant? Have you thought much about an older child or one who has a disability?

Stacked questions are confusing to clients. It is best to ask questions one at a time.

Leading questions are those that push or pull the client toward a certain response—for example, "Didn't you think that was wrong?" or "I assume that you explained to your boss why you missed work?" or "Isn't it true that you were hoping for a fight?" Leading questions are intimidating and insulting to clients. A leading question may prompt the client to lie rather than openly disagree with the worker.

Another common error is to ask *"why" questions*—for example, "Why do you get so angry when Maria spills food?" Essentially, "why" questions ask the client to justify his or her behavior, and this tends to produce defensiveness. Moreover, most people do not know the "whys" of their behavior, so, when asked, they simply guess or give socially acceptable answers. Instead of asking why, use questions that focus on the what, where, when, and how of the client's behavior and situation.

Active Listening

In active listening, the worker attends to both the client's verbal and nonverbal messages. The worker also reflects back to the client what has been heard so that the client will know that his or her message has been accurately understood. When engaged in active listening, the social worker should remember the following:

- Pay attention to the client's underlying feelings rather than only the literal meaning of the client's words.
- Use a clear, calm, and interested tone of voice.

- Use body language that communicates attentiveness and demonstrates openness and concern.
- Ask questions that clarify what is being said by the client.
- Speak in order to better understand the client, and not primarily to make a point or offer an opinion.

The skills of active listening are those of using encouragers, clarification, paraphrase, reflection, summarization, and exploring silences.

An ***encourager*** (also called a *prompt*) refers to single words, short phrases, and nonverbal gestures that encourage the client to continue talking. Examples of verbal encouragers are "Uh-huh," "Tell me more," "Please go on," and the repetition of a key word just uttered by the client. Nonverbal encouragers would include nods of the head and hand gestures that signal an invitation to say more.

Clarification refers to asking a question designed to encourage a client to become more explicit or to verify the worker's understanding of what the client has said. Such questions might begin with "Are you saying that . . . " or "Do you mean that . . . " and end with a rephrasing of the client's words. For example:

> ***Client:*** My life is a disaster. I thought I could get things squared away, but it doesn't look like that will be possible.
>
> ***Worker:*** I am not sure I am following you. Are you saying that things are changing more slowly than you expected or that your situation is now worse than before?

Another example follows:

> ***Worker:*** I am not sure what you mean when you say that you and your wife had a fight. Did this involve hitting?

When a worker becomes confused by what a client is saying, it is best to acknowledge the confusion and seek clarification. Here are a couple of examples:

> ***Worker:*** You have been talking very fast. I cannot keep up and I am getting confused. Please start over, one point at a time. Also, try to slow down so I will not miss anything that you have to say.
>
> *or*
>
> ***Worker:*** I am sorry, but I didn't follow that. Please tell me once more.

A skilled social worker focuses on both the client's words and on the affect associated with those words. To do this, he or she will make frequent use of the paraphrase and reflection. The skill known as ***paraphrase*** is a rephrasing of the literal meaning of the client's statement, whereas the skill termed ***reflection of feeling*** is an expression of the feeling or emotional component of the message. Examples of paraphrase and reflection are as follows:

Client: That guy down at the employment office is a real jerk. How does he get away with treating people like that? I feel three inches tall when I go down there.
Worker: I hear you saying that when you go to that office you are treated badly. (paraphrase)

or

Worker: It sounds like you feel shamed and humiliated at the employment office. (reflection of feeling)

The skill of ***summarization*** refers to pulling together the content and affective components of several messages. For example, a worker might use summarization to draw together the key affective and content elements of what was discussed during the previous five minutes. Here is an example of summarization:

Worker: From what you have been saying, I am hearing a number of things. You are desperate for a job and feel a mix of anger and depression because you haven't found one. You have been going to the employment office but that adds to your feelings of frustration and humiliation. On top of that, you have begun to feel deep regret for having dropped out of high school. Is that an accurate summary of what you have been saying?

Active listening also requires careful attention to times when the client is silent. Silence is a behavior that has meaning, and sometimes it is important to discover that meaning. The skill of ***exploring the client's silence*** refers to efforts to gently probe the silence. For example:

Client: (thoughtful silence)
Worker: You appear to be puzzling over something. Can you tell me what you are thinking about?

or

Client: (thoughtful silence)
Worker: Our discussion about your mother's illness seems to be pretty hard on you. Am I asking you to talk about something that is too painful to discuss?

An error commonly made by beginning social workers is to respond to silence with a change of topics. This happens because the worker becomes uncomfortable when the client is quiet. A brief silence is best responded to with polite quietness. If the silence is a long one, the worker should attempt to explore the silence.

Displaying Empathy, Genuineness, and Warmth

Item 8.2 of this chapter described the importance of the social worker's capacity for empathy, genuineness, and personal warmth in a helping relationship. A number of skills or techniques are used to display these qualities to the client. The skill of ***dis-***

playing understanding refers to verbal and nonverbal communication intended to demonstrate that the social worker comprehends and can identify with the client's thoughts and feelings. For example:

> ***Client:*** Having to place Susan in foster care is one of the most difficult decisions I have ever made.
>
> ***Worker:*** It must be hard to make a decision that is going to be very upsetting to Susan. It seems like this decision is tearing you apart inside.

It is especially important to acknowledge and display an understanding of a client's negative feelings such as anger and resentment. For example:

> ***Client:*** I am sick of this place. I don't need to be in a treatment program. I feel like punching the next person who asks me about my drinking.
>
> ***Worker:*** Well, I am part of this treatment program and you know that I will ask about your drinking. I guess that means you want to hit me. I am not sure how to respond to your threat. What are you expecting me to do?

The skill of ***putting the client's feelings into words*** refers to the articulation of what the client is feeling but has stopped just short of expressing in words. For example:

> ***Worker:*** How did the visit with your mother go?
>
> ***Client:*** OK, I guess, but I don't know if I can take this much longer.
>
> ***Worker:*** Watching your mother die is putting you under a lot of stress. It sounds like you hope death will come soon, but I assume that such a thought makes you feel guilty. Is that the way you are feeling?

This helping skill gives the client a supportive invitation to express what he or she is feeling but is reluctant to say aloud. Here is another example:

> ***Worker:*** Do you have any other questions about adoption or our agency's adoption program?
>
> ***Client:*** No, I don't think so. You explained it pretty well. I guess it's just a lot different from what I expected.
>
> ***Worker:*** I have the impression you were disappointed with what I had to say. You looked quite sad. Can you tell me how you are feeling about what I have told you?

It is important to recognize that encouraging a client to express feelings is appropriate only when those feelings are directly related to the overall goals of the professional relationship and intervention.

The helping skill of ***self-disclosure*** refers to a worker's statements that reveal some of his or her own thoughts, feelings, or life experiences. When properly used, self-disclosure has the effect of making it easier for the client to talk about a sensitive topic and to feel more at ease with the worker. On the other hand, the improper use of self-disclosure can cause the client to question the worker's emotional stability and professional competence and even cause the client to feel manipulated.

In some instances of self-disclosure, a social worker may elect to reveal feelings. These may be either positive or negative, as shown in these examples:

> ***Worker:*** I feel disappointed and angry when I think about all the time we spent looking for your job and now, after just one week, you are talking about quitting.

or

> ***Worker:*** I really feel good about what you have done. When we first met, I was worried about your financial situation. I feel proud and happy that our agency's training program helped you find that job.

At other times, a social worker may elect to share information about some life experience. For example:

> ***Worker:*** I am sorry about how I reacted on the phone. I guess you noticed that I become sad when we talk about your mother's death. That touches me deeply. I had a real hard time adjusting after my mother died of cancer two years ago.

As a general rule, the use of self-disclosure should be avoided in the early stages of relationship building and used sparingly at other times. The information revealed by the worker should always have a clear connection to the client's concern. It is inappropriate for the worker to talk about personal experiences that are unrelated to the purpose of the interview.

Sustaining Client Motivation

In Chapter 7, motivation was described as a type of hope-discomfort balance. In order for people to make a change, they must feel hopeful about the possibility of change as well as feel some discomfort or dissatisfaction with their current behavior or situation. Several skills can be used to increase or sustain a client's motivation for change.

Displaying a belief in the potential of work (Shulman 1981) refers to statements intended to convey the worker's belief that professional intervention can be helpful. It is an offer of realistic hope to the client. For example:

> ***Worker:*** The problems you have described are serious. I can understand why you feel overwhelmed. But I think you can successfully deal with these problems if we work together and start chipping away at the problems, one at a time. It won't be easy, but I believe we can make some progress over the next few weeks.

The skill of ***recognizing client strengths*** refers to expressions of confidence in the client's ability to accomplish some specific tasks or to cope with a difficult situation. Here are two examples:

> ***Worker:*** I know it is going to be difficult and painful for you to visit your kids in their foster home, but your visits are important to them, and I think you can handle it because you have been through this experience once before.

or

> ***Worker:*** You faced this problem in the past, and somehow you weathered the storm. I know you just want to run away from the whole thing, but you are an intelligent person and I really believe that you can figure out a solution.

(See Item 12.7 for more information on client strengths.)

The skill of ***pointing out negative consequences*** refers to statements that remind the client that change is needed in order to avoid undesirable consequences. For example:

> ***Worker:*** When you talk about wanting to drop out of the sex offender treatment program, I feel that I must warn you of the consequences. If you do not work on your problems and demonstrate a capacity to control your attraction to children, the judge will revoke your probation and you will go to prison.

or

> ***Worker:*** When we first met, you were frantic because you owed so much money on your credit cards. Over the past months, you have made some real progress on controlling your spending. Now, you are talking about a very expensive vacation. I am concerned that you might slip back into your old habits.

Maintaining Progress toward Change

Effective helping involves much more than understanding the client's problem or situation. The client needs to be helped and encouraged to make decisions and take action. Realistic, gentle, and supportive demands for change are necessary. Change usually involves having to reexamine one's assumptions and reevaluate past behavior; this can be painful and embarrassing. Change also involves trying out new behaviors and completing unfamiliar tasks; this can be frightening because it requires risk taking. It is important to recognize that a degree of fear, ambivalence, and resistance is a normal part of change. In fact, a lack of ambivalence and resistance may indicate that what looks like an effort to change is, in reality, only an illusion. Shulman (1981) explains that

> the worker must make a consistent ***demand for work***. The demand may be expressed in many ways, but it is generally experienced by the client as the worker saying "I mean business." It is a critical skill because it conveys to the client the worker's belief in the client's strength and the worker's willingness to deal with even the toughest problems and feelings faced by the client. It is precisely this additional pull that clients need at that moment to mobilize their strength and to take their next steps. . . .
>
> The demand for work needs to be linked closely to the empathic skills. . . . A worker who is demanding, but not empathic, will be seen by the client as rejecting. On the other hand, the worker who is empathic, but makes no demands, will appear to the client as easy to put off. It is a critical synthesis of these two behaviors that will lead to effective work. (p. 20)

Several skills are helpful in maintaining momentum in the change process. One of these, ***partialization***, refers to breaking down a seemingly insolvable problem into smaller, more manageable components. Clients often feel overwhelmed or helpless when faced with large, complex problems. When a problem is broken down into several smaller concerns, it seems less frightening, and the client is better able to focus his or her attention and energy. For example:

Client: I cannot believe what is happening. Jimmy cut his head and I took him to the hospital. That crazy doctor notified child protective services and accused me of abusing Jimmy. Then my oldest son got into a fight with the landlord, and now the landlord has asked me to find another apartment. I cannot afford a lawyer, my child support check is late, and, on top of everything else, our car won't start. Things are so screwed up I cannot even think straight. All of a sudden the whole world has fallen in on me.

Worker: I think we better talk about your concerns one at a time. Otherwise, we will get confused and feel even more frustrated. Let's first focus on the child abuse report. We will return to the other problems later. First, tell me more about Jimmy's injury and the abuse report. For now, let's talk only about that problem, OK?

The skill of ***staying on track*** involves worker statements intended to keep the client's attention focused on a specific concern or objective. This is especially important if the client tends to ramble or wants to avoid work on a relevant concern. For example:

Worker: Because your boss has threatened to fire you, I think we better focus on that problem.

Client: Yeah. I guess so. I really wish I could get a transfer. But the company has such old-fashioned policies on things like that. I'm surprised they make any money at all. With the economy the way it is, you would think they would change the whole operation. They are not prepared for global markets. I recently read an article on new styles of management and . . .

Worker: I think we better come back to the conflict between you and your supervisor. You have lost other jobs because of conflict. I know you need this job, so I think we better figure out a way of dealing with the problem between you and your supervisor.

The skill of ***building a communication link*** refers to efforts by the worker to establish a connection between the client and those with whom he or she needs to communicate. For example:

Worker: This is the third time you have told me that you haven't been able to tell your doctor about your concerns. What do you think about me giving her a call and explaining that I know you have something to talk to her about? I think that might cause her to spend more time with you when she visits you in the hospital tomorrow. Is that OK with you?

Sometimes a client will outwardly agree to take a certain course of action but inwardly have no real commitment to that plan. It is also fairly common for a client to decide on an action without being fully aware of the difficulties he or she will encounter. The skill of ***checking for acquiescence*** refers to efforts aimed at flushing out a client's resistance to or ambivalence regarding a certain decision or action. For example:

Worker: I certainly agree that you should talk to your math teacher about your failing grade. That needs to be done and I am pleased to hear that you intend to do it. But I also know that you often feel intimidated by that teacher. Don't you think this is going to be a difficult step for you?

Because genuine personal change is often an emotional struggle, the helping process and the content of the client-worker communications are usually emotionally charged. If, over a period of several sessions, there is little or no affectively charged discussion and no significant change in the client's behavior or situation, it is likely that the client is not really engaged in the change process. This needs to be discussed with the client. The skill of ***challenging the client's avoidance of change*** is a type of confrontation aimed at pointing out the client's resistance. The next example illustrates the use of this challenge during a marriage counseling session:

Worker: There is something that concerns me. When you two first came to the agency a few weeks ago, you requested help with your marriage. We have met three times. However, both of you have spent most of our time talking about your jobs, your kids, and your wish for a new house. You have said that there have been times when you were close to a divorce. Yet you seem to be avoiding any discussion of your marriage relationship. Unless we focus on your interaction, we are not going to make any progress.

(See Item 14.11 for additional information on challenge and confrontation.)

Sometimes a client's movement toward change is blocked because he or she does not want to grapple with painful feelings. The skill of ***identifying emotional blocks*** refers to messages aimed at increasing the client's awareness of how these feelings are getting in the way of progress. For example:

Client: I know I said I wanted to visit my kids more often, but I have been too busy at work to get away for a visit.

Worker: You are a hard worker and your job demands much of your time, but I suspect the anger and guilt you feel about your divorce is also causing you to avoid visiting your kids. Perhaps we need to discuss those feelings and how they keep you from doing what you want to do.

Another example follows:

Worker: I have noticed something, and I think we need to talk about it. We started meeting together because you wanted help in learning how to handle your children. Yet each time I ask about Gloria, you become tense and start talking about the other children. What is it about your relationship with Gloria that makes you so uncomfortable?

In some cases, the change process is blocked when a client has unusual difficulty talking about an important but embarrassing topic such as sexual behavior, spending habits, or irresponsible behavior. The skill of ***supporting the clients in taboo areas*** (Shulman 1981) refers to communication intended to assist the client in discussing sensitive topics. For example:

Client: I always feel nervous when I get to the topic of sex. It's hard for me to talk about it because of the way I was raised.

Worker: You are not alone. Many of us were raised the same way. But I want you to try. You and your husband need to discuss your sexual relationship. That area in your marriage is causing you some real problems. It's difficult to discuss, but let's keep at it.

Some clients have had difficulties with authority figures (e.g., parents, employers, police, etc.) and view the social worker as one more authority wanting to control their life. It is important to invite the client to talk about this concern. The skill of ***addressing the authority issue*** refers to worker communication that invites the client to express concerns or complaints about the worker or the helping process. Consider this illustration:

Client: I think things are a lot better now at home. I don't think we need to set up another meeting.

Worker: I hope things are better, but I think something else is going on here. I have the impression that you think my job is like that of a parole officer and that I am trying to catch you doing something wrong. How about that? Are you scared of me and the trouble I might cause you?

(See Item 11.6 for more information on authority and the helping process.)

Bringing Things to a Close

Not infrequently, clients will wait until the last few minutes of a session before bringing up an important issue. There are several possible motives behind this *doorknob communication,* such as fear of the topic, wanting to inform the worker of a concern but not wanting to discuss it, and so on. The skills of ***setting time limits*** and ***giving a 10-minute warning*** are ways of encouraging the client to bring up difficult topics and to stay focused on high-priority topics. Here are a couple of examples:

Worker: Before we begin, I want to remind you that we can talk until 4:00 P.M. I say that because I want to make sure that we use our time to discuss issues that are of greatest importance to you.

or

Worker: I just noticed that we have to end this session in 10 minutes. Have we gotten to all the topics you wanted to discuss or is there something else that you wanted to talk about today?

The skill of ***looking ahead to the end*** is designed to remind the client of a planned ending for the intervention so the best possible use can be made of the remaining sessions. For example:

Worker: When we began meeting a month ago, we agreed to meet for eight times. We have three sessions left. Let's discuss what remains to be done so we use those three sessions to focus on high-priority concerns.

The client–social worker relationship may end either because their work together is finished or because the social worker must transfer the client to another worker. If the relationship has been a meaningful one, the ending can be difficult. Because so many clients have experienced losses during their lives, the ending may be painful because it reactivates feelings attached to prior losses. These feelings must be addressed directly by the worker. Shulman (1981) explains that

> because of the general reluctance to face endings, both on the part of the worker and the client, endings often are handled too quickly, without an opportunity for the client and worker to deal with the complex feelings involved. . . . Since the client needs time to deal with the ending, encompass it, and not experience it as a sharp rejection by the worker, it is important for the worker to point out the ending well in advance in order to allow the process to become established. . . . It is only when workers can come to grips with their own feelings that they can begin to help the client in this important phase. (pp. 26–27)

The worker can help the client deal with the separation by voicing feelings about termination. This is termed ***sharing ending feelings*** (Shulman 1981). For example:

Worker: I have been thinking about our relationship. Since you came to this hospital in September, we have gotten to know each other very well. I am glad you are finally able to go home, but I want you to know that I will miss our discussions and your positive attitude.

The review of what the client and worker have done to address the client's concerns is an important element in termination. This skill is referred to as ***reviewing progress.*** Here is an example:

> *Worker:* Altogether, we have been meeting for about four months. A lot has happened since you were reported for child abuse. You have made some positive changes in how you deal with your son, Michael. What have you learned from this whole experience?

It is important to encourage the client to express his or her feelings about termination. These feelings may be positive or negative or a mix of both. The skill of ***reaching for ending feelings*** (Shulman 1981) refers to worker communication that helps the client articulate his or her feelings. For example:

> *Worker:* I know you are pleased about getting off probation. You are no longer required to see me. But I also sense that you have mixed feelings about our meetings coming to an end. I wonder if it will be difficult for you to say good-bye. How about that?

(See Item 15.6 for more information on termination.)

SELECTED BIBLIOGRAPHY

Egan, Gerald. *The Skilled Helper*, 6th ed. Pacific Grove, CA: Brooks/Cole, 1998.

Kadushin, Alfred. *The Social Work Interview*, 4th ed. New York: Columbia University Press, 1997.

Murphy, Bianca, and Carolyn Dillon. *Interviewing in Action.* Pacific Grove, CA: Brooks/Cole, 1998.

Shulman, Lawrence. *The Skills of Helping: Individuals, Families and Groups*, 4th ed. Itasca, IL: F. E. Peacock, 1999.

———. *Identifying, Measuring and Teaching Helping Skills.* New York: CSWE, 1981.

Sommers-Flanagan, John, and Rita Sommers-Flanagan. *Foundations of Therapeutic Interviewing.* Boston: Allyn and Bacon, 1993.

8.4 Nonverbal Communication

PURPOSE: To understand and use nonverbal messages.

DISCUSSION: Some researchers suggest that about 50 percent of every message in face-to-face communication is sent by facial expression alone, especially through the eyes, and about 30 percent is expressed by voice tone, pitch, and resonance. A social worker must be alert to the messages he or she may be sending by way of nonverbal communication. By paying attention to the client's nonverbal communication, the social worker can determine how he or she is being perceived by the client. Observing nonverbal behavior also tells the worker if what the client is saying in words reflects his or her thoughts and feelings.

Eye contact is a powerful means of communication. Eyes reveal much about our emotional state. Eye contact usually indicates a willingness to engage in communication and is an indicator of sensitivity and understanding. A lack of eye contact suggests a lack of interest or lack of sincerity. It is important to maintain eye contact with the client; however, intense eye contact is considered inappropriate within some cultures.

Tone of voice reveals feelings. A loud, forceful tone suggests aggressiveness, control, and strength. A meek, scarcely audible tone suggests withdrawal, fear, and weakness. A monotonous or flat voice suggests a lack of interest.

Facial expressions—such as smiles, frowning, nodding the head, shaking the head, lip quivering, and blushing—send messages to the observer. Quite often, facial expressions reveal that the person is saying one thing but thinking or feeling another. And it is often facial expressions that reveal a worker's disapproval of a client, even when the worker is trying hard to be nonjudgmental.

Arm and hand movements frequently communicate strong emotions. Crossed legs, arms folded across the chest, and body rigidity usually suggest defensiveness, whereas arms and hands at the body's side or in an outreached position suggest openness to others. Clenched fists indicate anger or anxiety. Fidgety movements, toe and finger tapping, leg bouncing, and similar movements suggest impatience, nervousness, or preoccupation.

Body positioning conveys various attitudes and intentions. It is best to face the client at a 90-degree angle, since this suggests both safety and openness. Facing the client directly may communicate aggressiveness. A desk separating the client and worker inhibits closeness and openness and also suggests the worker is in a superior position. Leaning slightly toward the client communicates interest and acceptance. Physical closeness invites trust and involvement, but being too close is threatening. Each client has his or her own sense of personal space. The worker can avoid invading this space by reading the client's body movements and adjusting his or her chair to accommodate the client's comfort level.

Dress and appearance are important forms of nonverbal communication. Our choice of clothing and accessories (e.g., jewelry) and our hairstyle sends a message about who we are or who we want to be and reveals information about our identity and membership in a social class, group, or subculture. The worker must give careful thought to his or her choice of clothing and hairstyle. A well-groomed appearance connotes a seriousness about one's professional role and responsibilities. Dress that would be appropriate in an agency serving children may be inappropriate in a hospital or court setting. Likewise, dress that is acceptable to adolescent clients may be offensive to elderly clients. Some agencies have dress codes. The new worker should consult his or her supervisor for guidance on selecting appropriate dress.

SELECTED BIBLIOGRAPHY

Morris, Desmond. *Body Talk: The Meaning of Human Gestures.* New York: Crown Trade Paperback, 1994.

Leathers, Dale. *Successful Nonverbal Communication,* 3rd ed. Boston: Allyn and Bacon, 1997.

8.5 The "I-Statement"

PURPOSE: To send a clear and direct message.

DISCUSSION: The term *I-statement* refers to a type of message structure that increases the effectiveness of communication. This structure makes it possible to send a clear, direct message and reduce the chance that the person receiving the message will be put on the defensive. It is especially useful in situations of confrontation and conflict because it allows the sender to express disappointment, anger, or frustration while minimizing the chance that the discussion will turn into a fruitless argument.

All too often, the messages we send are "You-statements"; for example, "You should clean up your room," "You need to have more confidence in yourself," or "You are driving me crazy." Such messages, even when well intended, cause the person on the receiving end to feel put down. The intention of a You-statement may be to bring about a needed change in the behavior of another, but it usually ends up creating added resistance to change. Other forms of the You-statement are orders and commands (e.g., "Stop doing that!"), blaming or name-calling statements (e.g., "You are acting like a baby"), and statements that give solutions (e.g., "You better forget that idea and take my advice"). Perhaps the most disturbing form is the "if-then threat" (e.g., "If you don't . . . , then I will . . . ").

In contrast to the You-statement, which usually blocks communication, the I-statement allows the person bothered by the behavior of another to describe, in a noncritical or nonaccusatory manner, the impact the behavior is having, while leaving the responsibility for modifying the behavior with the person exhibiting the troublesome behavior. In effect, the I-statement says, "This is my concern, this is how it bothers me, this is how I feel." The I-statement does not accuse or blame; instead, it says implicitly, "I trust you to decide what change in your behavior is necessary." An I-statement consists of three parts:

1. A brief, clear description of a *specific behavior*
2. The *resulting feeling* experienced because of that specific behavior
3. A description of the *tangible impact* the behavior has had

For example, a social worker using an I-statement might say to a client:

Worker: When you did not show up for our scheduled appointment (specific behavior), I felt upset and put down (feeling) because I don't like having to wait around and because it disrupts my work schedule (tangible impact).

The I-statement is a technique that has wide applicability. The typical social worker will use it many times each day with clients and other professionals. It can be taught to clients as a method of helping them deal with interpersonal problems, such as those that occur between parent and child, husband and wife, and so on.

SELECTED BIBLIOGRAPHY

Ivey, Allen, and Mary Ivey. *Intentional Interviewing and Counseling,* 4th ed. Pacific Grove, CA: Brooks/Cole, 1999.

8.6 Understanding Emotions and Feelings

PURPOSE: To assist the client in understanding and appropriately expressing his or her feelings.

DISCUSSION: A social worker's capacity to understand and communicate with others depends on his or her ability to accurately "read" and "tune in" to human emotions and feelings. Many of the clients served by social workers are confused, frightened, or overwhelmed by their emotions and many have not learned to express their feelings in a healthy manner. A social worker must be able to discuss the nature of emotions in ways that clients can understand and in ways that help clients learn how to gain greater control over troublesome feelings and emotions.

Emotions are complex, physical, biochemical, and psychological responses to conscious and unconscious interpretations of an event or experience. Neuroscience is just beginning to understand how emotions arise within us and how normal emotions can go awry, as when, for example, fear grows into a phobia or sadness turns into a disabling depression.

The word *emotion* means "to move." Our emotions move or motivate us to take action. They are a type of innate and primitive survival wisdom that is programmed into our very being. Emotions warn us of danger and push us away from or pull us toward activities that are likely to protect us from harm or assist us in meeting our basic needs. For example, the emotion of fear moves us to withdraw from a dangerous situation, whereas anger moves us to attack those who threaten harm. The emotion of anticipation moves us to persist in efforts to reach a goal, whereas the emotion of sadness attracts the attention and caring of other people. The emotion of remorse or guilt moves us to correct misbehavior, to rebuild damaged relationships, and make amends for harm we have caused.

Emotion is also a type of communication that signals our intentions and reactions to others. The facial representations of certain emotions such as sadness, fear, anger, disgust, joy, and so on, are recognizable around the world, regardless of culture.

Each emotion can vary in intensity. For example, joy can range from serenity to ecstasy, fear can range from apprehension to terror, and anger from annoyance to rage. While all emotions involve some level of physiological change, the bodily reactions that accompany the primitive fight-flight emotions such as fear, anger, panic, and terror are the most intense of all. Strong emotional reactions can overpower one's capacity to reason and maintain self-control; they can interfere with the ability to concentrate, remember, and learn.

Although the words *emotion* and *feeling* are often used interchangeably, it is useful to define an *emotion* as a particular physiological and psychological response and a ***feeling*** as one's subjective awareness of that response. As explained earlier, emotions motivate us to take action when our physical or psychological survival or our well-being is perceived by us to be threatened or when the satisfaction of our needs is perceived to be blocked. It is critically important to understand that our emotions are a response to our perceptions of what is happening at a particular time and that these perceptions may or may not be an accurate interpretation of what is really happening.

The usual sequence between perception and thought and emotional and behavioral responses is as follows:

1. An event or situation occurs.
2. We notice, interpret, and think about the event.
3. Depending on our interpretations and thoughts, we experience a certain emotion.
4. The emotion moves us to engage in a certain behavior.

Some emotional reactions are immediate and do not involve thinking or cognition at a conscious level. For example, no real thought or analysis is necessary to interpret the danger of an attacking dog, elicit the emotion of fear, and move us to escape. Also, because of past "conditioning" (learning), we may interpret certain experiences in a habitual and almost automatic (unconscious) manner that involves little or no conscious thought. Thus, learning associated with prior painful life experiences may cause us to "misread" a situation or event and thereby elicit emotions and behaviors that are seen as inappropriate by others. An example would be a woman who feels fearful around all men because during childhood she was sexually abused by one man.

It is important to recognize that we respond emotionally not only to our interpretations of events and situations but also to our own feelings and behavior. For example, as we experience an emotion, we often think about whether it is "right" or "wrong" to be feeling as we do, and these thoughts may, in turn, elicit still other emotions. Similarly, we frequently pass judgment on our own behavior, and these judgments may give rise to still other emotions and behaviors or perhaps prompt us to reinterpret the situation in a different light. Thus, our thoughts, emotions, and behaviors are interrelated and interactive.

Because of the interplay between thought and emotion, we can, to a degree, alter and control our emotions and feelings by striving to change the usual ways we think about and interpret events and experiences. Several steps are involved in this learning process:

1. ***Noticing our feelings.*** People who are aware of their feelings are, by definition, in touch with their bodies, since all emotions have physiological correlates. Certain bodily sensations inform us that an emotional response is occurring. However, many of us tend to ignore or deny these sensations. Consequently, we may need help in learning to recognize the bodily reactions associated with emotion. One approach is to stop periodically throughout the day and reflect on our body's reactions and ask, for example, "What part of my body is experiencing emotion?" "Does some part of my body feel tense or strange?" "Is my body trying to get my attention?" "Why?" "What thoughts and interpretations are giving rise to these emotions?" Our bodily reactions during difficult interpersonal encounters or during times of stress are important windows to our underlying assumptions about self and others and our habitual ways of interpreting experiences.

2. ***Naming our feelings.*** Assigning a name to emotions and feelings helps us to accept them as real and provides a beginning sense of control. But attaching a label to something as subjective and nebulous as feelings is more difficult than it sounds. Many people lack a vocabulary for feelings. A list of feeling words may be of assistance in this naming process (see Item 14.23). If we reflect on an emotion, locate it in our body, and give it a name, it becomes more familiar and is less upsetting.

3. ***Owning our feelings.*** Before we can really examine an emotion or feeling, we need to claim it as ours. Taking ownership of a feeling can be difficult if we are in the habit of denying and ignoring our feelings. Owning and accepting a feeling can be made easier if its name is spoken aloud, possibly to another person (e.g., "I am afraid" or "I am feeling sad"). Many people are surprised to discover that this simple verbalization helps them cope with troublesome feelings.

4. ***Examining our habits of thought.*** Our ways of interpreting and thinking about events and situations are often habitual. To a large degree, those patterns are learned during childhood and carried into adulthood. Thus, in order to understand and modify troublesome thoughts and feelings, it may be necessary to reevaluate what we were taught during our childhood—a time when we uncritically form beliefs about ourselves and others. We must then decide if what we came to believe years ago as a child is still valid.

5. ***Looking under and behind our emotions.*** It is useful to think of our emotions as windows through which we can view the underlying and often unconscious interpretations of events and situations. For example, when feeling anxious or fearful, we might ask ourselves, "Why does this situation seem frightening or threatening?" "Is it really so or am I interpreting it this way out of habit or because of a prior painful experience?" "Are there alternative ways of interpreting this situation or experience?" By looking at things from a different angle or coming up with other interpretations, we can often gain some control over the direction and intensity of our emotions and feelings.

6. ***Choosing a course of action.*** Even when we cannot significantly change our emotional reaction to a particular situation or event, it is still possible to make choices about how to behave. We begin to gain control over our behavior by asking ourselves, "When I feel this way, what choices do I have?" "Is my instinctive response (e.g., running if I am afraid, attacking if I am angry) an appropriate one under the circumstances?" "What destructive responses must I avoid?" "What responses would hurt me or others?" "Which response would be most positive for me and others?"

SELECTED BIBLIOGRAPHY

Ekman, Paul, and Richard Davidson, eds. *The Nature of Emotion: Fundamental Questions.* New York: Oxford University Press, 1994.

Greenberger, Dennis, and Christine Padesky. *Mind over Mood.* New York: Guilford, 1995.

Lewis, Michael, and Jeanette Haviland, eds. *Handbook of Emotions.* New York: Guilford, 1993.

8.7 Responding to Defensive Communication

PURPOSE: To reduce the client's defensiveness.

DISCUSSION: The social worker must be skilled in reducing a client's need to be defensive and guarded. Schlosberg and Kagan (1988, 7) identify a number of common defensive maneuvers used by clients: "We do not have a problem" (denial); "It's all Greg's fault" (blaming); "She can't help it, she's retarded" (labeling); "If I get one more pressure, I'll go crazy" (being fragile); "My husband couldn't come today!" (avoidance); "Johnny was in another fight and I must talk about it!" (using crisis or distraction); and "What's the use, nothing will ever change" (helplessness). In addition, some clients use their physical environment (e.g., drawn shades, vicious dogs, terrible smells) and even their style of dress as a means of intimidation and keeping people at a distance. Still others use cursing, aggression, and threats.

Often, the client is defensive before he or she even meets the social worker, but sometimes the worker's behavior or style can add to the problem. Behaviors that increase client defensiveness include appearing rushed, being brusque or insensitive to a client's feelings, making judgmental statements, using jargon or quoting agency rules and policy without explanation, failing to identify yourself and your role clearly, calling an adult by his or her first name without permission, being authoritarian, and creating long waits and delays. By following several guidelines, the social worker can reduce a client's defensiveness:

1. Remember that defensiveness is an attempt to protect oneself from real or imagined danger. Within a context of social service delivery, the dangers or threats perceived by clients are those of embarrassment, humiliation, loss of control over one's life, loss of privacy, or failure to receive a desired social provision. Thus, do not respond to the defensive behavior as such but rather focus on what might be the client's underlying fear. Determine what is causing your client to feel threatened and try to remove that cause. Acknowledge those aspects of the situation that may cause your client to feel awkward, threatened, or humiliated (e.g., "I know it can be embarrassing to have to ask for financial assistance"). Use a generous amount of active listening (see Item 8.3) and make it as easy as possible for your client to verbalize feelings, but do not pressure him or her to do so.

2. Expand your tolerance of your client's defensive behavior by understanding that it may have served a purpose in the past. If the client's defensiveness is a long-term pattern rather than situational behavior, hypothesize how it may have protected the client from pain associated with some fundamental disruption (e.g., rejection by a parent, breakup of one's family, or separation from loved ones) or a frightening event (e.g., major personal problem, family violence, or a life-threatening illness). Patterns of defensiveness often develop in response to such fear and pain. Your gut reactions to the client will often provide clues as to the function served by the defensiveness. For example, if you feel a strong desire to walk away

from the client, the client's defensiveness may serve as protection against interference by outsiders. If the client's sad and helpless behavior makes you feel sorry and want to protect the client, this defensive pattern may help the client avoid a frightening responsibility.

3. If your client exhibits a positive or nondefensive behavior, respond with reinforcement and use the technique of ***mirroring.*** This technique is similar to *pacing,* which Cormier and Cormier (1998) describe as speaking at the client's pace and in a subtle manner matching the client's nonverbal behavior. In other words, follow a nondefensive conversational exchange with a vocal tone and cadence, posture, and nonverbal behavior that mirrors or imitates the client's verbal and nonverbal behavior. On the other hand, if your client assumes a defensive posture or tone of voice, respond with exactly the opposite (e.g., an open, nondefensive posture and a soft comforting tone of voice). If your client's conversation speeds up as a result of anxiety or anger, respond with a slow and nurturing manner; this usually has a calming effect on the client.

4. To the extent possible, use words and phrases that match your client's dominant mode of receiving information. The three basic modes are visual, auditory, and touch. A client reveals his or her dominant mode in the frequent use of certain predicates in phrases such as "I see what you mean" (visual), "I hear what you are saying" (auditory), or "That idea is beyond my reach" (touch). If you can identify your client's dominant mode, try to match your phrases to his or her mode—for example, "Do you have a clear picture of what I am suggesting?" (visual), "Does this plan sound OK to you?" (auditory), or "I don't think this plan is going to hurt you—do you feel the same way?" (touch).

5. Whenever possible, give your client opportunities to make choices and remain in control of what is happening in his or her life. Use words such as *we, us, together,* and *it will be your decision;* these imply cooperation, respect, and choice.

6. Consider using the technique of ***joining the resistance*** by aligning yourself with the client's feelings—for example, "After such a long wait, you deserve to be angry. I would be angry also." Such an alignment with the client's hurt feelings reduces resistance by removing the client's need to keep defenses up and it gives the client permission to vent feelings.

7. Do not label or categorize your client (e.g., "All Medicaid recipients have to fill out this form"). People become defensive when they experience a loss of individuality. Also, do not embarrass or back your client into a corner, either physically or psychologically. Arrange your office and your own seating position so your client does not feel trapped. Allow your client to save face in embarrassing situations.

8. A defensive or resistant individual may attempt a number of maneuvers to block a worker's engagement efforts. In situations where it is critically important to engage the resistant client (e.g., in cases of child abuse), you will need to be assertive and deal directly with the issue. For example, if your client is silent, you might say something like, "I can see you do not want to talk to me about how your child was injured, but I am going to stay here until we have discussed it." If your client appears overly agreeable to what you have said, you could say, "I certainly hope you will take the actions you have promised, but how will I know that you have followed through on those plans?" Some defensive clients attempt to divert attention away from the real issue. When that happens, you might say, "I can sense you do not want to focus on the child abuse report, but that is why I am here and we have to get back to that topic." If your client attempts to avoid the central issue by talking about secondary concerns, you may need to take control by saying something like, "You have mentioned at least five other problems and I can understand that they are of concern to you, but we have to come back to the question of how Joey got those bruises—that must be the primary focus of this interview." Sometimes clients defend themselves by trying to make the worker feel guilty. When that happens, you may need to say, "I know you are upset and I don't like to see people cry, but your child has been seriously injured and it is my job to find out what happened. Take a few minutes to compose yourself and then we must get to the bottom of this. If you cannot talk to me I will ask someone from the prosecutor's office to speak with you." If your client verbally or physically threatens you, you will need to say something like, "I have no intention of harming you. I will not argue with you and I cannot continue the interview under these conditions. If you are too angry to talk now, I will come back this afternoon with a police officer. Do you prefer to talk now or later?" (see Items 11.6, 11.7, 11.9, and 11.10).

9. If your client uses obscene or abusive language, remain calm and do not respond in ways that might reinforce the behavior (e.g., shock, attention, etc.). Respond immediately with verbal and nonverbal attention and reinforcement to any part of the client's communication that is appropriate and constructive.

10. If the client persists in verbal attacks, consider using the technique termed ***fogging***. This name comes from the notion that rocks thrown into a fog bank have no effect. If the person under verbal attack can mentally and emotionally behave like the fog, the verbal "rocks" have no impact and, hopefully, the attacker will soon abandon his or her efforts to cause discomfort. This technique works because the person under attack offers no resistance and avoids responding with either anger or defensiveness and because it calmly acknowledges that the angry person may have a point and is possibly accurate in his or her criticism and judgments. For example:

Angry Client: All you ever do is talk!
Worker: You're right. I do talk a lot.
Angry Client: If you would pay attention to what I have been saying, you wouldn't have to ask these dumb questions!
Worker: That may be true. I could be more attentive to what you say.
Angry Client: You are just like all the other lazy government employees and state social workers! You are always telling people what to do and butting into things that are none of your damn business.
Worker: I am a state employee. It does make sense that all state employees would do their job in similar ways.

SELECTED BIBLIOGRAPHY

Cormier, Sherry, and William Cormier. *Interviewing Strategies for Helpers,* 4th ed. Pacific Grove, CA: Brooks/Cole, 1998.

Rooney, Ronald. *Strategies for Work with Involuntary Clients.* New York: Columbia University Press, 1992.

Schlosberg, Shirley, and Richard Kagan. "Practice Strategies for Engaging Chronic Multi-Problem Families." *Social Casework* 69, No. 1 (January 1988): 3–9.

8.8 Cross-Cultural Helping

PURPOSE: To become sensitive to the importance of cultural differences and minority group status in the helping process.

DISCUSSION: Social workers interact with many individuals and families who have cultural, ethnic, religious, and socioeconomic backgrounds different from their own. In these relationships, they must guard against ***ethnocentrism,*** which is the tendency to assume that one's own way of life is superior and an appropriate standard for judging the beliefs and behavior of other people.

Culture refers to the learned patterns of thought and behavior that are passed from generation to generation. Our own culture is like a lens or a screen through which we view our relationships, life experiences, and the world around us. However, that particular lens has become so internalized and feels so normal and natural that we have a hard time even recognizing its existence and its power in shaping the way we perceive, think, and behave. Fundamentally, a culture consists of a set of interrelated beliefs, values, patterns, and practices that strongly influence how a group of people meet their basic needs, cope with the ordinary problems of life, make sense out of their experiences, and negotiate power relationships, both within and outside their own group.

Differences between cultures are expressed in many ways: language, religion and spirituality, art, family customs, rhythms of everyday life, preferred foods and leisure activities, clothing and body decoration, facial expressions and gestures during communication, manner of emotional expression, and so forth. Cultures are constantly changing; some change slowly while others change rapidly. These changes always occurs within a political, historical, and economic context. Something new (e.g., another language, television, computers, drug use, etc.) cannot be added to a culture without displacing or distorting other facets of that culture.

Related to the concept of culture is ethnicity. An ***ethnic group*** is a segment of a larger population who defines itself and is regarded by others as being a distinct people because they share a common culture, language, religion, ancestry, physical appearance, or some combination of such characteristics. The ethnic group's sense of identity is valued by its members and passed from generation to generation. Green (1995, 19) explains that ethnicity is primarily about "perceptions of boundaries, with how contrasts [perceived differences] are manipulated, managed, denied, asserted, and proclaimed." Social workers must appreciate differences in how people might perceive themselves as different from others, even when differences are not readily apparent. If people believe and feel that they belong to a particular group and are somehow different than other people and groups, those perceived differences are important and they will effect communication, interactions, and professional relationships.

The word ***race*** refers to our physical characteristics whereas *culture* and *ethnicity* have to do with how people think and behave. Although the notion of race has no scientific standing as a biological concept for classifying people, the widely held assumption that there are distinct biological types of people has a profound negative effect on intergroup relations. The term ***racism*** refers to the judgment of others solely on the basis of characteristics (e.g., skin color, facial features, size, language patterns) common to a people. Like many societies around the world, our society is racist in its prevailing attitudes. We still fall far short of Martin Luther King's dream of a society where people "would not be judged by the color of their skin, but by the content of their character."

Some ethnic, racial, and religious groups are also a ***minority group,*** which Schaefer (1996, 5) defines as a "subordinate group whose members have significantly less control or power over their own lives than that held by the members of the dominant or majority group." Schaefer (1996, 7) further explains that the members of a minority group typically have five things in common:

1. Physical or cultural characteristics distinguish them from the dominant group.
2. They experience prejudice and discrimination.
3. Membership in the minority group is not voluntary.
4. They experience a strong sense of solidarity with others of the group.
5. Members usually marry those from the same group.

Minority group status has a powerful impact on individual behavior and on a person's opportunity for socioeconomic advancement.

It is helpful to distinguish between prejudice and discrimination. ***Prejudice*** (i.e., to prejudge) refers to a person's unfavorable beliefs and attitudes toward a particular group or category. ***Discrimination*** refers to behavior and actions that are unfavorable toward a group and that deprive them of certain basic rights and opportunities. Given this distinction between beliefs (prejudice) and behavior (discrimination), one sees that being prejudiced does not always lead to discrimination. Also, it is possible to engage in discriminatory behavior without being prejudiced, such as when a person acts out of ignorance or when one's behavior is directed by an insensitive organizational policy or procedure. Discrimination can exist at two levels: personal and institutional. In *personal discrimination,* an individual acts out his or her negative views toward members of a group. In *institutional discrimination,* the negative behavior is a reflection of values, norms, and assumptions embodied in the laws, systems, and structures of a society. As such, institutional discrimination is more complex and subtle.

Prejudice and discrimination may exist within an ethnic or cultural group. For example, some members of the group may be predjudiced or discriminate against others of the group on the basis of differences of gender, education level, religion, and socioeconomic status. These intragroup dynamics may have a significant impact on how a member of the group views himself or herself in relation to other members of the group.

It is difficult to completely rid ourselves of the prejudices we all acquire during our upbringing. However, it is possible and necessary for social workers to become aware of their prejudices and refrain from acts of discrimination. Certain behaviors are characteristic of professional helpers who are racist and prejudiced in their thinking:

- Stereotyped explanations are given for the behavior of people of a specific ethnic or minority group.
- The same helping strategies are used for all clients who are members of a particular ethnic or minority group.
- The importance of culture and ethnicity in a person's life are easily dismissed or, on the other extreme, they are used to explain nearly all behavior.
- Discussions of race and culture are avoided or are talked about continuously.

Social workers must strive to learn about their clients' cultures and ethnicities, but also must recognize that one can seldom acquire more than a superficial knowledge of another culture. It is very difficult to understand another culture, especially when differences of language are involved. In fact, most of us have little awareness of our own culture until we travel in a foreign country and have an opportunity to examine our way of life from a distance and with some objectivity. Every attempt to describe a group of people requires the use of generalizations. Even when a member of a particular group attempts to describe the beliefs, values, and behaviors common to his or her own culture , ethnic, or religious group, he or she is forced to make generalizations. Of course, all general statements about a group—whether it be people of the White middle class, people who are blind, people who are African Americans, or people who are Democrats—give rise to the dangers of stereotyping and overgeneralization. Among the people of a particular group, there are always significant individual differences.

Social workers and administrators must be alert to the possibility that their agency's policies and programs might, in some way, discriminate against an ethnic or minority group. An openness to this possibility, ongoing self-studies, and reviews by persons from outside the agency who are members of various ethnic and minority groups are of critical importance in identifying and eliminating discrimination.

Because most social agencies and social programs are created by decision makers representing the most powerful or dominant groups in society, the social workers employed by these programs may be viewed with fear or suspicion by clients who are members of a minority group. Whittaker and Tracy (1989, 158) explain that a major obstacle in working with a member of an ethnic minority is the "differing expectations as to what constitutes 'help,' making it extremely difficult to select appropriate and effective intervention methods." Whittaker and Tracy also warn that some of the most popular and commonly used techniques may not be effective when working cross-culturally. For example:

- Self-disclosure may be particularly difficult between dominant-culture workers and discriminated minority groups, since it presumes a degree of trust which may not exist initially.
- Short-term, task-oriented styles of social work may be ineffectual with clients who feel that extended periods of time "just talking" is an appropriate way to enter a relationship. . . .
- Reflection, reaching for feeling, or asking for insights may appear inappropriate or intrusive.
- Some ethnic groups, for example Asian-Pacific Americans, may view help-seeking as a shame-inducing process and will be extremely reticent to disclose personal problems. . . .
- Many ethnic minority groups (e.g., Puerto Rican, Hispanic) expect a more active helping relationship with the worker offering advice and tangible assistance.
- Techniques that rely on intrapersonal solutions versus social resolutions may be less appealing.
- Cognitive behavioral or rational emotive techniques . . . [e.g., managing self-talk, imagery, challenging irrational beliefs, etc.] may run counter to important cultural values and beliefs. (pp. 158–159)

Closely related to ethnic sensitivity is the need to adapt practice to the client's religious beliefs and spirituality. In fact, one's ethnicity, culture, and religion are usually interwoven. The social worker should be aware that the lives and decisions of a large portion of the clients they serve are influenced by particular religious and moral beliefs. Practice that neglects the client's religion may miss opportunities to be helpful to the client. Loewenberg (1988), for example, observes that

> avoiding one segment of a person's life, such as religion, will handicap the interaction, even if it is a professional relationship between a social worker and client. One may wonder whether a social worker can really have a meaningful or helpful relationship with clients who have a strong religious commitment when such a social worker avoids the religious aspects of their lives. (p. 86)

In work with all clients, but especially with clients of a different cultural or ethnic background, the social worker is advised to individualize the client. The social worker must be alert to human diversity and never assume that a client's physical features or ethnic identity will predict the client's values, beliefs, or behavior patterns.

Other guidelines that a social worker should keep in mind are the following:

1. Appreciate the subjectiveness involved in how people see themselves and others. Remember that human differences are whatever people define them to be and their relevance is whatever people believe them to be.

2. Self-awareness is of critical importance. Constantly examine your attitudes and behavior and be alert to the possibility that you are making judgments based on racism, prejudice, and stereotypes, or perhaps behaving in a discriminatory manner. Frequently ask yourself, "What is my attitude toward people of different cultural backgrounds?" "How do I feel about people who have a different skin color or speak a different language?" "How do I feel about people who have religious beliefs different from my own?"

3. Early in the relationship with a client, you should acknowledge the existence of differences of ethnicity or race as a way of giving the client permission to talk about these matters and express concerns about not being accepted or understood. Encourage the client to identify perceived differences and to explain how these differences might be addressed in the professional relationship and service delivery.

4. Show a special interest in your client's name, place of birth, and home community, for these topics are good icebreakers and lead naturally to a discussion of the client's cultural background and ethnic identity. A client who might experience difficulty with the English language should be asked if an interpreter is needed.

5. Overlooking client strengths, misreading nonverbal communication, and misunderstanding family dynamics are among the most common errors made in cross-cultural helping. Behaviors motivated by religion and spirituality, family obligation, and sex roles are often misunderstood. Because of the difficulty in reading nonverbal cues cross-culturally, the worker should move slowly when reaching for feelings and putting the client's feelings into words. Overlooking strengths results when the worker does not fully appreciate the situation—especially the contextual and systemic aspects—with which the client must cope.

6. Be alert to the fact that in many ethnic families, certain members are the key decision makers and other family members will not make an important decision without consulting that member. For example, in many Hispanic families, the husband and father typically has considerable authority and his wife and even his adult children may feel obligated to obtain his approval before taking a course of action. Also, within the extended families common to the American Indian tribal cultures, certain individuals perform the role of advisor and other family members will delay making a decision until they have obtained his or her advice on the matter. Thus, it is always a good idea to ask the client if he or she wants to invite others to the interview or somehow involve them in decision making. Not infrequently, clients will simply bring these respected individuals to important meetings.

7. Be alert to the subtleties and the limitations inherent in the use of language. Recognize the influence of language on how one thinks or is able to think about certain matters. Whenever we use a word, we call up in our minds a concept or "picture" of what that word means. A given word may call forth somewhat different thoughts and ideas, depending on one's culture. Clearly, it is in our use of language that we encounter differences in how people think and interpret experiences.

8. Because members of many ethnic minority groups have suffered from discrimination, it is to be expected that they will be somewhat distrustful of professionals and agencies that represent and reflect the dominant groups in society. They will enter a helping relationship with caution as they size up the social worker. For example, they may evaluate the worker's trustworthiness by asking, directly or indirectly, about his or her life experiences, family, children, and opinions. The worker needs to respond to these probes with honest, nonevasive answers. Because visiting people in their own home is usually seen as an indication of caring and respect, the home visit may help the worker build trust.

9. Ask your clients to explain their beliefs and culture and ask for their advice in how you might adapt your helping methods to their values, traditions, and customs. Do not be afraid to say that you do not understand. If you genuinely care for the clients and demonstrate concern for their situation, most will explain what you need to understand about their way of life. It often helps to use a bit of self-effacing humor (i.e., laughing at your own ignorance) when asking questions about things you do not understand. This display of humility makes you less threatening.

10. When you need to better understand certain cultural or ethnic factors, seek appropriate consultation. Also, contact leaders in the ethnic community and express your desire to learn about their values, beliefs, and way of life. They will usually offer their assistance if they perceive your interest to be genuine. Also, attend celebrations, ceremonies, and other cultural and religious events sponsored by the group.

11. Be alert to the fact that societal or systemic problems (poverty, unemployment, poor housing, lack of access to health care, etc.) bring ethnic minorities to agencies more often than do psychological problems. Thus, the provision of concrete services and the practitioner roles of broker and advocate are of special importance.

SELECTED BIBLIOGRAPHY

Cox, Carole, and Paul Ephross. *Ethnicity and Social Work Practice.* New York: Oxford University Press, 1998.

Devore, Wynetta, and Elfriede Schlesinger. *Ethnic Sensitive Social Work Practice,* 4th ed. Boston: Allyn and Bacon, 1996.

Ewalt, Patricia, Edith Freeman, Stuart Kirk, and Dennis Poole, eds. *Multicultural Issues in Social Work.* Washington, DC: NASW, 1996.

Green, James. *Cultural Awareness in the Human Services,* 2nd ed. Boston: Allyn and Bacon, 1995.

Harper, Karen, and Jim Lantz. *Cross-Cultural Practice.* Chicago: Lyceum Books, 1996.

Leigh, James. *Communicating for Cultural Competence.* Boston: Allyn and Bacon, 1998.

Loewenberg, Frank. *Religion and Social Work Practice in Contemporary American Society.* New York: Columbia University Press, 1988.

Lum, Doman. *Culturally Competent Practice.* Pacific Grove, CA: Brooks/Cole, 1999.

Ponterotto, Joseph, J. Manuel Casas, Lisa Suzuki, and Charlene Alexander, eds. *Handbook of Multicultural Counseling.* Newbury, CA: Sage, 1995.

Schaefer, Richard. *Racial and Ethnic Groups,* 6th ed. New York: HarperCollins, 1996.

Whittaker, James, and Elizabeth Tracy. *Social Treatment,* 2nd ed. New York: Aldine de Gruyter, 1989.

9 Workload and Caseload Management

INTRODUCTION

The new social worker learns quickly that there is not enough time to do all that needs to be done. Faced with that reality, the worker must make the best possible use of limited time and focus on matters of highest priority. Time and workload management skills are essential.

Paperwork and recordkeeping consume much of a social worker's time. Most workers dislike these tasks, but they are an essential component of service provision. Professional records must be complete, concise, legible, and accurate. Ideally, an agency's recordkeeping system will create documentation useful for the following purposes: (1) provide an accurate account of services provided; (2) provide data that can be used to identify needed changes in policy, service delivery, and staff deployment; (3) provide data for retrospective and prospective research; (4) provide data that reveal the judgments behind key decisions and are therefore useful in staff development and professional education; (5) provide data needed to meet relevant legal and policy requirements; and (6) provide information that is understandable to and will withstand scrutiny by external reviewers (e.g., accreditation bodies, ombudsmen, lawyers, insurance companies, quality control personnel, etc.).

In our litigious society, social workers are increasingly named in lawsuits alleging professional negligence or misconduct. Proper documentation is of critical importance in defending oneself against such suits. From a legal perspective, "If it is not documented in the record, it was not done." In other words, in the absence of documentation, there is no evidence that a particular action was completed or that a decision was appropriate and justified.

This chapter discusses report and letter writing as well as recordkeeping. Also included are guidelines and techniques that can help workers increase their efficiency on the job: time management, using a telephone, incorporating information technology, and refusing and accepting added work. The chapter ends with a section on testifying in court. With increasing frequency, social workers in all fields are called to be witnesses in court proceedings.

The social worker must strive to be efficient. Efficiency can best be improved through using better tools of workload management, such as computers, and improving the paper flow in an agency. Social workers should be cautious, however, about actions in the name of efficiency that would compromise the requirements of an effective helping process.

9.1 Managing Time at Work

PURPOSE: To make the best possible use of limited time.

DISCUSSION: Nearly every social worker is faced with the problem of having too much work and too little time. Thus, the worker must use time-management skills as a way of increasing efficiency on the job. Consider these guidelines:

1. Come to terms with your resistance to using time-management principles. Do not hide behind the claim that you are too busy to get organized. Some people appear busy because they are always in motion, but activity does not always mean that something is being accomplished. Make sure your activity is productive.

2. Understand your agency's mission and your job description. Unless you are clear about what needs to be done, you cannot figure out ways to do it effectively and efficiently. If your assignments and responsibilities are not clear, discuss them with your supervisor or administrative superiors. Find out what tasks and assignments are of highest priority within the agency.

3. Recognize that in order to be effective and efficient, your job must be consistent with your personal and professional values, goals, and style. A mismatch between what your agency expects and what you can do or want to do is a recipe for frustration for both you and your colleagues at work.

4. Be proactive, not reactive. Anticipate the tasks that need to be accomplished and the problems that may arise in completing those tasks and then take action. Do not procrastinate.

5. Use "to-do" lists. Good managers of time use a *"things-to-do" checklist* that they carry with them. Estimate how long it will take to complete each task on the list, so adequate time can be budgeted. Anticipate deadlines and begin tasks early enough to meet them. It is usually best to tackle lengthy tasks before those that can be completed in a short time. It is also best to work on the most difficult tasks when your energy level is highest (e.g., first thing in the morning). Save some time at the end of each day for clearing your desk and taking care of last-minute activities.

6. Plan your work and set priorities. Develop both daily and weekly plans. At the end of each day, as well as at the end of each week, write down what you plan to accomplish the next day and the next week. Prioritize this list of tasks by using, for example, the ABC Priority System. Write an *A* next to those tasks that are most important and have highest priority. Write a *C* next to tasks that are of least importance and a *B* next to tasks in the middle range. Next, prioritize each *A* task in order of importance, labeling them *A–1, A–2, A–3,* and so on. The *B* tasks can be labeled in the same way: *B–1, B–2,* and so on. At the beginning of the working day, start at once on task *A–1* and stay with it until it is completed. Then move to *A–2* and on down the list.

A less complex approach is to classify all tasks into three categories: (1) tasks that must be completed today, (2) tasks that should be started today, and (3) tasks that can wait a few days. Realize that priorities may change over the course of a day or week. Thus, it is necessary to continually review your "to-do" list. Also, cultivate equanimity about priority setting. If a task you thought was a low priority suddenly becomes a pressing high-priority task, do not chastise yourself for poor planning. Accept such shifts as inevitable.

7. Plan for the unexpected. Allow time in your schedule for emergencies. Remember Murphy's Laws: "Nothing is as simple as it seems," "Everything will take longer than you think," and "If anything can go wrong, it will."

8. Reduce interruptions to a minimum. When you are interrupted, maintain control of the situation by giving the interruption full attention, avoiding irritation, and, where appropriate, setting a time limit on the interruption. Drop-in clients are often less of a problem than staff who interrupt other workers. Being able to say no to the question, Do you have a minute? is an important time-management skill. Closing your office door or standing up to converse with someone who just stopped by can help control unnecessary interruptions.

9. Make decisions in a timely manner. Some workers are too afraid of making mistakes; as a result, they delay making decisions. Some avoid making decisions because they cannot arrive at a perfect solution. There are few, if any, perfect solutions in the real world of social work practice. One must strive for excellence, but striving for perfection will result only in frustration. Everyone makes mistakes. When you make a mistake, learn from it; do not waste time brooding over it. A "good" mistake is one from which you learn and do not repeat. A "bad" mistake is one you will repeat again.

10. Keep your agency's policy and procedures manual up to date. As changes occur, insert the new information and discard the old. Much time can be lost in fervid search for misplaced information or when you erroneously follow an outdated procedure.

11. Develop a *tickler file* to keep track of deadlines for submitting monthly reports and other tasks that must be completed according to a schedule. A tickler file can be as simple as notations on a calendar, or a complex system, such as a desktop file or computerized calendar.

12. Develop a system for the storage and rapid retrieval of frequently used information such as e-mail addresses, telephone numbers, and mailing addresses of professionals and agencies you contact frequently (e.g., a Rolodex). As you learn of new programs and meet human services personnel, place their names and other relevant information in the file for future reference.

13. When appropriate, delegate a task to staff at the next lowest level within the organization (e.g., a secretary, case aide, or paraprofessional). However, be careful not to overburden others or make assignments they are not prepared to carry out.

14. Limit the time spent in meetings. The following suggestions are helpful:

- Consider alternatives to a meeting (e.g., conference phone calls, exchange by e-mail).
- Define the purpose clearly before scheduling the meeting so all participants understand why they are attending and can properly prepare.
- Choose a convenient time and location for the meeting.
- Attend only for the time needed to make your contribution.
- Prepare an agenda and follow it. Start on time and end on time. Control interruptions. Stay on task; accomplish the purpose of the meeting.
- Evaluate the success of the meeting and agree on necessary changes in future meetings.

(See Items 14.41 and 14.44 for additional guidelines on meetings.)

15. When possible, structure your day by using scheduled appointments for interviews, collateral contacts (contacts with other service providers), and the like. Reduce travel time by scheduling all meetings in a given locality for the same day.

16. Organize your desk and eliminate clutter in your workspace. Keep those things you are working on in front of you, but clear your desk of other materials. This will help keep your attention on the task at hand. Focus on one thing at a time until you either complete the task or reach a preset time limit for that activity. Avoid jumping from task to task.

17. An important rule in managing paperwork is to handle each paper only once. If you pick up a letter, report, or request, take the action required or discard it if no action is necessary. Do not set it aside; do not let papers pile up on your desk.

18. Learn to use the office machines and communications systems that can increase your efficiency (e.g., word processor, e-mail, the fax, the agency's computer, etc.). If a lack of skill or knowledge is slowing you down or causing you to make mistakes, request the training you need. Ask experienced workers to help you devise an efficient approach to the tasks of preparing agency records and routine reports (see Item 9.4).

19. Practice clear communication. Much time is wasted trying to deal with problems caused by poor communication. Learn to use the telephone effectively and efficiently. Poor telephone communication technique causes confusion and wastes time (see Items 8.1 and 9.5).

20. Avoid being drawn into doing someone else's work. Nothing reduces your energy or motivation more quickly than trying to compensate for someone's incompetence. This does not preclude helping others on occasion but do not make a habit of rescuing others.

21. Keep track of how you spend each day and week. Once you have this information, analyze it and identify those areas in which you can make time-saving changes.

SELECTED BIBLIOGRAPHY

Culp, Stephanie. *Conquering the Paper Pile Up.* Cincinnati: Writer's Digest Books, 1990.
Glesson, Kerry. *The Personal Efficiency Program.* New York: John Wiley and Sons, 1994.
Hemphill, Barbara. *Taming the Paper Tiger,* 4th ed. Washington, DC: Kiplinger Books, 1997.
Winston, Stephanie. *Best Organizing Tips.* New York: Simon and Schuster, 1995.

9.2 Report Writing

PURPOSE: To prepare a clear and useful professional report.

DISCUSSION: A social worker must write many reports. Reports that are inaccurate, incomplete, or unclear create misunderstanding, antagonism, and costly errors. A number of guidelines can improve the quality of reports:

1. A report is always addressed to someone; thus, it is important to analyze the report's audience and determine what information they need and expect. Also determine whether the report may be passed on to other organizations and possibly clients. Keep these readers in mind as you write. Always think about how the readers will interpret your words or perhaps misinterpret what you have written.

2. Decide whether a formal report or just a memo is required. A formal report usually follows the format prescribed by the agency. A copy of a report—one judged by others in the agency as a good model—can be used as your guide. A memo may contain abbreviations, first names, and jargon, but such shorthand should be avoided in a formal report.

3. Before you begin to write, organize the information to be presented in a logical structure. Construct an outline. If you present your ideas in an orderly way, the reader will be more likely to understand.

4. Two or three drafts or revisions may be needed before the final version is produced. Ask peers to review your draft. If they are not sure of what you are trying to say, you can be certain that the intended reader will not understand either. Also read the draft aloud; if it does not sound right, revise it.

5. Use language that is simple and clear. Select your words carefully, using only those your reader will understand. Avoid words that have different meaning in different contexts. Also avoid using slang or phrases that might offend the reader. For example, consider the following series of words: *inebriated, intoxicated, drunk, stoned; portly, stout, obese, fat; firm, obstinate, stubborn, pig-headed.* Each of the words in a given series has the same basic meaning, but each strikes the reader in a different way.

6. Do not use "weasel words"—words or phrases that let the writer avoid responsibility for his or her statements. The weasel words *feel* and *seems* appear frequently in social work reports. Instead of saying, "I feel placement is necessary," it would be better to say, "I believe placement is necessary." Also avoid language such as, "It would appear that . . . ," "There may be a tendency toward . . . ," "It seems as though . . . ," "There is some reason for believing that . . . ," or "I feel there might be . . . ." Such wishy-washy language gives the reader the impression that the report writer is unsure of what he or she is talking about. This causes the reader to doubt the validity of the report and question the worker's competence.

7. Avoid hackneyed expressions such as, "It certainly merits study . . . ," "The matter is receiving our closest attention . . . ," "We will explore every avenue . . . ," or "Naturally, the child's interest is our concern . . . ." Such trite phrases suggest that the writer is insincere or responding as a mere formality.

8. Use the number of words necessary but no more. Wordiness lessens the force of expression and distracts the reader from the point you want to make. Also avoid redundant phrases such as, "first beginnings," "the present time," "join together," and "point in time."

9. Keep your sentences short, usually 20 words or less. Most often, the straightforward subject-verb-object sentence is the best arrangement because it can be read quickly and is seldom misunderstood. Consider these two sentences:

- After much discussion, not all of which was productive, a foster home placement—the agreed upon arrangement—was made for the child.
- The child was placed in a foster home.

The second sentence is easier to read and understand; it is short and it follows the subject-verb-object structure.

10. Use active verbs whenever possible. The passive voice adds unnecessary words, weakens the statement, and makes the meaning less clear. For example, "Don hit John" has a clearer, stronger impact than "John was hit by Don."

11. Give special attention to paragraph construction. Each paragraph should focus on a single idea. The outline for a good paragraph is as follows:

- In the first sentence, state the central point of the paragraph.
- If necessary, restate the central point in other words or provide additional clarification.
- Present evidence or background supporting the central point, including examples, where appropriate. Draw conclusions.
- Finally, draw the paragraph to a close, summarizing the key point in a single sentence.

By reading only the first and last sentence of a paragraph, the reader should be able to pick up much of what you are trying to communicate. In general, a page of double-spaced typewritten copy should contain two or three paragraphs. If there is only one paragraph per page, it is likely that too many ideas have been crammed into a single paragraph.

12. Use the dictionary to determine the exact meaning of a word, the correct spelling, whether a word should be capitalized, correct word forms for different parts of speech, how a word should be divided at the end of a line, correct punctuation (i.e., hyphens, apostrophes, accents), and whether a hyphen should be used in a compound word. Most dictionaries contain a section that lists the basic rules of pronunciation, capitalization, and spelling; some contain information on grammar. A thesaurus, which contains synonyms and antonyms, will help the writer add variety and freshness in word selection.

13. The word processor has dramatically changed the tasks of writing and editing. Computer programs now include a thesaurus, spelling checks, and grammar checks. Because writing is so much a part of social work practice, all social workers must be skilled in using a word processor.

SELECTED BIBLIOGRAPHY

Hairston, Maxine, and John Ruszkiewicz. *The Scott Foresman Handbook for Writers,* 3rd ed. Reading, MA: Addison-Wesley, 1993.

Houp, Kenneth, and Thomas Pearsall. *Reporting Technical Information,* 9th ed. Englewood Cliffs, NJ: Prentice Hall, 1997.

9.3 Letter Writing

PURPOSE: To communicate ideas and information clearly and concisely in letters.

DISCUSSION: Most of the principles that guide report writing (see Item 9.2) also apply to letter writing. In addition, the following guidelines will improve correspondence:

1. Plan carefully before you write even the shortest letter. If it is worth doing, it should be done well. Your image as a professional person is shaped by the appearance of your letter.

2. Revise and polish all drafts of letters and proofread the final version. All letters to other agencies and professionals should be typed on letterhead stationery. Ordinarily, letters to a client should also be typed. If you know the client well, short notes may be handwritten.

3. A copy of all letters and notes should be retained for agency files. Use certified or registered mail when necessary to document that a letter was delivered.

4. Always use proper titles, such as "Mr.," "Mrs.," "Miss," "Ms.," "Dr.," "Rev.," and so on. The use of "Ms." is appropriate when a woman's marital status is unknown. First names should be used only when addressing children or persons with whom you have a close relationship.

5. Develop several model or sample letters based on situations commonly encountered in your agency. Use these as a starting point when preparing new letters.

6. Remember that a professional letter will have at least the following parts: letterhead, date, inside address, reference line or subject line, salutation, body, complimentary close, typed signature, and written signature. When appropriate, there should also be an enclosure notation ("enc.") and a copy notation ("cc") that names others receiving copies of the letter.

7. In some letters, you will be complaining or making demands. You can usually make your point clearly and emphatically without being too aggressive. On the other hand, do not go to the opposite extreme by humbling yourself or avoiding an important issue. Write with directness, clarity, and authority.

8. Humanize and personalize your letters, especially those to clients. The recipient of your letter should feel that he or she is dealing with a real person, not an impersonal representative of an organization.

9. When writing to people in important positions, avoid sounding too friendly. Use a businesslike tone. Be pleasant but not folksy.

10. Be cautious about using the "I" point of view. This occurs when the writer constantly refers to himself or herself, especially by beginning sentences with the word *I*. Employing an *I* two or three times in an ordinary letter will not hurt; even starting an occasional sentence with it is all right, but do not overdo it.

11. Do not include material that would violate confidentiality or prove embarrassing if read by persons other than the intended recipient of the letter. Be alert to the fact that an agency's name and address on an envelope may reveal the client's involvement with an agency.

SELECTED BIBLIOGRAPHY

Berger, Arthur. *Improving Writing Skills: Memos, Letters, Reports, and Proposals.* Newbury Park, CA: Sage, 1993.

Davidson, Wilma. *Business Writing.* New York: St Martin's Press, 1994.

9.4 Using Information Technology

PURPOSE: To employ various forms of information technology for increasing practice effectiveness and workload efficiency.

DISCUSSION: As computers have become smaller, more powerful, less expensive, and more user-friendly, social workers have increasingly incorporated information technology into their practice. An increasing array of software that support both the administrative functioning of human services agencies and private practice, as well as providing tools for practice assessments and efficient communication, have opened electronic technology to social workers. Although highly technical skills are required to create computer equipment and software programs, to make use of existing technology the social worker needs only a "functional computer literacy." Familiarity with three aspects of information technology (i.e., the hardware, software applications, and online resources) provides the base for becoming computer literate.

Hardware refers to the physical or machine components of information technology. The hardware serves three distinct purposes: the input of data, its processing (or throughput), and the final product (output). *Input* is accomplished through a keyboard, mouse, touch screen, computer disk or tape, scanner, CD-ROM, or other data-entry forms. *Throughput* is accomplished by the "brains" of the computer, the central processing unit (CPU), which receives instruction and data from the input devices, performs arithmetic and logical operations, and stores the results in its memory. It is the speed with which the CPU can process large amounts of information that makes information technology a valuable asset to the social worker. *Output* takes several forms, including images appearing on a monitor, hard copy from a printer, or storage on a disk or magnetic tape.

Computers vary greatly in their size and capacity. *Mainframe computers* with multiple terminals often are used by statewide human services agencies to collect large amounts of standardized data for reports of agency activity. *Microcomputers* (i.e., desktop computers) are used by midsized and small agencies. By using a local area network (LAN), these agencies can link workers to the agency's central database to aid interagency communication and collect data for program evaluation. They can also be linked to resources throughout the world over telephone lines and through electronic mail (e-mail) programs.

The term ***software*** refers to the programs that can be purchased or developed to provide the instructions to the computer. Typically, the program for each ***application*** (e.g., word processing, spreadsheet, etc.) is stored on the computer's hard disk to be called up by the operator when needed. The social worker needs only to know which programs to use for the intended purpose and how to access those programs.

The most frequent use of information technology by social workers is ***word processing.*** Word processing is used for composing and editing case summaries, correspondence with clients and other agencies, agency information sheets, news releases, letters to legislators, and so on. A specialized form of word processing is *desktop publishing* software, which provides templates that facilitate the creation of newsletters, flyers, and brochures. Similarly, *presentation packages* assist in the creation of text and graphics for preparing professional-looking overheads and slide shows that can be used in making presentations at professional meetings (see Item 10.4) or in interpreting agency services.

Spreadsheets (and accounting application programs based on spreadsheets) allow users to work with mathematical and accounting data. The primary advantage of spreadsheets is their ability to use formulas so that when one value is changed, all other numbers based on that value change accordingly. For example, in developing an agency budget it is possible to quickly see the effects of an across-the-board 3 percent reduction or increase in funds. Most spreadsheet programs incorporate presentation graphics allowing the data to be viewed as charts or graphs.

Database programs are recordkeeping systems—the electronic equivalent of the filing cabinet and file folders. For a social worker, a database will typically contain client demographic characteristics, social histories, intake information, treatment plans, and progress notes. These data can be readily accessible to the social worker to track the progress of an individual client, review report data, schedule appointments, identify items due and pending, and reduce paperwork. For the agency, a database can provide aggregate data for planning and accountability purposes, forecast demand for services, monitor the impact of services on clients, and compare anticipated outcomes with those actually achieved. Another form of database is *The Social Work Reference Library* (NASW 1995) on a CD-ROM that combines the entire social work encyclopedia, social work dictionary, and social work almanac into a single database that can search for information about social work and social work practice.

When using a database program in either an agency or a private practice setting, the social worker is ethically and legally responsible for making reasonable effort to maintain the confidentiality of case records that are stored on a computer. The worker's password is the first line of defense in protecting client confidentiality. Some guidelines for making a password secure include:

- Do not use a password that can be found in any database or dictionary.
- Use a mixture of numbers, letters, symbols, and punctuation.
- Use both upper- and lowercase letters.
- Memorize your password and do not write it down or share it with anyone.

Decision support systems utilize the data in an agency information system to assist professionals in making decisions. A decision support system, for example, might prompt a worker to obtain additional client information regarding a specific problem. It would then provide the worker with a description of similar cases and how they were resolved, offer suggestions for use of further diagnostic tests, provide a list of actions followed in similar cases that were successfully resolved, or give a list of abstracts of studies or articles related to the client's problem or culture.

Computerized assessment instruments facilitate assessment of individual and family case situations and assist in ongoing monitoring of cases. A variety of intake, social history, and problem assessment inventories are available, as well as scales to assess such factors as depression, eating disorders, grief, anxiety, marital satisfaction, spouse abuse, suicidal ideation, and others. (See Item 12.16 for a discussion of standardized instruments.) Research suggests that having tests available on computer has resulted in more use of assessment tests, better professional performance, and higher client satisfaction (Nurius and Hudson 1993).

Research-related software also serves an important function in social work. Such software can be used to select a sample size, construct data-entry forms, calculate the margin of error for given return rates, suggest and perform appropriate statistical tests, analyze qualitative data, and present the results in graphic format. Research-related software can also assist in practice activities ranging from testing hypotheses about the relationship between various client variables and practice outcomes to conducting agency program evaluations and community needs assessments.

Software programs have also been developed for worker ***education and training.*** Computer-based education and training activities range from relatively simple text-based programs to multimedia programs that incorporate text, graphics, sound, and video. In addition to self-paced programs for agency staff regarding client assessment, policy interpretation, and so on, computer-based training has been designed to provide clients with parent education, relaxation training, and sex education. Similarly, ***computer games*** have been used with children, adolescents, and the elderly to enhance self-concept and feelings of success, to provide art therapy, and to stimulate social interaction.

Social workers use ***on-line resources*** as a communication tool for networking, information sharing, consultation, and social support among geographically dispersed human services professionals, agencies, and client self-help groups. Through on-line resources, workers can access e-mail, search for government and library documents and have them delivered, and examine databases of local and national information through bulletin board systems (BBS). Private companies such as America Online, Compuserv, and Prodigy, and the vast resources of the Internet link thousands of computers in universities, human services agencies, government, and other sources in a worldwide network.

Several on-line resources are particularly useful for social workers. ***Electronic mail,*** for example, provides each worker with an "electronic mailbox" to which messages can be sent and stored. It is especially helpful for busy workers who must coordinate the activities of many people in order to serve their clients. The same message can be sent to several people at once, time and energy are not lost in "telephone tag," messages can be read and answered at one's convenience, and the messages can be printed and saved for case records. It is an effective, fast, and inexpensive way of communicating information among staff members that can be accessed from home or office. ***E-mail–based discussion groups*** (also known as e-mail groups, special-interest groups [SIGS], newsgroups, USENET groups, or LISTSERVs) permit people to discuss specific topics with experts from around the world. Such groups relate to various topics as welfare reform, gay rights, AIDS, Alzheimer's disease, adoption, community revitalization, gangs, and child maltreatment. One popular e-mail discussion group that addresses general social work issues is maintained by the University of Arkansas. To subscribe, address an e-mail message to LISTSERV@ UAFSYSB.UARK.EDU and for the message write SUBSCRIBE SOCWORK and add (your) Firstname Lastname.

Another resource for social workers is ***computer-based self-help/mutual aid groups.*** These groups provide support to thousands of people with a variety of concerns including, for example, physical and sexual abuse, addictions, AIDS, disabilities, catastrophic illness, mental illness, and care giving. These groups are especially useful for persons who wish to participate in a self-help group anonymously, who have limited verbal communication skills, who are homebound due to disability or caregiver responsibilities, and those in rural areas or other places where local groups are not available (Finn 1993; Finn and Lavitt 1994).

The Internet also makes it possible to access ***files and databases of social work information*** without leaving one's home or office. Using ***FTP (File Transfer Protocol)*** software allows transfer of files from a remote computer site, whereas ***Telnet*** allows a worker to search over 700 professional journals on the Educational Resources Information Center (ERIC) and have articles faxed (for a fee).

Finally, perhaps the most useful information technology resource for the social worker is the ***World Wide Web (WWW),*** which links Internet information through web pages. As opposed to print material, as soon as information is entered on a web page, it is available to anyone who accesses that page at no cost. Many government agencies, human services organizations, universities, and individuals maintain web pages. Often, the creators of the web pages will provide links to related web pages, making it relatively easy for a social worker, even in a location remote from a well-stocked library, to get the latest information on a topic. Figure 9.1 provides a listing of particularly useful web resources for a social worker.

As information technology increasingly becomes part of social work practice, practitioners at all levels within the service organization must participate in shaping the technology of human services computing rather than permitting the technology to shape and drive practice (Nurius and Hudson 1993). Social workers should understand both the potential benefits and dangers in these changes. They must also address the associated ***ethical issues*** such as making sure disenfranchised groups will have access to information technology and protecting the accuracy, security, and confidentiality of social work records when agencies share records via telecommunications (Finn 1990). In the end, however, social workers must recognize that electronic technology only provides tools to assist practice; it is the workers themselves who must ultimately decide how to use this technology in an appropiate and responsible manner.

SELECTED BIBLIOGRAPHY

Finn, Jerry. "An Exploration of Computer-Based Self-Help/Mutual Aid Groups." In *Human Welfare and Technology,* edited by Bryan Glastonbury. The Netherlands: Van Gorcum, 1993.

———. "Security, Privacy, and Confidentiality in Agency Microcomputer Use." *Families in Society* (formerly *Social Casework*) 71 (May 1990): 283–290.

Finn, Jerry, and Melissa Lavitt. "Computer-Based Self-Help/Mutual Aid Groups for Sexual Abuse Survivors." *Social Work with Groups* 17, 1/2 (1994): 21–46.

Marson, Steven M. "A Selective History of Internet Technology and Social Work." *Computers in Human Services* 14(1997): 35–49.

National Association of Social Workers. *The Social Work Reference Library* (CD-ROM). Washington, DC: NASW Press, 1995.

Nurius, Paula S., and Walter W. Hudson. *Human Services Practice, Evaluation, and Computers: A Practical Guide for Today and Beyond.* Pacific Grove, CA: Brooks/Cole, 1993.

FIGURE 9.1 Useful Web Resources for Social Workers

The sources available to social workers through websites change rapidly. For a social worker to obtain up-to-date information, it is necessary to access the several websites that provide updated links to online materials.

Professional Organizations

National Association of Social Workers *http://www.naswdc.org*

Council on Social Work Education *http://www.cswe.org*

Canadian Association of Social Workers *http://www.intranet.ca/~casw-acts/info-e.htm*

International Federation of Social Workers *http://www.ifsw.org*

Award-Winning Links to Listservs, Client Resources, Social Work Education Programs, and Topics and Issues of Concern to Social Workers

Association of Baccalaureate Program Directors (BPD) *http://www.rit.edu/~694www/bpd.htm*

University of South Carolina (SWAN) *http://www.sc.edu/swan*

Colorado State University *http://www.colostate.edu/Depts/SocWork/web%20links.html*

New York University *http://pages.nyu.edu/~gh5/gh-w3-f.htm*

Government Sources

U.S. Government Information *http://www.access.gpo.gov/su_docs/aces/dcff001.html*

U.S. Legislation on the Internet *http://thomas.loc.gov*

U.S. Statistics *http://www.fedstats.gov*

U.S. Library of Congress *http://lcweb.loc.gov/homepage/online.html*

Canadian Government Information *http://canada.gc.ca/programs/pgrind_e.html*

Miscellaneous Sources

Allyn and Bacon Books and Hot Links *http://www.abacon.com/socwk/swhome.html*

Internet Nonprofit Center *http://www.nonprofits.org*

Licensing of Social Workers *http://www.aasswb.org/license.html*

Social Work Joke Page *http://dolphin.upenn.edu/~prentice/swjokes.html*

Printed Sources

Grant, Gary B., and Linda May Grobman. *The Social Worker's Internet Handbook.* Harrisburg, PA: White Hat Communications, 1998.

Yaffe, Joanne, ed. *Allyn and Bacon Quick Guide to the Internet for Social Work, 1998 Edition.* Boston: Allyn and Bacon, 1998.

9.5 Effective Telephone Communications

PURPOSE: To communicate clearly and concisely when using the telephone.

DISCUSSION: Many social work transactions occur over the telephone, making this a frequently used tool in social work practice. However, the telephone is not always the most effective method of communication.

The telephone should be used when a quick response is needed and the matter under discussion is relatively uncomplicated. It is important to remember that a phone call does not establish a permanent record of the transaction. A letter or memo may be preferred when time is not critical, when a record must be established, or when the message involves many details. The following guidelines will help improve telephone use:

1. The task of communicating over the telephone has to be accomplished by your voice. The person to whom you are speaking does not have the advantage of being able to observe your body language. Take care to enunciate distinctly. Use a normal speaking voice.

2. When making and receiving calls, always fully identify yourself by name, organization, and department.

3. Jot down the major points you wish to cover before placing the call. Take notes while on the phone. Before saying goodbye, it may be appropriate to summarize the information you intended to convey and the information you received.

4. If the person on the other end is talking at some length, interject a brief comment at intervals: "Yes, I see" or "I understand." This lets the other person know that you are still listening. If your caller gets sidetracked, steer him or her back to the main point of the call.

5. Answer the telephone on the first or second ring—and immediately respond to the caller. Do not just pick up the receiver and hold it while you finish a conversation with another person; this would be rude.

6. If you must leave a message for a person you did not reach by phone, keep the message short (e.g., your name, phone number, and reason for calling) and assume there is a good chance that the message will get garbled or lost. Suggest a specific time for the person to return your call. You will probably save time by calling back yourself rather than waiting for your call to be returned.

7. When you leave your office, always tell the office secretary where you can be reached or when you will be back. If needed, establish a regular time of day to receive telephone calls.

8. Master the skills of using your agency's phone system such as transferring calls, using voice mail, and so on. When transferring calls to other lines, let callers know what you are doing: Tell them the name and title of the person to whom they will be speaking and why you are transferring their call. When you must leave the phone, explain why: "Please hold on for a few seconds while I get that file." Unless you are sure you will be away for only a few moments, tell your caller that you will call back. If you have left the phone, alert your caller to your return before resuming the conversation: "Hello" or "Thanks for waiting" or "I have that file now."

9. Realize that the voice mail systems used in many agencies can be confusing and frustrating to callers. Appreciate the fact that the caller may be upset after having to carefully listen to a recorded voice and perform numerous dialing maneuvers. Instruct your clients and other frequent callers how to use the system.

SELECTED BIBLIOGRAPHY

Tarbell, Shirley. *Office Basics Made Simple.* New York: Learning Express, 1997.
Timm, Paul. *Winning Telephone Tips.* Franklin Lakes, NJ: Career Press, 1997.

9.6 Controlling Workload

PURPOSE: To manage workload by refusing and accepting additional work assignments.

DISCUSSION: Given the demands placed on a social worker, the worker must view his or her time as a limited resource. If the worker does not control workload, he or she will be spread too thin and effectiveness will diminish. There are only a couple ways to control an ever-growing workload—say no to additional work assignments or ask other staff for their assistance.

Saying no is difficult for many people. When someone asks you to take on additional work, it may seem easier to say yes in order to avoid conflict or feeling guilty. Nevertheless, you must take responsibility for managing your workload and this requires saying no to some requests. Follow these guidelines:

1. Decide if the proposed assignment or request for your time is reasonable, given your job description and current workload. Ask yourself: Is this a matter of high priority? Am I responsible for this matter or is someone else? If I say yes, will I soon regret it and feel angry and put upon? Am I tempted to say yes mainly because I want to avoid a conflict or the appearance of selfishness?

2. When unsure if the request is reasonable, obtain more information before saying yes or no. If still in doubt, ask for time to think about the request and set a deadline for making the decision (e.g., "I'll let you know in a half hour").

3. If you must refuse, say no firmly and calmly. It may be appropriate to give a straightforward explanation of why you must say no. But say no without saying "I'm sorry" or offering excuses and rationalizations. If you have a good reason for refusing, there is no need to apologize.

Whenever you ask others for assistance, explain why you think it is an important and reasonable request and why you are asking them to take on the task. If your request is refused, adhere to three guidelines.

1. Accept the answer graciously. Do not put pressure on the person and do not make the individual feel guilty for having refused.
2. Be pleasant and appreciative. Respond with something like, "I understand; thank you for your consideration."
3. If appropriate, ask if your request might be acceptable under other circumstances, such as at a later time or date.

It is important to note that this brief discussion of refusing and accepting additional assignments presumes a situation in which there is room to negotiate. Such a situation does not always exist. Within an agency, a supervisor or administrator has the authority to assign tasks, even when he or she knows you are already overloaded. In other words, a worker does not always have the freedom to refuse.

SELECTED BIBLIOGRAPHY

Alberti, Robert, and Michael Emmons. *Your Perfect Right,* 6th ed. San Luis Obispo, CA: Impact, 1990.

Mcbride, Patrica. *The Assertive Social Worker.* Brookfield, VT: Ashgate, 1998.

9.7 Maintaining Casenotes for Narrative Recording

PURPOSE: To improve efficiency in creating narrative case recordings.

DISCUSSION: Each social agency develops its own procedures for recordkeeping. What is recorded and the format used will depend on factors such as the agency's mission, relevant state and federal laws and regulations, type of service provided, and who has access to the records.

Narrative recording is still a fairly common format in direct-service agencies even though many have moved to the use of brief progress notes, computer-assisted systems, problem-oriented recording, and other structured and concise formats. The narrative format is often used because of its flexiblity—anything deemed important can be written into the record. The major disadvantages are that it is a time-consuming method, an individual may need to read several pages of the record in order to find a specific piece of information, and these types of records can grow large and bulky.

Two steps are involved in the preparation of a narrative record: The worker creates many handwritten notes and then, at a later date (sometimes weeks or even months later), the worker reviews these notes and prepares a summary of his or her work with the client. The handwritten notes record the day-to-day actions and activities related to a specific case (e.g., "Mr. Smith, Richard B's teacher, called to say . . .") and help the worker keep track of what has happened. Some notes are merely reminders (e.g., "Contact Mrs. Jones's attorney and request . . .").

In order for the worker to do the summary efficiently, he or she must develop a system of notetaking that (1) keeps all casenotes in one place so this information is always at hand, (2) maintains a chronological record of activities, and (3) facilitates summarization. One such method is to utilize a loose-leaf notebook filled with sheets specifically designed for brief handwritten and chronological entries. The sheets can be constructed to facilitate the recording of statistics kept by the agency (e.g., number of office interviews). Figure 9.2 is a sample with several typical entries. All of the notesheets are kept in one place and used as a basis for the periodic (e.g., once a month or bimonthly) dictation of a summary entry into the agency record.

SELECTED BIBLIOGRAPHY

Kagle, Jill. *Social Work Records,* 2nd ed. Belmont, CA: Wadsworth, 1991.
Wilson, Suanna. *Recording: Guidelines for Social Workers.* New York: Free Press, 1980.

FIGURE 9.2 Sample Recording of Casenotes

Client Jimmy Jones   Case Number 321   Cross Reference L. Smith Foster home

Type of contact										Date			Notes
Client (child)	Client (adult)	Foster parent	Collateral	Other	Office	Out-of-Office	Telephone	Letter	Other		Time spent	To Do	
		✓					✓			Jan 27			Mrs Smith called to say Jimmy ran away. He did not come
													home from school. She will call his friends and will
													inform Jimmy's probation officer. (Leland Green)
		✓					✓			1/28			I called Mrs. S. Still no word on Jimmy. Police have been informed.
				✓			✓			•••			Learned from L. Green that Jimmy was picked up. No charges.
✓		✓				✓				•••			Jimmy returned to Smith home. Jimmy having trouble in school.
													Failing math. Picked on by other kids. Wants to quit school.
												✓	(set up meeting with math teacher + school counselor. Is tutor possible?)
		✓					✓			1/29			Mr. + Mrs Smith and I will meet at school for conference, 4 pm today. Room 104
✓						✓				1/29			Spent hr with Jimmy. He is angry with math teacher. Feels he is not
													treated fairly because he is "foster kid." Also upset because mother
													forgot his birthday. "She is probably drunk again." He
													cried as he talked about mother. He cares for her and worries
													about her but "hates her when she drinks." He wants to
													visit older sister, Mary. "Mary helps me understand Mother."
												✓	(arrange meeting between Jimmy and Mary.)

9.8 Problem-Oriented Recording (POR) and the SOAP Format

PURPOSE: To facilitate concise recordkeeping that focuses on the client's problem and the professional interventions to deal with that problem.

DISCUSSION: *POR,* Problem-Oriented Recording, is a method of recordkeeping often used in hospitals and medical programs. Its use has spread to many social agencies. POR has a number of advantages, such as the following:

- It permits the worker, agency supervisor, outside consultants, or researchers to review the way in which a particular problem was approached by the worker or agency.
- It displays the multiplicity and interrelatedness of problems experienced by a client, yet it permits focused attention on each specific problem.
- It promotes case coordination and teamwork because it facilitates interprofessional communication and clarity of direction.
- It provides continuity of professional attention on specific problems, even when there is personnel turnover in the agency.
- It provides a mechanism for follow-up and the monitoring of progress toward problem resolution. A review of a problem-oriented record will quickly reveal inaction or actions unrelated to the client's problem.
- It encourages concise recording. Because specific problems are kept in focus, irrelevant information is kept out of the record.

POR consists of four components, which are related to the basic steps of the problem-solving process: (1) establishment of a database; (2) listing of specific problems, each of which is assigned an identifying number; (3) development of an action plan to address each problem; and (4) implementation of the plan.

The database consists primarily of the information collected during the intake phase and includes a description of the problem that brought the client to the agency. Much of the data appear on the record facesheet. These data should be systematically collected, organized, or recorded, for they provide a foundation for identifying and conceptualizing the client's problems and yield a preliminary problem list.

A problem can be anything of concern to the client, the social worker, or both. All problems become part of the problem list. Each problem is assigned a number and described in behavioral language. Diagnostic labels are avoided, if possible. The problem list serves to focus case planning and intervention. What the social worker does should be logically related to a specific problem in the list. As problems are resolved, they are removed from the list. However, the resolved problem's number is not reassigned; each number is used only once. Thus, the intervention and progress on a specific problem can be traced throughout the case record. In a sense, the numbering system serves as a audit trail. It is important that the problem list be on a separate page in the case record; this makes it easy for the user to find the list and provides a ready reference point for a review of progress and planning.

Figure 9.3 is a sample problem list for Mrs. Brown, a mother of three, who was reported to a protective services agency for child neglect. Note that each numbered problem is dated according to when the problem was first identified. If additional problems were identified, they would be added to the list. Problems 2 and 3 have been resolved, but problems 1 and 4 continue to receive the worker's attention.

Some agencies have adopted the concept of a master problem list, which utilizes a standard nomenclature and numbering system. For example, the number 15 might be assigned to the problem of unsafe housing. This uniformity of problem numbering facilitates research and program evaluation.

POR requires some type of action or response to each item on a client's problem list. Basically, three actions are possible: (1) intervention, (2) secure additional information in order to more fully understand the problem, or (3) do nothing except monitor the situation and wait for further developments. The social worker records his or her action in the main body of the case record and is careful to utilize the problem number to reference the action to a specific problem.

When intervention is required, it is helpful to use the SOAP format to describe this action. The acronym ***SOAP*** can be explained as follows:

S: *Subjective information* describes how the client feels about or perceives the situation. It is derived from client self-report. By definition, subjective information does not lend itself to independent or external validation.

O: *Objective information* is that which has been obtained by way of direct observation by professionals, clinical examinations, systematic data collection, and the like. As compared to subjective information, this category of information can be independently verified.

A: *Assessment* refers to the professional's conceptualization or conclusions derived from reviewing the subjective and objective information.

P: The *Plan* spells out how the professional intends to address or resolve the specific problem.

FIGURE 9.3 Problem List for the Brown Family

Problem Number	Problem	Date	Inactive or Resolved	Date Resolved
1.	Crowded housing	4/10		
2.	Short of food money	4/10	Client enrolled in food stamp program	4/20
3.	Johnny (age 8) needs glasses	4/15	New prescription issued by Dr. Green at Clinic	4/25
4.	Ann (age 10) failing in school	4/28		

FIGURE 9.4 Sample SOAP Entry

Subjective: Mrs. Brown states she worries about children's diet. The children complain of being hungry and to her embarrassment they have asked neighbors for food. Since Mrs. B grew up on welfare, she has vowed "never to go on the dole." She says she is in a "panic" about the thought of losing her children.

Objective: Her part-time job earns $200 take-home pay per week. Rent is $400 per month. It is hard to follow Mrs. Brown in conversation; she jumps from topic to topic. Agency records indicate that she was herself neglected as a child and placed in foster care for two years.

Assessment: Family does not have enough money for food. Mrs. Brown is probably eligible for food stamps. Much of her disorganization is due to her anxiety about losing children to foster care, which is, in turn, related to her own experience in foster care. She fears that accepting welfare will label her as a "bad parent."

Plan: (Problem #2) Need to support Mrs. Brown's application for food stamps and show her that application is a way to be a "good mother" under these very trying circumstances. Need to assure her that agency has no plans to place her children. Begin effort to help Mrs. B find higher-paying job. Complete food stamp application by 5/25.

The POR requires the use of the SOAP format; however, the SOAP format can be used apart from the POR system.

Figure 9.4 is a SOAP entry related to problem 2 (lack of money for food) in the Brown case (Figure 9.3). Note the deadline set for making the application. It is important to set a deadline for accomplishing a particular task; this encourages implementation and action.

Once the plan has been formulated, intervention follows. Clients are only helped by *action,* not by *plans,* no matter how logical or well written.

SELECTED BIBLIOGRAPHY

Burrill, George. "The Problem-Oriented Log in Social Casework." *Social Work* 21 (January 1976): 67.

Hartman, Barbara L., and Jane M. Wickey. "The Person-Oriented Record in Treatment." *Social Work* 23 (July 1978): 296–299.

Schmitt, Barton. "The Problem-Oriented Record and Team Reports." In *Child Protection Team Handbook,* edited by B. Schmitt. New York: Garland STPM Press, 1978, pp. 175–185.

9.9 Process Recording

PURPOSE: To establish a record of the social worker's practice so the process of helping and client-worker interaction can be studied.

DISCUSSION: Process recording is a detailed form of recording often used to assist students and new workers in learning basic skills. It is also used when a worker is having unusual problems with a client and wants to create a record that can be examined by his or her peers, supervisor, or consultant as a basis for making suggestions on how the worker might overcome the problems.

A social work student's process recording might include the following components.

1. Names of those in attendance at interview or meeting
2. Date, location, and length of session
3. Purpose of session (i.e., why client and student were meeting and how this session fits within goal of intervention)
4. Student's plan for session (i.e., what student hoped to accomplish and how)
5. Description of interaction and content—for example:
   - how session began
   - significant exchanges during session (e.g., what client said and how student responded; what student said and how client responded)
   - specific topics discussed, decisions reached, plans made
   - new facts and information obtained by student
   - mood and feeling tone of session
   - how session or meeting ended
6. Student's role and activities (e.g., techniques and skills used during session; roles and responsibilities taken on by student during session)
7. Student's assessment of client's concern, situation, or problem and client's current response and reactions to student social worker and to helping process
8. Student's assessment of his or her own performance during the session (e.g., problems encountered, strengths, limitations)
9. Student's plan for next interview or meeting with client

A process recording is an excellent teaching tool because it encourages the worker to analyze his or her practice behavior and decisions. A major disadvantage is that it requires a great deal of time to prepare. Many experienced social workers recommend the process recording of at least one case in a worker's caseload. A careful and detailed study of even one case can prove valuable for skill development and increase self-awareness.

Audio- or videotape recordings are, in many respects, superior to process recording as a teaching tool. However, many agencies do not have video equipment; even if they do, it often requires that the interview take place in a studio atmosphere in order to escape background noise. Compact camcorders may expand opportunities for students and workers to study their own performance. Although audiotaping an interview can be useful, listening to a tape is tedious.

SELECTED BIBLIOGRAPHY

Kagle, Jill. *Social Work Records,* 2nd ed. Belmont, CA: Wadsworth, 1991.

Urbanowski, Martha, and Margaret Dwyer. *Learning through Field Instruction.* Milwaukee: Family Service America, 1988.

9.10 Testifying in Court

PURPOSE: To prepare for a court appearance as a witness.

DISCUSSION: Social workers employed in child protective services, probation, and parole settings make frequent appearances in court. Sooner or later, nearly every social worker—regardless of agency setting—will serve as a witness. The following guidelines can help the worker perform effectively on the witness stand:

1. Prepare for the court appearance. Consult with the attorney who will call you as a witness and learn about the questions he or she will ask, as well as the questions you are likely to be asked by the attorney who will cross-examine you.

2. Inform the attorney representing the side for which you are testifying of any uncertainty and gaps in what you will be describing. He or she should know of these problems before you get on the witness stand.

3. Tell the truth, regardless of how you think it will affect the case. Remember that you will be under oath. Any exaggeration or departure from facts will be uncovered and your credibility as a witness will suffer.

4. Appearance and demeanor are critical. You should be properly dressed and well groomed to reflect the solemnity of the courtroom. When seated in the witness chair, you should be attentive and courteous.

5. Your testimony will probably fall into one or more of three categories:
   a. *Personal observations.* Prepare to testify with little, if any, reference to your notes. If your observations occurred over a long period of time, you can prepare a chronology or list of events to refresh your memory and keep your recollections organized. The opposing counsel and judge will probably look at your list, but it will not usually be introduced as evidence unless it differs from your oral testimony. Memorize the facts, but avoid sounding as though you are giving a recitation.
   b. *Reading reports.* Portions of your case record may be admitted into evidence. If so, you may be asked to read aloud segments of the record. Prepare by being thoroughly familiar with the content and organization of the record. Make sure you can read any handwritten parts. You should be able to explain the method for producing, transcribing, and storing a case file in your office.
   c. *Expert conclusions.* An individual who the judge has designated as an expert witness is permitted to offer opinions as to the meaning of facts and observations. All other witnesses must confine their testimony to facts and observations. Opposing attorneys often argue over whether a person should be qualified as an expert. If an attorney plans to qualify you as an expert witness, be prepared to explain:

- your professional qualifications (e.g., degree, experience, special training, publications, memberships in professional associations, etc.)
- the knowledge base, theories, and principles you used in forming an opinion
- your mode of practice and how it is similar to or different from that of other social workers or professionals in your field
- the opinions you formed and why (the major portion of your testimony as an expert)

6. Speak clearly and avoid using slang and jargon. Much of the jargon used by social workers is incomprehensive to judges, attorneys, and juries.

7. Listen carefully to the questions you are asked. If you do not understand a question, ask that it be rephrased or explained. If you do not know the answer, say so. Never speculate or guess. Answer only the question that is asked. Answer questions in a confident manner. Phrases such as "I feel" or "I guess" weaken the impact of your testimony.

8. If an objection is made during the course of your testimony, stop speaking immediately. If the judge overrules the objection, you will be told to answer the question. If the objection is sustained, you will not be permitted to answer and a new question will be asked.

9. When being cross-examined by the opposing attorney, keep in mind that he or she is not your friend. Even a polite and friendly cross-examiner is looking for ways to trip you up and discredit your testimony. Do not volunteer information that is not asked for. Do not explain why you know something unless you are asked. And finally, remember that the attorney offering your testimony has a chance to follow up and ask additional questions after the other attorney's cross-examination. This may help clear up any problems in your testimony.

10. Many times, cross-examiners ask compound questions. When responding to a compound question, divide it into sections and then answer each part. Do not agree with a partially untrue statement, because the attorney may cut you short and not allow you to complete your response, thus giving an erroneous impression of your actions or beliefs.

11. When being cross-examined, do not lose your temper at questions you consider impertinent or offensive. Exercise absolute self-control. If you maintain your composure, you will be less likely to become confused and inconsistent. If the questioning is truly improper, your attorney will object. Pause before answering a provocative question to allow the objection to be made, but not so long that you appear hesitant or unsure. All questions should be handled with tact and truth. Fortunately, judges are familiar with the histrionics of some trial attorneys and are rarely impressed by them.

12. Do not get caught in the "yes-or-no" trap. If, on cross-examination, the attorney asks a question and ends it with "Answer yes or no," don't feel obliged to do so if you believe such an answer will be misleading. Instead, begin your answer with "Well, that needs explaining." The attorney may again push you to answer yes or no and the judge may require you to give a yes or no answer, but the jury will understand your position and look forward to your explanation when your attorney clarifies the situation on redirect examination.

13. Often, a witness will be asked a question regarding sympathy for one side or the other in the case. If asked, admit your beliefs or sympathies honestly. It is absurd to deny an obvious sympathy, and an honest admission will not discredit a witness.

SELECTED BIBLIOGRAPHY

Barker, Robert, and Douglas Branson. *Forensic Social Work.* New York: Haworth, 1993.
Haralambi, Ann, and Donna Rosenberg. "The Expert Witness: Social Work, Medical, Psychiatric." In *The New Child Protection Team Handbook,* edited by Donald Bross et al. New York: Garland, 1988, pp. 396–413.
Saltzman, Andrea, and Kathleen Proch. *Law in Social Work Practice,* 2nd ed. Chicago: Nelson-Hall, 1999.

9.11 Dealing with Managed Care

PURPOSE: To adapt social work practice to requirements and restrictions of managed care arrangements.

DISCUSSION: Corcoran (1997) explains that usually the term ***managed care*** refers to "any effort to control the costs of services while—at least ostensibly—ensuring the quality of care. Although originally it was concerned with health and mental health care costs and quality, managed care has begun to influence other social services, including family services, child welfare services, and a variety of public programs" (p. 191).

Managed care efforts have taken several forms such as health maintenance organizations (HMOs), Employee Assistance Programs (EAPs), preferred provider organizations (PPOs), prospective payment systems (PPSs), and various approaches to utilization review. The mechanisms used in managed care to control treatment costs are usually one or more of the following: (1) to control or influence the decision on whether an individual will receive treatment, (2) to control or influence the decision on the type (or length) of treatment to be provided, (3) to control or influence the decision on what professional or facility will provide the treatment, (4) to minimize the length of stay in an expensive treatment facility and move the patient to a less expensive facility as soon as possible, (5) to determine how much the provider is to be paid, and (6) to cease payment for certain types of treatment when the patient or client is no longer making progress.

For several decades, the term *third-party payer* has been used to refer to the organizational entity (e.g., an insurance company, Medicare, Medicaid, CHAMPUS) that is paying for the services provided by a professional and received by a client or patient. The managed care company is now a fourth-party in this already complex arrangement.

Typically, the managed care company works under a contract with the third-party payer such as an insurance company or a governmental agency. The job of the company's employee, the case manager, is to monitor the use of insurance or program benefits and, where possible, reduce the costs of patient care and treatment. The provider of the treatment and the company's case manager are often separated by hundreds of miles, and their communication will be by phone and through the exchange of patient records and progress notes by surface mail, FAX, or e-mail. In rare situations, the case manager will speak face to face with the provider and patient, but most often the case manager will base his or her decisions on the written materials submitted by the provider.

The advent of managed care has raised many complex legal and ethical questions for social workers and other providers of health and human services. The provider of the treatment continues to be ethically and legally responsible for making sure that the patient receives needed and appropriate care even though many of the key treatment decisions are in the hands of a company case manager or dictated by fiscal considerations. Many of the social worker's ethical concerns relate to such issues as confidentiality, client self-determination, and the client's right to be fully informed about various treatment options.

As agencies and social workers attempt to adapt their practice and programs to the realities of managed care, the following guidelines may prove helpful:

1. Decisions and actions related to referring an individual for treatment and accepting a referral must consider whether and how managed care requirements and restrictions may affect service delivery. In many cases, it will be necessary to help the client seek information about possible managed care implications so that the client can make an informed decision on whether and from whom to seek services (see Item 11.3).

2. Learn about the procedures used in diagnosis. For the most part, third-party payers only pay for the treatment of disease and pathological conditions. A diagnosis is required to establish the existence of the disease or disorder. In mental health, this requires classification according to the *DSM* (see Item 12.22). The third-party payer will cover certain conditions, but not others, often tempting the provider to manipulate a diagnosis in order to maximize client service. However, it is important to understand that the crime of insurance fraud is committed by a provider who knowingly assigns the wrong diagnostic label in order to secure payment from an insurance company.

3. Conceptualize treatment plans as the best possible and most reasonable outcomes with full awareness of the costs involved and how managed care will limit the type and length of services that will be reimbursed.

4. Because the managed care company's case manager will agree to pay for treatment only so long as need can be justified and progress can be documented, it is important to use assessment tools and outcome measures that are understandable to and acceptable to the case manager (see Chapter 15). Also, the client's record and progress notes must document treatment efforts and client progress in ways required by the case manager to approve of and justify continuing the treatment.

5. Be prepared to assume the role of client advocate and develop the skills of persuasion and negotiation in order to secure the case manager's approval of treatment you consider important to your client.

6. Anticipate significant change in managed care. The outcome of lawsuits, new legislation, and innovations in managed care arrangements will bring about change. Join with other professionals and advocacy groups to shape the future of managed care so it will better serve social work clients.

SELECTED BIBLIOGRAPHY

Corcoran, Kevin. "Managed Care: Implications for Social Work Practice." In *1997 Supplement, Encyclopedia of Social Work,* 19th ed., edited by Richard Edwards. Washington, DC: NASW, 1997, pp. 191–200.

Jackson, Vivian, ed. *Managed Care Resource Guides—Agency Settings.* Washington, DC: NASW, 1995.

Lightburn, Anita, and Gerald Schamess, eds. *Humane Managed Care?* Washington, DC: NASW, 1998.

Lohmann, Roger. "Managed Care: A Review of Recent Research." In *1997 Supplement, Encyclopedia of Social Work,* 19th ed., edited by Richard Edwards. Washington, DC: NASW, 1997, pp. 200–206.

National Asociation of Social Workers. *Third-Party Reimbusement for Clinical Social Work Services.* Washington, DC: NASW, 1997.

10 Personal and Professional Development

INTRODUCTION

Social work is a difficult and demanding profession but also a rewarding one. However, the rewards are mostly intrinsic. By selecting social work as a career, one is virtually assured of never attaining wealth or prestige. Social work is about caring, sharing, and social responsibility; these are not the values rewarded by our economic system. Gordon Allport, a respected social psychologist, once observed that the low status given to social work in the United States may be due to the emphasis social workers place on compassion and cooperation within a society that places high value on competition and individualism.

From its beginnings, the social work profession has demonstrated special concern for those who are powerless, stigmatized, and devalued—the people who others tend to avoid or ignore. Because social workers are in a position to see so many people in need and see the inadequacy of professional, agency, and societal resources, they frequently suffer the anguish of knowing that no matter how hard they work, efforts will fall short of the mark. This is a frustration with which the social worker must learn to live.

Because many clients are economically poor, few are in a position to pay directly for services. For this reason, most social workers are employed by governmental or nonprofit agencies. This means that most workers find themselves in resource-poor organizations—ones with few perks and with limited opportunities for continuing education and in-service training.

This chapter provides social workers with guidance aimed at helping them develop their skills and cope with work-related frustrations. More specifically, it offers guidance on using supervision, making a presentation, writing an article, coping with bureaucracy, managing job-related stress, developing self-awareness, making ethical decisions, avoiding malpractice suits, improving the image of social work, dealing with sexual harassment and misconduct, and analyzing and interpreting research reports and statistical data.

10.1 Getting a Social Work Job

PURPOSE: To secure employment as a social worker in a human services organization.

DISCUSSION: Once a social worker has completed professional education, the next task is to secure employment in the capacity of a social worker. That usually takes time and effort, as agencies are necessarily careful in their selection of staff to serve their clientele. (To examine this process from the viewpoint of the agency, see Item 11.12.) It is important, therefore, for the social worker who is seeking a job to present himself or herself in a manner that ensures the best chance of being hired.

The first step in finding employment is to discover the job openings. In most communities, several sources of information might be examined. Agencies with good affirmative action plans will advertise their positions. The classified advertisements in the local newspaper and/or the *NASW News* should be read on a regular basis. The personnel departments of city, county, or state agencies will post job openings on agency bulletin boards. Those should be checked periodically. The local United Way staff will frequently be aware of current and future job openings in its member agencies. Finally, informal networks among professionals are an excellent source of information. Attending local NASW meetings is a good way to tap into the professional network in most communities.

Once an open position is located, an application must be prepared. The application typically has two parts: a cover letter and a professional resumé. The ***cover letter*** should focus on the particular job being applied for and should stress the applicant's qualifications for that position. It should be approximately one page in length and must be carefully written with no spelling, punctuation, or grammatical errors. The letter should clearly indicate that it and the resumé represent an application for the position, describe why the applicant is interested in that job, and discuss qualifications for the position. The cover letter is not the place to discuss salary expectations or reasons for leaving past jobs. Indicate that a list of references will be provided on request (unless the job announcement asks that references be supplied as part of the application). Be sure to obtain advance permission from the people named as references. The letter should be upbeat and positive about the position for which one is applying.

The professional ***resumé*** is more generic than a cover letter and might be used when applying for several positions. It is an organized summary of one's professional qualifications. Its purpose is to present the applicant's background in a manner that will convince the employer to invite him or her for an interview. There is no prescribed format or style for a resumé. Rather, use a creative approach to attract the attention of members of a screening committee who may be selecting a few finalists from a large number of applications; however, avoid being cute or clever. Often, photocopy shops provide layout consultation, have laser printers available, and can recommend good quality paper, making it relatively inexpensive to prepare an attractive resumé. In addition, many colleges or universities have offices that provide workshops and consultation to students in preparing job applications.

At a minimum, the following information should be included in a resumé; other items may be added at one's discretion:

- *Personal data.* Include your name, address, and phone number. If you have a number where you can be reached during working hours, be sure to include it to facilitate scheduling an interview.
- *Education.* Give the name of your degree(s), your major, the colleges or universities you attended, and graduation dates. List all schools you have attended (listing in reverse order) and possibly add grade-point average, honors,

special projects, or any special skills or training that might be relevant to a social work job (e.g., computer, foreign language, etc.).

- *Experience.* List employment in reverse order (i.e., beginning with your current or most recent job), giving the job title, name of organization, dates of employment, and job duties. It is also helpful to list any volunteer experience that might have contributed to your social work competencies.
- *Activities and interests.* Identify your professional interests as well as those that extend beyond social work. Note membership in professional organizations, your participation in various clubs or organizations and any offices held, and any hobbies or special interests.
- *References.* A statement such as "References Available On Request" is usually best to place on a resumé. If a job announcement calls for references, they should be listed in the cover letter. This flexibility allows for selecting the most appropriate references for each position. In general, the persons selected as references should be able to comment on your skills and might include a faculty member, a field instructor, and/or job supervisors or persons who supervised volunteer experiences. In many instances, an agency will contact the references by telephone rather than by letter, so give telephone numbers.
- *Other information.* It may be desirable to add other information such as publications, travel experiences, and unique experiences that may enhance your competence as a social worker.

If the application is successful, the applicant will be invited to an ***interview.*** Typically, the interview process will involve appearing before a panel of interviewers, although there will usually be some one-to-one discussions, as well. Many review panels will present the applicant with hypothetical situations or case vignettes and ask how he or she would handle the situation. The interviewing procedures used by government agencies are usually highly structured and many require a written exam in addition to oral interviews.

Preparation is essential. First, research the agency thoroughly. Know the services it offers, its target clientele, and something about its structure and goals. This information might be obtained by stopping by the agency in advance to pick up informational materials, by talking with the receptionist about the agency, or by discussing the agency with clients and/or other social workers in the community. Second, dress professionally and be as relaxed as possible during the interview process. Third, be prepared for questions about your personal and professional interests, as well as your preparation for the specific job duties. Grobman (1994, 16) identified seven questions that are commonly asked in an interview:

1. What are your qualifications for this job?
2. What are your strengths?
3. What are your weaknesses?
4. Why do you want this job?
5. What are your career goals?
6. What would you do in the following situation? (For example, a client tells you he wants to hurt himself. What is your response?)
7. Why should I hire you?

Finally, be prepared with your own questions about the agency and the job. Remember that an interview is a two-way street—both the applicant and the agency are deciding if there is a good match between one's skills and interests and the requirements of the job.

If offered the position, be sure to know what will be expected of you on the job, and negotiate the salary or other benefits with the employer. Before accepting a new position, (1) you should obtain a letter of appointment that states the starting salary, duties, and other pertinent information; and (2) you should review the agency's personnel manual to be sure the provisions of the agreement are understood.

SELECTED BIBLIOGRAPHY

Doelling, Carol. *Career Development: A Handbook for Job Hunting and Career Planning.* Washington, DC: NASW, 1997.

Ginsberg, Leon. *Careers in Social Work.* Boston: Allyn and Bacon, 1998.

Grobman, Linda May. "Job Recruiters: What Do They Really Want?" *The New Social Worker* 1 (Spring 1994): 16–21.

10.2 Elements of Professional Behavior

PURPOSE: To clarify the nature of professional behavior.

DISCUSSION: It has been said that a professional is "someone who knows what to do and can be counted on to do what needs to be done, even when he or she does not feel like doing it." There is much wisdom in that description. It suggests that a professional knows what can and should be done, can be trusted to do it, and does not let matters of personal convenience or personal feelings interfere with his or her performance.

It is important for social workers to continually examine their performance and make sure their behavior is of a professional nature. Consider the following comparison of professional and nonprofessional behavior:

Professional Behavior	*Nonprofessional Behavior*
Decisions and actions are based primarily on a body of knowledge learned through a process of formal education and training.	Decisions and actions are based primarily on personal opinions and personal preferences, or agency rules and regualtions.
Principles of good practice are followed, regardless of other pressures.	Political and fiscal pressure and other forces are allowed to dictate decisions and actions.
Objectivity is employed and decisions are based on the facts of the situation.	Subjectivity rules and decisions are based mostly on personal bias and personal convenience.

Professional Behavior	*Nonprofessional Behavior*
The profession's values, principles, and *Code of Ethics* are used to identify and resolve ethical issues.	Only personal moral judgments are used to resolve ethical questions; many ethical issues go unrecognized or are ignored.
Knowledge and skills are continually developed so that services to clients can be improved.	Only what is required to keep the job is learned.
The relationship with the client is purposeful, goal oriented, and time limited.	The relationship with the client lacks a sense of direction and resembles a friendship.
The well-being and needs of the client are of primary concern; the worker does not expect to meet personal needs within work-related relationships.	The well-being and needs of the worker are of primary concern; the worker expects to have personal needs met through contact with the client and within work-related relationships.
Review of performance by peers is expected and invited.	Peer review is threatening and is avoided.
Self-discipline in decision making and action is excercised; when with an angry or frustrated client, emotional reactions are under control; personal feelings are expressed in a helpful and purposeful manner.	Emotions shape decisions and actions; when with an angry or frustrated client, the worker reacts with anger and frustration; feelings may be expressed in a thoughtless and hurtful manner.
The client's expressions of negative emotion are not taken personally; the worker seeks to understand the reasons behind the client's frustration and anger.	The client's frustrations and anger are taken personally.
Accurate and complete records of decisions and actions are kept.	Recordkeeping is avoided; records are incomplete or inaccurate.
Responsibility is taken for seeking new knowledge and information and for sharing it with peers.	The worker does not see self as responsible for the development of new knowledge or for teaching peers.
Personal responsibility is assumed for examining the quality of services provided and for working to make the agency, program, or policy changes that would improve services to the client.	The worker is concerned only about doing the job as assigned or described by others; the worker does not see self as responsible for agency, policy, or program changes.
Social work is regarded as a lifelong commitment; the occupation and work are seen as a "calling."	Social work is seen as a job that can be easily abandoned if something better comes along; another occupation or type of work could easily be sought.

SELECTED BIBLIOGRAPHY

Lauffer, Armand. *Working in Social Work.* Newbury Park, CA: Sage, 1987.

Morales, Armando, and Bradford W. Sheafor. *Social Work: A Profession of Many Faces,* 8th ed. Boston: Allyn and Bacon, 1998.

Reid, P. Nelson, and Philip Popple. *The Moral Purpose of Social Work.* Chicago: Nelson-Hall, 1992.

10.3 Using Agency Supervision

PURPOSE: To obtain knowledge and learn skills through guidance provided by an agency supervisor.

DISCUSSION: In order for a social worker to learn job-related tasks and procedures and develop as a skilled professional, he or she must make effective use of the social work supervision provided within his or her practice setting. According to Kadushin (1992), a social work supervisor is

> an agency administrative-staff member to whom authority is delegated to direct, coordinate, enhance, and evaluate on-the-job performance of the supervisees for whose work he is held accountable. In implementing this responsibility the supervisor performs administrative, educational and supportive functions in interaction with the supervisee in the context of a positive relationship. The supervisor's ultimate objective is to deliver to agency clients the best possible service . . . in accordance with agency policies and procedures. (pp. 22–23)

Guidelines for Agency Social Workers

Several guidelines can help the social worker make appropriate and effective use of supervision.

1. Realize that your supervisor will expect you to:
   - Be effective and get results consistent with the agency's mission, program, goals, and your job description.
   - Follow agency policy, procedure, and specific instruction.
   - Consult with your supervisor when you are unsure about how to proceed or when a course of action is raising unforseen issues or encountering unexpected problems.
   - Immediately inform your supervisor when you become aware of an ethical, legal, or procedural violation that could give rise to a formal complaint or in some way harm the agency or its clients.
   - Demonstrate an eagerness to learn the details of your job, to become more efficient and effective, and to accept constructive criticism and suggestions on how you could improve the quality of your work.
   - Take initiative and assume responsibility for work that needs to be done.
   - Work cooperatively with and be respectful of colleagues and engage in behaviors that improve staff morale.
   - Maintain accurate and up-to-date records of your work with clients.

2. Expect your supervisors to:
- Provide needed on-the-job training.
- Keep you informed of changes in agency policy or procedure and any changes in your responsibilities.
- Explain the reasons behind agency policy and procedure.
- Provide encouragement and support when your work is particularly difficult and frustrating.
- Evaluate your performance on a regular basis and offer specific suggestions on how it can be improved.
- Give you a clear warning when your performance falls below standards.

3. Establish a regularly scheduled time to meet with your supervisor. This should be at least once a week. Having adequate time to discuss work and job-related concerns is of critical importance.

4. Seek your supervisor's assistance in formulating an individualized training plan that will build on your personal and professional strengths and address limitations in your performance. Such a plan should be in writing. Identify specific tasks and objectives to be accomplished over the next 6 and 12 months, and list specific learning activities (reading, study, conferences, workshops, etc.).

5. The newly hired social worker and the student beginning a practicum must recognize that agency staff often adopt a "wait and see" attitude toward newcomers. The staff may be offended if the newcomer criticizes the agency's programs or makes suggestions for "improvement" without appreciating or understanding why the agency operates as it does. Shulman (1993, 72) observes that if recent graduates of a school of social work "articulate highly theoretical positions or arguments that tend to denigrate the services of the agency, they put the supervisor on the defensive and this often leads to an initial battle of wills."

6. Recognize that the recommendations of experienced and respected supervisors are usually pivotal to your effort to secure a promotion or career advancement. When making such a recommendation, a supervisor will be especially attentive to the quality and quantity of your work, your understanding of the agency and the work to be done, your ability to formulate a feasible plan and carry it out, your leadership skills and the ability to win the respect of others, your time-management skills, your capacity to learn and adapt to change, your initiative and willingness to assume responsibility, and your emotional stability and dependability.

Guidelines for Social Work Students

Horejsi and Garthwait (1999, 12–13) explain that the social work student has a special set of responsibilities to his or her practicum agency. Among these are the following:

1. Meet with the practicum instructor (field instructor) on a regular basis (at least weekly).
2. Prepare for all meetings with the practicum instructor and inform him or her of the topics that need to be discussed during the upcoming meeting.

3. Be present at the agency on days and at times agreed upon by the student and practicum instructor. If unable to attend, notify the agency supervisor prior to or at the start of the workday.
4. Behave in a professional manner, taking responsibility as an adult learner to understand and carry out assigned duties, meet all deadlines, and seek direction when needed.
5. Carry out agency-related assignments, tasks, and responsibilities in a manner consistent with agency policy and procedures and prepare all records and reports in accord with prescribed format.
6. Identify learning needs and, if required, prepare an agreement that identifies learning outcomes and learning activities.
7. Provide proof of having professional malpractice insurance, if required by the school or agency.
8. Complete all practicum monitoring and evaluation forms and reports required by the agency and school (e.g., time sheets).
9. Discuss with the practicum instructor and or the school's practicum coordinator any areas of significant disagreement, dissatisfaction, or confusion related to the practicum experience.
10. Devote the required number of hours to the practicum.

SELECTED BIBLIOGRAPHY

Holloway, Stephen, and George Brager. *Supervising in the Human Services: The Politics of Practice.* New York: Free Press, 1989.

Horejsi, Charles, and Cynthia Garthwait. *The Social Work Practicum.* Boston: Allyn and Bacon, 1999.

Kadushin, Alfred. *Supervision in Social Work,* 3rd ed. New York: Columbia University Press, 1992.

Munson, Carlton. *Clinical Social Work Supervision,* 2nd ed. New York: Haworth, 1993.

Shulman, Lawrence. *Interactional Supervision.* Washington DC: NASW Press, 1993.

10.4 Presenting to a Professional Audience

PURPOSE: To organize and plan a speech or other oral presentation to communicate professional information.

DISCUSSION: Because social workers make numerous presentations to decision makers and professional colleagues, it is important that they develop the skills of public speaking. Making a good presentation can be an effective way of improving services to clients. For example, a single speech to a group of community or political leaders can have far-reaching effects if that speech moves the group to modify a policy or create a needed program. Similarly, throughout their careers, social workers will be expected to make presentations at workshops or conferences in which they exchange information and describe new insights or developments in order to improve the quality of services provided to clients. To make these presentations as effective as possible is an important responsibility of the professional social worker.

Speeches can vary considerably in structure. At one extreme is an "off-the-cuff" presentation; at the other extreme is reading from a prepared paper. Neither is usually effective. The former is likely to be difficult to follow and the latter can easily lull the audience to sleep. Somewhere between the two extremes is the recipe for a effective oral presentation.

Considerable planning is required for an effective oral presentation. The presenter must keep in mind the fact that the audience must grasp the material when it is presented. As opposed to reading a book or article, members of the audience do not have the luxury of skimming the outline to understand where the author is headed, skipping over sections of material that are not of interest, or rereading to be sure material is understood. The presenter, then, must carefully plan the speech to be sure the communication is accurately received.

The first step in preparing for a presentation is to know the content and be familiar with the audience. Second, one must select and adapt the content to be presented to the interests of the audience being addressed. For example, a presentation on the tasks performed by social workers would be quite different at a junior high school career day than when presenting to a state personnel board. Third, it is essential to carefully organize the flow of information. In broad terms, the speech should include three major components: a preview of the topic, the main body of the speech, and a summary pointing out the conclusions reached about the topic. Last, the presenter should consider creative ways to make the presentation interesting and understandable to the audience.

Careful preparation and a relatively relaxed presenter are the two essential conditions for successful speeches. The following guidelines can be helpful in achieving these conditions:

1. *Be clear about the purpose of the speech.* Is the intent to inform or persuade? If the purpose is to *persuade,* the presentation should be planned to (a) identify the nature and extent of the problem using facts or case examples, (b) identify the consequences of not changing the situation for the individuals affected and the society (including the members of the audience) in general, (c) suggest solutions, and (d) propose actions the audience can take to help. If the purpose is to *inform* (e.g., a professional presentation), the presenter should (a) identify the relevance of the information to be presented, (b) explain the status of the current knowledge about the subject based on a review of the literature, (c) give a summary of the manner in which the data or concepts were developed, and (d) provide an analysis of the practice implications or conclusions drawn from the information.

2. *Carefully analyze the audience—both when preparing the presentation and just before presenting.* When planning what to present and how to present it, form a clear picture of the people who will be in the audience. It is often useful to visualize a particular person who is expected to be in attendance and prepare a presentation that will interest that person. A practice run-through and critique by a colleague can

help identify areas that need reworking. To reduce anxiety and provide information to help fine-tune the presentation about to be delivered, it is often helpful for the presenter to mingle with the audience before the session begins. Introducing oneself to audience members who arrive early, asking what they hope to get from the session, and simply cultivating a few familiar and responsive faces in the audience can increase the comfort level of the presenter considerably.

3. *Be enthusiastic about the topic.* If the audience can feel that the presenter is excited and interested in the material being presented, they too will look at the material in a positive light. A little of the "salesperson" in each of us should be used to capture the attention of the audience.

4. *Be responsive to the ability of the audience to absorb the content.* The time of day, length of available time for both presentation and discussion, size of audience, atmosphere of the room, and other factors all can affect audience attention. In general, it is best to be as brief as possible. After all, the mind can absorb only what the seat can endure. A good rule is to cover the content as efficiently as possible in the presentation and to reserve time for the audience to explore the material that is of most interest to them in a question-and-answer period.

5. *Use 5 × 7 notecards to help maintain the planned organization of the presentation.* The notecards should be numbered in case they get out of order and should be prepared in large and legible print.

6. *Use language and visual aids that will help the audience follow the organization of your presentation and comprehend the data that are presented.* One way to help the audience remember the key points is to put together key words that spell something (acronyms). Visual aids may take the form of handing out hard-copy materials, presenting information on an overhead projector, or using videotaped materials. Given the availability of portable overhead projectors and the ease of preparing charts, figures, and tables on home computers, the well-prepared presenter can readily present considerable information while holding the attention of his or her audience.

7. *Examine your mannerisms while speaking.* Words and phrases such as "you know" and "uh" are annoying and distracting, as are physical mannerisms such as elaborate hand movements or pacing while presenting. Practice delivering the speech before a mirror to get a sense of the time required (although the time it takes to deliver a speech is often underestimated), and then try not to depend too heavily on notes when actually presenting. An audiotape or videotape of a practice run or the honest critique of a colleague can help to minimize distracting behaviors. Also, be sure to dress appropriately for the nature of the meeting, as attire that is out of place can be distracting to the audience.

8. *Present with an aura of confidence.* If the presenter knows the material, is well organized and enthusiastic, and responds effectively to the discussion with the audience, most errors will be forgiven. It is the message, not the messenger, that is most important.

SELECTED BIBLIOGRAPHY

Cook, Jeff. *The Elements of Speech Writing and Public Speaking.* New York: Macmillan, 1996.
Kushner, Malcolm. *Successful Presentations for Dummies.* Foster City, CA: IDG Books, 1996.
Sprague, Jo, and Douglas Stuart. *The Speakers Handbook,* 4th ed. New York: Harcourt Brace, 1996.

10.5 Writing to a Professional Audience

PURPOSE: To share one's knowledge in written form with colleagues in order to strengthen the quality and effectiveness of social work practice.

DISCUSSION: When a social worker develops or discovers some new knowledge that will enhance the practice of social workers, he or she is obligated to share that knowledge. The *Code of Ethics* (NASW 1997) is clear about this expectation. This knowledge might be shared through a conference presentation (see Item 10.4) or through preparing an article for publication in a professional journal.

Oral presentations have the advantage of allowing the presenter to tailor the presentation to a specific audience and to have the benefit of feedback from that audience. However, the number who can benefit from such a presentation is limited to those who are able to attend the meeting. Written presentations are less dynamic and flexible than speeches but can reach large audiences. Each issue of *Social Work,* for example, is mailed to nearly 160,000 members of NASW and is maintained for many years in hundreds of libraries. A single social worker can have a substantial effect on practice through the preparation of journal articles and other written materials.

When preparing a journal article, it is important to remember that the reader ultimately decides if the material will be read at all and, if so, how it will be approached. Some readers will begin with the first paragraph and read each word as the author has presented the material. Some will skim and return to read carefully the parts that most interest them. Others may read the introduction and conclusion and, if their interest is not captured, move on to other materials. The author, then, must write to help the reader determine if it will be worth the time to read the material and to keep the interest of those who decide to read the article carefully. The following guidelines are useful when preparing written materials:

1. *Have a clear and important message.* Although some articles are built on original ideas and data, most update and expand existing information, synthesize or combine available knowledge in a unique way, or simply express something already known in a form that makes it more understandable. The author must help the reader understand how this message relates to what is already known and why reading this article could enhance the social worker's practice. Since articles are limited in length, the scope of the article cannot be too broad nor the content too complex. A good test of scope is to see if the key ideas can be stated in a single paragraph. If it is not possible to be this succinct, the topic is probably too broad and may need to be broken into subparts and presented in more than one article.

2. *Select an appropriate journal.* A large number of journals address matters of interest to social workers. Some publish articles on a wide range of topics (see "generic" journals next), but most specialize. The NASW *Author's Guide* contains information about publishing requirements for over 130 different journals. Each has its own focus and will attract a specific readership. Some journals in which social workers frequently publish are the following:

Generic Topics

Journal of Applied Social Sciences
Journal of Baccalaureate Social Work
Journal of the National Association of Black Social Workers
Journal of Sociology and Social Welfare
New England Journal of Human Services
New Social Worker, The
Smith College Studies in Social Work
Social Service Review
Social Work

Specialized Fields, Methods, and Settings

AFFILIA: Journal of Women and Social Work
Child and Adolescent Social Work Journal
Child Welfare
Clinical Social Work Journal
Families and Society (formerly *Social Casework)*
Health and Social Work
Human Services in a Rural Environment
Journal of Community Practice
Journal of Family Social Work
Journal of Gay and Lesbian Social Services
Journal of Gerontological Social Work
Journal of Independent Social Work
Journal of Law and Social Work
Journal of Multicultural Social Work
Journal of Specialists in Group Work
Pediatric Social Work
Public Welfare
School Social Work Journal
Social Thought: The Journal of Religion and Social Work
Social Work in Education
Social Work with Groups: A Journal of Community and Clinical Practice
Social Work in Health Care

Research

Computers in Human Services
Journal of Social Service Research
Research on Social Work Practice
Social Work Research

Administration and Supervision

Administration in Social Work
Clinical Supervisor, The
Journal of Social Work Supervision
Nonprofit and Voluntary Sector Quarterly

Social Work Education

Journal of Continuing Social Work Education
Journal of Social Work Education
Journal of Teaching in Social Work

International and Foreign

British Journal of Social Work
Canadian Welfare
European Journal of Social Work
Indian Journal of Social Work
International Child Welfare
International Social Work
Journal of International and Comparative Social Welfare
Social Work and Christianity
Social Work Today
Social Worker-Travailleur Social

Before beginning to write, examine several issues of the journal most appropriate for the content and make an assessment of the probable readership, type of articles accepted for publication, and typical format of the articles (e.g., research based, theoretical, case applications). Each journal will periodically include a statement of its publishing requirements and provide information on preferred topics, length, style, and procedures for submitting articles. Increasingly, journals are using the APA style (American Psychological Association 1994) and typically have a maximum length of 12 to 15 double-spaced pages.

3. *Picture the audience.* It is helpful to write to an individual rather than an unknown audience. Select someone who would be likely to read the article, and write to that person. Use language that communicates your ideas clearly to him or her, and use concepts familiar to that person.

4. *Prepare an abstract.* Most journals require a 75- to 100-word abstract to accompany the article. Although it is often easier to write an abstract after the article is completed, preparing a first draft before writing the article can help focus attention on the most important points. The abstract should be clear, concise, and factual, as it may ultimately appear in *Social Work Abstracts,* on *Social Work Abstracts Plus* (CD-ROM), or on other databases.

5. *Develop an outline.* How well the readers will be able to comprehend the information is influenced by the organization of the article. Think through the logical connections between elements to be included. Preparing an outline will help achieve smooth and understandable transitions between the various parts of the article.

6. *Write the introduction.* The opening two or three paragraphs should tell what the article is about, explain why it is important, and suggest which social workers might be especially interested in this material. A good introduction maintains the reader's attention and stimulates continued reading. Tying the subject to a current issue or including a short case example related to the topic may help the reader see the benefit in reading the entire article.

For many writers, getting started is the most difficult part of writing. Do not let frustration over the introduction block the process. Some writers find it helpful to write a rough introduction with the intent of completely rewriting it later.

7. *Set the context or background.* It is important to let the reader know where this material fits in social work (e.g., practice theory, practice techniques, social welfare policy issues, etc.). The reader also needs to know the theoretical context in which this material is placed. A literature review or even clarification of its relationship to a particular concept or school of thought helps provide this background information. However, this contextual material cannot be extensive and must be focused clearly on the topic of the article.

8. *Prepare the body of the article.* Concisely report the facts and observations that are the heart of the article. It is helpful to supplement narrative material with alternative means of presenting the information (e.g., charts, figures, tables, and lists). If case examples are used, be sure that they are presented in a way that helps the reader generalize from that example to other situations.

Make frequent use of headings and subheadings so the reader can easily follow the flow of ideas and information. Articles are most readable when they contain short paragraphs with clearly focused content.

Write simply and clearly and avoid social work jargon. Omit gender-specific language and any terms that might reflect bias or stereotyping based on race, ethnicity, gender, age, handicapping conditions, or sexual orientation.

9. *Prepare a summary and/or conclusion.* End the article with a short statement that pulls together the key points and presents conclusions that can be drawn from this material. If relevant, point out additional research that is needed to further develop the subject.

10. *Collect and format references.* Using the format appropriate for the selected journal, list the references that support the ideas and information presented. Endnotes or some type of reference list are most often used.

11. *Choose a good title.* The title will be the first clue the reader will have about the article, so be sure it clearly identifies the subject. A creative or provocative title can attract reader interest.

12. *Rewrite, rewrite, rewrite.* Expect to revise and rewrite a number of times before concluding that the article is completed. Polishing the structure, content, and language time and time again is an essential part of good written communication.

13. *Let it cool.* Avoid sending an article to a journal as soon as it comes out of the word processor. A week or two away from the material provides a fresh perspective and may yield alternative ideas for presenting the material or strengthening the way ideas are expressed. It may be helpful to use this time to get colleagues to review the work and offer comments. Remember, however, that it is your article, and you must own the final result. Do not feel obligated to incorporate all suggested changes. Also, do not allow this "cooling" period to become an excuse for procrastination. You may never be completely satisfied with your writing, but one simply must stop refining it at some point.

14. *Mail the manuscript.* Send the required number of copies to the selected journal. Typically, the publisher will acknowledge receipt of the manuscript and send it on to two or three reviewers. The review process may take several months.

15. *Dealing with acceptance or rejection.* Reviewers will usually offer comments on the strengths and limitations of the article and how it does or does not fit the focus of that journal. Reviewers will typically conclude with a recommendation to (a) reject, (b) accept if revised in specific ways, or (c) accept the article for publication. Some journals will, on request, provide the reviewers' comments if the article is rejected. If that occurs, seriously consider those comments and either revise and resubmit the article, send it to another journal, or drop the plan to publish it.

If the article is accepted, you will work with the professional editors who will offer suggestions for strengthening the presentation. You will have the opportunity to be sure that their editing does not misrepresent the content. Depending on the backlog, it may take as much as a year for the article to appear in print. When it is printed, most journals will send the author several copies of the issue in which the article appears or provide reprints of the article.

When an article is accepted, the author will be required to assign the legal rights to this material to the publisher. It will then be necessary for the publisher to approve any subsequent reprinting or extensive quoting of the article in other books or articles, including your own.

SELECTED BIBLIOGRAPHY

American Psychological Association. *Publication Manual of the American Psychological Association,* 4th ed. Washington, DC: APA, 1994.

Beebe, Linda, ed. *Professional Writing for the Human Services.* Washington, DC: NASW, 1993.

Henson, Kenneth T. *The Art of Writing for Publication.* Boston: Allyn and Bacon, 1995.

National Association of Social Workers. *Author's Guide to Social Work Journals,* 4th ed. Washington, DC: NASW, 1997.

———. *Code of Ethics.* Washington, DC: NASW, 1997.

10.6 Coping with Bureaucracy

PURPOSE: To function effectively within a large, complex organization.

DISCUSSION: Every day, many social workers go home from their jobs feeling frustrated. Their complaints are usually not about their contact with clients but rather about the bureaucratic aspects of the agencies and service systems in which they work. Some complain that a myriad of laws, agency rules, regulations, and policies stifle their creativity and keep them from practicing good social work. Others complain that political manipulations, self-serving superiors, and power struggles between departments and divisions interfere with the delivery of service to clients.

Being part of a bureaucracy is unavoidable for most social workers because most social work jobs exist within large organizations. To find satisfaction in their work, social workers must develop the attitudes and skills needed to function and get things done within a large organization. Here are several suggestions:

1. Large agencies are by nature bureaucratic and political. This is a reality. It is important that you learn to maneuver and negotiate within this political and organizational arena. Develop the fine art of reframing the agency context of practice in ways that turn a negative into a positive. For example, do not view policies, rules, and regulations as barriers and constraints. Rather, view them as guidelines to be managed and as opportunities to be exploited in order to achieve important goals and objectives.

2. Study your agency. An in-depth knowledge of one's work setting is a form of organizational power. If you understand your agency's history, mission, goals, structure, culture, budget, policies, and procedures, you are better able to address problems and bring about needed changes (see Item 11.11).

3. It is important to view yourself as a partner with your agency and not just an employee. Carefully examine your own values, beliefs, and professional goals. They must be compatible with the mission and the goals of your agency. In order to be effective within your agency, you must believe in the agency's purpose.

4. Identify your personal and professional strengths and seek a niche within the organization where those strengths can be utilized and rewarded and where you can obtain a sense of job satisfaction. Think seriously before accepting a promotion or a transfer that would take you away from the type of work you really enjoy. Maintain direct contact with agency clients even as you rise to a supervisory or administrative level, for this provides you with a constant reminder of the agency's purpose and what needs to be changed to improve service to clients.

5. Acquire the skills needed and valued by your agency. Examine your agency's programs and operations and then strive to develop your knowledge or skills in an area that is especially valued by the agency (e.g., computer operations, report writing, public speaking, work with a special client group, etc.). Having a special competency not only contributes to job satisfaction but it also increases your power and influence within the agency.

6. Respect the chain of command. Your superiors will want to be informed about any situation that could have an impact on the unit for which they are responsible. They will need to decide when and how their own superiors are to be informed. Thus, any attempt to go around or over the head of your immediate superior is a risky move. Violating the chain of command is likely to have negative repercussions.

7. When frustrated by a specific rule or procedure, seek answers to the question of why it exists. Many rules, procedures, and policies come into existence as a reaction to some problem and remain in force even when no longer necessary. Knowing the history behind a certain rule will at least make it more sensible, and if you should discover that it has outlived its usefulness, you have taken the first step toward eliminating unnecessary requirements.

8. Although a bureaucracy can be changed, the rate of change is slow. Many months—even years—of effort may be needed to achieve a significant change. Only frustration results when you expect to see rapid change. Focus your limited time and energy on only one or two issues at a time. Do not try to change things that are clearly outside your scope of activity or responsibility. Do not waste time on insignificant or petty concerns. Work for changes that are realistic and feasible. And always work as part of a group; a group has more influence and more knowledge than an individual.

9. When working toward change, select your tactics with care. Be attentive to the question of who has power within the organization and who stands to gain or lose from a particular change in structure, policy, or procedure. Always assess the risks associated with a proposed change. Those who challenge well-entrenched power groups and those who acquire a reputation within the organization for being troublemakers are likely to be stripped of their power or squeezed out of the organization. Be a diplomat rather than a combat soldier. Aggressive tactics seldom work.

10. As an agency employee, you have no choice but to work cooperatively and respectfully with other agency employees, committees, and departments, even when you disagree with their approaches and even when you do not personally like the people with whom you must work. Employment within a large agency requires that you make accommodations and adapt to administrative and organizational requirements. If you lack this personal flexibility and are unable or unwilling to make concessions, you will always be dissatisfied with your job and become a source of conflict within the agency.

11. Maintain a proper perspective and a sense of humor about your job and your place within your organization. Work hard and be a responsible employee but do not take yourself or your agency too seriously. Realize that the modern bureaucracy is incapable of providing a sense of meaning in life or of meeting other emotional or spiritual needs. Look elsewhere for the activities and relationships that can meet those needs.

SELECTED BIBLIOGRAPHY

Lauffer, Armand. *Working in Social Work.* Newbury Park, CA: Sage, 1987.

Russo, Robert. *Serving and Surviving as a Human-Service Worker.* Prospect Heights, IL: Waveland Press, 1993.

10.7 Stress Management

PURPOSE: To cope effectively with the stress common to social work practice.

DISCUSSION: Social work is a demanding and stressful profession. Job-related stress can have three sources. First, there is the stress that is simply a part of a particular job. Everyone placed in a high-stress job will feel stressed—it comes with the territory. Second, there is stress caused by a lack of skills necessary to do the job. For example, a particular job may not be stressful for most people but will be for the individual who is poorly prepared. Third, some individuals create their own stress. For example, an individual may feel stressed because he or she has unrealistically high expectations or takes on an excessive number of responsibilities.

Every social worker responds to the demands of the profession in a unique manner; some thrive while others become emotionally drained. The term ***burnout*** refers to a state of physical, mental, and emotional exhaustion caused by an inability to cope with work-related stress. Burnout is not inevitable; it can be prevented if the professional is committed to taking care of himself or herself and develops a strategy for stress management. The following guidelines suggest ways to handle stress:

1. The key to preventing negative stress reactions is to find your proper niche in the world of work. There must be a good fit or match between you as a person and the demands of your job. As a social worker, you must feel positive about your chosen profession and feel that you are effective in what you do. If not, you will experience much distress and dissatisfaction. A century before stress reactions were studied in the laboratory, an unknown author wisely stated, "In order that people may be happy in their work, these three things are needed: they must be fit for it, they must not do too much of it, and they must have a sense of success in it."

2. Make an honest attempt to recognize stress in your own life. Listen to those who care about you for clues that you may be under more stress than you think (e.g., "You're so crabby when you get home," "You're not as much fun as you used to be," "You never go anywhere with us anymore," and "You've looked so tired lately"). Other signs of dangerous stress levels include low-level and persistent soreness in the muscles, joints, and tendons; frequent mild colds and sore throats; skin eruptions among nonadolescents; excessive nervousness, depression, and irritability; headaches; inability to relax or sleep; fatigue and sluggishness that lingers from day to day; aching stomach, often accompanied by loss of weight; diarrhea or constipation; unexplained drop in performance levels; and disinterest in normally interesting and exciting activities.

3. Examine the fit between your work and your values. Are you spending your time and energy on activities you consider important? For example, if you value family and friends, are you making choices that enable you to be with them? On the other hand, if you find that life on the job is more exciting than your personal or family life, that, too, must be faced with honesty. As a general rule, people find time for what they really want to do and for that which they truly value. Part of stress management is to become clear about what you value.

4. Take time to recognize and enjoy the positives in both your personal and professional lives. Avoid dwelling on the negatives and on what is lacking in your work. Cultivate a sense of humor. Take your work seriously and do the best job you can, but do not take yourself too seriously.

5. Develop hobbies and outside interests that lead you into activities that are very different from what you do at work. Doing something different can be like a minivacation. And do not underestimate the genuine pleasure that can come from the simple and ordinary things in life.

6. Exercise, good nutrition, and adequate sleep build natural defenses against the harmful effects of stress. Reduce or eliminate the use of alcohol, nicotine, caffeine, and other drugs. Obtain regular medical checkups and take action concerning the treatable conditions that you may have, such as hypertension, obesity, and depression. In our sophisticated but fragmented health care system, assuming responsibility for one's own health is essential.

7. Take several breaks during your workday. Keep the break simple but enjoyable. For example, take a walk at lunch and notice the changing seasons, read something that makes you laugh, or watch children at play. Take brief physical exercise breaks while doing paperwork; try isometric exercises or climb a few flights of stairs.

8. Learn to manage your time. Time management is, in effect, stress management. When we properly manage our time, we accomplish more and are more effective. This contributes to a feeling of satisfaction at work (see Item 9.1).

9. The feeling of not being in control is a major source of stress. If you are unable to gain some sense of control at work, consult with an experienced worker who seems to enjoy what he or she does. What is he or she doing that you might try? Unless you start making changes, the problem will only get worse. Setting priorities is the first step; the next step is making your time and energy fit your priorities.

10. Build a support group of friends or colleagues with whom you are able to share your frustrations. Find enjoyable ways to spend time together—eat out, see a movie, take a walk, or travel together. Talk a co-worker into trying a new physical activity with you so you can encourage each other, but do not get competitive.

11. Recognize that perfection is not required in most work-related tasks. Realize that you and all others have made mistakes and will continue to make them. Help yourself recover from a setback or mistake by thinking of prior accomplishments.

12. Like a long-distance runner, set your pace at a rate you can maintain without wearing down. For most people, it is better to do a few things well than to do many things poorly. Arrange work activity so you accomplish at least one important thing each day; this can produce a surprising amount of satisfaction.

13. If you are having personal problems, seek help from trusted friends or professionals. The longer you avoid getting needed help, the more areas of your life will be negatively impacted.

14. Listen for thoughts or sayings that have special meaning for you or that soothe or lift your spirit. For example, from *The Desiderata:* "Nurture strength of spirit to shield you in sudden misfortune. But do not distress yourself with dark imaginings. Many fears are born of fatigue and loneliness. Beyond wholesome discipline, be gentle with yourself."

15. Learn stress-management techniques and begin making needed changes. Do not try to make large changes too quickly, however. Small steps in the right direction will add up. Apply to yourself the techniques you use with clients. For example, when faced with a stressful interpersonal task, use techniques of role-playing or behavioral rehearsal to reduce anxiety and build confidence (see Items 14.5 and 14.7).

16. As a technique for handling your fears, try exaggerating them out of proportion. For example, if you fear being embarrassed, visualize yourself blushing to the point of turning beet red, sweating profusely, and shaking so hard your watch vibrates off your wrist. Exaggerating your fears to the point of being ludicrous may help you laugh at yourself and put your fear into perspective.

17. Apply problem-solving and organizational change techniques to the stressors common to most work settings: poor working conditions, unreasonable deadlines, heavy workloads, interruptions, and problems with co-workers and supervisors. Serious problems require careful analysis and intervention. They will not go away without intervention. Do something about them!

18. Visitors to the United States often observe that our life-style is characterized by a fast pace, complexity, materialism, and a "coolness" in our human interactions. These characteristics contribute to the stress we experience but often we are not even aware of their influence. Look for ways to simplify your life and slow its pace by reducing the number of decisions you must make each day. For example, simplify your wardrobe and your meals so you have fewer decisions to make about what to wear and what and where to eat. Give up nonessential possessions and activities that demand your attention and consume your time and money but provide little in the way of joy and relaxation. Replace the "things" in your life with meaningful relationships with family and friends.

SELECTED BIBLIOGRAPHY

Maslach, Christina, and Michael Leiter. *The Truth about Burnout.* San Francisco: Jossey-Bass, 1997.

Newton, Timothy. *Managing Stress.* Thousand Oaks, CA: Sage, 1995.

Potter, Beverly. *Overcoming Job Burnout.* Berkeley, CA: Ronin, 1998.

Turkington, Carol. *Stress Management for Busy People.* New York: McGraw-Hill, 1998.

10.8 Using Humor in Social Work

PURPOSE: To make use of humor as a counterbalance to the grimness and frustration often experienced in professional practice.

DISCUSSION: In recent years, humor has been recognized increasingly as an appropriate tool for use within professional helping relationships. Hageseth (1988, 18) notes that positive humor (i.e., that which is loving and healing) can "help you deal with grief, interpersonal strife, marital conflict, workplace stress, life threatening illness, baldness, excess adipose, and teenage children." It is recommended that professionals view the use of humor as any other technique and realize that what may be helpful, appropriate, and effective with one client may be offensive to another. Factors such as a client's age, culture, ethnicity, education, or gender may determine whether a particular use of humor is perceived as funny or offensive. It is recommended that the professional helper conduct a "humor assessment" before attempting to use humor in a practice situation. Such an assessment might include questions or requests such as the following:

- Tell me about the last time you had a good laugh.
- Can you recall something funny that happened in recent weeks?
- Would you tell me your favorite joke?

The client's response to such questions will indicate his or her receptivity to humor and capacity to perceive humor in a practice situation.

It is also important for social workers to allow humor to become part of the office atmosphere. A number of activities can encourage humor in the workplace. Consider the following:

- Devote the first five minutes of each agency staff meeting to sharing jokes or to describing "this week's most embarrassing moment."

- Create a humor bulletin board on which staff can tack jokes, cartoons, comic strips, and so on. Create a second board and invite clients to post humorous items.
- Design a staff training session on how to use humor to handle stressful situations or the effective use of humor in work with clients.
- Develop a lending library of humorous books, articles, and tapes.
- Keep a file of jokes, anecdotes, and humorous agency stories from which ones can be selected and shared with staff at times when comic relief is especially needed.

Poking fun at our professional shibboleths and sacred cows is a first step toward developing a social work humor. For example, one might ask: How many social workers does it take to change a lightbulb? Responses might include the following:

> "I hear you saying that you are concerned about the lightbulb. Tell me more about that."
>
> "Is the lightbulb the thing you most want to change about your situation?"
>
> "Only one—but the social worker will need a M.S.W. degree and two years' experience."
>
> "I am sorry but I cannot answer that question; it is confidential."
>
> "We will let you know as soon as our agency's study committee finishes its report."

An irreverent look at our professional jargon will also uncover some humor. For example, Brown (1976) offers the following definitions:

> *Crisis Intervention:* Technique for rapid transfer of anxiety from client to social worker.
>
> *Unmotivated*: Frequently stated reason for termination of services. What is not clear, however, is who is being described—the client or the social worker?
>
> *Intake*: The process by which clients are screened out or screened in—depending on what is needed for the agency's annual report.

Here is another example of poking fun at our profession. In this case, it is a tongue-in-cheek letter from a recent social work graduate:

> Dear Social Work Faculty:
>
> Thank you for your letters of recommendation. I did get the job and by now I have been a professional social worker for one full month.
>
> I don't want to sound critical but I must take this opportunity to say that my social work education did not prepare me for what I am facing in my new job. I have become very confused and I can hardly speak anymore.
>
> I have discovered that the social workers in my office get real uptight about language and words. They are striving to be "politically correct." That means, I believe, that they are careful to select just the right word so they won't offend anyone. But that is really hard to do since we spend so much time talking about other people—who they are, what they believe, and how they behave.

Personally, I like political correctness because I don't like conflict, so I avoid offending anyone. But it is getting harder and harder to keep from accidentally using the wrong word. My relationships are becoming like mine fields and it's so easy to step on the wrong word. Nevertheless, I guess we should try. So, for example, rather than offend a man who is dead and call this limitation to his attention, it is probably best to refer to him as "metaphysically challenged."

We cannot be too careful about the words we use because words do strange things to people. Take, for example, the word welfare. This is a really great word. It represents a wonderful idea. According to my dictionary, welfare is defined as "health, happiness and general well-being." Yet, when I read the newspaper, I find that nearly everyone wants to do away with welfare. No one wants welfare and no one wants to pay for it. How can such a nice word upset so many people? People are really strange—I mean interesting.

I am also told I should avoid using the word problem. I am told I should use a word that is more positive. My dictionary defines a problem as "a question or situation that presents uncertainty, perplexity or difficulty." Actually that doesn't sound bad to me. I certainly have had a lot of perplexity and I don't think I have been terribly damaged so far.

Some in the helping professions manage to avoid the word problem by substituting the word dysfunctional. Seemingly, it is better to refer to a person or family that has a problem as a dysfunctional person or a dysfunctional family. My dictionary defines dysfunction as "disordered or impaired." I don't know about you, but I would rather have a problem.

Still other professionals are able to avoid the word problem by referring to a person's questions, perplexities, and difficulties as issues, challenges, or concerns. Thus, instead of saying "Tell me about your problem," they would say "Tell me about your issues, your challenges, and your concerns." Or perhaps they would say "Tell me about your unresolved issues" or "areas of concern" or "personal and family dilemmas."

Some say that I shouldn't focus at all on people's problems (i.e., uncertainties, perplexities or difficulties) and should instead focus on their strengths. I like that idea. However, the problem—I mean the challenge—with this suggestion is that when I look in my dictionary for a definition of strength I find that it means "(1) the state, quality or property of being strong; physical power; muscularity (2) the power of resisting force, attack, strain or stress; durability; solidity; impregnability."

Given that, I am not sure what to think of all this emphasis on a person's strengths. Being relatively small myself and out of shape, I think I would prefer to be around people with problems.

I am told to be very careful around children, especially children who have problems—I mean issues. It can be harmful to label a child with the wrong word. For example, instead of saying that a boy has a "problem" or a "serious problem," it is preferable to describe the child as being "at risk" or perhaps "seriously at risk." Such words have a nice ring but they are a bit confusing to me; I am never sure what "risk" we are talking about. And what about the word at in "at risk"? Does that mean the boy is approaching a risk, is about to meet the risk, or has now engaged the risk? Or does it mean he has a problem?

As I said, I am a bit confused about professional words and language. You might want to mention this to the students in your classes.

Sincerely yours,
Ben Goode, M.S.W.
(Class of 99)

SELECTED BIBLIOGRAPHY

Blumenfeld, Ester, and Lynn Alpern. *Humor at Work.* Atlanta: Peachtree Publications, 1994.

Brown, H. S. *Some of My Best Friends Are Social Workers.* Bloomfield, CT: H. S. Brown, 1976.

Fry, W. F., Jr., and W. A. Salameh, eds. *Handbook of Humor and Psychotherapy*. Sarasota, FL: Professional Resource Exchange, 1987.

Hageseth, Christian. *A Laughing Place: The Art and Psychology of Positive Humor in Love and Adversity.* Fort Collins, CO: Berwick, 1988.

Robinson, Vera. *Humor and the Health Professions.* Thorofare, NJ: Slack, Inc., 1991.

10.9 Making Ethical Decisions

PURPOSE: To clarify ethical issues and make practice choices that are consistent with social work's ethical principles and professional values.

DISCUSSION: Each day, social workers make decisions concerning complex ethical issues. Sometimes the task is to help clients sort out their own ethical concerns, and at other times it involves the social worker determining if an action he or she is about to take is appropriate from an ethical perspective. Sometimes all possible practice options will cause harm or distress to someone, creating an ethical dilemma for the social worker. Essentially, an ***ethical dilemma*** is a situation wherein the worker has two or more ethical obligations but cannot follow or adhere to one without violating another. For example, ethical dilemmas faced by social workers increasingly involve decisions on how best to allocate scarce resources in times of budget cutbacks or staff shortages. In such cases, the decision to provide services to one client may result in limiting or withholding the services needed by others.

A first step toward resolving such ethical dilemmas is to find answers to several questions that supply important background information and clarify the matter under consideration. For example, consider the following:

- What aspects of the agency's activity or worker's roles and duties give rise to the dilemma (e.g., legal mandates, job requirements, agency policy, questions of efficient use of limited resources, possible harm caused by an intervention, etc.)?
- Who can or should resolve this dilemma? Is it rightfully a decision to be made by the client? Other family members? The worker? The agency administrator?

- For each decision possible, what are the short-term and long-term consequences for the client, family, worker, agency, community, and so on?
- Who stands to gain and who stands to lose from each possible choice or action? Are those who stand to gain or lose of equal or of unequal power (e.g., child vs. adult)? Do those who are most vulnerable or those with little power require special consideration?
- When harm to someone cannot be avoided, what decision will cause the least harm or a type of harm with fewest long-term consequences? Who of those that might be harmed are least able to recover from the harm?
- Will a particular resolution to this dilemma set an undesirable precedent for future decision making concerning other clients?

Once those questions have been answered, the worker must answer three additional questions:

- What ethical principles and obligations apply in this situation?
- Which, if any, ethical principles are in conflict in this situation and therefore create an ethical dilemma?
- Would certain ethical obligations be more important than others?

To answer these questions, the social worker must be very familiar with the National Association of Social Worker's ***Code of Ethics*** (1996), which lists and describes ethical standards and principles and provides general guidelines for professional conduct. Perhaps nothing is more prescriptive in social work than the requirement to adhere to the *Code of Ethics.* Also, the *Code* is NASW's basis for evaluating and responding to any charges of unethical conduct that may be made against a social worker. To join NASW, a social worker must sign a statement indicating that he or she will abide by the *Code,* and each year, when membership is renewed, the social worker once again commits to uphold the *Code.* A copy of the *Code* should be on the desk of every social worker.*

NASW's *Code of Ethics,* therefore, is an important benchmark that may be used to survey a practice situation to determine if a specific alternative or action is ethically responsible. Since creative social workers regularly examine various alternative intervention strategies, the *Code* serves as an ethical screen or filter through with the acceptable practice alternatives should pass.

The Ethics Worksheet (see Figure 10.1) is offered here as a tool for comparing the ethical dimensions of practice alternatives. To use the Ethics Worksheet, the worker should first list each practice option (e.g., each possible action or decision). For example, Option A might be "I will prevent my client from making a serious mistake by pressuring him to follow my advice" and Option B might be "I will respect

*In the United States, the latest version of the *Code of Ethics* can be obtained from the National Association of Social Workers, 750 First Street, NE, Washington, DC 20002-4241, or can be downloaded from NASW's website (http://www.naswdc.org). The Canadian Association of Social Workers' *Code of Ethics* can be obtained from MYROPEN Publications, 383 Parkdale Ave, Suite 402, Ottawa, ON K1Y 4R4 and information on that code can be obtained from CASW's website (http://www.intranet.ca/~casw-acts/code2-e.htm).

FIGURE 10.1 Ethics Worksheet

What options, actions, or decisions are being considered as a practice intervention?

List and briefly describe the practice option(s) being considered.

Option A: ______________________________

Option B: ______________________________

Option C: ______________________________

Does the option potentially place you in violation of any of the following ethical areas identified in the *NASW Code of Ethics?* If so, make a brief note regarding the potential violation.

1. **Standards related to the social worker's ethical responsibilities to clients.**
   This section of the *Code of Ethics* is concerned with such factors and principles as: the worker's primary responsibility is to the client; respect for client self-determination; securing client's informed consent; worker's competence to provide needed services; worker's cultural competence; avoiding conflict of interest; respecting clients' right to privacy and confidentiality; the prohibition of sexual involvement, sexual harassment, inappropriate physical contact, and abusive or derogatory language; special considerations when clients lack decision-making capacity; avoiding the interruption of services; careful termination of services.

   Potential issues and problems to consider:

   Option A: ______________________________

   ____

   ____

   Option B: ______________________________

   ____

   ____

2. **The social worker's ethical responsibilities to colleagues.**
   Section two of the *Code of Ethics* is concerned with social workers' responsibility to treat colleagues with respect; concern for maintaining confidentiality among professionals; appropriate collaboration and teamwork; proper handling of disputes and disagreements; appropriate consultation relationships; proper referral of clients to colleagues; the prohibition of sexual harassment and sexual involvement with one's supervisees or students; and the requirement for responsible action in relation to a colleague who is impaired, incompetent, or is unethical in his or her practice.

   Potential issues and problems to consider:

   Option A: ______________________________

   ____

   ____

   Option B: ______________________________

   ____

   ____

(continued)

FIGURE 10.1 Continued

3. **The social worker's ethical responsibilities in practice settings.**
This section of the *Code of Ethics* relates to services performed in relation to social workers and other professionals, and only indirectly relates to clients. The items addressed include competence in providing supervision, consultation, education, and training; evaluating the performance of other workers; maintaining proper client records and billing properly; carefully evaluating client needs before accepting transfers; assuring an appropriate working environment and providing on-going education and training in human services agencies; demonstrating commitment to agency employees; and acting responsibly in labor disputes.

Potential issues and problems to consider:

Option A: ______________________________

____

____

Option B: ______________________________

____

____

4. **The social worker's ethical responsibilities as a professional.**
This section of the *Code of Ethics* includes items related to the social worker accepting employment and job assignments when he or she may not be competent to perform that work; practicing, condoning, or participating in any form of discrimination; engaging in private conduct that compromises the ability to fulfill professional responsibilities; engaging in dishonesty, fraud, and deception; addressing one's own problems if impaired; clarification of public statements regarding whether acting as a professional or a private citizen; making uninvited solicitations for business; and properly acknowledging any contributions to one's written or other work made by others.

Potential issues and problems to consider:

Option A: ______________________________

____

____

Option B: ______________________________

____

____

5. **The social worker's ethical responsibilities to the social work profession.**
Section 5 of the *Code of Ethics* concerns issues related to the social worker promoting high standards for social work and contributing time and energy to its growth and development, as well as items related to social workers monitoring and evaluating social policies, programs, and their own practice interventions.

Potential issues and problems to consider:

Option A: ______________________________

____

____

Option B: ____

____

____

6. **The social worker's ethical responsibilities to the broader society.**
In this section of the *Code of Ethics,* social workers are charged with promoting the general welfare of the society and the realization of social justice; participating in public debate to shape social policies and institutions; providing services in public emergencies; and actively engaging in social and political action.

Potential issues and problems to consider:

Option A: ____

____

____

Option B: ____

____

____

my client's decision even if he makes a choice that will make his problems even worse." There could be other options (e.g., Options C, D, E, etc.). Second, the worker should make notes of issues and concerns that might arise for each option directly on the Ethics Worksheet. This worksheet is built on the NASW *Code*'s six areas of ethical consideration—that is, the social worker's ethical responsibilities (1) to clients, (2) to colleagues, (3) to practice settings, (4) as professionals, (5) to the social work profession, and (6) to the broader society. The Canadian *Code of Ethics* is organized differently, but could readily be placed in a similar format. The 10 areas addressed in the Canadian *Code* are (1) primary professional obligation, (2) integrity and objectivity, (3) competence, (4) limits on professional relationships, (5) confidential information, (6) outside interests, (7) limits on private practice, (8) responsibilities to the workplace, (9) responsibilities to the profession, and (10) responsibilities for social change. Third, once potential issues are identified, the worker should examine the specific language in each *Code of Ethics* for clarification and eliminate any specific issues that no longer seem relevant after this closer scrutiny. Finally, for each practice option, the worker should prepare a summary of the *Code of Ethics* items that may be compromised if that option is selected.

A limitation of the *NASW Code of Ethics* as a tool for resolving ethical issues is that all standards in the *Code* are given equal weight. Thus, it is useful for the worker to apply a second tool when making ethical decisions: the Ethical Issue Priority Checklist (see Figure 10.2). This checklist is derived from a ranking of ethical priorities developed by Loewenberg and Dolgoff (1996, 58–62). It lists seven guiding principles, with Principle 1 (i.e., the protection of life) viewed as most important and

Principle 7 (i.e., telling the truth) considered least important among the seven. Although an individual social worker might identify additional principles or develop a different ordering of the priorities, the ranking by Loewenberg and Dolgoff provides a useful starting point.

FIGURE 10.2 Ethical Issue Priority Checklist

What options, actions, or decisions are being considered by the social worker?

Option A: ______________________________

Option B: ______________________________

Option C: ______________________________

Answer the following questions for each of the options you have identified with yes, no, or cannot determine. (Note: Avoid making too many assumptions about possible but unlikely long-range implications of the action.)

1. Does this option/action threaten or risk someone's life, physical well-being, or chances of survival?
   Option A Yes No Cannot Determine
   Option B Yes No Cannot Determine
2. Does this option treat someone in a fundamentally unjust, unfair, or unequal manner and/or violate basic human rights?
   Option A Yes No Cannot Determine
   Option B Yes No Cannot Determine
3. Does this option significantly and unreasonably limit someone's self-determination or autonomy?
   Option A Yes No Cannot Determine
   Option B Yes No Cannot Determine
4. Does this option cause someone significant personal distress or economic hardship?
   Option A Yes No Cannot Determine
   Option B Yes No Cannot Determine
5. Does this option decrease the quality of life for those of a neighborhood, community, or society as a whole?
   Option A Yes No Cannot Determine
   Option B Yes No Cannot Determine
6. Does this option cause someone to lose his or her right to privacy and confidentiality?
   Option A Yes No Cannot Determine
   Option B Yes No Cannot Determine
7. Does this option involve distorting or withholding the truth from an individual or a community?
   Option A Yes No Cannot Determine
   Option B Yes No Cannot Determine

The process followed in using the Ethical Issue Priority Checklist begins with identifying the various practice options in a manner identical to completing the Ethics Worksheet. In this case, however, the worker then responds to questions 1 through 7 on the checklist by circling an answer "yes," no," or "can't determine" for each option. If a circled yes answer appears higher among the priorities (i.e., higher on the page) for one option as opposed to others, the worker should seriously question the appropriateness of using that practice option.

When the two checklists are completed and analyzed, the worker should be prepared to make a decision regarding which option to exercise—at least as far as the ethical issues are concerned. If the action selected violates a provision of the *Code of Ethics,* it is suggested that the worker write out the rationale for that decision and include such a statement in the client's file, as this documentation may useful if the worker is subsequently charged with a *Code* violation as a result of this decision.

SELECTED BIBLIOGRAPHY

Corey, Gerald, Marianne Schneider Cory, and Patrick Callanan. *Issues and Ethics in the Helping Professions,* 5th ed. Pacific Grove, CA: Brooks/Cole, 1998.

Loewenberg, Frank M., and Ralph Dolgoff. *Ethical Decisions for Social Work Practice,* 4th ed. Itasca, IL: F. E. Peacock, 1996.

National Association of Social Workers. *Code of Ethics.* Washington, DC: NASW, 1996.

Reamer, Frederic G. *Ethical Standards in Social Work: A Critical Review of the NASW Code of Ethics.* Washington, DC: NASW Press, 1998.

Steinman, Sarah O., Nan Franks Richardson, and Tim McEnroe. *Ethical Decision-Making Manual for Helping Professionals.* Pacific Grove, CA: Brooks/Cole, 1998.

10.10 Avoiding Malpractice Suits

PURPOSE: To minimize the possibility of being named in a lawsuit alleging professional negligence or misconduct.

DISCUSSION: A growing number of social workers are being sued for malpractice or professional negligence. Most social workers probably underestimate their legal vulnerability. Broadly speaking, a worker may be held liable if he or she did something or neglected to do something and these acts or omissions caused harm or injury to a client.

In general, the plaintiff in a successful malpractice suit must prove four points:

1. The defendant (e.g., the social worker) was obligated to provide the plaintiff with a particular standard of care or professional conduct.
2. The worker was derelict because he or she breached that obligation (or duty) by some act or omission that had a foreseeable consequence.
3. The client suffered some injury or harm (physical, financial, emotional, etc.).
4. The worker's conduct was a direct or proximate cause of the client's injury or harm.

Whether a breach of duty has occurred is determined by measuring the allegedly harmful act or omission against published standards of practice, agency policy, and the performance of social workers in similar settings. The client's injury must be one that would not have occurred had it not been for the social worker's negligence. Despite this traditional "proximate cause" requirement, juries are increasingly finding liability without fault (i.e., finding providers of services negligent even when they are not the proximate cause of the injury).

The professional duties that, if breached, place social workers and social agencies at greatest risk of legal liability are the following:

- Duty to avoid sexual misconduct
- Duty to warn others when a client discloses intent to harm them (i.e., the Tasaroff Decision)
- Duty to prevent a client's suicide
- Duty to properly diagnose and treat a client
- Duty to ensure continuity of service to a client under the care of a worker or agency
- Duty to maintain and protect confidentiality
- Duty to maintain accurate professional records and a proper and legal accounting of payments and reimbursements

In addition to allegations of misconduct based on the preceding duties, there can be many others, such as:

- Providing or arranging the transportation that involves a client in a vehicular accident causing bodily injury
- Failing to report or properly investigate suspected abuse or neglect
- Inappropriately placing of a child or adult into foster care, an institution, a hospital, or jail
- Inappropriately or prematurely releasing a client from foster care, a hospital, an institution, or another protective setting
- Placing or contributing to the placement of a client into a facility or foster home in which he or she is subsequently abused or neglected (i.e., failing to properly select or supervise the placement)
- Practicing while impaired by use of drugs or alcohol or failure to report a colleague known to be impaired
- Failing to inform a client of eligibility rules or regulations, resulting in avoidable financial costs to the client
- Failing to consult with or refer a client to a specialist
- Failing to recognize an obvious medical problem and not referring the client to a physician
- Practicing medicine without a license (e.g., suggesting changes in the client's use of medications)
- Misrepresenting one's professional training and qualifications

- Using a radical or untested approach, technique, or procedure
- Providing inaccurate information or advice to a client
- Providing birth control information or abortion counseling to a minor without consent of the parent
- Acting in a prejudicial manner in the selection of an adoptive home or in the licensing of a foster home, day-care facility, or the like
- Failing to be available to a client when needed (e.g., failing to provide professional coverage during the worker's vacation)
- Inappropriately or prematurely terminating a treatment relationship
- Causing alienation between parent and child or husband and wife
- Failing to supervise a child or a person with a mental disability while he or she is participating in an agency program
- Failing to supervise the work of others, including the work of volunteers and students

Of course, there is a big difference between being named in a lawsuit alleging negligence and actually being found negligent by a jury. But even if the suit is eventually dropped or dismissed for a lack of evidence, the worker and/or the agency will have incurred legal expenses during their defense. Most of these lawsuits are settled out of court.

Most lawsuits name as defendants both the social worker and the employing agency because the agency is assumed to be indirectly responsible for the harm caused by an employee. A social worker employed by an agency can be found personally liable, although this is not likely if the worker was acting within his or her job description, was following agency policy, and did nothing of a criminal nature.

In some cases, a social worker is held liable for harm caused by a person under his or her supervision (e.g., another social worker, volunteer, or student). Also, a worker might be held liable if he or she somehow contributed to the harm caused by another professional. An example of this is when a worker refers a client to an incompetent professional or when a worker provides a social assessment report to a psychiatrist who then makes a poor decision based on that report.

A social worker who learns that he or she has been named in a malpractice suit should immediately contact an attorney (the worker's agency may provide legal representation) and also notify his or her supervisor, agency administrator, and insurance company. The social worker should not speak with anyone about the allegations before securing legal counsel. The worker must never alter case records or other documents related to the case. Such changes are easily detected and may constitute a crime. An attempt to alter a record will be viewed as an effort to destroy evidence and cover up a wrongdoing.

Legal experts explain that the key to avoiding a malpractice suit is adherence to reasonable, ordinary, and prudent practices. In order to defend one's self against allegations, the worker must show that his or her actions were fair, in good faith, and consistent with how other properly trained professionals would behave under similar circumstances. One of the best defenses is to be able to show that the client gave his or her informed consent to the professional's intervention. This underscores the need to document client involvement in problem identification, assessment, and case planning and the value of written service agreements (see Item 13.5).

A number of additional guidelines will help the social worker avoid a malpractice suit or at least minimize its damage. Consider the following:

1. Because of the growing number of social work malpractice suits, the social worker should secure malpractice insurance. It can be purchased through the National Association of Social Workers by NASW members and from some insurance companies.

2. Adhere to the *Code of Ethics* and the *NASW Standards of Professional Practice* relevant to your area of practice. Also adhere to your agency's policies and procedures, as well as state and federal laws and regulations affecting your agency's program and services.

3. Do not become sexually or romantically involved with a client. Sexual misconduct toward a client is one of the most common allegations giving rise to malpractice suits in social work. Sexual involvement with a client is a clear violation of the *NASW Code of Ethics,* a violation of state professional licensing statutes, and, in some states, a violation of criminal law. Avoid situations that could be misinterpreted as sexually inappropriate or give rise to false allegations of sexual misconduct. For example, male workers should be very cautious about visiting a female client in her home. A third party (potential witness) should be within earshot whenever a male worker interviews a female adult or a child.

4. Do not engage in or create dual relationships. A dual relationship is one in which a second set of obligations or expectations is introduced into the social worker–client relationship. Examples include dating a client, renting an apartment to or from a client, loaning money to or borrowing money from a client, hiring a client to perform some service (e.g., repair worker's car), selling some item or product to a client, and so on. Dual relationships must also be avoided in supervisor-worker and faculty-student interaction.

5. Know your level of skill and practice within those limitations. Secure the training and supervision needed to perform your job-related tasks and activities responsibly. Become aware of the types of clients or situations that touch your personal issues and lessen your ability to be objective. Obtain supervision and/or consultation when you are having unusual difficulties with a client. Consult with your peers, supervisor, and/or attorney when faced with difficult ethical or legal issues.

6. Be especially careful when dealing with clients or situations that present high legal risk. Examples include clients who may attempt suicide, clients who are violent and a threat to others, clients who have a history of filing lawsuits, clients who are very manipulative, and clients who always find fault or perceive bad intentions in the behavior of others.

7. Base your practice on a professionally recognized theory or model. Keep your client fully informed of decisions, plans, and any risks associated with the intervention. Be careful not to give your client false hope about what you will be able to do. Convey a realistic picture of what you and your agency's services can accomplish. Maintain records that document your actions and any events or circumstances that might have had an adverse impact on the client.

8. Inform clients of any circumstances that may affect confidentiality. Confidentiality must be broken in order to report suspected abuse or neglect, to warn others of your client's intention to harm them, and to alert others of your client's intention to commit suicide.

9. Reach out to the client who has been angered by your actions and attempt to rebuild the relationship and address his or her complaint. Many malpractice suits could have been prevented if only the worker or agency had followed up on client complaints. If you work for a fee-charging agency, make sure that financial arrangements are handled in a completely businesslike manner so as to minimize the possibility of misunderstanding regarding cost and the collection of insurance payments.

10. Adhere to agency policy whenever a client presents you with a gift. As a general rule, food and inexpensive gifts valued at not more than a few dollars can be accepted, but a more expensive gift should not be accepted before consulting with your supervisor.

11. Be very cautious about giving any advice that could have a significant impact on the client's life (e.g., advising a client to get a divorce, how to invest money, etc.).

12. Do not transport a client in your private car unless this is keeping with agency procedure and allowed under your auto insurance policy.

13. Adhere to rules and policies concerning confidentiality. If you receive a request from an attorney (or anyone else) for information about a client, say nothing before considering whether the information sought might be confidential. Even revealing that a record exists or that the client is, in fact, a client may violate the client's right to confidentiality.

14. If served a subpoena to release client records, immediately consult with your supervisor and agency attorney. It is important to understand that you must respond to the subpoena, but one possible response by your attorney is to claim confidentiality and contest the request to release the records. Contesting the request will result in a court hearing on the matter and then a decision by the judge on whether your claim is valid or if you must indeed turn over the records.

15. Never agree to a interview with an attorney or other investigator before first consulting with your own attorney. (It is a common practice for attorneys to attempt to secure statements or information before you are even aware that you are the target of a lawsuit.)

16. Before accepting a job with an agency, check into the agency's record of providing legal defense for employees who are named in a lawsuit.

SELECTED BIBLIOGRAPHY

Bullis, Ronald. *Clinical Social Worker Misconduct.* Chicago: Nelson-Hall, 1995.

Dickson, Donald. *Confidentiality and Privacy in Social Work.* New York: Free Press, 1998.

Houston-Vega, Mary, Elane Nuehring, and Elizabeth Daguio. *Prudent Practice: A Guide for Managing Malpractice Risk.* Washington, DC: NASW Press, 1997.

Reamer, Frederic. *Social Work Malpractice and Liability.* New York: Columbia University Press, 1994.

Saltzman, Andrea, and Kathleen Proch. *Law in Social Work Practice,* 2nd ed. Chicago: Nelson-Hall, 1999.

Schroeder, Leila. *The Legal Environment of Social Work,* revised ed. Washington, DC: NASW Press, 1995.

10.11 Developing Self-Awareness

PURPOSE: To examine one's attitudes, personal habits, and interactional patterns to identify those that may obstruct work with clients.

DISCUSSION: The social worker uses himself or herself as a tool or an instrument in the helping process. Just as a physician must be attentive to the condition of medical instruments, the social worker must constantly examine the self to identify barriers to his or her effectiveness. Professional social workers have always emphasized the need to develop their self-awareness and self-knowledge. The term ***self-awareness*** refers to an accurate perception of one's own beliefs, attitudes, and behavioral habits and their usual effects on one's own decision making and behavior in social work practice. Efforts to develop self-awareness should focus on identifying both strengths and limitations. Many of the strengths that are of importance in social work practice are discussed in other parts of this book. Chapter 3, for example, describes the qualities of courage, compassion, hopefulness, empathy, genuineness, warmth, creativity, imagination, flexibility, energy, good judgment, knowledge, and so on (also see Chapters 2 and 8). In this section, the focus is mostly on factors that can interfere with effective practice. This is not to suggest that strengths are of less importance but rather to counter, in a straightforward manner, our human tendency to deny and ignore personal limitations. Several actions will help the worker increase his or her self-awareness:

- Keep a daily journal or log. This helps one sort out and think about experiences and get in touch with feelings.
- Ask for constructive criticism. Seek feedback and evaluations from trusted and experienced colleagues familiar with your performance, responsibilities, and agency setting.
- Obtain and then study audio or video recordings of your interviews, group sessions, and other work-related meetings. (*Note:* Secure permission of others before making such a recording; clients should sign a written authorization.)
- Use role-play. Practice and evaluate your performance in simulated sessions that focus on or act out situations that are especially difficult.

Many individuals are drawn to the helping professions (social work, nursing, medicine, counseling, etc.) because they believe the problems they have faced in life give them a special understanding or sensitivity to the problems of others. Indeed, life's problems can be a powerful teacher and provide a degree of empathy that others do not have. However, this will be the case only after one has honestly examined those experiences and successfully worked through the residual feelings associated with them. If a professional denies or suppresses the emotions connected to painful life experiences and cannot come to peace with the past, efforts to help others will be plagued by misunderstanding, self-doubts, and feelings of failure.

Growing up in a dysfunctional family typically produces an individual who has low self-worth and a fear of strong emotions. According to Wegscheider (1981, 223–225), a professional helper with this family background and these characteristics will have serious problems in their work with clients:

- Because they fear emotion, they only give advice . . . rather than lead the client through their pain to find answers for themselves.
- Because they are not comfortable with certain feelings, they avoid topics that their client needs to discuss.
- Because they are preoccupied with defending their own fragile self-worth and defending against their own suppressed emotion, they cannot fully attend to the client nor hear the client's subtle messages. At the other extreme, they are unable to control their own emotions and they react inappropriately to their client's feelings.
- Because they have such a strong need to be liked by clients, they are unable to confront a client when necessary and they tell the client what he or she wants to hear and not what needs to be said.
- Because of their low self-worth, they are terribly afraid of being seen as incompetent in their work and may hide behind a facade of false professionalism and the use of endless jargon and intellectualizing in an attempt to convince others of their competence.

When a social worker becomes aware of some factor that interferes with client service, he or she must be willing to correct the problem or, if change is not possible, to seek a practice setting where the factor will not have a negative impact on clients. The following list outlines some of the factors that can interfere with the formation of a professional helping relationship and client service; use it as an aid in self-examination:

1. *Personal hang-ups and emotional problems.* To a considerable degree, one's beliefs and behavior have been shaped by one's childhood and early family experiences. Most people carry a certain amount of emotional "baggage" into their adult lives, including unresolved parent-child conflicts, prejudice, aftereffects of traumatic events, and so on. Sometimes this "baggage" is carried to the workplace, where it has a negative impact on clients and work performances. For example:
   - Preoccupation with personal problems, resulting in an inability to give one's full attention to the client
   - Inability to control one's reactions or exercise self-discipline when in an emotionally charged situation or when under the ordinary pressure associated with direct social work practice

- Inability to demonstrate warmth, empathy, and genuine caring for clients served by the agency
- Inability or unwillingness to work cooperatively with persons in positions of authority (e.g., judges, physicians, administrators, supervisors, etc.)
- Difficulty separating personal experience (e.g., having been a victim of child abuse, growing up with alcoholic parents, etc.) from the concerns and problems presented by clients
- Extreme defensiveness that prevents a critical examination of one's own job performance
- Avoiding certain clients or difficult tasks
- Personalization of client anger and frustrations (i.e., inability to maintain an appropriate level of objectivity)
- Imposing one's values, political beliefs, religious beliefs or life-style on clients
- Inability to respect the religious beliefs and cultural values of a client
- Alcohol or drug abuse
- Misuse or abuse of one's authority over clients
- Extreme level of shyness or nonassertiveness resulting in an inability to express one's opinions and engage in the give-and-take of client work, peer supervision, and team decision making

2. *Appearance, clothing, and grooming.* To a large extent, people form impressions of others—especially the powerful first impression—on the basis of physical appearance. Thus the social worker must pay attention to his or her clothing and grooming because it matters to clients and will affect how they respond to the worker and their utilization of agency services. Of course, what is offensive to one client may be acceptable to another, and what is appropriate dress in one agency setting may be inappropriate in another. The staff in a particular setting must make decisions on what is acceptable. Many agencies and most hospitals establish dress codes as a way of providing guidance to staff. When examining your appearance and its possible impact on clients, remember the following:

- Some choices of clothing, hairstyle, makeup, perfume, or jewelry may offend or distract clients served by the agency.
- Deficiencies in grooming and personal hygiene may offend clients.
- Uncovered infections, skin irritations, and similar conditions may distract the client or cause him or her worry and anxiety.

3. *Behaviors that devalue or degrade others.* Social work values dictate that every client should be treated with respect. The social worker must avoid behaviors that are disrespectful, including the following:

- Using words, phrases, or gestures that are in bad taste or known to offend clients and staff (e.g., cursing, sexual overtones, etc.)
- Telling sexist or ethnic jokes
- Telling disrespectful and disparaging stories about clients
- Demonstrating prejudice against particular client groups
- Making sarcastic, insulting, cruel, or disrespectful comments about clients

4. *Distracting personal habits.* Most people have some undesirable mannerisms and habits that their friends and families have learned to accept. However, the social worker must be willing to modify habits that annoy clients, including the following:

- Fidgeting, pencil tapping, knuckle cracking, nail biting, and the like
- Scratching, pulling, or twisting hair
- Chewing gum or tobacco and smoking
- Scowling, frowning, or other facial gestures that seem to express scorn
- Excessive nervous laughter, frequent clearing of throat, or other distracting mannerisms

5. *Difficulties in cognitive functioning.* A social worker must absorb information quickly and apply complex principles. A capacity for abstract thinking is essential. The following examples illustrate insufficient cognitive functioning:

- Cognitive deficits that interfere with attention, memory, and judgment
- Inability to explain the assumptions and inferences behind one's judgments, conclusions, and decisions
- Difficulty processing new information, drawing logical inferences, and solving problems
- Lack of reading speed and comprehension needed to understand records and reports, agency policy, and professional books and journals

6. *Difficulties in verbal communication.* The social worker's verbal communication must be understandable to clients and other professional persons. The following problems could hamper work with clients:

- Mumbling, speaking inaudibly, loud or penetrating voice tones, halting or hesitant speech, rapid speech
- Frequent use of slang not understood by or offensive to clients
- Errors of grammar or awkward sentence construction that confuse clients
- Inability or unwillingness to adjust vocabulary to client's age or educational level
- Uncorrected vision or hearing problems

7. *Problems in written communication.* Because so much of the social worker's service to a client involves the exchange of information with other professionals, the worker must be able to communicate in writing. If letters, reports, and agency records are carelessly written and difficult to understand, those attempting to read them will conclude either that the worker does not care enough to communicate clearly or is incompetent. The worker's effectiveness is seriously damaged if the client or other professional persons form such negative impressions. Serious writing problems that merit correction include the following:

- Inability to prepare letters, reports, and records that are understandable to clients, agency staff, and other professionals
- Not recognizing and correcting errors of spelling, grammar, and syntax
- Difficulty selecting words that adequately express thought
- Inability to write at a speed sufficient to manage required paperwork

8. *Poor work habits.* Poor work habits may have a direct or indirect impact on the clients served by an agency. Some of the commonly observed problems are:

- Being late for client appointments, team meetings, case conferences, and other scheduled events
- Missing deadlines for the completion of written reports that are important to clients or other agencies and professionals serving the client
- Incomplete or sloppy recordkeeping
- Lack of preparation for meetings with clients and other professionals
- Not following through on assignments or tasks
- Distracting other staff members or keeping them from their work
- Unwillingness to seek and utilize direction from the supervisor
- Blaming clients or others for one's own ineffectiveness; inability or unwillingness to acknowledge mistakes or limitations of knowledge and skill
- Being more interested in diagnostic labels and theoretical issues than with clients as real people
- Unwillingness to follow established agency policies and procedures
- Behaviors occurring outside work hours that draw negative attention to the social worker and thereby lessen client and public respect for the social agency and/or the worker

In order to grow in self-awareness, we need to examine our beliefs, assumptions, and behavioral patterns. We must remember, however, that our most significant advancements in self-awareness do not come from self-scrutiny but rather are "gifts" from others, such as comments made by our clients, the constructive criticism offered by a supervisor, and suggestions from our professional peers and from others who care about us and our performance as social workers.

SELECTED BIBLIOGRAPHY

Cory, Marianne, and Gerald Cory. *Becoming a Helper*, 3rd. ed. Pacific Grove, CA: Brooks/Cole, 1998.

Kottler, Jeffery. *Growing a Therapist.* San Francisco: Jossey-Bass, 1995.

Munson, Carlton. *An Introduction to Clinical Social Work Supervision,* 2nd ed. New York: Haworth, 1993.

Wegscheider, Sharon. *Another Change: Hope and Health for the Alcoholic Family.* Palo Alto, CA: Science and Behavior Books, 1981.

10.12 Dealing with Sexual Misconduct

PURPOSE To prevent or address issues of sexual misconduct and sexual harassment in the context of social work practice or education.

DISCUSSION The structure of professional relationships is inherently unequal, making clients vulnerable to exploitation. Clients enter the relationship in order to receive assistance from a competent professional and trust the worker to treat their needs and interests as primary. In turn, it is expected that the professional will be responsible to avoid any misuse of this trust and will not exploit the client in any form (i.e., financial, sexual, or in any other way of personal gain). In addition, professional responsibility requires that any social worker in a position of power avoid manipulating that situation for personal advantage. For example, a supervisor should not manipulate a supervisee, an administrator should not take advantage of workers for personal gain, or a teacher or a field instructor should not manipulate a student.

The *NASW Code of Ethics* (1996) provides guidance in several areas in which there is a potential conflict of interest for a social worker in practice or employment situations. In recent years, there has been growing recognition that the potential for sexual exploitation in the human services is high and professions have begun to take strong positions when sexual misconduct occurs. Section 1.09 of the *Code of Ethics* is explicit in prohibiting sexual contact with clients, the relatives of clients, and former clients, as well as providing services to persons with whom the social worker has previously had a sexual relationship. In addition, Section 2.07 of NASW's *Code of Ethics* clearly prohibits sexually exploiting colleagues in a vulnerable position in the workplace (i.e., supervisees, students, trainees, or others for whom there may be a conflict of interest).

A study of 10 years of violations of the *Code of Ethics* by the National Association of Social Workers (1995) indicated that the largest number of code violations that were upheld during NASW's grievance process (29.2 percent) related to sexual misconduct by social workers. Evidence that social workers are concerned about this problem is found in the fact that more than one-half of the complaints were filed by other social workers. Those wishing to discuss the process for making a complaint regarding a *Code* violation should contact the local chapter of NASW. Current information for reaching state chapters is found on NASW's webpage, http://www.naswdc.org/CHAPTERS.HTM

A particular form of sexual misconduct is sexual harassment. "Sexual harassment is an old problem but a new issue . . . (and) society is finally willing to acknowledge the existence of this problem and victims are increasingly willing to confront the problem directly" (Shank 1994, 12). The federal government's definition considers ***sexual harassment*** as any unwelcome sexual advances, requests for sexual favors, and other verbal or physical conduct of a sexual nature when:

- Submission to such conduct is explicitly or implicitly made a term or condition of an individual's employment or participation in an education program or activity.
- Submission to or rejection of such conduct by an individual is used as the basis for academic or employment decisions affecting that individual.
- Such conduct has the purpose or effect of substantially interfering with an individual's academic or work performance or creating an intimidating, hostile, or offensive working or educational environment. (Equal Employment Opportunity Commission, 1980)

Sexual harassment includes both heterosexual and homosexual advances.

Two strategies are available for dealing with sexual harassment: organizational and individual. At the *organizational* level, it is important to create agency policy that clearly prohibits sexual harassment and identifies procedures for making a complaint. That policy should be published in the agency's personnel manual, and the agency director should periodically post or circulate the statement. Periodic training also helps to sensitize all staff to the problem and can help prevent harassment.

At the *individual* level, if you feel that you are being harassed, you should first speak directly to the harasser, directing him or her to stop the offensive behaviors. If you are not able to directly confront the harasser, an effective strategy is to send a letter that specifies the nature of the harassing incidents and when they occurred, how you were affected, and how the conduct should change in the future. If the harassment persists, it is advisable to keep a diary of events and a list of any witnesses, as well as consulting with other workers, informing your supervisor, and seeking resolution using agency procedures. (*Note:* Some employers require an official complaint within 30 or 60 days of an incident.) If the situation is not resolved within the agency, consultation with a lawyer is suggested. Options include contacting your state human rights commission or the U.S. Equal Employment Opportunity Commission—making an official complaint within 180 days of the incident. If you file a complaint, be prepared for possible negative reactions from the harasser and others in the organization.

SELECTED BIBLIOGRAPHY

Equal Employment Opportunity Commission. "Guidelines on Discrimination Because of Sex, Title VII, Section 703." *Federal Register* 45 (11 April 1980): 2505.

National Association of Social Workers. *Code of Ethics.* Washington, DC: NASW, 1996.

———. "Overview of a Decade of Adjudication," mimeo. Washington, DC: NASW, 1995.

Paludi, Michele, and Richard Barickman. *Sexual Harassment, Work, and Education.* New York: SUNY Press, 1998.

Shank, Barbara W. "Sexual Harassment: Definitions, Policy Frameworks, and Legal Issues." In *Sexual Harassment and Schools of Social Work: Issues, Costs, and Strategic Responses,* edited by Marie O. Weil, Michelle Hughes, and Nancy R. Hooyman. Alexandria, VA: CSWE, 1994.

Singer, Terry. "Sexual Harassment." In *Encyclopedia of Social Work,* 19th ed., Vol. 3, edited by Richard L. Edwards. Washington, DC: NASW Press, 1995, pp. 2148–2156.

10.13 Understanding Qualitative Data

PURPOSE: To make sound judgments about the appropriateness of qualitative research studies reported in the social work literature.

DISCUSSION: In recent years, qualitative research has increasingly been viewed as a respectable form of data collection in the social sciences. As opposed to *quantitative research,* which is focused on counting and statistically analyzing data (see Item 10.14), ***qualitative research*** is more concerned with describing the factors being studied.

Quantitative research typically collects an enormous amount of data from a large and representative sample of respondents. Statistical analysis may then be used to summarize and reduce those data to understandable generalizations and to identify relationships among the data. Qualitative research, by contrast, has the capacity to secure an in-depth understanding of the thoughts, values, and experiences of a smaller group of respondents.

Although some tend to view qualitative and quantitative research as competing methods, it is more useful to consider them as ends of a single continuum of approaches used in the development of knowledge. Qualitative research is most appropriate when the basic characteristics of the phenomenon being studied are still unclear and poorly defined. On the other hand, qualitative research is most appropriate when the phenomenon is understood well enough to know what specific categories or types of information are needed to advance understanding of that phenomenon.

Several principles and concepts are unique to qualitative research. First, when formulating questions for inquiry, the researcher delays the in-depth literature review until the data have been collected, lest the researcher develop a bias or a predisposition in regard to what information is really important and what meaning should be assigned to the data. Second, the researcher acknowledges and owns up to his or her own perspectives on the matter under study as a means of providing the consumers of the research with evidence of possible bias that might have influenced how the data were collected and interpreted. In this approach, there is no pretense that the researcher is a completely objective or neutral party. Third, although it is hoped that the respondents will reflect a true cross-section of opinions and viewpoints, they need not be a systematically selected sample nor is it necessary to have large numbers of respondents. Fewer respondents are asked to provide more in-depth data. In this approach, no preset limits determine when data collection is complete. Rather, the researcher continues to collect information until repetition is apparent. Finally, the concept of triangulation is central. *Triangulation* refers to the use of multiple (usually three) data-gathering methods, multiple observers or investigators, and/or multiple perspectives applied to the same data set. A particular interpretation of the data is accepted when a congruence emerges from these various ways of examining and thinking about the data.

The methods of data collection used in qualitative research are varied. The most basic is *interviewing* respondents to obtain their perceptions. Interviews with individuals will vary in the amount of structure allowed, but will always allow the freedom to follow tangents in a respondent's discussion in order to capture the description as fully as possible. When interviewing groups of respondents, the *focus group* technique (see Item 12.28) is commonly utilized. In both individual and group interviews, process notes and audio recordings are typically used to document the descriptions for later analysis.

A second method commonly used is *case study research,* which involves carefully documenting the experience of a single individual, family, organization, or community over time and identifying patterns, themes, and so on that emerge. In *ethnographic research,* the researcher gains an in-depth understanding of the perceptions, values, and experiences of others by immersing himself or herself in the respondent's physical, social, and cultural environment. *Sociometry* is a procedure used to examine the relationships (e.g., likes and dislikes, affinity and disdain) among people. A tool commonly used in such sociometric studies is the *sociogram,* which maps the content and frequency of interactions among people. When using the *Delphi Technique,* a statement about a subject (i.e., the research topic) is presented to a panel of experts. Each member of this panel comments, the statement is revised and circulated again along with comments, and a rating of relative agreement or disagreement with the statement is made. A Delphi study usually involves at least three cycles of this process until sufficient consensus among the respondents is achieved. Finally, a number of *unobtrusive measures,* such as archival data from existing records or recorded observations that do not require direct interaction with the subjects, provide another method of qualitative data collection.

Content analysis of the documented data is used to organize the data into categories. A first step is to code the data to form categories (i.e., *open coding*) combined with *axial coding* that is intended to facilitate discovering linkages among the categories. Several computer software programs have been developed to facilitate the reduction of massive data into categories for analysis. In addition, a goal of qualitative research is to buttress the summary results with sufficient description, usually in the respondent's own words, to make clear its meaning.

SELECTED BIBLIOGRAPHY

Berg, Bruce L. *Qualitative Research Methods for the Social Sciences,* 2nd ed. Boston: Allyn and Bacon, 1995.

Padgett, Deborah. *Qualitative Methods in Social Work Research.* Thousand Oaks, CA: Sage, 1998.

Sherman, Edmund, and William J. Reid. *Qualitative Research in Social Work.* New York: Columbia University Press, 1995.

Weitzman, Eban A., and Matthew B. Miles. *Computer Programs for Qualitative Analysis.* Thousand Oaks, CA: Sage, 1995.

10.14 Understanding Quantitative Data

PURPOSE: To make sound judgments about the appropriateness of quantitative research studies and to accurately interpret statistical data reported in the social work literature.

DISCUSSION: Much of the knowledge in social work is based on ***quantitative research.*** Quantitative methodologies seek to imitate the scientific approach used in the hard sciences. If, for example, one were to use this approach to evaluate the effectiveness of a particular intervention, the steps might include: (1) formulate a hypothesis about the impact of the intervention; (2) identify, define, and isolate the various factors and elements of the intervention that must be examined in order to test the hypothesis; (3) select a statistically valid sample from the population being studied; (4) utilize control groups to reduce the influence of other factors on the outcome; (5) apply the intervention to an experimental group; (6) collect and apply appropriate statistical analysis; and (7) draw conclusions. In Western society, where science is highly valued, this approach is often viewed as the most valid way to gain knowledge.

In research regarding human beings, it is always difficult and sometimes inappropriate to adhere rigidly to the principles of scientific inquiry. For example, can one ethically encourage or require a person to remain in an abusive family in order to be part of a control group during the study of a domestic violence intervention? Certainly not. Also, consider how difficult it is to adequately match the people selected for a control and an experimental group; individuals, their life experiences, and their situations are very diverse. Despite the difficulty of using rigorous study designs, it is possible to gain understanding of the relationships between professional actions and client outcomes by collecting sufficient data from clients who have and have not had the opportunity to experience a particular intervention or helping method. The application of statistical analysis is central to the task of sorting through such data and discovering and explaining the connections between various client characteristics, life experiences, circumstances and situations, the actions of a professional, the services of an agency, and client outcomes.

Many journal articles present statistical analyses that must be understood if one is to base practice decisions on research. Like foreign languages, one must use statistical procedures on a regular basis before they become easy to read and interpret. Statistics are tools that help make decisions, but should not dictate practice choices. In other words, judgment is required to determine the appropriateness of any statistical analyses.

Statistics are numerical representations of the characteristics of individual cases—in social work, those cases are usually people. *Characteristics* or *variables* are attributes or properties of the cases that the researcher has chosen to define and observe in order to increase understanding of how that variable acts under certain conditions. The groups of cases selected for study may be either *samples* (part of a population) or the *populations* themselves (i.e., the total cases to which the researcher may want to generalize the results). At times, information about the total population actually exists and can be compared to a sample of the population. At other times, characteristics of the population are theoretical or estimated as part of the statistical analysis.

Statistical analysis involves assembling, analyzing, summarizing, and interpreting numerical data. Knowledge of relatively few statistical tests will allow the social worker to read most research reports that appear in professional journals. In fact, a review of three years' issues of NASW's journal, *Social Work,* indicated that knowledge of just 15 statistical procedures (see below) would make it possible to understand most of the research reported in the profession's primary journal. To interpret accurately this statistical information, it is useful to keep three guideposts in mind.

Guidepost 1: The Purpose of the Statistical Procedure

The reader of research reports should be aware of the reason the statistical procedure was applied. The most frequent reason statistics were used in the articles in *Social Work* was to describe respondents or their responses. Those ***descriptive statis-***

tics permit the summarization of raw data into a more useable and communicable format. Descriptive statistics are often referred to as *data-reduction tools* because they reduce data from many responses to a single summary statistic. Statistics consistently reported in the literature are frequency distributions, percentages, measures of central tendency (i.e., reflections of the most typical response from a group of respondents), and measures of variability (i.e., descriptions of the spread in the data or how the subjects are disbursed).

A second, and more complex, set of statistical tools are known as ***inferential statistics***. They permit the researcher to draw certain conclusions from a randomly selected sample about the larger population from which the sample was drawn. These statistics include *measures of difference* that determine if the results from a sample were sufficiently different from an expected result to conclude that the finding was not due to chance and thus could be interpreted as being "statistically significant." Tests of significance are either reported at the exact level (e.g., $p = .02$, or the likelihood is 2 in 100 that the result would occur by chance) or that the result was greater or less than an established criterion for judging the result significant. In the social sciences the typical criterion for accepting a finding as significant is $p = .05$, meaning that the probability is equal to or less than 5 in 100 that the outcome would occur by chance.

A second frequently used set of inferential statistics are *measures of association*. Such tests measure the correlation between two or more variables. In social research it is seldom possible to clearly establish a cause and effect relationship but it is possible to identify patterns of interaction among variables. If the relationships are completely random, they would show zero (0.00) correlation and one would conclude that the variables are unrelated. If there is a positive relationship (i.e., one variable increases when the other increases), the correlation coefficient would be somewhere between +0.01 and +1.00. When a negative relationship exists (i.e., one variable increases when the other decreases), the correlation coefficient would fall between –0.01 and –1.00. Although there is no established rule for interpreting correlation coefficients, Elifson, Runyon, and Haber (1990) suggest the following guidelines:

+ or – 0.01 to 0.30	=	a weak relationship
+ or – 0.31 to 0.70	=	a moderate relationship
+ or – 0.71 and above	=	a strong relationship

These guidelines for interpretation are predicated on the relationship having been judged "clinically significant" from one's practice knowledge as well as on the basis of a test of significance or a statistic derived from the measure of association. Further, depending on the nature of the data being examined and previous inquiries on this topic, these interpretations might appropriately be adjusted and should be noted by the author(s) of the research report.

In addition to the bivariant (two variables or two samples) statistical tests described later, there are additional tests for significant difference and measures of association that can be used when there are three or more variables or samples. These *multivariant statistical procedures* include multiple regression analysis, cluster analysis, and factor analysis. Except for the description of the Analysis of Variance (ANOVA) statistic (provided later), a presentation of these more complex statistical tests is beyond the scope of this book; the reader is referred to a statistics text for further information.

Guidepost 2: Level of Measurement

The application of many statistical tests depends on the level of the data being analyzed. At the most basic level, data are simply grouped into different mutually exclusive categories. One category is not considered to have more or less value than another. Such information is termed ***nominal data.*** Gender, ethnicity, and various yes or no questions (e.g., parent or nonparent) are examples of nominal-level data. ***Ordinal data*** represent information that can be ranked from low to high, but for which it would not be reasonable to assume that there is equal value in each category. For example, many scales used in the social work literature are three- or five-point ratings of a factor (e.g., frequently, occasionally, seldom) but there is no assumption of equal intervals between ratings—only indication of more or less, or higher or lower. For example, a rating scale may be used to indicate that Client A has higher self-esteem than Client B, but in measuring a variable like self-esteem, one is not able to say that Client A has three times more self-esteem than Client B. ***Interval or ratio data,*** on the other hand, assume the categories are divided into equal units and thus permit more precise measures. Interval-level data might include client age or the population of the community served by social workers. As the consumer of a research report or article, it is important to be sure that the statistical procedures selected were appropriate for the level of data collected in the study. Otherwise, the statistic may misrepresent the outcome.

Guidepost 3: Type of Sample

The type of sample (in combination with the level of measurement) determines which statistical procedures can be appropriately used. The most powerful (i.e., more rigorous in a mathematical sense) statistical tests are ***parametric tests,*** which require independent or random samples and interval- or ratio-level data for at least one variable. For a sample to meet the sampling criteria for parametric tests, the different cases being compared must have been independently assigned to groups or randomly selected and there must be reason to assume that the population from which the sample was drawn has a normal distribution. ***Nonparamatric statistics,*** in contrast, are less powerful predictors but allow work with data that are nominal and ordinal. Also, since they compare the outcomes observed in the study with expected outcomes for those respondents, they do not assume a normal distribution. Nonparametric statistics fit almost all research situations and are frequently used in social work research.

Some of the statistics commonly reported in the social work literature are described here. The reader is urged to see the Selected Bibliography or other statistics books to acquire more in-depth knowledge of these and other statistical tests. Each procedure is identified by the symbol that is commonly used in journal articles.

ANOVA — *Analysis of Variance.* This test examines the variation in the means of two or more independent or predictor variables to determine the likelihood that the results could have occurred by chance. This parametric test requires that the dependent variable is measured by interval-level data, while the predictor variable or variables may be nominal or ordinal. The ANOVA is similar to the *t*-test (see below) but can also be applied when three or more groups of data are being compared. By consulting an *F* table, the probability (e.g., $p < .05$) of a distribution occurring by chance can be estimated.

DF — *Degrees of Freedom.* *DF* indicates the number of cells in a set of data that are free to vary. This freedom to vary is an important factor in estimating the probability of an outcome occurring by chance. *DF* is computed by multiplying the number of rows minus one in a table by the number of columns minus one. Thus a 2×3 table would have 2 *DF*, whereas a 3×4 table would have 6 *DF*. *DF* is reported to allow the reader to understand how the researcher interpreted the probability tables for the different statistical tests.

f — *Frequency.* An *f* will usually be reported in a table and simply reflects the number of responses in each category or interval.

F-ratio — *F.* Usually based on an ANOVA or a multiple regression analysis, this parametric test of significance is a measure of variability that requires interval or ratio data. It tests for difference between the standard deviations of two variables or samples. The *F*-ratio compares estimates of variance *between* the samples with variance *within* the samples. If the between-group variance is higher than the within-group variance, increasing the likelihood that the variance did not occur by chance, the *F*-ratio will be larger. The *F* value has little meaning until it is applied to a table that identifies the probability of that distribution occurring by chance.

Mdn — *Median.* This is a measure of central tendency that may be used with ordinal- or interval-level data. It is the midpoint in a distribution (i.e., the score above which and below which 50 percent of the cases lie).

Mo — *Mode.* This is a measure of central tendency that may be used with all levels of data. It reflects the category that includes the most cases in a distribution and thus can be applied to nominal data. In some distributions more than one category may have the same number of cases, resulting in a bimodal or multimodal distribution.

N — *Number.* The *N* reports the total number of cases that are being considered in the statistical procedure. The *N* may vary in different analyses of a data set due to incomplete responses or test requirements that may necessitate the exclusion of some cases.

% *Percent.* A percentage is a reflection of the share of the cases that would fall into a category if the total were 100. It is computed by dividing the frequency (f) in a category by the total number of cases (N) and multiplying by 100.

p *Probability.* A p-value reports the likelihood of a particular distribution occurring by chance if a normal distribution is assumed. Thus, the lower the likelihood of a distribution occurring by chance, the more confidence can be placed in the assumption that the variables being tested indeed affected the outcome.

r *Pearson Product-Moment Correlation Coefficient.* The r is a correlation coefficient (i.e., a number that represents the association between two variables). It reflects the tendency of high or low scores for one variable to regularly be associated with high or low scores for another variable. Therefore, it is possible to predict the value of one set of scores by knowing another. The nearer the r-score is to +1.00 or –1.00, the greater is the likelihood that the items vary together (i.e., are associated with each other). The r is a parametric test that requires interval-level data. (*Note: The Spearman Rank Order Correlation Coefficient* (r_s) is a similar nonparametric test that can be applied to ordinal or ranked data. It examines the association between pairs of variables and can be computed with a relatively small number of pairs [i.e., less than 30] in the sample.)

Range *Range.* The range is a measure of variability that reports the span between the lowest and highest scores of the cases in the sample. Data must be at least ordinal to compute the range.

SD *Standard Deviation.* SD tells how much dispersion from the mean exists in the scores of the sample or population being studied. The more the scores deviate from the mean, the greater the standard deviation score. When comparing samples or groups as part of a study, the ones with the largest SD scores have the greatest variability in distribution, whereas the respondents in groups with smaller SDs are more like the mean (or average) and thus are more homogeneous. In a normal distribution, about 68 percent of all cases fall within one standard deviation from the mean (34 percent above and 34 percent below) and 95 percent fall within two standard deviations from the mean.

t-test *Student's t.* The t-test is a parametric test of significant difference between the means of two samples (or a sample and the population from which the sample was drawn). At times it is also used to test the significance of the difference between two coefficients of correlation. If the means differ substantially (i.e., a higher score), it is likely that the difference was not a result of sampling error or chance, and it is reasonable to assume that the difference is associated with actual variations in the factors being examined. A *t* table provides statistical estimates of the probability that the results might be due to chance (e.g., $p < .05$).

$\overline{X}$ *Mean.* The arithmetic mean is a measure of central tendency that requires interval- or ratio-level data. It is the sum of the values for a variable divided by the number (*N*) of cases.

χ^2 *Chi Square.* χ^2 is a nonparametric test of significance that may be applied with nominal data. In essence, it compares the observed and expected frequencies for a variable to determine if the differences found could be explained by chance. Until the chi square value is translated to a probability score (e.g., $p < .05$), it has little meaning.

SELECTED BIBLIOGRAPHY

Craft, John L. *Statistics and Data Analysis for Social Workers,* 2nd ed. Itasca, IL: F. E. Peacock, 1990.

Elifson, Kirk W., Richard P. Runyon, and Audrey Haber. *Fundamentals of Social Statistics,* 2nd ed. New York: McGraw-Hill, 1990

Mark, Raymond. *Research Made Simple: A Handbook for Social Workers.* Thousand Oaks, CA: Sage, 1996.

Pilcher, Donald M. *Data Analysis for the Helping Professions: A Practical Guide.* Newbury Park, CA: Sage, 1990.

Vogt, W. Paul. *Dictionary of Statistics and Methodology: A Nontechnical Guide for the Social Sciences.* Newbury Park, CA: Sage, 1993.

Weinbach, Robert W., and Richard M. Grinnell, Jr. *Statistics for Social Workers,* 4th ed. New York: Longman, 1997.

10.15 Improving the Social Work Image

PURPOSE: To build public understanding and a more positive image of social workers.

DISCUSSION: Social work suffers from public misunderstanding and a negative image. The typical citizen has little understanding of what social workers actually do and the impressions they have are often erroneous or incomplete. On TV and in the movies, the social worker is often portrayed as either a judgmental and mindless busybody or someone who breaks up families by removing children for no good reason. All too often, the only newspaper or magazine articles that mention social workers are ones describing how the acts or omissions of an agency or a social worker contributed to a client's harm or distress. Additional image problems are created when the media uses the term *social worker* in a generic manner and applies it to all human services workers.

Social workers want a better image and want to be appreciated and understood by the public. They would also like the higher pay that comes with a high-status profession. However, such changes will not result from wishful thinking; they must be made to happen. The image will change in a positive direction when it becomes evident to the public that social workers are truly experts in what they do and are able to get results that nonsocial workers are unable to match. The financial rewards and the status associated with certain other professions (e.g., medicine, engineering, accounting) came about not through exhortation but rather because their members completed long and difficult training, acquired a definite expertise, and assumed a legal responsibility for the outcome of their decisions and actions.

Social work's image problem is, in part, rooted in its history and its association with devalued groups (e.g., the poor) and with controversial and unpopular causes (e.g., the expansion of governmental programs to address social problems). However, individual social workers, by their own acts and omissions, also contribute to the problem. For example, many avoid describing themselves as social workers; they prefer to use titles such as therapists, counselors, administrators, and so on. Consequently, whatever the public finds positive and praiseworthy about their performance is associated with some other occupational title. In other words, by avoiding the title of social worker, they miss opportunities to inform the public about social work and to correct public misperceptions. Social workers cannot expect the public to change its attitude until social workers themselves are openly proud of their profession. In order to promote a greater public understanding, social workers should adhere to certain guidelines, such as the following:

1. Use the title of social worker. If you must also use words such as *counseling* or *psychotherapy* to clarify your role, describe yourself as, for example: "I am a social worker—I provide psychotherapy to troubled youth," "I am a social worker specializing in the planning and development of services for persons with AIDS," "I am a social worker who administers a family support program," "I am a social worker who teaches at a university," and so on.

2. Assume a personal responsibility for improving the profession's image. Three actions are essential. First, provide the highest quality service possible—get results. Second, behave in a highly professional and completely responsible manner when dealing with clients and the public. Third, inform those observing your performance that you are a social worker.

3. When being interviewed for a news story, make sure the reporter understands that you are a social worker and that you have a degree in social work, and perhaps describe the special training that has prepared you for the work you do. Always operate on the assumption that reporters and the public at large have little or no idea that social work is a distinct profession. Otherwise, you will probably be termed a *sociologist, welfare worker, counselor,* or *agency worker.*

4. Speak of your work with respect. If you truly value what you do, others are more likely to adopt a positive attitude toward both you and your work. Avoid any action or association that would damage your credibility and trustworthiness.

5. Be very careful and thoughtful about what you say in public. Always anticipate how your words, manner, and actions will be perceived by the public and by the clients served by social workers and social agencies. Public statements must be accurate, clear, and respectful of others.

6. Work with other social workers and professional associations (e.g., the NASW) to plan and implement a media and public relations campaign aimed at educating the public about social work and social workers in your community.

7. Whenever a news story uses the term *social work* or *social worker* in an erroneous manner, send the newspaper, magazine, or radio or TV station a letter that explains the error. Also send a packet of informational materials that describes the nature of the profession and social work activities.

SELECTED BIBLIOGRAPHY

Barker, Robert. *Social Work in Private Practice.* Washington, DC: NASW, 1991.

Bromley, D. B. *Reputation, Image and Impression Management.* New York: John Wiley and Sons, 1993.

Hopps, June, and Pauline Collins. "Social Work Profession Overview." In *Encyclopedia of Social Work,* 19th ed., Vol. 3, edited by Richard Edwards. Washington, DC: NASW, 1995, pp. 902–908.

Part IV Techniques and Guidelines for Phases of the Planned Change Process

Many social work supervisors have heard practicum students and new social workers ask a question such as "Well, I think I understand the basic theory and the general principles of working with people, but what specifically should I do when I see Mrs. Jones and her daughter this afternoon?" Obviously, these social workers have discovered that there is a difference between the *knowing* and the *doing* in social work practice. They sense the need for some specific direction on what to do with the client.

Part IV of this book addresses this need. As was explained in the Preface, the authors chose to prepare a book focusing mostly on techniques and guidelines rather than on theory. This decision reflects their belief that many texts do an excellent job of presenting the theoretical frameworks of practice, yet few provide the concrete guidance so often requested by students and new workers.

Many social workers engage in some combination of both direct and indirect practice. The term ***direct practice*** refers to those activities that involve frequent face-to-face interaction with an individual or family who has requested a service or is experiencing some difficulty. The activities of direct social work practice might include, for example, individual and family counseling, case assessment, case management, referral work, group treatment, guiding a support group, advocating for the services needed by a specific individual, and so on. By contrast, the term ***indirect practice*** is used to describe social work practice activities that do not involve extensive contact with the clients or consumers of services but indirectly serves or benefits those who need various types of services or forms of assistance. Examples of such practice activities include agency administration, staff supervision, program planning, program evaluation, fund-raising, public education, work with community groups and coalitions of agencies that are concerned about a particular social problem or condition, advocacy on behalf of a large group of persons in need, and efforts to enact legislation and change public policy that would benefit agency clients and consumers of human services.

The five chapters of Part IV correspond to the five phases of the change process as described in Chapter 7. The reader will notice that each of these chapters has a Section A and a Section B. Techniques and guidelines related to direct social work practice are found in Section A, whereas Section B contains techniques and guidelines used in indirect practice.

Chapter 11, "Intake and Engagement," is concerned with start-up activities or the beginning phase of work with clients. Also included is information on new beginnings that are part of joining an agency and starting work in a new community.

Chapter 12, "Data Collection and Assessment," provides a sampling of techniques and guidelines for gathering information about the client situation and assigning meaning to that information. Some form of data gathering and assessment is required, whether the social worker's client is an individual, a family, a neighborhood, or a community.

Chapter 13, "Planning and Contracting," presents techniques and guidelines for helping the client and worker arrive at a set of agreed upon goals and objectives for their work together. The failure to secure such an agreement and to formulate a clear plan for the change effort or intervention is one of the most common errors made by human services professionals, whether working with a family or an agency committee.

Chapter 14, "Intervention and Monitoring," provides a sampling of direct practice and indirect practice techniques and guidelines for encouraging and facilitating the process of change and for bringing about specific types of change. The selection included in this chapter alerts the student and new worker to the wide variety of techniques available to the practitioner and the wide range of situations in which they might prove useful.

Finally, Chapter 15, "Evaluation and Termination," anticipates the practical problems associated with finding a valid and feasible means of measuring whether the change effort has been effective. Figuring out how to evaluate one's practice is a difficult task for most social workers. This chapter also includes information on the termination of a professional relationship.

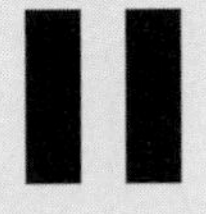

Intake and Engagement

INTRODUCTION

This chapter presents guidelines and techniques for use during the beginning or start-up phase of the change process. During this phase, a client, whether an individual or even an organization, is typically ambivalent about entering a helping relationship and beginning the change process. Making a favorable first impression on the client and setting a positive tone for working with the client can have a powerful influence on all that follows. Although the activities differ somewhat when providing direct services (Section A) as opposed to indirect services (Section B), the intent is essentially the same.

During this initial period of interaction, the social worker should undertake three sets of activities. First, several ***preparatory activities*** should be conducted. For example, the worker should prepare for the first contact by reviewing the history of the situation; selecting a meeting time and place that will be convenient, comfortable, and supportive; determining who should be involved in this meeting; and being sensitive to factors that may affect clients' perspectives on and investment in the process.

Second, the worker should begin the process of ***engagement*** by establishing rapport and helping clients articulate and clarify the nature of their concerns or requests. Usually, individuals or families have already unsuccessfully attempted to deal with their issues through friends or other professional helpers when they come to a social worker. If the client is an agency or community, they too have often unsuccessfully attempted to deal with the matter of concern. In these situations, people are likely to approach the social worker and the change process with some degree of skepticism and ambivalence. It is important, therefore, to quickly help the client become truly invested in this process by starting to build trust and actively engaging the client in working toward meaningful change.

Third, the worker must determine if he or she can appropriately address the client's need or request. In short, some form or ***intake*** or screening decision must be made. In most communities, the human services delivery system is complex and those in search of service may begin with an agency or worker who will not be able to address the client's concern. Or, at the indirect-service level, the initial group created to address an agency or community issue may not, on more thorough examination of the matter, be the best structure or set of actors to proceed with the change process. A decision to be made by the social worker, then, is whether it is appropriate to continue the contact or relationship or to make a referral to another organization or professional that is better suited to address the situation.

SECTION A

TECHNIQUES AND GUIDELINES FOR DIRECT PRACTICE

Many clients are anxious and ambivalent during the start-up phase of a helping relationship. They may wonder, for example: Will I be treated with respect? Will this social worker be able to help? Will he or she really care about me or just treat me as another "case"? Will this worker listen to what I have to say? Is there a good chance that my concern or situation can be resolved in a reasonable amount of time at a reasonable cost to me?

Preparatory Activities. When providing direct services, it is not always possible to plan for the initial meeting, as sometimes a social worker first meets a client under crisis conditions when there is not an opportunity to adequately prepare. However, since the first contact is critical in setting the tone for a helping relationship, the worker should carefully plan for that meeting whenever possible.

One useful preintake activity is to reflect on the fact that the typical client has already unsuccessfully sought assistance and may be skeptical, discouraged, or distrustful of entering still another professional relationship. If the client is *involuntary* (pressured to see the worker by someone else), he or she may be angry, resentful, and unmotivated. To prepare for issues that might arise at a first meeting, it is useful, especially for the inexperienced social worker, to review guidelines for working with clients who are involuntary, hard to reach, chemically dependent, manipulative, or dangerous (see Items 11.6 through 11.10).

It is also important to consider a number of factors when planning the first meeting, such as carefully establishing the time and place for that critical contact. Some clients cannot conveniently leave work to see a social worker during usual business hours and thus weekend or evening appointments may be necessary. These meetings might be conducted in the worker's office, the client's home (see Item 11.5), or some other location such as a hospital, jail, group home, neighborhood center, or other convenient location for both the client and worker. When the meeting is held, it is the social worker's responsibility to attend to such concerns as comfort, privacy, freedom from distractions, and accommodation to special needs (e.g., space for a wheelchair, arrangements for an interpreter, etc.). The worker, too, should be concerned with personal preparation for the contact such as wearing appropriate clothing, being on time, and being prepared to guide the session.

The social worker should also be sensitive to factors about the agency that might affect the helping relationship, such as: Is the receptionist courteous and helpful when the client telephones or stops by the agency to initiate contact? Is there a comfortable reception or waiting area for clients? Is child care available if needed? Is the worker's office or a group meeting room appropriately furnished to create a favorable environment for interacting with clients? Agency atmosphere sets the stage for what is to follow.

Engagement Activities. A critical factor in successful helping is involving the client in the change process. The following activities can help clients take the risk to invest themselves in a helping relationship:

- Greet and speak with the client in a way that is nonthreatening and puts the client at ease.
- Demonstrate genuine interest in the client and concern for his or her request, problem, or situation.
- Explain any legal or ethical obligations the social worker may have regarding the confidentiality of information divulged by the client.
- Help the client articulate and clarify his or her request or concerns.
- Learn about the client's expectations of the agency and worker.
- Identify any fears or misunderstandings the client may have about the social worker, the agency, or its services.
- Explain pertinent eligibility requirements that may affect service provision.
- Address the client's possible ambivalence about receiving services.

During this phase of helping, the worker should be particularly sensitive to the client's fear of the unknown and people's inherent *resistance to change*. Clients usually begin a helping relationship feeling some conflict over whether the perceived need for change outweighs the disruption it may cause. Even a small amount of change can create discomfort or fear for clients, especially if they hold rigid beliefs, are inflexible in their thought processes and behaviors, or are fearful about risking change in their relationships with others. The social worker's role is to help clients examine new ways of thinking, believing, and behaving that may result in improved functioning and to help them determine if various options are sufficiently benefical and feasible to risk an effort at change. The social worker should also recognize that the client is likely to become somewhat defensive regarding his or her thoughts, decisions, and behaviors. In the context of a supportive helping relationship, these prior patterns must be examined and challenged if the client is subsequently to make changes that will replace the problematic ways of functioning.

Intake Activities. A decision a social worker must make during the intake and engagement phase is concerned with the continuation of service. The worker must rapidly determine if there is a fit between agency eligibility criteria requirements and the client's need or request. If so, the next decision is whether the worker should provide continuing services (i.e., guide the remainder of the process) or transfer the matter to another worker in the agency. That decision will depend on the division of labor in the agency and the competence of the worker to address the client's specific issues. If it is determined that the worker should continue to provide services to the client, some actions that should be taken are:

- Assess the urgency of the client's needs or presenting problem and attend to the emergency if one exists.
- Explain the responsibilities that both the client and worker will assume during the helping process.
- Explain to the client that he or she will need to provide information (in some cases, very personal information) needed to assess the problem or situation.
- Secure the client's signed release of confidential information (if one is needed).
- Reach tentative agreement on the minimum and, if possible, maximum number of meetings that probably will be necessary.

- Explain procedures to be followed or fees to be paid in order to receive services. If approval to provide services must be given by a managed care company (see Item 9.11), begin the process of acquiring approval and learning of any associated restrictions on practice activities.
- Reach agreement on the time, place, and frequency of future meetings.

If the client's needs do not match this agency's programs, a referral to appropriate source of help must be made. Social workers are the professionals who are typically expected to be most well-versed in the human services resources available to clients. However, making successful referrals is difficult and only about one-half of the referral efforts have been found to succeed (see Item 11.3). When making a referral, the social worker should approach the task with as much care as in other aspects of practice.

11.1 The First Telephone Contact

PURPOSE: To engage the person contacting the agency by phone.

DISCUSSION: The first contact between the worker and client is often by telephone. Most clients feel nervous; many are confused and uncertain about what to expect. Others have a distorted idea about what the agency can or will do for them. Thus, the worker must use the time on the telephone to lessen the client's fears, secure at least a general understanding of what the client expects from the agency, and, if appropriate, arrange for the first face-to-face interview. Several guidelines should be kept in mind:

1. Remember that, during a telephone conversation, you cannot read the client's nonverbal behavior. You will not always know if the caller is becoming confused or fearful in response to what you are saying. Keep your messages clear and simple.

2. If speaking with a voluntary client, briefly explore the client's presenting concern or request so you can evaluate the appropriateness of this referral to your agency. However, avoid gathering detailed intake information by phone; that is best done during a face-to-face interview. Also, avoid overwhelming the client with extraneous information about your agency and its services and procedures. Explanations of complex or detailed concerns should also be saved for a face-to-face meeting.

3. If speaking to an involuntary client, it is usually best to confine the phone conversation to arranging the first face-to-face interview unless explanations and encouragement are needed to get the client to attend such a meeting. The involuntary client often has strong negative feelings about having to meet with a social worker. Such feelings are much easier to read and effectively addressed during a face-to-face interview (see Item 11.6).

4. When arranging the first office visit, make sure the client knows the location of your office and your name. Some clients may need guidance on how to use public transportation to reach the agency. In some cases, a follow-up letter should be sent to the client, repeating the time and place of the appointment.

5. Be aware of the client's relationships and roles (e.g., child, spouse, parent, etc.) and assess how family or household members will be impacted by the caller's decision to seek professional assistance. When taking a call from one member of a family or household, ask if others in the home know about the caller's request for assistance. If the call is being kept secret from others, ask why secrecy is important. Determine if making the call places the caller in physical danger. Except in situations where secrecy is necessary to protect the caller, encourage the caller to consider involving others (e.g., spouse) in at least the beginning phase of the helping process. Explain that the assessment of the problem will be more accurate and intervention more effective if all persons affected share their perceptions of the problem or concern, their thoughts on what might be helpful, and their views on what changes are possible. Discuss how some agency services and interventions may be ineffective unless family members or significant others also become clients. If it sounds as if others might be willing to participate, hold out for such a meeting. If the caller insists that others will not or should not participate, respect his or her wishes and set up a meeting with the caller alone. Later in the helping process you should again try to involve the client's significant others.

SELECTED BIBLIOGRAPHY

Gorden, Raymond. *Basic Interviewing Skills.* Itasca, IL: F. E. Peacock, 1992.

Hepworth, Dean, Ronald Rooney, and Jo Ann Larsen. *Direct Social Work Practice.* Pacific Grove, CA: Brooks/Cole, 1997.

11.2 The First Face-to-Face Meeting

PURPOSE: To conduct the initial interview in a manner that lays the foundation for a good working relationship.

DISCUSSION: It is quite common to feel a bit nervous when meeting a client for the first time. It can be safely assumed that the client has similar feelings. It is during this first meeting that the worker and client size up each other and form initial impressions. Several guidelines can help the social worker get the interaction off to a good start:

1. Before beginning the first face-to-face session, anticipate what the client might be thinking and feeling. Be prepared to respond in an understanding way to the client's fears, ambivalence, confusion, or anger during a first meeting with a stranger whom the client may perceive as an authority figure.

2. Create a physical arrangement conducive to good communication. For a two-person meeting, chairs should face each other. Chairs for a family interview should be arranged in a circle. Make sure the room temperature is comfortable. Be aware that your body language, how you are dressed, your posture, facial expressions, and gestures all send messages to the client. Try to send a message of respect, caring, and professionalism.

3. If the client requested the meeting, begin with some introductory remarks and possibly some small talk, but soon move on to the concerns that brought the client to the agency. If you initiated the interview, begin by explaining who you are, who you represent, and why you need to speak to the person.

4. Explain the rules of confidentiality that apply and inform the client if what he or she says cannot be held in complete confidence. For example, you might say, "Before we begin, I want to make certain you understand that I will be preparing a report for the court that is based on our meetings. So, what you tell me may end up in my report to the judge. Do you understand that?"

5. If you have only limited time to spend with a client, explain this at the beginning of the session so those things of highest priority will receive sufficient attention.

6. Give serious attention to what the client describes as his or her concerns, but realize that many clients will test your competency and trustworthiness before revealing the whole story or the real problem. Begin with whatever the client considers important and wants to talk about.

7. Do not jump to conclusions about the nature or cause of the client's presenting concern or problem. Check out your assumptions and perceptions. Do not display surprise or disbelief in response to what the client tells you.

8. Do not rush the client. Respect his or her need to be silent and pause before speaking. Convey the message, "I will give you the time necessary to develop your thoughts and decide what you want to say."

9. Adapt your language and vocabulary to the client's capacity to understand. If you do not understand what the client is saying, ask for clarification or examples.

10. Use open-ended questions, unless you need specific data. Do not ask a question that you believe the client will be unwilling to answer. This may force the client to lie and that may obstruct the further development of a working relationship.

11. When you do not know the answer to a service-related question asked by the client, explain this in a nonapologetic manner and offer to find the answer for the client. Be careful not to make promises that you may not be able to keep.

12. Some notetaking during the intake phase is usually necessary and appropriate. Writing down pertinent client information can demonstrate concern and a desire to remember important details. Notetaking can be distracting, however. If the client is bothered by notetaking, show him or her your notes and explain why they are needed. If the client still objects, cease taking notes. If you are completing an agency form, give the client a copy to follow along as you talk.

13. Plan the next meeting with the client, if one is necessary. Be sure the client has your business card that lists your name and phone number and that you have his or her full name, address, and phone number.

The social worker will encounter a number of ***clients who have significant physical or sensory disabilities.*** The place and usual patterns of first meetings may need to be altered in order to accommodate their special needs and limitations. A few guidelines should be kept in mind:

1. When interviewing a person in a hospital bed or using a wheelchair, sit or position yourself so that you directly face the client. Do not stand over him or her. Not only would this place the client in a psychologically inferior position but it may also force the client to strain his or her neck or body in order to look at you. If the client moves about in a wheelchair or by using crutches, a cane, or a walker, respect his or her wish to remain in control and move independently. Do not offer assistance unless it is needed, and respect the client's right to decline your offer of assistance. Be patient if it takes him or her longer to complete tasks and movements. Avoid focusing on the client's medical equipment or prosthesis.

2. When you meet with a person who is blind and in an unfamiliar physical environment, you may need to provide information he or she needs to move about. When walking with a person who is blind and using a cane, simply stay at his or her side and let the person maneuver. Never grab or move the individual, for this is both insulting and frightening. If the client wants your assistance, he or she will ask or reach out; respond by offering your elbow to hold and then walk about a half-step ahead. It is appropriate to alert the person to an unusual obstacle or danger he or she might not detect and to mention things like overhead obstructions, sharp turns, or stairs. If the person is using a guide dog, do not touch, feed, or speak to the dog. Guide dogs are trained to walk down the center of a sidewalk or hallway.

3. An individual with a hearing loss will easily confuse similar sounds and have difficulty accurately hearing the human voice, especially if there is background noise. Group conversations may be particularly troublesome. If possible, move to an area away from background noise. Since most hearing aids amplify all sounds, these limitations may exist even if the client is wearing an aid. If the client seems to be having difficulty, slow your pace slightly, speak as clearly as possible, but do not exaggerate your words, since this makes speech reading (lip reading) more difficult. To facilitate speech reading, be sure to position yourself so he or she can see your face and do not speak while looking away or down at papers. Do not position yourself in front of a window or a bright light, for this too interferes with speech reading. Also, a heavily mustached mouth may impede lip reading. Check often to see if the person is able to follow the conversation. Do not mistake simple nodding and smiling as a sign of comprehension, for this may be the person's response to embarrassment and reluctance to say that he or she cannot understand. A person who is totally deaf is usually prepared to communicate in writing. Be aware that some people who are deaf use "hearing dogs"; these dogs usually wear an orange collar and leash. If the individual uses a sign language, find out what system he or she uses and secure the services of an interpreter who knows that system.

4. Increasingly, governmental offices, hospitals, and other essential services are equipped with devices that can be used by persons who have difficulty communicating because of blindness, hearing loss, or speech impairments. A social worker likely to encounter clients with these limitations should become familiar with amplifiers, signaling devices, puff-blow devices, electronic artificial larynx devices, telebraille, TDD (telecommunications device for the deaf), and TTY (teletypewriter).

SELECTED BIBLIOGRAPHY

Marziali, Elsa. "The First Session: An Interpersonal Encounter." *Social Casework* 69, No. 1 (January 1988): 23–27.

Murphy, Bianca, and Carolyn Dillon. *Interviewing in Action.* Pacific Grove, CA: Brooks/Cole, 1998.

Shulman, Lawrence. *The Skills of Helping,* 4th ed. Itasca, IL: F. E. Peacock, 1999.

11.3 Making a Referral

PURPOSE: To link a client with an agency, program, or professional person that will provide the service needed by the client.

DISCUSSION: An important social work activity is to link the client with the community resources, services, and opportunities that he or she needs, wants, and can use. Many people view referral as a relatively simple task. However, studies indicate that many attempted referrals end in failure. This high rate of failure, possibly 50 percent, indicates that referral is actually very complex. By following these guidelines, the worker can increase the rate of success in the referral process:

1. A *referral* is a action intended to help a client address some specific problem or concern. Thus, it is only after you and the client have clearly identified and explored the client's concern, that you can hope to make an appropriate referral. Unless the client views the problem or concern as a high priority and one on which he or she wants to work, an attempted referral will fail.

2. View the client as an expert on his or her problems and situation, on what services are needed, and on what will or will not work. Honor and respect the client's opinions and preferences.

3. Referral is appropriate when your agency cannot provide the service needed and wanted by a client. Referral is also appropriate when you do not have the knowledge or skills needed to work with a particular client and when you have reason to believe your own values, attitudes, religious beliefs, or language will be a barrier to developing an effective helping relationship. Attempting to rid yourself of responsibility for dealing with a difficult client is never an acceptable reason for referral. "Passing the buck" or "dumping" a client on another agency is unprofessional and unethical.

4. Before concluding that referral to another agency is necessary, make sure you have considered all sources of assistance available within your own agency. Because any attempted referral carries a risk of failure and may add to the client's frustration, the social worker should first use the resources of an agency to which the client is already linked.

5. Be realistic about what other agencies and professionals have to offer your client. Some workers tend to overestimate the worth of yet untapped resources and to undervalue the resources that the client is already using. Also, be sure to consider the client's friends, relatives, neighbors, natural helpers, and other informal resources as a possible source of assistance.

6. In this era of managed care, careful consideration must be given to the question of whether the client's private insurance or public medical program (e.g., Medicaid) will, in fact, cover the services needed and whether a particular professional is on the list of providers acceptable to the managed care company. Helping a client secure the proper preauthorization from the managed care company is now an important step in making a proper and effective referral to a health care provider.

7. When helping a client select a provider of a professional service, such as counseling or psychotherapy, the social worker should ask himself or herself the following question: Would I refer my mother or my own child to this professional? The social worker must strive to help the client locate a service provider known to be competent and ethical.

8. Make sure you know of all the agencies already involved with a client before considering a referral. Some problems are best handled through interagency case coordination and improved case management rather than by expanding the number of agencies involved with the client. Professionals and other agencies already working with a client should be consulted prior to referring a client to yet another agency. The client's permission will usually be needed before this discussion can take place. Whenever necessary, obtain releases of information signed by the client prior to engaging in the referral process.

9. Whenever appropriate, the client's family and other significant individuals should be involved in the decision making related to a referral. This will, of course, increase the number of persons who have opinions about the referral, which may bog down the process. However, it will avoid having others unexpectedly throw up obstacles because they "felt left out." In the long run, full involvement increases the chance that the referral will be successful.

10. Whenever considering a particular service that might prove beneficial to the client, give special attention to the practical problems that may be a barrier to its utilization (e.g., client's lack of transportation or phone, inability to read, lack of child care during appointments, fearfulness associated with travel in a high-crime area, inability to take time away from job, etc.).

11. Agency decisions concerning eligibility for services, benefits, and entitlement are usually tied to questions about whether the applicant fits into a legally defined category and meets established criteria. Thus, referral work requires skill in gathering information and documents related to, for example, citizenship, marriage, parent-child relationships, prior employment, income, household composition, medical conditions, and so forth. It is important to know how to verify information and obtain key documents such as citizenship papers, birth certificates, marriage certificates, divorce decrees, death certificates, Social Security numbers, tribal enrollment numbers, and military service papers.

12. Help the client tell his or her story about the agencies and resources he or she has used or rejected in the past. Also determine how the client approached and interacted with these resources; this will provide clues as to what needs to be done to facilitate the referral. A prior negative experience with an agency can contribute to referral failure. Anticipate possible barriers and take action to lay the groundwork for success.

13. Assume that the client is ambivalent about the referral. Although the client may see the logic of using the services of another agency or professional, he or she may be fearful. It is important to explore this ambivalence and help him or her express fears or concerns about using a particular resource.

14. The referral process can be stressful and frustrating for many clients. They may encounter a harried agency receptionist, an overwhelmed intake worker, waiting lists, red tape, and confusing eligibility requirements. Some clients need a great deal of emotional support during the referral process and some will need to be carefully coached on how to approach an agency and apply for services.

15. Acknowledge that the client has already invested time and energy in relating to you. A successful referral may mean terminating a satisfying and secure partnership. Be aware of these feelings and be prepared to deal with feelings of separation from you and a familiar agency.

16. If possible, the client should be given several options from which to choose the agency or professional he or she wishes to utilize. It is appropriate to recommend the one or two that you think will best meet the client's needs. If the client asks for advice on whether to use a particular resource, you have an obligation to give your honest assessment of its appropriateness and quality.

17. Ordinarily, when telling a client about services available through another professional or agency, you should explain both the advantages and limitations of those services. However, with clients who are confused, fearful, or highly dysfunctional, it is best not to focus on the limitations. Doing so could create an added barrier to the client's use of a needed service.

18. View the referral as the first step in a new helping process. It sets the stage for what will follow. If done well, the referral process itself will be an empowering and therapeutic experience for the client. Because the referral process involves the use of problem-solving skills such as problem definition, gathering information, and decision making, your involvement with the client during the referral process gives him or her an opportunity to learn these skills and how to secure needed resources.

19. All agencies and private practitioners have their own procedures, policies, and eligibility criteria. Do not expect them to suspend their ordinary procedures as a favor to you or your client. Be careful not to tell a client that he or she is eligible for a particular service unless you have the authority to make such eligibility decisions. Do not speak for another professional or agency.

20. When a client is in need of a professional or agency service for which there is a fee, the issue of cost and the client's ability to pay must be addressed. Some clients will need much detailed direction and assistance in obtaining information from the providers of the service, the health insurance companies, managed care organizations, or public programs (e.g., Medicaid) in order to determine whether they have a way of paying for a particular service.

21. Whenever possible, clients should make their own arrangements for the services they want. In some cases, however, the frightened, immature, or overwhelmed client will need help in setting up an appointment, securing transportation, arranging child care, and the like. As a general rule, the client should be expected to assume as much responsibility as possible, without, of course, placing the success of the referral in jeopardy. If a referral is critically important to a client, you should do whatever is needed to establish the linkage. Sometimes you will need to accompany clients if they are confused or fearful about going to an agency. Family members, friends, or volunteers may also be able to provide this support.

22. In order to make an effective referral, you must understand existing community resources. Because much of social work practice involves linking people to needed resources, a social worker must invest the time and energy necessary to learn about resources and keep up with the constant change that occurs within the community resource system. Just knowing that a resource exists is seldom sufficient. It is important for the worker to know someone on the agency staff who can be used as a contact point. Use agency visits as well as NASW and other professional meetings as an opportunity to meet people working in the agencies to which you will be referring clients. Most communities have a clearinghouse and/or computerized database designed to help the user identify existing health and social service agencies, programs, and providers. Know how to access these listings.

23. Make sure the client becomes linked to the resource. Weissman (1976) describes a number of techniques he calls ***connection techniques*** that can increase the likelihood that a referral will be effective:

> *Writing out* the necessary facts: the name and address of the resource, how to get an appointment at the resource, how to get to the resource and a specific explanation of what the client may expect to occur once he arrives. . . .
>
> Providing the client with the name of a specific *person to contact* at the resource. . . .
>
> Providing the client with a *brief written statement* addressed to the resource, describing in precise terms the nature of the problem and what the client would like done. The client should be involved in the composition of this statement. . . .
>
> [Having the client call] the resource to make an appointment while he is in the worker's office. Alternately, the worker may place the call to ensure that the appropriate person is contacted, but the client then takes over the phone conversation. (p. 52)

With this last technique, it is important to remember that all too often the agency person on the other end of the phone does not really listen to the client and instead launches into a explanation of the service program, eligibility, and so on. Some instruction, support, and modeling for the client may be necessary to prepare the client to ask the right questions and be assertive during the phone conversation.

These connecting techniques have several advantages:

- The client has support during the introductory contact.
- The social worker can assist with drawing out needed information and clarification from both sides, serving to repeat and reinforce instructions given, as well as express immediate appreciation to the accepting agency.
- The client and social worker share the experience. This can be especially valuable if the contact turns out to be disappointing, rude, abrupt, or inappropriate.

24. Even after the client has had a first interview with the other agency, take action to firm up this connection. Weissman (1976) describes several ***cementing techniques*** designed to increase the chances that a client will continue with the agency beyond the first contact:

> *Checkback:* the client is asked to call the worker after the initial contact at the resource to summarize what has been accomplished so far.
>
> *Haunting:* the worker, with the client's approval, plans to contact the client by telephone after the initial contact at the resource and after each subsequent contact.
>
> *Sandwiching:* a planned interview with the client before he or she goes for the initial interview at the resource and immediately after the interview.
>
> *Alternating:* a planned series of interviews held intermittently during the period in which the client is involved in interviews at the resource. (p. 53)

These cementing techniques will uncover any misunderstandings or problems the client may be having with the agency. If detected early, they can be corrected before causing the client to withdraw from the agency.

25. Evaluate your referral work. It is important to do a follow-up evaluation on referrals to assess whether the client actually received what he or she wanted from the agency, if the client is making progress, and if additional information is available to help guide the referral experience with other clients in the future.

SELECTED BIBLIOGRAPHY

Abramson, Julie. "Six Steps to Effective Referrals." In *Agency-Based Social Work,* edited by Harold Weissman, Irwin Epstein, and Andrea Savage. Philadelphia: Temple University Press, 1983, pp. 65–71.

Matthews, R. Mark, and Stephen Fawcett. *Matching Clients and Services: Information and Referral.* Beverly Hills: Sage, 1981.

Weissman, Andrew. "Industrial Social Services: Linkage Technology." *Social Casework* 57 (January 1976): 50–54.

11.4 Obtaining Information from Other Agencies

PURPOSE: To secure client information from records maintained by other agencies and professionals.

DISCUSSION: It is often during intake that the social worker decides it is important to obtain client information contained in the records maintained by another agency or professional. For example, a social worker may conclude that it would be helpful to read a child's school record or medical report or perhaps read a child welfare agency record that describes how the child adjusted in a prior foster care placement. The process of gaining access to those records is controlled by a variety of federal and state laws and regulations. Different laws and regulations apply in different settings (e.g., hospitals, schools, adoption agencies, substance abuse programs, child protection agencies, etc.). Information concerning a client's treatment for drug and alcohol is very tightly controlled by federal law and regulation.

Generally speaking, client records belong to the client and therefore he or she can determine to whom they are released. Thus, if you want this information, it is necessary to secure the client's written permission. Similarly, you must not release client information to another agency or a professional outside your own agency without first receiving the client's written permission. There are, however, exceptions to this basic principle. For instance, a court order or a protective services agency investigator (i.e., investigation of child or elder abuse or neglect) may gain access to client records without the client's permission. In rare instances, the social worker will need to reveal selected client information when necessary to protect the client or others from imminent and serious physical harm.

The permission statement signed by the client is often called a ***Consent for Release of Confidential Information.*** Most agencies have developed a standard form for this purpose. A sample is presented in Figure 11.1. Parents or legal guardians control the release of information concerning minor-age children.

The client's permission must constitute an *informed consent.* Thus, before signing a release, the client should:

- Know what information is being requested, by whom, and for what purpose.
- Have an opportunity to read the material to be released or, if necessary, have it read and explained in words he or she can understand.
- Have an opportunity to correct any errors in the record before it is released.
- Know whether the professional or agency that will receive the information is being given permission to pass it on to a third party (the client must be given the opportunity to prohibit this transfer).
- Be informed of any negative consequences that might occur if he or she decides not to sign the consent.
- Understand that when the consent form is signed, he or she has a right to revoke this consent at a later date.

FIGURE 11.1 Sample Release Form

DEPARTMENT OF HEALTH AND HUMAN SERVICES
PUBLIC HEALTH SERVICE
INDIAN HEALTH SERVICE

AUTHORIZATION FOR RELEASE OF INFORMATION

Each section must be completed.

I. I, ______________________ , hereby request the disclosure of information from my record.
(Name of Patient)

II. The information is to be released **from:**

Name of Facility ______________________

Address ______________________

City/State ______________________

and is to be provided **to:**

Name of Person/Organization/Facility ______________________

Address ______________________

City/State ______________________

III. The purpose or need for this disclosure is: ______________________

IV. The information to be released is from my: *(Check one)*

☐ Medical Record ☐ Personnel Record ☐ Other *(specify):* ______________________

and includes: *(Check as appropriate)*

☐ The entire record, including any information on alcohol or drug abuse contained therein.

☐ Only information related to *(specify):* ______________________

____

☐ Only the period or events from: ______________ to ______________

V. I understand that I may revoke this authorization in writing at any time, except to the extent that action has been taken in reliance on this authorization. If this authorization has not been revoked, it will terminate one year from the date of my signature.

Signature of Patient: ______________________ ______________
(Date)

Signature of Parent, Guardian
or Authorized Representative *(if necessary):* ______________________ ______________
(Date)

Source: Privacy Act Procedures, Public Health Service, U.S. Department of Health and Human Services, Washington, DC: U.S. Government Printing Office, 1990.

In recent years, federal and state laws and regulations concerning client records have grown more complex. Their purpose is to provide citizens with greater privacy and make professionals and agencies more accountable for the records they keep. In general, they give social agency clients and hospital patients greater access to their own records, some control over what the record contains, and control over who else can read the record. In some instances, however, these laws and regulations may have the unintended effects of reducing confidentiality within the client-worker relationship, decreasing the usefulness of the professional record as a means of interprofessional communication, and decreasing interagency coordination.

The rules surrounding the release of client information can make it difficult for professionals and agencies to share information needed for an accurate diagnosis or assessment and can create an added barrier to effective case management and the coordination of services provided to the client by several different agencies. Laws giving clients easy access to their agency records have had a profound effect on what is placed into the record. Professionals may be reluctant to document information that could be upsetting or damaging to the client or family if they were to read the record. A school social worker, for example, may be reluctant to record the content of a discussion with a student about the parent-child relationship if the worker knows that the parent can review the school record and challenge what has been recorded. In reference to just such a situation, Kagle (1991, 188) observes that "it is ironic that in an effort to establish an important privacy safeguard (that is, by allowing parents to know what is in the record and therefore, know what is being communicated within the organization), the confidentiality of the worker-student relationship has been undermined."

The Federal Privacy Act of 1974, which applies to agencies receiving federal funds (except correctional agencies), assures a client access to his or her own records. The act defines a *record* as "any item, collection, or grouping of information about an individual that is maintained by an agency, including, but not limited to, his [or her] education, financial transactions, medical history, and criminal or employment history and that contains his [or her] name, or the identifying number, symbol, or other identifying particular assigned to the individual."

Deciding what is and is not part of an official agency record is more difficult than it might appear. For example, is a report prepared by a private psychologist part of the agency record just because it has been placed in the file? Or what about a report the social worker obtained from a school? The social worker must clearly understand agency policy and procedure concerning such questions before responding to a written request to release a client record.

In the absence of legal and policy guidance to the contrary, it is best to presume that records and reports prepared by and obtained from a third party (e.g., a doctor, another agency) are not a part of your own agency's record. In other words, the authors suggest that an agency record be defined as only the material written by agency staff. Thus, you should not release reports that were prepared by someone outside your own agency, even if your client previously gave you permission to obtain them from the third party. Also, when documenting service to a client, the social worker should always operate on the assumption that clients have a right to be told exactly what records are being kept, have full access to his or her record, and may copy, question, and correct the record.

Within the context of this discussion concerning the protection and release of client information, it is important that the reader understand a related concept. Some professional licensing laws provide for what is termed *privileged communication.* The extent of the privilege is governed by state statutes. It usually applies to doctor-patient, attorney-client, husband-wife, and priest-penitent relationships. Some laws might also extend the privilege to the social worker–client relationship. This privilege belongs to the client, not to the professional; it can be claimed by the client when he or she learns that information covered by the privilege has been subpoenaed and could be disclosed in a trial. The client then asks the judge to recognize the privilege and prevent the disclosure. The judge makes the decision on the basis of whether there is a compelling need to reveal the information.

SELECTED BIBLIOGRAPHY

Dickson, Donald. *Confidentiality and Privacy in Social Work.* New York: Free Press, 1998.

Gothard, Sol. "Legal Issues: Confidentiality and Privileged Communication." In *Encyclopedia of Social Work,* 19th ed., vol. 2, edited by Richard Edwards. Washington, DC: NASW, 1995, pp. 1579–1584.

Kagle, Jill. *Social Work Records,* 2nd ed. Belmont, CA: Wadsworth, 1991.

Public Health Service. *Privacy Act Procedures.* Washington DC: U.S. Department of Health and Human Services, August 1990.

11.5 The In-Home Interview

PURPOSE: To engage and deliver services to the client who cannot or will not meet in an office setting and/or to secure a more accurate assessment by observing the client in his or her natural environment.

DISCUSSION: The terms *in-home interview* and *home visit* refer to a meeting between social worker and client in the client's home. In the early days of social work, home visiting was the *modus operandi* of the worker. In later years, the home visit was abandoned by many because it did not seem "professional" and did not fit the popular office-based models of therapy. Of course, the home visit has always been used heavily by social workers in child protection and public health agencies and by those providing services to the elderly. The home visit is an essential component in all outreach activities and of critical importance in work with the hard-to-reach client (see Item 11.7).

Despite its usefulness and necessity in many cases, the in-home interview is a source of anxiety for many social workers. A number of guidelines can help the worker make proper use of this valuable diagnostic and treatment tool:

1. Understand the rationale for observing clients in their usual environment. Sherman and Fredman (1986) explain that

> information which is not readily presented in office visits may come across as the therapist interacts in a setting that is more natural to the family. Arranged home visits have the potential for decreasing family defensiveness and promoting the involvement of the entire family. It is a more natural setting for the family's functioning. It may also be possible that behavior change achieved in the home environment is both more adaptive to the family's reality and more likely to be retained. (p. 238)

The home visit is especially valuable in helping the worker develop empathy for the client and in understanding how the environment impinges on the client.

2. Appreciate the depth of understanding that can be gained from an in-home interview. Ebeling and Hill (1983) explain that a person's home is his or her "sacred" space and a reflection of the individual's personality and life-style:

> Within the walls of a home, people experience the intimate moments of their lives. They sleep, wake up, bathe, eat, drink, make love, raise children. They fight, scream, and rejoice; they cry, laugh, and sing. They may experience the warmth of positive object relationships, the anguish of negative ones, or isolation and loneliness. . . .
>
> Their outer space reflects their inner space. The way the homes are decorated and furnished can reveal either the chosen life-style of the occupants or their economic position. It can also indicate depression, despair, and disorganization. (p. 64)

3. Do not confuse the in-home interview with a purely social or friendly visit. This technique, like all others, is to be used in a purposeful manner. When it is the social worker who requests an in-home interview, the client should be given a clear explanation as to how and why it will make the service more effective.

4. An in-home interview should be scheduled at a mutually convenient time. Unannounced visits should be avoided but may be necessary when the client does not have a phone or is unable to read a letter, or when prior attempts to reach the client have failed. If you must stop by a client's home unannounced, explain immediately your previous efforts to reach him or her and use the conversation to set up a scheduled visit. (Often, the client will immediately invite you in.)

5. When you enter the home of a client, extend the same respect and courtesy you expect when someone enters your home. Ask where you are to be seated. Accept an appropriate offer of food or drink. Convey a genuine interest in family pictures and household furnishings that are an expression of the client's identity, interests, and culture. Ebeling and Hill (1983, 66) remind us that it is essential that the social worker never show shock or disapproval as he or she enters the client's home—their sacred space: "No matter what the condition of the building, . . . regardless of the number of dogs, the darkness of the halls, or the odors of the stairways; no matter how barren or cluttered or 'hospital' clean; even no matter what signs of impulsivity, violence, or sexual acting out are encountered."

6. Obtaining sufficient privacy is often a problem during a home visit—children may run in and out of the house, neighbors may stop by, the telephone may ring, and the TV may be blaring. This will be distracting to you but possibly not to your client. On the positive side, such distractions provide an accurate picture of the family's real-life functioning and their ecosystem. Significant distractions are best dealt with directly by expressing a need for privacy and for attention to the interview's purpose. When friends or neighbors are in the home, the client should be asked if it is permissible to discuss private matters in their presence. Some clients may invite their informal helpers and supportive friends to sit in on the interview and this choice should be respected.

7. If your client lives in a high-crime neighborhood, it is important to schedule the home visit for a time when the risks are at a minimum. Ask your client if you should take some special precautions and to describe the safest route.

SELECTED BIBLIOGRAPHY

Ebeling, Nancy, and Deborah Hill, eds. *Child Abuse and Neglect.* Boston: John Wright, PSG, Inc., 1983.

Sherman, Robert, and Norman Fredman. *Handbook of Structured Techniques in Marriage and Family Therapy.* New York: Brunner/Mazel, 1986.

Wasik, Barbara. *Home Visiting: Procedures for Helping Families.* Newbury, CA: Sage, 1990.

Weiss, Marc. "Using House Calls in a Psychotherapy Practice." In *Innovations in Clinical Practice: A Source Book,* vol. 9, edited by Peter Keller and Steven Heyman. Sarasota, FL: Professional Resource Exchange, 1990, pp. 229–238.

11.6 Engaging the Involuntary Client

PURPOSE: To begin building a working relationship with a client who was forced into contact with a social worker and agency.

DISCUSSION: The term ***involuntary client*** refers to an individual who is required or mandated to seek and make use of professional help. The external pressure bringing the person into contact with the worker may be a legal authority such as a judge, probation officer, or child protection agency; a powerful family member; or an employer. Such a client is often resentful, angry, and sometimes belligerent. Needless to say, social workers would much rather work with a client who asks Who am I? rather than the client who asks Who are you? What are you doing here? and When are you going to get out of here? It is a challenge to engage the involuntary client in the helping process, but it can be done.

In most cases involving an involuntary client, the social worker will possess some degree of official authority. For example, social workers employed in child protection, probation, and parole are granted authority by law to impose a certain course of action on a client. Many social workers are uncomfortable with such authority and avoid using it; others overuse or misuse legitimate authority. Workers who are in positions of legal authority must use it in ways that are helpful to the client. A worker's compassionate and fair exercise of legitimate authority can be a therapeutic experience for clients who associate authority with abuse and exploitation. An experienced probation and parole officer (Hardman 1960), offers the following advice on the appropriate use of authority:

> I will make crystal clear, in defining my role, where my authority begins and ends, and I will consistently function within these limits. I will avoid veiled threats, bluffing, or any behavior that might be so interpreted, since this clouds, rather than clarifies my limits. This rule will eliminate a vast amount of testing by the client. I will further clarify which decisions are mine to make and which the client must make. . . . Once I have made a decision, I will steadfastly resist all client efforts to alter my decision by threats, tantrums, seduction, illness, etc. I will just as steadfastly defend his right to make his decisions and stand by them. By the same token, if a client shows me rational evidence that I have made a hasty or unwise decision, I will alter it and will tell him so. Common terms which [clients] . . . use to describe authority are "arbitrary, inconsistent, and unfair." For this reason I must demonstrate that authority can be considerate, consistent and fair. (p. 17)

Filip, McDaniel, and Schene (1992) remind child protection workers (CPS) of the therapeutic use of authority with the following:

- Use your authority in a warm, personal, supportive manner and show an understanding of the parents' feelings about the problem.
- A family may feel less fearful of your authority if you demonstrate a non-threatening and non-coercive attitude.
- Help your client to see that you represent a reasonable authority so that (s)he can learn that other authority figures can also be reasonable.
- Demonstrate your authority in a manner which indicates that you have no hidden agenda, that is, be honest.
- Clarify your protective service role and function. Do not retreat from your responsibility; make the family aware of the expectations for change and the consequences of no change in their behavior. Make them aware that you will develop a plan for your work together and that there are consequences should the changes in their behavior not occur and their child be considered at-risk.
- Make the family aware of your knowledge that CPS intervention can be traumatic and you will do your best to minimize that trauma. Remember the experience may be traumatic for both children and parents. . . .
- Avoid insensitivity to parental feelings since insensitivity may create anger, hostility, and resistance and will make it difficult for you to establish a helping relationship.
- Avoid excessive reliance on your legal authority. (p. 45)

Consider the following guidelines when working with the involuntary client:

1. Prepare yourself for the session by anticipating how the client may respond and recalling how it feels when you are forced to do something you do not want to do.

2. When you first meet with your client, reveal the factual information you have about why the client is involved with your agency, and ask the client to correct any misunderstandings you may have about this information. Seek clarification from the referring source if there is a significant discrepancy between what the client has been told about why he or she must seek professional help and what you have been told by the referring person.

3. Provide a clear and completely honest explanation of both your role and responsibility and what you or your agency expect of the client. Also, explain the rules of confidentiality that apply. For example, if you are expected to prepare a report to the court, the client has a right to know that what he or she tells you may end up in this report and be discussed by the judge and attorneys in open court.

4. Inform the client of any adverse consequences that may occur if he or she does not cooperate. However, respect the client's right to choose the consequences rather than your services. Remind the client who decides not to cooperate that he or she is, in effect, giving up the control he or she has to influence the outcome.

5. Assume that the client has negative feelings about being forced into contact with a social worker. Be prepared to encounter hostility, anger, shame and embarrassment, and a number of defensive reactions (see Item 8.7). Foremost, you need to address the client's negativism. Do not ignore or avoid these feelings; deal with them directly. Use basic interviewing skills to help the client express negative feelings. Do not ask questions that could be construed as an attempt to trap the client or catch him or her in a lie.

6. Discuss the client's previous experience with professionals or the "system," along with any preconceived notions he or she has about social workers, counselors, or other professional helpers. Be aware of the client's cultural background or experience with discrimination and how this might add to his or her feeling of being overpowered by or alienated from social institutions.

7. Within the limits and legal constraints placed on the client, give him or her as much choice as possible. Allowing the client to make some choices and have some degree of control over even minor details will usually lower his or her resistance—for example: "We have to meet each Wednesday for the next six weeks. We can meet either at 2:00 P.M. or 4:00 P.M. What is your choice?"

8. Consider trying the "Let's make a deal" tactic. In this approach, the worker agrees to do something that will lessen the client's discomfort or help the client get something he or she wants (something legal and legitimate) in exchange for the client's cooperation or the client's completion of certain specified tasks.

9. There is no such thing as an unmotivated client. All clients are motivated—all have wants, needs, and preferences. When a social worker labels a client "unmotivated," he or she is simply acknowledging that what the client wants is different from what the worker wants for the client. Successfully engaging the involuntary client requires that the worker tap into the client's own needs and wants and establish intervention goals that are at least partially consistent with the client's own wishes and inclinations. Some workers call this "moving with the motive." Work hard to identify something that both you and the client agree is a goal or a desirable course of action. Once there is an agreed upon goal, you can more easily engage the client in problem solving. For example, you might say, "Well, we both want you to get off probation so you won't have to see me each week. What ideas do you have on how we can work together to reach that goal?"

10. Highlight the client's strengths and make frequent use of the reframing technique (see Item 14.12). Use the problem search technique (see Item 13.2) if you and the client cannot agree on the problems that need to be addressed.

11. With most clients, some degree of self-disclosure by the worker has the effect of breaking down client defensiveness. However, when working with a prison inmate population, sociopathic individuals, or persons who are skilled manipulators, you should avoid sharing personal information (see Item 11.9). The use of self-disclosure with these individuals will usually have unwanted consequences, as many have an uncanny ability to spot and exploit a helper's personal weakness. For similar reasons, you must never break or even bend agency rules as a favor to the client; even a minor concession quickly leads to further requests or a "blackmail" situation (e.g., "Look, if you won't do . . . for me, I'll tell your supervisor that you violated program rules when you allowed me to. . .").

SELECTED BIBLIOGRAPHY

Filip, Judee, Nancy McDaniel, and Patricia Schene, eds. *Helping in Child Protective Services.* Englewood, CO: American Humane Association, 1992.

Hardman, Dale. "The Functions of the Probation Officer." *Federal Probation* 24 (September 1960): 3–10.

Harris, George, ed. *Tough Customer: Counseling Unwilling Clients.* Laurel, MD: American Correctional Association, 1991.

Ivanoff, Andre, Betty Blythe, and Tony Tripodi. *Involuntary Clients in Social Work Practice.* New York: Aldine de Gruyter, 1994.

Rooney, Ronald. *Strategies for Work with Involuntary Clients.* New York: Columbia University Press, 1991.

11.7 Engaging the Hard-to-Reach Client

PURPOSE: To build a working relationship with a client who is distrustful and reluctant to become involved.

DISCUSSION: The term ***hard to reach*** is used here to describe a client with whom it is extremely difficult to build a relationship. Most of these clients are socially isolated, fearful, and distrustful. Many suffer from serious mental illness and/or are extremely uncomfortable in interpersonal relations. The term *hard to reach* should not be confused with the term *involuntary client;* some hard-to-reach clients are, in fact, voluntary, and many involuntary clients are actually quite easy to engage. In working with the hard to reach, the greatest challenge is to break through the client's distrust. Several guidelines should be followed:

1. You must be willing to use unconventional methods. The techniques that are most effective are usually not ones drawn from the traditional approaches to psychotherapy and counseling, nor ones used by conventional mental health and social service agencies. Homebuilders, a program operated by Behavioral Sciences Institute based in Federal Way, Washington, established a remarkable record of effective work with highly dysfunctional, multiproblem, and hard-to-reach families in imminent risk of having a child placed into foster care. Among the methods and principles that contributed to that success are: (a) reaching out to families while they are in crisis; (b) responding to the family within 24 hours of referral; (c) being available to families 24 hours a day, seven days a week; (d) meeting with families in their home, not in an office setting; and (e) a willingness and ability to provide a wide variety of services (e.g., helping to clean the kitchen floor, meeting basic needs for food and shelter, case coordination, and applying the most sophisticated of psychotherapeutic techniques, such as individual and family therapy, assertiveness training, behavior management, etc.).

2. Remember that first impressions are extremely important to these clients. They are quick to form judgments; more often than not, they interpret situations in the most negative way possible. To be effective, you must be a warm, giving, and dependable person. Use a liberal dose of self-disclosure to help the client see you as a real and genuine person. In many ways, you must become a good parent figure to the client—loving but firm. That firmness and concern may express itself in the gentle setting of limits on what is and is not acceptable behavior.

3. Be prepared to tolerate a great deal of testing behavior, and be patient when progress is slow. Many hard-to-reach clients have been so beaten down by life that they feel hopeless about ever making a change in their situation.

4. Be very tactful. The feelings of hard-to-reach clients are easily hurt and many are supersensitive to any hint of rejection. Do nothing that could be construed as criticism. If you accidentally do something that is hurtful to the client, discuss it immediately and repair the damaged relationship; if you do not, the client may withdraw from the relationship, once again convinced that no one can be trusted.

5. In the early stages of relationship building, you will probably need to do many things *for* the client before reaching the point where you do things *with* the client. Strive to demonstrate your good will and usefulness to the client in a concrete way. Home visits, sending birthday cards, sharing food, and other tangible expressions of concern are usually necessary. By doing things for the client and by "feeding" the client's dependency needs, you provide assurance that you are "safe." By becoming useful to the client, you become attractive and thereby gain some psychological leverage. Unless you become attractive and a reinforcer, the client's distrust will keep him or her from entering into even a superficial relationship. Do not worry about creating overdependency. That problem can be addressed later. Remember, your first objective is simply to build a human bond or connection.

6. Encourage frequent contacts. As a general rule, the more often people interact, the more important they become to each other. Use frequent phone calls and brief letters to supplement face-to-face interviews.

7. Place only minimal demands or expectations on the client until you have developed a meaningful relationship. This does not mean you should be completely permissive, however. You need to help the client understand that the two of you are to work on the client's problems and that you will not tolerate destructive or manipulative behavior.

8. If the client announces that he or she does not want to talk about certain topics, explain that his or her decision is acceptable and that you will not ask the client to talk about those topics. But then follow up with an effort to engage the client in a discussion of general reasons why some topics might be hard for people to discuss and why people often want to withhold and protect certain information. These reasons might include feelings of shame and embarrassment, not knowing what words to use, not knowing how the social worker will react, not knowing if the worker would understand, fear that the worker might be judgmental, fear of a lack of confidentiality, fear that the information will be used to exploit the client, and so on. Very often this general discussion of common fears and concerns will reveal to the client that the worker can be trusted and the client will then decide to talk about previously protected topics.

SELECTED BIBLIOGRAPHY

Harris, George, and David Watkins. *Counseling the Involuntary and Resistant Client.* Laurel, MD: American Correctional Association, 1987.

Kaplan, Lisa. *Working with Multiproblem Families.* Lexington, MA: Lexington Books, 1986.

Kinney, Jill, David Haapla, and Charlotte Booth. *Keeping Families Together: The Homebuilders Model.* New York: Aldine, 1991.

Rothman, Jack, and Jon Simon Sager. *Case Management,* 2nd ed. Boston: Allyn and Bacon, 1998.

11.8 Engaging the Client Who Is Chemically Dependent

PURPOSE: To engage the chemically dependent client in a way that increases the chances he or she will seek treatment.

DISCUSSION: Many of the individuals receiving services from social agencies suffer directly or indirectly from the effects of alcoholism and drug abuse. The abuse of chemicals is contributing factor in other problems such as marital discord, parent-child conflict, spouse abuse, child abuse and neglect, suicide, homicide, financial problems, crime, and auto accidents. Substance abuse also contributes to the spread of AIDS due to intravenous injections and indiscriminate sexual behavior related to the disinhibiting effects of drugs and alcohol. The use of alcohol and drugs by a pregnant woman can damage the fetus and result in various birth defects and neurological and developmental problems.

Most social workers consider the actively drinking alcoholic and drug user to be difficult clients, in part because of the extreme denial, rationalization, and self-centeredness that is a part of the addictive process. A social worker's response to this type of client must be based on an understanding of how these chemicals affect mind and body and on the realization that it is nearly impossible for an individual to break an addiction without specialized treatment.

Some professionals find it useful to distinguish between dependency and abuse. *Chemical abuse* or *substance abuse* refers to occasional use that causes problems in only one or two areas of functioning. In contrast, *chemical dependency* refers to a pattern of frequent use that is affecting several areas of personal and social functioning.

A ***chemical dependency*** can be defined as a pathological relationship with a mood-altering substance. The dynamics of this relationship resemble those of a neurotic love affair, but in this case the love object is a chemical. Each time the chemical is used, its mood-altering effects reinforce usage, and over time this learning process results in *psychological addiction.* In addition, many drugs alter body chemistry, and this can lead to a *physical addiction* and such symptoms as craving and withdrawal. Central to the physical addiction process is the gradual development of *tolerance* (i.e., more and more of the chemical is necessary to create its desired mood-altering effect).

Generally speaking, the chemicals most sought after are those with the most rapid onset of action. Onset of effect is related to chemical properties, dose, method of intake, and characteristics of the user. The effect of a chemical is also influenced by the psychosocial setting of its use.

There are local and regional differences in the popularity of certain chemicals, terminology, and preferred methods of intake. There are continual changes in the street lingo applied to illegal substances and new chemical combinations appear frequently. Provided here are brief descriptions of the legal and illegal substances most often abused and that serve as the basic ingredients for new combinations.

Nicotine

The nicotine found in tobacco is highly addictive. Because this stimulant is so widely used and is a contributing cause in cancer and heart and lung disease, nicotine may lead to more illness and death than all of the illegal street drugs combined. Tobacco is usually smoked but is also chewed or placed next to the gums in the form of "snuff."

Alcohol

If one considers the number of individuals and families affected, the number of injuries and deaths caused by drunken driving, and the number of health problems either caused or exacerbated by drinking, the abuse of alcohol (a legal drug) is the number one drug problem in the United States. Because alcohol depresses the central nervous system (CNS), it can be very dangerous when used with other drugs or medications that also depress the CNS.

In 1990, the National Council on Alcoholism and the American Society of Addiction Medicine approved the following definition of ***alcoholism:***

> A primary, chronic disease with genetic, psychosocial, and environmental factors influencing its development and manifestations. The disease is often progressive and fatal. It is characterized by continuous or periodic: impaired control over drinking, preoccupation with the drug alcohol, use of alcohol despite adverse consequences, and distortions in thinking, most notable denial.

There is no cure; at best, alcoholism can be controlled through complete abstinence. Experts generally agree that it is not possible for an alcoholic to become a social drinker; if the alcoholic tries, he or she soon slips back into a pattern of problem drinking.

In its early stage, alcoholism is difficult to recognize because symptoms are subtle. However, one may observe that the person drinks a lot and that alcohol has a part in many of his or her activities. The incipient alcoholic can consume a great deal without showing the effects; this phenomenon may be genetic in origin. At this early stage, the consumption of alcohol does not significantly interfere with job or family functioning and may be almost indistinguishable from the person who only occasionally drinks too much.

In the middle stage, the alcoholic is physically addicted. When his or her blood alcohol level is lowered, the alcoholic will experience withdrawal symptoms, including anxiety, agitation, and tremors. Family and job functioning are now affected. It is common for family and friends to pressure the alcoholic to cut back. Concerned family members may reach out for help, but typically the alcoholic denies there is a problem. He or she may quit for weeks or months at a time but eventually starts again. These short periods of abstinence convince the alcoholic that he or she can quit at any time and that alcohol is not a problem.

In the later stage of alcoholism, the existence of a serious problem is apparent to all but the alcoholic. Although family, job, and health are affected, the denial continues, at least until some major crisis occurs (e.g., an accident, loss of job, health problems, divorce, etc.). It may take from 5 to 15 years of drinking for an adult to develop alcoholism. This illness may develop in an adolescent after only 6 to 18 months of heavy drinking.

The following list identifies a number of the ***symptoms of alcoholism.*** Usually, the alcoholic will display several of these:

- Inability to stop at one or two drinks; increase in the amount of alcohol consumed; "gulping" drinks
- Increased dependency on alcohol; hiding and protecting liquor supply
- Inability to remember what occurred while drinking (blackouts)
- Drinking alone; needing a drink the next morning
- Lateness and absenteeism at work; neglect of financial obligations
- Neglect or indifference to personal appearance
- Deterioration of moral and ethical behavior
- Family quarrels and family tensions over drinking
- Lateness in returning home (growing number of excuses or none at all)

- Changes in eating and sleeping habits; grandiose beliefs; hallucinations; persistent remorse; increased irritability
- Suspiciousness of family and friends; loss of friendships
- Hostile and belligerent behavior when drinking
- Hand tremors and increased nervousness; falling and stumbling
- Angry denial that there is a drinking problem, usually accompanied with a strong "alibi system" to excuse or minimize drinking
- In its terminal phases, health problems affecting such vital organs as the brain, liver, and gastrointestinal system

Amphetamines

There are several forms of amphetamines. All are CNS stimulants. Some (e.g., Dexedrine and Benzedrine) are manufactured by pharmaceutical companies and prescribed in the treatment of narcolepsy, brain dysfunction, and obesity. When these prescription drugs are sold illegally on the street, they are often called "uppers," "dexies," "bennies," and so on. As new laws placed tight controls on the prescription use of these drugs, related forms (i.e. the methamphetamines) were produced illegally and are now widely used because of their strength, low cost, and the ease with which they can be manufactured in simple laboratories.

Among the forms of methamphetamine are methamphetamine sulfate (i.e., "crank"), methamphetamine hydrochloride (i.e., "crystal meth"), and dextromethamphetamine (i.e., "ice"). These chemicals produce an intense and long-lasting euphoria and have been called the "poor man's cocaine." Depending on their form, they may be snorted, swallowed, smoked, or injected.

The abuse of these stimulants is indicated by hyperactivity, nervousness and anxiety, dilated pupils, irritability, and going for long periods without sleep or food. Some users experience a dry mouth, sweating, headache, blurred vision, dizziness, and sleeplessness. High doses can cause dangerously rapid or irregular heartbeat, tremors, loss of coordination, and physical collapse. Long-time and heavy use can lead to malnutrition, skin disorders, ulcers, weight loss, kidney damage, depression, and speech and thought disturbances. A methamphetamine injection causes a sudden increase in blood pressure that can precipitate a stroke or heart failure.

Heavy use can result in a psychosis involving hallucinations (seeing hearing, and feeling things that do not exist), delusions (having irrational thoughts or beliefs), and paranoia (feeling as though people are out to harm himor her). In such a state, the person may exhibit bizarre and sometimes violent behavior. Methamphetamine use is a major factor in some cases of child abuse, domestic abuse, and other forms of violence.

Related to the amphetamines are the so-called designer drugs—drugs whose molecular structure has been modified in order to produce a stronger effect or escape legal sanctions.

Cocaine

Cocaine, like the amphetamines, is a CNS stimulant. It is smuggled into the United States as a fine, white, crystalline powder (cocaine hydrochloride). This powder is then diluted, or "cut," to increase its bulk and stretch the supply for sale.

The most common method of administration is intranasal, or "snorting" the diluted powder. When snorted, the euphoric effects begin within a few minutes, peak within 15 to 20 minutes, and disappear within about 45 minutes. During this brief period, the user often feels confident, energetic, talkative, and omnipotent.

Chemical procedures can be used to separate or free the pure cocaine from the other usual additives in powdered cocaine. This results in "freebase" that can be smoked—a more direct and rapid way to transmit the chemical to the brain. Smokeable "crack" or "rock cocaine" is particularly potent and highly addictive.

The smoking of "crack" produces a short but very intense "high." Whereas the users of powdered cocaine may develop their addiction over many months or even years, "crack" smokers can become addicted in a matter of days.

Since freebase cocaine is water soluble, it can also be injected. This is the most dangerous method of administration. Because it produces an immediate and intense euphoria, intravenous use is highly addictive.

Regular users of cocaine often report feelings of restlessness, irritability, anxiety, and sleeplessness. Cocaine causes physical and mental damage similar to that caused by the amphetamines. High doses over a long period may precipitate a "cocaine psychosis" with hallucinations of touch, sight, taste, or smell. Because cocaine stimulates the body and its nervous system, it is not uncommon to experience a physical "crash" and a mental depression following a period of use. The depressions can be debilitating and last from a few hours to several days.

Marijuana

Marijuana is the common name for a drug made from the plant *cannabis sativa.* The main psychoactive ingredient in marijuana is THC (delta-9-tetrahydrocannabinol). The amount of THC in the marijuana determines how strong its effects will be on the user. Hashish, or hash, is made by taking the resin from the leaves and flowers of the plant and pressing it into cakes; it contains more THC than crude marijuana. Marijuana and hash are usually smoked but sometimes taken orally.

Research and the clinical experience of drug treatment programs identify several adverse effects. Some individuals become psychologically addicted and heavy users may develop "amotivational syndrome," a general loss of interest in life's activities and an increase in passivity and sluggishness.

An individual "high" on marijuana or hashish will feel euphoric and may speak rapidly and loudly and have dilated pupils. Some individuals experience sensory distortions. The drug can impair short-term memory, alter sense of time, and reduce the ability to do things that require concentration and quick reactions such as in driving a car. A possible response to marijuana is an acute panic reaction.

PCP

PCP (phencyclidine) was developed as an anesthetic but later taken off the market for human use because it sometimes caused hallucinations. It continues to have use in veterinary medicine. PCP is easily manufactured and is available in a number of forms (i.e., white crystal-like powder, tablet, or capsule). It can be swallowed, smoked, sniffed, or injected. PCP is sometimes sprinkled on marijuana and smoked.

It is sometimes sold as mescaline or THC, thus the user of those drugs may get PCP by mistake.

The sought-after effect is euphoria. For some, small amounts act as a stimulant. For many users, PCP changes how they perceive their own bodies and things around them; movements and time are slowed. The effects of PCP are unpredictable, and for this reason many "experimenters" abandon its use. Others, unfortunately, become dependent. Negative effects include increased heart rate and blood pressure, flushing, sweating, dizziness, and numbness. When large doses are taken, effects include drowsiness, convulsions, coma, and sometimes death. PCP, sometimes called "angel dust," can produce violent or bizarre behavior. Regular use affects memory, perception, concentration, and judgment. Users may show signs of paranoia, fearfulness, and anxiety. When under the drug's influence, some become aggressive; others withdraw and have difficulty communicating. A PCP-induced psychosis may last for days or weeks.

Hallucinogens

Hallucinogens, or psychedelics, are drugs that affect a person's perceptions, sensations, thinking, self-awareness, and emotions. Hallucinogens include such drugs as LSD, mescaline, psilocybin, and DMT. *LSD* is manufactured from lysergic acid, which is found in a fungus that grows on grains; it is one of the most potent mood-changing chemicals. LSD is sold on the street in tablets, capsules, or occasionally in liquid form. It is usually taken by mouth but sometimes is injected. *DMT* is similar to LSD. *Mescaline* comes from the peyote cactus and, although it is not as strong as LSD, its effects are similar. Mescaline is usually smoked or swallowed in the form of capsules or tablets. *Psilocybin* comes from certain mushrooms. It is sold in tablet or capsule form or the mushrooms themselves may be eaten.

The effects of psychedelics are unpredictable and depend on dosage as well as the user's personality, mood, expectations, and the surroundings. Usually, the user feels the first effects 30 to 90 minutes after taking it. The person's sense of time and self change. Several different emotions may be felt at once or swing rapidly from one to another. Sensations become mixed and seem to "cross over," giving the user the feeling of hearing colors and seeing sounds. For some, these strange sensations are frightening and cause a "bad trip" that may last a few minutes or several hours and involve confusion, suspiciousness, anxiety, feelings of helplessness, and loss of control. Physical effects include dilated pupils, higher body temperature, increased heart rate and blood pressure, and often sweating, irregular breathing, and tremors. Some users sit in a stupor, whereas others become agitated.

Taking a hallucinogen can unmask mental or emotional problems. Flashbacks, in which the person experiences a drug's effects without having to take the drug again, can occur. Heavy users sometimes develop impaired memory, loss of attention span, confusion, and difficulty with abstract thinking.

Sedative Hypnotics

Sedative hypnotics are prescription drugs often referred to as sleeping pills, sedatives, and tranquilizers (antianxiety medications). Two major categories are the barbiturates and the benzodiazepines. Because they depress the central nervous systems, they have a calming effect and promote sleep. An individual who has taken a higher than prescribed dosage may give the appearance of being drunk (e.g., staggering, slurred speech, sleepiness, etc.) but not smell of alcohol. When taken with alcohol (also a depressant), these drugs can cause unconsciousness and death.

The sedative-hypnotic drugs can cause both physical and psychological dependence. When regular users suddenly stop, they may develop withdrawal symptoms, ranging from restlessness, insomnia, and anxiety to convulsions and death. Barbiturate overdose is a factor in many drug-related deaths; these include suicides and accidental poisonings.

Inhalants

Inhalants are chemicals that produce psychoactive vapors. They are grouped into four classes (1) volatile solvents (e.g., certain glues, gasoline, paint thinner, nail polish remover, lighter fluid); (2) aerosols (e.g., spray paints); (3) anesthetics (e.g., ether, chloroform, nitrous oxide); and (4) amyl and butyl nitrates. Nearly all of the abused inhalants act to depress the body's functions. At low doses, users may feel slightly stimulated and some, like butyl nitrite, produce a "rush" or "high" lasting for a few seconds or a couple of minutes. Young people are likely to abuse inhalants, in part because these chemicals are readily available and inexpensive.

Possible negative effects include nausea, sneezing, coughing, nosebleeds, fatigue, bad breath, lack of coordination, and a loss of appetite. Solvents and aerosols decrease the heart and breathing rates and affect judgment. Deep breathing of the vapors may result in a loss of self-control, violent behavior, and unconsciousness. Inhalants can cause death from suffocation by displacing oxygen in the lungs and by depressing the central nervous system to a point that breathing stops. Long-term use can damage the brain, liver, kidneys, blood, and bone marrow.

Opiates

Opiates (narcotics) are a group of drugs used medically to relieve pain, but they also have a high potential for abuse. Some opiates (opium, morphine, heroin, and codeine) come from the Asian poppy. Others, such as meperidine (Demerol), are manufactured. Heroin accounts for most of the opiate abuse in the United States.

Opiates are ingested, snorted, smoked, or injected intravenously. After causing an initial rush, they tend to relax the user. Indicators of opiate abuse include needle scars on the arms and the backs of hands, drowsiness, frequent scratching, red and watering eyes, sniffles, and a loss of appetite overall but an attraction to sugar and candies. In contrast to the effects of most other abused drugs that dilate the eye's pupils, the opiates constrict the pupils. When an opiate-dependent person stops taking the drug, withdrawal symptoms begin within 4 to 6 hours; symptoms include anxiety, diarrhea, abdominal cramps, chills, sweating, nausea, and runny nose and eyes. The intensity of these symptoms depends on how much was taken, how often, and for how long. Withdrawal symptoms for most opiates are stronger approximately 24 to 72 hours after they begin but subside within 7 to 10 days.

Most of the physical dangers of opiate abuse are caused by overdose, the use of unsterile needles, contamination of the drug by other chemicals, or combining the drug with other substances. Over time, opiate users may develop infections of the heart, skin abscesses, and congested lungs.

Guidelines

Social workers should follow a number of guidelines during their initial contact with the chemically dependent individual and his or her family:

1. Because the abuse of alcohol and other drugs is such a pervasive problem in our society, assume that it will be a contributing cause to many of the individual and family problems you encounter in direct practice. The existence of a chemical dependency must be considered a possibility even when there has been no mention of the problem by the client and his or her family.

2. Drugs and alcohol are used because they make people feel better, even if but for a short time. Curiosity and peer pressure also play a role. The powerful reinforcement provided by the chemical's mood-altering effects often leads to dependence. No one starts using a drug with the intention of becoming dependent or addicted; in fact, beginners usually believe they are invulnerable to addiction. There is a steady supply of both legal drugs (e.g., alcohol) and illegal drugs because so much money can be made in this market.

3. Never underestimate the psychological power of alcohol and drugs. The addictive process can turn an otherwise kind and honest person into a self-centered individual who is willing to lie, cheat, and even injure loved ones in order to protect and maintain his or her love relationship with a chemical. Typically, the user is adamant in denying any dependence on a substance and denies any connection between his or her problems in life and his or her use of alcohol or a drug.

4. Be alert to ***signs of abuse and dependency.*** An individual with a significant drug (or alcohol) problem will probably exhibit several of the following behaviors and patterns:

- Takes more of the substance and takes it for a longer period of time than was intended
- Experiences frequent intoxication and withdrawal symptoms that interfere with performance of work, school, or family roles
- Uses substance to relieve withdrawal symptoms
- Develops tolerance to drug (i.e., more and more of substance is needed in order to attain the desired mood-altering effect)
- Has a persistent desire to quit and/or has experienced one or more unsuccessful efforts to quit
- Spends much time securing, protecting, and taking the substance
- Gives up previously valued and important activities (e.g., family, work, recreation, etc.) in favor of drinking and drug use
- Continually uses substance even though aware that its use is causing family, social, or health problems
- Neglects appearance and bodily hygiene
- Experiences a decrease in physical and intellectual capacities (e.g., ability to concentrate, stay on track, think logically)
- Participates in illegal activities (e.g., stealing, prostitution, etc.) when there has been no prior history of such activities

- Makes efforts to cover needle scars on arms
- Uses sunglasses to protect dilated eyes from light

5. Assess the degree to which your client's psychosocial functioning is impaired by his or her drug use. If it is a problem, referral to a treatment program is imperative. Consult with treatment specialists on how best to overcome the client's denial and resistance.

6. Learn about the 12-step recovery programs by attending "open" meetings and talking with members. Members are usually eager to consult with professionals who are trying to decide how best to approach problems presented by the chemically dependent client.

7. Be patient and nonjudgmental but do not be afraid to be confrontive in your communications. You will not help the chemically dependent client by accepting his or her denials, alibis, rationalizations, or manipulations—all of which are part of the addictive process.

8. If you are a recovering alcoholic or drug abuser, share this fact with the client. Emphasize that you know from personal experience that controlling the problem is a difficult, day-by-day struggle, but that it is possible.

9. Do not lend the client money, and do not become part of the enabling system that "covers" for the client by protecting him or her from the real-life consequences of chemical abuse.

10. If your client comes to an interview intoxicated, there is no point in trying to gather psychosocial data or to engage the client in a counseling process. Explain in a polite but firm manner that you need accurate information to do your job and must therefore postpone the interview, rescheduling it for a time when the client is sober. Expect the client to become angry but remain calm and firm.

11. If an intoxicated individual appears at your agency, secure basic identifying information (name, age, address, etc.) and then attend to the individual's physical condition. Be alert to the life-threatening dangers of delirium tremens or drug overdose and the need for detoxification under medical supervision.

12. Encourage family members to make use of Al-Anon and Alateen groups, along with other resources such as COA (Children of Alcoholics), ACOA or ACA (Adult Children of Alcoholics), and programs that address the problem of codependency.

13. Learn about the behavioral pattern of *codependency* that develops as a result of living for many years with someone who is chemically dependent. Typically, the codependent assumes responsibility for the behavior of others (e.g., the alcoholic) while neglecting his or her own needs. Persons who have taken on a pattern of codependency are often hostile because of how they have been treated by someone they love, controlling because their situation is so out of control, manipulative because manipulation seems to be the only way to get things done, and indirect and vague in their communication because they live in a family system that cannot tolerate honesty.

14. The assistance and support of the client's family and friends will probably be needed in making a referral to a treatment program. Thus, it is important to reach out to these individuals and engage them in the assessment, planning, and helping process. However, be alert to the possibility that they too may have a substance abuse problem and/or may be contributing to your client's problem through denial, enabling, or codependency behaviors.

When appropriate, consult with family members and others concerned for the person who is chemically dependent and determine if they would participate in a professionally guided confrontation of the individual. This procedure (known as an ***intervention***) is used to convince the person who is locked into the denial pattern that he or she has a major problem and that there will be serious and immediate consequences if he or she does not immediately enter treatment. If it is well planned and properly implemented, it can break through the denial and help the individual accept treatment. The intervention must be planned under the direction of an experienced chemical dependency counselor who is skilled in using this procedure.

The intervention requires detailed preparation and rehearsal by the people who mean most to the client or those who exert power or control (e.g., spouse, children, employer, close friends, etc.). Each person prepares a list of specific incidents of destructive drinking or drug-related behavior and vividly describes how he or she and the client are being hurt by the chemical abuse. It is important that these feelings be conveyed in a nonjudgmental and caring manner. During several practice sessions, each person reads his or her list and rehearses the presentation until he or she feels confident enough to directly face the chemically dependent person. Such rehearsals are critical to the success of the emotionally charged encounter. The group decides when to confront the chemically dependent person. It must be unannounced and arranged at a time when the individual will be as sober and lucid as possible. Those involved insist that the individual listen and hear them out. The individual's usual denials and promises are not accepted, and no one comes to the person's rescue. Instead, everyone insists that the chemically dependent person must immediately—today—enter a treatment program. Prior to the confrontation, necessary arrangements are made so a treatment program is ready to accept the individual on the very day of the confrontation. Thus, all details (cost, insurance coverage, leave of absence from work, etc.) must have been worked out in advance.

If the use of an intervention is not feasible and if the chemically dependent person engages in behavior very dangerous to self or others, a court-ordered involuntary commitment to a treatment facility should be considered.

15. Realize that successful treatment usually involves three phases: (a) detoxification in a hospital or as an outpatient (i.e., supervised withdrawal from drug, either with or without medication); (b) inpatient treatment within a highly structured therapeutic community where the client's denial system can be broken down and he or she begins to use counseling and self-help groups; and (c) outpatient, drug-free programs that provide counseling and self-help groups using the 12-step approach. Following these three phases, the client enters the most difficult and most important part of his or her recovery: the day-by-day and life-long struggle to rebuild his or her life and remain drug free. To be successful, the chemically dependent person must take responsibility for his or her own recovery.

The various ***12-step programs*** (e.g., Alcoholics Anonymous, Cocaine Anonymous, Narcotics Anonymous, etc.) have the best record of success in facilitating this long-term recovery process. These self-help programs provide encouragement and teach methods of day-by-day coping. They emphasize the development of one's spirituality and help the individual reorient his or her life-style.

16. Once the individual stops using chemicals, special attention must be given to planning for relapse prevention. This involves helping the individual develop a plan for coping with those times and situations when he or she will be at highest risk of resuming the use of alcohol and drugs.

17. Because drugs alter mood, individuals with low self-esteem, feelings of powerlessness or loneliness, and emotional pain are especially prone to misuse drugs. Because they do not value themselves, they do not believe they are capable of changing their situation, so they look to things outside themselves (e.g., drugs) for relief from life's problems and pain. Effective recovery programs counteract these beliefs and help the individual develop self-esteem, learn problem-solving skills, rely on inner resources, and create drug-free relationships with others.

18. Be aware that hundreds of over-the-counter medicines and grocery store products contain alcohol (e.g., vanilla extract, certain cough syrups, cold medicines, and some mouthwashes). This fact may be important in the identification of substance abuse problems and especially for recovering alcoholics who are using *anabuse* in their treatment and will, therefore, have a violent physical reaction to alcohol in any form.

19. Be alert to problems caused by the misuse of other drugs and medications. For example, it is estimated that about one million individuals, mostly male, use *anabolic steroids* to boost their athletic strength and physical appearance; more than half of these people are under age 18. Steroids are not addictive like the other drugs discussed in this section, but they do pose a serious problem. Steroids are attractive because they build muscles, but they also cause tumors, high blood pressure, shrunken testicles, liver and kidney disorders, and erratic sleep disorders. In young users, steroids can retard growth. In some cases, steroid use leads to violent mood shifts, aggression, and violence. Steroids are easy to obtain and inexpensive.

SELECTED BIBLIOGRAPHY

Doweiko, Harold. *Concepts of Chemical Dependency,* 3rd. ed. Pacific Grove, CA: Brooks/Cole, 1996.

Fisher, Gary, and Thomas Harrison. *Substance Abuse.* Boston: Allyn and Bacon, 1997.

Grilby, David. *Drugs and Human Behavior.* Boston: Allyn and Bacon, 1998.

Inaba, Darryl, and William Cohen. *Uppers, Downers, All Arounders,* 3rd ed. Ashland, OR: CNS Productions, 1996.

McNeece, C. Aaron, and Diana Dinitto. *Chemical Dependency: A Systems Approach,* 2nd ed. Boston: Allyn and Bacon, 1998.

Miller, William, and Stephen Rollnick. *Motivational Interviewing: Preparing People to Change Addictive Behavior.* New York: Guilford, 1991.

Van Wormer, Katherine. *Alcoholism Treatment: A Social Work Perspective.* Chicago: Nelson-Hall, 1996.

11.9 The Manipulative Client

PURPOSE: To respond appropriately to the client who frequently manipulates other people.

DISCUSSION: Most people, at least occasionally, attempt to manipulate others as a way of getting what they want. However, some individuals rely on manipulation and "conning" as a primary means of coping with life. These individuals can be difficult clients, primarily because they are so skilled and subtle in "using" other people. Social workers who are unable to detect a manipulation may quickly find themselves in legal, ethical, and moral difficulties.

Some of the most practiced manipulators are labeled as "sociopaths," "psychopaths," or as having an "antisocial personality disorder." Many have a long history of criminal activity. Hare (1993) explains that the hallmark of psychopaths is their lack of a conscience; they do not experience genuine remorse or guilt. They also lack empathy and are unable to appreciate the feelings of other people. Additional common characteristics include a glib and superficial manner of relating, egocentric and grandiose thinking, shallow emotions, impulsiveness and poor self-control, a strong need for excitement and risk taking, and antisocial behavior. For them, truth is whatever fits their purpose at the moment. Many grew up in environments where manipulation was the key to their physical and psychological survival; thus, it is useful to view manipulation as the continuation of behavioral patterns that proved effective in the past. Included here are a few guidelines:

1. The manipulative client, like all clients, is deserving of respect. With this client, however, you need to be much more cautious, deliberate, and careful in your actions. You must be explicit in outlining your role, what you can and cannot do as a professional person, and your expectations of the client. You must demonstrate firmness and strength of conviction. Yochelson and Samenow (1985) remind us that the habitual manipulator is always behaving in ways that help him or her gain control of others:

> He tries to determine what others want to hear and feeds it to them. He finds and uses opportunities for digression and diversion. He discloses as it suits his purposes. He slants his version of events to make himself a victim and blames others for his plight in life. He tries whatever he thinks will impress the [change agent], enlist his sympathy and compassion, or convince him of a particular point of view. Failing this, he uses a variety of tactics to put [the change agent] on the defensive. These may be couched in highly intellectual terms as the criminal argues the meaning of a word, disputes a philosophic issue, and generalizes a point to absurdity. However, there are also open power plays as he intimidates, threatens, ridicules and erupts with angry reactions.
>
> The agent of change has no hope of being successful if he allows a criminal to set the conditions of a meeting. . . . The [agent of change] must stand firm. . . . [A professional] who is indecisive or lacks confidence does not instill confidence or respect in a criminal. Nor can [a professional] who is permissive later establish himself as a firm authority. Many criminals have had experience with permissive change agents and have exploited them. A person who is shy, timid, or reserved may do well in many endeavors, but he will fail to effect change in criminals. (p. 541)

2. Suspect a manipulation whenever your client takes an inordinate interest in your personal life or your feelings about your job. Be especially cautious when your client says such things as, "You are the only person who really understands me," "No one else has ever been as helpful as you," "You are the most caring person I have ever met," "If you could just do this one thing for me (often something illegal or unethical), I can get my life straightened out," "I have a wonderful opportunity to pull my life together—I just need a small loan," or "I need to tell you something but you must promise not to tell this to anyone else." Also, be alert to the possibility of manipulation if your client makes frequent use of the word *but* as a way of avoiding responsibility or downplaying the seriousness of a behavior (e.g., "Well yes I did steal some money but only 30 dollars" or "I hit him with a chair but not very hard").

3. If you suspect that you are being drawn into a manipulation, consult with another professional and examine your actions and feelings. If you are part of a team, raise your concerns with team members. Often you will find that the client is saying very different things to other team members. An elevated level of communication and coordination is necessary to keep team members from being drawn into a manipulation where one is played against another.

4. Inform your client that, above all else, you do not want him or her to lie. Say, for example, "I want to be very clear on one point. If I ask you a question that you do not want to answer, tell me so. Do not lie to me. If you lie, it will only confuse our relationship; it will not help you and it will not help me." Remember that there are no completely reliable ways of knowing when a person is lying. It is very difficult to detect a lie offered by a person who is practiced in the art of lying. It is especially difficult if you have not previously observed this person with others in a variety of situations; however, we offer a few observations about lying:

- Most people feel at least a bit uncomfortable when they lie. Consequently, when lying, their voices often become higher in pitch and they are more likely to stumble over words.
- When lying, people tend to use fewer descriptive phrases and fewer hand motions than when they are not engaged in deception. Also, when lying, they are more prone to frequent blinking and fidgeting.
- Engage the person in several minutes of friendly small talk before addressing a topic about which they may lie and before asking pointed questions aimed at detecting a deception. An obvious change in voice, facial expressions, or other body language suggests a deception.
- Even a clever, confident, and experienced liar cannot completely control his or her facial expressions. Thus, they may exhibit a momentary look of panic when they fear they have been detected.
- The experienced liar has prepared and practiced responses to commonly asked questions, but his or her response often sounds emotionally flat. A really unusual or unexpected question may catch such a person off guard.

5. Be fair but unwavering in your expectations of these clients. Hold manipulative clients responsible for their behavior and do not rescue them from the natural consequences of their choices. Before deciding to change their behavior, they usually need first to experience the punishing consequences of their actions.

6. Professionals who are usually nonjudgmental in their relationships with clients may become judgmental when they encounter the manipulative client, especially one who knows how to "work the system"—meaning that the client can accurately predict how agencies, social workers, and other professionals will respond under certain circumstances. You can increase your tolerance for these clients and decrease your judgmentalness by remembering that manipulation is essentially a coping strategy. This client uses manipulation because it works better than anything else he or she knows how to do. Although there may be something particularly irritating about people who use deception and lies to manipulate caring professionals, it is important to remember that in other areas of society, being able to "work the system" is a mark of competence. For example, the lawyer, businessperson, or social worker who knows how to get the "system" to do what he or she wants is viewed as someone with great skill.

SELECTED BIBLIOGRAPHY

Allen, Bud, and Diana Bosta. *Games Criminals Play.* Sacramento: Rae John Publishers, 1981.

Doren, Dennis. *Understanding and Treating the Psychopath.* New York: Wiley, 1987.

Hare, Robert. *Without Conscience: The Disturbing World of the Psychpaths Among Us.* New York: Simon and Schuster, 1993.

Yochelson, Samuel, and Stanton Samenow. *The Criminal Personality,* vol. II. Northvale, NJ: Jason Aronson, 1985.

11.10 The Dangerous Client

PURPOSE: To respond to a potentially violent client in a manner that reduces the danger inherent in the situation.

DISCUSSION: Social workers in correctional settings and child protective services, more than those in other fields of practice, are frequently in contact with people who are potentially violent. For example, the removal of a abused child from an abusing parent always carries some risk of being physically assaulted. When interacting with an extremely angry and potentially violent person, the social worker should adhere to the following guidelines:

1. Never enter a situation believed to be dangerous without first consulting with others about your plans. Consider the situation to be high risk whenever you are to meet with individuals who have a history of violence or who possess firearms or other lethal weapons, and whenever you are to meet an unfamiliar client in a nonpublic or isolated place. An inadvertent encounter with illegal activity such as drug dealing is also dangerous. If you must enter a dangerous environment or situation, do not hesitate to call for police protection.

2. A history of violent behavior is the best predictor of future violence. Statistically speaking, individuals with certain characteristics and certain life experiences are more likely to commit violent acts, such as:

- Has a history of committing violent acts
- Is violent when under the influence of alcohol or drugs
- Is or was the target of violence and/or observed family violence during childhood
- Is or was the target of violence in his or her community
- Has been publicly humiliated
- Is part of a violent peer group
- Is experiencing a high level of stress
- Is a male teen or a young adult
- Has experienced a traumatic brain injury

3. An agency's recordkeeping system should utilize color coding or some other method of flagging the case record of a potentially dangerous client so the social worker who is to meet the client for the first time can take appropriate precautions. Your agency should have a preestablished emergency communication code so all staff will recognize a disguised request for assistance. For example, in a telephone message such as, "Hello, Bob. This is Jim. Would you please send a copy of our red resource book to my office?" the phrase *red resource book* might be code for "send the police to my office."

4. When making a home visit that could develop into a dangerous situation, always keep your office aware of your concern and informed of your itinerary, and check in by phone according to a prearranged schedule. Before entering a home or building, take a few seconds to look around and think about your safety. Are you alone? Where are the escape routes? Do you hear a violent argument in process? Do the people inside sound out of control?

5. Never move through a doorway as a response to an invitation to "come in" unless you can see the person who is speaking and he or she has seen you. (Being mistaken for someone else can be dangerous.) When entering a room containing an angry person, move in slowly. Remain on the periphery until you can assess the situation and then move in slowly. Do not move into the person's space. Intrusive movement may trigger violent behavior.

6. Be alert to anything about the situation that feels or looks unusual or out of place. We all possess an unconscious "danger detector." Thus, trust your "gut feelings." If you feel afraid, assume that you are in danger even if you cannot pinpoint why you are feeling this way.

7. Most people who are very angry will vent for 2 or 3 minutes and then begin to calm down. However, some individuals are further stimulated and aggravated by what they are saying and thinking. If an angry individual is not calming down after a few minutes, assume that the situation has become more dangerous.

8. Do not touch an angry person; do nothing that could be interpreted as a threat. If possible, sit rather than stand, because sitting is a less aggressive stance. Also encourage the client to sit, as it usually has a calming effect. However, avoid sitting in a overstuffed chair or sofa because it can be difficult to rapidly get up and out of a well-cushioned chair. Rather, pick a hard, movable chair that could be used for protection if you are attacked.

9. Be alert to signs of imminent attack such as flaring nostrils, rapid breathing, dilated pupils, pulsing veins, grinding teeth, pointing fingers, clenching fists, choppy movements and speech, crouching upper body, and bobbing or dipping movements of the body. Do not turn your back to an angry or distraught person nor let that person walk behind you. If the danger of the situation escalates, leave.

10. When in the home of a potentially violent person, be alert to the fact that guns are usually kept in the bedroom and that the kitchen contains numerous potential weapons. If the person has threatened you and then moves quickly to one of these rooms, leave immediately.

11. An attack on others is often a reaction to being afraid; thus, do what you can to lessen the person's need to be afraid of you. Remain composed and speak in a gentle and soothing manner. Do not argue, accuse, or give advice. Demonstrate empathy for the person's feelings of frustration and anger. Use active listening skills (see Item 8.3) to secure an accurate understanding of his or her feelings. If an inappropriate statement on your part causes the client to become angry, admit your error and apologize. Use I-statements (see Item 8.5) when expressing your concerns or explaining your intentions, role, and responsibilities. Allow the angry client to ventilate; this can drain off some of the emotional intensity.

12. Aggressiveness and attacks often arise out of a feeling of being controlled by others. Thus, for an office interview, position your furniture and yourself so you have easy access to an escape route; make sure that the client also has easy access to the door so he or she does not feel trapped. To the extent possible, increase the client's sense of being in control by offering options and choices and using language such as, "Of course, it is up to you to decide what is best" or "Think about what we have discussed and decide which course of action you want to follow."

13. Select clothing and shoes that permit running and rapid movement. Do not wear long earrings that can be easily grabbed. Maintain a neat, well-groomed appearance and an attitude of confidence that projects the impression that you take your job seriously and are able to handle the situation. An angry person is more likely to attack someone who appears weak, afraid, and insecure.

14. Do not attempt to disarm a person with a weapon. Leave that to the police! If your client has a weapon, calmly explain that you intend no harm and then slowly back away or otherwise extricate yourself from the situation.

15. The social worker's family (e.g., spouse, children) may become the target of a client's anger and violence. Thus, family members should be informed and prepared for that possibility.

16. If you work in a dangerous neighborhood, secure guidance from experienced peers, local merchants, and the police on how to protect yourself. If you are likely to encounter dangerous clients, ask your agency for in-service training on nonviolent self-defense. You must be able to protect yourself from harm without inflicting physical injury on your clients. If you secure training in self-defense be sure to select an instructor who has had personal experience with violent persons. Remember, even excellent training does not adequately prepare you for the real thing. Never overestimate your ability to handle a situation or underestimate the paralyzing effect of fear.

SELECTED BIBLIOGRAPHY

Cambell, Jacquelyn, ed. *Assessing Dangerousness.* Thousand Oaks, CA: Sage, 1995.

Griffin, William. "Social Worker and Agency Safety." In *Encyclopedia of Social Work,* 19th ed., vol. 3, edited by Richard L. Edwards. Washington, DC: NASW, 1995, pp. 2293–2305.

Kaplan, Stephen, and Eugenie Wheeler. "Survival Skills for Working with Potentially Violent Clients." *Social Casework* 64 (June 1983): 339–346.

SECTION B

TECHNIQUES AND GUIDELINES FOR INDIRECT PRACTICE

At the indirect-service level, the change process usually involves the social worker in activities aimed at affecting a person or group that has authority to take action. These actions might target, for example, an agency administrator or legislator, an ad hoc group that comes together to consider an issue, or a formal committee that has been designated to decide or recommend action regarding a particular policy, program plan, or budget proposal. Unless highly invested in the outcome, participants in this process may be less than enthusiastic about spending the necessary time and energy to bring about change. Getting the potential participants involved in the change process requires thoughtful effort by the worker. The social worker, or another change agent, should consider that it is usually very busy people who are key actors in bringing about change and they may be thinking about such questions as: Do I really have time to get involved another issue or committee? What are the chances that this endeavor will be more successful than past efforts to resolve the matter? Will my input be valued? Will I personally have to give up something I value for the good of the whole?

Preparatory Activities. Social workers attempting to facilitate organizational or community change must know their "turf" or territory. Even new social workers must be able to assess the agency where they are employed (see Item 11.11) and the dynamics of their community (see Item 11.14). That foundation is prerequisite to any effort to facilitate change in an agency or community.

Typically, the work of the social worker involves bringing together groups of people from within an agency or from a community to address new problems or ones that have not been successfully resolved in the past. Gaining knowledge of past efforts, barriers that existed, and the people or organizations that were involved is a necessary part of one's homework. When providing indirect services, it is rare that the worker faces an emergency or crisis situation that does not allow time for gathering this background information. Such preparation is expected.

Also, to maximize the chances of having a productive first meeting, the worker should carefully select, invite, and recruit participants; identify a meeting time that accommodates as many potential participants as possible; select a convenient meeting place and arrange the meeting room to facilitate interaction; and have a prepared agenda that includes ample opportunity for participants to discuss the issue at hand.

Engagement Activities. It is infrequent that a social worker will have the power or authority to individually resolve problematic issues in an agency or community. Rather, the worker must secure support and resources from others in order to solve problems. It is important, then, that the first meeting of a group or committee is structured to involve the participants in identifying concerns and issues from their own perspectives and encouraging the expression of differing viewpoints. Also, participants should leave the meeting having some responsibility for an action to be reported at the next meeting as a means of maintaining their involvement.

Intake Activities. The first meeting of a group or committee must, among other things, reach a decision regarding the desirability of this group continuing to address the matter, deferring to another group that may already be addressing this topic, joining a parallel effort to deal with the matter, or dissolving. The social worker's role, as convenor of the group, is to help the group decide which of these options should be followed.

For the social worker involved in administration, the intake phase takes on a second meaning. It also may involve selecting and training personnel, the most essential resource for human resource delivery, to work in a human services agency. This activity includes selecting staff members (see Item 11.12) or, as is more likely to be the task of the new worker, the selection of volunteers (see Item 11.13) to perform needed services that are appropriate for unpaid personnel.

11.11 Learning about Your Agency

PURPOSE: To become knowledgeable about an agency's purpose, structure, and procedures.

DISCUSSION: Most social workers are employed by either a private or a public agency. ***Public agencies*** (whether at the city, county, state, or federal level) are established by legislation adopted by elected officials and are funded by tax dollars. By contrast, most

private agencies (also called *voluntary agencies*) are nonprofit corporations funded primarily by voluntary contributions and possibly by fees, grants, or contracts. It should be noted that some of the organizations providing mental health and substance abuse treatment may be ***for-profit corporations*** designed to yield income for investors and stockholders. Some private agencies enter into the purchase of service contracts with public agencies and are paid to deliver specified services; thus, such private agencies are funded, in part, by tax dollars. The term ***membership agency*** refers to a private agency that derives a significant portion of its funds from membership fees (e.g., a YMCA). The term ***sectarian agency*** is often used to describe a private agency that is under the auspices of a specific religious body (e.g., Jewish Community Services, Catholic Social Services, etc.).

In order to deliver social services and programs effectively, the social worker must understand the agency's mission, structure, funding, policies, and procedures. The following activities will help the worker learn about his or her agency:

1. Ask your supervisor and experienced agency staff for guidance on how best to become familiar with the agency's purpose, policies, and operation. Study the agency's organization chart and determine how you and your department or unit fit into the agency structure.

2. If your agency is a *public agency,* read the law(s) that established the agency and those describing the specific programs that the agency is to administer (e.g., state child protection laws) and examine relevant state and federal administrative rules and regulations. If your agency is a *private agency,* read the bylaws that describe the agency's purpose and the functions of the board of directors and its officers and committees and how board meetings are to be conducted. The bylaws will also describe the responsibilities assigned to the executive director.

3. Examine your agency's manual of policies and procedures. Pay special attention to any ethical guidelines that prescribe employee behavior. For example, many agencies will have guidelines for such potential issues as:

- Use of time at work for personal matters or a private practice
- Use of agency property (e.g., telephones, fax, automobiles, copy machines, computer, office space) for personal use or private practice
- Receipt of gifts from clients, other employees, or persons who are in a position to receive referrals of fee-paying clients from agency employees
- Use of the agency's name or the worker's affiliation with the agency in outside activities
- Provision of agency services to friends and family
- Situations wherein personal or financial interests might conflict, or appear to conflict, with official duties
- Publication and dissemination of research reports or other information prepared or developed during agency employment
- Sale of materials prepared on agency time or with agency resources

4. Read documents that describe your agency's history, mission, and philosophy. Find out how the agency has changed during the past 5 to 10 years and what community or political forces are having a significant impact on the agency. Seek information about the agency's goals and objectives for the current year and its goals and plans for the next 3 to 5 years.

5. Examine the agency's personnel policies, the tools or forms that will be used in the evaluation of your job performance. Read the union contract, if one exists.

6. If your agency must conform to standards issued by a national accrediting organization (e.g., Child Welfare League of America, Council on Accreditation of Rehabilitation Facilities, etc.), review those portions of the accreditation standards that apply most directly to your areas of service.

7. Examine your agency's budget. Pay special attention to the sources of income, because the agency must be responsive to these sources if it is to continue to attract needed funding and remain solvent. Also, review any purchase of service agreements, interagency agreements, or protocol statements that tie the services and operation of your agency to other agencies or funding sources. If your are working on a project funded by a grant or a contact, read the relevant documents so you know what the funding source is expecting of the project.

8. Examine annual reports and statistical data compiled by your agency and determine which of its programs and services are most used and least used by clients and consumers. Also, examine data that describe the people served by your agency in terms of their ages, genders, socioeconomic status, races, ethnicities, religions, and so on.

9. Determine what procedures are used to evaluate agency performance and the quality of services provided. Also determine how the agency's clients and consumers are involved in evaluation and planning services and programs.

10. Identify the agencies and organizations with which your agency frequently interacts. Determine what community or state planning agencies have an impact on your agency and how the services and programs provided by your agency are to be coordinated with other agencies in the community.

11. Determine what specific roles, tasks, and activities are assigned to the agency's social work staff and those assigned to persons of other disciplines and professions (see Chapter 5). Also, find out what practice frameworks guide service delivery (see Chapter 6).

12. Talk to community leaders and professionals outside your agency to ascertain how your agency and its programs are perceived by others. Determine the public image attached to your agency and how it acquired that reputation.

SELECTED BIBLIOGRAPHY

Netting, F. Ellen, Peter M. Kettner, and Steven L. McMurtry. *Social Work Macro Practice,* 2nd ed. New York: Longman, 1998.

Weinbach, Robert. *The Social Worker as Manager,* 3rd ed. Boston: Allyn and Bacon, 1998.

11.12 Staff Recruitment and Selection

PURPOSE: To conduct a fair and effective search for agency staff.

DISCUSSION: The quality of staff is critically important in the provision of human services. Thus, the skill or ability to provide the agency's services should be the key consideration in selecting new staff. Social work values require that a search is open, fair, and does not discriminate on the basis of race, national origin, gender, age, disability, or sexual orientation. It is important, therefore, that social workers who participate in recruiting and selecting new staff be familiar with the elements of a good affirmative action search. This understanding is also valuable because social workers too are individuals being hired for positions in human services organizations and knowledge of the search process helps them to successfully compete for available positions (see Item 10.1).

The Search Committee

One of the most important elements of a search is the membership of the search committee. If the members are too much alike, it is more likely that the person selected for the position will also reflect those characteristics and associated perspectives. Thus, the membership should include a mix of people in ethnic background, age, and gender. It should also reflect a range of perceptions of the agency, including those of staff, board, and clientele. Usually a committee of four or five people is sufficient; it is small enough to be efficient yet large enough to represent a range of perspectives.

Contents of a Position Announcement

The search committee (often with input from other staff and board members) typically prepares a position announcement. It should be prepared very carefully, as it must serve to attract qualified applicants and, at the same time, become the basis on which applicants will be evaluated. At a minimum, a position announcement should contain the following:

1. *A description of the major tasks of the position.* In most cases, this can be adapted from the job description. Any changes in that description should be identified before the position announcement is finalized. Applicants are expected to prepare a cover letter that specifically identifies their preparation for this job.

2. *A statement of legitimate requirements for the position.* In order to avoid discriminating against potential applicants, and particularly against population groups that have less access to advanced education, it is important that the qualifications are appropriate to the work to be performed. For example, a M.S.W. degree should not be required when a B.S.W. is sufficient; five years of practice experience should not be required of an entry-level position; and so on. It is important to separate those characteristics that are *required* from those that are *preferred.*

3. *The closing date for applications.* Provide enough time between the date the announcement is published and the closing date to allow potential candidates to learn of the opening, prepare application materials, get permission from potential references, and permit the mail to reach the search committee. A minimum of four weeks is suggested.

4. *A description of how to apply.* Clearly identify the materials that will constitute a completed application. Usually, this will include a resumé, names and addresses of three to five persons who could be contacted as references (or letters of reference supplied with the application), and sometimes an application form. The announcement should include the name, address, and phone number of the person responsible for the search or a person who can be contacted for answers to questions.

5. *The salary range and starting date.* If these factors are known, include them, as they help to screen out applicants who would not consider the position if this information were known. Such self-screening saves time and energy for both the applicant and the selection committee.

Advertising

It is important to advertise the position widely. The most commonly used sources are the local newspaper, the *NASW News* (national), and the state chapter or local program unit of NASW's newsletter. It may also be productive to circulate a flyer to local agencies and to contact any coalitions of minority social workers that exist in the community or region. In addition, the committee, board, and staff should identify and encourage applications from qualified persons with whom they are familiar. It takes only one strong applicant to conclude a successful search, but the chances are vastly improved when selection can be made from a pool of strong candidates.

Paper Screening

When the closing date has passed, the completed applications are reviewed by the committee. This "paper screening" involves independently reading the candidates' files and evaluating each according to the criteria identified in the position announcement. Prior to examining individual files, the committee should develop an evaluation form to score the applications. This form should list the required and preferred characteristics, and sometimes numerical weights are assigned to represent the importance of a specific characteristic for the job. A narrative statement of impressions of the candidate should be recorded to serve as a basis for committee discussion and as documentation in case the search process is challenged by an unsuccessful candidate.

When this review of applications is completed, the committee is then prepared to meet, compare evaluations, discuss differences in perception, eliminate unacceptable candidates from consideration, and develop a priority list to invite for interviews. It is a professional courtesy to inform applicants not placed on the priority list that they are no longer under consideration.

Interviewing

Usually, three to five candidates are interviewed for a position, although the priority list may include backup candidates. The interviews should be carefully planned and hosted by members of the committee. However, other members of the staff and board should participate in the interviews. A list of questions to be asked of all candidates should be prepared by the committee in order to provide a fair comparison between the finalists. All people involved in interviews should be warned against asking *inappropriate personal questions* about a candidate's marital status, plans for having children, child care arrangements, sexual orientation, and other such topics. It should be assumed that professionals will make appropriate provision for their personal lives and keep that separate from professional responsibilities. The interview should be a time of give and take between the candidate and the agency. It is important to remember that not only is the agency determining if the candidate is suitable for the job but the candidate is also making a decision about accepting the position, should it be offered.

Selection

Following the interviews, feedback from the various participants should be collected and reviewed by the committee. At this point, the committee should be prepared to conclude the search and recommend one or more persons (preferably in rank order) to the executive director or those responsible for hiring. The committee's frank evaluation of the candidates' strengths and limitations should be shared with this person. The job can then be offered and negotiated. When the position is filled, all applicants left from the priority list should be informed of the decision and thanked for their interest. Records of the search should be maintained for a minimum of three years.

SELECTED BIBLIOGRAPHY

Pecora, Peter J. "Personnel Management." In *Encyclopedia of Social Work,* 19th ed., vol. 3, edited by Richard Edwards. Washington, DC: NASW, 1995, pp. 1828–1836.

Pecora, Peter J., and Michael J. Austin. *Managing Human Services Personnel,* 3rd ed. Newbury Park, CA: Sage, 1987.

11.13 Selecting and Training Volunteers

PURPOSE: To screen and prepare volunteers to provide human services as caregivers and as an adjunct to the agency staff.

DISCUSSION: Social workers often have the responsibility to recruit, train, and supervise the work of volunteers. Throughout the history of social welfare in the United States, volunteers have played a central role. Volunteers can help to maximize scarce agency and professional resources and sometimes bring specialized skills not otherwise available to the agency. In addition, experienced and informed volunteers often become effective advocates for the agency and its programs. Volunteers can perform a wide variety of important tasks, ranging from office work and fund-raising to activities involving client contact. The key to using volunteers successfully is being able to match the tasks to the volunteers' special interests and abilities. However, if volunteers are not carefully selected, prepared, and supervised, they become frustrated and may quit. In some cases, they may harm agency clients and damage the agency's reputation.

Volunteers are especially active in the area of youth services. Examples include the work of volunteers in YMCA/YWCA and Big Sister/Big Brother programs, Scouting, 4-H, foster care, tutoring programs, and so forth. Increasingly, the various forms of caregiving are popular areas of volunteer activity. Typically, these volunteers are assigned duties that will support or supplement the services provided by professionals. Examples include providing transportation, companionship, or personal care to people who are elderly or disabled, helping such an individual write letters and pay bills, delivering or preparing meals, and so on. Such volunteer-supported home care is far less expensive than nursing home or other forms of institutionalized care.

Recruitment

Reaching out to the community and attracting volunteers to the work of the agency must be an ongoing activity. Because there is always some turnover, new volunteers must be found to replace those who leave. In general, volunteers are the best recruiters of other volunteers. If agency volunteers enjoy their work, they will tell their friends and attract them to the idea of volunteering. On the other hand, if an agency treats its volunteers poorly, it will soon have a bad reputation and will find it very difficult to recruit volunteers.

Screening

Screening volunteers is a difficult and sensitive task. Maintaining the goodwill of people who express an interest in volunteer work must be balanced against the agency's responsibility to protect its clients from harm and exploitation. This is especially true when the agency's clients are highly vulnerable, such as children and the frail elderly. It must be remembered that the agency assumes a legal liability for the work of its volunteers; improper screening can leave the agency open to a costly lawsuit.

Several questions might be asked to assess a person's motivation and capacity for volunteer work, such as:

- Why are you interested in being a volunteer in this agency?
- What type of activity is of greatest interest?
- Are there certain tasks or activities that are of little or no interest?
- Are you hoping to have direct contact with agency clients? If yes, with what type of clients? What type of relationship do you want to have with clients?
- What do you expect to gain personally from this experience?
- Have you been a volunteer for other agencies? If yes, when and where? Can you provide references?

- For about how long do you expect to serve as a volunteer?
- How much time can you contribute each week or month? Can you commit to being at the agency on certain days of each week or month?
- What special skills and experience would you bring to the agency? Do you have certain limitations that the agency should know about?
- What type of training and supervision do you expect from the agency?
- How will you maintain confidentiality concerning the agency and client information you may obtain while working as a volunteer?

Throughout the screening process, special attention needs to be given to the person's attitudes toward the agency's clients and the problems or concerns the clients bring to the agency. References should be obtained and checked on those volunteers who will have direct contact with clients. Police checks for a history of child molestation are important on volunteers who will work with children.

Job Description

Being able to provide a clear description of the agency's expectations and the volunteer's duties is critical to successful recruitment and selection. The agency should prepare a written job description for the position to be filled by a volunteer. That description should address at least the following:

- Specific tasks and activities to be performed
- Time required each week or month and perhaps the duration of the activity (e.g., volunteer must commit to one year)
- Training and skills needed by the volunteer
- Name and title of person who will supervise the volunteer

A signed contract with the volunteer may be used to further define duties and responsibilities.

Training

Volunteers must be adequately trained for the specific tasks and work they are assigned. The staff member to whom the volunteer is responsible is usually the best person to provide this training. Demonstrations of how the tasks should be performed and ongoing coaching are often necessary. Volunteers need to be constantly reminded of the importance of confidentiality.

New volunteers should be oriented to the agency's structure, operations, and programs. Part of this orientation can be conducted with groups of volunteers. In these sessions, it is helpful to use case examples and allow the volunteers to share ideas and interact with agency staff. Staff observations may be useful to the screening and selection process.

Support and Monitoring

Volunteers must be supervised and supported to make sure they are meeting agency expectations, are properly prepared for their work, and are finding satisfaction in their work. Because volunteers are not paid, they must receive recognition for the work they do. They must feel appreciated. Many volunteers quit because they do not receive the recognition, support, and supervision they expect of agency staff.

Some types of volunteer work is stressful. For example, those who work in hospice programs, nursing homes, or foster-care programs find their work to be emotionally draining. Such volunteers may become too attached to their clients and experience a sense of loss and grieving when a client dies or is transferred to another facility. Agency staff must be able to help the volunteers work through painful experiences.

SELECTED BIBLIOGRAPHY

Navarre, Ralph G. *Professional Administration of Volunteer Programs.* Madison, WI: "N"-Way Publishing, 1986.

Pearse, Jane L. *Volunteers: The Organizational Behavior of Unpaid Workers.* London: Routledge, 1993.

11.14 Learning about Your Community

PURPOSE: To conduct an informal assessment of a community in order to understand the context in which an agency's services are delivered.

DISCUSSION: A *community* is a group of people who feel a bond with each other because they share an identity, common interests, a sense of belonging, and usually a common locality. Thus, one can think of a community of people who share a common interest (e.g., the social work community, the African American community, etc.) or as a geographic community such as a neighborhood, town, or city. Communities are expected to perform one or more of the following functions:

- *Provision and distribution of goods and services.* Water, food, housing, garbage disposal, medical care, education, transportation, recreation, social services, information, and the like are provided.
- *Location of business activity and employment.* Commerce and jobs exist from which people earn the money needed to purchase goods and services.
- *Public safety.* Protection from criminal behavior and hazards such as fires, floods, and toxic chemicals is provided.
- *Socialization.* Opportunities are available to communicate and interact with others and to develop a sense of identity and belonging beyond that provided by the family system.
- *Mutual support.* Tangible assistance and social supports beyond those provided by one's family are available.
- *Social control.* Rules and norms necessary to guide and control large numbers of people (e.g., laws, police, courts, traffic control, pollution control, etc.) are established and enforced.

- *Political organization, and participation.* Governance and decision making related to local matters and public services are in place (e.g., streets, sewer, education, public welfare, public health, economic development, zoning of housing and businesses, etc.).

For the social worker who is new to a geographic area, conducting an informal study of the community where he or she is employed is an important part of moving into a new job. Such an assessment has three purposes:

1. *To understand the context of one's practice.* The social worker must become knowledgeable about the community's history, as well as its economic and political structures and the prevailing values, norms, and myths that affect decision making and intergroup behavior.

2. *To evaluate the existing human services system.* The social worker needs to know what services are available and to understand community attitudes toward people who have psychosocial problems and utilize the human services. Communities differ in their willingness to respond to human needs and fund social agencies. Communities also differ in regard to how well the local professionals and agencies work together.

3. *To acquire understanding of the community decision-making structure.* At some point, the social worker's desire for more adequate human services should lead to efforts to bring about changes in the community's response to a particular problem or need. To succeed in those efforts, the social worker must understand the power structure operating in the community, the beliefs and values of the leaders and key actors who decide what programs and services will be provided and funded, and the formal and informal processes used to reach those decisions.

The social worker's study and assessment of his or her community is an ongoing activity that must be continually updated as new information surfaces. However, it is essential that this process be initiated when beginning work in a new community. This might be done in collaboration with several other professionals who are also new to the community.

Information that describes a community and its functioning can be gleaned from documents such as census data, economic forecasts, public health reports, prior studies of a community problem, reports related to community planning projects, directories of health and human services agencies, and the like. Helpful documents may be available from the local library, Chamber of Commerce, United Way, and government offices. Supplemental data might be obtained by reading historical accounts of how the community grew and developed and how it responded to recent problems, by interviewing long-time residents, and by closely following current issues and controversies reported in the local news. It is important to record the names of the organizations and individuals who are important decision makers, especially those associated with human services concerns.

Although the social worker's area of practice will determine the nature and depth of information sought in relation to particular aspects of the community and its service systems, certain general information is essential. The following points will help the social worker develop a profile of the community in which he or she is working:

1. *Identifying information*
   - Names used to refer to neighborhoods, sections, or areas of the community
   - Social, legal, and physical boundaries that define the community
   - Distance from other cities or communities

2. *Demographics*
   - Total population and number per square block or square mile
   - Age distribution (e.g., number of preschoolers, number in grade school and high school, number of people over age 65, etc.)
   - Minority and ethnic groups; languages spoken by various groups
   - Size of families and types of households (e.g., married couples, single parents, people living alone)

3. *History of area*
   - When, why, and by whom was area developed
   - Major events that shaped area's development and the attitudes of its people
   - Changes in characteristics of population over time
   - Reasons why newcomers move to area; reasons why people move away

4. *Geography and environmental influences on community*
   - Effect of climate, mountains, valleys, rivers, lakes, and so forth on local transportation patterns, economic development, and population distribution
   - Effect of highways, railroads, truck routes, and other corridors and barriers on neighborhood patterns, social interaction, agency location, and service delivery
   - Effect of natural resources and environmental concerns on current and future development (e.g., water supply, pollution, sewage treatment, sources of electricity and energy, distance from markets)

5. *Beliefs and attitudes*
   - Dominant values, religious beliefs, and attitudes of population and its various subgroups
   - Types of human services agencies and programs that are valued and respected and that attract community support, favorable publicity, and funding
   - Types of agencies and programs that have been rejected by the community or viewed in an unfavorable light
   - Residents' sense of "belonging" to the community
   - Identification with and a sense of loyalty and responsibility toward the community

6. *Local politics*
   - Form of local government
   - Relative power and influence of political parties and various interest groups
   - Level of voter participation
   - Types and level of taxes used to secure public funds
   - Current debates, issues, and controversies at local level

7. *Local economy and businesses*
   - Major industries, businesses, and products of area
   - Area's businesses and corporations that are locally owned and those controlled from outside the community
   - Types of jobs and work available in area (wages; part time or full time; seasonal or year-round; hours and times of work)
   - Job skills required by major employers
   - Reasons why new businesses move to area; move away from area
   - Percentage of labor force employed; unemployed
   - Forecast of future economic growth and job opportunity

8. *Income distribution*
   - Median income for women; for men; for minority groups
   - Number of persons/families below official poverty line
   - Number of persons/families/children receiving various types of public assistance such as AFDC, Medicaid, food stamps, etc.

9. *Housing*
   - Most common types of housing (e.g., single-family dwellings, apartments, public housing)
   - Cost and availability of housing
   - Percentage of housing units occupied and vacant
   - Percentage of units overcrowded or substandard

10. *Educational facilities and programs*
    - Locations and types schools (i.e., public, private, neighborhood, magnet, etc.)
    - Sufficient and appropriate school programs for children with special needs
    - Schools sensitive to problems and strengths of persons from minority and ethnic groups; schools with bilingual programs
    - Minority and ethnic groups of the community represented on school boards, school staffs, etc.
    - Dropout rate for all students; for members of various socioeconomic and minority groups
    - Availability of college-level, adult education, vocational, and job-training programs

11. *Health and welfare systems*
    - Names and locations of providers of health care (e.g., emergency services, acute care, home health programs, long-term care, public and private hospitals, public health programs, private clinics, etc.)

- Names and locations of agencies providing social and human services (e.g., housing, substance abuse treatment, child welfare, protection from child abuse and domestic abuse, financial assistance, etc.)
- Comprehensiveness, availability, accessibility, and adequacy of local health and human services programs; organizations exist to promote the improvement and coordination of these services
- Service providers sensitive to special needs or concerns of minority and ethnic groups; bilingual staff members; clients treated with respect
- Self-help groups and informal helping networks exist in the community
- Numbers of children and youth in out-of-home placements

12. *Public safety and justice system*
    - Adequacy of police and fire protection and public health safeguards
    - Public attitudes toward local police, courts, and correctional programs
    - Responsiveness of these agencies to concerns of minority groups in community
    - Numbers of adults in jail or on probation and parole
    - Numbers of youth in correctional facilities and juvenile justice programs
13. *Sources of information and public opinion*
    - Influential TV and radio stations and newspapers to which the people look for information and perspectives on current events
    - Key leaders and spokespersons for various segments of the community, including racial or ethnic and religious groups
14. *Major problems and concerns in community*
    - Assessment of major social problems within the community (e.g., inadequate housing, inadequate public transportation, lack of jobs, youth gangs, crime, poverty, racism, teen pregnancy, domestic abuse, etc.)
    - Efforts underway to address these concerns; leaders in these efforts
    - Major gaps among existing social, health care, and educational services

SELECTED BIBLIOGRAPHY

Devore, Wynetta, and Elfriede G. Schlesinger. *Ethnic-Sensitive Social Work Practice,* 4th ed. Boston: Allyn and Bacon, 1996.

Fellin, Phillip. *The Community and the Social Worker,* 2nd ed. Itasca, IL: F. E. Peacock, 1995.

Homan, Mark. *Promoting Community Change.* Pacific Grove, CA: Brooks/Cole, 1994.

Rubin, Herbert J., and Irene S. Rubin. *Community Organization and Development,* 2nd ed. New York: Macmillan, 1992.

12 Data Collection and Assessment

INTRODUCTION

The worker's focus during the second phase of the planned change process is on collecting sufficient information from the client and others to comprehend the problem or situation, understand the client's goals and motivation, and assess the capacity and opportunity to make needed changes. In this phase, the worker brings an expertise not usually possessed by the general public, including skill in determining what data are needed, where they can be obtained, and how they should be interpreted.

Data collection is the activity of securing the information needed to understand the practice situation as a prerequisite to formulating a plan of action. It is important to gather factual information from the client, other involved people, and, in some cases, other sources such as medical records, school reports, probation records, and so on. Also, the worker should identify the subjective perceptions, assumptions, and beliefs regarding the situation held by the client, family members, teachers, employers, and perhaps even a referring agency (e.g., a court, school, spouse, etc.). Depending on the situation, the worker may need skills ranging from interviewing to data compilation in order to obtain the needed impressions or facts to assess the problem or case situation.

When does data collection end? To some degree, new data are always being collected. Certainly, it is essential that a social worker obtain sufficient information to have a clear picture of what is occurring in the client's life before arriving at an assessment. However, it is equally important to avoid delaying or stalling the change process by collecting too much data or irrelevant data.

Assessment is the thinking process by which a person reasons from the information gathered to arrive at tentative conclusions. During assessment, the available information is organized and studied to make sense of the client's situation and lay a foundation for a plan of action. When the assessment is complete, the social worker should be able to describe the problem or situation accurately and identify what needs to be changed to improve the client's situation.

The best assessments are multidimensional (i.e., they are drawn from numerous sources that reflect varying perceptions and points of view). If the perceptions and conclusions of the worker, client, and other people involved in the situation are too varied when they are compared, it may be necessary to return to data collection and bring more information to bear on the analysis that will eventually inform the intervention plan.

Social workers must guard against unconsciously making the client's situation fit a particular theory or diagnostic category. One protection against the worker's own biases having undue influence on the assessment is to have the client actively involved in sorting through the information when arriving at an assessment. Further, when a conclusion is reached, the worker should view that as tentative and be open to revising that assessment as additional information is obtained during other phases of the change process.

SECTION A
TECHNIQUES AND GUIDELINES FOR DIRECT PRACTICE

In direct practice with individuals, families, and small groups, a social worker's emphasis should be on gathering and interpreting information that allows the worker, client, and others to understand the situation from the *person-in-environment* framework (i.e., the needs, wants, and abilities of the person as well as the demands and constraints of his or her external world). Ultimately, it is finding a suitable match between the person and his or her environment that becomes the focus of the intervention (see Chapter 14).

Data-Collection Activities. A social work assessment should give some attention to the whole person and the relevant factors that impinge on that person's social functioning. Some aspects of the client's functioning about which the worker should seek information are the following:

- *Volitional* (e.g., personal choices and decisions; how one spends one's time and money; impact of such choices on self and others)
- *Familial* (e.g., relationships to one's parents, siblings, spouse, children, and close relatives; sense of loyalty to and responsibility for family members; one's personal history and traditions; one's ethnic and religious identity)
- *Social* (e.g., interaction with network of friends and peers; special interests and recreational activity)
- *Community* (e.g., one's sense of belonging to a group beyond family and friends; sense of loyalty to and responsibility for others in neighborhood and local area; one's place or social status in the community; one's use of formal and informal resources to meet personal and family needs)
- *Spiritual* (e.g., one's deepest core beliefs concerning "who am I" and the meaning and purpose of life; relationship with one's Creator; views as to what is right and wrong; meaning assigned to disappointment and suffering)
- *Emotional* (e.g., feelings and moods such as joy, love, sadness, anger, fear, and shame; inclination to move toward or away from certain experiences and persons)

- *Intellectual* (e.g., ideas, knowledge, and beliefs used to understand self, others, and the world; ability to interpret and give conceptual order to one's experiences; use of information and knowledge to make decisions)
- *Work/Employment* (e.g., one's occupation and source of income; relationships with others in work organization or same profession; the place and meaning of work in one's life)
- *Economic* (e.g., one's material resources and capacity to secure money needed to purchase goods and services)
- *Physical* (e.g., one's level of energy; health; illness, disabilities, pain, ease of movement; nutrition)
- *Legal* (e.g., one's rights, responsibilities, protections, and entitlements as a citizen)

There are several different modes of data collection. Since each method of data collection has limitations, the social worker should use more than one whenever possible to increase the accuracy of the inferences that result from these data. Data-collection modes a social worker might use include the following:

- Direct verbal questioning, such as the face-to-face interview or a group interview (see Chapter 8)
- Direct written questioning, including the use of problem checklists and questionnaires (see Item 12.14)
- Indirect or projective verbal questioning, such as the story completion or the use of case vignettes (see Item 12.14)
- Indirect or verbal written questioning, such as sentence completion
- Observation of the client in the client's natural environment, such as home visits (see Item 11.5), visits to a classroom, and so forth
- Observations of the client in a simulated situation that is analogous to real life, including such techniques as role-playing a job interview
- Client self-monitoring and self-observations by means of written recording tools, such as a personal log, journaling, or recording information about one's actions, feelings, or beliefs
- The use of existing documents, such as agency records, newspapers, school records, and physician reports

Assessment Activities. An assessment tool combines data collection with a format that facilitates interpretation. Often, this format provides a way to compare the client's responses to those of a larger collective to whom the instrument has been administered (i.e., a standardized assessment tool; see Item 12.16). Literally hundreds of such instruments are available to the social worker. Sometimes, it is useful for the worker to develop an assessment tool that is tailored to fit the manner of communication and experiences of an individual client or family (see Item 12.15). Techniques for organizing data to maintain an ongoing assessment of practice achievements are reported in Chapter 15.

Particular attention needs to be given to assessing client strengths. Too often, both the client and worker become preoccupied with the presenting problem and all that is wrong. This can generate a sense of pessimism and yield an incomplete or distorted intervention plan. Including an analysis of client strengths builds hopefulness and uncovers possibilities for dealing with a problem.

Value preferences also affect assessments. The client and the social worker will hold beliefs about the way things ought to be, and these views affect the way a problem is defined and the outcomes one would want to achieve. To the extent possible, these values and beliefs should be made explicit and discussed during the assessment process.

Finally, during assessment (but hopefully earlier) there must be clarity as to who is the client and who will become the target system. In other words, who is asking for and expects to benefit from the social worker's services (the *client system*) and who is expected to change (the *target system*). They are not always the same. For example, when a mother requests counseling for a rebellious daughter who is forced to attend the counseling sessions, who is the client? We would probably conclude that the mother is the client and the daughter is the target of intervention.

12.1 The Social Assessment Report

PURPOSE: To convey to other professionals a basic understanding of relevant social information about a particular individual or family.

DISCUSSION: A ***social assessment report*** (often called a *social history*) is frequently prepared by social workers in direct practice. As contrasted, for example, to a report prepared by a physician that focuses on physical functioning, the report prepared by a professional social worker focuses primarily on social functioning—the social, relational, or interactional aspects of the client's functioning and his or her situation. The word *social* refers to the interactions between and among people and between people and the significant systems of their social environment (e.g., family, school, job, hospital, etc.). Social workers are particularly concerned about the match (or lack thereof) between client needs and the resources (formal and informal) available to meet those needs. A good report will reflect this focus.

Past behavior is the best predictor of future behavior; this fact is the rationale for compiling a social history. If a social worker can gather accurate descriptions of how a client previously reacted to new situations, felt, behaved, handled stress, and coped with problems, and can also identify patterns in those prior responses, the worker can then make an informed prediction about how the client will respond to various situations in the future. A social history or assessment is especially useful to professionals responsible for making decisions concerning the type of program or service that would be most appropriate for a particular client and to those responsible for facilitating a client's adjustment to a new environment (e.g., treatment program, foster home, nursing home).

Most reports contain two types of information: (1) the social data and (2) the worker's assessment or thoughts about the meaning of that data. Social data are the basic facts; the social assessment is a statement summarizing the worker's impressions and hypotheses that give added meaning to the data and their implications for social work intervention. The information presented in a report should lay a foundation for doing something with the client about his or her problem or situation.

The organization, format, and content of a report will vary from agency to agency and reflect the agency's purpose and program. Also, the content will vary depending on the audience for which it is prepared: doctors, judges, psychologists, school personnel, interdisciplinary teams, and so on. A good report is characterized by a number of qualities, such as the following:

1. *Shortness.* The report should say no more than needs to be said to those who will use the report. Everyone is busy. Do not ask others to read more than is necessary.

2. *Clarity and simplicity.* Select the least complicated words and phrases. Avoid jargon and psychiatric labels. Rather than use labels, describe and give examples of the behavior you are discussing.

3. *Usefulness.* Keep the report's purpose in mind while you are preparing it. Ask yourself who will read the report and what they need to know. Do not include information merely because it is interesting or sensational.

4. *Organization.* Use numerous headings to break the information into easy-to-find topical categories. Here are some of the headings commonly used in social assessment reports:

- Identifying Information (name, date of birth, address, etc.)
- Reason for Report
- Reason for Social Work or Agency Involvement
- Statement of Client's Problem or Concern
- Client's Family Background (family of origin)
- Current Family Composition and/or Household Membership
- Relationships to Significant Others
- Ethnicity, Religion, and Spirituality
- Physical Functioning, Health Concerns, Nutrition, Home Safety, Illness, Disabilities, Medications
- Educational Background, School Performance, Intellectual Functioning
- Psychological and Emotional Functioning
- Strengths, Ways of Coping, and Problem-Solving Capacities
- Employment, Income, Work Experience, and Skills
- Housing, Neighborhood, and Transportation
- Current and Recent Use of Community and Professional Services
- Social Worker's Impressions and Assessment
- Intervention and Service Plan

The sample social assessment report presented in Figure 12.1 illustrates the use of various topical headings.

FIGURE 12.1 Sample Social Assessment Report

Greystone Family Service Agency

Identifying Information

Client Name: Shirley McCarthy
Case Record #: 3456
D.O.B: July 4, 1979 Age: 20
Date of Referral: Oct. 8, 1999
Soc. Security #: 505-67-8910
Social Worker: Jane Green, BSW
Address: 2109 B Street, Greystone, MT 09876
Report Prepared: Oct. 13, 1999
Phone: 591-0123

Reason for Report

This report was prepared for use during consultation with Dr. Jones, the agency's psychiatric consultant, and for purposes of peer supervision. (The client is aware that a report is being prepared for this purpose.)

Reason for Social Work Involvement

Shirley was referred to this agency by Dr. Smith, an emergency room physician at City Hospital. Shirley was treated there for having taken an unknown quantity of aspirin in an apparent suicide attempt. She is reacting with anxiety and depression to her unwanted pregnancy. The father is a former boyfriend with whom she has broken off. She does not want him nor her parents to learn that she is pregnant.

She does not want an abortion and does not want to care for a child. She has thought about adoption but knows little about what would be involved. She agreed to come to this agency in order to figure out how she might deal with her dilemma.

Source of Data

This report is based on two one-hour interviews with the client (Oct. 9 and 11) and a phone conversation with Dr. Smith.

Family Background and Situation

Shirley is the youngest of three children. Her brother, John, age 30, is a chemical engineer in Austin, Texas. Her sister, Martha, age 27, is a pharmacist in Seattle. Shirley does not feel close to either sibling and neither knows of her pregnancy.

Her parents have been married for 33 years. They live in Spokane, Washington. Her father, Thomas, is an engineer for a farm equipment company. Her mother, Mary, is a registered nurse.

Shirley describes her parents as hard-working, honest people who have a strong sense of right and wrong and a commitment to family. The family is middle class and of Irish heritage. The McCarthy's are life-long Catholics. The three children attended Catholic grade and high schools. Shirley says that if her parents knew of the pregnancy "it would just kill them." Her wish to keep her parents from learning of the pregnancy seems motivated by a desire to protect them from distress.

Physical Functioning and Health

Shirley is 5'7" tall and weights 105 pounds. She is about three months pregnant. Dr. Smith reports that she is underweight but otherwise healthy. He has concern about her willingness to obtain proper prenatal care; he had referred Shirley to Dr. Johnson (an OB/GYN physician), but she did not keep that appointment.

Shirley says that she is in good health, eats well, exercises minimally, and reports no medical problems. She is not taking any medication.

Intellectual Functioning

Shirley completed two years at the University of Washington and then transferred to the University of Montana where she is currently a junior in computer science. She has an overall GPA of A–. Despite her good grades, Shirley describes herself as a "mediocre student."

She is attracted to subjects where there is a clear right and wrong answer. She does not like courses such as philosophy, which seems "wishy-washy" to her. Although she values the logical and precise thinking that is part of computer science, she explains that she tends to make personal decisions impulsively and "jumps into things without considering the consequences."

Emotional Functioning

Shirley describes herself as "moody." Even before the pregnancy, she had bouts of depression when she would sit alone in her room for hours at a time. She never sought treatment for the depression. In describing herself, Shirley uses the words *childish* and *immature;* she has always felt younger than others her age.

She often feels anger and sadness, but tries to keep her feelings from showing. In this sense, she is like her father, who always keeps things to himself until he finally "blows up."

In spite of her accomplishments, Shirley seems to have poor self-esteem and focuses more on her limitations than her strengths.

Interpersonal and Social Relationships

Shirley has no "close friends." She says it is difficult for her to interact with others and she wishes she had better social skills. She has held various part-time jobs during high school and college, but socialized only minimally with co-workers. In college, Shirley had trouble getting along with her roommates in the dorm, so she moved to an apartment so that she could be alone.

When she drinks alcohol, she feels more outgoing and friendly. However, this fact scares her because several uncles are alcoholic. For the past year, she worked hard at not drinking at all. She was not drinking when she took the aspirin.

Her former boyfriend, Bob (father of her baby), was the first person she ever dated for more than a few months. The relationship ended one month ago. Bob is also a student.

Religion and Spirituality

Shirley was raised as a Catholic and retains many of the beliefs and values she learned as a child. She describes herself as a spiritual person and one who prays quite often. She has clear ideas of right and wrong but also feels she is in a stage of life when she is trying to decide what she really believes and is in the process of constructing a system of values, morals, and ethical principles.

(continued)

FIGURE 12.1 Continued

Strengths and Problem-Solving Capacity

Although Shirley tends to minimize her strengths, she exhibits intelligence, an ability to work hard, a desire to make friends, a loyalty to her family while also wanting to make her own decisions, and a moderate motivation to deal with her situation constructively. She displays a good vocabulary and expresses herself in a clear manner.

She tends to avoid making hard decisions and lets things pile up until she is forced by circumstances to follow the only option still open to her. She usually knows what she "should do" but does not act; she attributes this to a fear of making mistakes. When faced with interpersonal conflict, she is inclined to withdraw.

Economics/Housing/Transportation

Shirley's parents are assisting her with the costs of her education. She also works about 30 hours per week at the Baylor Department Store, earning minimum wage. With this money, she pays rent and keeps her eight-year-old car running.

Aside from her college student health insurance, she has no medical coverage. She does not know if that policy covers pregnancy. Shirley lives alone in a two-room apartment which she says is located in a "rough area" of town. She is afraid to be out alone after dark.

Use of Community Resources

This is the first time Shirley has had contact with a social agency. During our sessions, she asked many questions about the agency and expressed some confusion about why she had been referred here by Dr. Smith. She acknowledged that feelings of embarrassment and shame make it difficult for her to talk to about her concerns.

Impressions and Assessment

This 20-year-old is experiencing inner conflict and depression because of an unwanted pregnancy. This gave rise to a suicide attempt. In keeping with her tendency to avoid conflict, she has not told others of the pregnancy, yet the father (Bob) will need to be involved if she chooses the legal procedure of relinquishment, and her parents' involvement may be needed for financial support. Prenatal care is needed, but it too has been avoided. Abortion is not an acceptable solution to Shirley, and she is ambivalent about adoption and how to manage her life while pregnant.

Goals for Work with Client

In order to help Shirley make the necessary decisions to deal with this pregnancy, I hope to engage her in pregnancy options counseling. Issues to be addressed include making a further assessment of her depression and suicide attempt, obtaining and paying for medical care, and deciding on whether to inform Bob and her own parents. She will need emotional support, some structure, and a gentle demand for work so she can overcome her avoidance, make decisions, and take necessary action.

Note: The names in this report are fictitious.

5. *Confidentiality and client access.* Respect the client's privacy. Assume that the client may want to read the report and has a right to do so. Do not include information that you would not want the client or family (or their lawyer) to read.

6. *Objectivity.* Select words that express your observations in an accurate and nonjudgmental manner. Beware of value-laden words and connotative meanings such as, for example, "welfare mother," "chauvinist," "The client admits she doesn't attend church," and "He claims to have completed high school." Label your opinions and personal judgments as such and support your conclusions with data. Do not present an opinion as if it were a fact. The best way to do this is to place your conclusions, opinions, and hypotheses under a separate topical heading called "Worker's Impressions and Assessment."

When it is necessary to include information or draw conclusions that might offend the client/family, do so, if possible, by using the client's own words. Note these examples:

Inappropriate: It is apparent that Jane is a hostile and uncaring individual who is too self-centered and immature to cope with the demands of her elderly father.

Acceptable: While I was talking with Jane, her father requested a glass of water. She responded in a loud voice and said, "Go to hell, you old fool. I hope you dry up and blow away."

7. *Relevance.* The information included in the report should have a clear connection to the client's presenting concern and/or the reason the social worker and agency are involved with the client.

8. *Focus on client strengths.* Avoid preoccupation with psychopathology and family disorganization, personal weakness, and limitation. To the extent possible, emphasize whatever strengths exist. Focus on what the client/family can do, not on what they cannot do. Successful intervention is built on client strength; the social assessment report must identify these strengths (see Item 12.7).

SELECTED BIBLIOGRAPHY

Kagle, Jill. *Social Work Records,* 2nd ed. Belmont, CA: Wadsworth, 1991.

Zuckerman, Edward. *The Clinician's Thesaurus: The Guide for Wording Psychological Reports,* 4th ed. Sarasota, FL: Professional Resource Press, 1995.

12.2 The Dual Perspective

PURPOSE: To graphically depict barriers and supports that affect a person's interactions with his or her social environment.

DISCUSSION: Among the helping professions, one of social work's unique contributions is its emphasis on understanding the client within the context of his or her social environment. Norton's (1978) dual perspective brings this conceptualization alive in practice. She identifies two distinct sets of influences that make up a person's social environment: the nurturing environment and the sustaining environment.

One's ***nurturing environment*** (or immediate environment) is composed of family, friends, and close associates at work or school. These are people with whom a person interacts frequently and often in an intimate manner. It is in and through these relationships that a person develops a sense of identity, belonging, and self-worth. These relationships have a profound effect on one's functioning.

A person's ***sustaining environment*** is made up of the people one encounters and learns to deal with in the wider community and broader society, including, for example, political organizations, work settings, labor unions, the media, educational systems, health care facilities, and human services programs. (A social worker and a social agency are also part of this sustaining environment.) Ideally, the individual is accepted, respected, and supported within both his or her nurturing and sustaining environments, but this is often not the case.

Of special concern during the assessment phase of the change process is the question of whether an intervention should be directed toward elements of the nurturing environment or toward the sustaining environment. The dual perspective helps to answer that question. For example, if the nurturing system is positive but the messages from the sustaining system are negative (e.g., a minority child from a supportive family who feels devalued when in school), the social worker needs to focus on changing aspects of the school experience. If the messages from the nurturing system are negative (e.g., the child abused by his parents), arranging a positive sustaining system experience can help compensate for these negative influences but the social worker must focus primarily on changing interactions within the family. Finally, and most difficult, are those situations where both the sustaining and nurturing environments give negative messages to the person. An example of this double negative would be a gay or lesbian adolescent who is rejected by his or her family, by peers at school, and by the wider society. In that situation, change efforts would need to be simultaneously directed toward helping the adolescent cope with the rejection, helping the family understand and accept the adolescent, and changing community attitudes toward gays and lesbians.

The concepts of a nurturing and a sustaining environment can be translated into a simple assessment tool for identifying the location of both the supports and problems a person experiences in the social environment. To make a dual perspective assessment, one begins by recording on a chart (see Figure 12.2) the positives and negatives in the client's situation as you understand them. Begin with the person. List in the inner-most circle the characteristics and capacities of the client and indicate with a (+) or (–) the effects they have on his or her functioning. Make a few notes in the margins to explain the reasons for arriving at this conclusion. Next, move to the center circle—the nurturing environment. Write in the names of key actors in the client's situation and again indicate if they are a positive, negative, or neutral (0) influence. Once again, add some description to clarify the rationale for your judgments. Finally, do the same for the circle representing the sustaining environment. Some social workers have found it useful to conduct a dual perspective as-

FIGURE 12.2 Dual Perspective Worksheet

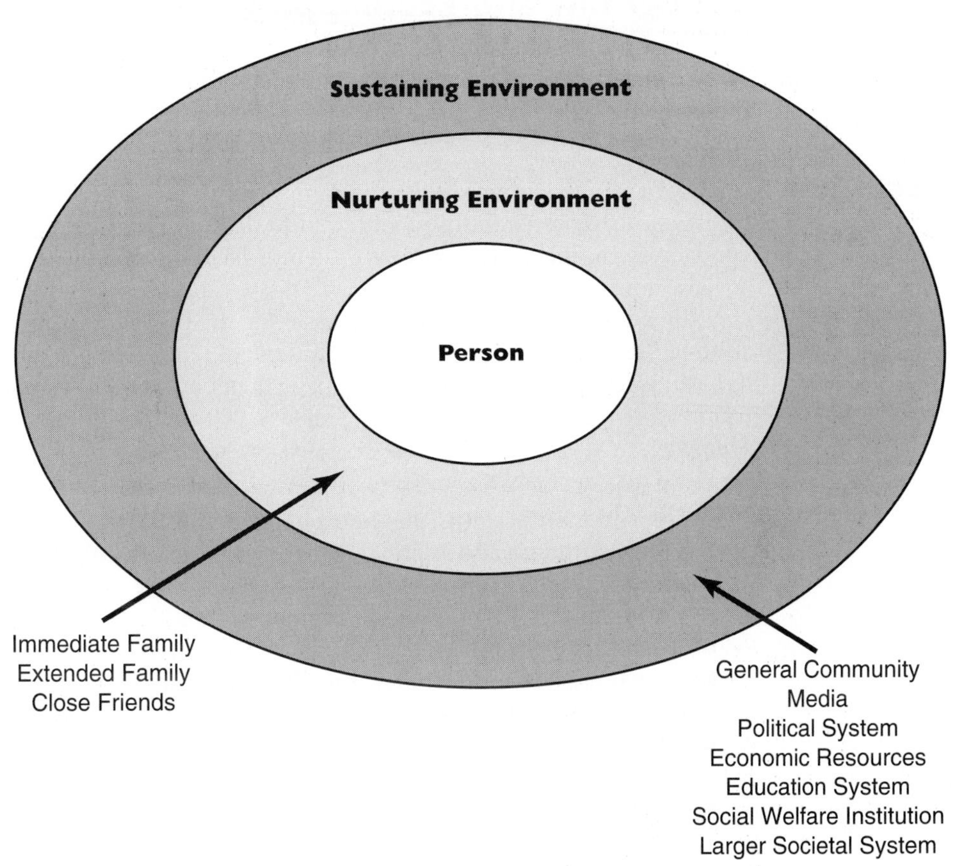

sessment directly with clients to check the accuracy of the judgments and help clients gain insights into the issues they face.

Examination of the completed dual perspective worksheet will reveal both the areas that need to be changed (i.e., the – notations) and the areas of strength (i.e., the + notations) that might be resources for accomplishing change. With an accurate problem and resource assessment completed, it is then possible to begin planning appropriate interventions.

SELECTED BIBLIOGRAPHY

Norton, Dolores. *The Dual Perspective: Inclusion of Ethnic Minority Content in the Social Work Curriculum.* New York: CSWE, 1978.

———. *Plurality and Ecology.* Alexandra, VA: CSWE, in press.

12.3 Genograms and Ecomapping

PURPOSE: To graphically depict family and interactional data as an aid in the social assessment process.

DISCUSSION: A *genogram* is a diagram similar to a family tree. It can describe family relationships for two or three generations (an attempt to depict more than three generations becomes very complex). The ***ecomap*** drawing places an individual or a family within a social context.

In addition to their value in assessment, the genogram and ecomap can shorten the case record. Descriptions that might require two or three pages of narrative can often be reduced to a single page of genogram and ecomap diagrams. For example, a typical record or social history will include information such as the following:

- Age, sex, marital status, and household composition
- Family structure and relationships (e.g., biological children, stepchildren, parents, etc.)
- Job situation, employment, and responsibilities
- Social activities and interests (hobbies, recreational activities, etc.)
- Formal associations (church membership, participation in union, membership in service club, etc.)
- Sources of support and stress in social interactions (between people and between people and community systems)
- Utilization of community resources (Medicaid, economic assistance, public health, mental health, schools, Social Security, doctors, etc.)
- Informal resources and natural helpers (extended family, relatives, friends, neighbors, self-help groups)

All of these data can be "drawn" into a one-page ecomap.

Although the user of these diagrams can create his or her own symbols and abbreviations, certain symbols are commonly used, as shown in Figure 12.3. Words and notations—such as "m" for "married," "div" for "divorced," and "d" for "died"—may also be used in the family diagram and ecomap.

Figure 12.4 is a diagram of a reconstituted family, which appears within the dotted circle (boundary). It indicates that a man (age 45), his wife (age 33), and three children (ages 3, 1, and 10) live in the household. The 10-year-old is from his mother's former marriage; the boy's biological father died in 1987. The 45-year-old husband was divorced from his former wife (age 42) in 1986. Also, we see that he has two daughters (ages 20 and 18) by this former wife and is now a grandfather, since his 20-year-old daughter has a 1-year-old daughter. The former wife is now married to a man who is age 44.

An ecomap places the family or client within their social context by using circles to represent organizations or factors impacting their lives. Various symbols or

70
female, age 70
15
male, age 15
78
deceased male, died at age 78
marriage
separation
divorce
sibling link
boundary of family or household
parents plus two daughters and twin sons
foster or adoptive children
miscarriage or abortion
a stressful, conflict-laden relationship
a tenuous, uncertain relationship
a positive relationship (the thicker the line, the stronger the relationship)
arrow's direction depicts give and take of a relationship (e.g., client may give more than he or she receives from a relationship)

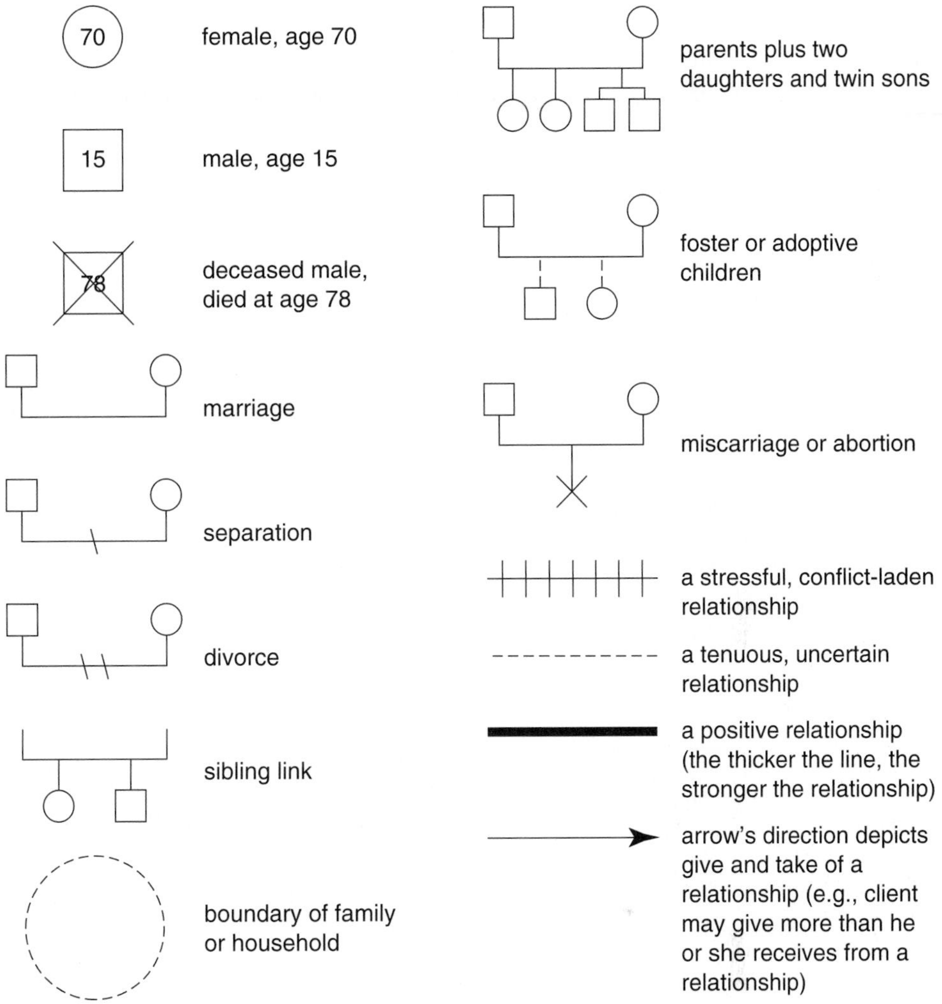

FIGURE 12.3 Symbols for Ecomaps and Genograms

44
42
m. 1971
div. 1986
45
m. 1989
33
died 1987
21
20
18
3
1
10
1

FIGURE 12.4 Genogram of a Reconstituted Family

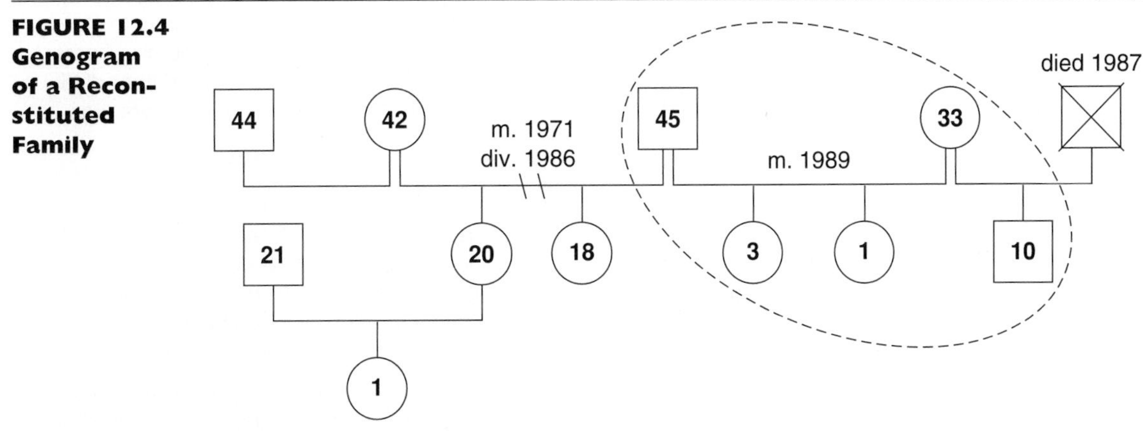

short phrases are used to describe the nature of these interactions. Figure 12.5 is an ecomap of Dick and Barb and their two children, John and June.

Usually, an ecomap is developed jointly by the social worker and client and helps both to view the family from a system's or ecological perspective. Ecomapping can be used by the worker to build a relationship and demonstrate a desire to learn

FIGURE 12.5
Ecomap

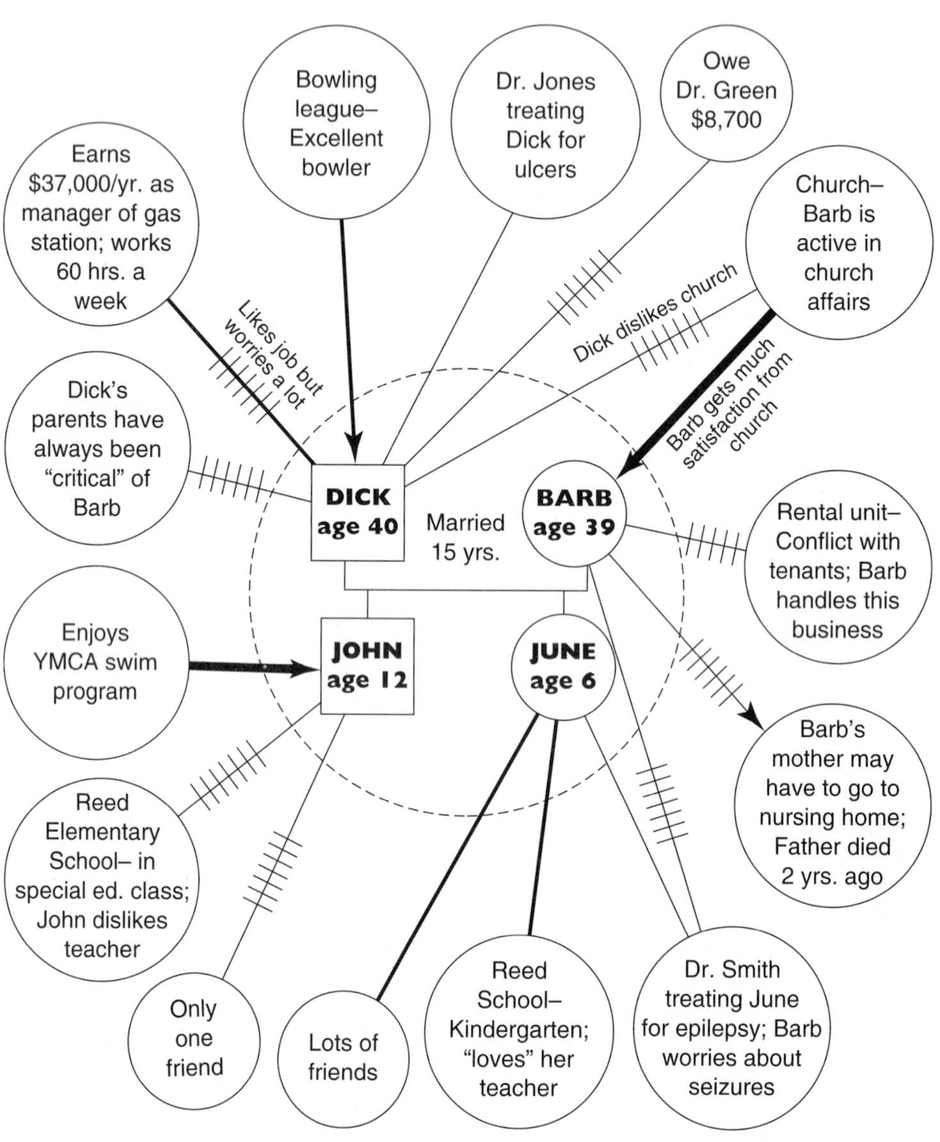

about the client and his or her situation. It has been used in adoption and foster-care home studies and in marriage and family counseling. Many clients report that doing an ecomap helps them see their situation more clearly.

When examining an ecomap, consider a number of basic questions: Does the family have an income adequate to cover basic needs such as food, shelter, transportation, and health care? Are family members employed? Do they enjoy their jobs? Does the family live in a neighborhood that is safe? Does the family interact with relatives, friends, and neighbors? Does the family participate in social, cultural, religious, and community activities? Are the family's values, beliefs, or life-style in conflict with those dominant in the neighborhood? Do the children have access to needed educational resources? Do they enjoy their school experience? Are some of the family members experiencing high levels of stress? Answers to such questions yield important information for assessment and intervention.

SELECTED BIBLIOGRAPHY

Mattaini, Mark. *More than a Thousand Words: Graphics for Clinical Practice.* Washington, DC: NASW Press, 1993.

McGoldrick, Monica, and Randy Gerson. *Genograms in Family Assessment.* New York: W. W. Norton, 1985.

12.4 Social Support Assessment

PURPOSE: To identify people to whom a client might turn for various types of social support.

DISCUSSION: The term ***social support*** refers to the information, encouragement, and tangible assistance that is offered to a person, by others, and is perceived by the person as being beneficial to his or her functioning. Such social supports are a component of one's larger ***social network***—those individuals and groups with which he or she interacts on a regular basis. Although social supports and one's *social support network* exert a positive and helpful influence, other parts of a person's social network may add to his or her stress or have a harmful impact on functioning.

In order to help clients make appropriate and effective use of social supports, it is necessary to engage them in the identification and assessment of potential social supports. The ***Social Network Map*** (Figure 12.6) and its accompanying ***Social Network Grid*** (Figure 12.7) are tools for that purpose. This assessment process was developed and piloted by Tracy as part of the Family Support Project based at the University of Washington (Whittaker, Tracy, and Marckworth 1989). The map and the grid are especially attractive because they use sort cards that draw the client into a visual and tactile activity. Tracy (undated) presents the following sample script as a way of describing how a social worker might communicate with a client as they work together on the Social Network Map and the Social Network Grid:

FIGURE 12.6
Social Network Map

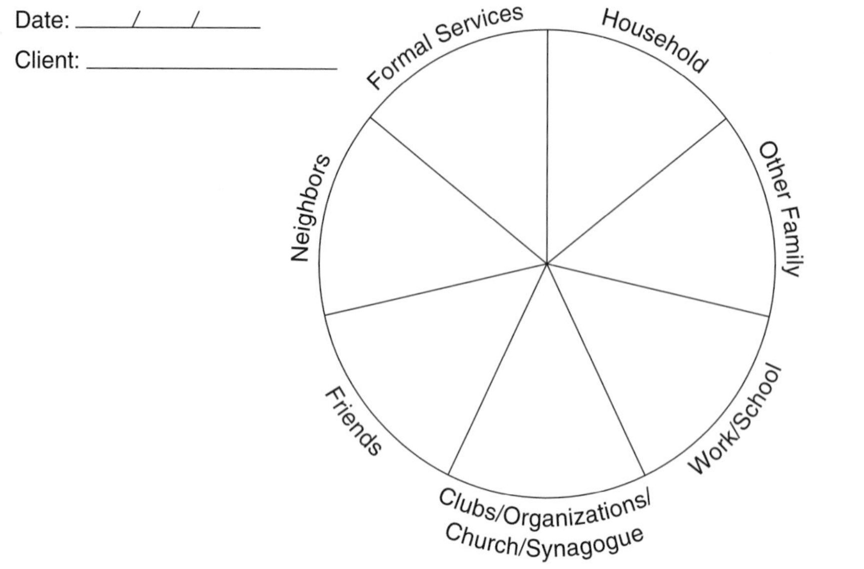

Source: Family Support Project, University of Washington, School of Social Work and Behavioral Sciences Institute. James K. Whittaker, Principal Investigator; Elizabeth M. Tracy, Project Coordinator. Reproduced with permission of Elizabeth M. Tracy.

*Step One: Developing a Social Network Map**
Let's take a look at who is in your social network by putting together a network map. [Show network map—Figure 12.6.] We can use first names or initials because I'm not that interested in knowing the particular people and I wouldn't necessarily be contacting any of the people we talk about.

Think back to this past month, say since [date]. What people have been important to you? They may have been people you saw, talked with, or wrote letters to. This includes people who made you feel good, people who made you feel bad, and others who just played a part in your life. They may be people who had an influence on the way you made decisions during this time.

First, think of people in your *household*—that includes who?

Now going around the map, what *other family members* would you include in your network?

How about *people from work or school?*

People from clubs, organizations or religious groups? Who should we include here?

Other friends that haven't been listed in the other categories?

Neighbors? (Note: Local shopkeepers may be included here.)

Finally, list professional people or people from formal agencies [name] that you have contact with.

Look over your network. Are these the people you would consider part of your social network this past month? (Add or delete names as needed.)

*Reproduced with permission of Elizabeth Tracy.

FIGURE 12.7 Social Network Grid

CLIENT ________ NAME	#	Area of Life 1. Household 2. Other Family 3. Work/School 4. Organizations 5. Other Friends 6. Neighbors 7. Professionals 8. Other	Concrete Support 1. Hardly Ever 2. Sometimes 3. Almost Always	Emotional Support 1. Hardly Ever 2. Sometimes 3. Almost Always	Information/ Advice 1. Hardly Ever 2. Sometimes 3. Almost Always	Critical 1. Hardly Ever 2. Sometimes 3. Almost Always	Direction of Help 1. Goes Both Ways 2. You to Them 3. Them to You	Closeness 1. Not Very Close 2. Sort of Close 3. Very Close	How Often Seen 0. Does Not See 1. Few Times/Yr 2. Monthly 3. Weekly 4. Daily	How Long Known 1. Less Than 1 Yr 2. From 1–5 Yrs 3. More than 5 Yrs
	01									
	02									
	03									
	04									
	05									
	06									
	07									
	08									
	09									
	10									
	11									
	12									
	13									
	14									
	15									

Source: University of Washington, School of Social Work and Behavioral Sciences Institute. James K. Whittaker, Principal Investigator; Elizabeth M. Tracy, Project Coordinator. Reproduced with permission of Elizabeth M. Tracy.

Step Two: Completing the Social Network Grid
(If there are more than 15 people in the network, ask the client to select the "top fifteen," and then ask the questions about only those network members. For each of the questions, use the appropriate sorting guide card. Once the client has divided up the cards, put the appropriate code number for each person listed on the network grid.)

Now, I'd like to learn more about the people in your network. I'm going to write their names on this network grid [see Figure 12.7], put a code number for the area of life, and then ask a few questions about the ways in which they help you. Let's also write their names on these slips of paper too; this will make answering the questions a lot easier. These are the questions I'll be asking (show list of social network questions), and we'll check off the names on this grid as we go through each question.

The first three questions have to do with the *types of support* people give you.

Who would be available to help you out in real *concrete ways*—for example, would give you a ride if you needed one, or would pitch in to help you with a big chore, or would look after your belongings for awhile if you were away? Divide your cards into three piles—those people you can hardly ever rely on for concrete help, those you can rely on sometimes, and those you'd almost always rely on for this type of help.

Now who would be available to give you *emotional support*—for example, to comfort you if you were upset, to be right there with you in a stressful situation, to listen to you talk about your feelings? Again, divide your cards into three piles—those people you can hardly ever rely on for emotional support, those you can rely on sometimes, and those you almost always can rely on for this type of help.

Finally, who do you rely on for *advice*—for example, who would give you information on how to do something, help you make a big decision, or teach you how to do something? Divide your cards into the three piles—hardly ever, sometimes, and almost always—for this type of support.

Look through your cards and this time select those people, if any, in your network that you feel are *critical* of you (or your lifestyle, or you as a parent). When I say "critical," I mean critical of you in a way that makes you feel bad or inadequate. Divide the cards into three piles—those people who are hardly ever critical of you, sometimes critical of you, and almost always critical of you. Again we'll put the code numbers next to their names.

Now look over your cards, and think about the *direction of help*. Divide your cards into three piles—those people where help goes both ways (you help them just as much as they help you), those where it's mostly you helping them, and those where it's mostly them helping you. OK, let's get their code numbers on the grid.

Now think about how *close* you are to the people in your network. Divide the cards into three piles—those people you are not very close to, those you are sort of close to, and those you are very close to—and then we'll put a code number for them.

Finally, just a few questions about *how often* you see people, and *how long* you've known the people in your network.

Divide the cards into four piles—people you see just a few times a year, people you see monthly, people you see weekly, and people you see daily. (*Note:* If you see someone twice or more than twice a week, count that as "daily.") OK, we'll put their numbers on the grid.

This is the last question. Divide the cards into three piles—those people you have known less than a year, from 1–5 years, and over 5 years.

Now we have a pretty complete picture of who is in your social network.

It is important to remember that the Social Support Map and the Social Network Grid do not objectively describe the client's support but rather reflect the client's perceptions and beliefs. It is quite possible that a client may exaggerate or underestimate the importance of some people and simply forget to name others.

Once the map and grid have been completed, the social worker engages the client in a discussion of how the client might reach out to and use identified social supports. Whether the supports are likely resources will depend on the nature of the client's problem or needs and the client's willingness to use them.

SELECTED BIBLIOGRAPHY

Kemp, Susan, James Whittaker, and Elizabeth Tracy. *Person-Environment Practice.* New York: Aldine de Gruyter, 1997.

Tracy, Elizabeth. *Social Support Assessment.* Seattle: University of Washington School of Social Work, Family Support Project (mimeograph, undated).

Tracy, Elizabeth, and James Whittaker. "The Social Network Map: Assessing Social Support in Clinical Practice." *Families in Society* 71 (October 1990): 461–470.

Whittaker, James, Elizabeth Tracy, and Peg Marckworth. *The Family Support Project: Identifying Informal Support Resources for High Risk Families.* Seattle: School of Social Work, University of Washington, 1989.

12.5 Life History Grid

PURPOSE: To graphically depict significant events in a client's life and/or the development of significant problems through time.

DISCUSSION: The ***life history grid*** is a method of organizing and presenting data related to the various periods in a client's life. The grid is especially useful in work with children and adolescents, where an understanding of life experiences during a particular stage of development may shed light on current functioning. Data from a variety of sources (interview, agency records, hospital records, etc.) are brought together in a life grid.

Figure 12.8 is a grid prepared on David, a 14-year-old referred to a social worker because of behavior problems. When one examines David's life history grid, it becomes apparent that his problems have grown worse in reaction to his parents' escalating marital conflict and eventual divorce. Also, there appears to be a relationship between his asthma attacks and significant family changes. Thus, we see that a life history grid can help a social worker formulate hypotheses about the origin of problem behavior and suggest focal points for intervention.

SELECTED BIBLIOGRAPHY

Anderson, James, and Ralph Brown. "Life History Grid for Adolescents." *Social Work* 25 (July 1980): 321–322.

FIGURE 12.8 Sample Life History Grid

Client: David

Year	Age	Location	Family	School	Health	Activities	Problems
1985	DOB: 3-23-85	Chicago, IL	Father 21, Mother 18	—	Normal birth	—	—
1986	1						
1987	2		Karen born				
1988	3	Billings, MT			Asthma, hospital, 3 days		
1989	4						
1990	5	Denver, CO	Donald born	K—Lewis & Clark School	Asthma, in hospital 3 times		
1991	6		Dad drinking a lot	I—very fearful of school	Car accident, broken leg		Did not like school Frequently sick
1992	7	Butte, MT		II—new school			Lots of fights at school
1993	8		Dad fired from job	III		Cub Scouts	
1994	9		Mother takes job	IV—poor grades	Asthma attack		Steals money from mother
1995	10			V	Appendec-tomy		Ran away from home
1996	11	Denver, CO	Parents separate and mother moves	VI—poor grades	Asthma attack/ hospital		Breaks classmate's nose in fight
1997	12			VII—truancy		Paper route	Alcohol & fighting
1998	13	Mother & kids move to Helena, MT	Parents divorce	VII—new school			Hits teacher, suicide gesture
1999	14		Dad killed in car accident	Freshman at Big Sky HS		Tried out for football; did not make team	Pot smoking, arrest for shoplifting, poor grades

12.6 Life Cycle Matrix

PURPOSE: To graphically depict the developmental stage of all persons in a household.

DISCUSSION: An assessment should consider the client's stage in the life cycle and the developmental tasks common to that stage. This is especially important in work with families because the various members are at different points in the life cycle. The use of a matrix can help the social worker organize his or her thoughts about the family members and the physical, psychological, social, and spiritual needs associated with a particular stage of life.

Figure 12.9 depicts a household made up of a father, mother, three children, and a grandmother. The importance of considering the developmental stage of each member of a household becomes apparent when we recognize that certain tasks need to be accomplished and certain developmental crises must be resolved during each stage. Within a family system, the developmental struggles of one member may interfere with the developmental tasks and crises faced by another.

Table 12.1 presents an overview of life cycle stages intended to remind the social worker how developmental tasks change over time. The concept of developmental crisis reflects the belief that psychosocial development proceeds by stages; each stage represents a time to decide between hanging on to the old or letting go and moving on to a new way of thinking and behaving.

SELECTED BIBLIOGRAPHY

Berk, Laura. *Development through the Life Span.* Boston: Allyn and Bacon, 1998.

Kaplan, Paul. *The Human Odyssey: Life-Span Development,* 3rd ed. Pacific Grove, CA: Brooks/Cole, 1998.

FIGURE 12.9 Sample Life Cycle Matrix

	Developmental Stage								
Family Member	0–1	2–4	5–7	8–12	13–17	18–22	23–34	35–60	61+
Margaret (Grandmother)									✗
John								✗	
Mary								✗	
John (Jr.)					✗				
Jimmy			✗						
Mary		✗							

TABLE 12.1 The Life Cycle

Stage	Common Developmental Tasks	Developmental Crisis
Prenatal (conception to birth)	■ In utero physical development	
Infant (birth–2 years)	■ Bonding and attachment ■ Differentiation of emotions ■ Maturation of nervous and motor systems ■ Concept of object permanence ■ Beginning understanding of causality	Basic trust versus mistrust of others
Toddler (2–4 years)	■ Fantasy and play ■ Language ■ Self-control ■ Locomotion ■ Use of symbols in thought	Basic sense of worth and autonomy versus shame and self-doubt
Early school age (5–7 years)	■ Group play ■ Early gender identification ■ Beginning moral standards ■ Learning of classification, combination, and other basic intellectual skills	Taking initiative versus only reacting to or imitating others
Middle school age (8–12 years)	■ Cooperation with others ■ Team play ■ Same sex peer identification ■ Introspection	Self-confidence and industry versus inferiority
Early adolescence (13–17 years)	■ Physical and sexual maturation ■ Membership in peer group ■ Boy-girl relationships ■ Abstract thought processes ■ Coping with strong emotions	Group identity versus sense of alienation
Late adolescence (18–22 years)	■ Dating and mate selection ■ Sex-role identity ■ Internalization of moral principles ■ Career choice ■ Separation from parent	Individual identity versus role diffusion and confusion
Early adulthood (23–34 years)	■ Marriage ■ Childbearing ■ Work ■ Developing life-style apart from parents	Intimacy versus isolation
Middle adulthood (35–60 years)	■ Childrearing ■ Career development ■ Management of home and financial resources	Expansion of life experience and concern for society versus stagnation and self-absorption
Late adulthood (61+ years)	■ Coping with physical change and health problems ■ Acceptance of one's own life choices ■ Redirection of energy after retirement ■ Developing a perspective on one's death	Integrity versus despair

12.7 Identifying Client Strengths

PURPOSE: To identify individual and family strengths.

DISCUSSION: A social worker's assessment of a client's functioning and situation should emphasize strengths rather than weaknesses and pathology. It should identify positive and functional patterns rather than only the dysfunctional ones. In short, the assessment should focus mostly on what the client can do and wants to do, rather than on what the client cannot do or will not do. This is not to suggest a Pollyannaish approach that ignores or overlooks real problems, but it does ask the worker to search for strengths even in the most dysfunctional, difficult, and chaotic of cases. The reason for this emphasis is simple: To be successful, *an intervention must be built on and around client strengths.* If the worker focuses only on problems and on what is going wrong in the client's life, the client will soon feel even more frustrated and discouraged and the worker will feel pessimistic about being able to be of help.

For many in the helping professions, focusing on client strengths requires a paradigm shift—a whole new way of thought and analysis. Several forces encourage and reinforce a focus on problems and limitations rather than on strengths. Consider the following:

- *Agency policy and funding.* Most human services agencies are created for the purpose of addressing or correcting some personal or family problem, pathology, deficiency, or dysfunction. Thus, agency staff may assume that their primary "duty" is to identify and focus on problems.
- *Diagnostic labels.* Commonly used terminology and reference books (e.g., *DSM IV*) focus attention on pathology and on all that is wrong and troublesome in a person's life. Frequent use of this terminology creates a rather negative mindset that looks for and finds only problems and pathology.
- *Lack of skill.* Identifying personal and family problems can be described as a beginning level or elementary skill. Most people can do it with little or no training. On the other hand, identifying strengths is an advanced or high-level skill. It is a skill that many seem unable to learn.
- *Personality and temperament.* Many people tend to be negative in their outlook. They see the glass as "half empty" rather than "half full." They just naturally focus on what is missing and on what is wrong. Some sociobiologists believe that the human tendency to notice quickly what is wrong and out of place has a survival or protective value for animals and the human species. Consequently, evolution has "wired" our senses and perceptual processes so we will quickly notice things that are unusual, because doing so helps us to detect and avoid dangers in our environment.

As suggested earlier, a strength is something positive and important that an individual or a family can do and will do. The social worker can identify strengths by carefully observing individual and family behavior. Examples of ***individual strengths*** include the following:

- Assuming responsibility for one's actions
- Taking reasonable risks in order to make needed changes
- Demonstrating loyalty and a sense of duty to family, relatives, and friends
- Showing affection, compassion, and concern for others; demonstrating a willingness to forgive others
- Assisting and encouraging others; protecting others from harm
- Seeking employment, holding a job, being a responsible employee, meeting one's financial obligations
- Exercising self-control and making thoughtful decisions and plans; choosing not to engage in problem or self-defeating behavior (e.g., an angry youth wanted to beat up another teen but chose to walk away)
- Being trustworthy, fair, and honest in dealing with others
- Experiencing true and appropriate sorrow and guilt; making amends or restitution for having harmed others
- Seeking to understand others and their situations and accepting differences among people
- Willingness to keep trying despite hardship and setback
- Participating in social, community, or religious organizations and working to improve one's neighborhood and community
- Expressing one's point of view and standing up for one's own rights and the rights of others
- Making constructive use of special abilities and aptitudes (e.g., mechanical, artistic, interpersonal, athletic, etc.)

Important ***family strengths*** include the following:

- Members trust, respect, and enjoy each other.
- Members listen to and respect each other's opinions, even when they disagree. Their communication is clear, positive, and productive.
- The family has clear and reasonable rules that govern behavior and interaction.
- Each member's ideas, preferences, and needs are considered before making a decision that would affect the family.
- The family has traditions, rituals, and stories that provide a sense of history, belonging, and identity.
- Family members share what they have and make personal sacrifices in order to help each other; members stick together and support each other in times of adversity.
- Conflicts are acknowledged and resolved.

Additional client strengths are listed in Item 12.17.

Strengths can be identified by asking the client questions such as: Can you tell me about times when you successfully handled problems similar to those you now face? Where did you find the courage and energy to deal with those problems? How have you managed to cope up to this point? What kept you going? Despite your current problems, what parts of your life are going fairly well? What do other people like about you? What strengths or advantages do others see in your approach to life? What would you not change about yourself, your situation, and your life?

Building on client strengths may require looking at a client's problems from a different angle. For example, consider the man who has been labeled uncooperative and unmotivated. If one views this so-called uncooperative behavior from another perspective, one uncovers a strength: He is asserting his rights to disagree and resist doing what does not make sense. In other words, he is being logical and assertive. When problems are reframed in ways that reveal strengths, one usually also discovers more effective ways of helping. (See Item 14.12 for other examples of redefining a problem as a strength.)

Another way of orienting your approach to one that recognizes and builds on client strengths is to operate on the assumption that within all people, there are innate tendencies toward psychological health and prosocial behavior. Just as there are natural healing processes that are constantly repairing the human body, there appears to be natural forces that, over time, tend to heal and repair psychological damage, ruptured relationships, and the many other hurts that are part of human life and living. If such a belief is a reasonable one, it lends hope to the worker's helping efforts. It informs the social worker of the importance of supporting those natural forces and creating conditions and environments that allow the client's natural healing processes to work.

Drawing on some suggestions made by Cowger (1994), several guidelines are offered that will help the worker maintain a focus on strengths:

1. Believe the client. Assume that he or she is honest and trustworthy, unless it is proven otherwise. Assume that all people are capable of making positive changes in how they cope with the challenges of life and in how they interact with others.

2. Display an interest in strengths. Listen for and call to the client's attention all indicators of the client's competence, skill, resourcefulness, and motivation to make his or her situation better.

3. Assume that the client is an "expert" on his or her behavior, life, and situation, and knows best what will and will not work in a change effort or treatment plan. Give primary attention to the client's own perceptions and understanding of his or her situation. View the client as the "director" of the helping process.

4. View the assessment and the service planning processes as joint worker-client activity. Both the client and the professional share responsibility for determining what concern or issue needs to be addressed and how this can be done.

5. Assess but do not diagnose. Avoid the use of diagnostic labeling, for it draws attention away from client strengths and places the focus on pathology and deficits.

6. Avoid discussions of blame and what the client or others should or should not have done previously. Attempts to assign blame lead nowhere and use time and energy better spent on problem solving. Rather, focus on what can be done now. Also, avoid pointless discussions of cause and effect. Typically, problems of social functioning arise from many complex and interrelated factors. Trying to figure out the exact cause of a problem is usually nonproductive. Time is better spent on here-and-now problem solving.

7. Assume that within the client's family, social network, and community there is an "oasis" of potential resources, both formal and informal, that can be drawn into the helping process. Every family, every neighborhood, and every community contains people who are willing and capable of being helpful and supportive of others.

8. Formulate an intervention plan that is specific and individualized to the client and his or her situation. Because every individual and every family is unique and unlike every other one, all treatment plans or service plans should be unique.

SELECTED BIBLIOGRAPHY

Cowger, Charles. "Assessing Client Strengths: Clinical Assessment for Client Empowerment." *Social Work* 39 (May 1994): 262–268.

McQuaide, Sharon, and John Ehrenreich. "Assessing Client Strengths." *Families in Society* (March 1997): 201–212.

Saleebey, Dennis, ed. *The Strengths Perspective in Social Work Practice,* 2nd ed. New York: Longman, 1997.

12.8 Coping Strategies and Ego Defenses

PURPOSE: To identify a client's usual methods of coping and defenses in order to anticipate how the client will respond to difficult situations.

DISCUSSION: Some people use the terms *coping strategy* and *ego defense mechanism* interchangeably, but the authors find it useful to make a distinction based on the degree to which the response is under conscious and voluntary control and whether self-deception and reality distortion is involved. A ***coping strategy*** is a fairly deliberate and conscious effort to solve a problem or handle personal distress. By contrast, an ***ego defense mechanism*** is often a habitual or unconscious problem-avoiding maneuver.

Coping strategies have two functions: to solve a problem (task-focused coping) and to reduce the emotional discomfort caused by stressors (emotion-focused coping). Often, an individual must first deal with emotional reactions before moving on to problem solving, but emotion-focused and task-focused coping frequently occur simultaneously.

Individuals vary widely in the type of emotion-focused strategies they use to cope with painful feelings and stressful situations. For example, given a situation that causes much anxiety, some individuals might elect to go off by themselves, others might visit friends, some pray and meditate, and still others might engage in a brisk physical workout. Other coping strategies—some functional, some not so functional—include ignoring the problem, sleeping more, eating more, and becoming absorbed in work. Since an individual tends to use certain coping strategies habitually, the social worker can get a pretty good idea of a client's usual coping strategies by asking how he or she behaved previously in response to stressful situations.

In their initial reactions to intense emotional pain, people, regardless of culture, use certain ***emotion-focused coping strategies,*** such as the following:

- *Crying.* Crying is a common and normal means of alleviating tension and responding to loss. It is a necessary part of successful grief work.
- *Talking it out.* People who have undergone traumatic experiences often need to repeatedly describe and talk about the experience. As a result of this natural desensitization process, they eventually learn to accept and tolerate the painful thoughts and feelings associated with the traumatic experience.
- *Laughing it off.* Joking and viewing painful experiences with a sense of humor serves to release tension and place the matter in perspective. In successful grieving, for example, there is often a good mix of crying and laughter among those adjusting to the death of a loved one.
- *Seeking support.* It is natural for both children and adults to seek support, attention, and affection from others as a means of regaining emotional equilibrium.
- *Dreaming and nightmares.* These do not fit the authors' definition of a coping strategy (i.e., conscious and voluntary) but they are a common reaction to traumatic experience. These dreams and nightmares are often repetitive. And, like the desensitization process involved in talking it out, the recurring dream encourages the individual to consciously grapple with the experience.

If a client has recently had a traumatic experience (rape, death of a loved one, etc.), the social worker should be especially attentive to the coping strategies just mentioned and, where possible, facilitate their utilization by the client. In working with clients who have moved beyond these initial, emotion-focused responses or who have not had a recent traumatic experience, the social worker's assessment should give more attention to task-focused strategies.

The more ***task-focused coping strategies*** involve deliberate action to make changes in one's self, one's environment, or both. As compared to the emotion-focused strategies, these are more rational and planned. Listed here are coping strategies of a rather general nature, but they illustrate what the social worker would be looking for in data collection and assessment. A client with good task-oriented coping strategies will have the motivation, the capacity, and the opportunity to:

- Express thoughts and feelings in a clear, positive, and, when necessary, assertive manner.
- Ask questions and gather new information, even when the new information may challenge current beliefs.
- Identify one's personal needs and learn socially acceptable means of meeting those needs.

- Model one's own behavior after persons who behave in an effective and responsible manner.
- Recognize that one does have choices and can exert influence on one's own behavior, feelings, and life events.
- "Cut one's losses" and withdraw from relationships or situations that are unhealthy or stressful and unchangeable.
- Examine the religious and spiritual dimension of life and draw on one's beliefs for insight, strength, and direction.
- Identify early signs or indicators of a developing problem so action can be taken before the problem becomes serious.
- Take positive and appropriate steps to solve problems even when such actions are a source of fear and anxiety.
- Release pent-up emotion in ways that do not verbally or physically harm self or others.
- Take care of one's body and maintain one's health.
- Delay immediate gratification in order to stick with a plan that will attain a more distant but desired goal.
- Use mental images of future actions or events to mentally rehearse how to handle anticipated difficulties.
- Make fair and appropriate changes in one's daily activities of living so as not to interfere with the needs of others.
- Ignore unjustified criticism by others and remove one's self from situations that lead to self-defeating or harmful outcomes.
- Seek out and use additional skills training and needed professional services.

If the assessment reveals that a client lacks necessary coping strategies, the intervention plan should focus on helping the client learn specific *coping skills.* Of course, the skills needed will depend on the client's problem, situation, and goals. For example, an abusing parent may need to learn parenting skills, an individual in need of a job will need to focus on job finding skills, a married couple in conflict may need communication skills, and a youth leaving the foster-care system will need to acquire independent living skills.

Defense mechanisms frequently mentioned in the professional literature include denial, projection, repression, reaction formation, rationalization, displacement, intellectualization, fantasy, and acting out. The *DSM-IV* (American Psychiatric Association 1994, 765) defines ***defense mechanisms*** as "automatic psychological process that protects the individual against anxiety and from awareness of internal or external stressors or dangers."

We all use defense mechanisms as we cope with anxiety, stress, and the problems of living. It is clear, however, that defensiveness impairs a person's ability to accurately perceive reality and get along with others. The rigid or excessive use of defenses is a barrier to realistic problem solving. High levels of defensiveness and distortions of reality are characteristic of disturbed personalities.

An individual who uses the ego defense of ***denial*** screens out certain realities by refusing to acknowledge them. Denial is often used in combination with ***rationalization,*** which involves the justification of inappropriate behavior by manufacturing logical or socially acceptable reasons for the behavior. An example is the abusing parent who justifies physical abuse on the basis that "the only thing he understands is pain." Although clearly a distortion of the truth, a rationalization is not the same as a lie because the defensive pattern is so habitual that the person is not consciously and deliberately trying to fabricate a falsehood. Denial and rationalization are predominant defenses used by people who are chemically dependent.

In ***projection,*** others are seen as being responsible for one's own shortcomings or unacceptable behavior. For example, the child molester may believe that he was seduced by the young child and sees himself as the victim rather than the offender.

Repression refers to a mental process in which extremely threatening and painful thoughts or experiences are excluded from consciousness. For example, a child may repress experiences of sexual abuse and not remember them until years later.

Emotional insulation is a maneuver aimed at withholding an emotional investment in a desired but unlikely outcome. This defense creates a shield that protects the individual from loss or a recurrence of pain and disappointment. For example, a child who is moved frequently from foster home to foster home may use emotional insulation as a defense against the pain of separation and loss; unfortunately, such a child often carries this pattern into adulthood and is then unable to develop emotional attachments to a marriage partner or to his or her own children. This defense is closely related to the concept of "learned helplessness"—after a long period of frustration, many people simply give up and quit trying to escape their misery. These are the "broken" individuals who become passive recipients of whatever life brings them. Emotional insulation is commonly used by persons who have grown up in extreme deprivation.

Intellectualization involves the use of abstractions as a way of distancing one's self from emotional pain. The impact of disappointment and hurt is softened by theoretical explanations and platitudes. For example, the individual who is turned down for a much desired job may avoid feelings of disappointment by discussing the country's economic theory and global markets.

Regression involves a retreat from one's present level of maturity to one that has fewer demands and stressors. For example, when a new child is born to a family, the 5-year-old may begin behaving like an infant (e.g., wetting pants, sucking thumb, etc.) as a way of getting more attention and coping with fears of being overlooked by his or her parents. Regression is common among physically ill persons who are experiencing much fear or pain.

When using ***reaction formation,*** a person defends against troublesome thoughts, feelings, or impulses by rigidly adhering to exactly the opposite set of thoughts and behaviors. An example is an individual who discovers he is sexually attracted to children. In response, such a person becomes obsessed with the dangers of child sexual abuse and campaigns endlessly for prevention programs.

Displacement refers to transferring troublesome emotions (often hostility) and acting-out behaviors (e.g., violence) from the person(s) who arouses the emotion to another less threatening and less powerful person or thing. The classic example is the man who kicks his dog because he is angry with his boss.

When using ***fantasy*** as a defense, a person daydreams imaginary achievements and pleasant situations as a way of meeting personal needs or counteracting painful feelings of inadequacy. Serious problems develop when the person finds his or her reality so painful that much of the time is spent in a fantasy world. Excessive fantasy and the inability to distinguish between fantasy and reality are often symptoms of serious mental illness.

Acting out is not a defensive maneuver like the mechanisms just described, but it is a pattern of thought and behavior designed to alleviate stress and inner conflict. For example, an angry and frustrated individual may seek release from inner tension by attacking the person he or she views as the source of trouble. An example of another form of acting out is the battered wife who feels the tensions build and knows she will soon be beaten by her husband, so she proceeds to provoke him so she can "get it over with." Combat soldiers who can no longer handle the stress of waiting for an attack have been known to leave the safety of their foxhole and blindly charge the enemy.

Several guidelines can be offered to assist the social worker in assessing and responding to a client's defense mechanisms. Consider the following:

1. When using defense mechanism terminology, certain precautions are necessary. The patterns we call defenses are only hypothetical constructs inferred from the way people behave. At best, they are a shorthand language for describing behavior. Simply labeling a client's behavior as projection or rationalization, for example, in no way explains nor changes the behavior. You must look behind the surface behavior and identify and address the unmet needs and pain that cause the client to rely on the defense mechanism.

2. Because defenses are mostly learned and habitual, an individual tends to utilize those defenses he or she has used in the past. For example, if, in the past, an individual frequently used denial and rationalization, you can expect him or her to use those same defenses when again faced with anxiety or conflict.

3. People hold tightly to their defensive patterns. The more anxiety they experience, the more rigidly they use the defense. People do not easily give up these habits of thought and behavior. It is usually only within a relationship characterized by empathy, warmth, and genuineness that a person can feel safe enough to let down his or her defenses and examine the underlying pain.

4. Sometimes it can be difficult to tell where a true description leaves off and rationalization begins. Behaviors that suggest rationalization by a client include: (a) groping for reasons to justify an action or belief, (b) inability to recognize inconsistencies in his or her own "story," and (c) unwillingness to consider alternative explanations and becoming angry when one's "reasons" are questioned.

SELECTED BIBLIOGRAPHY

American Psychiatric Association. *Diagnostic and Statistical Manual of Mental Disorders (DSM-IV)*, 4th ed., rev. Washington DC: American Psychiatric Association, 1994.

Conte, Hope, and Robert Plutchik. *Ego Defenses: Theory and Measurement.* New York: Wiley and Sons, 1995.

12.9 Assessing a Client's Role Performance

PURPOSE: To clarify and describe the nature of a client's difficulty in performing role-related behaviors.

DISCUSSION: As used here, a problem in role performance refers to a significant discrepancy between a client's behavior and that considered appropriate to one of his or her assigned roles (e.g., employee, parent, spouse, etc.). A number of concepts borrowed from role theories can help the social worker assess and describe role behavior. These concepts are especially useful because they bridge psychological and social perspectives on human behavior and deepen the understanding of social functioning.

The concept of ***social role*** derives from the observation that within a society's social structure and institutions, certain behaviors and norms are prescribed for certain relationships. For example, in the parent-child relationship, the parent is expected to provide the child with food, shelter, supervision, guidance, and so on. In a teacher-student relationship, the teacher is expected to teach, and the student is expected to learn that which the teacher judges to be important. The term *role,* borrowed from the world of theater, implies that a script, an actor, and an audience are components of interactional behavior.

The term ***role expectation*** suggests that for a given role (e.g., parent, social worker), there is a cluster of behaviors that are deemed appropriate and acceptable by a reference group or by society as a whole. In other words, the reference group (e.g., a peer group, organization, or community) expects the individual to behave in a certain way and will either approve or disapprove of the person, depending on whether he or she conforms to those norms or expectations. Role expectations define the limits or the range of acceptable and tolerated behavior.

Role performance (or role enactment) refers to a person's actual behavior, which may or may not conform to role expectations. ***Role conception*** (or subjective role) is an individual's beliefs about a role and how he or she expects to behave in that role. One's expectation of self in a particular role may or may not conform to role expectations, as defined by other social systems and wider society. The term ***role demands*** refers to the specific knowledge, values, skills, physical and mental abilities, and other personal attributes necessary to perform a particular role successfully.

A number of terms are used to describe problems in role performance. ***Interrole conflict*** refers to an incompatibility or clash between two or more roles. For example, a woman may experience a conflict between her role as parent to a young child and her role as a corporate executive who is expected to make frequent out-of-town business trips. ***Intrarole conflict*** exists when a person is caught up in a situation where two or more sets of expectations are assigned to a single role. For example, a high school boy may not be able to reconcile the role of student as defined by his teacher with how the role is defined by his peers. ***Role incapacity*** exists when, for some reason, an individual cannot adequately perform a role; possible reasons include physical or mental illness, lack of needed knowledge or skills, drug addiction, mental retardation, and so on. ***Role rejection*** occurs when an individual refuses to perform a role; an extreme example is when a parent abandons his or her child.

A problem of ***role ambiguity*** (or role confusion) exists when there are few clear expectations associated with a role—a condition most likely to occur in times of rapid social change. Consequently, the individual is unsure of what is expected and is unable to evaluate his or her own performance. ***Self-role incongruence*** exists when there is little overlap between the requirements of a role and the individual's personality. For example, an individual may occupy the role of a professional but not feel comfortable in that role. Another example is when an individual finds that his or her values, ethics, or life-style is at odds with the expectations of a role. The problem of ***role overload*** exists when a person occupies more roles than he or she can perform adequately. In reality, most individuals are unable or do not choose to conform to the expectations of all their social roles. Thus, most people live with some degree of ***role strain,*** a situation that necessitates making compromises and trade-offs, setting priorities, and using the various defense mechanisms and coping strategies to reconcile role demands with limited time, energy, and commitment.

A number of questions can help the social worker analyze problems of role performance and make decisions concerning the type of intervention needed. The questions are based, in part, on ones proposed by Mager and Pipe (1970) for the analysis of job-related performance problems. Consider the following:

1. *What is the nature and degree of the discrepancy between actual performance and role expectation?*

- How does the client's behavior differ from that considered appropriate or "normal" for persons in this particular role?
- What observations, events, or experiences have caused you and/or the client to conclude that a discrepancy exists?
- Why are you and/or the client dissatisfied or concerned about the client's role performance? Why is this role important? What will happen if there is no change in the client's role performance?

2. *Is the discrepancy caused by a lack of knowledge or skill?*

- Does the client possess the knowledge or skill needed to perform this role?
- Could the client adequately perform this role if he or she really had to or really wanted to? Could he or she do it if life depended on it?

3. *If the discrepancy is caused by a lack of knowledge and skill, how best can the problem be addressed?*

- Was there a time when the client could perform this role? If so, what experience or condition has caused the client to lose the capacity or motivation to perform this role?
- What can be done to help the client regain a capacity that has deteriorated?
- Is the client now able to learn the behaviors needed to perform the role?
- What teaching methods or techniques will help the client learn the behaviors needed to perform this role?

4. *If the discrepancy is caused by a rejection or a lack of interest in the role, how can the problem be addressed?*
   - Does this role really matter to the client? Is it important to the client?
   - What roles or activities does the client consider more important?
   - Does the client see any benefits in performing this role?
   - Is the client rewarded or reinforced for the performance of this role? If not, how can rewards be increased?
   - Is the client punished by others or the social environment for attempting to perform this role? How can the client be helped to avoid this punishment?

SELECTED BIBLIOGRAPHY

Davis, Liane. "Role Theory." In *Social Work Treatment,* 4th ed., edited by Francis Turner. New York: Free Press, 1996, pp. 581–600.

Mager, Robert, and Peter Pipe. *Analyzing Performance Problems.* Belmont, CA: Pitman Learning, 1970.

12.10 Assessing a Client's Self-Concept

PURPOSE: To understand a client's perceptions and thoughts about herself or himself as a person.

DISCUSSION: The term *self* refers to that private world of perceptions and thoughts that each of us has about ourselves and our life experiences. Basically, one's sense of self answers the question: Who am I? Meador and Rogers (1984, 158) explain that the term ***self-concept*** refers to a "set of perceptions of the characteristics of the 'I' or 'me' and the perceptions of the relationship of the 'I' or 'me' to others and to various aspects of life, together with the values attached to those perceptions." This sense of self is of critical importance to our social functioning because how we respond to others and to events is strongly influenced by how we think and feel about ourselves. However, Nurius and Berlin (1995, 517–518) remind us that each of us has not one, but rather "multiple concepts about who she or he is, sometimes is, was, should be or could be." They also state that the concept of self that is activated is, to some degree, responsive to the situation and the circumstances or tasks most salient at that time.

Several other terms and concepts are used to explain and describe various aspects of the private, inner world of the self. ***Self-identity*** is how we define and describe ourselves to ourselves and differentiate ourselves from other people. It is important to recognize that what we think about ourselves (our private thoughts) may be different from the image we present to other people. Thus, we have a private self and a public self. Others may view us quite differently than we view ourselves. ***Self-efficacy*** has to do with our feelings of being competent and effective and in control of one's life. The term ***self-worth*** (self-esteem) refers to our evaluation of our own value or adequacy as human beings. Self-worth is a very subjective evaluation, not an objective one. The term ***self-acceptance*** can be thought of as the degree to which we are satisfied and at peace with our qualities and attributes, assets and limitations. The term ***ideal-self*** (self-expectation) refers to our inner thoughts about who we could be, should be, or want to be. ***Body image*** refers to our perceptions of our bodies. Deeply personal thoughts and the core beliefs that are part of the self have much to do with the meaning and purpose we assign to our lives and our life experiences; thus, a person's sense of self is closely related to his or her ***spirituality.***

To a large degree, one's sense of self is formed during early childhood but experiences during adolescence also exert a strong influence. However, experiences throughout one's lifetime can lead one to reevaluate and modify the answer to the questions: Who am I? and How did I come to be the person I am?

Whether a particular aspect of a client's self-concept needs to be discussed during the assessment process depends on the client's concern and situation and the reasons why the client and social worker are meeting together. The exploration of a client's sense of self must be approached with great sensitivity. However, because people generally want to tell their story and describe meaningful life experiences, many clients respond nondefensively to questioning that is organized around five dimensions of experience that are common to the human condition. These dimensions are love, loss, fear, being hurt, and hurting others:

1. *Who and what do you love?* Who do you really care for? What is most important to you? For whom do you make personal sacrifices? For what purposes do you donate your time and money? Are you able to love others as you want to?

2. *Who and what have you lost?* Have you lost parents, children, and close friends to death or separation? Have loved ones become disabled or seriously ill? Have you lost your hopes and dreams because of divorce, abandonment, or relocation? Have you lost some physical abilities as a result of illness or injury (e.g., mobility, vision, hearing, etc.)? Have you lost your sense of emotional security and personal safety as a result of abuse, exploitation, violence, or war? Have you lost purpose and meaning in life? Have you lost contact with your homeland or native language? Have you lost touch with meaningful religious and cultural activity? Have you lost a home or important possessions to a flood, fire, or natural disaster?

3. *Who and what do you fear?* Do you live with a fear of hunger, violence, illness, pain, disability, or death? Do you fear that no one cares for you? Do you fear that you are incapable of loving others? Do you fear the loss of respect and status? Do you fear the loss of important relationships, a job, money, or a home?

4. *How have you been hurt in life?* How and when were you hurt by others (physically, emotionally, financially, etc.)? How do you explain these painful life experiences? Who is responsible? Have these past hurts given rise to fears of being hurt again or a desire for revenge? How have these experiences affected the way you think and feel about yourself and others?

5. *Whom have you hurt?* How and when have you hurt others, deliberately or inadvertently? Why did it happen? How do you explain these experiences? How has your hurting of others shaped the way you think and feel about yourself? What have you done to correct or make amends for the pain and injury you caused?

Included next are some other lines of questioning that might be used, in one form or another, to explore a client's sense of self:

1. *Family membership.* Who is your family (tribe or clan)? For whom do you feel responsible and obligated to care for, help, or look after? With whom do you live? Where do other family members live? How often do you talk to with these family members? To which members of your family do you feel especially close? Are you comfortable with your membership in this family?

2. *Identity.* How do you define yourself in terms of the groupings and labels commonly used to describe people? (For example: Gender? Sexual orientation? Occupation? Nationality? Ethnicity? Religion? Socioeconomic class? Language? Political orientation?)

3. *Body image.* What do you notice most about your body? What do others see when they look at your body? Are you satisfied with your body? To what extent do you worry about illness and a loss of physical capacity? What specifically do you worry about?

4. *Self-acceptance.* To what degree are you comfortable with your answer to the question: Who am I? Do you enjoy times when you are alone? When by yourself, are you comfortable with your thoughts and feelings? Are you usually at ease or usually tense when you are with people you know? If you could change yourself, what, if anything, would you change?

5. *Self-worth.* What criteria do you use when you judge the worth or value of another person? How do you measure up on those same criteria? Do you like yourself? What are your major strengths, talents, and abilities? In what ways are you a unique person?

6. *Ideal-self.* To what degree are you doing or accomplishing what you expect of yourself? Are your hopes and dreams within reach? How do you define personal success? In what areas are you successful? In what areas are you falling short of your expectations? What do you want to accomplish or achieve in your lifetime? What contributions do you want to make to others, your family, or your community? How do you want to be remembered after you die?

7. *Self-efficacy.* Do you feel that you are in control of your life? Which has more influence in your life: the decisions that you make or the decisions that others people make? Do you usually respond to change with anticipation and enthusiasm or with fear? Are you hopeful about your future? Is what you expect to happen mostly good or mostly bad?

8. *Spirituality.* Do you have spiritual or religious beliefs or particular moral standards that I should know about in order to better understand your concerns and situation? Do you have a set of beliefs that help you find meaning and purpose in your life? How do you explain or make sense out of the pain and suffering that you and others experience in life?

9. *Past self and future self.* Do you see yourself as about the same or somewhat different from who you were one year ago? Five years ago? Ten years ago? Do you

have regrets or guilt feelings about the past? Do these feelings have a significant impact on your life? Do you expect that you and your life situation will be different in five years? Will this be a desirable or an undesirable change?

10. *Sense of place.* In what kind of a physical environment are you most comfortable? To what degree are you satisfied with your home? Your neighborhood? Your community? Is there some place you really want to live? Where? Why?

SELECTED BIBLIOGRAPHY

Bracken, Bruce, ed. *Handbook of Self-Concept.* Somerset, NJ: John Wiley and Sons, 1995.

Meador, B. D., and Carl Rogers. "Person-Centered Therapy." In *Current Psychotherapies,* 3rd ed., edited by R. J. Corsini. Itasca, IL: F. E. Peacock, 1984, pp. 142–195.

Nurius, Paula, and Sharon Berlin. "Cognition and Social Cognitive Theory." In *Encyclopedia of Social Work,* 19th ed., vol. 1, edited by Richard Edwards. Washington, DC: NASW Press, 1995, pp. 513–524.

12.11 Family Dynamics and Family Functioning

PURPOSE: To identify the nature and structure of interactions among those who make up a family system.

DISCUSSION: Given the dramatic societal changes of recent decades, it is increasingly difficult to define the term *family.* The U.S. Census Bureau defines a *family* as "two or more persons related by birth, marriage or adoption who reside in the same household" and it defines a *household* as "all the persons, related or not, occupying a housing unit." For purposes of planning human services and maintaining a family-centered approach in the delivery of these services, the authors prefer a definition based on family functions. Thus, the authors define a ***family*** as a group of persons related by biological ties, a legal relationship, and/or long-term expectations of loyalty and commitment, often comprising at least two generations and usually inhabiting one household; moreover, some of the adults of this group must have the intention and also the capacity to carry out all or most of the ***functions common to a family,*** as in the following:

- *Provide for the rearing and socialization of children* (e.g., prepare children for adulthood; teach children what they need to know in order to function within a particular culture and society; teach and model basic values, morals, and social skills such as honesty, responsibility, cooperation, compassion, trust, sharing, communication, and self-acceptance).
- *Provide its members with intimacy and a sense of belonging* (e.g., acceptance and love).
- *Provide an emotionally secure environment for sexual expression among consenting adults.*

- *Provide its members with a place of privacy and respite* (e.g., respite from other and more formal and more public social roles such as those related to community, work, and school responsibilities).
- *Provide its members with a legal and social identity* (e.g., an identity and location for the purposes of legal transactions, especially those related to parental rights and responsibilities).
- *Serve as an economic unit* (e.g., make decisions concerning the purchase of goods and services, budget and plan for future, and manage and care for possessions and property).
- *Protect, assist, and care for those family members who are vulnerable or cannot care for themselves* (e.g., young children, the frail elderly, the sick or disabled).
- *Serve as an advocate for family members in need of community resources* (e.g., parent identifies her child as being ill or disabled and seeks out medical care, parent makes sure his child gets a proper education, etc.).

In addition to nuclear and extended family structures, other variations in family form are increasingly common. These include *single-parent families* (i.e., one biological parent or adoptive parent or foster parent plus children), *blended families* or stepparent families (i.e., two married adults plus each one's children from a prior marriage and possibly children born to them as a couple), and *functional families* (i.e., two or more unmarried and unrelated adults plus their children). We are also seeing a growing number of families headed by what some call *second-time-around-parents,* referring to grandparents who have assumed primary responsibility for rearing their grandchildren. In part, this is due to the growing number of biological parents who have been incarcerated or whose functioning is seriously impaired by addiction to drugs and alcohol.

As people create or join a new family, there is a tendency for them to repeat the behavioral patterns they learned as a child in their family of origin. Moreover, when people live together for an extended period, their interactions become habitual. Once the patterns are well established, there is a tendency for family members to preserve the status quo and repeat that which is familiar, even when there are obvious problems in the family's functioning.

The family is indeed a complex system and it is a challenging task to identify and assess its interactional patterns. Following are questions that the social worker should keep in mind as he or she gathers information about a family's functioning:

1. ***How is family membership defined?*** One can view membership in a number of ways. For example, who are members of the *biological family* (e.g., bio-parents, biological offspring)? Who are members of the *legal family,* as defined by marriage, divorce, and adoption laws and by court orders affecting child custody? What is the composition of the *functional family* (i.e., who is part of household and who assumes responsibility for child care and other tasks of daily living)? Who belongs to the *perceived family* (i.e., those who the members consider as belonging to the family regardless of biological and legal ties)? And finally, who belongs to the *family of long-term commitments,* as defined by an expectation of lifelong loyalty, duty, and "being there for me" regardless of changes in household composition or legal definitions?

2. ***What facts and realities describe the family?*** What are the names, sex, and ages of the members? How is the family's functioning affected by the various developmental stages of its members, such as the presence of young children, teens, and the elderly? How does the family's functioning relate to the family life cycle? Does the family have a particular religious, ethnic, or cultural identity? What is the source of income? Are family members employed? Where? What are their occupations? How do the demands of these jobs affect family roles and functioning? What personal and social circumstances surrounded the marriage or the formation of the family and the birth of the children? Is there a history of divorce, abandonment, or violence? Is the family's functioning affected by a member's physical or mental illness, disability, or addiction?

3. ***Is family functioning supported by the community?*** In what neighborhood and community does this family live? How is the family affected by living there? Is it a safe place to be? Is decent and affordable housing available? Are jobs available? Are basic public utilities and services available (e.g., police protection, sanitation services, transportation, library)? Do the local schools provide the educational programs needed by the children?

4. ***How well are family functions performed?*** How does the family function as an economic unit (i.e., secure income, pay bills, etc.)? Does it successfully manage tasks of daily living (e.g., cooking, cleaning, laundry, etc.)? Does the home serve as a place of rest, recuperation, and privacy for its members? Does the family provide its members with a sense of identity and belonging? Does it provide nurturing, love, companionship, and intimacy? Do the children receive the encouragement and guidance needed to prepare for success in school and work roles? Does the family provide appropriate socialization experiences for its children so they learn the interpersonal and social skills they will need in adulthood? Is the family able to adhere to customs, traditions, and religious beliefs it considers important?

5. ***What are the boundaries, subsystems, rules, and roles governing family interaction?*** A family system may consist of four subsystems: the *spouse subsystem* (i.e., two adults that usually involves a sexual relationship); the *parental subsystem* (i.e., those family members responsible for childrearing); the *parent-child subsystem* (i.e., a special closeness between a particular parent and child); and the *sibling subsystem.* The various rules, communication channels, and behavioral patterns that define and regulate these subsystems are termed *boundaries.* In a healthy family, these boundaries are fairly clear and in keeping with societal norms. By contrast, for example, in an incest family, the child has been drawn into the spouse subsystem. In many cases of physical child abuse, a child will move into the parental subsystem and engage in role reversal behavior wherein the child cares for his or her parent—often in an effort to keep the parent calm.

When boundaries are unclear and defuse, members become intrusive and overly involved in the lives of family members. Such family relationships are termed *enmeshed,* fused, or merged. The opposite condition is where there is little meaningful interaction among family members or between the family's subsystems. Such families are said to have a *disengaged* pattern of relationships. A boundary also exists between a family and its social environment. The nature of that boundary determines whether the family will be *open* or *closed* to outside influences. (See Chapter 6 for more on systems theory.)

Special attention must be given to the family's *role structure.* Roles are those patterns of thought and action that define who we are, how we behave toward others in the family, and, of course, how they behave toward us. Certain role sets guide the common tasks of living, such as who drives the car, who pays the bills, and who cares for the children. It is important for the social worker to determine why such tasks are assigned to certain family members. The role structure may be strongly influenced by the family's culture and religion. The family-related roles we take on during the course of growing up in a family tend to be more permanent, less flexible, and less conscious than other social roles, such as those of student, employee, social worker, or supervisor. Pet expressions for common family roles include "black sheep," "the happy one," "peace maker," "the banker," "golden boy," "disciplinarian," "family worrier," "lone wolf," and "daddy's little girl." In professional literature, one often finds references to the family roles of scapegoat, identified patient, infantalized child, parentified child, hero, mascot, lost child, rescuer, and message boy.

Essentially, *family rules* are explicit or implicit principles that maintain the family's organization or "systemness" and that govern member interaction. Rules are reflected in the seating arrangement during meals and in family regulations, such as "always clean the bath tub when finished." Most family rules are necessary and innocuous and some can appear silly to the outsider, such as "Don't take a trip in the car without first changing your underwear." By contrast, it is the unspoken or hidden rules that contribute most to family dysfunction. Rules that suppress emotion, cover up irresponsible behavior, promote dishonesty, or generate feelings of shame are especially harmful. Examples include: "When Dad is drinking, never mention his brother Ed" or "Pretend you don't see Mom and Dad fighting" or "Only an evil person would ever feel anger toward a parent." The children of parents who are alcoholic often grow up with the rules of "don't talk" (about the drinking or other real issues), "don't feel" (suppress all feelings), and "don't trust" (always be on guard and keep people at a distance). The social worker must identify family rules and, more importantly, observe whether they can be openly discussed and what happens when rules are broken.

The boundaries, rules, and roles at work within a family can only be inferred after careful observation. Some family members may be able to articulate family rules, but most of these patterns are so ingrained that they seem natural and normal and are never questioned.

6. ***How well does each member fit within the family system?*** Although there is great value in viewing the family from a systems perspective, it is important to remember that this dynamic system is made up of separate human beings, each of which has a unique genetic makeup, biology, personality, and life experience. Thus, the worker needs to be cognizant that each member has his or her own thoughts and feeling; hopes, expectations, and obligations; talents; sense of identity; spirituality; coping strategies and ego defenses; special emotional needs; and physical or mental limitations. It is useful to consider whether there is a good match or a possible mismatch between each family member and the norms, values, and rules of his or her family system.

7. *What are the moral and ethical dimensions of the family's functioning?* This dimension of family dynamics refers to issues such as obligation, loyalty, fairness, sacrifice, accountability, and entitlement that relate rather directly to a person's moral standards, religious beliefs, notions of good and evil, and spirituality. Many of the conflicts among family members revolve around moral and ethical issues.

8. *What aspects of life are considered beyond human control?* In order to understand a client's behavior and decisions, it may be necessary to understand his or her sense of the sacred—that which is in the sphere of the mysterious, the awesome, the uncontrollable, and the supremely important. These views and beliefs are in contrast to views concerning aspects of life that one can control or at least attempt to control. An individual's or family's sense of the sacred is closely related to their religious beliefs, spirituality, concepts of God, and the meanings assigned to life, death, and human suffering.

9. *How does the family make decisions?* All families develop patterns or styles of decision making. In some families, all members can express opinions and participate in decision making. On the other extreme are families in which one member makes all major decisions. Some practitioners learn about a family's way of making decisions by meeting with the whole family and asking them to perform a task (e.g., plan a vacation or family outing) and then observing how they reach a decision.

10. *What is the mood of the family?* Much like an individual, a family is often characterized by a prevailing mood. Is the family warm and caring? Optimistic? Pessimistic? Excitable? Outgoing? Depressed? Fun loving? Angry? Controlled? Spontaneous?

11. *How do family members handle "differentness"?* Everyone is unique and everyone must learn to live with others. A common source of interpersonal difficulty is the inability to accept others as being different from one's self and/or the inability to accept one's self as being different from others. Thus, when assessing a family, consider how each member deals with differentness. There are four basic ways of handling differences:

- *Eliminating others.* Attempting to deal with differentness by beating down or suppressing the individuality of others (e.g., finding fault with others, blaming, attacking, etc.)
- *Eliminating self.* Handling differentness by suppressing one's individuality (e.g., always agreeing, submitting to others, accommodating, hiding one's true feelings, etc.)
- *Avoiding issues.* Attempting to handle differentness by denying or avoiding issues that would reveal differences (e.g., keeping family communication on "safe" topics, etc.)
- *Open and honest communication.* Dealing with differentness by acknowledging the existence of differences, discussing them in a respectful manner, and working to resolve whatever conflicts exist

Systems theory postulates the existence of system forces that resist change and maintain a state of dynamic equilibrium. When other maneuvers do not work, a family may attempt to preserve itself and protect its systemness by scapegoating one family member. A related phenomena, often termed *re-peopling,* refers to the family system's efforts to regain stability by either adding or excluding a member. A request by parents to have their disruptive teenager placed in foster care can be viewed as a re-peopling maneuver.

12. ***How clearly do family members communicate their own expectations and needs?*** In order for family members to respond appropriately to each other's needs, there must be communication concerning those needs. Sometimes we are unwilling or unable to communicate our wants and needs but still feel angry and disappointed when others do not respond in the desired way. Problems arise when family members expect others to be skilled at mind reading.

13. ***What communication patterns exist within the family?*** A pattern of verbal and nonverbal communication develops whenever two or more people interact on a regular basis; certain unwritten rules begin to guide interaction. The pattern reveals how each member regards himself or herself in relation to the others. There are many forms of workable communication patterns. What is functional for one family may not work for another. As with so many aspects of family functioning, culture and ethnicity have a strong impact on family communication and on what works for the family. To decipher this pattern, the worker needs to observe: Who speaks to whom? Who speaks first? Who responds? Who listens to whom? Who speaks most? Who speaks least? Who speaks last? Who sits next to whom? Are messages directed to one person but meant for someone else? Are the messages clear? Do the words say one thing but mean another? Are the family's communications characterized by respect, openness, and honesty or by evasiveness, denial, double messages, blaming, threats, hurtful jokes, interruptions, or defiance?

14. ***Do family members allow other members to get close emotionally?*** Everyone has a need for intimacy, but at the same time most of us have some fear of closeness. Sometimes people avoid getting close to others because they fear that if they reveal their vulnerabilities, others will take advantage of their weakness. Some people hide behind a facade because they fear others will not care for the "real" them. Even within a family, members may keep others at a distance. Within a well-functioning family, members are able to reveal many of their inner thoughts and feelings but also maintain a comfortable level of privacy.

15. ***To what tasks and activities do the adults and older children devote their time?*** For example, how many hours each week are devoted to paid employment? Travel to and from work? Child care? House cleaning and laundry? Cooking? Shopping? Medical and health care? Education and training? Study and homework? Clubs and organizations? Religious activities? Recreation and leisure? Reading? TV? What portion of each day and week is spent at home and with other family members?

16. ***What are the interpersonal payoffs of "troublesome behavior"?*** To understand a troubled family, the social worker must see beyond the problem behavior and develop working hypotheses about why members repeatedly engage in interac-

tions that create so much distress and misery. Two interrelated themes of family interaction explain many problem and nonproblem behaviors: the desire by a member for closeness versus his or her desire for distance and the member's desire for belonging versus his or her desire for independence. People want intimacy but not to be oppressed by the closeness. Also, people want to be part of a family but not to be consumed or controlled by family loyalty. When observing the family's struggle with a problem, the worker should constantly ask: How does this behavior bring the family members closer emotionally or create a feeling of belonging? How does this behavior promote a sense of separateness and independence?

17. ***Who supports and who opposes change?*** Whenever a change is being considered, some degree of resistance can be expected. However, family members will differ in the degree to which they will oppose change. In order to assess support and opposition, the social worker might ask the family members to speculate on the effects of a hypothetical change.

SELECTED BIBLIOGRAPHY

Karpel, Mark. *Evaluating Couples: A Handbook for Practitioners.* New York: W. W. Norton, 1994.

Kaslow, Florence, ed. *Handbook of Relational Diagnosis and Dysfunctional Family Patterns.* Somerset, NJ: John Wiley and Sons, 1996.

Walsh, Froma, ed. *Normal Family Processes,* rev. ed. New York: Guilford, 1993.

12.12 Multiworker Family Assessment Interviews

PURPOSE: To secure an understanding of how each family member views the family's presenting problem or concern by utilizing more that one social worker during family interviews.

DISCUSSION: Kinney, Haapala, and Gast (1981) report that a multiworker model of assessment is particularly helpful when providing intensive family crisis services designed to prevent out-of-home placements. Such an assessment interview is conducted after the social worker assigned to the case (i.e., the primary worker) has conducted an initial interview with the family. If this worker decides to use a multiworker assessment, it is explained to the family. Once the family agrees, secondary social workers are temporarily assigned to each family member (e.g., if there were four family members, four additional workers would be needed). Each secondary worker then spends an hour or so listening to their assigned family member's perspective on the family's problem and attempts to understand how that member sees himself or herself within the context of the family system. After these individual interviews are completed, the secondary social workers and the primary social worker meet for about an hour and share what they have learned about each family member. Meanwhile, the family members spend this time together without a social worker being present.

Next, all of the social workers and all of the family members meet together. Each secondary social worker sits next to his or her family member and speaks for that person; each speaks as if he or she were the family member and uses I-statements to describe his or her thoughts and feelings about the family's functioning. During this phase, the family members are not to speak. If a family member does not like what is being said, he or she and the social worker can leave the room, discuss the difference, and then rejoin the group. After all of the social workers have spoken for the family members, the family members are asked to react to what they have heard.

The last part of this session is used to plan the next steps in the family's effort to secure help with their problem. After this multiworker assessment, the primary social worker continues to provide service.

Although this assessment process may take from three to five hours, it has important advantages, such as the following:

1. A great deal of information is gathered and each family member's point of view is expressed and explored. The workers are often able to say things that the family member is afraid of saying, thus the issues are out in the open.

2. The family members usually leave this lengthy assessment session feeling they have been listened to and understood. Typically, the process yields a firmer commitment by the family members to work on the problem, a feeling of hopefulness, and ideas on how to make changes.

3. The process has the effect of creating several consultants who have firsthand knowledge of the family, which can be helpful to the primary social worker.

SELECTED BIBLIOGRAPHY

Kinney, Jill, David Haapala, and Elizabeth Gast. "Assessment of Families in Crisis." In *Treating Families in the Home,* edited by Marvin Bryce and June Lloyd. Springfield, IL: Charles C. Thomas, 1981.

12.13 The ABC Model and the Behavior Matrix

PURPOSE: To achieve greater precision in observation and the analysis of behavioral interactions.

DISCUSSION: Social workers often look to behavioral analysis and behavior modification for techniques of helping clients learn new behaviors or eliminate problem behaviors. The influence of behavior-oriented approaches has done much to help practitioners be more precise in data gathering and assessment. Two tools commonly used in behavioral analysis, the ABC model and the behavior matrix, are particularly useful.

The ABCs of Behavior

In the ***ABC model,*** the letter *A* stands for *antecedent, B* for *behavior,* and *C* for *consequences.* For example, when assessing a problem behavior, such as a child's temper tantrum, the worker first clearly identifies and operationally defines the behavior under study. In this example, the tantrum is the *B* (i.e., target behavior).

Next, the worker looks for the *A,* or the antecedent, which are the various situational factors or cues that set up the behavior. In the tantrum example, it might be a particular action by the parent that sets the stage for the child's tantrum; perhaps the parent begins to work in the kitchen or turns on the TV news.

Finally, the worker looks for the immediate consequences of the behavior, which is the *C* in the model. This may identify factors that reinforce or reward the behavior. For example, once the tantrum starts, the parent may try to comfort the child and, in the process, reinforce the tantrum behavior. By using the ABC model, the worker may be able to identify those factors that can be changed in order to reduce or eliminate a problem behavior.

Behavior Matrix

A second tool, actually an observational aid, is a three-cell matrix known as the ***Behavior Matrix*** (see Figure 12.10). After observing the interactions of an individual client, family, or small group, the worker records his or her observations in the appropriate cell. What emerges will be a picture of what positive behaviors should be reinforced, what negative behaviors should be extinguished, and what new behaviors will need to be learned by the client.

As an example, assume that the worker is attempting to help a man who is developmentally disabled learn to interact more appropriately when greeting other adults. While observing and using the matrix, the worker sees that when introduced to another person, the client giggles, reaches for a handshake, and fails to look directly at the person he is greeting. The worker would record his or her observations as follows:

1. The giggle is an existing inappropriate behavior—enter comment in cell 3.
2. The handshake is an existing appropriate behavior—enter comment in cell 1.
3. Eye contact when shaking hands is a nonexisting appropriate behavior—enter comment in cell 2.

FIGURE 12.10 Behavior Matrix

	Behavior Exists	Behavior Does Not Exist
Positive or Appropriate Behavior	1	2
Negative or Inappropriate Behavior	3	

TABLE 12.2 Behavioral Observations and Intervention Techniques

Observation	Possible Intervention
Desired behaviors do not occur at all	Instruction, modeling, prompting, shaping
Desired behaviors occur but infrequently	Additional reinforcement, shaping behavioral rehearsal
Behaviors occur but not at appropriate time	Behavioral contracting, prompting, and other reminders
Desired behavior occurs so frequently as to be inappropriate	Reduce frequency of reinforcement, differential reinforcement, removal from reinforcing environment
Behaviors that occur are dangerous to self or others	Removal from reinforcing environment, reinforcement of an incompatible behavior

Having made such observations, the next step is to develop an appropriate intervention strategy. Table 12.2 matches recommended behavioral techniques to findings derived from the matrix. (See Items 14.4, 14.5, and 14.6 for information on behavior techniques.)

SELECTED BIBLIOGRAPHY

Mattaini, Mark. *Clinical Practice with Individuals.* Washington, DC: NASW Press, 1997.

Sundel, Sandra, and Martin Sundel. *Behavior Modification in the Human Services,* 3rd ed. Newbury Park, CA: Sage, 1993.

Thyer, Bruce, and John Wodarski. *Handbook of Empirical Social Work Practice.* New York: Wiley, 1998.

12.14 Using Questionnaires, Checklists, and Vignettes

PURPOSE: To create data-gathering questionnaires, checklists, vignettes, and other data-gathering tools for use with clients in a particular practice setting.

DISCUSSION: A social worker can design a number of tools that will engage clients in discussion of important matters and facilitate data gathering. Such tools can take several forms.

Some clients have difficulty verbalizing their concerns, either because they feel confused or embarrassed or because they do not have the words to express their thoughts. In such cases, some type of checklist may prove useful. A *problem checklist* is simply a list of the concerns commonly reported by a particular group of clients served by a particular agency. It is compiled by a worker familiar with how people with these concerns think and feel. If a client is having difficulty articulating concerns, he or she is presented with the list and asked to mark those statements that come close to describing those concerns. Because the list probably includes some of the client's private thoughts, it reassures the client that he or she is not alone in having a particular problem or worry.

Consider the case of a 15-year-old who has just given birth to a baby in a hospital and will be dismissed in one day. In such a case, the hospital social worker would like to meet with the young mother, do a quick assessment, and refer the mother to relevant community resources. Many such clients may be reluctant to verbalize their worries, and the worker's task is further complicated because there is so little time to build a relationship. Figure 12.11 is a checklist that could be used with this client. In addition to helping the youth identify and express her concerns, it focuses the communication so that she and the worker can make the best possible use of very limited time together.

Frequently, clients are unaware of the services that can be offered by the social worker. If a worker and a client examine a problem checklist together, the client begins to understand how the worker or agency might be of assistance. In this sense, the checklist serves as an educational tool. A checklist can also help to structure interviews with clients who are easily distracted. In addition, the completion of the checklist might be assigned as "homework" between the first and second meeting (see Item 14.15).

Figure 12.12 is a *questionnaire* developed by a social worker who provides counseling to married couples in conflict. Its purpose is to help the clients quickly identify those aspects of the relationship that are troublesome. Because the questionnaire is simple and brief, clients can complete it in only a few minutes and they do not find it burdensome. By substituting another set of questions, the basic format illustrated in this example can be adapted for use with other groups of clients in other practices settings.

In some practice situations, the worker needs a type of information that cannot be elicited by specific questions such as those written into questionnaires. For example, social workers often need to gather information about a client's values and attitudes but recognize that direct questioning is not likely to yield complete or accurate information. Consider a child welfare worker faced with the task of deciding whether an individual should be licensed as a foster parent. Among other things, the worker needs to gather information about the person's beliefs and attitudes related to child care. The worker could ask direct questions such as: Do you believe in spanking a child who misbehaves? and How would you respond if a 10-year-old frequently wets the bed? Such direct questions are likely to elicit answers that the individual thinks the worker wants to hear and may not reveal much about the person's underlying attitudes that are so central to parenting.

An alternative approach is for the worker to write a set of vignettes and use them as springboards for discussion and exploration. Basically, a *vignette* is a brief story to which the client is asked to respond. Thus, this techniques is an indirect or a projective method of gathering information that draws feelings and beliefs from the

FIGURE 12.11
Sample Problem Checklist

Concerns of Young Mothers: A Checklist

The birth of a baby is a time of happiness and joy. But along with the good feelings are concerns about the changes in lifestyle and responsibility that lie ahead. A new mother often feels uncertain and a bit scared about the responsibility of caring for a baby. If we know about your concerns, we may be able to help you find ways to address them.

Below is a list of worries and concerns that have been expressed by other new mothers who have had babies in this hospital. Please read through this list and place a check (✓) by all statements that are similar to the concerns you now have. Your responses will be held in strict confidence.

1. ____ Have worries about paying hospital and doctor bills.
2. ____ Have worries about my baby's health and physical condition.
3. ____ Have worries about my own health and physical condition.
4. ____ Uncertain about how to feed and care for an infant.
5. ____ Uncertain where to turn when I have questions about child care.
6. ____ Afraid I may become pregnant before I am ready to have another child.
7. ____ Worried about not having enough money to care for my baby.
8. ____ Concerned about whether I can finish school.
9. ____ Worried about getting or keeping a job when I have a baby to care for.
10. ____ Concerned when I feel resentment or anger toward my baby.
11. ____ Worried about the effects of drugs or alcohol on me and my baby.
12. ____ Worried that my friends will not accept me and my baby.
13. ____ Worried about my relationship with my baby's father.
14. ____ Concerned that I do not feel love toward my baby.
15. ____ Feeling sad and depressed about my situation.
16. ____ Worried that I will be a burden to my own parents.
17. ____ Worried about living alone with my baby.
18. ____ Concerned that my own parents and family will not accept me and my baby.
19. ____ Afraid I am going to lose my independence and freedom.
20. ____ In the space below, please describe or list any other concerns not covered by the checklist.

____

____

Now, look over all of those items you have checked and draw a circle around the one or two that seem most important. Please feel free to discuss these concerns with a hospital social worker.

Source: Charles Horejsi and Gloria Horejsi, "Practice Oriented Social Assessment Tools," paper presented at the Sixth Biennial National Association of Social Workers Professional Symposium, San Antonio, Texas, 1979.

FIGURE 12.12 Sample Questionnaire

Questionnaire on the Husband-Wife Relationship

Explanation: Below are questions about how satisfied you are with what goes on between you and your spouse. Your answers will help us understand and clarify your concerns. To the right of each statement, place a check (✓) to indicate if you are mostly satisfied, or mostly dissatisfied, or perhaps unsure and confused about this aspect of your marriage relationship. If a statement does not apply to your situation, write NA next to the statement.

	Mostly Satisfied	Mostly Dissatisfied	Unsure or Confused
The way we make decisions	______	______	______
The way we divide up responsibility for child care	______	______	______
The way we handle and budget money	______	______	______
The way we divide up housework and other home-related jobs	______	______	______
The way we talk to the children	______	______	______
The amount of money we earn	______	______	______
The way we resolve conflict	______	______	______
The way we discipline our children	______	______	______
The way we get along with in-laws and other relatives	______	______	______
The way we use our free time	______	______	______
The way we talk to each other	______	______	______
The way we care for our home	______	______	______
The amount of time we have together	______	______	______
The way we help and encourage each other	______	______	______
The amount of privacy we have	______	______	______
The way alcohol or drugs affect our relationship	______	______	______
The way we handle birth control	______	______	______
The sexual part of our relationship	______	______	______
The way we plan for our future	______	______	______
The way we get along with the neighbors	______	______	______
The way we deal with moral or religious concerns	______	______	______
The way we handle anger and frustration	______	______	______

Please list here any other concerns you may have about your relationship:

____

What do you consider to be the major strengths in your marriage?

____

What do you consider to be the one or two major problems in your marriage?

____

____

client. Figure 12.13 presents two examples that were written for use in the foster home-study process. Needless to say, the worker using this tool must create vignettes that will elicit the type of information needed to better understand the client.

In general, social workers underutilize aids such as questionnaires, checklists, and vignettes in their data collection. The reader is encouraged to develop and experiment with these tools. Here are some guidelines that will help:

1. Be clear about the purpose to be served by the tool, the reasons for using it, the type of information sought, and the type of client for whom it is being prepared. Rather than attempt to develop one all-purpose questionnaire, it is better to design several, each with a specific purpose or focus.

2. The completion of the questionnaire should be a relatively easy task and not tax the client's physical or mental capacity. A simple, short, and focused questionnaire is more likely to be completed than a long one. In general, the higher the client's level of education and motivation, the more likely he or she is to deal successfully with a written data-gathering tool. Remember that many people lack basic reading skills.

3. The writing of questions for a questionnaire or checklist requires knowledge of possible responses by clients to certain types of questions. Open-ended questions will be necessary when it is difficult to anticipate or to list the full range of likely responses. However, written responses to open-ended questions are often difficult to read and understand. Consequently, a data-gathering tool with many open-ended questions will have few advantages over verbal questioning.

FIGURE 12.13 Sample Vignettes

The Peterson Family: A Situation to Discuss

The Petersons have been foster parents to 15-year-old Sharon for about six years. Religion is very important to Mr and Mrs. Peterson. They attend church services and participate in several church-related activities on a regular basis. Until about two months ago, Sharon also attended the Petersons' church even though she had been raised in another religious denomination. Sharon now refuses to attend church and tells her foster parents that religion is a bunch of superstition and foolishness. The Petersons are worried and upset by Sharon's attitude because religion is so central to their life and family.

1. What could have caused this situation?
2. How should the Petersons respond to Sharon?

The Allen Family: A Situation to Discuss

Mr. and Mrs. Allen have three children. In order to celebrate Mrs. Allen's birthday, the whole family goes to a restaurant. During the meal, 6-year-old Jimmy throws a tantrum—he cries and throws food at his parents. Others in the restaurant stare at the Allens and obviously disapprove of what they are seeing.

1. What is your evaluation of Jimmy's behavior?
2. How should the parents respond to Jimmy?

4. Each question or item should focus on a single idea. The wording should be simple, clear, concise, and free of bias. Avoid using jargon or acronyms. When possible, the wording should adhere to a uniform or consistent format and structure because this helps the client move easily from question to question and minimizes the chances of misinterpretation.

5. The sequence of the question should follow a logical order. The most sensitive or probing questions should usually appear toward the end of the questionnaire or checklist.

6. A pretest should be used to determine whether clients can understand all items in the questionnaire or checklist, can complete it in a reasonable amount of time, and whether the data obtained are indeed useful.

SELECTED BIBLIOGRAPHY

Horejsi, Charles. *Foster Family Care.* Springfield, IL: Charles C. Thomas, 1979.

———. *Assessmnet and Case Planning in Child Protection and Foster Care Services.* Englewood, CO: American Humane Association, 1996.

Horejsi, Charles, Anne Bertsche, and Frank Clark. *Social Work Practice with Parents of Children in Foster Care: A Handbook.* Springfield, IL: Charles C. Thomas, 1981.

Jordan, Cathleen, and Cynthia Franklin. *Clinical Assessment for Social Workers.* Chicago: Lyceum Books, 1995.

12.15 Developing Individualized Rating Scales

PURPOSE: To prepare a scale, unique to an individual client or client group, to measure the frequency, duration, or intensity of an action, event, behavior, emotion, or attitude.

DISCUSSION: Social workers often need to measure various factors that are related to client conditions or situations that are the focus of practice. Accurate assessment of the duration, intensity, frequency, severity, and so on, of a client's condition is prerequisite to determining if an emergency exists, if the client or someone else is at risk, or if a referral should be made. The assessment is also an indicator for selecting an intervention technique.

Another reason for developing ways to measure factors affecting the client is to be able to track the amount and direction of change that occurs as the helping process unfolds. This allows the worker to correct the course of service if the selected interventions do not accomplish the desired goals.

Finally, measurements taken at the beginning and end of a service period can help a social worker examine his or her practice effectiveness (e.g., Did my client's condition improve? How much? In what practice issues and with what practice approaches am I most effective? Least effective? etc.). The answers to those questions can lead to a professional development plan to strengthen one's competence or, if applied to a number of workers, to accumulate data that can help an agency design its staff development plan.

In short, accurate measurement can benefit clients, workers, and agencies alike. How does a social worker accurately measure a client condition or situation? In truth, measurements of human behaviors, attitudes, feelings, and interactions are rarely completely accurate. Yet, with careful selection of appropriate indicators and a rigorous process of data collection, usually a good approximation of the factor being measured can be achieved.

Two basic forms of measurement are available to the social worker. One approach is to select one of the many "standardized" scales available to social workers (see Item 12.16). These scales have already been developed with careful attention to the psychometric properties of the scale so that they will give a valid approximation of the construct (e.g., stress level, quality of family interaction, sexual satisfaction with partner, etc.) the social worker wants to measure.

The second fundamental approach to measuring factors related to the client's actions and feelings is to construct an ***individualized rating scale*** that is developed or adapted to fit the client's unique situation. A homemade scale is particularly useful if the client can be involved in the process of developing the scale. Often, clients become more clear about their situations and what it might take to bring about change in a situation by working on a scale in which abstract feelings or concerns are translated into concrete statements that describe degrees of change. Thus, the development of the measurement tool becomes a part of the practice activity. Further, when scales reflect the client's own descriptions of the variables, the face validity of the scale is high and repeated measurements can be relatively accurate indicators of the client's experience. Finally, some factors that social workers help clients address defy standardized descriptors that can be universally interpreted for the purpose of measurement. For example, how does one standardize a person's feeling of grief, or a spouse's level of listening, or someone's motivation to change? With individualized scales, it is possible to "start where the client is" and construct measures of change from the perspective of that client.

Several steps should be followed when constructing an individualized rating scale:

1. *Help the client recognize the value in measuring behaviors, attitudes, or feelings.* Unless the client is invested in measuring his or her condition, the results are unlikely to be very helpful. Measurement of one's condition, however, should be a familiar experience for most clients. Other professionals, such as physicians, routinely utilize indices of a patient's physical health by measuring blood pressure, temperature, weight, and so on, as part of a physical examination. Similarly, social workers require indices of a client's social health to perform most effectively in providing assistance. Many clients want such indicators and find the results confirming of their own observations.

2. *Carefully identify what is to be measured.* Many times, the problem or concern being addressed cannot directly be measured. If measured indirectly it is critical that the items selected for measurement are valid or logical indicators of the problem being addressed. Just as an elevated temperature might be an indicator of infection, the number of arguments a couple has might be an indicator of marital discord. It is also important that each scale is designed to measure only one dimension of client functioning. If more than one dimension in involved, multiple scales that measure each dimension should be created. Further, if there are multiple indicators for a single dimension, the use of several indicators can help to confirm or raise caution about the outcome of any one indicator.

3. *Develop a scale where the client's status on a continuum from negative to positive functioning can be designated.* When developing a scale, one task is to determine how many points on a continuum will be identified. There can be as few as 2 points (e.g., yes or no, more or less), whereas other scales typically range anywhere between 3 and 10 points. A general guideline is to have only as many points as the client can clearly distinguish—usually 3 to 7 points. Whether to have an odd or even number of points depends somewhat on the item being scaled. For some items, it is appropriate to have a midpoint, but often that creates a situation in which the respondent simply takes a noncommittal middleground that provides little useful information. An even-numbered scale, by contrast, forces the respondent to at least lean one direction or the other.

Once the number of points on the scale is determined, anchoring statements can be developed that describe each point. One method is to describe the most negative point on the scale (e.g., "I lost my temper at least once each day") and then define the most positive anchor point (e.g., "I did not lose my temper at all during the week"). With the two ends of the continuum identified, some or all of the points between them can be defined. Care should be taken that the client can identify differences in the increments between points. Another method for developing anchor points is to begin describing the client's functioning at the current time and making that description the midpoint. A description of what it would be like if things should get worse (a worst-case scenario) would become the negative end of the continuum and progressive levels to the midpoint on the negative side identified. Then the process is repeated on the positive side of the continuum.

When the anchor points use the client's own words (e.g., "I feel encouraged," "I am furious," "My thoughts are fuzzy," "I flew off the handle," etc.) the scale is referred to as a *self-anchored scale.* The face validity of the scale is enhanced. At other times, it is helpful to use anchor points that have been utilized in other scales and are known to reflect differing scale values. Some frequently used response categories are:

- *Frequency*
  rarely > seldom > occasionally > frequently > almost always
  none > 1 or 2 times > 3–5 times > 6–7 times > more than 7 times
  never > rarely > sometimes > often > very often > always
- *Duration*
  0-20% of the time > 21–40% > 41–60% > 61–80% > 81–100% of the time
  never > some of the time > most of the time > almost always
- *Intensity*
  strongly agree > disagree > agree > strongly agree
  totally disagree > disagree slightly > neutral > agree slightly > totally agree
  not at all > slightly > moderately > very much > extremely

- *Change*
  about the same > a little less > less > much less > a great deal less
  strong decrease > some decrease > no change > some increase > strong increase

One last decision is whether to present the scales horizontally or vertically. Most people are accustomed to horizontal scales, as they are convenient to produce on a typewriter or computer and are regularly used in survey instruments. Usually, the negative end of the continuum is placed on the left side of a page and the progressive steps (i.e., identified by the anchor points) flow from left to right. For some clients, however, a vertical scale communicates the more or less dimension more clearly. Children, for example, sometimes find a scale that looks like a thermometer or a height chart more understandable.

4. *Determine how the data will be collected.* Determining a process for completing the scales is the next step. Who should do the rating? The client? The worker? A teacher? A relative? When should the rating be made? The rating scale might be completed just before each counseling session, first thing each morning, Sunday evenings, and so forth. Where should the rating be done? At home? In the agency's waiting room? In the worker's office with the worker participating? There are any number of suitable places where the client can give thoughtful responses. Perhaps the most important general guideline is to attempt to achieve consistency regarding the conditions under which the ratings are made.

5. *Present the data in a form that make the data easily interpreted.* Just marking before and after scores, possibly in different colors, on the scale itself is often sufficient visual evidence of change. However, if a series of measurements are taken to reflect change over time or to compare changes in two or more variables, it is useful to create simple line graphs or bar charts to track the progression. Such organization of the data can provide a useful basis for discussion of change, or lack of change, with clients.

For additional information on more systematic ways to organize data from both standardized and individualized scales, see Chapter 15. In that chapter, such direct practice research tools as goal attainment scaling, task achievement scaling, and the various single-subject designs are described.

SELECTED BIBLIOGRAPHY

Bloom, Martin, Joel Fischer, and John Orme. *Evaluating Practice: Guidelines for the Accountable Professional,* 2nd ed. Boston: Allyn and Bacon, 1995.

Judd, Charles M., Eliot R. Smith, and Louise H. Kidder. *Research Methods in Social Relations,* 6th ed. Ft. Worth: Holt, Reinhart and Winston, 1991.

Monette, Duane R., Thomas J. Sullivan, and Cornell R. DeJong. *Applied Social Research: Tool for the Human Services,* 3rd ed. Fort Worth: Harcourt Brace, 1994.

Nurius, Paula S., and Walter W. Hudson. *Human Services: Practice, Evaluation, and Computers.* Pacific Grove, CA: Brooks/Cole, 1993.

12.16 Selecting Standardized Rating Scales

PURPOSE: To use predeveloped and tested scales to measure various dimensions of client functioning.

DISCUSSION: In many instances, the social worker can measure a client's social functioning by using one of the many standardized measuring instruments. ***Standardized rating scales*** are indices of behaviors, attitudes, feelings, and so on, that represent a set of questions to measure a clearly defined construct and that have been subjected to sufficient testing to confirm the instrument's reliability when used with various populations. As opposed to individualized rating scales that are designed for a specific individual client or client group (see Item 12.15), standardized indexes can be used to measure the experiences of many different clients.

Social workers use standardized scales for three reasons. First, because they have already been developed and tested, standardized scales are ready for immediate use and can be applied in a practice situation even before the client and worker have established the repertoire necessary for an ongoing professional relationship. Thus, they can be used for diagnostic purposes in many case situations where it is necessary to assess the severity or intensity of a client's situation.

Second, periodic application of standardized assessment scales when working with a client can identify changes as they occur during the intervention. Known as *formative research,* a social worker can organize the scores from these measurements to inform practice decisions regarding the desirability of continuing or changing the intervention plan. Methods for organizing the information derived from these scales to inform practice decisions are described in Chapter 15.

Finally, these scales can be used as *summative research* to help a social worker sum up the results of the intervention with one client (i.e., comparing the client's score on the scale before the intervention begins and at the conclusion of service) or to summarize the results for some or all of the clients served by a worker. The scores can also be accumulated for a number of workers through an agency or unit of an agency. In addition to the social worker's general ethical obligation to be accountable to clients and agencies for the quality of services provided, empirical analyses of practice outcomes as reflected by standardized measurement tools are increasingly requested by managed care companies. Today, 59.0 percent of all master's-level social workers are involved with managed care companies in their practice (Teare, Sheafor, and Shank 1997), making the use of such scales a necessary part of much of social work practice.

Although standardized scales vary in length, most contain between 15 and 30 one-sentence statements that a client is asked to rate on a 3- to 7-point scale. Therefore, these scales can be completed in a short period of time. One set of scales, known as the *WALMYR Assessment Scales,* illustrates a typical format used to measure constructs applicable to social work practice. For example, one of the *Walmyr* Scales, the *Index of Self-Esteem (ISE),* is designed to measure the extent of a client's problems with self-esteem; 5 of 25 items on that scale are the following:

1. I feel that people would not like me if they knew me really well.
4. When I am with others I feel they are glad I am with them.
8. I feel that I need more self-confidence.
16. I feel very self-conscious when I am with strangers.
20. I feel I get pushed around more than others.

The client then rates each item on a 7-point scale with (1) none of the time, (2) very rarely, (3) a little of the time, (4) some of the time, (5) a good part of the time, (6) most of the time, and (7) all of the time. To prevent respondents from falling into a pattern of responses in which each item is not carefully considered, some of the items are presented as a positive statement and others as negative. In these cases, the responses must be "reverse scored." To illustrate, an answer of "most of the time" on Item 1 (above) would be a negative statement about the client's self-esteem, while on Item 4 a response of "most of the time" would reflect a positive attitude. Clear instructions are provided with the scales to guide the worker in reverse scoring.

A well-established research methodology underpins the development of standardized instruments known as *psychometrics*. During the process of development, the scales are examined to assure that they not only represent the meaning of the construct being measured (validity) but that the scale would also yield approximately the same result each time it is administered (reliability). In the development phase, the scales are administered to a large number of respondents and the responses are statistically analyzed. The scale is then revised and adjusted until it meets the required criteria for a valid measure.

The descriptions provided with the scales inform the social worker when making a selection. For example, data should always be available on the instrument's validity and reliability. Although there are no strict guidelines, generally when judging a scale's validity in the human services area, a correlation coefficient of +.60 or greater when compared to other indicators is acceptable. For reliability, an Alpha score of +.80 or greater is sufficient. Some scale descriptions will specify the age and reading levels for which the measure is acceptable. Finally, the worker must decide if it is feasible to use the instrument in the particular practice situation. For example, the worker should determine if the measure has been normed with the cultural or age group that includes the client, is of appropriate length to use in the practice situation, is sensitive to the issues on which the practice is focused, and does not take an inordinate amount money to secure or time to score.

Another feature of some scales is that cutting scores can be established. *Cutting scores* indicate the point on a scale where a client's score reflects a very serious problem or, at the other end of the continuum, does not represent a problem that would require professional intervention. Many of the Walmyr Scales, for example, measure the severity of problems with scores ranging from 0 (low severity or intensity) to 100 (extremely high level). A cutting score of 70 on these scales has been standardized to indicate the level of severity at which the client begins to be at high risk to self or others. Similarly, a score below 30 is an indication that intervention is probably not required.

Reports on standardized scales are scattered throughout the social work and psychology literature and are often difficult to locate. Two excellent resources for finding useful scales are described in Figure 12.14.

FIGURE 12.14 Basic Sources of Standardized Scales for Social Workers

Fischer, Joel, and Kevin Corcoran. *Measures for Clinical Practice: A Sourcebook*, 2nd ed. New York: Simon and Schuster, 1994.

This two-volume handbook of measures appropriate for social work practice describes 320 different standardized instruments. Volume 1 contains scales for use with children, couples, and families; Volume 2 is focused on scales for measuring adults. A partial list of topic areas for which multiple scales are reported includes:

Anger and hostility	Marital/couple relationships
Anxiety and fear	Parent/child relationships
Assertiveness	Phobias
Children's behaviors/problems	Satisfaction with life
Depression and grief	Self-concept and esteem
Family functioning	Social support
Health issues	Substance abuse
Interpersonal behavior	Treatment satisfaction

For each scale, a short description is provided, its psychometric properties presented, and sources for obtaining permission to use the scale (with or without a fee) included.

Hudson, Walter W. *WALMYR Assessment Scales Scoring Manual* (and disks). WALMYR Publishing Co., P.O. Box 6227, Tallahassee, FL 32314-6229, e-mail to scales@walmyr.com, or website http://www.syspac.com/~walmyr/

This collection of nearly 30 paper-and-pencil short self-report scales computer software (now in Windows) computes the composite score for each scale, prepares charts of the scores of repeated measurements, and helps manage case records. The scales include "personal adjustment measures" that assess levels of depression, stress, anxiety, substance abuse, and so on; "problems with spouse or partner" such as marital discord, physical or nonphysical abuse; "family relationship problems," including a child's attitude toward mother or father, sibling relations, and family relations; and measures of "organizational outcomes" such as a person's job-related distress or a client's satisfaction with the services provided. The psychometric properties and a description of the construct being measured by each scale are also included with the set of scales.

SELECTED BIBLIOGRAPHY

Bloom, Martin, Joel Fischer, and John G. Orme. *Evaluating Practice: Guidelines for the Accountable Professional*, 2nd ed. Boston: Allyn and Bacon, 1995.

Jordan, Cathleen, and Cynthia Franklin. *Clinical Assessment for Social Workers.* Chicago: Lyceum Books, 1995.

Jordan, Cathleen, Cynthia Franklin, and Kevin Corcoran. "Standardized Measuring Instruments." In *Social Work Research and Evaluation,* 4th ed., edited by Richard M. Grinnell, Jr. Itasca, IL: F. E. Peacock, 1993.

Nuris, Paula S., and Walter W. Hudson. *Human Services Practice, Evaluation, and Computers: A Practical Guide for Today and Beyond.* Pacific Grove, CA: Brooks/Cole, 1993.

Teare, Robert J., Bradford W. Sheafor, and Barbara W. Shank. "National Task Analysis of Social Work Practice II," Unpublished data. Tuscaloosa, AL: School of Social Work, University of Alabama, 1997.

12.17 Assessing a Client's Social Functioning

PURPOSE: To examine and assess the various dimensions of a person's social functioning.

DISCUSSION: As explained in Chapter 1, the social work profession seeks to enhance social functioning and to prevent and correct problems of social functioning. The concept of social functioning, when applied to an individual, can be thought of as the person's motivation, capacity, and opportunity to meet his or her basic needs and perform his or her major social roles such as those of parent, spouse, partner, family member, employee, citizen, and so on.

At a fundamental level, assessing a client's social functioning involves the client and social worker examining various facets of the client's need-meeting activity and role performance and then drawing conclusions about his or her current level of functioning. Depending on the client's presenting concerns or problem, some areas are examined in more depth than others.

The following statements serve to remind the social worker of the various dimensions of an individual's social functioning. Each one describes a desirable and prosocial behavior or situation. If a client's current behavior or situation departs significantly from the descriptions, it is likely that he or she is facing some special challenges in social functioning. However, a client's social functioning always exists within a wider environmental context. Thus, the social worker's intervention plan may focus on helping the client change and adjust, on changing the environment in which the client must function, or both.

Several of the statements listed here are based on categories of functioning identified by MacNair (1981) and MacNair and McKinney (1983), Heimler (1982), and the Daniel Memorial Institute (1993). Because the items are written in positive form—rather than focusing on client problems and limitations—this set of statements is a list of possible client strengths. Also, this list can serve as a starting point for the selection and writing of goals and objectives to be included in a service agreement or treatment plan (see Items 12.7, 13.4, and 13.5).

Adults

Fundamentals of Independent Living

- The client manages basic self-care tasks such as bathing, toileting, eating, and food preparation.
- The client is sufficiently mobile, has the range of body movement, and possesses the energy necessary to safely care for self.
- The client recognizes and responds to dangerous situations (e.g., criminal activity, gas leak, malfunctioning electric circuit, etc.) and knows how to call police and fire department, request emergency medical assistance, and alert neighbors of danger.
- The client understands his or her situation and can process information, make decisions, and take action needed to complete ordinary tasks and activities of day-to-day living.

- The client speaks, reads, and writes the language(s) needed in his or her community for such activities as shopping, work, school, obtaining medical care, and calling for help.
- The client has the time and energy needed to perform his or her key social roles and fulfill his or her responsibilities.
- The client takes personal responsibility for own behavior, decisions, and choices.
- The client initiates interactions with others and influences them to cooperate or assist in meeting his or her own legitimate needs.
- The client has positive self-image and self-confidence and expresses feelings of self-worth. He or she does not overlook or underestimate abilities and strengths and does not deny or ignore real limitations.

Citizenship and Legal Concerns

- The client has a basic understanding of right and wrong as well as legal and illegal activity, and strives to live in accord with existing laws and basic moral principles that recognize the rights and needs of others and the common good.
- The client understands his or her basic rights and responsibilities as a citizen and the functions of police, lawyers, and the court system.
- The client has a basic knowledge of laws related to ordinary concerns such as marriage, parent-child relationships, contracts, insurance, leases, loans, taxes, driving an automobile, use of alcohol and drugs, firearms, and so on.
- The client expresses his or her views on public policy and legislation through such activities as voting and participation in political and advocacy organizations.
- The client avoids situations, associations, and activities that could draw him or her into dangerous or illegal conduct.

Use of Community Resources

- The client is aware of and knows how to access common resources such as those providing medical care, mental health services, legal counsel, consumer counseling, recreation, employment services, library services, and so on.
- The client knows of some agencies and organizations that provide services pertinent to his or her special concerns and life circumstances and knows how to access those resources, if needed.
- The client knows how to use Yellow Pages, directories of community services, and information and referral agencies in order to identify and contact needed resources.
- The client knows how to use telephone, letters, and other means of communication necessary to obtain needed services and resources.
- The client has access to transportation, child care, and other types of support or assistance that are prerequisites to the use of most community resources.

Family Life

- The client has a relationship with a spouse or partner that is mutually satisfying and meets his or her need for intimacy and companionship.

- The client experiences mutual and nonexploitative sexual activity that is satisfying to self and partner.
- The client behaves toward his or her children in a manner that is accepting, supportive, and encouraging. He or she recognizes and is able to meet a child's need for nurturing, guidance, protection, and limits.
- The client has an income sufficient to meet the needs of his or her family.
- The client has family members who care for each other, help each other, and are a source of support and encouragement for each other.
- The client is willing to make sacrifices for his or her family and put the needs of the children before his or her own needs and wants.
- The client has children who consider the provided guidance, limits, and discipline to be fair and reasonable.
- The client experiences adults in his or her family who encourage each other and their children to participate in community, school, job, recreation, religious, civic, or other activities and to build healthy relationships with people outside the family.

Friendships and Social Supports

- The client maintains satisfying and lasting relationships with family, friends, neighbors, and co-workers.
- The client has access to and is willing to utilize a social support network that can provide encouragement, information, and some forms of tangible assistance.
- The client selects companions who provide acceptance and encouragement and who have qualities of warmth and genuineness. He or she avoids companions who are discouraging, manipulative, or exploiting.
- The client can build and maintain new friendships that are age appropriate, positive, and satisfying.

Spirituality and Religious Activity

- The client possesses values, beliefs, and perspectives that provide meaning, purpose, and direction in life.
- The client possesses and uses a framework of moral principles for making responsible and ethical decisions.
- The client is part of a group or faith community that provides a sense of hope, encouragement, and guidance, especially in times of difficulty.
- The client is able to attend religious services of his or her choice.

Interaction with Community

- The client lives in a community and neighborhood that meets basic standards of public health and safety.
- The client is not limited by forces of discrimination or oppression within community or society in his or her efforts to work and care for self and family.
- The client participates in social, recreational, and political activities of the neighborhood and community.
- The client participates in activities intended to benefit and improve his or her community and the lives of its people.

- The client feels accepted in and has a sense of belonging to a positive and prosocial neighborhood and community.
- The client takes initiative to help neighbors and is willing to be helped by others in the neighborhood.

Personal Appearance and Hygiene

- The client maintains the level of personal hygiene needed to prevent illness and infections.
- The client is able to obtain those items and services needed to maintain appropriate appearance (e.g., hair care, deodorants, shampoos, washing machine, dry cleaning, etc.).
- The client selects clothing, accessories, and body decorations that are appropriate to the occasion or situation and that enhance personal appearance and social acceptance.

Education and Training

- The client is free of any cognitive or sensory difficulties that impede or seriously limit learning or is able to effectively compensate for these limitations.
- The client explores new areas of knowledge that stretch and challenge self in order to discover new interests and abilities.
- The client is aware of and has access to types of education and training needed to maintain and develop needed job skills.
- The client is interested in and stimulated by the education and training needed to prepare for and maintain a job.
- The client assesses own learning needs, seeks out instruction, and then learns what is needed in order to perform social roles and fulfill responsibilities at work, home, and school.
- The client has realistic understanding of his or her capacity to learn and to complete programs of education and training.

Employment and Job Performance

- The client knows about various types of jobs, how to apply, and how to conduct self during job interviews, and can determine if a particular job matches his or her skills and financial needs.
- The client has a satisfying job that provides an adequate level of income and is appropriate to his or her level of skill and experience. Working conditions and environment are safe. If the client is a parent, he or she has access to suitable and affordable day care.
- The client is a responsible employee, is able to perform assigned work, is on time for work, dresses appropriately, gets along with most others at work, and understands employment-related policies and procedures.
- The client prepares for and works toward those job changes and promotions that expand opportunity, increase job satisfaction, and provide needed income and benefits.

Money Management and Consumer Awareness

- The client monitors spending and financial transactions by using some type of budgeting and bookkeeping effort.
- The client plans and budgets for unanticipated emergencies, for seasonal expenses, and so on.
- The client understands the difference between necessities and wants and has sufficient self-discipline to avoid unwise expenditures and debt.
- The client understands basic money concepts such as interest, debt, charge accounts, loans, and late payment penalties, and understands that the purpose of commercial advertising is to encourage spending.
- The client understands payroll deductions such as those for taxes, FICA, and insurance.
- The client understands basic eligibility requirements for assistance (e.g., unemployment insurance, SSI), reporting rules, and time limitations.

Recreational and Leisure Activity

- The client participates in enjoyable recreation or leisure activity that provides a respite from the demands of other responsibilities.
- The client is aware of various forms of recreation and leisure and is willing to explore some of them in order to expand opportunity for physical exercise, new learning, and new friendships.
- The client selects recreation and leisure activities that are safe and wholesome and does not expose self to social influences that could prove harmful (e.g., excessive drinking).

Housing and Housekeeping

- The client has housing that provides adequate space and privacy and offers basic protection from fire, cold weather, excessive heat, break-in, and so forth.
- The client has safe drinking water and a safe method of food storage.
- The client keeps the living area and especially the food preparation area clean and sanitary.
- The client has access to and knows how to safely use the various tools, soaps, and household chemicals needed to keep the living area and kitchen area free of disease-causing microbes, roaches, and rodents.

Nutrition and Health Care

- The client plans, shops for, and prepares a variety of nutritious meals within his or her food budget.
- The client engages in health-building behaviors (e.g., adequate sleep, proper diet, exercise) and avoids misuse of medicines, harmful foods, street drugs, and alcohol.
- The client has access to and capacity to pay for appropriate treatment of illness or injury.
- The client avoids high risk or daredevil activities that could result in injury.

Coping with Ordinary Problems of Living

- The client completes assigned tasks and carries out responsibilities in various areas of life (e.g., home, job, school) even when they are a source of frustration. He or she is able to stick with and follow through in order to complete important tasks.
- The client recovers at a reasonable rate from anxiety or depression brought on by an upsetting event or life disruption such as a death in the family, loss of job, and so on. He or she resumes responsibilities without serious or unusual interruption.
- The client carefully and purposely rebuilds alternate intimate relationships following a loss such as a divorce, separation, or death of significant other. Overall feelings of self-worth and self-confidence are not permanently damaged by loss and disruption.
- The client is comfortable with own identity, self-concept, ethnicity, gender, sexual orientation, economic situation, and life circumstances.
- The client is able to set priorities and reasonable limits on demands by others for his or her time and energy.
- The client uses knowledge of past experiences to decide how best to cope with current difficulties and to anticipate challenges.

Coping with Mental Health Problems or Addiction

- The client recognizes the nature of his or her problems and their present and future consequences. He or she does not deny the existence of significant problems.
- The client makes full and appropriate use of effective therapies, medications, and support groups.
- The client who has prior problems with addiction has the addiction controlled and monitored in order to prevent relapse.
- The client interacts with a wide variety of people. (Current relationships and activities are not limited to ones with people having similar problems.)

Adjustments to Physical Disability

- The client makes full and appropriate use of rehabilitation programs, medications, and assistive technology (e.g., communication devices, artificial limbs, wheelchair, etc.) to minimize the impact of the disability.
- The client's expressions of frustration and concerns over his or her disability are reasonable and do not offend or drive away family members, friends, relatives, and other helpers.
- The client is able to discuss the disability and the need for assistance without embarrassment or apology. The client lets others know what he or she can and cannot do.
- The client recognizes disability-related risks and vulnerabilities and plans how to reduce risks and handle possible emergencies or accidents.

Children and Adolescents

School Performance

- The youth performs in school at a level consistent with his or her ability, as indicated by reasoning abilities evident during discussion and problem-solving activities, and by standardized achievement and intelligence tests.
- The youth effectively communicates with teachers and other school personnel and desires and enjoys these exchanges.
- The youth participates in both planned school-related social activities (e.g., sports, dances, and clubs) and in spontaneous activities involving other students and peer group.
- The youth (in keeping with age level) is interested in learning about job possibilities and educational requirements and opportunities related to various career choices.
- The youth is able to attend school without concern for personal safety.

Relationship to Parents, Siblings, and Family

- The youth usually does what is expected by the parent. He or she performs household chores and other assigned duties that are appropriate to age and ability (e.g., taking care of clothing, cleaning room, supervision of younger siblings, etc.).
- The youth frequently joins in the family's recreational, social, or spiritual activities, such as family gatherings, going to church, shopping, and so on.
- The youth regularly interacts with extended family members such as grandparents, aunts, uncles, and cousins.
- The youth joins with friends and peers in activities intended to improve the neighborhood or community.

Child or Adolescent Sexuality

- The youth is comfortable with the biological, social, and psychological aspects of his or her own sexuality.
- The youth (consistent with age level) has basic knowledge of sex. He or she seeks out accurate information about sexual matters and expresses comfort with this information.
- The youth often talks with parents about feelings, thoughts, and questions related to sexual matters.
- The youth is respectful of his or her dating partner and makes decisions concerning sexual activity accordingly. Sexual activity is kept within the limits of the partner's and own sense of morality. Participation in sexual activity is not compulsive nor forced; he or she does not coerce or force others to participate.

Ordinary Problems of Childhood and Adolescence

- The youth is able to express feelings and emotions without letting them interfere with the activities of everyday living or seriously disrupt relationships at home and in school.

- The youth (if necessary to adjust to new parent figures) accepts the emotional support and guidance offered by the new parent figures such as stepparents, guardians, or foster parents.
- The youth acknowledges and faces up to his or her problems. He or she can recognize a problem that is blocking positive interactions and neither underestimates nor exaggerates its effect.
- The youth plans clear and specific actions intended to avoid a recurrence of prior problem behavior.

SELECTED BIBLIOGRAPHY

Heimler, Eugene. *Heimler Scale of Social Functioning, Revision III.* Calgary, Canada: University of Calgary, School of Social Welfare, 1982.

MacNair, Ray. *Assessment of Social Functioning: A Client Instrument for Practitioners. Vol. 6, Human Service Series.* Athens: Institute of Community and Area Development, University of Georgia, 1981.

MacNair, Ray, and Elizabeth Mckinney. *Assessment of Child and Adolescent Functioning: A Practitioner's Instrument for Assessing Clients.* Athens: Institute of Community and Area Development, University of Georgia, 1983.

Daniel Memorial Institute. *Independent Living Skills Assessment.* Jacksonville, FL: Daniel Memorial Institute, 1995.

12.18 Assessing a Client's Mental Status

PURPOSE: To determine if the client's thought and behavior indicate serious mental illness and the need for a psychiatric referral.

DISCUSSION: Regardless of agency setting, the social worker will encounter clients who suffer from mental illness. Thus, it is important to be able to recognize symptoms so that the client will be promptly referred for a competent psychiatric examination. Because some symptoms may be caused by dramatic changes in the brain (e.g., tumors, neurological diseases, etc.), a proper referral can sometimes mean the difference between life and death (see Items 14.34 and 14.35).

Mental status exams consist of a set of simple questions aimed at gauging orientation to time and place, short- and long-term memory, and appropriateness of affect. Typical questions are: How old are you? In what year were you born? What did you have to eat at your last meal? Can you count backwards from ten? What is the name of the building we are in?

When gathering information for purposes of assessing mental status, it is important to work the questions into the ordinary flow of conversation. If asked one question after another, the client may be offended, and if the client cannot answer the questions, he or she will feel embarrassed. Engaging the client in a description of his or her typical day—from awaking to bed time—provides a context for asking specific questions. Following are 11 categories of information that should be considered in assessing mental status:

1. ***General appearance and attitude*** considers whether the client's appearance is appropriate and consistent with his or her age, social, and economic status. The client's dress, hygiene, speech, facial expressions, and motor activity provide information about his or her self-perception and awareness of others. Marked inappropriateness in appearance may be associated with psychological disturbance, particularly if these characteristics have changed over a short period of time.

2. ***Behavior*** is concerned with the appropriateness of the client's conduct during the interview and with any reports of bizarre behavior by others or the client. Irrational behaviors, such as compulsions (repeated acts that the client feels compelled to do) and phobias (avoidance of places, persons, or objects because of unfounded fears), are characteristics of many disorders.

3. ***Orientation to time and place*** refers to whether the client is aware of who he or she is, where he or she is, and what time it is (year, month, date, and day). Disorientation is a symptom of brain dysfunction.

4. ***Memory*** deficits may be associated with psychiatric as well as physical disorders. Four types of memory may be assessed:
   - *Immediate recall* refers to the ability to recall things within seconds of their presentation.
   - *Short-term memory* is generally defined as covering events transpiring within the last 25 minutes.
   - *Recent memory* refers to the client's recollection of current events and situations occurring within the few weeks preceding the interview.
   - *Remote memory* refers to the recollection of events occurring months or years ago and of a significant life happening, such as marriage, first job, high school graduation, and so on.

Immediate and short-term recall are generally assessed by instructing the client to remember something (a word, number, or object) and then asking him or her to recall that item after the lapse of a few minutes. Recent memory can be tested by asking questions such as: Where do you live? and How long have you lived there? Remote memory can be tested by asking: Where were you born? Where did you go to school? and Who was president of the United States when you got married?

5. ***Sensorium*** refers to an individual's ability to utilize data from his or her sense organs (hearing, vision, touch, smelling, and taste) and more generally to his or her overall attentiveness and alertness to the surroundings. If a client cannot comprehend visual symbols (and has no visual impairment), touch, or ordinary conversation (and has no hearing impairment and can be presumed to understand the language) or otherwise demonstrates an inability to respond to sensory stimuli, he or she may have an organic brain disorder.

6. ***Intellectual functioning*** is screened by evaluating the client's abilities to read, write, and follow simple instructions, to do simple arithmetic, to think abstractly (e.g., How are an apple and orange alike?), and the client's awareness of common knowledge consistent with his or her level of education. Poor comprehension as well as deficits in abstract thinking and intellectual performance are commonly noted as

symptoms of various psychological disorders. Gauging educational attainment is important because low levels of intellectual functioning may be attributable to a lack of education. Poor intellectual functioning among educated persons, however, may be indicative of organic disorders. Intellectual deterioration is most apparent among individuals with central nervous system disorders but may also be evident in other disturbed individuals.

7. ***Mood and affect*** refer to the client's prevailing emotional state and the range of emotions displayed during the interview. Moods include such emotions as anger, irritability, elation, exhilaration, anxiety, fear, depression, sadness, apathy, and indifference. In assessing mood and affect, two questions are important:

- Is the client's emotional state a reasonable response to his or her situation? For example, it is important to determine whether a client's depression is the result of recent events (e.g., the death of a spouse).
- Does the client show emotions that correspond to the topic being discussed? Inappropriate smiling or laughter when talking about sad events or rapid changes in emotional expression, such as laughing or crying without relevance to the conversation or circumstances, may be indicative of a psychiatric disorder. Emotional lability can also have an organic origin (e.g., after a stroke).

8. ***Perceptual distortions*** may be exhibited by some psychologically impaired individuals. Two of the most significant perceptual problems are illusions and hallucinations. Illusions are misinterpretations of actual stimuli. Hallucinations are perceptual experiences in the absence of external stimuli (e.g., hearing voices).

9. ***Thought content*** refers to the logic and consistency of an individual's attitudes, ideas, and beliefs. Examples of thought content problems include delusional thinking (false beliefs that cannot be altered by logical arguments) and obsessions (fixed or repetitive ideas that the client cannot get out of his or her mind).

10. ***Insight*** can be evaluated by asking questions that determine whether the client understands and is aware that he or she has a problem or is exhibiting behavior that is of concern to family members, the social worker, or a physician, and whether the client can describe reasons why he or she might be having this problem. Ironically, the more severe the disorder, the more likely it is that the client will be unaware of that his or her behavior is unusual or symptomatic of a mental disorder.

11. ***Judgment*** refers to the individual's ability to make responsible and rational decisions in relation to obvious problems. It also refers to a client's mental capability to make decisions related to daily living and particularly his or her physical well-being and survival.

SELECTED BIBLIOGRAPHY

Kaplan, Harold, and Benjamin Sadock. *Synopsis of Psychiatry,* 8th ed. Baltimore: Williams and Wilkins, 1998.

Sommers-Flannigan, John, and Rita Sommers-Flannagan. *Foundations of Therapeutic Interviewing.* Boston: Allyn and Bacon, 1993.

12.19 Identifying Developmental Delays in Young Children

PURPOSE: To identify possible developmental delays in a young child.

DISCUSSION: A social worker in contact with families is often in a strategic position to observe preschool-age children and conduct a cursory assessment of the child's physical and mental development. The early identification of possible developmental delays and proper referrals for further evaluation and intervention are of critical importance. Once children enter school, teachers will usually identify developmental delays.

Children who are malnourished or chronically ill, many who are abused and neglected, and, of course, those who have mental retardation or sensory or neurological problems will fall behind developmental norms. However, there can be considerable variation among children at a given age. Moreover, for a given child, it is not unusual to find some degree of unevenness across the various domains of development. For example, a child may be quick to walk but slow to talk.

Figure 12.15 lists a number of easily observed developmental "markers" that can be used to judge a child's developmental progress. If it appears that a child cannot perform the motor, mental, language, and social skills and tasks expected of a given age, he or she should be referred to a specialist for further screening or an in-depth evaluation.

The following are some early warning signs of a sensory problem or a developmental delay:

Indicators of Vision Problem

- Holds head in strained or awkward position when trying to look at a person or object
- Is often unable to locate and pick up small objects within reach
- Has one or both eyes crossed

Indicators of Hearing Problems

- Exhibits delays in speech and language development
- Does not turn toward source of strange sounds or voices by six months of age
- Has frequent earaches or runny ears
- Talks in a very loud or very soft voice
- Does not respond when you call from another room
- Turns the same ear toward a sound he or she wishes to hear

Indicators of Delays in Speech Development

- Cannot say "Mama" and "Dada" by age 1
- Cannot say the names of a few toys and people by age 2
- Cannot repeat common rhymes or TV jingles by age 3
- Does not talk in short sentences by age 4
- Cannot be understood by people outside the family by age 5

FIGURE 12.15 Developmental Markers

At about 1 month, child will:
- Turn eyes and head toward sound
- Cease crying if picked up and talked to
- Lift head when lying on stomach
- Follow a moving light with eyes
- Stretch limbs and fan out toes and fingers
- Display pupil response when a flashlight is moved in front of eyes

At about 3 months, child will:
- Make cooing sounds
- Respond to loud sounds
- Turn head toward bright colors and lights
- Move eyes and head in same direction together
- Recognize bottle or breast
- Make fists with both hands
- Grasp rattles or hair
- Wiggle and kick with legs and arms
- Lift head and chest while on stomach
- Smile in response to others

At about 6 months, child will:
- Babble
- Recognize familiar faces
- Turn toward source of normal sound
- Follow moving object with eyes when head is held stationary
- Play with toes
- Roll from stomach to back
- Reach for objects and pick them up
- Transfer objects from one hand to other
- Help hold bottle during feeding
- Bang spoon on table repeatedly
- Look for fallen object

At about 12 months, child will:
- Have a 5- to 6-word vocabulary
- Sit without support
- Pull self to standing position
- Crawl on hands and knees
- Drink from cup
- Wave bye-bye
- Enjoy peek-a-boo and patty cake
- Hold out arms and legs while being dressed
- Put objects into container
- Stack two blocks

At about 18 months, child will:
- Use 8 to 10 words that are understood
- Feed self with fingers
- Walk without help
- Pull, push, and dump things
- Pull off shoes, socks, and mittens
- Step off low object and keep balance
- Follow simple directions ("Bring the ball")
- Like to look at pictures
- Make marks on paper with crayons

At about age 2 years, child will:
- Use 2- to 3-word sentences
- Say names of favorite toys
- Recognize familiar pictures
- Carry an object while walking
- Feed self with spoon
- Play alone and independently
- Turn 2 or 3 pages at a time
- Like to imitate parents
- Point to own hair, eyes, ears, and nose upon request
- Build a tower of four blocks
- Show affection toward others

At about age 3, child will:
- Use 3- to 5-word sentences and repeat common rhymes
- Walk up stairs or steps alternating feet
- Jump, run, climb
- Ride a tricycle
- Put on shoes
- Open door
- Turn one page at a time
- Play with other children for a few minutes
- Name at least one color correctly
- Use toilet with occasional accidents

At about age 4, child will:
- Ask "what," "where," "who" questions
- Give reasonable answers to simple questions
- Give first and last names
- Show many different emotions
- Say "no" or "I won't" with intensity
- Balance on one foot for 4 to 8 seconds
- Jump from a step and maintain balance
- Dress and undress with little help
- Cut straight with scissors
- Wash hands alone
- Play simple group games

At about age 5, child will:
- Speak clearly,
- Print a few letters
- Count 5 to 10 objects
- Skip, using feet alternately
- Catch a large ball
- Bathe and dress self
- Draw a body with at least five parts
- Copy familiar shapes (e.g., square, circle, triangle)

Indicators of Delays in Motor Development

- Unable to sit up without support by age 1
- Cannot walk without help by age 2
- Does not walk up and down steps by age 3
- Unable to balance on one foot for a short time by age 4
- Cannot throw a ball overhand and catch a large ball bounced to him or her by age 5

Indicators of Delays in Social and Mental Development

- Does not react to his or her own name when called by age 1
- Does not play games such as peek-a-boo, patty cake, and waving bye-bye by age 1
- Unable to identify hair, eyes, ears, nose, and mouth by pointing to them by age 2
- Does not imitate parents doing routine household chores by age 2 to 3
- Does not understand simple stories told or read by age 3
- Does not enjoy playing alone with toys, pots and pans, sand, and so on, by age 3
- Does not plan group games such as hide-and-seek, tag-ball, and so on, with other children by age 4
- Does not give reasonable answers to such questions as "What do you do when you are sleepy?" or "What do you do when you are hungry?" by age 4
- Does not seem to understand the meanings of the words *today, tomorrow,* and *yesterday* by age 5
- Does not share and take turns by age 5

SELECTED BIBLIOGRAPHY

Berk, Laura. *Infants, Children, and Adolescents.* Boston: Allyn and Bacon, 1996.
Chess, Stella, and Alexander Thomas. *Know Your Child.* Northvale, NJ: Jason Aronson, 1996.

12.20 Referral for Psychological Testing

PURPOSE: To make appropriate use of psychological testing in the assessment of client functioning.

DISCUSSION: Not infrequently, the social worker will refer a client to a psychologist for testing. Such testing can provide information on the client's intellectual capacity, patterns of motivation and coping behavior, self-concept, level of anxiety or depression, and general personality integration. It is important to remember that psychological tests focus on certain variables while neglecting others that may be of importance. Cronbach (1990), an authority on testing, reminds us that the value of test information should be judged by how much it improves decisions over the best possible decisions made without the test. A psychological test can provide valuable information on which to base a decision, but one should not rely exclusively on test results, especially if based on a single test instrument. Presented here are brief descriptions of some of the tests administered by psychologists:

Infant Development Scales

- *The Brazelton Neonatal Behavioral Assessment Scale* tests an infant's (1) neurological intactness, (2) interactive behavior (including motoric control such as putting the thumb in the mouth and remaining calm and alert in response to stimuli such as a bell, a light, and pinprick), and (3) responsiveness to the examiner and need for stimulation.
- *The Bayley Scales of Infant Development* test mental abilities, including memory, learning, and problem-solving behavior; motor skills; and social behaviors, such as social orientation, fearfulness, and cooperation.
- *The Gesell Developmental Schedules* test for fine and gross motor behavior; language behavior; adaptive behavior, including eye-hand coordination, imitation, and object recovery; and personal/social behavior, including reaction to persons, initiative, independence, and play response.
- *The Denver Developmental Screening Test* is widely used and can be administered by a person with only limited training. It is a screening tool, not a dianostic test. It is used to discover possible developmental delays in the four areas of personal/social, fine motor/adaptive, language, and gross motor skills that should be more carefully evaluated with other tests.

Intelligence Tests for Preschool- and School-Age Children

- *The Wechsler Scales* include separate forms for preschool- and school-age children. The preschool form is called the *Wechsler Preschool and Primary Scale of Intelligence* (*WPPSI-R*), and the school-aged form is called the *Wechsler Intelligence Scale for Children* (*WISC-III*). The WISC III is the test most likely to be used to assess the cognitive functioning of school-age children. It has six verbal and six performance subtests.
- The *Stanford-Binet IV* can be used with both preschool- and school-age children. Examples of tasks include remembering where an object was hidden, building a block tower to match an existing tower, explaining the use of common objects, and identifying pictured objects by name. The Stanford-Binet may not provide an accurate assessment of bilingual or bicultural children.

Intelligence Tests for Adults

- *The Wechsler Adult Intelligence Scale* (*WAIS-III*) is usually considered to be the best general intelligence test for persons age 16 and older. Six subtests (information, digit span, vocabulary, arithmetic, comprehension, and similarities) make up its verbal scale, and five subtests (picture completion, picture arrangement, block design, object assemble, and digit symbol) make up the performance scale.

Special Abilities Tests

- *The Bender Visual Motor Gestalt Test* is used to assess visual perceptual skills and eye-hand coordination. The client is given nine geometric figures, one at a time, and asked to copy each.
- *The Peabody Picture Vocabulary Test* assesses familiarity with vocabulary words without requiring the child to speak. The client is shown four pictures at

a time and must point to the one that corresponds to the word the examiner says. The test was originally designed to be used with persons who are nonverbal, mentally retarded, and/or have cerebral palsy.
- *The Detroit Test of Learning Aptitude* measures auditory and visual memory and concentration.

Testing for Cognitive Delay

An IQ score below 70 indicates that a client may have cognitive delay or mental retardation. However, a low IQ score by itself is not sufficient for diagnosis; the client's adaptive behavior must also be measured. *Adaptive behavior* refers to the person's ability to carry out everyday living skills, such as dressing, eating, washing, playing, functioning independently, and cooperating with others. Several instruments measure age-appropriate adaptive behavior: *The Vineland Adaptive Behavior Scale (VABS), The American Association on Mental Retardation's (AAMR) Adaptive Behavior Scales,* and *Scales of Independent Behavior.*

Personality Tests

Objective-type personality tests such as the following are pencil-and-paper tests designed to determine predominant personality traits or behaviors:

- *The Minnesota Multiphasic Personality Inventory (MMPI-2)* is probably the most often used objective personality test. It consists of 567 self-descriptive statements to which the client answers either true, false, or cannot say. It is used with persons 16 years of age or older.
- *The Personality Inventory for Children (PIC)* is one of the few objective tests for children. It has forms for both the parent and the youth.

Projective tests provide a stimulus (e.g., inkblots, a set of pictures, or incomplete sentences) and ask the client to respond to the stimulus. These tests rest on the assumption that the client's responses will reveal his or her unique view of the world, troublesome thoughts, and inner conflicts. Another type of projective test provides instructions for the client to draw a picture, again with the idea that the drawing will reveal information about the inner self. The *Rorschach Test,* the first inkblot test, is the most commonly used projective test for adults. The *Holtzman Inkblot Technique* may substitute for the Rorschach. The most common picture-story type tests are the *Thematic Apperception Test (TAT),* the *Michigan Picture Test,* the *Tasks of Emotional Development Test,* and the *Make-a-Picture-Story Test.*

Referring a Client for Psychological Testing

1. Before deciding on a referral, be very clear about why you are seeking a psychological evaluation of your client.
2. When making a referral to a psychologist for testing, explain how and why you and your agency are involved in providing service to this client, the case management decisions you face, and the type of information that would be helpful. List the questions you would like the psychologist to answer.

3. Provide the psychologist with information concerning the client's age, sex, education, occupation and employment history, ethnicity, and any special disabilities, such as hearing or visual problems or physical limitations. Also provide the results of any previous testing, including the dates of testing and the names of the tests used.
4. After consulting with the psychologist who will do the testing, prepare the client by giving him or her basic information on what to expect, where the testing will be done, and about how long it will take.
5. Have realistic expectations of psychological testing. In many cases, the results of testing will simply confirm the conclusions already reached by people who have observed the client for a matter of weeks or months.
6. Ask the psychologist to explain the strengths and limitations of the testing procedures used with your client, so you can decide how much faith to place in the results.

SELECTED BIBLIOGRAPHY

Anastasi, Anne. *Psychological Testing,* 7th ed. New York: Macmillan, 1997.

Cronbach, L. J. *Essentials for Psychological Testing,* 5th ed. New York: Harper & Row, 1990.

Olin, Jason. *Rapid Psychological Assessment.* New York: Wiley, 1998.

Wodrich, David. *Children's Psychological Testing: A Guide for Nonpsychologists.* Pacific Grove, CA: Brooks/Cole, 1997.

12.21 The Person-in-Environment System (PIE)

PURPOSE: To describe, classify, and code problems in adult social functioning.

DISCUSSION: The PIE system is designed for use by social workers and is built around two key social work concepts: social functioning and the person-in-environment construct (see Chapter 1 for discussion of these concepts). According to Karls and Wandrei (1994a), the PIE provides social workers with the following:

- common language . . . to describe their clients' problems in social functioning.
- a common capsulated description of social phenomena that could facilitate treatment or amelioration of the problems presented by clients.
- a basis for gathering data required to measure the need for services and to design human services programs and evaluate effectiveness.
- a mechanism for clearer communication among social work practitioners and between practitioners and administrators and researchers.
- a basis for clarifying the domain of social work in the human services field. (p. 7)

The PIE system groups client problems into four classes or "factors." Basically, a factor is a category or a general type of problem. The terminology used for Factor I (*social functioning problems*) and Factor II (*environmental problems*) is unique to social work practice. Factor III (*mental health problems*) utilizes the clinical syndrome and personality and developmental disorders terminology found in the *DSM-IV.* Factor IV (*physical health problems*) records diseases and health problems that have been diagnosed by a physician or reported by the client or others. It should be noted that the PIE is not intended as a substitute for the *DSM-IV* but rather is a complementary system (see Item 12.22 for information about the *DSM-IV*).

An abbreviated outline of Factor I and Factor II categories and subcategories is presented here.

PIE Factor I: Social Functioning Problems

1. Social role in which each problem is defined (four categories and numerous subcategories):
   - Familial roles (parent, spouse, child, sibling, other family member, and significant other)
   - Other interpersonal roles (lover, friend, neighbor, member, and other)
   - Occupational roles (worker-paid, worker-home, worker-volunteer, student, and other)
   - Special life situation roles (consumer, inpatient/client, outpatient/client, probationer/parolee, prisoner, immigrant-legal, immigrant-undocumented, immigrant-refugee, and other)
2. Type of problem in social role (nine types: power, ambivalence, responsibility, dependency, loss, isolation, victimization, mixed, and other)
3. Severity of problem (rated on a 6-point scale)
4. Duration of problem (six categories)
5. Ability of client to cope with problem (six levels)

PIE Factor II: Environmental Problems

1. Social system where each problem is identified (six major systems and numerous subcategories):
   - Economic/basic needs system problems
   - Education and training system problems
   - Judicial and legal system problems
   - Health, safety, and social services problems
   - Voluntary association system problems
   - Affectional support system problems
2. Specific type of problem within each social system (71 subcategories; number varies for each of six social systems. Examples of social system problem subcategories: lack of regular food supply, absence of shelter, lack of culturally relevant education, discrimination, lack of police services, unsafe conditions in home, regulatory barriers to social services, absence of affectional support system, lack of community acceptance of religious values, etc.)
3. Severity of problem (rated on a 6-point scale)
4. Duration of problem (six categories)

SELECTED BIBLIOGRAPHY

Karls, James, and Karin Wandrei. "Person-in-Environment." In *Encyclopedia of Social Work*, 19th ed., vol. 3, edited by Richard Edwards. Washington, DC: NASW Press, 1995, pp. 1818–1827.

———, eds. *Person-In-Environment System.* Washington, DC: NASW Press, 1994a.

———. *Pie Manual.* Washington, DC: NASW Press, 1994b.

12.22 The Diagnostic and Statistical Manual of Mental Disorders (DSM-IV)

PURPOSE: To use proper terminology and classifications when exchanging information about a client's mental disorder.

DISCUSSION: In order to communicate accurately with other professionals about a client's mental disorder and to understand reports prepared by psychologists and psychiatrists, the social worker must be familiar with a book titled the *Diagnostic and Statistical Manual of Mental Disorders*, or the *DSM-IV*, published by the American Psychiatric Association (1994). An increasing number social workers and agencies look to third-party payments (e.g., Medicaid, Medicare, private health insurance, etc.) as sources of payment for the psychotherapy they provide to clients; prior to submitting a claim for such payments, the client must be assigned to a specific diagnostic category from the *DSM-IV*.

In the *DSM-IV* system, over 200 disorders are classified within 17 broad categories, Each disorder is described in terms of symptoms, diagnostic criteria, age of onset, prevalence, level of impairment, and so on. The major categories are the following:

1. Disorders Usually First Diagnosed in Infancy, Childhood, or Adolescence
2. Delirium, Dementia, and Amnestic and Other Cognitive Disorders
3. Mental Disorders Due to a General Medical Condition
4. Substance-Related Disorders
5. Schizophrenia and Other Psychotic Disorders
6. Mood Disorders
7. Anxiety Disorders
8. Somatoform Disorders
9. Factitious Disorders
10. Dissociative Disorders
11. Sexual and Gender Identity Disorders
12. Eating Disorders
13. Sleep Disorders
14. Impulse-Control Disorders Not Elsewhere Classified
15. Adjustment Disorder
16. Personality Disorders
17. Other Conditions That May Be a Focus of Clinical Attention

The American Psychiatric Association (1994) warns of the inherent difficulties of assessing the behavior of a person from an ethnic or cultural group different from that of the clinician: "A clinician who is unfamiliar with the nuances of an individual's cultural frame of reference may incorrectly judge as psychopathology those normal variations in behavior, belief, or experiences that are particular to the individual's culture" (p. xxiv).

Many social workers question the appropriateness of this diagnostic manual for social work practice. They are bothered by the labeling inherent in the *DSM* system, by the manual's exclusive focus on pathology, and by its lack of attention to environmental context. Fortunately, the *Person in-Environment System* (*PIE*) is now available as a supplement to the *DSM-IV* (see Item 12.21).

SELECTED BIBLIOGRAPHY

American Psychiatric Association. *Diagnostic and Statistical Manual of Mental Disorders (DSM-IV)*, 4th ed., rev. Washington, DC: American Psychiatric Association, 1994.

Kutchins, Herb, and Stuart Kirk. *Making Us Crazy: DSM—The Psychiatric Bible and the Creation of Mental Disorders.* New York: Free Press, 1997.

Morrison, James. *DSM-IV Made Easy.* New York: Guilford, 1995.

12.23 Assessing and Responding to Suicide Risk

PURPOSE: To assess risk of suicide and take preventive action.

DISCUSSION: Given the high rate of suicide among teenagers, young adults, and the elderly, the social worker will encounter clients who are at risk of taking their own lives. The ***warning signs of suicide*** include depression, preoccupation with death and pain, giving away prized possessions, unexplained changes in behavioral patterns, sudden increase in the use of drugs and alcohol, and impulsive or reckless behavior. Clinical data indicate that most suicide victims have consulted with a physician within six months of their suicide. Although not all people who end their lives are clinically depressed, studies reveal that depression is often present. The ***symptoms of depression*** include pervasive sadness, feelings of hopelessness, lack of interest in activities once enjoyed, inability to concentrate, thoughts of suicide, unexplained aches and pains, fatigue and restlessness, changes in appetite and sleep habits, withdrawal from others, early waking from sleep or erratic sleep patterns, irritability, and unexplained crying. Whereas depression in adults usually results in a retardation of activity, depression in children and youth is often expressed in agitation.

Legally and ethically, the social worker must make every reasonable effort to prevent a client's suicide. This includes providing counseling, staying with the person during times of high risk, and, if necessary, calling the police and arranging involuntary hospitalization. State laws dictate when police can detain a suicidal person and when involuntary hospitalization is permitted. An individual who acknowledges thinking about suicide is at high risk for suicide if he or she:

- Has a history of prior attempts
- Is in a troublesome or painful situation that is growing worse, more complex, and more painful
- Has a clear plan for suicide and access to the chosen means of suicide (e.g., has a gun or a supply of sleeping pills)

- Has changed rather quickly from being distressed and talking a lot about suicide to being apparently at ease and content
- No longer has access to a person who was previously an important source of support and encouragement

The following guidelines will help the social worker in assessing suicide potential and responding to situations that pose a risk of suicide:

1. Take every message about suicide seriously. It is very significant that the person is talking about harm to self rather than expressing his or her frustration in other ways. It is a myth that people who talk about suicide will not kill themselves. Unfortunately, the message may be subtle and, in some cases, it is not until after the death that its meaning becomes clear. In 10 to 20 percent of suicides, there are no noticeable warnings prior to the death.

2. If you believe that a client is at risk of suicide, consult with other professionals on how best to proceed. Do not allow yourself to be "hooked" by the suicidal client into a promise of complete confidentiality. Ordinary rules of confidentiality must be broken in order to prevent a death.

3. Listen for indirect statements of suicidal intent such as: "I won't be around much longer," "There is nothing worth living for anymore," or "I just can't stand the pain any longer." Be especially concerned about such statements if the person has recently experienced the loss of an important relationship, a loss of status among peers, an episode of family violence, or is in the throes of adjusting to chronic pain, a life-threatening illness, or a serious physical limitation.

4. Keep in mind that the person thinking about suicide is experiencing intense feelings of ambivalence—the desire to live and, at the same time, the desire to escape pain, even if by death. The person does not really want to die but wants desperately to get away from his or her pain. Thus, assume that the person talking about suicide is ambivalent and hoping for your assistance. Reach out and support that part of the person holding to life.

5. Ask simple and direct questions when communicating with the suicidal person. Do not be afraid to ask if he or she is thinking about suicide. Speaking openly will not increase the likelihood of suicide. Direct questioning tells the suicidal person that you are concerned and not afraid to talk straight. Also, questioning is a way of eliciting the information needed to be of help. Examples of questions include: Are you thinking of killing yourself? Can you tell me why suicide seems like the answer? and Who else knows you are thinking about suicide?

6. Try to understand why life seems so painful and futile to the individual. Suicide is seen by the person as a solution to a problem. Thus, it is of critical importance to identify the problem as it is perceived by the individual. Do not argue or become judgmental—the suicidal person already feels helpless and hopeless. Do nothing that would add to his or her feelings of inadequacy of shame.

7. Determine whether the person has worked out a specific suicide plan. Suicide is seldom an impulsive action. Ask questions such as: Do you have a plan for killing yourself? How do you plan to get the gun you intend to use? Where do you plan to kill yourself? and What time of day or night do you plan to kill yourself? The more detailed and specific the person's plan, the higher the risk of suicide. Many suicidal people have thought much about their suicide plans, but most have not thought about an alternative or a "plan B." Thus, if you can interfere with a key element of their plan, you can often thwart their suicide.

8. Determine whether the person has chosen a specific method (shooting, hanging, pills, etc.) and if he or she has access to the method. The person who has selected a method and has access to it is at high risk.

9. Determine the lethality of the method. Highly lethal methods include shooting, jumping, hanging, drowning, carbon monoxide poisoning, car crash, or taking high doses of barbiturates, sleeping pills, or aspirin. Less lethal methods include wrist cutting, gas stove, or tranquilizers and nonprescription drugs (excluding aspirin and Tylenol). The more lethal the method, the higher the risk and the greater the chance that a suicidal gesture will result in death.

10. Determine whether the person has attempted suicide in the past. Ask questions such as: Have you attempted suicide in the past? How did you try to kill yourself at that time? Did you seek professional counseling? and Was it helpful? A history of prior attempts elevates the risk.

11. Determine what has happened recently that causes the person to think more and more of suicide. For example, ask: What has happened over the past days or weeks that has increased your sense of hopelessness? Determine what this event means to the person: Is his or her perception realistic? Is the person too upset to understand the situation clearly? Will the event or situation continue to trouble the individual or will things change in time? Ask: Why do you believe your situation will not improve? and How might your situation be different six months from now?

12. Most suicidal people have "tunnel vision"—they can think only about their pain and helplessness. It is important to help them identify and consider alternative methods for dealing with the situation. How has the individual managed stressful situations in the past? Will any of these methods work in the present situation?

13. Determine whether the suicidal person has anyone to rely on during a time of crisis. Many of the people who commit suicide feel ignored or cut off from the people around them. The risk of suicide increases when a person is widowed, divorced, or separated. It is important to help significant others come to the support of the suicidal person.

14. Help the person see that suicide is a permanent solution to a temporary problem. Identify other possible solutions to dealing with the pain the individual is experiencing but do not lie or offer false hope. Ask the client to immediately enter counseling as an alternative to suicide. If necessary, ask him or her to agree not to commit suicide for a specific period (e.g., two weeks) or to promise not to commit suicide before talking to you one more time. If a referral for counseling is made, you or someone else should accompany the client to the initial interview. Follow-up is necessary to ensure that the client is making use of the service.

15. In extreme situations and when nothing else seems to be working, attempt to engage the person in a discussion of what will happen after he or she is found dead. Sometimes this will jar the person into thinking more clearly about the consequences of a suicide. For example: What kind of a funeral service do you want? Who should be notified? Should the people to be notified of your death be approached or talked to in a certain way? Can we make a list of all the people who should be contacted and invited to your funeral? Who do you want to have your favorite possessions?

16. Realize that it may not be possible to prevent the suicide of a person who is genuinely committed to taking his or her own life. Counseling, close monitoring, and hospitalization may delay a suicide but such efforts will not always prevent a suicide.

SELECTED BIBLIOGRAPHY

Hack, Thomas. "Suicide Risk Assessment and Intervention." In *First Steps in the Art of Intervention*, edited by David Marlin and Allan Moore. Pacific Grove, CA: Brooks/Cole, 1995.

Jacobs, Douglas, ed. *Suicide Assessment and Intervention*. San Francisco: Jossey-Bass, 1998.

Silverman, Morton, and Ronald Maris, eds. *Suicide Prevention*. New York: Guilford, 1995.

12.24 Assessing a Child's Need for Protection

PURPOSE: To identify a child who has been abused or neglected and to determine if the child is at risk of further harm.

DISCUSSION: State laws require social workers to report cases of suspected abuse or neglect. (Many states also mandate the reporting of elder abuse.) The observation of several of the physical and behavioral indicators suggest the possible existence of child abuse or neglect. These indicators are summarized here.

Indicators of Physical Abuse

- Unexplained bruises or welts, especially if on both sides of face or body, or on back, buttocks, or torso
- Bruises in different stages of healing
- Multiple bruises clustered in one area, forming symmetrical patterns or reflecting the shape of an instrument (e.g., loop marks, lineal or parallel marks, punch marks, etc.)
- Bruises regularly appear after a weekend or a visit
- Bruises on shoulders or neck displaying shape of hand and fingers (e.g., grab marks)

- Unexplained burns, such as those caused by cigarettes, and especially if on palms, soles, back, or buttocks
- Hot water immersion or dunking burns (e.g., socklike, glovelike, or doughnut shaped on buttocks or genitalia)
- Burns patterned like electric stove burner, hot plate, curling iron, etc.
- Rope burns on wrists or ankles (i.e., tie marks)
- Unexplained mouth injuries such as frenulum tears or broken teeth (caused by rough feeding)
- Human, adult-size bites to child's body
- Unexplained broken bones or head injuries such as skull fractures or subdural hematoma
- Retina detachment or whiplash injuries to neck caused by violent shaking
- Internal injuries caused by punch
- Poisoning caused by ingestion of street drugs, alcohol, prescription medicines, or household chemicals
- Attempts by child to hide injuries with clothing; embarrassment or shame over injury, reluctance to talk about injury (nonabused children proudly display injuries)
- Hyper-vigilant, fearful, and guarded around adults; avoids physical contact with people including his parents (i.e., fearful of human touch).
- Overly adaptive behavior in an attempt to meet parents' needs (i.e., by taking care of and comforting parent, the child seeks to keep things calm and prevent abusive episodes)
- Becomes uneasy when another child cries or acts up (i.e., has learned to associate crying with pain of abuse)
- Serious behavioral problems at young age (e.g., runs away, self-mutilation, suicide attempts, violent, withdrawn, etc.).

Indicators of Neglect

- Begging, stealing, or hoarding food; underweight; failure to thrive; bald patches on scalp
- Poor school attendance (sometimes the neglectful parent is so lonely he or she keeps the child home for company; sometimes the child remains home to care for younger siblings)
- Untreated medical and dental problems, even though parent has resources to get medical services
- Unsocialized and primitive in eating and toilet behaviors
- Unusual fatigue and listlessness; falling asleep at unusual times
- Stays at school, in public places, or at other homes for extended periods
- Poor hygiene, filthy clothing, clothing inappropriate for weather
- Child not supervised or protected from dangerous activity

Indicators of Sexual Abuse

- Bruises, scaring, or tissue tears around vagina and anus; bruised or swollen penis (caused by rough fondling and masturbation)
- Blood on child's underwear

- Redness or rash in genital area in child not wearing diaper (caused by frequent fondling)
- Redness or abrasions between upper legs (caused by penis placed between child's legs)
- Recurrent bladder infections (i.e., bacteria from rectum introduced into vagina when there is both anal and vaginal intercourse)
- Pregnancy or a sexually transmitted disease in younger child
- Semen in vagina, rectum, or mouth (can be detected by medical exam within three days of intercourse)
- Inappropriate masturbation that has a driven or compulsive quality
- Unusual sexual play and exploration of pets or dolls
- Aggressive and forced sexual activity with other children, usually of a younger age
- Inappropriate sexual behavior toward adults
- Unusual level of knowledge about sexual activity (e.g., can describe sexual movement, smells, taste, feelings, etc.)
- Preoccupation with sexual matters or unusual fear of anything sexual
- Unusual fear of showers, bathrooms, bedrooms
- Unwilling to change clothes for gym or to expose body (caused by extreme shame of body)
- Frequent and patterned absences from school that are justified by one adult, the offender
- Unusual or bizarre sexual themes in artwork
- Wearing many layers of clothing (protection of body)
- Frequent use of dissociation as coping mechanism
- Unusually close relationship with adult that has secretive or sexual overtones
- Extreme protectiveness of child by an adult who keeps child from talking to or getting close to responsible adults

In the United States, over 50 percent of all cases of child maltreatment are cases of neglect. Moreover, about one-half of all child maltreatment–related fatalities are caused by neglect. A high percentage of the neglect cases occur in families where the parents are abusing alcohol or addicted to drugs.

Many parents believe in and utilize corporal punishment as discipline. Thus, in assessing a situation, the social worker must be able to differentiate physical abuse from ordinary spanking or corporal punishment. That decision will, of course, be tied to the definition of physical abuse found in a states legal code. In addition, we offer three criteria for making that distinction:

1. In corporal punishment, the child experiences some pain and discomfort. In abuse, there is injury to body tissue.
2. In using corporal punishment, the parent maintains self-control and is aware of where and how hard the child is being hit. In an abusive situation, the parent loses control over his or her emotions and strikes the child with excessive force or hits the child in places that are easily injured.

3. Nonabusive parents using corporal punishment may occasionally get carried away and hit too hard but they quickly realize what has happened and are able to make changes in how they discipline the child so this does not happen again. In situations of abuse, there are repeated episodes of excessive corporal punishment and injury because the parents are unable to gain control of their anger and make changes in how they respond to the child.

It is tragic but true that child sexual abuse is not an uncommon occurrence in our society. Most children who are sexually abused do not tell anyone because they are either afraid or feel great shame. Most cases of child sexual abuse involve fondling and masturbation but *not* penetration. Penetration might be of the child's mouth, vagina, or rectum. Even if there has been penetration of the vagina or rectum there will be no physical evidence in most cases.

It is also important to understand that the majority of sexually abused children do *not* exhibit unusual sexual behavior. However, sexually abused children are more likely than nonabused children to display adultlike sexual behavior.

The social worker must report suspected cases of child sexual abuse. However, he or she must also be alert to the fact that false or mistaken accusations do occur. Both children and adults are suggestible and may misinterpret facts, and occasionally false accusations are used as a means of hurting someone. False allegations by a child are relatively rare but the rate increases if the child's accusation is being encouraged by a parent and the rate becomes even higher in cases involving child custody fights between parents.

Once a case of abuse or neglect has been identified, the question of risk must be addressed. In other words, is the child at risk of serious harm and in need of immediate protection? Presented here are factors that should be considered in the assessment of risk.

Child-Related Factors

- Child's young age and/or presences of serious illness or physical or mental disability (i.e., vulnerable and unable to protect self, need for medication, etc.)
- Prior history of being target of abuse
- History of severe or frequent abuse or neglect
- Injuries to child at vulnerable body locations (e.g., head, face, genitals, etc.)
- Injuries that require medical attention or hospitalization
- Child's behavior and special needs (e.g., disability or illness) place great and stressful demands on caregiver
- Perpetrator has access to child
- Child's relationships with siblings or others in the household are strained or troubled (i.e., decreasing chances that others will offer protection)

Parent/Caregiver-Related Factors

- Presence of condition that limits ability of caregiver to care for or protect child (e.g., existence of a serious physical or mental illness, mental retardation, extreme immaturity, etc.)
- Presence of serious drug or alcohol dependency

- History of domestic violence (e.g., spouse abuse) or other violent criminal activity
- History of having abused or neglected other children
- Lack of basic parenting skills or knowledge
- High levels of anger, hostility, or rejection toward child
- Existence of other serious family problems that place added stress on family (e.g., marital conflict, financial, health, chaotic life-style, etc.)
- Unrealistic and unreasonable expectations of child
- Denial of problem; evasiveness or refusal to cooperate with agency personnel or other helpers
- Prior efforts to work with family have been rejected or ineffective

Environmental Factors

- Physical conditions of home presents serious danger to child (e.g., exposed electrical wiring, unprotected household chemicals, etc.)
- Family is socially or physically isolated from social supports and other forms of assistance in times of emergency

In some cases, the removal of the child from his or her own home is necessary. However, because the separation of parent and child is so traumatic to the child and so disruptive to the family, an out-of-home placement should be used only in those cases where the child is at high risk of serious harm and there is no less drastic method of protecting the child. The following principles should guide placement decisions:

- If a child must be placed into foster care, it is to be done for one reason only: to protect the child from harm. For example, it would be unethical and unprofessional to place a child in order to coerce the parent into taking some action.
- A child should be placed in the least restrictive alternative; moreover, the parent(s) and child should, to the extent possible and appropriate, participate in the placement decision and the preparation of the child for the placement.
- Efforts to assure protection for child are to be those that are the least intrusive and least disruptive for both the child and family.
- During the placement, respect and maintain the child's cultural heritage and religious beliefs (*Note:* See the special requirements and provisions of the Indian Child Welfare Act.)

SELECTED BIBLIOGRAPHY

Briere, John, Lucy Berliner, Josephine Bulkley, Carole Jenny, and Theresa Reid, eds. *The APSAC Handbook on Child Maltreatment.* Thousand Oaks, CA: Sage, 1996.

Haynes-Seman, Clara, and David Baumgarten. *Children Speak for Themselves.* New York: Brunner/Mazel, 1994.

Monteleone, James. *Recognition of Child Abuse for Mandated Reporters.* St. Louis: G. W. Medical Publishing, 1994.

Tower, Cynthia. *Understanding Child Abuse and Neglect,* 4th ed. Boston: Allyn and Bacon, 1999.

Yakpo, Michael. *Suggestions of Abuse: True and False Memories of Childhood Sexual Trauma.* New York: Simon and Schuster, 1994.

12.25 The 4 Ps, 4 Rs, and 4 Ms

PURPOSE: To assist the social worker in assessing the client's behavior and functioning within a social context.

DISCUSSION: For many years, Perlman's (1957) ***4 Ps*** (person, problem, place, and process) have proven useful to many social workers as a way of organizing their thoughts about a client, his or her situation, and the agency context of social work intervention. Doremus (1976) suggests the ***4 Rs*** (roles, reactions, relationships, and resources) as a way of conceptualizing assessment in health care settings. In addition, the authors offer the ***4 Ms*** (motivation, meanings, management, and monitoring) as further reminders of important elements in social work intervention. A blending of the 4 Ps, 4 Rs, and 4 Ms results in a 12-item, easily remembered conceptual tool that can help a worker sift through available data, organize it, and begin formulating an intervention plan. As used here, the word *client* refers to an individual. However, the underlying ideas that make up the 4 P/4 R/4 M can be applied to work with other client systems, including couples, families, or small groups.

The 4 Ps

1. Problem
   - What is the nature of the client's problem or concern? Its cause, intensity, frequency, and duration?
   - How does the client define or describe it? How do others who know the client define it? How does the worker define it?
   - Can this problem or situation be changed? What part or what aspects of the problem can feasibly be addressed in a change effort by the worker and client?
   - How effective have previous efforts by the client, agency, or worker been in dealing with the client's problem or concern?
   - Is the problem or situation an emergency that requires a rapid response?
   - What would the consequences be if the worker or agency does nothing for or with the client?

2. Person
   - How are the various dimensions of the whole person (e.g., physical, emotional social, economic, and spiritual) related to or affected by the client's problem, concern, or situation?
   - What client strengths or assets can be used as a foundation on which to build an effective helping and change process?
   - How might the client's usual ways of thinking and behaving become barriers to dealing effectively with the problem or concern?

3. Place
   - What meaning does the client assign to his or her involvement with the agency (e.g., hopefulness, stigma, fear, humiliation, etc.)?

- Can the agency provide the services needed by the client? If not, is referral to another agency likely to be effective?
- Are the agency's own procedures and policies somehow contributing to the client's problems?

4. Process
   - What type of helping approach, method, or technique is the client likely to find acceptable?
   - What approach, method, or technique is likely to work and be effective?
   - How will the requirements of the helping process (time, fees, scheduling, etc.) affect the client's current roles and responsibilities and that of others (e.g., family, friends, employer, etc.)?

The 4 Rs

5. Roles
   - What roles and responsibilities does the client have in life (e.g., parent, spouse, employee, etc.)?
   - What do others (e.g., family, employers, etc.) expect of the client?
   - How satisfied is the client with his or her role performance?

6. Reactions
   - What are the client's reactions (e.g., physical, behavioral, and emotional) to his or her problems, concerns, and situation?
   - How do these reactions compare to his or her usual patterns? Is the client in a state of crisis?

7. Relationships
   - What people are a significant and meaningful part of the client's life (e.g., family, peers, friends, etc.)?
   - How are they being affected by the client's problem or situation?
   - What is the relationship between the behavior of significant others and the client's current problem or situation?

8. Resources
   - What formal and informal resources has the client used in the past to cope with various problems? Are these still available to the client?
   - What new or additional resources are now needed by the client? Are they available? Is the client willing to use them?
   - Is the client eligible for needed services and programs?

The 4 Ms

9. Motivation
   - What does the client want to do about his or her problem or situation?
   - What discomfort or aversive factors are pushing the client toward action?
   - What factors of hope and optimism are pulling the client toward action?
   - What can be done to increase client motivation?

10. Meanings
    - What meaning does the client assign to his or her situation, and problems?
    - What ethnic, cultural, and religious beliefs and values are important to the client and relevant to the current problem or situation?
11. Management
    - How can the worker best use his or her limited time, energy, and resources to help the client deal with the problem or situation?
    - What overall plan or strategy will guide the worker's activity with the client?
    - How will work with this client affect the worker's other responsibilities?
12. Monitoring
    - How will the worker monitor his or her impact on the client and evaluate the effectiveness of the intervention?
    - How can the worker use peers, supervisors, or consultants to monitor and evaluate intervention?

SELECTED BIBLIOGRAPHY

Doremus, Bertha. "The Four R's: Social Diagnosis in Health Care." *Health and Social Work* 1 (1976): 121–139.

Perlman, Helen. *Social Casework: A Problem Solving Process.* Chicago: University of Chicago Press, 1957.

SECTION B

TECHNIQUES AND GUIDELINES FOR INDIRECT PRACTICE

When working to change organizations and communities, the social worker should be especially thorough in data collection and assessment before proceeding to action. Not suprisingly, large system change is difficult and time consuming; consider how rare it is when a single person, or even a few people, can decide on changes to be made and implement the actions to bring about that change. It takes careful planning, education, negotiation, and patience to achieve meaningful changes, such as in agency policies and programs or the legislative changes that affect the larger community.

Data-Collection Activities. The first step in preparing for agency or community change is to collect sufficient information to be well informed. In an agency, for example, change requires working through, or sometimes around, the agency's or community's decision-making structure. To do this, the worker needs to learn about the feasibility of various options, the costs (in dollars and the expenditure of human resources) of changing the current situation, and the most effective ways to bring about change.

Like direct-practice data collection, indirect practice requires that the worker be skilled at interviewing people to obtain information regarding their experiences and attitudes about the situation being considered for change. However, these impressions typically are obtained from a number of people who have knowledge of the situation or may be affected by change. The worker must also be able to accumulate data regarding differing perceptions and accurately summarize the information obtained.

Often, this data collection occurs in a staff meeting, in a board meeting, or from members of a committee appointed to consider the situation. On other occasions, focus groups (see Item 12.28) are created where intensive verbal interaction is stimulated in order to air various opinions on a topic. Another format for data collection involves creating a standardized questionnaire that invites written responses to a series of questions that can be tabulated and summarized to yield a description of the thoughts and opinions of the respondents. Finally, data collection may mean securing relevant reports and documents and then writing a report that organizes these data so that they might be readily analyzed.

Assessment Activities. Once data are collected and summarized, the social worker must have some tools to help interpret the meaning of the data and to arrive at conclusions. When working at the organizational level, a social worker is typically concerned with issues such as understanding alternative ways to structure the work to be done in a human services agency (see Item 12.26) or ways to organize data that leads to an assessment of needs that clients typically experience (see Item 12.27).

At the community level, a social worker needs to be able to assess the factors that impinge on decision makers in that particular community (see Item 12.29). Also, before moving to action, the social worker must accurately assess the social policies that are in place and understand the ramifications of various changes that may be proposed. Having at least a general sense of the elements of a sound policy analysis (see Item 12.30) is important for any social worker.

12.26 Assessing Agency Structure

PURPOSE: To identify alternative ways to structure staff roles and responsibilities in order to achieve efficient and effective agency operation.

DISCUSSION: The organizational structure of an agency has a significant impact on the ability of the social worker to provide effective services. In any type of organization, the structure can be expected to vary according to the complexity of the tasks being performed, the amount of authority reserved for central decision making, and the degree to which policies, rules, and procedures are formalized. For example, many successful industrial organizations are based on the *bureaucratic model.* That model is most viable when the work requires the performance of relatively simple tasks (e.g., putting together parts on an assembly line) that are coordinated through a carefully structured process and very specific rules of operation. The bureaucratic organizational model, however, is much less viable in human services agencies where the work (i.e., the practice activities) is complex and must be adapted to the unique needs of clients. This work requires individualized judgments by professionals that cannot be readily subjected to centralized control and formalized rules and procedures.

In human services agencies, a variety of structures exist that range from highly bureaucratized operations to those that permit considerable worker autonomy. For example, public agencies are relatively inflexible because they are constrained by the laws that establish and sanction their operation, are dependent on a budget allocation from a legislative body, tend to be large with multiple functions, and are governed by elected or politically appointed boards that are often only vaguely familiar with the agency's day-to-day operation. Consequently, these agencies tend to be bureaucratized, allowing the policymakers and program administrators to maintain a high degree control over agency functioning. Private nonprofit agencies, by contrast, are usually smaller, offer fewer programs, and are governed by volunteer boards that are at least moderately familiar with the internal operation of the agency. These agencies tend toward decentralized authority and a minimum of rules and regulations, thus allowing staff members more control over their practice activities and substantial flexibility in how they perform their jobs.

For social workers in all types of human services organizations, it is useful to recognize that various degrees of bureaucratization can exist and that adaptations can be made that create a balance between management and worker in order to facilitate the provision of high-quality services. At times, workers must advocate for structural changes when they find that the agency's structure interferes with service to clients. To inform these advocacy efforts, it is useful to examine several structural formats commonly found in human services agencies.

Bureaucratic Model

At one end of the continuum of organizational structures is the ***bureaucratic model.*** In their pure form, bureaucracies have an elaborate *division of labor* in which work activities are clearly defined and assigned to specialized workers: A *hierarchy* of several of layers of managers, supervisors, and front-line workers is developed; a formalized set of very specific *rules and regulations* is rigidly applied; and the work is carried out in a *spirit of impersonality* that is not adjusted to accommodate individual uniqueness. Bureaucracies are characterized by fairness and equal treatment, but they suffer from lack of flexibility and the ability to individualize. They are stable and consistent, yet slow to change.

Adhocracy

At the other end of the continuum of organizational structures is the ***adhocracy*** (i.e., the organization that forms internal structures on an issue-by-issue basis with various collectives of staff members addressing each issue). The ad hoc groups have considerable authority and operate with few agencywide rules and regulations. These organizations have a "flat" administrative structure in which all staff positions are somewhat equal. Ad hoc agencies are weak on both structure and stability, but are able to respond to new issues and undergo change rapidly. They are particularly effective when the nature of the work is dynamic or fluid.

Other Organizational Structures

In reality, most human services agencies fall somewhere between a fully developed bureaucracy and a completely ad hoc structure. In smaller agencies, it is possible to have a relatively flat structure with an executive director heading the organization (e.g., representing the staff with the board and community) and the other staff member reporting directly to that executive.

As agencies become larger and more complex and when the span of control or number of contacts becomes too great for one person to manage, the work must be divided into segments. In this situation, a functional structure is likely to serve the agency well. In the ***functional model,*** a second-level administrative layer reports to the director and also leads a program unit or supervises a group of workers. A family services agency, for example, might have a counseling unit, a day treatment unit, a social action unit, and an administrative support unit—each with its own unit manager. The executive director would facilitate coordination of these units and oversee the work of the unit managers.

At times, an agency may temporarily supplement one of these structures with a ***project-team approach.*** This model provides for groups of staff to be organized around specific tasks for limited periods of time. In addition to being assigned to a specific unit or supervisor for their primary job, workers may be temporarily assigned on a full- or part-time basis to a team that cuts across units to address a specific problem. For example, staff from a family agency's clinical and day treatment units may temporarily join with a staff member from the social action unit to plan and carry out a strategy of public education and legislative advocacy to reduce the incidence of spouse abuse.

SELECTED BIBLIOGRAPHY

Brueggeman, William G. *The Practice of Macro Social Work.* Chicago: Nelson-Hall, 1996.

Kettner, Peter, Robert M. Moroney, and Lawrence L. Martin. *Designing and Managing Programs: An Effectiveness Based Approach.* Newbury Park, CA: Sage, 1990.

Weiss, Richard M. "Organizational Structure in Human Service Agencies." In *Managing Human Service Organizations,* edited by Lynn E. Miller. New York: Quorum Books, 1988.

12.27 Assessing Human Services Needs

PURPOSE: To provide data on the utilization of and/or need for specific human services offered in a community or region, or to an identified population group.

DISCUSSION: Although the perspective of the agency board and staff is a valuable source of information for determining agency goals and services, it is also important that decisions be based on a formal evaluation of the need for these services. Agencies should periodically conduct needs assessments.

The Minnesota State Planning Agency (Franczyk 1977, 4) observes that the term ***needs assessment*** usually refers to "the process of identifying the incidence, prevalence and nature of certain conditions within a community or target group. The ultimate purpose is to assess the adequacy of existing services and resources in addressing those conditions. The extent to which those conditions are not adequately addressed denotes a need for different services or resources."

When conducting a needs assessment, two judgments must be made by those conducting the analysis and those who will use the findings (e.g., agency board, city council, United Way). First, there should be agreement about what constitutes a need. Second, there must be a willingness to take action if an unmet need is identified. It is not a good use of time or resources to conduct a needs assessment if there is not recognition in advance that if needs are discovered some corrective action is both possible and probable.

Methods and Steps of a Needs Assessment

Several methods may be used to gather needs assessment data:

1. Community forums attended by concerned and interested members of the community
2. Caseload counts (i.e., counts of persons utilizing various services)
3. Opinions expressed by experts or other professionals having relevant knowledge or experience
4. Public opinion and attitude surveys
5. Social indicators (e.g., suicide rates, poverty rates, divorce rates, etc.)

Franczyk (1977) identifies six steps in the needs assessment process:

Step 1. *Selecting units and topics for analysis.* This step involves the identification of target groups (populations at risk) and/or the geographical area about which information is to be gathered. These target groups and geographical areas are known as the units of analysis. The kinds of information desired about each of these units are the topics of analysis.

Step 2. *Selection of one or more methods for gathering data.* On one level, a choice must be made between establishing an ongoing, agency based, informational system and implementing a short-term data collection project. On another level, the advantages of using existing data must be weighed against the costs of generating new data.

Step 3. *Gathering data/generating information.* Information about the needs of the specific units of analysis is generated from the aggregation and analysis of the individual bits of data collected.

Step 4. *Identifying unacceptable social or human conditions.* Having formulated a composite picture of the conditions experienced by the units of analysis, certain conditions are judged to be in violation of acceptable standards.

Step 5. *Comparing observed conditions to existing services.* Step five involves the gathering of information about the availability, adequacy and effectiveness of existing services in meeting identified needs.

Step 6. *Recommending changes in existing services.* The product of a well done needs assessment should be a confirmation of existing services as adequate or recommendations for change to cope with the observed inadequacy. (p. 6)

Guidelines for Conducting a Needs Assessment

The following guidelines should be kept in mind when conducting needs assessment:

1. It is essential to have a clear understanding of the policy issues and administrative concerns that prompted the decision maker to recommend the use of a needs assessment. In other words, what problems do the decision makers hope to solve through the use of a needs assessment?

2. The goals and objectives of the needs assessment must be clear before it is possible to select appropriate methods of data collection and analysis. All too often, those planning a needs assessment jump ahead to the question of "What questions should we ask the people we are going to interview?" before they are clear on exactly what kind of data they can and will use in the planning of new services or the modification of existing services.

3. It is helpful to know how other communities or agencies have approached the task, but it is usually a mistake to borrow someone else's objectives and methodology. Those who are in a position to use the data should decide what approach would be useful and work best in their community. Such decisions should not be made by outside consultants or by persons or agencies that have a vested interest in seeing the assessment yield certain findings.

4. In planning a needs assessment, it is important to anticipate possible reasons why situations of unmet need might exist. For example:

- No services are available in the community.
- Existing services are not accessible because of transportation problems, eligibility criteria, and the like.
- Persons in need are not aware that services exist.
- Existing services are not integrated to provide a continuity of service to multiproblem individuals and families.
- Existing programs do not have adequate resources to provide quality service.
- Existing services are unacceptable to residents of a particular community. For example, they may be perceived as degrading, threatening, or in conflict with existing ethnic, religious, or cultural norms and values.

5. A needs assessment should not only identify unmet service needs but also shed light on the quantity, quality, and direction of existing services. For example:

- *Quantity.* Does the level of service meet the need? This involves some assessment of the number of persons in need of service compared with the capacity of providers to serve those persons.
- *Quality.* Are the services effective? Do they accomplish what they are intended to do? Do they work?
- *Direction.* Are the approaches used in service delivery appropriate or possibly out of touch with the real needs of clients? Does the philosophy that gave rise to existing programs coincide with the generally accepted philosophy espoused by current experts in the field?

6. Do not attempt a needs assessment until there is evidence that the agency(s) and community possess the administrative and political readiness to use the data once it is gathered. If they are not ready, the report will gather dust on a shelf.

SELECTED BIBLIOGRAPHY

Franczyk, James J. *Needs Assessment: A Guide to Human Service Agencies.* St. Paul: Minnesota State Planning Agency, 1977.

Slaght, Evelyn, and Janice H. Schopler. "Are Quick and Dirty Needs Assessments Better than No Needs Assessments?" In *Controversial Isues in Communities and Organizations,* edited by Michael J. Austin and Jane Isaacs Lowe. Boston: Allyn and Bacon, 1994, pp. 142–157.

Soriano, Fernando I. *Conducting Needs Assessments: A Multidisciplinary Approach.* Newbury Park, CA: Sage, 1995.

Witkin, Belle Ruth, and James Altschuld. *Planning and Conducting Needs Assessment.* Newbury Park, CA: Sage, 1995.

12.28 Focus Groups

PURPOSE: To acquire in-depth responses from a group of human services consumers or research subjects regarding an agency, program, service, or other topic.

DISCUSSION: Human services agencies and qualitative researchers have followed the marketing branch of the business community in the use of focus groups as a technique for collecting valuable information. A ***focus group*** is a small group of people (usually 8 to 12) who have had a common experience or share common knowledge and are led through a one- to two-hour discussion of a particular topic. The goal is to explore the topic by allowing the ideas of participants to create a synergy that promotes in-depth discussion until the points of agreement or disagreement emerge and become clear. Focus groups are particularly useful in identifying why the participants think or feel as they do about the subject.

When used for administrative purposes, focus groups can supply information that may be helpful in activities such as planning new services, assessing the needs of current consumers of services, developing marketing strategies, or identifying the implications of terminating a particular program. This technique might be used with existing groups such as agency boards, advisory committees, and staff members or with groups of clients or community members. In research, focus groups are used in association with qualitative approaches (see Item 10.13) in which content analysis of transcriptions of the meetings serve as a data source for the identification of important themes and fleshing out the meaning participants attribute to them. In addition to the snowball effect of members extending their thinking from the ideas presented by others, focus groups are a relatively inexpensive and, usually, a readily available source of data.

There are four essentials of a successful focus group meeting. First, the participants should be selected carefully. They should represent a broad range of the people who are familiar with the topic and should be people willing to speak their minds. The atmosphere of the meeting and the meeting place should be conducive to freewheeling discussion, and the participants should be protected from retribution for any remarks they might make. It is not usual procedure to follow a scientific sampling process in selecting the participants. Thus, the results should be viewed cautiously and considered only one data source for making decisions.

Second, the moderator should be well prepared. It is the leader's responsibility to introduce the topic without suggesting a bias and to facilitate open discussion of the topic. The moderator must listen carefully and explore the meaning behind the participants' statements, constantly probing for greater depth and clarity. He or she must also be flexible in allowing the group to explore the topic as the flow of their discussion leads, but at the same time be able to bring the group back to the topic when tangents are no longer productive. The moderator must assure that no one member dominates the session and that everyone has a opportunity to speak on each dimension of the topic being explored.

Third, there should be a carefully developed plan for the meeting that includes the preparation of a series of open-ended questions or statements that stimulate discussion of the topic. The persons planning the focus group meeting should develop an outline known as a "moderator guide" that introduces the subject matter in a logical order (i.e., usually from the most general areas to the most specific) and probes for what the participants perceive to be the relevant diminsions of the topic. The "moderator guide" can be used as a checklist during the meeting to assure that all important aspects of the topic are addressed before the meeting is concluded. Time should be reserved at the end of the meeting for participants to add topics that may have been omitted and for the moderator to summarize what he or she saw as important themes in the discussion, allowing participants to reply to that summary.

Finally, the information provided by the group members must be recorded and accurately interpreted. Often, audiotapes or videotapes of the sessions are used, along with notetaking by observers, to record the information that emerges in the meeting. Again, it is important to minimize any biases or self-interests when interpreting the information.

SELECTED BIBLIOGRAPHY

Krueger, Richard A. *Focus Groups: A Practical Guide for Applied Research,* 2nd ed. Newbury Park, CA: Sage, 1994.

Toseland, Ronald W., and Robert F. Rivas. *An Introduction to Group Work Practice,* 3rd ed. Boston: Allyn and Bacon, 1998.

Webster, Susan. *Focus Groups: An Effective Marketing Research Tool for Social Service Agencies.* Portland, ME: National Child Welfare Resource Center for Management and Administration, 1992.

12.29 Community Decision-Making Analysis

PURPOSE: To assess the factors that influence the actions of elected officials and other decision makers.

DISCUSSION: As social workers seek to influence decisions that affect the quality of human services in a community, they must develop a strategy for convincing the person or persons in authority that a particular course of action is the best choice among the possible options. Ideally, decisions should be made on the merit of the proposal; in reality, however, decision makers usually respond to external pressures and various personal considerations. The social worker must be alert to the factors and forces that may sway a decision maker.

Research on community decision making and community power structures does not yield a consistent picture of the forces that lead to these decisions. However, several generalizations can be made regarding variables that at least partially explain why some communities tend to center the decision making in a small, elite group of people while others are more pluralistic and involve a broader spectrum of the community:

1. *Size.* Large cities tend to be pluralistic. They are likely to become more diverse and competitive as they grow, resulting in a greater range of people and interest groups involved in making decisions.

2. *Population diversity.* Communities that have more varied and complex class and ethnic structures develop more special interest groups and more community organizations that compete for power and resources. Consequently, there are more challenges to any dominant elite group and a tendency to increase pluralism in decision making.

3. *Economic diversity.* More diversified communities in terms of varied sources of employment, high levels of industrialization, and the presence of absentee-owned industry (as opposed to local people owning the major industries) all tend to make communities more pluralistic in how decisions are made.

4. *Structure of local government.* Reformed governments (i.e., cities with council-manager format, nonpartisan-at-large elections) tend to be more elitist than those partisan governments with representatives elected by districts. Further, the greater the competition or balance among political groups, the more likely the community will have a pluralistic decision-making structure.

Increasingly, communities in the United States have a pluralistic type of decision-making structure, and only small rural communities tend to maintain elite power structures. The worker in most communities, then, should be aware that the task of influencing decisions requires a careful assessment of the people who are authorized to make the decisions. For example, the critical ***decision maker*** regarding an issue of interest may be an agency board member, an elected official, or the manager or management team for a social program. In most cases, relatively few people are involved in making a decision, and they will tend to be focused on particular issues where they have a self-interest (e.g., realtors and bankers focused on housing and economic issues, physicians and other health care professionals focused on health care, etc.).

One task for the social worker is to assess the various factors that may affect a decision maker's choice. As identified in Figure 12.16, *personal charactistics* of the person or persons attempting to influence the decision maker, as well as the *institutional power* the influencer represents, will potentially affect the decision. Also, *personal considerations* such as the repercussions of the decision on one's finances, self-esteem, judgment about the merits of the proposed change, and so on, will af-

FIGURE 12.16 Factors Influencing Community Decision Makers

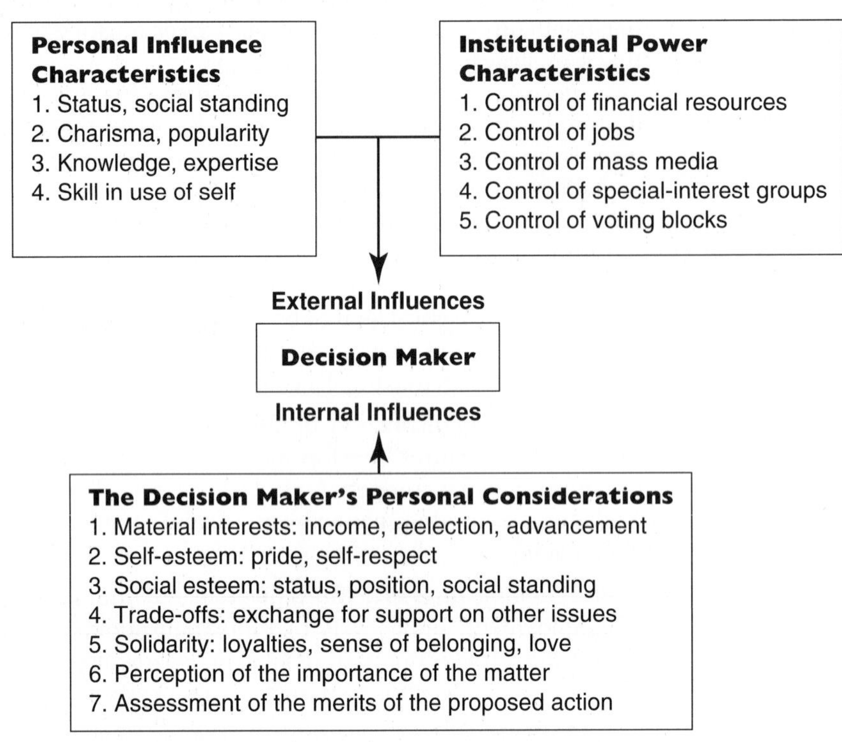

fect the choice. An assessment of the sources for influencing the decision makers for both the proponents and opponents of the change, as well as the personal issues that might affect the decision, should serve as the basis for mapping a strategy for change.

SELECTED BIBLIOGRAPHY

Rubin, Herbert J., and Irene S. Rubin. *Community Organization and Development,* 2nd ed. New York: Macmillan, 1992.

12.30 Social Policy Analysis

PURPOSE: To make an accurate assessment of social policy and program issues in order to guide community change activities.

DISCUSSION: The analysis of public social policy issues can be a difficult and time-consuming task. Fortunately, several good models that can guide such an analysis exist within the social work literature. Depending on the social worker's role and preparation for making an analysis, it is possible to approach this task in greater or lesser depth. Social workers who are not engaged in full-time community change activity usually do not have the time or resources available to apply the more complex models.

When examining a public social policy, it is important to recognize that social policies and social programs are a response to some social problem as perceived by those groups who formulate program proposals and have the political power to pass the laws or write policies. To a large extent, every policy and program reflects the beliefs, values assumptions, and self-interests of those able to influence the process of program design and policy development. Also, it is helpful to recognize that a policy is a reflection of how a problem is understood at a particular point in time. As knowledge of a problem accumulates, existing policies may become outdated and require revision.

Chambers (1993, 7–49) has developed an approach to public policy analysis that is relatively simple and straightforward. As such, it is helpful in identifying the key questions that should be addressed by the occasional policy analyst. Consider the following:

1. *Social problem analysis.* The first step in the analysis of a social policy or program is to have a clear understanding of the problems that created the situation requiring such a policy. To make this assessment, it is useful to undertake the following activities:

- *Identify how the problem is defined and locate estimates of its magnitude.* For example, what definition of poverty, mental illness, or unemployment is commonly used? Are there other definitions that might be more appropriate? How many people experience this problem as it is defined? What particular subpopulations are most likely to experience this problem?
- *Determine the causes and consequences of the problem.* What forces or factors have caused the problem? Are there multiple causes? Are there multiple consequences from a single cause?
- *Identify the ideological beliefs or basic principles embedded in the description of the problem.* The definition of a problem is influenced by beliefs about what "ought to be," or the values one holds. Is there a difference of opinion about the seriousness of the problem? Do different groups hold varying views about the nature and cause of the problem?
- *Identify the gainers and losers in relation to the problem.* Who gains from the existence of the problem? What do they gain and how much? Who loses? What do they lose and how much? How serious are the negative consequences on the lives of the losers?

2. *Social policy and program analysis.* Once the problem is understood, the second step is to assess the social policy and/or program being considered as a means of addressing the problem or offering relief to the victims of the problem. The following are useful for this analysis:

- *Search out the relevant program and policy history.* Is this a new problem? Have conditions, values, or perceptions changed over time? What is different about the proposed program or policy from past efforts to deal with the problem?

- *Identify the key elements or operating characteristics of the proposed policy or program.* What are the goals and objectives of the proposal? Who would be eligible to benefit from the plan? What benefits or services would be delivered if this proposal gains approval? What administrative structure would be required and how would it work? How would the program be financed and how much money would be required? Are there any undesirable consequences from interactions among the characteristics already listed?

3. *Draw conclusions.* After the preceding information has been collected, it is necessary to judge the merits of the policy or program under analysis. Ultimately, it is the weight of the evidence matched with one's beliefs about what the quality of life should be for members of the society that results in a recommendation favoring or opposing the proposal—or suggesting modification.

Answers to the following questions might be considered in arriving at conclusions about this program or policy proposal: Is it appropriate for addressing the problem identified? Does the remedy proposed adequately deal with the causes as well as the consequences of the problem? Will it yield an outcome different from ones attempted in the past? Would the costs associated with the proposed remedy justify the possible outcomes? Are there better remedies that might be proposed?

When addressing a social policy, it is particularly important to be conscientious about using accurate data. If challenged by those with competing interests, credibility can be lost by not having sufficient and accurate data to support conclusions and underpin recommendations for change.

With a solid analysis of the policy or program proposal in hand, the social worker is prepared to influence the legislation that would impact the problem under consideration. At times, the social worker will work through committees or other groups to affect these decisions; on other occasions, it is appropriate to contact a legislator directly and express a position on the proposal.

SELECTED BIBLIOGRAPHY

Chambers, Donald E. *Social Policy and Social Programs: A Method for the Practical Public Policy Analyst,* 2nd ed. New York: Macmillan, 1993.

DiNitto, Diane. *Social Welfare Politics and Public Policy,* 4th ed. Boston: Allyn and Bacon, 1998.

Ginsberg, Leon. *Understanding Social Problems, Policies, and Programs.* Columbia: University of South Carolina Press, 1994.

Meenaghan, Thomas M., and Keith M. Kilty. *Policy Analysis and Research Technology: Political and Ethical Considerations.* Chicago: Lyceum Books, 1994.

Popple, Phillip R., and Leslie Leighninger. *The Policy-Based Profession: An Introduction to Social Welfare Policy for Social Workers.* Boston: Allyn and Bacon, 1998.

13 Planning and Contracting

INTRODUCTION

Once the client and social worker have completed the assessment of the situation, they move on to formulating an action plan and entering into a formal or informal contract for implementing the plan. During this phase, the people and organizations with whom the client and worker will work to achieve the goals are identified and actions to be taken for accomplishing the needed changes are agreed upon.

Planning is the bridge between assessment and intervention. It begins with (1) specifying goals the client hopes to achieve, then (2) identifying what changes need to be made to achieve those goals, (3) selecting from among alternative change strategies the interventions most likely to reach the goals, (4) determining which actions will be taken by the client and the worker, and (5) establishing timelines for completing those actions. Clients, and sometimes inexperienced workers, may want to shortcut this planning activity. However, action without a clear plan is a sure recipe for failure. In efforts to change complex systems such as organizations and communities, the length of the planning phase will often exceed the time required for the intervention itself.

Effective planning places a special demand on the creativity of the social worker and the willingness of the client to consider alternative courses of action. Each possible option must be evaluated in an effort to predict any helpful or harmful impacts on the client or others, to identify the resources required, and to estimate the time frame for carrying it out. The worker must also determine the most appropriate practice frameworks—perspectives, theories, and models—that might be used to guide the process (see Chapter 6). Recognizing that some methods of securing change may be effective but unethical, the *Code of Ethics* should be considered at this point, as it is an effective screen or filter when planning intervention strategies (see Item 10.9). Finally, to the extent possible, the worker should base the planning decisions on hard facts and objective evidence that was collected during the data collection and assessment phase.

Once a plan has been developed, it is important for the worker and clients to develop a ***contract*** (i.e., an agreement between the worker and client that spells out the activities to be conducted by each, along with a timetable for action during the intervention phase). A contract can be written, oral, or even an implied agreement, although the more specific the contract, the more likely it is to prevent misunderstandings. A written contract, in particular, is useful because it provides an explicitness that helps clarify points of agreement and disagreement between the worker and client; it serves as a basis for demonstrating accountability to both the client and the agency; and it can be an effective tool in facilitating the transfer of cases to another worker, should that become necessary.

The language and format of contracts may vary, but the content is essentially the same whether working at the individual, family, group, organization, or community level. At a minimum, a contract should delineate the following:

- Problems or concerns to be addressed
- Specific goals of the intervention
- Activities the client will undertake
- Tasks to be performed by the worker
- Expected duration of the intervention (in weeks or months)
- Schedule of time and place for interviews or committee meetings
- Identification of other persons, agencies, or organizations expected to participate and clarification about what they will be expected to contribute to the change process

Recognizing that even the most carefully developed plan may need to be modified as the intervention evolves, the worker and client must be open to revising the contract.

SECTION A

TECHNIQUES AND GUIDELINES FOR DIRECT PRACTICE

When working with individuals, families, and groups during the planning and contracting phase, the social worker should pay particular attention to the social work principles of maximizing client participation and self-determination. After all, it is the clients who must live with the outcome resulting from the plans selected and the accompanying interventions. Specifically, the worker should recognize that the client should have the following rights:

- Make decisions and have input concerning the intervention goals and objectives, as well as the general approach to be used to reach those goals.
- Know what approach the worker proposes to use, the likelihood of success, and if there are any anticipated risks or adverse effects associated with the proposed intervention.
- Know how long the intervention will last and/or about how long it will take to achieve the agreed upon objectives.
- Know how much time and money (if any) will be required of the client.
- Know any consequences for terminating the intervention against the advice of the social worker or agency.
- Know what rules of confidentiality apply and who else (e.g., court, probation officer, school officials, parent, etc.) will have access to information about the client's participation and the outcome of the intervention.

- Know how the success of the intervention will be evaluated.
- Know about appeals or grievance procedures that can be used to challenge a decision made by the social worker or agency.

Planning Activities. Some of the most critical decisions a social worker must make occur as part of planning. These can have lifelong consequences for a client—for example, whether to plan the separation of an abused child from his or her parents, whether to recommend probation or incarceration for a youth, and so on. Therefore, it is important to avoid making mistakes.

Some mistakes can be prevented by an awareness of common errors in reaching these decisions. One common error is to spend too little time in defining the problem and identifying what needs to be changed to improve the situation. Another error is to make decisions on the basis of surface concerns or issues and not probing for underlying facts or factors that may contradict the client's or worker's assumptions about the situation. Also, mistakes often result because the worker may consider only a narrow range of alternative strategies for change. This can occur because of hurried decision making, laxness, or rigid interpretation of agency policy. The creativity that is an essential part of the "art" of social work (see Chapter 3) is particularly important when identifying a range of possible interventions. Finally, the routine or uncritical application of a particular practice theory or model can lead to bad decisions. Conceptual frameworks tend to create mindsets about the nature and causes of problems, and a person too committed to a certain way of thinking may overlook or disregard important information that does not "fit" his or her preferred theory.

During the planning phase, the worker must be alert to balancing the need for information with the requirement to move the process forward with a clear plan of action. Some tools the worker might use to facilitate planning are reported in Items 13.1 through 13.5 in this chapter.

Contracting Activities. The best plans are of little value if there is not clear agreement and understanding about how they will be implemented. The greater the specificity about who will do what, when, and how, the greater the chances of the plan being fully implemented. The temptation for the social worker who has been through the change process many times is to assume that the client, too, knows what lies ahead. The discipline of carefully developing a contract is often reassuring to clients, while also encouraging the social worker to rethink steps that may have become routine.

Of the three forms of service contracts—implied, oral, and written—implied contracts typically offer the least clarity and are probably the least beneficial for the client. Oral contracts between the client and worker add an element of clarity, but the details of oral communication can be quickly forgotten and it is difficult to document the degree to which both the client and worker have been accountable. Although more time consuming to develop, written contracts (see Item 13.5) are the most useful for both the client and worker. They can be reviewed between sessions to remind the participants of their responsibilities and serve as the basis for future evaluation and accountability reporting. As suggested by Items 13.7 and 13.8, implied or oral contracts are also important when using group processes and in work with various informal helping resources.

13.1 Selecting Target Problems and Goals

PURPOSE: To select the target problems and goals that will give direction to the social work intervention.

DISCUSSION: A ***goal*** is a desired end toward which an activity is directed. Thus, the goal of a social work intervention is the end sought by the client and his or her social worker. This goal logically flows from the data gathering and assessment phase. Direct-service goals can take many forms. For example, the social worker may help the client with the following:

- *Learn a skill or acquire needed knowledge* (e.g., learn how to interview for a job, manage time, make decisions, resolve interpersonal conflict, manage stress, take care of a child, etc.).
- *Make an important decision* (e.g., decide on a college major, whether to get a divorce, whether to relinquish custody of a child, whether to seek help for an emotional problem, etc.).
- *Gather the information* needed to make a plan or make a decision.
- *Assess a problem or concern* (e.g., conduct a careful assessment of some concern in order to decide if it is a serious problem needing attention, what the nature of the problem is, etc.).
- *Make a plan* (e.g., formulate a plan on how best to address some concern or problem).
- *Change a behavior* (e.g., increase a desirable behavior, decrease or eliminate a troublesome behavior).
- *Alter feelings and attitudes* about self or about some other person(s).
- *Gather information about availability of certain types of services or programs.*
- *Become linked to or enrolled in a program or service* provided by some agency or professional.
- *Rebuild a damaged relationship* (e.g., reach out to and reestablish relationship with estranged parent or child, improve husband-wife relationship, etc.).
- *Change the way life circumstances or a life event is perceived or interpreted* (e.g., learn to assign new meaning to events and circumstances, view things from a different angle, develop new perspectives, etc.).

Sometimes the social worker and client can quickly agree on the goal. This is likely when the client's need or problem is readily apparent to both the client and worker. However, in many cases, the social worker and client will see things differently and must actively discuss and struggle to reach agreement on the nature of the problem and on what can and should be done about it. Often, the worker and client must also devote considerable time to the task of priority setting in order to decide which of the client's many problems and concerns should become target problems for intervention. Until those decisions are made, they cannot formulate a feasible intervention plan.

The principle of *client self-determination* dictates that the client has the right to select the concerns to be addressed. There are also practical reasons related to motivation for expecting the client—rather than the social worker—to select the target problems and goals. Epstein (1992, 174) observes, "It is unlikely that a client's motivation can be readily enhanced, or that [he or] she can be maneuvered into a genuine commitment for a personal change not wanted, not sought, and not accepted. [However] clients seek and value help help that makes sense to them, is useful in their daily lives, and gets or keeps them out of trouble." Even with the nonvoluntary client, it is important to give the client as much choice as possible. In such cases, the worker or agency might mandate one target problem but allow the involuntary client to select the second or third.

Many of the clients served by social workers have multiple and complex problems and concerns. Both research and practice wisdom suggest that, in order to be effective, the helping process must concentrate available time and energy on just one, two, or three problems at a time. If priorities and a clear focus are not established, the helping effort flounders and usually ends in frustration for both client and worker. The following steps will help the client and worker set *priorities:*

1. The client identifies and lists what he or she sees as problems or concerns (i.e., what client wants to change).

2. The social worker offers his or her recommendations, if any, and explains why they also need to be considered. The worker makes sure that any mandated problems are included (mandated problems are ones imposed on the client by some legitimate authority such as a court, probation officer, or child protection agency).

3. The problems and concerns are reviewed and sorted into logical groupings or combinations so that interrelatedness is identified.

4. The client examines the list and selects the two or three problems or concerns of highest priority.

5. The worker selects the two or three items he or she considers to be of highest priority.

6. Together, the client and worker discuss the concerns identified in steps 4 and 5 and examine them against the following criteria:

- Which ones weigh most heavily on the client's situation (e.g., which ones cause the most worry and anxiety)?
- Which ones, if not addressed and corrected, will have the most negative and far-reaching consequences for the client?
- Which ones, if addressed and corrected, would have the most positive effects on the client (e.g., provide the client with greatest sense of relief, make it easier to solve other problems, etc.)?

- Which ones are of greatest interest to the client (e.g., which ones the client is most motivated to work on at this time)?
- Which ones can be addressed and corrected with only a moderate investment of time, energy, and other resources?
- Which ones are relatively unchangeable or would require a extraordinary investment of time, energy, or resources?

7. After considering these criteria, the three problems of highest priority are selected. As mentioned earlier, it is usually counterproductive to try to address more than three concerns at one time. Task-centered practitioners have termed this principle *the rule of three.*

8. It is important for the social worker to remember that the client's problems and concerns will almost always affect or involve significant others (e.g., spouse, children, parents, close friends, employer, etc.). Unless these individuals, who are either part of the problem or part of the solution, are considered in the intervention planning, there is good chance that they will—knowingly or unknowingly—become an obstacle to the change process. In some cases, they may actively sabotage the client's attempt to make desired changes.

SELECTED BIBLIOGRAPHY

Epstein, Laura. *Brief Treatment and a New Look at the Task-Centered Approach.* New York: Macmillan, 1992.

Reid, Kenneth. *Social Work Practice with Groups: A Clinical Perspective,* 2nd ed. Pacific Grove, CA: Brooks/Cole, 1997.

Toseland, Ronald, and Robert Rivas. *An Introduction to Group Work Practice,* 3rd ed. Boston: Allyn and Bacon, 1998.

13.2 The Problem Search

PURPOSE: To engage the reluctant client in a process designed to identify a problem on which he or she is willing to work.

DISCUSSION: The ***problem search*** can be viewed as a "minicontract" or an agreement to spend a couple of sessions trying to determine whether a problem exists and, if so, whether it should be addressed. It is used either when (1) the client has been referred by an authoritative agency (court) or by his or her family but does not acknowledge the existence of a problem as defined by others or (2) the client has requested a specific agency service but, in the worker's opinion, it is desirable to help the client expand that request or redefine the presenting problem. In this later situation, the social worker is concerned that the client's definition of the problem is not accurate or realistic and/or that his or her request for a specific service will not resolve the problem. An example might be the father who requests foster care placement for his children because he and his wife are having marital problems.

Essentially, the problem search asks the reluctant client to participate in one or two additional sessions in order to explore the situation in more depth. The client is asked to withhold judgment about the need for service and the worker's usefulness until after these meetings. In using this technique, the social worker moves through several steps:

1. *Explain why you are suggesting a further exploration of the client's situation.* Briefly identify your concerns and the advantages of an additional session or two. For example: "I realize that you see no problems that deserve my attention, but what you have said about getting fired leads me to believe that you really try to get along at work but for some reason you and your supervisors often clash on how best to do the job. Because of that, I suggest we meet two times and talk more about your job experiences. If, after the second session, we cannot figure out what might be done to improve the situation, we will stop meeting."

2. *Solicit the client's thoughts and feedback on the proposal.* For example: "What do you think about my suggestion that we meet two times to review and discuss the stress you experience on the job?" (If client responds with a no, say, for example, "Well, I can understand your reluctance and I will respect your decision, but let me give you one other reason why I think it is a good idea. . . .")

3. *Set up a plan for a future meeting.* For example: "I am glad that you agreed to meet again. As I said, we will meet two times. If it proves useful, that will be great. But, if after the second session, it doesn't seem useful, then we will not continue. How about meeting the next two Wednesdays at 4 P.M.?"

4. *Identify two or three topics to be discussed.* For example: "When we meet next week, let's start with a discussion of the jobs you have really liked and why. Second, I would like to discuss the type of supervision you expect to get on the job. Does that sound like a reasonable place to begin?"

SELECTED BIBLIOGRAPHY

Doel, Mark, and Peter Marsh. *Task Centered Social Work.* Brookfield, VT: Ashgate, 1992.

Epstein, Laura. *Brief Treatment and a New Look at the Task-Centered Approach.* New York: Macmillan, 1992.

13.3 Using Checklists in Goal Selection

PURPOSE: To assist the client in identifying and selecting intervention goals.

DISCUSSION: Some clients have difficulty articulating their concerns and identifying their goals for change. In such cases, some type of goal checklist may be useful. Basically, this tool is a list of possible intervention goals from which the client can select ones that are relevant to his or her situation. For example, Figure 13.1 is a goal checklist developed for use in work with parents who had abused their children. A worker familiar with

FIGURE 13.1 Sample Goal Checklist

A List of Goals for Parents

Explanation: Having a clear goal in mind is one important step in dealing with problems and concerns. Once there is a goal, it is possible to develop a plan for reaching that goal. Below is a list of goals that have been mentioned by parents. Place a check (✓) by those that are similar to your goals. This checklist can help you and your social worker formulate a workable plan of action.

_____ Talk to people about my concerns, problems, and worries.

_____ Budget my money and keep track of bills.

_____ Prepare meals that are healthy.

_____ Clean and take care of my apartment or house.

_____ Find and make use of services such as day care, counseling, and legal services.

_____ Cope with daily pressures and demands on my time.

_____ Show greater affection toward my child.

_____ Make friends, mix, and feel comfortable with people.

_____ Learn skills needed to get a job.

_____ Have good visits with my child in foster care.

_____ Get along well with my spouse or partner.

_____ Learn to recognize when I am at risk of doing something I may regret.

_____ Find a better and safer living arrangement.

_____ Talk with my child in ways that make him or her feel secure.

_____ Discipline and control my child without hitting him or her.

_____ Talk to and plan with the foster parents who are taking care of my child.

_____ Talk with my social worker and make use of the help he or she can provide.

_____ Learn to calm myself down when I start to get angry or agitated.

_____ Find friends or a support group that will understand my situation and help me deal with problems.

_____ Learn what to expect from children and what is "normal" behavior for a child of a certain age.

_____ Be more assertive and direct in making my thoughts and feelings known to other people.

_____ Get along without alcohol or drugs.

_____ Learn how to deal with conflicts with my parents and relatives.

_____ Learn how to deal with emergency situations and with times when I feel overwhelmed.

_____ Learn to cope with strong emotions such as guilt, sadness, fear, and anger.

the problems and concerns of a particular client group can easily construct a goal checklist and tailor it to the type of client served and a particular practice setting or type of service (also see Item 15.1).

SELECTED BIBLIOGRAPHY

Horejsi, Charles. *Assessment and Case Planning in Child Protection and Foster Care Services.* Englewood, CO: American Humane Association, 1996.

Horejsi, Charles, Ann Bertsche, and Frank Clark. *Social Work Practice with Parents of Children in Foster Care: A Handbook.* Springfield, IL: Charles C. Thomas, 1981.

13.4 Formulating Intervention Objectives

PURPOSE: To develop objectives that are measurable and relevant to the client's concerns.

DISCUSSION: Unless there are clear objectives for an intervention, the helping process will flounder and its evaluation will be impossible. Unless the client and social worker are very clear about what they are trying to achieve, they cannot determine when or whether they achieved it. Although the terms *goals* and *objectives* are often used interchangeably, they do not mean the same thing. A *goal* is usually a broad and rather global statement (e.g., "to better cope with the demands of a child who has a disability"). Not infrequently, a goal is simply a restatement of a problem in a way that suggests a solution. For example, if a family's lack of money creates stress that erupts in violence against children, a logical goal would be to increase that family's financial resources in order to reduce stress.

As compared to a goal, an *objective* is more specific and concrete. An objective is a statement written in a manner that allows and facilitates measurement and evaluation. Consider these examples:

Statements Prepared by a Hospital Social Worker

Goal: Improve responsiveness of social work staff to new referrals.

Objective: To conduct at least 80 percent of initial patient or family member interviews within four hours of receiving a referral from a doctor or nurse.

Statements Prepared by the Administrator of a Big Brother/Big Sister Program

Goal: Obtain more Big Brothers and Big Sisters for our children.

Objective: To recruit, train, and match 35 new volunteers before August 1.

Statements Prepared by a Child Welfare Worker

Goal: To enhance the development of parent-child relationships.

Objective: To encourage and facilitate parental visitation so that by January 15 at least 70 percent of parents in my caseload visit their children in foster care at least once a month.

A properly written objective will answer a five-part question:

1. Who . . .
2. will do what . . .
3. to what extent . . .
4. under what conditions . . .
5. by when?

When an objective is complex and cannot be written in a single sentence, it will be necessary to attach to a general statement a list of conditions and criteria as a means of further clarification. *Conditions* describe the situation or context in which the desired behavior or action is to take place; *criteria* are the rules or the definitions that will be used to decide whether the desired behavior or action has occurred at an acceptable level.

Inherent in the writing of an objective is the use of verbs that describe an action to be taken, such as the following:

attend	contact	answer	write	demonstrate	list
decide	discuss	plan	select	purchase	obtain
bring	supervise	practice	arrange	utilize	apply
implement	display	recognize	join	contribute	transport

When developing an objective, it is important not to confuse *input* with *outcome*. This common error results in statements like "Mr. Jones is to obtain counseling," which describes an input (counseling) but says nothing about the intended outcome. In this example, counseling is presented as an end, but in reality, it is only a means to an end. What is the intended outcome of the counseling? What is the counseling to accomplish? A better statement would be "Mr. Jones will obtain counseling focused on his physical abuse of his son, Johnny, and designed to help him learn to use time out and positive reinforcement as alternatives to harsh spanking and screaming as discipline."

In writing an objective, *positive language* should be used whenever possible; the words used should describe what the client will do, not what the client will not do (e.g., "learn and follow table manners" versus "stop being so messy when eating"). Also, it is important that objectives be formulated in *behavioral language*—using words that describe observable actions in terms of their frequency, duration, and intensity.

A *timeframe* is an essential part of an objective. In interpersonal helping, for example, an objective should not take more than a few weeks to accomplish. Thus, an objective that would probably take many months to accomplish should be broken down into several smaller ones. This is important because the client needs to see evidence of progress. If the client can perceive he or she is making concrete gains (i.e., reaching an objective), even if the steps are small, he or she will feel more hopeful and more motivated to continue.

The concept of *task*, as used by social workers favoring the task-centered approach, is both similar to and different from the concept of objectives, as presented here. Reid (1992) defines a task as a type of problem-solving action, sometimes of a general nature and sometimes highly specific, but always an activity that can be evaluated in terms of whether it was achieved or completed. Still another way of conceptualizing a task is to define it as one of the many highly specific and short-term activities necessary to achieve an objective. Thus, in working toward a single goal, a client may need to achieve several objectives, and in order to achieve objectives, he or she may need to complete numerous tasks (see Figure 13.2).

Generally speaking, an objective is something that a client might achieve in a matter of weeks (e.g., "Learn new methods of discipline with the help of a parent training program"), whereas a task is something that can be completed in a matter of days (e.g., "Call a friend to arrange transportation to the parent training program"). Regardless of the terminology used, the point to remember is that an intervention must have a clear purpose and direction.

Objectives are intended to give direction, structure, and relevance to the helping process, but objectives should never stifle the humanness and individualization that are essential ingredients in effective helping. A willingness to revise objectives to meet changing circumstances is critical to effective helping. In summary, a properly developed objective meets the following criteria:

1. It usually starts with the word *to,* followed by an action verb.
2. It specifies a single result or outcome to be accomplished.
3. It specifies a target date for its accomplishment.
4. It is as specific and quantitative as possible and, hence, measurable.
5. It is understandable by the client and others who will be contributing to or participating in the intervention.
6. It is realistic and attainable but still represents a significant challenge.
7. It is agreed to by both client and worker without pressure or coercion.
8. It is consistent with agency policies and with the social work *Code of Ethics.*

SELECTED BIBLIOGRAPHY

Pipe, Peter. *Objectives—Tools for Change.* Belmont, CA: Fearon, 1975.

Reid, William. *Task Strategies: An Empirical Approach to Clinical Social Work.* New York: Columbia University Press, 1992.

FIGURE 13.2 Relationship of Goals, Objectives, and Tasks

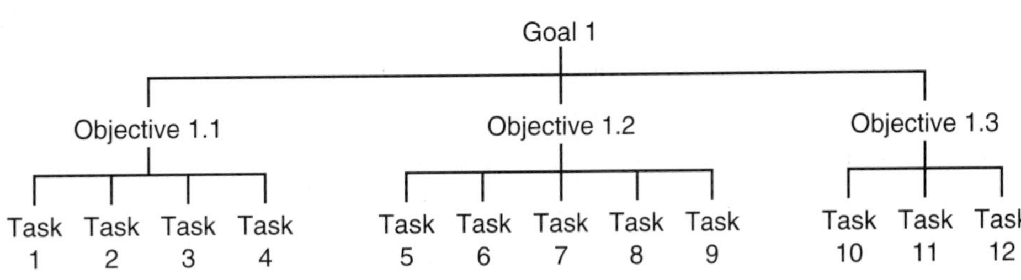

13.5 Written Service Contracts

PURPOSE: To provide direction and focus during intervention.

DISCUSSION: Arriving at an agreement on the service to be provided by the worker and used by the client is fundamental to social work practice. In most cases, a verbal agreement is sufficient. However, many social workers use written service contracts (or service agreements) in their work with clients. This is especially true in public agencies and in the fields of child welfare, developmental disabilities, and probation and parole. Some providers of psychotherapy and other mental health services use written contracts as a means of reducing the possibility of a serious misunderstanding and a malpractice suit.

The American Public Welfare Association (1979, 82) describes a ***written service agreement*** as a "document which specifies the behavioral objectives of service and describes, in concrete terms, the actions that will be taken within established time frames to facilitate accomplishment of the objectives. The agreement is signed by all those involved in the service planning process, as appropriate. . . . The agreement constitutes a non-legally binding commitment to pursue mutually agreed-upon goals." While the authors prefer the term *service contract,* other practitioners or agencies may use the terms *service agreement, case plan, treatment plan, intervention plan,* or *individual family support plan* when referring to this type of document. Often these terms are used interchangeably.

A service contract should answer the following questions:

- What is the desired outcome of the worker's and/or agency's service to the client?
- What is to be done by the client? By when?
- What is to be done by the client's significant others (family, friends, neighbors, etc.)? By when?
- What is to be done by the worker and other agency staff? By when?
- What services are to be obtained from other agencies? By when?
- What events will trigger a reassessment of the client's situation and/or a revision of the service contract?
- What are the consequences, if any, for not adhering to the plan?

Service contracts should not be confused with *behavioral contracts* (see Item 14.6). The two have similarities but also important differences. A behavioral contract is much more specific and covers a shorter period of time, often a matter of days or, a week or two. The period covered by a service contract may be several months, although it is ordinarily renegotiated and rewritten every three or six months.

Consider the following guidelines on the utilization of written service contracts:

1. Be very clear about your agency's policy and any legal requirements related to the use of written service contracts. The following statement, taken from a public agency manual concerning the handling of certain cases of child abuse and neglect, is fairly typical of agency policy on written service contracts:

> The tasks of identification, assessment and formulation of treatment recommendations rest primarily with the social worker working with the family. The results of these formulations are set forth in the written treatment plan to advise the parents and the court of the problems identified and the course of action recommended to remedy these problems. The treatment plan should contain the following elements:
>
> - Identification of the problems or conditions which resulted in the abuse or neglect.
> - Treatment goals for the family which address the needs identified and which, when attained, will assure the adequate level of care for the child.
> - Specific treatment objectives, or tasks, which outline in detail the series of steps which must be taken by each member of the household to reach the treatment goals. These objectives should clearly define the separate roles and responsibilities of all of the parties involved in the treatment process. Objectives should clearly state the actions which are necessary, and the time period in which the objective should be accomplished. The objectives should be reasonably attainable and designed to fit the capabilities and existing circumstances of the family involved.

In the fields of child protection and probation, it is common for a service contract to be incorporated into a court order.

2. Understand both the advantages and disadvantages of using written service contracts. A contract can clarify purpose and thereby reduce client-worker conflict, set priorities, delineate roles and responsibilities, and provide a means of measuring progress. Reid and Epstein (1977) point out that service contracts are especially important in work with involuntary clients:

> Contracting . . . works best when the client has an active interest in getting help and some notion of what he wants to accomplish. Unfortunately many if not most of the clients of social work do not fall into this category. Forming contracts becomes far more difficult when the client is reluctant to accept the services of a social worker or is uncertain about the nature of his problems or the kind of help he wants. Although contracts are hard to develop with such clients, we would argue that they are even more important with this group. . . . Most important, use of contracts with the unmotivated or uncertain clients provides some assurance that he will not be treated "behind his back" for conditions that have not been made clear to him. (p. 9)

An obvious disadvantage of such contracts is the time required to prepare a clearly written contact. Other problems associated with written contracts include their uncertain legal status, the possibility of concentrating on trivial but easily conceptualized objectives while avoiding complex objectives or ones that require risk taking in order to achieve success, and the danger of powerless clients agreeing to a contract out of a fear of being punished. This later danger is of special concern whenever a contract is written into a court order. Despite these potential problems, Epstein (1992) concludes that written contracts

> can and should be used in the bulk of ordinary practice. However, written contracts should not be viewed as a remedy for all difficulties nor as rigid machinery for pushing a case toward some hard and fast end. If a contract has been agreed upon and put into writing, it represents a degree of commitment to an arrangement worked out between the client and practitioner—a promising basis for positive movement. . . . Without mutual agreement and continuous work, the contract has little force for change. (p. 198)

3. Develop the contract only after a thorough social assessment during which you and the client study and agree on the problems to be tackled. The terms of the contract should be consistent with the client's capacities, the worker's skill, and the agency's mission.

4. By definition, a contract specifies what the client will do and what the worker/agency will do. A contract must never be one-sided and list only that which the worker or agency expects of the client. A statement that neglects to specify what the worker and agency will do should not be called a contract.

5. The contract should be phrased in simple, clear language so that the client will know exactly what it says. The wording should not confuse or intimidate the client. It may be necessary to prepare the contract in the client's first language (e.g., Spanish) if he or she has a poor understanding of English. In cases where the client cannot read, the worker should consider recording the agreement on a cassette tape, in addition to preparing a written statement.

6. A contract should be developed in a way that makes success probable without, of course, sacrificing relevance. If the worker believes that the client will be unable to meet the terms of a particular contract, that alone is an indication that its objectives are too ambitious, or the timeframe is too short.

7. The objectives identified in the contract must be realistic and worth achieving from the client's viewpoint. Since the purpose of the contract is to facilitate change, it must focus on behaviors or situations that can, in fact, be changed. Do not waste time on things that are beyond anyone's control.

8. When selecting and formulating objectives, logical sequences must be built into the plan. Some problems must be tackled one step at a time and in a certain order, and new behaviors may need to be learned in a particular sequence. For example, the client who wants a job must first learn how to complete a job application.

9. Do not propose to do something for the client if the client can do it himself or herself. Sometimes a busy social worker will do for the client rather than taking the time to teach or encourage the client to carry out the action. Unnecessarily doing things for a client can also occur when the worker is overly eager to be helpful or overlooks client strengths and abilities.

10. Provisions of the contract should be modified as necessary to stay in step with changing realities of the situation. This flexibility is important in maintaining the trust of the client.

SELECTED BIBLIOGRAPHY

American Public Welfare Association. *Standards for Foster Family Services Systems for Public Agencies.* Washington, DC: American Public Welfare Association, 1979.

Epstein, Laura. *Brief Treatment and a New Look at the Task-Centered Approach,* 3rd ed. New York: Macmillan, 1992.

Reid, William, and Laura Epstein. *Task-Centered Practice.* New York: Columbia University Press, 1977.

Rooney, Ronald. *Stratagies for Work with Involuntary Clients.* New York: Columbia University Press, 1992.

Rothman, Juliet. *Contracting in Social Work.* Chicago: Nelson-Hall, 1998.

13.6 Client Needs List

PURPOSE: To remind the worker and client of concerns and needs that should be addressed in a service contract or case plan.

DISCUSSION: A *needs list* is a tool used to guide case management activities related to a certain category of clients. This list is most often used with clients who are highly dependent of the services provided by health care and social agencies (e.g., the frail elderly, children in foster care, people who have serious developmental disabilities of mental illness, etc.). A needs list reminds all involved of the many concerns that should be addressed in a service plan. Those involved in formulating this plan—including the client—must decide how the client's needs and concerns can best be addressed and who will be responsible for doing so. It is especially useful when the case planning is being done by a multiagency or a multidisciplinary team because it helps to clarify assigned responsibility and reduce friction and conflict within the team.

Figure 13.3 is an example of a needs list used in work with adults who have developmental disabilities but are capable of living in a semi-independent living

FIGURE 13.3 Sample Needs List

Needs List for Independent Living

1. Housing suitable for client's level of mobility and physical limitations (consider stairs, wheelchair accessibility, etc.)
2. Safe heating and electrical system and usable toilet facilities
3. Home furnishing (chairs, tables, TV, radio, etc.)
4. Bed, blankets, sheets, etc.
5. Clothing for all seasons of the year
6. Food, food storage, stove
7. Telephone or other means of requesting assistance
8. Items needed for food preparation (e.g., utensils, pots, pans)
9. Items needed to maintain personal hygiene (razor, soap, sanitary napkins, etc.)
10. Financial resources/money management system
11. Transportation
12. Medical and dental care
13. Medication and monitoring of dosage, if needed
14. Social contacts and recreational activities
15. Concern and interest shown by family, friends, and neighbors
16. Protection from harm or exploitation
17. Appropriate level of supervision
18. Training (job-related, community, survival skills, etc.)
19. Employment or work-related activity
20. Adaptive aids (e.g., eyeglasses, hearing aids, leg braces, etc.)
21. Therapy and other special treatments (e.g., physical therapy, speech therapy, etc.)
22. Maintenance of cultural and ethnic heritage
23. Participation in spiritual or religious activities
24. Legal assistance

arrangement. Also, see Item 12.17 for ideas on specific areas of client functioning that might be included in a needs list.

SELECTED BIBLIOGRAPHY

Frankel, Arthur, and Sheldon Gelman. *Case Management.* Chicago: Lyceum Books, 1998.
Moxley, David. *Case Management by Design.* Chicago: Nelson-Hall, 1997.
Rothman, Jack, and Jon Simon Sager. *Case Management.* Boston: Allyn and Bacon, 1998.

13.7 Making Use of Informal Resources

PURPOSE: To assist the client in identifying and utilizing informal resources.

DISCUSSION: Whenever possible and appropriate, the intervention plan should draw on resources available within the client's social support network, such as the extended family, friends, neighbors, church groups, and service clubs. These resources are often termed ***informal resources,*** as contrasted to ***formal resources,*** such as agencies, hospitals, and trained professionals. Informal resources can provide emotional support, material assistance (e.g., money, loans, food, housing), physical care (e.g., child care, supervision of frail elderly persons living in their own home), information, and the mediation of interpersonal conflict.

A self-help group is usually considered to be an informal resource, even though some are affiliated with a state or national organization and may use professionals as advisors. Another important informal resource is the ***natural helper,*** an individual who has often resided in the community for a long time and is known for his or her ability to help others. An example is the "neighborhood Mom" to whom children gravitate for nurturing, advice, and friendship. Other natural helpers include respected elders, religious leaders, and healers. Another informal resource—one often overlooked by professionals—is other agency clients. Clients can often be of help to each other; however, in some cases, they can also exacerbate each other's problems.

Many people prefer to use informal resources over the formal ones, for several reasons:

- No stigma is attached to receiving help from an informal resource.
- Informal helping is available 24 hours a day, seven days a week, at no cost.
- One does not have to be categorized, labeled, diagnosed, or otherwise meet eligibility requirements in order to secure needed help.
- Informal helping involves a reciprocal relationship—the give and take among two equals or peers—rather than the expert-client relationship that is so often a part of the professional helping process.

Although informal resources are the oldest and most common form of helping activity, some professionals are reluctant to encourage or assist their clients in using these resources. Possible reasons include the following:

- They assume that formal resources and other professionals are inherently more effective than nonprofessionals, regardless of the client's problem or situation.
- They have little awareness of the informal helping networks and informal resources.
- They assume that the client has already thought about and considered using informal resources and for some reason rejected the idea.
- They doubt the capacity of informal resources to protect a client's right to confidentiality.

When considering the appropriateness of looking to informal resources as a source of help and assistance for a client, the social worker should keep the following guidelines in mind:

1. The goal of practice is to help clients improve their social functioning. The resources used—whether formal, informal, or a mix of both—are simply the means to that end.

2. Informal resources must never be viewed as a panacea or an inexpensive alternative to formal services. Both may be needed and both are important; one should support and supplement the other. A professional should not feel threatened by a client's use of or preference for informal resources.

3. During the assessment and planning phases, the client's social network should always be viewed as a potential source of assistance. The client's relationship—past and present—with relatives, friends, neighbors, churches, and service organizations should be explored to identify possible informal resources that are relevant to the client's current situation. If identified, the advantages and disadvantages of attempting to use the resource need to be discussed. In the final analysis, it is the client who decides which resources, whether informal or formal, he or she will use. Clients may need guidance on how to reach out to an informal resource, establish a relationship, and handle the expectation of reciprocity (see Item 12.4).

4. The ethical and legal codes concerning confidentiality need not be a barrier to the use of informal resources. Most often, the client first approaches the informal resources. Thus, the client is in control of what he or she chooses to reveal. In cases where the social worker needs to talk with an informal resource, he or she must, of course, first secure the client's permission, just as is done when the worker communicates with another professional or agency.

5. Do not attempt to "professionalize" informal resources. Generally, they work best when they are left alone. Efforts to train informal resources in the use of helping skills tend to disrupt the natural helping process.

6. Learn about self-help groups available in your community. You may wish to seek information from the National Self-Help Clearinghouse, 25 W. 43rd Street, Room 620, New York, NY 10036 (212/642-2944).

SELECTED BIBLIOGRAPHY

Gitterman, Alex, and Lawrence Shulman, eds. *Mutual Aid Groups, Vulnerable Populations and the Life Cycle.* New York: Columbia University Press, 1994.

Kurtz, Linda. *Self-Help and Support Groups.* Thousand Oaks, CA: Sage, 1997.

Maguire, Lambert. *Social Support Systems in Practice.* Washington, DC: NASW Press, 1991.

13.8 The Small Group as a Resource

PURPOSE: To develop groups that can be a resource to clients.

DISCUSSION: Small groups are an invaluable resource to clients. They can provide a sense of belonging and support, information, new perspectives, awareness that others have similar problems and concerns, role models for learning new behaviors, and opportunities to be helpful to others. Despite these advantages, many practice settings do not make groups available to their clients. One reason is that some workers presume that clients are not interested in being part of a group. Another reason is the difficulty of bringing several clients together at a convenient time and place. Still another barrier to the use of groups is the erroneous belief that the members of a group must all have the very same problem or concern; such a belief makes it nearly impossible to ever find enough participants for a group. And finally, some workers avoid groups because they fear that they will not be able to handle a group. While it is true that the development and utilization of a group experience can pose some challenges, the authors urge social workers to expand their use of groups in practice.

A group made up of individuals who meet several times and discuss some issue can be expected to move through various ***stages of group development:*** (1) preaffiliation, (2) power and control, (3) intimacy, (4) differentiation, and (5) separation. It is during the *preaffiliation stage* that members size each other up, consider what they have in common, and decide whether they want to belong to the group. Unless the members feel they have something in common and share the same goals for the group, they will resist further involvement. During this stage, members tend to be dependent on the leader for direction.

During the *power and control stage,* members test each other and the leader and come to a decision of where they fit in the group. They may challenge each other for position and leadership. Also, members tend to challenge the designated leader. At this time, a number of informal rules develop to govern what is and is not acceptable behavior within the group.

As the members get to know each other, they gradually let down their defenses and the group enters the *intimacy stage.* Members recognize and value what they have in common. Next, the group moves to the stage of *differentiation,* wherein differences of opinion and behavior are exhibited but respected and valued. Members begin to understand that each has a life and important roles outside the group and may behave quite differently in other settings. As the life of the group approaches its ending, it enters the *separation stage* and each member must struggle with the loss of meaningful relationships.

For those who want to make a group experience available to their clients, the following guidelines are suggested:

1. Before deciding to form a group, be clear as to its purpose and why it will be of benefit to your clients. Answers to most other questions about forming a group relate directly to the question of purpose and desired outcome.

As a general rule, the more focused and specialized the group's purpose, the better it serves the members. If all members share a common reason for being in the group and all agree on the group's purpose, they will feel more comfortable and better understood in the group and more willing to discuss issues in greater depth.

2. Decide which clients are to be offered the group experience. Some social group workers hold definite beliefs about the mix of personalities they want in the group (e.g., having outgoing and verbal members to offset members who are quiet and shy). Also, some group workers may want to eliminate from consideration those who are reputed to be resistant or uncooperative. However, in many practice settings, the worker does not have the luxury of using detailed selection criteria and must simply select for possible membership those who have a need for a group experience, have some ability to tolerate differences of opinion, and have at least a basic capacity to enter into relationships. Once in the group, a voluntary member should feel free to drop out if he or she feels uncomfortable or if the group is not meeting his or her needs.

When screening or selecting potential members, the group worker must balance the needs of the individual with the needs and safety of other members. People exhibiting bizarre or truly dangerous behavior should be eliminated from consideration for membership unless the meetings occur within an institutional setting that provides close supervision. In addition, individuals who are at high risk of suicide or who are actively using or selling illegal drugs may not be appropriate for inclusion.

3. It is often not possible to predict accurately how an individual will behave and function as a group member. As a general rule, however, people will behave in a formed group about as they do in other situations. For example, if an individual has difficulty demonstrating warmth or expressing positive feelings with family members, he or she will usually carry these same patterns into the group. Likewise, the person who controls and dominates others at work can be expected to try to dominate and control the group.

4. Decide what is an appropriate group size. Size depends on such factors as the age of the clients, concerns to be addressed by the group, and your experience as a leader or facilitator. You will want the group to be small enough so all members have a sense of belonging and a chance to participate, but large enough to yield a variety of opinions and minimize pressure on those who are fearful of interaction. You will also need to consider the developmental abilities of the members. For preadolescents, a group of only 3 or 4 is often workable. For adolescents, a group of 6 to 10 is preferred. Most adults seem comfortable in a group of about 8 to 10. You must also anticipate the inevitable problem of nonattendance and dropouts. In the beginning, the group must be large enough to continue functioning when some members miss a meeting and after a member or two decides to drop out.

5. Decide on the frequency of meetings and the length of each session. For most adults, a meeting lasting one and one-half to two hours is about right. Because of limited attention span, shorter but more frequent meetings are usually best for children and adolescents. The practice setting will also dictate the frequency of meetings. In an institutional setting, daily meetings are often possible and desirable. When members are drawn from the larger community, it may not be feasible to meet more often than weekly or monthly.

6. Decide when and where the group will meet. A meeting space should be quiet, private, comfortable, and large enough for people to move around and to accommodate a circle of chairs. The decision of when to meet must consider each member's work and family responsibilities, matters of personal convenience, and, of course, the availability of a meeting room..

7. Decide on the approximate number of times the group will meet. This is, of course, tied to purpose. An information sharing or training group might meet only once or twice, whereas a support or therapy group might meet weekly for several months or longer. Consider setting a limit (e.g., 3, 5, or 10 meetings) with the understanding that at the end of that period, you and the group will decide whether the meetings should continue. This can help keep members involved because they know there is a planned time to terminate and it can prevent a group from continuing to meet even when there is no longer a clear purpose.

8. Decide whether the group will be open or closed to additional members. This is sometimes a decision for the group to make. If it is to be decided by the group, the decision needs to be made during the first or second meeting. Incorporating new members into an already functioning group has the advantage of maintaining group size if some members drop out. Also, new members may bring fresh perspectives. However, the frequent introduction of new members is a barrier to the development of group cohesion and it may limit the intensity of interaction.

9. Decide if the group is for voluntary clients, involuntary clients, or both. Obviously, there are advantages to limiting membership to persons who want to attend. Although involuntary members can be forced by court order to attend, they cannot be forced to interact in a meaningful and productive manner. Nevertheless, the successful utilization of group methods in correctional, chemical dependency, and child abuse treatment programs demonstrates that groups made up of involuntary clients are feasible and can be effective. However, the leader of such groups must be strong and skilled in confronting resistant and manipulative members.

The addition of involuntary members to a basically voluntary group will usually work if the group has been functioning quite well for a time and the involuntary member is willing to cooperate to at least a minimal degree. On the other hand, it is not likely to work if the group is newly formed or has not been functioning well and/or if the involuntary member is highly resistant and disruptive. Before adding a new involuntary member, it is best to wait until the group has reached the intimacy stage. The addition of new members, especially resistant ones, should be avoided during the power and control stage.

10. When extending an invitation to join a group, be prepared to explain how the group will be of benefit, what will happen during the meetings, and the atmosphere you hope to create (e.g., informal, fun, learning, sharing, etc.). Also, be prepared to offer information that might raise interest and reduce fears about participating.

11. As the group moves through the usual stages of development, assess the functioning of each group member and consider the use of various techniques to deal with identified problems (see Items 8.3 and 14.44). The answers to the following questions will help the worker in this assessment:

- Is the member in agreement with the group's purpose and format?
- Is the member personally involved—sharing feelings, opinions, and experiences?
- Does the member attend on a regular basis and participate in discussion or activities?
- Does the member enjoy being with other members?
- Does the member engage in a mix of confrontation and support of others?
- How might the group's activities be modified to address the problems or concerns identified?

12. Be prepared to establish rules (possibly written) to govern the behavior of group members. Possible rules include the following:

- Members are expected to attend all meetings.
- Members are expected to maintain confidentiality.
- Members cannot smoke or do drugs during the meeting.
- Members are not allowed to remain at the meeting if they are under the influence of alcohol or drugs.
- Minor-aged members must have parents' written consent to participate.
- Members are to avoid dating and having sexual relationships with other members.
- Members who bring weapons, threaten violence, or engage in sexual harassment will be excluded.

13. Select activities (programs) for each meeting (e.g., introductions, ice breakers, refreshments, structured discussion, free and open discussion, role-play, guest speaker, etc.). These activities should be consistent with the group's overall purpose and encourage the type of activity relevant to the group's stage of development (see Item 14.21).

14. Anticipate how you can handle the numerous practical problems associated with a meeting, such as the room is too hot or cold or too large or small; the leader must miss a meeting; members arrive late; members bring uninvited friends; deciding if there will be refreshments and, if so, who will pay; conflict between smokers and nonsmokers; who will remind members of next meeting; and so on.

SELECTED BIBLIOGRAPHY

Anderson, Joseph. *Social Work with Groups.* New York: Longman, 1997.

Bertcher, Harvey, and Frank Maple. *Creating Groups,* 2nd ed. Thousand Oaks, CA: Sage, 1997.

Garvin, Charles. *Contemporary Group Work,* 2nd ed. Boston: Allyn and Bacon, 1997.

Greif, Geoffrey, and Paul Ephross, eds. *Group Work with Populations at Risk.* New York: Oxford University Press, 1997.

Henry, Sue. *Group Skills in Social Work,* 2nd ed. Pacific Grove, CA: Brooks/Cole, 1992.

Reid, Kenneth. *Social Work Practice with Groups: A Clinical Perspective,* 2nd ed. Pacific Grove, CA: Brooks/Cole, 1997.

Toseland, Ronald, and Robert Rivas. *An Introduction to Group Work Practice,* 3rd ed. Boston: Allyn and Bacon, 1998.

SECTION B

TECHNIQUES AND GUIDELINES FOR INDIRECT PRACTICE

It is especially important for social workers engaged in indirect service activities to give careful attention to the planning and contracting phase of the change process. As systems become more complex, it is increasingly difficult and time consuming to promote meaningful change in a system's ways of operating. When working with organizations and communities, one should be aware that a change in one system will reverberate not only through that system but through related systems, as well. Therefore, change efforts must be carefully planned and the responsibilities of each actor in the process should be clearly identified.

Planning Activities. Organization and community planning are forms of social work practice typically performed by social workers with specialized education and training. This book does not intend to address these more complex processes; rather, it provides some guidelines (see Items 13.9 through 13.12) that are useful for the front-line social worker (i.e., the direct practice worker whose job sometimes involves indirect practice activities).

Much of the front-line worker's planning activity related to organizations and communities involves the ability to assess various alternatives for remedying a problems, selecting the best alternative for achieving a positive outcome, and plotting the schedule of tasks and activities to make the change process as efficient and effective as possible. These planning activities should be based on a knowledge of how organizations can be changed from within, how ongoing agency planning should occur, the process of planning special projects, and understanding the requirements for developing a primary prevention program.

Contracting Activities. Once plans for organizational and community change have been developed, there must be explicit agreements among the participating parties about the responsibilities and timetable for carrying out the associated activities. In a community change effort, for example, once an assessment is made and a plan developed, individual or committee assignments for implementing the plan must be agreed upon. Typically, someone must prepare a position statement, someone must organize the people concerned with the issue to take action, someone must contact the media, someone must lobby the decision makers, and so on. These actions must be orchestrated to be sure that they are done in a timely manner, as subsequent actions may depend on those tasks having already been completed.

When the issues addressed are interagency in nature, the planning may take the form of ongoing contracts between organizations. Items 13.13 and 13.14 provide illustrations of contracts developed to facilitate the work among human services agencies.

13.9 Establishing and Changing Organizations

PURPOSE: To establish or modify agency goals, policies, and programs.

DISCUSSION: Social agencies stake their claim to specific areas of service provision. They must clearly state their mission, the goals they intend to achieve, the services they will provide, and the policies and procedures they will follow. Only then can the public be accurately informed about the nature of the agency, can clients know what services to expect, can unplanned duplication and overlap of services be minimized, and can staff members plan and coordinate their work.

An effective social agency is dynamic; it must constantly adapt to community and societal changes, to new knowledge about the nature of personal and social problems, to changes in public attitudes, and to ever-changing fiscal and political realities. Thus, a social worker can expect to participate, to some degree and at some level, in efforts to modify agency goals, structure, and operations.

Public agencies are particularly reactive to any change in the state and federal laws relevant to their areas of service and to budget modifications. In response to such changes, the agency's own policies and procedures may need to undergo significant change during a short period of time.

Private agencies, too, must be capable of responding to a variety of forces. When a private agency is created, the bylaws spell out its mission and decision-making structure. Although the original bylaws may capture the intent of the founders, such agencies must change over time to keep pace with changing community needs and new concepts of service. Leadership for needed change by a private agency often falls first to the executive director and the staff, with the board and/or a broader membership group subsequently amending the bylaws to reflect the proposed changes.

Although change is inevitable, an agency, like all social systems, will resist change; in fact, it may take considerable effort to make needed change. The following guidelines suggest several factors to consider when planning and initiating organizational change:

1. Begin by describing as precisely as possible the change that is needed and why. Then secure and study all documents that may pertain to the desired change. These may include, for example, federal and state laws and regulations, administrative and personnel manuals, union contracts, accreditation standards, agreements and contracts involving other agencies, agreements with national parent organizations, and so on. The information drawn from these sources will determine, to some degree, what changes are possible, how the change process must proceed, and who else must support or approve the change.

2. Assess the organization's readiness for change. Review its prior experience in accepting change. The people of an organization are likely to resist change if prior change efforts have been misguided, ineffective, or frustrating. On the other hand, they will tend to accept change if they trust those promoting or leading the change effort, when they believe the proposed change is needed and feasible, and when the proposal has addressed their questions, concerns, and fears about changing.

3. Determine if the desire for change is shared across the various levels, departments, and units of the organization. Pay special attention to the views of those who will be affected most directly by the proposed change. A common and serious error in planning change is to overlook or disregard the opinions of line workers and clerical staff—those who may know most about how the proposed change will have an impact on day-to-day agency operations and on agency clients.

4. Assess the degree to which the change is compatible with the agency's mission, traditions, and current goals. Determine the degree to which the change is desired and supported by top management and the board of directors.

5. Identify and assess the relative strength of the organizational subsystems and individuals who are likely to favor the change and those who will oppose it. Determine who stands to gain and who stands to be hurt by the proposed change. The strategy most likely to overcome resistance is one that either (a) increases the power of those within the agency that favor the change or (b) introduces new resources into the organization that will minimize the impact of the change on those who are resistant.

6. The agency, or a unit of the agency, is most likely to adopt a proposed change if it can be shown that the change will result in an increase in scope, authority, autonomy, or funds and other resources. A change that decreases power and resources will be resisted. People will favor a change that makes their work easier; they will resist a change that makes their work more complex or demands more of their time.

7. The members of an organization will strongly resist a change that they perceive as a threat to their jobs, advancement, or opportunities within the organization. Also, they will be resistant to change whenever they suspect others are withholding information about the true intentions of the change.

8. An organization will be more open to a proposed change if it can be demonstrated that other similar organizations have successfully made this change.

9. A change is most likely to be accepted by the organization after its advantages have been demonstrated in a trial run or as a demonstration project within only a part of the organization. Thus, it is desirable that the first phase of a more far-reaching change effort begin by focusing on a problem or situation of limited scope. It might, for example, involve a specific program, activity, or unit of the agency and should be achievable in a three-month period. Subsequent efforts would then deal with more complex changes. It is advisable to start small and then, by building on success, gradually widen the scope of the change effort.

10. Whenever possible, changes should be integrated into current structures and procedures so as to minimize the disruption of existing relationships and patterns.

SELECTED BIBLIOGRAPHY

Dalziel, Murray, and Stephen Schoonover. *Changing Ways: A Practical Tool for Implementing Change within Organizations.* New York: American Management Institute, 1988.

Frey, Gerald A. "A Framework for Promoting Organizational Change." *Families in Society* (March 1990): 142–147.

Netting, F. Ellen, Peter M. Kettner, and Steven L. McMurty. *Social Work Macro Practice,* 2nd ed. New York: Longman, 1998.

Schram, Barbara. *Creating Small Scale Social Programs.* Thousand Oaks, CA: Sage, 1997.

Weinbach, Robert. *The Social Worker as Manager,* 3rd ed. Boston: Allyn and Bacon, 1998.

13.10 The Process of Agency Planning

PURPOSE: To formulate plans to guide an agency's operations and to maximize its performance.

DISCUSSION: In order to operate in an effective and efficient manner and to grow and develop as an organization, a social agency must formulate both short-range and long-range plans that will guide its ongoing activity and decision making. All too often, agencies neglect long-term planning and then find that they must make hasty decisions and rapid changes in agency operations in response to a situation or crisis they did not anticipate and for which they were unprepared.

Ideally, an agency's planning process is proactive and forward looking. The plan it constructs will therefore be a truly useful and accurate description of how it will utilize its resources (i.e., staff time, money, knowledge, skills, etc.), how it can capitalize on its strengths and opportunities, how it will correct its weaknesses, and how it can respond to certain unwanted but possible future events such as a lawsuit, increased demand for service, loss of staff, or a reduction in funding.

A fruitful planning process is complex and time consuming. It can be especially difficult because all planning decisions rest on a set of predictions as to what will happen in future months and years. Unfortunately, few agencies are able to predict accurately the ever-changing political, economic, and public opinion forces that may affect an agency operation. Given these uncertainties, even the best of plans must be constantly reviewed and revised.

Despite all the challenges inherent in planning, an agency must devote time and energy to this activity. Broadly speaking, there are three types of planning processes: (1) problem-solving planning, (2) operational planning, and (3) strategic planning. They differ primarily in terms of the time period covered.

Problem-solving planning has a life span of 60 to 90 days. It focuses on some specific problem that is having an adverse effect on the agency's usual activity. The process involves (1) identifying and examining the problem, (2) selecting a set of corrective actions or measures, (3) planning the implementation of these measures, and (4) monitoring the effectiveness of the corrective action. If the agency is successful in its operational and strategic planning (discussed next), the need for problem-solving planning will be minimized.

Operational planning refers to short-range planning covering a period of 6 to 12 months or perhaps one budget cycle. This planning process formulates objectives, details performance standards, and prepares an action plan to reach the stated objectives.

Strategic planning may cover a period of 3 to 10 years. Basically, the strategic planning process strives to develop a plan for achieving the agency's mission or long-term goals. This type of planning calls for the identification and analysis of broad social and economic trends, for speculation on what challenges and opportunities the agency will face in several years, and for creativity in deciding how best to use agency resources. Strategic planning is based on the belief that it is important to have a plan that considers all conditions and factors that may have a significant impact on the agency, regardless how uncertain the future must be. Because it is so speculative and based on so many uncertain variables, a strategic plan must be revised if there are unexpected changes in the internal or external environment.

Adherence to the following guidelines will enhance the planning process:

1. Make certain that adequate and accurate data are readily available to those engaged in the planning process. Such data should describe:

- The agency's mission and goals
- Current and projected budgets and a history of the agency's fiscal condition
- Programs and services provided and the number of clients/consumers participating in each program or service area
- Characteristics of the persons served by the agency (e.g., age, income, ethnicity, religion, etc.)
- Profile of the agency staff (e.g., education, training, interests, skills, etc.)
- The agency's relationship with other agencies in the community
- Requests and concerns voiced by staff
- Requests and concerns voiced by clients/consumers and other agencies and community groups
- Trends and projections (i.e., demands for services, capacity to raise funds, demographic changes in the community)
- Special problems faced by the agency

2. Keep the planning process as simple as possible so that all those who should participate can do so despite the day-to-day pressures of their other responsibilities. Do not demand more of their time than is absolutely necessary. Keep the number of meetings and the paperwork requirement to a minimum.

3. Make sure that all who might be affected by a decision or proposed change are invited to participate in the discussion and encouraged to voice their thoughts and concerns. Avoid "top-down planning" (i.e., decision making and planning by only the upper-level administrative personnel).

4. Gather and organize ideas and promote creativity by performing a SWOPA analysis of the agency. The acronym ***SWOPA*** stands for Strengths, Weaknesses, Opportunities, Problems, and Action.

- *Strengths.* Identify the services, programs, and activities currently provided at a level of quality that meets or exceeds professional standards.
- *Weaknesses.* Identify the services, programs, and activities that fall below acceptable levels of quality or needed levels of quantity.
- *Opportunities.* Identify the service or program activities that are promising for development or expansion because of a favorable environment, growing demand, available funding, staff interest, and so on.
- *Problems.* Identify the areas of agency performance that are especially troublesome.
- *Actions.* Identify the possible activities or changes that would build on agency strengths, exploit opportunities, address areas of weakness, or better manage the problems faced by the agency.

5. Perform a *competition analysis.* This requirement asks those participating in the planning process to examine the activities of other agencies, organizations, or professional groups to determine how they compete with the agency's current programs and services. For example, are other organizations developing services that would attract your agency's clients or staff or are other agencies making requests for the funds now utilized by your agency?

6. Perform a *stakeholder's analysis.* As used here, stakeholders are those individuals, groups, or organizations that have an interest in the agency. Their beliefs, values, and possible reactions to changes in the agency must be given serious consideration. Examples of internal stakeholders are clients/consumers, agency staff, unions representing staff, members of the board of directors, and so on. Examples of external stakeholders include professional associations, politicians, other agencies, businesses and corporations, local newspapers, citizen groups, taxpayers, contributors, former clients, and the like.

7. Perform a *threat analysis.* A threat is some possible future circumstance or action by others that could harm the agency. Examples might include a lawsuit against the agency, an employee strike, loss of funding, loss of key staff, rapid change in community demographics, significant changes in the laws or regulations that affect the agency, damaging news stories, and so forth.

8. Make sure that the many facets of the planning process are coordinated and well integrated. For example, decisions concerning budget, staffing patterns, performance standards, and the programs and services to be offered are all interrelated. In particular, financial planning must be incorporated into all other areas of planning. If the many components of the process are not properly coordinated and integrated, much time will be wasted, much confusion will occur, and the planning process will be doomed to failure.

SELECTED BIBLIOGRAPHY

Kettner, Peter M., Robert M. Moroney, and Lawrence L. Martin. *Designing and Managing Programs: An Effectiveness-Based Approach.* Newbury Park, CA: Sage, 1990.

Porterfield, Gerald A. *A Concise Guide to Community Planning.* New York: McGraw-Hill, 1995.

Rapp, Charles, and John Poertner. *Social Administration: A Client-Centered Approach.* New York: Longman, 1992.

Weinbach, Robert. *The Social Worker as Manager,* 3rd ed. Boston: Allyn and Bacon, 1998.

13.11 Project Planning and Evaluation

PURPOSE: To plan, coordinate, and schedule project activities.

DISCUSSION: The introduction of a new service or special project into the day-to-day operation of a social agency can be disruptive unless it is carefully planned and integrated into the life of the organization. Efficient planning of new activities involves selecting the most effective strategy for accomplishing objectives, scheduling activities to maximize efficiency, and carefully planning the manner in which tasks are completed so as not to disrupt other parts of the agency.

Strategy Selection

Achieving the goals and objectives of a new project calls for the selection of the best possible course of action or strategy from among available alternatives. Craig (1978) identifies five criteria that should be considered in this selection:

1. *Appropriateness.* Is this strategy consistent with the agency's overall mission and goals? Is it consistent with the agency's experience and usual methods and standards of operation? Does the use of this strategy raise any legal or ethical concerns?
2. *Effectiveness.* Given the nature of the problem or issue being addressed by the project, is this strategy likely to be successful?
3. *Efficiency.* Given the agency's current resources (e.g., funding, available staff time, expertise), is this strategy an efficient use of those resources?
4. *Adequacy.* Are the actions called for by this strategy ones that will have a real and lasting impact on the problem or issues to be addressed by the project?
5. *Side effects.* What positive and negative side effects could result from using this strategy?

By charting each alternative according to these five criteria, it is possible to compare the advantages and disadvantages of each. Figure 13.4 is an example of a chart that might be developed to compare strategies for increasing the number of minorities and women on the staff of a human services agency.

Scheduling

A variety of techniques have been developed to help schedule specific project activities. One frequently used scheduling tool is the ***Gantt chart.*** This chart provides a visual means of depicting the relationship between the activities required for a project and the time frame for completing each. The activities are listed down the left column and the periods of work on each activity, charted by month or week, are across the top of the page (see Figure 13.5). The usefulness of a Gantt chart is that it helps to

FIGURE 13.4 Example of an Alternative Comparison Chart

Objective: To create a process for recruiting and promoting minorities and women that has the support of employee unions and minority/women's groups

	Appropriate	Adequacy	Effectiveness	Efficiency	Side Effect
Strategy	*Yes/No/Maybe*	*Hi/Med/Low*	*Hi/Med/Low*	*Hi/Med/Low*	*Good/Bad*
A. Develop task force of employees and advocates to write Affirmative Action plan.	Maybe	Hi	Hi	Med (probable benefits high, so is cost)	*Good*—precedent for better decision-making process. *Bad*—too much citizen involvement; time consuming.
B. Ask for suggestions first, then circulate plan, ask for comments.	Yes	Med	Med	Hi (probable benefits high, cost not so high)	*Good*—precedent for more input in decision making. *Bad*—hostility if we don't adopt their comments.
C. Write plan, then circulate for comments.	Yes	Low	Low	Med (probable benefits low, but so is cost)	*Good*—avoid direct confrontation. *Bad*—plan may not have real support.
D. Copy plan from another city where it was implemented without conflict.	Maybe	Low	Low	Low (low cost, but low benefit too)	*Good*—maybe no one would know we'd done a plan. *Bad*—plan might never be used.

Source: Craig 1978, p. 52. A Learning Concepts Publication, distributed by University Associates, San Diego.

FIGURE 13.5 Sample Gantt Chart

Activity

1. Collect literature on parent-effectiveness training.
2. Secure permission to initiate parent-effectiveness training group from supervisor.
3. Interpret parent-effectiveness training in staff meeting.
4. Request all workers in unit to nominate families for parent-effectiveness training.
5. Send letters to nominated families, inviting them to participate and asking for preference on which night to meet.
6. Set meeting times, reserve room, and notify families of first meeting.
7. Make day-care plans for children of the participants.
8. Prepare presentations and materials for parent-effectiveness training sessions.
9. Hold 12 weekly meetings with participants.
10. Assess the value of the sessions to the participants.
11. Report results to supervisor and other staff members.

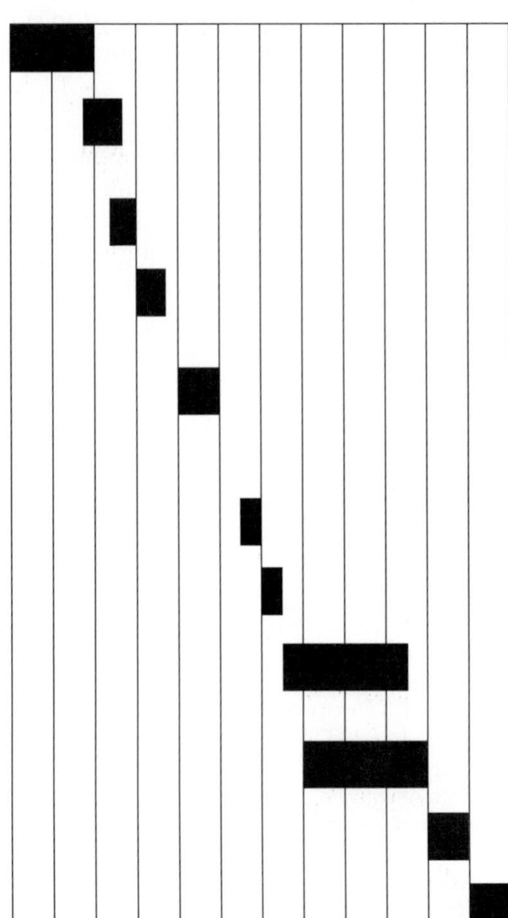

identify the sequencing required for the entire project and helps to keep track of the completion dates for specific activities.

The Program Evaluation and Review Technique (***PERT chart***) is a second useful scheduling tool. This chart is especially helpful for sorting out the proper sequencing of events and estimating the amount of time required to complete each activity or event. When developing a PERT chart, an *activity* is defined as requiring staff time to complete. Thus, by adding up the days or hours devoted to the various activities, it is possible to estimate the cost in staff time to carry out the project. An *event* is an action taken by someone other than staff on a target date that affects the timeline of the project. By first identifying the dates on which various events are likely to be completed and then charting the activities that must occur to prepare for each event, it is possible to start with the intended completion date for the project and work backwards to build the PERT chart. Figure 13.6 illustrates a section of a PERT chart developed for a client survey regarding the effectiveness of an agency's services.

Task Planning

A final step in completing a special project is to identify and carry out the activities required to implement the strategy that has been selected. This step involves identifying the tasks to be completed and the rationale for engaging in this activity, noting when it must be completed and who should be involved, and specifying the time or other resources required for completing the task. Figure 13.7 is an example of a chart that might be developed for this purpose when establishing a task force.

FIGURE 13.6 Sample PERT Chart for Client Survey Proposal

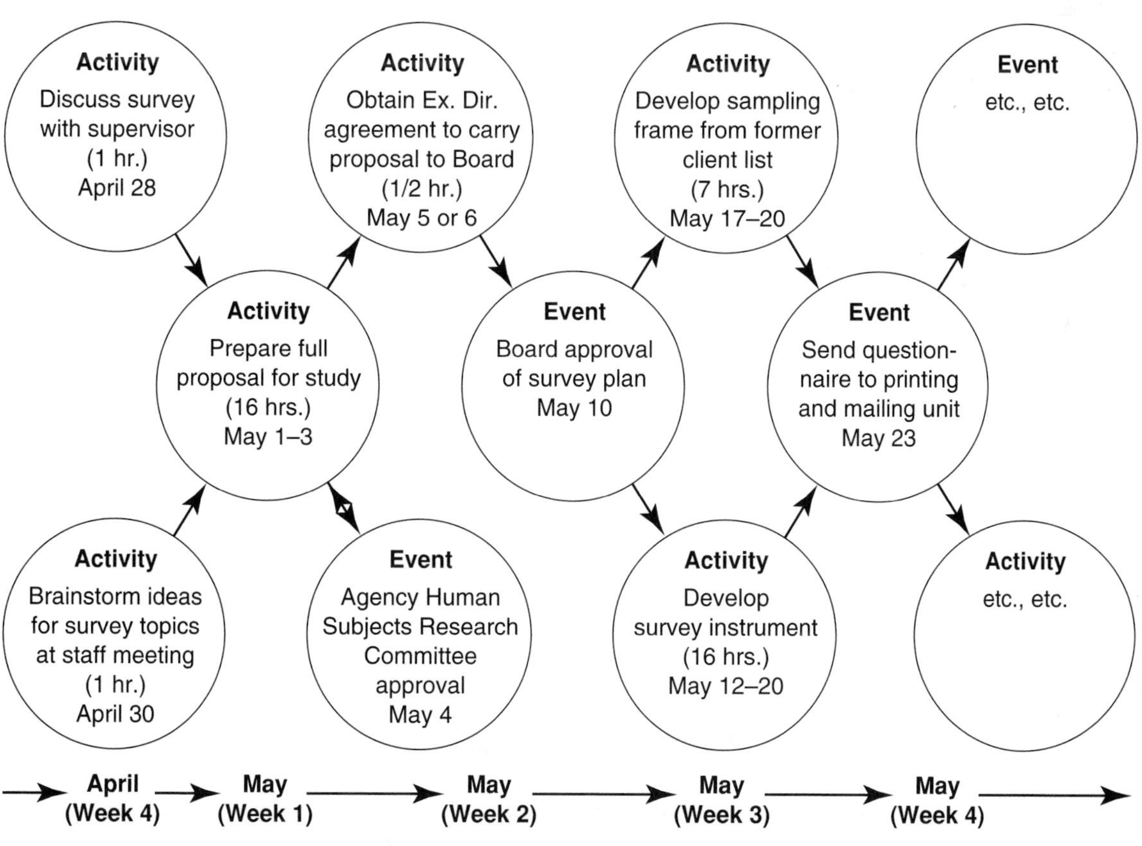

FIGURE 13.7 Example of a Task Planning Sheet

Staff Member: Personnel Manager

Strategy: Form task force to develop Affirmative Action Plan

Activity: Get agreement of members to serve on task force

Tasks	Why?	When?	Who?	Resources?
1. List key groups and potential task force members.	Make sure all possibilities are considered.	Jan. 3	Self	3 hrs.
2. Go over list with department director and agree on whom to approach.	Get director's perspective and approval.	Jan. 4	Self and director	2 hrs.
3. Review overall strategy with department director.	Make sure we're on same wavelength, confirm commitment to strategy.	Jan. 4	Self, director, and key clerical staff	same meeting as #2
4. Arrange meetings with some potential members for preliminary discussion.	Person-to-person, informal approach most likely to succeed.	Jan 15–22	Self and potential members	6 hrs.
5. Etc.				

Source: Craig 1978, p. 80. A Learning Concepts Publication, distributed by University Associates, San Diego.

SELECTED BIBLIOGRAPHY

Baker, Sunny, and Kim Baker. *The Complete Idiot's Guide to Project Management.* New York: Alpha Books, 1998.

Burch, Hobart A. *Basic Social Policy and Planning: Strategies and Planning Methods.* New York: Haworth, 1996.

Craig, Dorothy. *Hip Pocket Guide to Planning and Evaluation.* San Diego: University Associates, 1978.

Schaefer, Morris. *Implementing Change in Service Programs: Project Planning and Management.* Newbury Park, CA: Sage, 1987.

13.12 Planning a Primary Prevention Program

PURPOSE: To develop a human services program or change strategy intended to prevent problems in social functioning.

DISCUSSION: Most social programs are created as a reaction to an existing problem and are designed to offer treatment or assistance to the people who experience this problem. Equally important are programs designed to prevent the problem from developing in the first place. Prevention efforts are desirable and logical, but the actual design of an effective prevention program is complex and difficult.

Although many view prevention as essentially different from intervention, it is useful to treat prevention as a type of intervention. ***Primary prevention*** consists of a set of actions intended to intervene and modify those conditions or situations that will, if not changed, lead to the formation of a significant problem (see Chapter 1). Thus, those engaged in planning a prevention effort must be able to identify the specific factors, conditions, and situations that "cause" or give rise to a problem and then identify a set of actions and activities that will reduce or eliminate their impact.

Increasingly, primary prevention programs are built around ideas of risk and resiliency. In relation to children and youth, for example, considerable research identifies a high correlation between certain negative family, neighborhood, and community influences and the development of social problems such as delinquency, drug and alcohol abuse, school dropout, emotional disturbance, gang activity, and teen pregnancy. Among the corrosive influences that give rise to these problems are poverty, discrimination, lack of opportunity, family breakdown and dysfunction, feelings of low self-worth, easy access to drugs and alcohol, and poor schools. For reasons not well understood, some young people are more "resistant" to these influences than others. They have within their personalities, environment, and life experiences certain protective factors that shield them from the full force of negative influences. They are said to possess *resiliency* in that even when exposed to stress, trauma, and adversity, they do not develop serious problems. A variety of protective factors appear to contribute to resiliency in children and youth. Benard (1991), for example, believes that three protective factors are of critical importance:

- The child has a caring and supportive relationship with at least one adult (this may or may not be a parent).
- Some meaningful person(s) in the child's life communicates consistently high expectations of the child.
- The child has ample opportunity to participate in and contribute meaningfully to others in his or her social environment.

Resiliency-related research suggests that both children and adults are more adaptive and flexible than we often assume, and that the process of human development and adjustment includes many self-righting mechanisms that can compensate for trauma and life stressors. Some of these protective factors are found in the person's personality and behavior patterns (e.g., self-confidence, self-esteem, problem-solving skills, etc.), warm and supportive relationships within his or her family, the presence of caring people in the school or work environment, and/or supportive factors in one's ethnic, neighborhood, or community interactions. This is not meant to suggest that stages of human development do not exist, nor that what happens at one point in a person's development has no impact on what follows. Rather, it suggests that the developmental stages and the impact of significant events are more elastic than often assumed and it is possible for people to overcome serious problems that arise in their lives.

As part of their commitment to facilitating change in both the person and the environment, social workers must be skilled at designing and implementing primary prevention programs. A few general guidelines are offered to those planning to engage in primary prevention:

1. Enter the initial planning stage with caution and thoughtfulness; a poorly designed program is likely to fail. Early in the planning process, consult with those people who have experience in designing prevention programs and review the literature that reports efforts to address these target problems.

2. Clearly define and describe the problem or condition you are attempting to prevent. Without an operational definition of your target problem, you cannot design an effective program of prevention.

3. Identify the indicators of the problem you are addressing and its current level of seriousness so that you can later measure the impact of your prevention effort. Without a way of measuring success, your program is not likely to attract funding and support for more than a brief demonstration period. Make sure that these indicators are understandable, measurable, and important to those who are paying for this prevention program. Consult the literature and people skilled at program evaluation (see Item 15.9) early in the planning process.

4. Recognize that any plan you may select to prevent a problem rests on the knowledge, beliefs, and assumptions made about when, why, and how this problem develops, as well as judgments about which individuals or groups are most likely to experience this problem. In other words, a prevention program is built on a specific *theory of causation*. Thus, a critical step in planning is to formulate and articulate one's beliefs about the nature and causes of the problem to be prevented. This is a challenge because the social and behavioral sciences are seldom able to identify clear cause and effect relationships. Social problems are complex and a whole host of interrelated factors contribute to their development.

5. Once the theory of causation to be followed has been identified, it is necessary to decide which contributing factors, if any, can be influenced and changed. Identify the specific risk and protective factors related to the problem you want to prevent. A *risk factor* is a condition, situation, or set of circumstances that increases the likelihood that a person will develop the problem you seek to prevent. A *protective factor* is a condition or circumstance that reduces the chance that the problem will develop. The prevention program should be designed to weaken or reduce risk factors and, at the same time, strengthen or expand protective factors. As a general rule, a prevention program is most likely to be effective and efficient if it targets those at greatest risk of developing the problem.

6. Next, determine how the necessary changes can best be accomplished. In many cases, important contributing causes (e.g., large-scale economic and societal forces) are beyond the reach of community-based programs. A social worker may choose instead to engage in advocacy for change at the state or national levels. In other cases, the action plan would require intervention at the local level or at both the local and national levels.

SELECTED BIBLIOGRAPHY

Albee, George W., and Thomas P. Gullotta, eds. *Primary Prevention Works. Issues in Children's and Families' Lives,* vol. 6. Thousand Oaks, CA: Sage, 1997.

Benard, Bonnie. *Fostering Resiliency in Kids: Protective Factors in the Family, School, and Community.* Portland, OR: Western Regional Center for Drug-Free Schools and Communities, Northwest Regional Educational Laboratory, 1991.

Bloom, Martin. *Primary Prevention Practices. Issues in Children's and Families' Lives,* vol. 5. Thousand Oaks, CA: Sage, 1996.

Simeonsson, Rune, ed. *Risk, Resilience and Prevention.* Baltimore: Paul Brooks, 1994.

13.13 Establishing Formal Interagency Collaboration

PURPOSE: To improve services to clients through the exchange and sharing of agency resources.

DISCUSSION: It is useful to visualize the relationships among agencies as existing on a continuum, potentially ranging from competition to collaboration:

competition ↔ cooperation ↔ coordination ↔ collaboration

When in *competition* with other agencies, an agency engages in actions necessary to secure and hold on to the financial resources and the community and political support it needs to continue operation. It does not share resources or information with other agencies because doing so might place it at a disadvantage in the competition. Mattessich and Monsey (1992) distinguish between cooperation, coordination, and collaboration:

> *Cooperation* is characterized by informal relationships that exist without any commonly defined mission, structure, or planning effort. Information is shared as needed, and authority is retained by each organization. . . . Resources are [kept] separate, as are rewards.
>
> *Coordination* is characterized by more formal relationships and understanding of compatible missions. Some planning and division of roles are required, and communication channels are established. Authority still rests with the individual organizations. . . . Resources are available to participants and rewards are mutually acknowledged.

> *Collaboration* connotes a more durable and pervasive relationship. Collaborations bring previously separated organizations into a new structure with full commitment to a common mission. Such relationships require comprehensive planning and well defined communication channels operating on many levels. Authority is determined by the collaborative structure. Risk is much greater because each member contributes its own resources and reputation. Resources are pooled or jointly secured and the [rewards] are shared. (p. 39)

Although most agencies speak to the importance of working together, a number of factors keep them from doing so. These include the following:

- Competition is significant for scarce resources, especially when organizational or program survival depends on securing money that could be allocated to other agencies.
- Categorical funding and other restrictions on how funds can be spent make it difficult to share resources or assign them to some new purpose.
- An overburdened and underfunded service system severely limits the staff time and resources available for planning and implementing complex cooperative or collaborative activities.
- The desire for agency and professional status and power create "turf" problems that are barriers to cooperation, conflict resolution, and planning.
- Differences in agency philosophies, values, and practice frameworks become barriers to agreement on a common purpose and approach.

Indeed, finding ways to work together can be a challenge because each agency has its own special mission and constituency, its own policies and procedures, and its own restrictions on how its funds and staff time may be used. Despite these difficulties, coordination and collaboration are both necessary and possible. Here are some examples of areas where agencies can collaborate:

- *Purchase of services.* One agency contracts with another to provide certain services; for example, a public agency purchases group home services from a private agency.
- *Joint budgeting.* Two or more agencies commit a portion of their budgets to a specific activity, often for the purpose of creating the match needed to secure a grant.
- *Joint funding.* Two or more agencies pool their funds to achieve an objective beyond the reach of a single agency.
- *Joint studies.* Two or more agencies fund and or conduct research or a needs assessment desired by both.
- *Centralized information processing.* Two or more agencies share data-processing systems used in recordkeeping, program planning, grant management, or case management.
- *Public relations.* There is joint planning and dissemination of publicity and information about agency programs and community needs.

- *Procedural integration.* Two or more agencies adopt a uniform system of recordkeeping, utilize the same intake forms, use the same computer program, and so on, as ways of facilitating interagency communication, program planning, or the evaluation of services.
- *Shared program evaluation resources.* Several agencies hire a specialist to examine their interagency coordination or conduct evaluations of individual programs.
- *Centralized information and referral.* Several agencies operate and fund a centralized service needed to guide clients to the proper agency.
- *Interagency coordination of client services.* Several agencies agree to exchange information and share in the decision making necessary for case management, case coordination, the handling of grievances by clients, and so on.
- *Sharing of special services.* Several agencies pool resources in order for all to gain access to outside consultants, case assessments by specialists, transportation for clients, or needed staff training.
- *Standards and guidelines.* Several agencies jointly develop standards of service quality or staff performance.
- *Loaner staff.* A staff person with special expertise from one agency is "loaned" to another for a special project.
- *Outstationing of staff.* A staff member from one agency is housed in another agency in order to more easily reach certain clients or to better achieve interagency coordination of services.
- *Volunteer bureaus.* Several agencies share in the recruitment and training of the volunteers needed by the individual agencies.

Several preconditions are beneficial to successful interagency coordination and collaboration:

- A prior history of these agencies working together exists, as do mutual trust and respect.
- There is clear support for interagency cooperation and collaboration by the media or others who shape community opinion and by the decision makers who control the resources needed by the agencies.
- The group planning the cooperative or collaborative effort includes representatives from each agency and each segment of the community who will be affected by these activities.
- The agencies understand and agree with each other's goals, values, and methods of operation.
- Key administrators and participants know and trust each other and communicate clearly
- The staff of each agency involved truly believe that working together is in their self-interest.
- Agencies enter into a written agreement that specifies their roles, rights, and responsibilities in their joint activities (see Item 13.14).
- Agencies agree on concrete and attainable goals and objectives, but ones that are at least partially different from those held by each agency individually.

- Sufficient funds or in-kind contributions and staff time are available to support the needed effort and activity.
- At least one energetic, inspiring, and highly motivated individual is committed to making the collaborative arrangement work.

Those wishing to promote interagency coordination and collaboration should consider the following guidelines:

1. Carefully examine your agency's purpose and programs and its funding base in an effort to identify those areas of service or activity that require a competitive strategy and those areas that offer an opportunity for coordination and collaboration.

2. Identify the new programs or services that you want to see developed but that are beyond your own agency's capability, yet might be possible if several agencies worked together and shared resources. Bring together representatives from all the agencies that might be interested in discussing the idea of pooling resources in order to reach a goal that is desired by all but is beyond the reach of each agency acting alone. Identify how all these agencies and their clients stand to benefit.

3. Conduct the research necessary to answer the many fiscal, administrative, legal, organizational, and staffing questions that will arise in discussions of coordination and collaboration. Obtain information on how similar agencies in other communities have successfully addressed these issues.

4. Recognize that coordination and collaboration activities involve some degree of risk for your organization and for all others involved. Before entering any serious discussions or negotiations on how agencies might share resources, each one must be clear as to what resources it can and cannot afford to give up or reallocate.

5. Assemble a team of agency representatives that have the authority to sanction and plan the coordination or collaboration activity. It is critically important that this team secure suggestions and guidance from all of those affected by this plan and from those who will be expected to carry out its provisions.

6. Sign an agreement that describes in detail the goals and objectives of the planned activity and the rights and responsibilities of each agency affected. Included in the agreement is a plan for monitoring and evaluating the activity and making necessary improvements.

SELECTED BIBLIOGRAPHY

Haeuser, Adrienne. *Factors Influencing Successful Collaboration: Examples from the NCCAN Prevention Consortium Projects.* Chicago: National Committee to Prevent Child Abuse, 1994.

Mattessich, Paul, and Barbara Monsey. *Collaboration: What Makes It Work—A Review of Research Literature on Factors in Successful Collaboration.* St. Paul, MN: Amherst H. Wilder Foundation, 1992.

Rossi, Robert, Kevin Gilmartin, and Charles Dayton. *Agencies Working Together.* Newbury Park, CA: Sage, 1982.

13.14 Developing Protocol Statements

PURPOSE: To improve service to clients through the use of protocol statements that specify the responsibilities of participating agencies.

DISCUSSION: When two or more agencies are involved in a particular case or other practice activity, it is critical to the well-being of the client that each clearly understands its own responsibilities and those of others involved. Increasingly, agencies formalize such relationships by using protocol statements. A ***protocol*** is a concise, written description of the steps to be taken by a professional or agency in a situation where mistakes or omissions can have serious negative consequences. Levy (1980) explains the use of protocols by hospital social workers as follows:

> The protocols are designed to ensure consistent and complete provision and documentation of social work services. Separate protocols have been developed for the specific types of social work problems encountered at the medical center. Each protocol lists the necessary steps in social work intervention for a particular problem. Both the appropriate intervention process and the necessary documentation are indicated by the protocol; that is, the social worker is to perform each activity listed and also document those activities for which documentation is required. (p. 21)

The following excerpts are from a 13-step protocol developed by Bertsche, Francetich, and Horejsi (1985) for use in a state child protective services agency during the investigative phase of child sexual abuse cases. The key actors in this example are Child Protective Services (CPS), law enforcement, and the County Attorney's Office (prosecutor). Because criminal prosecution of the offender is common in sexual abuse cases, it is critical that these three agencies understand who is responsible for specific activities and know the preferred sequence of activities.

Protocol: Child Sexual Abuse Investigation

1. *Receive Referral* (i.e., report of alleged abuse)
   - CPS social worker speaks with referral source if possible. Obtain specifics (i.e., location of alleged incident, quotations from child). Make collateral contacts such as: individuals with knowledge of the sexual abuse as mentioned by referral source; school; doctors or other medical information sources; and the police department to discover if the offender named has a past arrest record for sexual molestation.
   - Contact County Attorney and advise of referral and that it will be investigated. If County Attorney is not available, a message left with the secretary.
2. *Interview with Child* CPS worker conducts interview with the child but obtains only enough information to determine that, most likely, abuse has occurred. Interview will be conducted in a manner appropriate to the developmental level of the child.
3. *Assessment* Based on information gathered from the child in Step 2, worker assesses need for:
   - Emergency placement.
   - Medical exam (non-offending parent may arrange this if parent believes and is supportive of child).
   - Action concerning other siblings in the home.

4. *County Attorney/CPS Consultation* CPS worker advises the County Attorney of action taken thus far. In conjunction with County Attorney, CPS worker arranges formal interview using one of the following:
   - Social worker and mental health therapist.
   - Social worker and law enforcement representative.
   - Any combination determined to be most appropriate.
5. *Formal Interview* (In some instances the non-offending parent is interviewed first, and if supportive of child, is present at the formal interview but seated behind the child.)
   - The interview is conducted in the manner determined most appropriate by the social worker and County Attorney. Emphasis should be on making this interview as non-threatening and non-traumatic for child as possible.
   - A tape recorder supported by written notes will suffice, if video equipment is not available. There should be two methods of recording used in case one malfunctions. Once taken, the report (tape, film, notes, etc.) forms evidence and needs to be appropriately protected. (Usually the Sheriff's Office or Police Department maintains the tapes.)
6. *Interview with Non-Offending Parent(s)* In this interview the worker assesses the non-offending parent's ability to protect the child from further abuse, the level of support for the child, and the need for out-of-home placement. If alleged offender is present, he/she is told that the referral will be made to law enforcement. (pp. 2.1–2.3)

The other steps in this 13-step protocol are (7) "Request for Legal Action Via Civil Court (when appropriate)," (8) "Separation of Alleged Offender from Child," (9) "Interview with Offender," (10) "Follow-Up," (11) "Prosecution," (12) "Ongoing Casework," and (13) "Treatment Plan."

SELECTED BIBLIOGRAPHY

Bertsche, Jon, Sherry Francetich, and Charles Horejsi. *Protocol Notebook for Child Welfare Workers.* Missoula: University of Montana, Department of Social Work, 1985.

Horejsi, Charles, Jon Bertsche, Sherry Francetich, Bill Collins, and Russell Francetich. "Protocols in Child Welfare." *Child Welfare* 66 (September/October 1987): 423–431.

Levy, Louis. "An Integrated Data Management System for Social Service." *Quality Review Bulletin* 6 (October 1980): 20–25.

14 Intervention and Monitoring

INTRODUCTION

The intervention and monitoring phase of the change process transforms all prior efforts to assess and plan into action (i.e., it is the time when the plans are implemented). At this point, the social worker is responsible for carrying out his or her part of the plan, helping the client perform agreed upon tasks, seeing that the necessary resources are brought to bear on the situation, monitoring progress, and helping stabilize any positive changes that occur.

Intervention is the most visible phase of the change process. Sometimes called the action phase, ***intervention*** is the time when people "do things" that are intended to change how they act, feel, or think about a troublesome situation in their lives or the way they interact with some aspect of their environments. Change, in and of itself, does not improve social functioning. To be worthwhile, it must be the correct type of change and the change must be sustained after the worker's services are terminated.

Perhaps because intervention requires concrete actions and typically takes up most of the time and energy expended during a change process, many helpful intervention techniques have been developed. In this book, for example, more than one-third of the techniques and guidelines selected for inclusion are related to intervention. Often, the greatest challenge for the social worker serving individuals, families, groups, organizations, and communities is to select the most appropriate approach to facilitate change.

As the interventive activities unfold, another task of the social worker is to ***monitor*** or keep track of what is happening and continuously evaluate the progress of the intervention. Depending on how well it is succeeding, the social worker must decide if the intervention should be continued, modified, or possibly aborted and a new plan and contract negotiated. Monitoring differs from evaluation in that monitoring occurs while the intervention is happening, whereas evaluation takes place at the end of the change process—looking back to assess what happened.

One often overlooked element of monitoring is continuing to examine the situation for a period of time before completely terminating the professional relationship and the change process. Whenever change occurs, various systems are disrupted, and progress will possibly deteriorate over time. The social worker should therefore attempt to determine if the change is more than a temporary accommodation to the interventive activities and ensure that the desired change become firmly established as part of the ongoing functioning for the client and/or the relevant environment.

SECTION A

TECHNIQUES AND GUIDELINES FOR DIRECT PRACTICE

When working with individuals, families, and small groups, the social worker's responsibility is to adapt the intervention approach to the uniqueness of the people involved and to support the clients as they take the necessary actions to bring about the planned change. The worker, too, must constantly monitor the client's response to the process and regularly assess progress toward the agreed upon objectives.

Intervention Activities. It is beyond the scope of this book to delineate all of the intervention activities in which a social worker might engage. As identified in Chapter 6, the worker must select an appropriate practice framework to address the specific client situation and choose from his or her repertoire of intervention techniques the appropriate ones to carry out the plan. Regardless of the techniques selected, the following "25 reminders" of factors that affect direct practice success are useful to consider:

1. A positive helping relationship is at the core of an effective change process. Successful intervention is more than the sterile application of techniques. It requires people (clients, social workers, and others) working together to change existing patterns. The process is never easy and takes time, energy, persistence, and a willingness to confront and struggle with complex problems.

2. The social worker's job is to facilitate problem solving by the client. The solution chosen by the client may not be the one that the worker would select, yet the worker must recognize that it is the client who will live with the decisions that are made.

3. Problem solving is mostly a process of searching for options and making hard decisions that lead to change. The decisions must grow out of the client's own values, belief system, and usual methods of coping.

4. A client is only motivated to change that which he or she perceives to be a real problem. The individual is motivated to work on a problem only when he or she feels hopeful that a solution is possible.

5. Remember that your client's behavior is always purposeful. Even dysfunctional behavior serves a purpose by meeting a need or mitigating some conflict or other problem.

6. View your client and his or her situation in context. People do not live in a vacuum. Everything affects everything else. Life is complex; do not proceed as if it were totally logical or completely controllable. Help your client to take control of those things he or she can control and to give up efforts to control those things over which her or she has no control.

7. Emphasize empathy. Strive to view the world through your client's eyes. Remember, his or her world is not your world, nor does it have to be. Realize that your client is probably doing the best he or she knows how.

8. Always demonstrate genuine respect and caring for your client, even if his or her behavior is abrasive, obnoxious, or repulsive. Do not be afraid to let your client know you care—if you do not care, then be afraid for yourself.

9. Remember that it is not your responsibility nor right to judge or punish a client for his or her problems or troublesome behavior. Most clients have already received an abundance of disapproval from others. Disapproval from you will only dampen communication and harm your relationship. Seek to accept and understand. Because acceptance and understanding are in such short supply, they will have great value to your client.

10. Do not moralize or preach. You do not need to argue the "rightness" of your choices in life. If your moral character is worthy of emulation, your client will be influenced by your behavior; explanations will not be necessary.

11. Reach for and explore your client's feelings. Struggling with confusing and conflicting feelings is what helping is all about. Do not be afraid of emotion. If feelings scare you, work with things, not people.

12. Maintain confidentiality. Respecting your client's desire for privacy is critical to the establishment of trust. Trust is essential to effective helping.

13. Expect a client who is struggling with serious psychosocial problems to feel frustrated and overwhelmed. His or her anger may be directed toward you, even when you are not the true source of the frustration. When this happens, do not take it personally nor react defensively.

14. Develop self-awareness and self-discipline. Do not allow your own needs or problems to distort the helping process. Meet your emotional needs and handle your problems outside your professional relationships. Your client already has a fair share of life's problems; do not ask him or her to worry about yours.

15. Listen more than you talk. What your client has to say is much more important than what you have to say to your client. Keep your own message short, simple, and clear. Leave the jargon in your textbooks and at professional conferences.

16. Do not take sides in your client's conflicts with others. If you do, you will almost always destroy the relationship you have with your client.

17. Search for your client's strengths and for positives in the situation. Build on those strengths. Give more attention to what your client can do rather than to what he or she is unable to do.

18. Do not allow yourself or your client to become discouraged by the labels others have attached to your client. View all labeling by professionals and diagnostic statements with a degree of skepticism.

19. Believe in the possibilities of change. Remain hopeful—especially when your client is feeling hopeless. Expect him or her to work toward agreed upon goals; do not be afraid to challenge and confront the client when reasonable progress is not being made.

20. A client should participate as much as possible in the professional and agency decisions that affect his or her life. Keep your client informed of what you are doing on his or her behalf.

21. To the extent possible, a client should be encouraged to make use of the informal resources that exist within his or her own social network (e.g., family, friends, neighbors, natural helpers, etc.).

22. Avoid creating dependence. Plan and conduct interventions so your client can learn problem-solving skills that will be useful and needed in the future. The help you provide should prepare and empower your client to function and cope without your assistance.

23. Recognize your limitations but do not underestimate your abilities. Consult with others when confronted with a situation you do not know how to handle. Refer your client to another professional when he or she has needs that are beyond the scope of your agency's program or your own skills.

24. Do not defend an agency procedure or policy that is illogical or unfair. Doing so only makes you look foolish and insensitive. It is best simply to acknowledge that the policy or procedure in question needs to be changed but that it cannot now be changed and therefore must be followed.

25. Remember that human beings are incredibly resilient and adaptive. They can put up with a great deal of pain and discomfort if they understand why it is necessary in order to reach a goal they desire.

In this chapter, nearly 40 direct-service intervention techniques are presented. Some are simple tools (e.g., the talking stick, envelope budgeting) and others are quite complex (e.g., dealing with the client on psychotropic medication). The reader is urged to view these techniques as a partial list of the range from which a social worker might select for a specific intervention. Social work literature, supervisors, and colleagues may be sources of still others. None, however, is likely to be successful unless it is used by a competent social worker.

Monitoring Activities. Monitoring involves keeping watch over the change process. To do this, the social worker must regularly interact in person or through other communication forms with the clients. The worker must be sensitive to how the change activities are affecting the client, but also to how other people or social institutions are being affected. If progress toward the agreed upon objectives is lacking, the worker then should suggest needed modifications in the intervention plan and possibly even cycle back to the beginning phases of the process to reexamine and clarify the issues being addressed and to look for other solutions.

Whenever possible, the social worker should share the results of this monitoring with the clients. Clients' ability to identify changes that are occurring, whether positive or negative, is an important factor in maintaining the effort to complete the intervention activities. Most often, these results are fed back to the client in an informal manner as part of regular counseling or therapy sessions. Increasingly, however, social workers are collecting empirical trend data about client change and feeding that information back to clients to assist them in understanding the affects of the services being provided. Some of the commonly used tools for organizing empirical data regarding changes that result from direct practice interventions can be found in Items 15.1 through 15.5.

14.1 Planning an Interview

PURPOSE: To formulate a tentative plan for an interview or contact with a client.

DISCUSSION: One of the most common errors made by new workers is to go into a session without a clear purpose. Just as there should be an overall intervention plan, there should be a plan for each contact with the client. This plan must be tentative and flexible in order to respond to client concerns that could not be anticipated. The following questions can help the worker formulate such a plan:

1. What are the overall goals and objectives of the intervention with this client? How will my next contact relate to these goals and objectives?

2. What needs to be accomplished during the interview or meeting? What decisions need to be reached during the session? Who needs to be present?

3. Should the next contact be a face-to-face or a telephone interview? One-on-one, family, or group session?

4. Will other professionals and/or concerned individuals participate in the session (e.g., a family conference in a medical setting)? What objectives do these other participants have and how might differences in expectations be resolved?

5. How much time do I have to devote to the interview or meeting? How much time can the client devote to the session?

6. Where and when will the interview take place? What arrangements are necessary prior to the interview (e.g., scheduling interviewing room, transportation, care for client's children)?

7. What techniques might be used during the session to complete important tasks and work toward intervention goals and objectives?

8. What factors related to the client's values or religious beliefs and social and family network need to be considered in preparing for the session?

9. What factors related to the client's current emotional state (e.g., anger, fear, confusion, depression, etc.) need to be considered in preparing for the session?

10. What factors related to the client's current physical functioning (e.g., mobility, pain, discomfort, hearing problems, effects of medication, etc.) need to be considered in preparing for the interview or meeting?

11. What documentation on this contact is necessary for the agency record?

SELECTED BIBLIOGRAPHY

Kadushin, Alfred. *The Social Work Interview*, 4th ed. New York: Columbia University Press, 1997.

Lukas, Susan. *Where to Start and What to Ask: An Assessment Handbook*. New York: W. W. Norton, 1993.

Murphy, Bianca, and Carolyn Dillon. *Interviewing in Action*. Pacific Grove, CA: Brooks/Cole, 1998.

14.2 Information and Advice

PURPOSE: To enhance the client's problem-solving capacity by providing needed information and guidance.

DISCUSSION: ***Information giving*** refers to providing a client with information he or she needs to make a decision or carry out a task. As used here, the term ***advice giving*** refers to worker statements that recommend what a client should do. In information giving, the client feels free to use the information as he or she sees fit; in advice giving, the client clearly senses the social worker's preference.

One of the common errors made by inexperienced social workers is to give advice when the client has not asked for it. This is an understandable error because often the worker has known other clients with similar problems or has had personal experience with the concern faced by the client, and, naturally, the worker wants the client to benefit from those experiences. However, there are many pitfalls in advice giving, and the worker needs to be very cautious in using this technique. Follow these ***guidelines for advice giving:***

1. Before giving advice, reflect on how you feel when someone gives you advice. Remember that most people do not follow advice, even when they have requested it. On those rare occurrences when someone does follow advice, it was usually offered by a person he or she has known for a long time and trusts completely.

2. Whether the giving of advice is appropriate depends largely on the purpose of the worker-client interaction. If it is a counseling-therapy relationship, giving advice is rarely appropriate. If the purpose relates to referral, brokering, or advocacy, advice giving may be appropriate and necessary.

3. Do not offer advice unless you have determined that the client genuinely wants your opinions and suggestions. Test the client's receptivity to advice by asking questions such as: Are you looking for some suggestions? or If you want, I could give you a few ideas about that.

4. When you do give advice, present it in a way that says, "This is what I would do" or "This is what others have done." But leave the responsibility for deciding what to do to the client. Explain the reasoning behind the guidance you offer. Never give advice on a topic outside your area of training and expertise.

5. Consider the issue of legal liability if you advise a client and he or she later suffers an adverse personal or financial consequence as a result of your recommendation. For example, beware of advising a client who asks questions such as: Do you think I should get a divorce? Do you think I should quit my job and look for another? Do you think it would be OK if I cut down on my medicine?

6. Be alert to the dangers of giving advice to a manipulative client, who may then hold you responsible if things do not turn out well (e.g., "I did what you said and it didn't work, so it's your fault"). Also be alert to the danger of encouraging dependency in a client who can and should take responsibility for decision making.

When providing information to a client, keep these ***guidelines for information giving*** in mind:

1. Carefully consider the client's current state of mind when giving information. Adapt what you say to his or her educational background, level of intelligence, command of the language, fears, and the like. If it is likely that the client will misunderstand, give the same information to the client's significant others.

2. Provide information or directions in a logical, organized, step-by-step fashion. Give the client time to think about what you are saying, and invite him or her to ask questions to clarify any uncertainty. Never assume that the client understands what you have said. Look for signs of misunderstanding. After giving information to a client, it is desirable to end your message with something like: "Now I want to make sure that I was clear in what I have been telling you. Would you please repeat back to me what you heard me say?" Do not simply ask, "Do you understand?" All too often, people will answer by saying that they understand even when they do not. It is important always to check that your message was understood.

3. Complicated, multistep instructions (e.g., how to get to another agency) may need to be written down. Also write out names, addresses, and phone numbers needed by the client.

4. Use pronouns (e.g., *it, this, that, those, them*) with caution. For example, the statement, "Fill out the form and take it to the person at the desk over there" could be very confusing to someone who does not know what the "form," "it," "person," or "over there" mean specifically. It is best to use the exact word rather than a pronoun, or provide sufficient description so there can be no mistake about what or to whom you are referring.

5. Speak distinctly. Avoid talking fast or using words the client may not understand. Remember that poor grammar and awkwardly constructed sentences result in confusion and misinterpretation.

SELECTED BIBLIOGRAPHY

Brill, Naomi. *Working with People,* 6th ed. New York: Longman, 1998.

Middleman, Ruth, and Gale Goldberg Wood. *Skills for Direct Practice in Social Work.* New York: Columbia University Press, 1990.

Shulman, Lawrence. *The Skills of Helping: Individuals, Families, and Groups,* 4th ed. Itasca, IL: F. E. Peacock, 1999.

14.3 Encouragement, Reassurance, and Universalization

PURPOSE: To enhance the client's problem-solving capacity by providing supportive and encouraging statements.

DISCUSSION: The interrelated techniques of encouragement, reassurance, and universalization are especially useful and important in work with children and with clients who lack self-confidence. ***Encouragement*** often takes the form of worker statements that express confidence in the client's capabilities. It is a means of recognizing and supporting client strengths (see Item 12.7). When using this technique, the worker must be genuine and send a clear, targeted message that explains why the worker has confidence in the client—for example: "On the basis of how you managed to learn three new responsibilities over the past six months, I think you are capable of handling this new task even though you are feeling scared."

Overgeneralizations such as "You're the greatest" or "I am sure you can do anything you want to do" are seldom perceived by the client as genuine because he or she knows they are exaggerations. At best, the client accepts such a statement as a gesture of politeness; at worst, he or she takes it as a put-down. By always being realistic and tying words of encouragement to some facts, the worker will avoid sounding phony.

Reassurance is used when the client is feeling doubtful about his or her thoughts or decisions when they are, in fact, reasonable and realistic. However, inexperienced workers are often too quick to use reassurance. Woods and Hollis (1990, 107) warn that reassurance "must be used with delicacy and discrimination. Yielding to the temptation to overuse reassurance in an attempt to build up a relationship or because the worker cannot endure the client's anxiety may merely leave the client with the feeling that the worker does not fully comprehend the reasons for guilt or anxiety, or that the worker is deficient in moral discrimination and therefore is not a person whose judgment matters."

Universalization is a form of reassurance that consists of statements explaining to the client that his or her thoughts, feelings, or behavior are similar to those of other people—for example: "I have known many people who had to place their parent in a nursing home and they described the same feelings you are expressing." This technique is intended to counteract the client's feelings of being different or deviant.

In every session, the worker should take some time to focus the discussion on client choices and experiences that make clients feel good about themselves. This is important because so many sessions end up focusing mostly on client problems and on things the client does not like about himself or herself or his or her situation. To counterbalance this attention to the negative, workers should create opportunities that encourage clients to recognize and verbalize their positive personal traits, strengths, and successes.

SELECTED BIBLIOGRAPHY

Gorden, Raymond. *Basic Interviewing Skills.* Itasca, IL: F. E. Peacock, 1992.

Woods, Mary, and Florence Hollis. *Casework: A Psychosocial Therapy,* 4th ed. New York: McGraw-Hill, 1990.

14.4 Reinforcement and Related Behavioral Techniques

PURPOSE: To modify the frequency, intensity, or duration of a specific behavior.

DISCUSSION: Behavioral techniques are some of the most powerful available to the social worker when the intervention objective is to help the client learn a new behavior or modify an existing one. The social worker usually employs behavioral techniques when trying either to strengthen (increase) or weaken (decrease) a particular target behavior. The term ***target behavior*** refers to an operationally defined and measurable behavior that is the focus of the intervention.

Reinforcement is any event or activity that increases the likelihood that a target behavior will occur more frequently than in the past. Thus, a reinforcer is anything that strengthens a target behavior. There are two forms of reinforcement: positive and negative. ***Positive reinforcement*** involves adding, presenting, or giving something to the client (such as attention, objects of value, or privileges) that has the effect of increasing the target behavior. Ordinarily, a positive reinforcer is a pleasurable event or an obvious reward, but sometimes even a painful event can prove to be a positive reinforcer. Thus, only by observing the effects of what you believe is a reinforcer can you know for sure that it is a reinforcer. For this reason, it is important to establish a *baseline measurement* that describes the frequency, intensity, or duration of the target behavior prior to intervention. As a general rule, what a person does when he or she does not have to do something else is an indicator of what is reinforcing for that person (e.g., how a person spends extra time and money).

There are two kinds of positive reinforcers: primary and secondary. *Primary reinforcers* are inherently rewarding and almost universally reinforcing. Examples include food, water, sex, warmth, and so on. *Secondary reinforcers* are learned, usually as a result of having been associated with primary reinforcers. Examples include money, tokens, and new clothes. Social reinforcers—such as praise, attention, and hugs—are usually considered to be secondary reinforcers, but there is some evidence that they are universally reinforcing.

Both positive and negative reinforcement increase the frequency, intensity, or duration of a target behavior. ***Negative reinforcement*** involves subtracting or removing some condition that is aversive or unpleasant to the client, which has the effect of increasing or strengthening the target behavior. Negative reinforcement is often confused with punishment, but they are not the same. Punishment weakens the target behavior, whereas negative reinforcement strengthens the behavior.

As a technique of behavior change, ***punishment*** involves the presentation of an unwanted or unpleasant stimulus that has the effect of suppressing a target behavior or reducing its strength. For ethical and legal reasons, the social worker must usually avoid the use of punishment. Most agencies and treatment programs prohibit the use of punishment for one or more of the following reasons:

1. Often, the results of punishment are short term. When the threat of punishment is not present, the target behavior often recurs.
2. The use of punishment provides a poor behavioral model for the client.
3. Punishment can become excessive or dangerous when administered by an angry or frustrated person.
4. Punishment may also suppress desirable behavior and make the client afraid to respond in normal ways.
5. The use of physical punishment may make the worker vulnerable to a civil lawsuit or criminal charges (e.g., assault).

A behavior that is not reinforced tends to decrease in frequency, duration, or intensity. The term *extinction* describes the planned withdrawal of whatever reinforces a target behavior so as to eliminate or weaken that behavior.

There are two basic ***reinforcement schedules:*** continuous and intermittent. *Continuous reinforcement* provides a reinforcer each time the desired target behavior occurs. In *intermittent reinforcement,* the target behavior is not rewarded every time it occurs. Continuous reinforcement is often used in the first stages of a program designed to teach a new behavior because it allows faster learning than intermittent reinforcement. However, a behavior that has been continuously reinforced is comparatively easy to extinguish. To make the newly learned behavior resistant to extinction, continuous reinforcement should be replaced by intermittent reinforcement.

A behavior that is maintained by *random reinforcement* (e.g., slot machine, bingo, fishing, etc.) or learned during a time of high emotion or personal crisis is highly resistant to change and difficult to extinguish.

When one behavior is described as being incompatible with another, it means that a person cannot perform both behaviors concurrently. For example, a child cannot play basketball and watch TV at the same time. A highly useful technique in planned behavior change is to recognize such an incompatibility and ignore an unwanted target behavior while at the same time reinforcing an incompatible desired behavior. This is called ***differential reinforcement.***

The techniques of chaining, prompting, fading, and shaping are useful when the objective is to help a client learn a new behavior. These are frequently used in training programs for people who are mentally retarded, in speech therapy, and in certain aspects of physical rehabilitation. ***Chaining*** refers to a procedure that breaks down a complex behavior (e.g., dressing) into many separate steps or components and teaches only one of these steps at a time. As new components are learned, they are "chained," or linked, to the ones already learned. The number of steps needed to teach a particular behavior will depend on the complexity of the behavior and the capacity of the client. There are two types of chaining: forward and backward.

In *forward chaining,* the first step in a chain is taught first. For example, in teaching a client to put on his trousers, the client would first be taught how to pick up and hold his pants. All subsequent steps are taught in order of their natural sequence. This sequence is determined by observing several people perform the behavior and noting the most common sequence of steps.

In *backward chaining,* the last step in the chain is taught first. Thus, all of the steps in the sequence would be done for the client except the one being taught. For example, in dressing training, the first step to be taught would be "pulls pants up to the waist." One advantage of backward chaining is that the last step in the chain is always the one that is reinforced. Thus, the client is always reinforced at the very end of the behavior chain (e.g., when he has finished putting on his pants). For some self-help skills, such as hand and face washing, backward chaining is not feasible.

The term ***prompting*** describes any form of assistance given by the worker to help the client perform the target behavior. A prompt may be a verbal cue or instruction, a gesture or other nonverbal cue, or physically moving or guiding the client through the behavior. Prompting should be used only when necessary.

Fading is the process of gradually withdrawing prompts and decreasing the frequency of reinforcement as the client begins to learn the desired behavior. In the first steps of a training program, the worker will use continuous reinforcement and frequent prompting to help establish the new behavior. Later, when the client regularly performs the target behavior, the worker will gradually "fade out" or decrease the frequency of reinforcement and prompting.

Shaping is a technique of building a new behavior by reinforcing close approximations of the desired response. For example, a speech therapist teaching a child to say "cookie" may reward the child when he says "gowk." Perhaps later, the child is reinforced for saying "gook-koo" and still later, "gookie." Finally, after many weeks of reinforcing the child for closer and closer approximations of the desired sound, the child is able to say "cookie."

Much of what one learns—especially social or interactional behavior—is learned by observing others and subsequently imitating their behavior. This learning process is termed ***modeling.*** Needless to say, both functional and dysfunctional behaviors are learned this way. A social worker can enhance the learning of functional behavior by keeping several principles in mind:

- Individual A is most likely to imitate the behavior of individual B if he or she views B as having some valued status (e.g., power, prestige, attractiveness, etc.) and if he or she observes B being rewarded for the behavior.
- In addition, individual A must in some way identify with B and feel similar. If A views B as being completely different, individual A may conclude there is no chance he or she could actually perform the behavior and/or that there was little or no chance that it would be rewarded.
- Individual A is most likely to learn B's behavior if he or she has an opportunity to perform or practice the behavior soon after observing it and is then rewarded for the behavior.

Under ordinary conditions, licensed foster parents and child care staff working in hospitals, treatment centers, and group homes are prohibited from using any form of physical punishment. The procedure termed ***time out*** is an alternative to physical discipline. Its purpose is to reduce or eliminate a problem behavior by temporarily removing the client from an environment that is reinforcing the unwanted behavior. Consider this set of instructions given to a foster parent who is learning methods of nonviolent child care for use with a 7-year-old, male, foster child:

1. Find an area in your home that can be used for time out. If he kicks, throws things, or has tantrums, be sure to choose an area that has no breakable or dangerous objects. You might use his bedroom or other quiet area that is well lighted and ventilated.

2. Identify the behaviors that will always result in time out (i.e., clearly define the target behavior). For example, you may decide to use time out whenever he hits other children or screams at you.

3. Each time a target behavior occurs, use the time-out procedure immediately. Walk up to the child, explain what rule was broken, and tell him what must now happen. For example, "Johnny, whenever you hit your sister, you must go on time out." Accompany the child to the time-out area; do not look at or talk to him on the way. If he resists, carry him there as quickly as possible.

4. Leave him in the time-out area for a preselected period of time. As a rule of thumb, use the formula of one minute per year of the child's age. At the end of the time period or when he is quiet and behaving well, go to the door and ask if he is ready to come out and behave correctly. For example, if Johnny threw toys, ask him, "Are you ready to come out and put your toys away?" If he hit his sister, ask, "Are you ready to come out and be friendly to your sister?"

5. If he answers this question "yes," have him come out and correct the earlier behavior. Reinforce the correct behavior with praise. For example, say, "I like the way you are picking up your toys."

6. If he does not answer "yes" or screams, cries, throws a tantrum, or displays other undesirable behavior, walk away from the door and wait until he is again quiet and behaving appropriately. Then go back and repeat the question.

7. At first, you may have to question him several times before he is ready to come out and correct the bad behavior. Do not be discouraged—just continue to follow these rules.

8. Try to arrange a special activity, privilege, or treat at the end of each day that he did not have to be taken to the time-out area, and tell him that the reward is for his good behavior.

SELECTED BIBLIOGRAPHY

Bellac, Alan, Michael Hersen, and Alan Kazdin, eds. *International Handbook on Behavior Modification and Therapy,* 2nd ed. New York: Plenum, 1990

Sanders, Matthew, and Mark Dadds. *Behavioral Family Intervention.* Boston: Allyn and Bacon, 1993.

Sundel, Sandra, and Martin Sundel. *Behavior Modification in the Human Services,* 3rd ed. Newbury Park, CA: Sage, 1993.

Thyer, Bruce, and John Wodarski. *Handbook of Empirical Social Work Practice.* New York: Wiley, 1998.

14.5 Behavioral Rehearsal

PURPOSE: To assist the client in learning a new behavior to better cope with a particular situation.

DISCUSSION: *Behavioral rehearsal* is a technique drawn from behavioral therapy that teaches a client how to handle a specific interpersonal exchange for which he or she feels unprepared. This technique helps reduce anxiety and builds the client's self-confidence about being able to handle the situation. Essentially, it is a form of role-playing that makes use of modeling and coaching. Like other forms of role-play, behavioral rehearsal provides the client with an opportunity to try out new behaviors in a protected environment and without risk of failure. For example, the technique can be used to prepare a client for a job interview (e.g., the social worker takes the role of the employer and conducts a simulated job interview). As the client practices the behavior, the worker provides feedback and offers suggestions and alternative ways of behaving. The worker may demonstrate or model the behavior, so it can be imitated by the client. Whether used during a one-to-one interview or during a group session, the steps are basically the same:

1. The client identifies the problem situation and then describes or demonstrates how he or she would usually behave in that situation.
2. The worker (and/or group members) makes suggestions on how the situation might be handled more effectively.

3. The client is given an opportunity to provide additional information about the problem or concern and to ask the worker (or group members) to further explain the suggestions.
4. A role-play is used to demonstrate the behavioral changes suggested to the client. The worker (or group members) will usually take the role of the client. However, the client may enact the behavior if he or she feels ready and understands the changes being suggested.
5. After the role-play, the worker (or members) first identifies the positive aspects of the performance, then makes additional suggestions for improvement. If necessary, the role-play is repeated to further illustrate the preferred way of behaving.
6. When the client understands how he or she ought to behave, he or she practices the behavior until satisfied with the performance.
7. Homework outside the session can be used to further the client's learning of the new behavior.

The major limitation of behavioral rehearsal is that the client may successfully learn what to do in the presence of the worker but may not be able to generalize it to the real world. Sometimes the real situation poses problems that cannot be anticipated during a practice session.

SELECTED BIBLIOGRAPHY

Curran, James, and Peter Monti, eds. *Social Skills Training.* New York: Guilford, 1982.
Garvin, Charles. *Contemporary Group Work,* 3rd ed. Boston: Allyn and Bacon, 1997.
Rose, Sheldon. *Group Therapy: A Behavioral Approach.* Englewood Cliffs, NJ: Prentice Hall, 1977.

14.6 Behavioral Contracting

PURPOSE: To modify a behavior through the mutual exchange of reinforcers.

DISCUSSION: A ***behavioral contract*** is an written agreement designed to bring about a change in a person's behavior. Usually, the contract involves an exchange of rewards or positive reinforcements between two or more persons. DeRisi and Butz (1975, 1–2) explain that behavior contracting "is a technique used to structure behavioral counseling by making each of the necessary elements of the process so clear and explicit that they may be written into an agreement for behavior change that is understandable and acceptable to everyone involved."

A behavioral contract can follow one or two forms: a contingency contract or a reciprocal behavioral contract. In a ***contingency contract,*** one person sets up a consequence associated with the behavior of another. For example, a group home manager may agree to take a resident to a movie if the resident cleans his or her room five days in a row. By contrast, the ***reciprocal behavior contract*** is an agreement between the members of a dyad (e.g., husband-wife), in which each agrees to reward the other for the performance of a desired behavior. For example, the husband agrees to take his wife to a movie of her choice if she will take the car to the repair shop, and she agrees to cook his favorite meal if he will clean the house.

Thus, we see that a behavioral contract might be negotiated between the social worker and the client, or the worker may help two or more clients (e.g., a husband and wife, parent and child) negotiate their own behavioral contract. Any behavior can become the focus or target of a contract so long as the behavior can be described clearly and is agreed to by everyone affected by the contract. Target behaviors should be described in positive terms. In other words, the contract should describe what a person *will* do rather than what he or she *will not* do. Also, the contract should be developed in a way that makes success likely, for success sustains motivation.

When helping to formulate a reciprocal behavioral contract to be used by a couple or family, the following guidelines are important:

1. Assist all parties to select tasks that will provide some immediate reward or relief from their problems. Make sure that each person stands to receive some desired payoff for participating and completing the tasks.
2. Select tasks that everyone agrees are worthwhile and possible, given the current circumstances.
3. Select tasks that are easily observed by others so there will be no disagreement as to whether a task was completed.
4. Select tasks that allow for approximation. It should be possible to observe even a partial success and a person's genuine effort to complete the task.
5. Set up a simple plan for recording task completion and the exchange of rewards. The plan should be one that can be easily monitored by the practitioner.
6. Before the participants leave the negotiation session, ask each one to describe and explain the contract and the tasks he or she has agreed to carry out. Make sure there is no misunderstanding.

Variations of the contingency behavioral contracting, often called *point systems* or *token economies,* are frequently used in special educational settings and residential treatment facilities. Under such systems, a client earns points or tokens for performing specific behaviors (e.g., completing homework, saying thank you, cleaning one's room) and can then use the tokens to "purchase" desired objects or privileges.

When using a contingency contract, the reinforcement (rewards) for compliance, along with any adverse consequences for noncompliance, should be clearly described and understood by all. Whenever noncompliance can have serious consequences for a client, the contract should be in writing. In other situations, a verbal agreement may suffice.

SELECTED BIBLIOGRAPHY

DeRisi, William, and George Butz. *Writing Behavioral Contracts.* Champaign, IL: Research Press, 1975.

Gambrill, Eileen. *Casework: A Competency Based Approach.* Englewood Cliffs, NJ: Prentice Hall, 1983.

Stuart, Richard. *Helping Couples Change: A Social Learning Approach to Marital Therapy.* New York: Guilford, 1980.

14.7 Role Reversal

PURPOSE: To assist the client in understanding the viewpoint and feelings of a significant other.

DISCUSSION: In a ***role reversal,*** a person is asked to assume the role of another and try to see things from the other person's perspective. The technique is especially useful during marriage or family counseling. The social worker may elect to use role reversal when two clients, such as husband and wife or parent and child, are in conflict, and when it is apparent that one or both has little awareness of how the other feels. The best time to use role reversal is when the two people have reached an impasse and keep repeating the same dialogue or when one is "stuck" on a particular perception.

The worker might initiate the role reversal by saying something like, "Joe and Susan, would you two be willing to try something? I would like you to reverse roles to see how it feels being the other person." The two people are then asked to switch chairs; if the clients do not change chairs, they often become confused as to which role they are playing. The worker should explain, "In this chair, you are yourself. In that chair, you are Joe."

Once they are in the role of the other, the social worker might get the discussion going by focusing attention on a particular line of repetitious or contentious dialogue. For example, "Joe, I want you to start playing Susan's part in this conflict and begin with the line 'Joe, you don't care about me.' And Susan, in the role of Joe, I want you to respond by saying how those words make you feel." As the discussion unfolds, the worker uses various interviewing techniques to encourage the expression of thoughts and feeling.

After a few minutes of role reversal, the worker has each person return to his or her own chair and perspective. The content of the role reversal is discussed in a way that helps each understand how and why the other thinks and feels about the issue that is causing the conflict.

When working with couples and families, the role reversal technique may be adapted for use as homework, asking the couple or family members to take a half hour at home prior to the next session and reverse roles. It also allows the individual to experience how his or her own behavior, as dramatized by another, affects others. It can provide insight and maybe even a little humor if the clients are instructed not to take the task too seriously.

SELECTED BIBLIOGRAPHY

Sherman, Robert, and Norman Fredman. *Handbook of Structured Techniques in Marriage and Family Therapy.* New York: Brunner/Mazel, 1986.

Sprafkin, Robert, N. Jane Gershaw, and Arnold Goldstein. *Social Skills for Mental Health.* Boston: Allyn and Bacon, 1993.

14.8 Managing Self-Talk

PURPOSE: To assist the client to manage emotional reactions by modifying distorted interpretations of reality.

DISCUSSION: Social work places much emphasis on viewing the client within an environmental context. The profession is particularly concerned about how the realities of life and external influences affect one's social functioning. However, in many situations, the client is more influenced by his or her interpretation than by reality itself.

The term ***self-talk*** refers to the messages that we give ourselves. What we "say" to ourselves reflects our unique interpretation of what we have experienced. Social workers who adhere to the theoretical assumptions of cognitive therapy emphasize that self-talk evokes emotional reactions, which, in turn, give rise to behaviors. Emery (1981) explains the basic principle of cognitive therapy:

> How you evaluate or think about your experiences determines how you react emotionally. If you think you've lost something, you'll feel sad; if you think you're in danger, you'll feel anxious; if you think others have treated you wrongly, you'll feel angry. Recent research has found that people with emotional disorders systematically distort their experiences. The direction and type of cognitive distortion determines the nature of the emotional disorder. (p. 23)

If a person habitually thinks about his or her experiences in distorting and irrational ways, he or she generates much inner turmoil and also creates problems in interpersonal relationships. Following are some common types of distortions:

- *All or nothing.* Experiences are evaluated in terms of the extremes of black and white, all right or all wrong; there is no grey area or middle ground (e.g., we conclude that a single mistake proves we are a complete failure).
- *Jumping to conclusions.* An unsupported and unrealistic conclusion is made on the basis of little or no evidence (e.g., we conclude that something is undesirable or unworkable even before we have gathered information).
- *Selective attention.* Attention is given to only those facts that support our preconceived ideas; facts that point to a different conclusion are dismissed.
- *Catastrophizing.* We anticipate and look for the worst possible outcome; we always expect something bad to happen.
- *Magnification of failure.* The meaning or importance of a setback or mistake is exaggerated (e.g., we have ten successes and one failure but we only think about the failure).
- *Minimization of success.* The importance of a positive experience or success is disregarded or played down (e.g., we attribute our success to dumb luck).
- *Negative beliefs about self, others, and the world.* We hold tightly to beliefs that everything and everybody, including ourselves, are bad, unchangeable, hopeless, and getting worse.

- *Personalization.* Every problem or negative happening is caused by our inadequacy. We take responsibility for things over which we have little or no control.
- *External locus of control.* We have no control over our lives; we believe that others control our lives or that whatever happens is a matter of fate.

McMullin (1986, 55–56) lists numerous examples of irrational thoughts that create problems for clients. These include beliefs such as: "Home is safe. Thus, the farther away from home I travel, the greater the danger"; "I must fit in with everybody else's values and behavior, otherwise I will be totally alone and rejected by everyone"; and "I must try as hard as I can in everything I attempt." By helping a client learn to think more critically, the worker can help him or her control troublesome emotions and behave more effectively. This is, of course, more difficult than it sounds. Patterns of thinking are habits; they are not easily changed and are themselves a barrier to change.

The social worker can use a five-step approach to help a client modify distortions in self-talk. Ask the client to do the following:

1. Identify what you are feeling and thinking right now.
2. Get in touch with your self-talk. Pay attention to extremes in thinking, as suggested by the use of words such as *never, can't, always, everybody, completely,* and so on.
3. Examine the objective reality of your situation. Once the facts have been identified, relax, take a deep breath, and repeat them out loud three times.
4. Notice that, when you hold to the facts and avoid using inaccurate words, you begin to feel differently and things do not seem as bad as before.
5. Keeping the facts of your situation clearly in mind, consider what you can do about it.

This five-step method is illustrated here in a dialogue between a social worker and a college student who has just learned that he failed a math exam:

Client: I cannot believe I am so stupid. I had a B average in math and got an F on the last test. I might as well leave school and get a job as a dishwasher. I am a complete failure. I don't deserve to be in school.

Worker: Wait a minute! You have said before you wanted to learn how to stop putting yourself down. Let's try something. Start by telling me again what you are feeling and thinking right now.

Client: Well, I just can't pass math tests. I'm stupid. I am embarrassed and I hate myself. I am never going to get through college. My parents are going to kill me for this. This is the worst possible thing that could have happened. My future is down the drain. Everything is just awful.

Worker: Let's take a look at that kind of self-talk. Try to recognize what you are saying to yourself; notice your extreme language. Let's take a look at the way things are in reality. Is it true you cannot pass math tests?

Client: Well, not really. I passed all of them before this one and I still have a B average in college.

Worker: Are your parents really going to kill you?

Client: Well, no, but they will be disappointed.

Worker: Is failing a test really the worst possible thing that could happen to you?

Client: Well, no, but it seems awful right now.

Worker: Does failing this test really mean you have no future?

Client: Well, I still have a future. I know what you are saying, and I agree that I am overreacting. But I don't know how to put a lid on those thoughts and feelings.

Worker: Do this for me. Repeat the truth—the reality—of your situation, which is as follows: I flunked one math test. My parents will be unhappy. I have a B average in college. I can remain in college. My life is not over.

Client: (repeats above)

Worker: Now take a couple of deep breaths and relax. Now say that again, three times.

Client: (client follows instruction)

Worker: How do you feel when you change your self-talk?

Client: Well, I guess it isn't as bad as I thought. I feel less upset than before.

Worker: Our emotions react to what we tell ourselves about our experiences. If your self-talk is distorted, your emotions are going to be more extreme and more negative than they need to be. You can use this technique yourself when your feelings start to get out of control. Certainly, your situation is not as bad as it seemed when you were telling yourself those awful things. But you still have to make some plans on how to prepare for your next math test. Now let's talk about that.

Once a client is able to describe his or her pattern of maladaptive self-talk, the cognitive restructuring techniques of self-instruction and visualization may prove helpful. ***Self-instruction*** (also termed *positive self-talk, covert speech,* and *countering*) refers to a set of statements that are repeated by the client on a regular basis, perhaps three times a day, and especially in times of distress. Often, they are said aloud in front of a mirror. These messages are incompatible with the client's habitual negative self-talk and are intended to counteract the dysfunctional pattern and to foster self-acceptance and self-confidence. The use of this technique rests on the observation that when an individual actively argues against his or her own irrational thoughts, those thoughts are weakened.

This technique should not be confused with blindly optimistic "positive thinking" that may gloss over important realities and allow self-deception. Rather, self-instruction requires that the messages be truthful and realistic, given the client's abilities and situation. Also, the messages should be as specific as possible and tied directly to the client's concerns. Self-instruction works but it works slowly. Frequent and consistent practice for a year or more may be needed to effect a significant and lasting change. Consider the client who avoids taking a better job because her dysfunctional self-talk tells her: "If I make a mistake on the job, people will think I am stupid and will criticize me." This woman might be taught to repeat the following message: "Each time I make a mistake on the job, I have an opportunity to learn something very important. If someone criticizes me, he or she is either right or wrong. If the person is right, I have learned something. If he or she is wrong, I can ignore it."

In using the technique of ***visualization,*** the client is taught to prepare himself or herself to deal with a worry-causing event by repeatedly imagining this event and mentally rehearsing the steps necessary to handle it successfully. It is important that the images are ones of action and activity; the more vivid and detailed, the better. For many individuals, visualization reduces their fear of the event and builds confidence in their ability to do what they know they must do. For example, a client might prepare for a frightening job interview by visualizing being asked hard questions and giving clear and appropriate answers. Such a visualization would need to be practiced dozens of times before the interview.

The technique of ***journaling*** asks the client to keep a daily log of significant thoughts and feelings. It is especially useful for clients who like to write. It helps them recognize recurring themes and patterns in the meaning assigned to their experiences. As a way of structuring this homework, the client might be instructed to respond in writing to specific questions such as the following: What have I learned about myself today? What feelings and moods did I experience? What thoughts gave rise to these feelings? What were the two most significant events of the day? What thoughts and feelings did I have in relation to these events? What personal strengths did I observe in myself today? What troublesome thoughts do I need to work on and what is my plan for doing so? How will my plan build on my personal strengths?

SELECTED BIBLIOGRAPHY

Borcherdt, Bill. *You Can Control Your Feelings.* Sarasota, FL: Professional Resource Press, 1993.
Emery, Gary. *A New Beginning.* New York: Simon and Schuster, 1981.
McMullin, Rian. *Handbook of Cognitive Therapy Techniques.* New York: W. W. Norton, 1986.

14.9 Building Self-Esteem

PURPOSE: To assist the client in coming to a more positive evaluation of self.

DISCUSSION: The term ***self-esteem*** refers to one's beliefs about one's own worth. Low self-esteem is an important contributing cause of unhappiness and problems of social functioning. Individuals who do not value or respect themselves lack self-confidence and struggle with a multitude of self-imposed limitations. Often, they engage in self-defeating behaviors and are vulnerable to exploitation and abuse by others.

Because the effects of low self-esteem are so far reaching, social workers have wished for a magic wand that could transform a client's negative self-evaluation into a more realistic and positive one. Unfortunately, no such magic exists. Movement toward self-esteem is a slow journey. By following these guidelines, the social worker can help the client along that journey:

1. It is important to help clients understand that one's feelings of personal worth is a perception—a subjective personal opinion about one's self. Consequently, Person A, who is violent and dishonest, may have high self-esteem; whereas Person B, who others view as a truly wonderful human being, may have low self-esteem.

2. Help clients understand that self-awareness and self-acceptance are the basic building blocks of self-esteem. We cannot come to know and accept ourselves without support and encouragement from others. We need other people. Thus, the client will need to form new relationships even when that is scary. Self-acceptance requires that we recognize our own goodness and also our weakness, woundedness, and incompleteness. To truly accept ourselves, we need to acknowledge our need to love and be loved. Self-esteem begins to grow when we begin to believe that our lives are valuable and valued, despite our imperfections.

3. Encourage clients to identify the specific conditions and circumstances they believe would elevate their feelings of self-worth. Then engage the clients in an examination of the underlying values reflected in those conditions and whether they are truly worthwhile and suitable criteria for measuring the worth of a person. For example, many people assume they would have higher self-esteem if they were more attractive, were better athletes, or had more money or higher social status. A closer look at those desires reveals that they are the values of a society obsessed with physical appearance, competition, and self-aggrandizement. Other values—such as generosity, compassion, friendliness, and honesty—are more appropriate and lasting measures of personal worth.

4. Low self-esteem often derives from unfavorable comparisons of self to others. People with low self-esteem tend to compare themselves with the "best in the field" (e.g., with the best musician, the best student, the most attractive person, etc.). Given that mode of thinking, they always suffer by comparison and this reinforces their beliefs that they are not as good as other people. Help clients understand that this is a self-defeating pattern of thinking. Encourage them to view others in a more realistic manner. For example, another individual may indeed be outstanding in a certain area but he or she is not outstanding in all areas.

5. A change in self-esteem must grow from within. Self-esteem cannot be taught, but it can be learned, and certain types of experiences encourage a growth in self-esteem. Efforts to help others elevate their self-esteem involves creating situations of cognitive dissonance wherein they must reconcile a seemingly positive outcome or experience with their negative opinions of self. A willingness to reevaluate one's beliefs about self is the first step toward a growth in self-esteem.

6. Encourage clients to participate in a support group, personal growth group, or church group where they will be accepted and respected by others, learn they have much in common with others, and learn that everyone has both strengths and limitations. Such group experiences are usually more effective than individual counseling but both may be necessary for some clients.

7. Encourage clients to take steps necessary to place themselves in new situations where they will have an opportunity to discover and develop their abilities and reassess their beliefs and assumptions about self; this may involve taking a job, changing jobs, returning to school, joining an organization, building a friendship, and so on. People with low self-esteem are inclined to reject the opportunities and avoid the experiences they need most.

8. Support clients in examining their tendency to see the negative rather than the positive, and how they are overly influenced by what others say and do. Also help clients understand that their value as a person is not dependent on the approval or actions of others and that they, not others, control how they will think and feel about life.

9. For some clients, low self-esteem is tied to one or more significant separation and loss experiences (e.g., separation from bio-family, loss of one's childhood through sexual abuse, loss of respect from valued others, etc.). Help these clients recognize and grieve for what they have lost (see Item 14.39).

10. Encourage and assist clients to develop a vision—a sense of purpose and meaning in life. Self-worth grows from knowing that you are living in accord with a set of ideals and values. For this reason, clients should be encouraged to do what they think and feel is the right thing to do.

SELECTED BIBLIOGRAPHY

Branden, Nathaniel. *Six Pillars of Self Esteem.* New York: Bantam Books, 1994.
Burns, David. *Ten Days to Self Esteem.* New York: Quill-William Morrow, 1993.
McKay, Matthew, and Patrick Fanning. *Self-Esteem,* 2nd ed. Oakland, CA: New Harbinger Publications, 1993.

14.10 The Empty Chair

PURPOSE: To help the client understand his or her feelings toward self or a significant other.

DISCUSSION: The ***empty-chair technique,*** sometimes called the *double-chair technique,* is borrowed from Gestalt therapy. It is usually used to clarify the issues involved in an interpersonal conflict. It helps the client view the conflict from a different angle and gain insight into why he or she is feeling and behaving in a certain way. Some skilled practitioners are able to use the technique to clarify intrapersonal conflict.

The social worker may elect to employ this technique after recognizing a specific conflict that needs to be explored with the client. To get started, the worker pulls up an empty chair and places it opposite the client. The chair becomes the person or situation with which the client is in conflict. The client is asked to speak to the chair, explaining his or her perceptions and feelings. The client is then asked to sit on the chair (assuming the role of that person or situation) and respond to what was just said. The client may move back and forth several times throughout this dialogue. The worker uses other interviewing techniques to explore the exchange as it unfolds.

As an example of application, consider Mary, a 40-year-old woman, who has exhaustingly high housekeeping standards. Even though she does not enjoy housework, she spends hours each day cleaning all rooms in her house, including her children's rooms and the garage. When asked how she became so devoted to cleaning and housework, Mary says that her mother emphasized the importance of housework. The worker pulls up an empty chair and asks Mary to sit on it, assume the role of her mother, and tell Mary about the importance of doing housework. In the role of her mother, Mary explains that cleanliness is next to Godliness, that the oldest child should take care of the younger ones, and that a good wife is devoted to her home. Then, the worker has Mary switch chairs, become herself, and respond to what her "mother" had to say. Her first response is, "Yes, ma'am." Exploration reveals that this response covers much hostility. What Mary really wants to say aloud is, "No, I don't want to do it. I am tired of working all the time. I am tired of doing things for other people." The worker then uses the empty chair to represent Mary's husband and invites Mary to express her feelings to him. During the course of this dialogue, Mary may realize that, as an adult, she now has choices that she did not have as a child. Moreover, she realizes that she has never told her husband how she feels.

The technique can be adapted to many situations. In the hands of a skilled social worker, it can be very powerful. It may also be combined effectively with behavioral rehearsal and role reversal techniques.

SELECTED BIBLIOGRAPHY

Cory, Gerald. *Theory and Practice of Counseling and Psychotherapy,* 4th ed. Pacific Grove, CA: Brooks/Cole, 1991.

Greenberg, Leslie, Laura Rice, and Robert Elliott. *Facilitating Emotional Change.* New York: Guilford, 1993.

Sherman, Robert, and Norman Fredman. *Handbook of Structured Techniques in Marriage and Family Therapy.* New York: Brunner/Mazel, 1986.

14.11 Confrontation and Challenge

PURPOSE: To increase the client's self-awareness, especially in regard to self-imposed barriers to change.

DISCUSSION: As used in counseling and psychotherapy, the technique of ***confrontation*** (also called a *challenge*) refers to gentle and respectful efforts to help the client recognize that he or she is using distortions, deceptions, denials, or manipulations that are self-defeating and getting in the way of desirable change. It challenges and invites the client take a careful look at a thought or behavior that is harmful to self or others and to take action to change it.

A challenge or confrontation is initiated by the social worker. Thus, its focus will depend on the worker's judgment as to what changes are essential for a client and what stands in the way of those changes. Most often the challenge will focus on the client's avoidance or self-deception, such as failure to acknowledge or "own" an obvious problem; rationalizations, evasions, and game playing; unwillingness to recognize consequences of one's behavior; discrepancies between what the client says and what he or she does; or unwillingness to take steps to correct a problem or deal with an important issue.

For a challenge to be effective, it must be used at a time when the client seems most ready to hear and consider the message. There is always some risk in using this technique. If used with a client who is depressed, the client may feel criticized and withdraw from the relationship. Clients who are highly defensive will usually reject the message by rationalizing, verbally attacking the worker, or minimizing the matter. Several guidelines need to be considered in the use of this technique:

1. Do not challenge when you are feeling angry. Unless you have a genuine concern for the client, its use may be little more than an expression of frustration or a desire to punish a difficult client.

2. Do not challenge or confront a client if you cannot or do not intend to become more deeply involved. Once offered, it is the responsibility of the worker to help the client deal nondefensively with the message, to understand it, and to consider what it means for future choices. Unless you have the time to help the client make use of the message, do not use this technique.

3. A challenge offered by someone for whom the client has no positive feelings will have no beneficial impact whatsoever. It will be effective only if the client feels care and respect from the social worker and if the client has similar feelings toward the worker. If those feelings are not there, the message will be discounted.

4. Couple the challenging message with positive observations about the client. In other words, present the message within a context of recognizing and supporting the client's strengths.

5. Make sure your message is descriptive and nonjudgmental. Be prepared to give a detailed description of the client's self-destructive or negative behavior, and provide concrete examples of how this behavior creates problems. Judgmental statements tend to trigger anger, whereas descriptive statements provide information that can be used in problem-solving efforts.

6. Always present the observations or data on which your message is based. For example, if the confrontation focuses on self-defeating behavior, present detailed descriptions of that behavior before trying to explain how the behavior is counterproductive for the client. Make sure the client understands the distinction between your observations and the inferences you have drawn from those observations. An *observation* can be stated directly: "I saw you . . ." or "Last Friday you specifically told me that . . ." or "I have had seven separate reports that describe your fights." An *inference* should be stated tentatively: "Because of what I have been told, I have concluded that . . ." or "Unless you can offer another explanation, I have to assume that . . . " Strive to use I-statements throughout the challenge (see Item 8.5).

SELECTED BIBLIOGRAPHY

Cormier, Sherry, and William Cormier. *Interviewing Strategies for Helpers*, 4th ed. Pacific Grove, CA: Brooks/Cole, 1998.

Egan, Gerald. *The Skilled Helper*, 6th ed. Pacific Grove, CA: Brooks/Cole, 1998.

Hepworth, Dean, Ronald Rooney, and Jo Ann Larsen. *Direct Social Work Practice*. Pacific Grove, CA: Brooks/Cole, 1997.

14.12 Reframing

PURPOSE: To assist the client in viewing the behavior from a different perspective and in a more positive light.

DISCUSSION: The technique known as ***reframing,*** sometimes called *relabeling* or *redefining,* is used to help a client modify the meaning he or she assigns to a particular event, behavior, or life experience. Its purpose is to gently persuade a client that the event or behavior can be viewed in a different and more positive light. Reframing recognizes the wisdom of the first-century philosopher Epictetus, who said, "It is not the things themselves which trouble us, but the opinions we have about these things."

This technique is especially useful in work with clients having interpersonal conflicts, such as a couple or family. It encourages family members to reexamine their definitions of the problem and their beliefs about why others are behaving as they do. It promotes interpersonal understanding and helps each person feel more favorable about the other. When a person perceives things in a new way, he or she usually feels differently and begins to behave differently.

The following example illustrates a social worker's use of reframing:

> ***Foster Parent:*** I get so upset with Anna (foster child). So often, she blows up and gets angry with me. But I haven't done anything to make her angry!
>
> ***Social Worker:*** That must be frustrating—to know you do not deserve to be the target of her anger. As you know, Anna is an angry child because of the severe abuse she experienced before you ever met her. But, in one way of looking at it, Anna is paying you a big compliment. When she gets angry in your presence, she is demonstrating that she feels safe when with you and trusts that you will not retaliate and hurt her.

Another example of reframing is illustrated in the following statement made to a 35-year-old client who has experienced a lifetime of physical and emotional pain related to a disabling car accident and having been physically and sexually abused as a child.

> ***Social Worker:*** I have been thinking about your life and all that you have experienced. Despite all you have been through, here you are at age 35 still alive and still struggling to do the best you can. In the school of life, you have received a very expensive and a very good education—much better than what a Harvard or a Yale could provide. You have learned things about people and about life that most people never learn, no matter how long they go to school, no matter how much money they spend on college tuition. Your tuition has been paid in the form of personal pain and suffering but in return you have received a high-quality education.

An alternative to the social worker providing the client with a new perspective is to encourage the client to brainstorm several different interpretations. For example, the worker might begin by explaining that there is a difference between the facts that describe a particular life experience and the story an individual tells himself or herself about that experience. The client will usually agree that five people will most likely tell five slightly different stories about the same experience. Using that agreement as a foundation, the worker can now encourage the client to come up with additional stories (interpretations) about the particular behavior or life experience being discussed. After thinking up several alternative perceptions, the client will usually soften his or her position and acknowledge that there may indeed be a different way to interpret his or her situation.

Still another approach to reframing is to redefine a client's problem or irresponsible action as a basically positive behavior taken to an extreme. In other words, a problem is redefined as a strength that is spinning out of control. For example, consider the young mother who has injured her 3-year-old child as a result of using excessive spanking as discipline. The discussion of her behavior might be approached by first recognizing that the mother wants to teach the child proper behavior but in this situation her motive to be a good mother jumped the track or went spinning out of control. When the worker can redefine a problem as a strength that went out of control or as a positive behavior that has jumped the track, the client feels less defensive and more hopeful. Somehow it seems easier to tone down or control a strength than to get rid of a problem behavior. The words a helper uses do make a difference.

SELECTED BIBLIOGRAPHY

Berg, Insoo Kim. *Family Based Services.* New York: W. W. Norton, 1994.

Minuchin, Salvador, and H. Charles Fishman. *Family Therapy Techniques.* Cambridge, MA: Harvard University Press, 1981.

Schuyler, Dean. *A Practical Guide to Cognitive Therapy.* New York: W. W. Norton, 1991.

14.13 Family Sculpting

PURPOSE: To help a client or family system understand their own feelings and behavior and those of other family members by acting out significant family events.

DISCUSSION: *Family sculpting* is a technique designed to help a client (within a group session) or a client family reenact and thus relive some important family event or aspects of their family's behavior. It is a tool for assessment as well as treatment. The term *sculpting* is an artistic analogy that describes how one of the family members physically arranges or molds the family in a way that conveys a certain meaning, much like a sculptor working with clay.

The social worker begins by explaining the technique to the family. Baron and Feeney (1976) offer a sample explanation:

> We're going to do something a little different today that will help us learn what's happening in the family. First of all, it involves everyone getting up out of their seats (worker stands as an example). Now we need someone who will make a family sculpture. What I mean is, I want someone, without talking, to arrange the family into a picture which if I were walking through the park would tell me something about who you are. Who's close to whom, who is far away, might be a way to start. The rest of the family has to let the sculptor sculpt. That means being as much like clay as possible. Some sculptors have sculpted the parents with Mom standing over Dad ruling the roost. Others show us kids who are still sitting on Momma's lap even though they are teenagers. You get the idea. Who wants to try it? (p. 82)

After such an explanation, someone will usually volunteer to do the first sculpture. In the beginning, this family member may need support and encouragement from the worker. The worker watches to make sure that the sculptor really sculpts and does not just verbalize instructions. Verbalizing can result in arguments and keeps members from touching. Playful touching and a bit of silliness are some of the positive aspects of this technique.

Hartman (1984) offers the following guidance on family sculpting:

> It may be suggested that the sculptor imagine the family at home in the evenings. Where will each person be? What will they be doing? Chairs and other props may be used. Placement of the members should include not only where they are in relationship to other members but also where they are looking and how their bodies are positioned.
>
> As the sculpture develops, family members may object because they see themselves in the family system in a different way. For example, if a child placed dad in the corner behind the newspaper he might not like that picture of himself, nor what his son or daughter is communicating through the sculpture. It is important, however, to allow the sculptor to finish without interruption and to assure other family members that they will be able to sculpt the family later in the way they see it if they so wish.
>
> The worker should give the sculptor support and help as needed, encouraging him or her to take whatever time is needed and asking enabling questions like, "Do you want mom to be looking in any particular direction?" or "Is that the way you want it? Are there any changes you want to make?"
>
> After the sculptor has completed the sculpture to his or her satisfaction, and taken his or her place in the tableau, the worker assumes the role of monitor and while the actors maintain their positions asks each member how they are experiencing their place in the sculpture. This invitation surfaces disagreements on the part of the family members as to how they see the family. It surfaces how they are feeling about current family structure and may expose points of stress and tension. (p. 24)*

In an elaboration of the basic technique, the sculpting member is instructed to give each person a sentence to say aloud—something that would illustrate that person's mood or attitude toward the others. This further reveals the sculptor's perceptions of the family.

The person doing the sculpture can be asked to depict the family as it now exists, as it once existed, or as it reacted to some event (e.g., the death of grandfather).

*Reprinted by special permission of CWLA from *Working with Adoptive Families: Beyond Placement,* 1984.

A sculpture might also be used to portray ideal family functioning or perhaps a future situation or set of circumstances that is feared by all.

The technique can be used as part of a group therapy session. In this application, the sculptor selects group members to play the roles of the members in his or her family, including the sculptor. Once the sculpture is developed, the worker asks the sculptor to assume his or her place in the family. Then the group discusses what they see in the sculpture and how it felt to be part of this family.

By using 3" × 5" name cards to represent family members, a form of sculpting can be conducted within a one-to-one interview. The basic procedure is as follows:

1. The client and worker identify all family members and write each of their names on a separate 3" × 5" card. The client's name is also written on one of the cards.
2. The client is asked to imagine being with his or her family members in a room and then to arrange the cards in a way that shows where each would be sitting or standing in relation to the others. This arrangement is then discussed.
3. The client is asked to rearrange the cards in a way that illustrates the various emotional ties, subsystems, and interpersonal conflicts within the family. This arrangement is then discussed.
4. The client selects one of the cards representing another family member and then rearranges all the other cards showing how that particular member experiences the family system. This step can be repeated with other cards.
5. The client is asked to rearrange the cards in a way that depicts the relationship he or she desires for his or her family. Discussion then focuses on what it would take to create this more desirable family interaction.

SELECTED BIBLIOGRAPHY

Baron, Roger, and Floyd Feeney. *Juvenile Diversion through Family Counseling.* Washington, DC: National Institute of Law Enforcement and Criminal Justice, U.S. Government Printing Office, 1976.

Hartman, Ann. *Working with Adoptive Families: Beyond Placement.* New York: Child Welfare League of America, 1984.

Vondracek, Fred, and Sherry Corneal. *Strategies for Resolving Individual and Family Problems.* Pacific Grove, CA: Brooks/Cole, 1995.

14.14 The Talking Stick

PURPOSE: To structure discussion within a group session or family interview.

DISCUSSION: For centuries, many American Indian tribes have used the "talking stick" to govern small group discussion and encourage listening behaviors. Instead of a decorated stick, some tribes use an eagle feather or other sacred object. During a discussion, the talking stick or special object is passed around the group, from person to person. Whoever holds it has permission to speak; all others are to give that person their undivided attention. This ensures that everyone has a chance to speak and is heard by the others. Reverence for the object serves to limit the verbose members and encourage the timid and those less inclined to speak.

This method of structuring discussion can be used with a small group or a family. It may be especially useful if members tend to talk all at once or do not listen to each other. In place of the talking stick or feather, a family might use some other object that illicits reverence and respect (e.g., a family picture, a Bible, etc.).

SELECTED BIBLIOGRAPHY

Locust, Carol. "The Talking Stick." Tucson, AZ: Native American Research and Training Center. (undated)

14.15 Homework Assignments

PURPOSE: To assist the client in learning a new behavior by assigning specific tasks and activities to be worked on between counseling sessions.

DISCUSSION: The term ***homework*** refers to various types of activities that the client is asked by the social worker to perform between sessions. Homework is often used when the objectives of the intervention involve teaching the client new skills that need to be practiced within the client's natural environment. For example, given a client whose problems revolve on low self-esteem, shyness, and an inability to interact comfortably with others, a homework assignment might be for the client to strike up at least two conversations a day while riding to and from work on the bus.

The homework assignment must be given with clear and precise instructions. Often, these need to be written instructions. Both the client and worker should have copies. Shelton and Ackerman (1974) explain that homework instructions contain one or more of the following:

1. *A do statement.* "Read, practice, observe, say, count . . . some kind of homework."
2. *A quantity statement.* "Talk three times about . . . ; spend thirty minutes . . . ; give four compliments per day . . . ; write a list of at least ten . . . ."
3. *A record statement.* "Count and record the number of compliments; each time he hits, mark a ________ on the chart; whenever that thought comes to you, write a ________ on the . . . ."
4. *A bring statement.* "Bring . . . your list; the chart; the cards; your spouse . . . to the next appointment."
5. *A contingency statement.* "Call for your next appointment after you have done . . . ; for each negative activity, one dollar will be deducted . . . ; each minute spent doing ________ will earn you ________; one-tenth of your penalty deposit will be forfeited for each assignment not completed." (p. 16)

Obviously, the homework assignment must seem possible and make sense to the client. The use of this technique presumes that the client is willing to accept direction from the worker.

SELECTED BIBLIOGRAPHY

Hecker, Lorna, and Sharon Deacon. *The Therapist Notebook: Homework Handouts, and Activities for Use in Psychotherapy.* New York: Haworth, 1998.

Schultheis, Gary. *Brief Therapy Homework Planner.* New York: Wiley, 1998.

Shelton, John, and J. Mark Ackerman. *Homework in Counseling and Psychotherapy.* Springfield, IL: Charles C. Thomas, 1974.

14.16 Envelope Budgeting

PURPOSE: To assist the client in money management.

DISCUSSION: Many of the clients served by social workers are economically poor. They find it difficult to stretch a very limited income to cover the bare essentials. Most of their money transactions are in cash; few have checking accounts. *Envelope budgeting* can be taught to clients who need a simple method for keeping track of their money and expenses.

The first step in setting up this budgeting system is for the client to identify the key categories of expenditure: rent, food, clothing, transportation, household supplies, and so on. The next step is to determine how many dollars need to be spent on each category during a spending cycle, such as a one-month or a two-week period. An envelope is then prepared and labeled for each category. In the "food envelope," for example, the client places the money allotted for food. All of the envelopes are kept together in a box.

As money is removed from an envelope and spent, the client has a tangible measure of cash outflow and can view the balance that remains. The client is encouraged to resist the temptation to shift money from one category to another, but this may sometimes be necessary. When the client obtains additional income, cash is again placed in the envelopes for the new spending cycle.

This technique can be used with clients who have limited computational skills. If the client can only count, he or she can usually use envelope budgeting. Subtraction and addition skills are helpful but not essential. This technique helps people plan and monitor expenditures but it is not a permanent solution for those who are overwhelmed by debt or have expenditures that far exceed their income. In such cases, more complex approaches—such as consumer credit counseling, debt consolidation, or even bankruptcy—may be necessary.

SELECTED BIBLIOGRAPHY

American Association of Retired Persons. *A Primer on Personal Money Management for Midlife and Older Women.* Washington, DC: AARP, 1991.

Vosler, Nancy. *New Approaches to Family Practice: Confronting Economic Stress.* Thousand Oaks, CA: Sage, 1996.

14.17 Managing Personal Debt

PURPOSE: To assist the client in handling large bills and debt.

DISCUSSION: An individual or family with too many bills and too little money experiences much stress. A shortage of money can be made up by borrowing or buying on credit, but this only makes the problem worse in the long run. Paying some bills while neglecting others may be necessary, but this soon results in a damaged credit rating and possible legal ramifications.

There is no easy way to climb out of debt, but several things can be done to gain control of the situation. The following suggestions may be relevant in work with a client who is trying to deal with financial problems:

1. Recognize that financial problems are often more complex that the simple lack of money. The problem is often rooted in a set of personal values, attitudes, and shopping behaviors that lead to overspending. The power of advertising, peer-group influences, and feelings of low self-esteem push many people into buying more than they need and can afford. The ease of obtaining credit cards is a pitfall for many. In order to get out of debt, some significant changes in behavior are required.

2. When bills always exceed income, you must find a way to decrease spending, increase income, or both. Begin immediately to cut spending. Since accumulating additional debts makes the problem even worse, avoid purchasing items on credit. Close out revolving credit accounts at stores, so you are not tempted to buy more than you really need when in these stores. If the overuse of credit cards is a cause of your financial problems, destroy the cards. If you must use credit cards, buy only what you can pay for within 30 days and avoid interest charges.

3. Make a careful analysis of what you owe. Begin by making four columns on a piece of paper. In column 1, list all of the items for which you are billed on a regular basis (e.g., loan and credit card bills, utilities, rent, car payments, dental and medical, phone, insurance, and the like). In column 2, list the expected monthly payment for each item in column 1. In column 3, list the amount you actually pay each month toward each item. In column 4, total the amount owed for all items. Begin your analysis by marking all items for which interest is charged; these should become high-priority targets for payment. If you must skip payments or reduce the amount paid toward a bill, do so on items that do not involve interest charges or overdue charges. Also, prioritize the interest-related bills according to the amount still owed; concentrate on paying off those on which the least amount is owed, which will eliminate all credit charges associated with that bill and free up money for other bills. Completely paying off a bill also provides a feeling of making progress on debt reduction and this record of progress can be used to argue for payment extensions because it demonstrates ability to pay bills.

4. If you cannot pay a bill, do not ignore the problem. Never miss a payment without first explaining the problem to your creditor. If they understand your situation, if your explanation is reasonable, and if they believe you intend to pay, they may be willing to make an adjustment. Be sure to describe the actions you are taking to solve your financial problems. Some lenders and businesses have emergency plans that provide temporary relief. They might rewrite your loan at a lower rate of interest or spread the loan over a longer period, both of which will lower the monthly payment.

5. Do not avoid bill collectors. A frank discussion may result in an acceptable solution. Remember that collection agencies do not really want your possessions. Moreover, they do not want to do anything that will cause you to lose whatever income you do have. What they want is money. If you can demonstrate a genuine desire to pay and actually pay even a little each month, often a creditor will find this acceptable. However, if you avoid bill collectors or show no effort to pay the bill, they seldom hesitate to do whatever is legal to recover something of value and make your life miserable.

6. Sell possessions you do not need. Consider selling your car unless it is needed for work-related transportation. Getting rid of a car is especially important if you are buying it on an installment plan. A car loan creates a cycle of debt because by the time it is finally paid off, the car must often be replaced. Look seriously for a less expensive means of transportation.

7. Make use of credit-counseling resources, but before using a particular program, be sure to find out (a) who sponsors the program; (b) what, if any, charges are involved; and (c) how the program operates. If possible, use the services offered by nonprofit agencies. Do not confuse the credit-counseling services available for little or no cost with the for-profit businesses that do debt adjustment for a high fee. A good consumer credit-counseling program can reduce your worry, help you develop the self-discipline needed to handle debt, and help you avoid bankruptcy.

8. When other less drastic methods fail to have an impact on the debt problem, loan consolidation or bankruptcy must be considered. When utilizing a ***consolidation loan*** strategy, you take out a new loan and immediately pay off all other loans and overdue accounts. The single payment on this new loan is designed to be smaller than the total for prior monthly payments, and it is easier to keep track of payments on just one loan. However, a consolidation loan stretches your payments over a longer period of time. You must still pay the whole amount before you are debt free, and you will be paying interest during the life of the consolidation loan. Another disadvantage of consolidation is that it is easy to forget how much is actually owed and you may be tempted to take on new credit obligations because the new monthly loan payment seems small in comparison to previous bills.

9. ***Bankruptcy*** may be necessary in cases of extreme financial difficulty, when creditors are unwilling to renegotiate debts, when a consolidation loan cannot be obtained, and when informal loans cannot be obtained from family or friends. For individuals and married couples, the Federal Bankruptcy Act provides two types of bankruptcy. The most common type is a Chapter 7—*straight bankruptcy* or liquidation proceeding. After a petition is filed with the U.S. District Court, a bankruptcy judge notifies the people to whom you owe money (i.e., your creditors) of their rights to file a claim against you and to question you on the witness stand. Creditors have an opportunity to object to your not having to pay what you owe. If there are no objections, the bankruptcy judge will grant what is called a "discharge in bankruptcy," which relieves you from legal liability for the payment of all debts owed at the time of bankruptcy. All of your possessions, with the exception of those exempt by law, are turned over to a trustee to be sold. The proceeds from this sale are distributed to the creditors who filed claims. The remaining debt is legally erased. Debts such as child support or alimony, taxes, unlisted debts, fines, and/or debts obtained under false pretenses cannot be discharged.

Another bankruptcy option, called a Chapter 13 or *wage earner plan,* allows you to keep your possessions while paying off your debts under an installment plan monitored by a court-appointed trustee. You develop a plan for repaying your debts over a period of three years (sometimes five years) and if your plan is approved by the judge, your creditors must stop all collection efforts. They must also stop charging you interest and late charges on most types of debts. Each payday, a fixed amount of your wage or other income is turned over to the trustee, who then pays your creditors. Creditors will usually agree to this plan because they are more likely to be paid under this arrangement than under straight bankruptcy.

Bankruptcy has a number of negative consequences. For example, a bankruptcy remains on your credit report for 10 years and will affect your credit rating. A person considering bankruptcy should seek the advice of an attorney and/or a credit-counseling agency. Information can be obtained from the Division of Bankruptcy, Administrative Office of the United States Courts, Washington, DC 20544.

SELECTED BIBLIOGRAPHY

Bamford, Janet. *Consumer Reports Money Book.* Novi, MI: Consumer Union of United States, 1995.

Leonard, Robin. *Money Troubles,* 3rd ed. Berkeley, CA: Nolo Press, 1996.

Tyson, Eric. *Personal Finance for Dummies,* 2nd ed. Foster City, CA: IDG Books, 1996.

14.18 Decision-Making Worksheets

PURPOSE: To assist the client in considering alternatives and making a decision.

DISCUSSION: Helping clients make difficult decisions is an important social work activity. A social worker familiar with key issues and common feelings surrounding a particular type of decision can facilitate the client's decision making by constructing a ***decision-making worksheet,*** which will focus the client's attention on important questions and factors that need to be considered before arriving at decision.

Figure 14.1 contains excerpts from a decision-making worksheet designed for use with pregnant teenagers considering whether to relinquish their babies for adoption. As can be seen from this sample, a worksheet is simply a format for raising questions and helping the client analyze his or her situation. Obviously, skilled interviewing could accomplish the same thing, but the worksheet can provide added structure and can be used as homework between sessions.

FIGURE 14.1 Sample Decision-Making Worksheet

Planning for My Baby

I. Questions about my relationship with my baby's father.
   A. Can I count on him for financial support?
   B. Can I count on him for emotional support?
   C. Has my relationship with him changed since I got pregnant?
   (and so on)

II. Questions about my relationship with my parents.
   A. What do my parents want me to do?
   B. Can I go against their wishes?
   C. If my mother helps take care of my baby, is it possible the baby will become "her baby"?
   (and so on)

III. Questions about my life after having the baby.
   A. If I keep the baby, how will this affect future dating, marriage, and children?
   B. If I give my baby up for adoption, how will this affect my future dating, marriage, and children?
   (and so on)

IV. A daydream exercise.
   A. If I could pick the ideal time for having a baby, when would it be? Where would I be? What would the baby's father be like?
   B. How does the above ideal situation compare with my real situation?
   (and so on)

V. Picturing myself.
   A. Draw a picture of yourself one year ago. Around your picture, indicate in words or pictures the things that were important to you then. What were your activities, how did you use your time? What were your goals and aspirations one year ago?
   B. Think about yourself now. Change the above picture of yourself one year ago to fit things today. Cross out those activities in which you are no longer involved. Have your goals and aspirations changed?
   C. Draw a picture of yourself one year from now. Again, around your picture, write in those things that you will be involved in one year from now. How will you spend your time? In one year, what will be your goals and aspirations?
   (and so on)

Source: Lutheran Social Services, mimeographed item (no date), pp. 1–2, 4–5.

SELECTED BIBLIOGRAPHY

Lutheran Social Services. "Decision-Making Plans for the Baby." Missoula, MT: Lutheran Social Services. (Mimeo.)

McClam, Tricia, and Marianne Woodside. *Problem Solving in the Helping Professions.* Pacific Grove, CA: Brooks/Cole, 1994.

Winkler, Robin, Dirk Brown, Margaret vonKeppel, and Amy Blanchard. *Clinical Practice in Adoption.* New York: Pergamon, 1988.

14.19 Distinguishing Means from Ends

PURPOSE: To assist the client in problem-solving efforts by making a clear distinction between the problem to be solved and possible solutions.

DISCUSSION: When helping a client solve a problem, it is necessary to distinguish between the problem and the means of solving that problem. Consider, for example, the client who asks for assistance in figuring out how to get money to buy a car because he needs to get to and from a new job. In this case, the client has confused means and ends. The client's problem is a lack of transportation, not the lack of a car. A car is only one means of transportation; others might include public transportation, paying a private car owner for a ride, walking, or taking a taxi.

A simple listing may help the client keep the ends and means separate. The following list was developed during an interview with a young single mother who had requested foster care placement for her child because she could not care for the child while holding a job:

End	*Means*
Child care while mother works to secure money to support self and child.	Licensed day-care center Paid babysitter Informal babysitting exchange with friend Babysitting (relative) Change jobs or hours of work Welfare assistance

As can be seen, once the client's presenting problem was redefined as a need for child care, rather than a need for placement, several new options emerged.

SELECTED BIBLIOGRAPHY

Nelson-Jones, Richard. *Lifeskills Helping.* Pacific Grove, CA: Brooks/Cole, 1993.

Priestley, Philip, James McGuire, David Flegg, Valerie Hemsley, and David Welham. *Social Skills and Personal Problem Solving: A Handbook of Methods.* London: Travistock Publication, 1978.

Sprafkin, Robert, N. Jane Gershaw, and Arnold Goldstein. *Social Skills for Mental Health.* Boston: Allyn and Bacon, 1993.

14.20 Indirect Discussion of Self in Small Groups

PURPOSE: To make it easier for group participants to discuss personal concerns.

DISCUSSION: This technique is designed to stimulate and structure small-group discussion of the participants' concerns while at the same time protecting individual privacy. It allows clients to discuss matters that they would not ordinarily share with others. Moreover, this technique can engage a reluctant client in group discussion. Essentially, the technique calls for each participant to respond to a set of questions by writing answers on 3'' × 5'' cards. The unsigned cards are collected, shuffled, and then randomly passed out to the group members. The members then discuss and analyze the responses, problems, or concerns found on the cards.

To begin the process, each participant is given three 3'' × 5'' cards; each card is labeled A, B, or C. The participant will use each card to write a response to a specific question: question A, question B, question C. Before they write, tell them exactly how the cards will be collected, shuffled, and then redistributed randomly for discussion. Warn participants against writing a response in a way that might reveal their identity. Encourage the group to be honest in answering the questions, since the identity of the person writing the card will be protected.

The social worker using the technique preselects the questions. The following is a sample set of stem sentences used in a group session with physically abusing parents:

On Card A: (complete the statement) "Before a hitting episode, I feel . . . "

On Card B: (complete the statement) "The thing I feel most after a hitting episode is . . . "

On Card C: (complete the statement) "One thing I could do to decrease the hitting episodes is . . . "

The technique is also useful in training sessions. The next sample is a set of stem sentences used in a training session for foster parents concerned with improving their work with the biological parents of children in foster care:

On Card A: (complete the statement) "In my work with biological parents, I find it most difficult to . . . "

On Card B: (complete the statement) "I know I shouldn't have this negative feeling toward biological parents, but I feel . . . "

On Card C: (complete the statement) "The thing that would help me to improve my work with biological parents is . . . "

After all of the participants have finished writing their responses, collect the cards in sequence: first, all of the A cards, then the Bs, then the C cards. Shuffle each stack separately. Then pass out all of the A cards randomly, then the Bs, then the Cs. This procedure ensures that each participant receives a response to each of the three questions or stem sentences.

The next step is to have groups of three or four members, if part of a large group, study and discuss the cards they have been given. They might be asked to summarize what the cards seem to be saying. For example, the foster parents might be asked to study the cards and answer the following:

1. Identify the difficulties experienced in work with biological parents.
2. Identify the possible causes of these difficulties.
3. Identify methods of improving relationships with biological parents.

After a small group has studied its cards, participants are encouraged to trade their cards with other small groups in order to obtain even more data. Typically, the participants discover that they share common worries, problems, and feelings. This can be reassuring. Use of the technique helps counteract feelings of isolation and the belief that "no one else feels like I do."

The technique works best in groups larger than about 15, but it can be adapted for use in smaller groups and even with families. When used with a small group, the social worker should also submit a set of cards. Sometimes, the worker can help things along by writing responses that are sure to provoke discussion.

SELECTED BIBLIOGRAPHY

Reid, Kenneth. *Social Work Practice with Groups: A Clinical Perspective,* 2nd ed. Pacific Grove, CA: Brooks/Cole, 1997.

Zastrow, Charles. *Social Work with Groups.* Chicago: Nelson-Hall, 1997.

14.21 Programming in Group Work

PURPOSE: To encourage individual and group development by selecting and arranging group activities that promote specific types of interaction.

DISCUSSION: The technique of ***programming*** originated within the group work tradition of social work. It refers to the planful selection and use of recreation, nonverbal media, and other activities to create opportunities for clients to learn new behaviors or experience positive interpersonal relationships and to move the group process in certain directions. Participation in an activity can have a profound effect on how members feel about themselves and each other and on the structure and norms that develop within the group.

A broad range of activities can be used in programming: camping, puppet shows, drama, care of animals, art, dance, music, crafts, basketball, parties, work tasks, and the like. Games can be useful in group work with all ages but they are especially important with children. Games are fun and engaging—they often allow for creativity and fantasy, they teach the importance of rules and boundaries, and they challenge the player to test himself or herself against others. Complex games may teach a variety of important skills such as self-control, problem solving, communication and cooperation, leadership, and handling feelings related to authority.

An individual's behavior during a group activity can provide important assessment and diagnostic information. For example, a child's interaction with peers during a game may garner insights into the child's behavior that could not be obtained from a battery of psychological tests.

The type of programming used will depend on the social worker's assessment of individual members, the functioning of the group as a whole, and the group's purpose. Guidelines include the following:

1. The usefulness of a particular activity is related to the stage of group development. For example, in the get acquainted stage, you would use activities that promote friendly interaction but avoid ones that would require a member to assume a leadership role (see Item 13.8).

2. The selection of an activity is always tied to the question: What behaviors do I want to encourage? Select an activity that elicits or teaches the behaviors you want to promote in the group. Activities should call forth and reinforce the behaviors and attitudes that benefit group members, advance the groups development, and help the group achieve its purpose.

3. When selecting an activity, consider such factors as the members' ages, developmental levels, physical capacities, motor skills, endurance, interests, attention spans, need for control and protection, social skills, and so forth. Also, group size must be considered.

4. A group activity should be attractive and interesting. For example, adolescents and young adults are often attracted to car repair and maintenance, woodworking, welding, cooking, and hiking because these are age appropriate and combine movement and the learning of useful skills with social interaction and purposeful communication. An activity should offer a challenge but not generate excessive frustration.

5. When selecting an activity, carefully consider what prerequisite skills or knowledge it requires. For example, does it require oral communication, writing, reading, cooperation, competition, movement, initiative, memory, judgment, self-control, ability to follow directions? Avoid activities for which members do not have prerequisite abilities.

6. Carefully consider what the activity will require of the social worker. For example, does the activity require the worker to function as a teacher, leader, advisor, planner, police officer, umpire, time keeper, transporter, supplier of food, or what?

7. Consider how the rules of the activity will affect the members. For example, does a game involve the selection or ranking of participants, the choosing of sides, or the elimination of a "loser" from further competition? Can the members cope with whatever frustration the rules may create?

8. Consider how the activity fits with scheduling constraints and the physical environment. How much time is required? How much space? Is it safe? Is it noisy?

SELECTED BIBLIOGRAPHY

Anderson, Joseph. *Social Work with Groups.* New York: Longman, 1997.
Garvin, Charles. *Contemporary Group Work,* 2nd ed. Boston: Allyn and Bacon, 1997.
Middleman, Ruth. *The Non-Verbal Method in Working with Groups.* New York: Association Press, 1968.

14.22 Resolving Interpersonal Conflict

PURPOSE: To assist people in resolving conflicts and disagreements.

DISCUSSION: The social worker is frequently in the position of trying to help clients resolve conflicts (e.g., between parent and teenager, husband and wife, etc.) and sometimes in the position of trying to help two professionals resolve their conflict. An important first step in helping others resolve a conflict is to realize that the dynamics of the conflict may be complex and that the conflict is often about issues no one is mentioning. People often fight over a minor issue because they are afraid to face the real one. If true resolution is to take place, the real issue must be identified.

Bisno (1988, 31) alerts us to various motives behind a conflict by identifying six types of conflict: those characterized by a clash of opposing interests or commitments; those created in order to achieve some hidden purpose; those related to errors of attribution and unknowingly misdirected to the wrong party or wrong issue; those deliberately directed to the wrong party or wrong issue in order to avoid the real issue; those based on misperceptions, misunderstandings, and poor communications; and, finally, those created for the purpose of expressing hostility or other strong emotion.

It is important to recognize the difference between a misunderstanding and a disagreement. All too often, we assume that a conflict is caused by a misunderstanding and that it can be resolved through better communication and a more complete understanding of the various points of view. However, improved and additional communication will not resolve a conflict caused by genuine disagreement. A true disagreement exists when both sides continue to hold different positions even after they have listened to each other and have thoroughly and clearly explained their own points of view. In a disagreement, each side understands the the opposing viewpoint but cannot accept it. If the conflict is caused by a basic disagreement, you need to seek a compromise or simply agree to disagree. A worker trying to mediate a conflict should keep several guidelines in mind:

1. Do not take sides. Be fair and respect the views and feelings of everyone involved. Remind the parties in conflict of the things they already agree on, such as certain values, concern for a third party, desire to avoid further pain, and so on.

2. Appeal for a demonstration of mutual respect and a willingness to at least listen and try to understand differences in perception and needs. Attempt to get those in conflict to agree that during the discussion, they will avoid issuing threats, name calling, moralizing, attacking sensitive spots, or bringing up past hurts and disagreements that are unrelated to the current conflict.

3. Urge those in conflict to ask themselves four questions before they speak:

- Do I really want to resolve this conflict or do I have another motive for what I am about to say?
- Is what I am going to say true, or is it an exaggeration or only a partial truth?
- Is what I am going to say relevant to the issue we are discussing?
- Is what I am going to say constructive—something that will move us closer to mutual understanding?

4. Help those in conflict to clearly identify and define the problems and issues. But urge them to avoid taking a definite stand on what they want as a solution, for doing so sets the stage for a struggle of wills. Ask each person to state briefly his or her concerns and needs. Ask the others to repeat what they have heard. If they have not understood, repeat this process. The objective here is to help each person understand what the other is saying and to gain empathy for each other's perspective and feelings.

5. Use techniques of reflection, clarification, paraphrase, and summarization to assist each to express his or her point of view, needs, and concerns. Help each to use I-statements in expressing his or her side in the conflict (see Items 8.3 and 8.5).

6. Once the issues are on the table and there is some degree of mutual understanding, use brainstorming to identify several potential solutions. Look for solutions or compromises that provide some benefits to both sides.

7. Throughout the discussion, recognize and reinforce efforts to control anger, to understand the other party, and to honestly express needs and concerns—even if these are only feeble efforts.

8. Remember that the person who is labeled a troublemaker or the one who is causing a problem is very often a person who feels powerless. People who feel powerless often strike out, directly or indirectly, at others. In response, others may strike back or withdraw from the relationship, thereby creating a vicious cycle. It is important to directly address the feelings of powerlessness.

9. Those who want to resolve an interpersonal conflict are advised to *do what comes unnaturally*. The person who feels the desire to retreat from the conflict really needs to directly confront the issue. The person who wants to talk actually needs to listen. The person who would like to vent frustration and inflict pain really needs to display compassion and empathy.

SELECTED BIBLIOGRAPHY

Bisno, Herb. *Managing Conflict.* Newbury Park, CA: Sage, 1988.

Kruk, Edward, ed. *Mediation and Conflict Resolution in Social Work and the Human Services.* Chicago: Nelson-Hall, 1997.

Leviton, Sharon, and James Greenstone. *Elements of Mediation.* Pacific Grove, CA: Brooks/Cole, 1997.

Wilmot, William, and Joyce Hocker. I*nterpersonal Conflict,* 5th ed. New York: McGraw-Hill, 1998.

14.23 The Feelings List

PURPOSE: To assist a client in the identification and expression of feelings.

DISCUSSION: Many of the clients seen by social workers grew up in dysfunctional families (e.g., alcoholic, abusive, etc.) where they learned to suppress their feelings. Often, they were punished for expressing emotion or for asking the "wrong" questions. Many were exposed to a childrearing pattern that invalidated or discounted the feelings that they did express (e.g., when a mother tells her angry child, "You're not really angry; you're just tired"). As these individuals grow older, they carry with them a tendency to suppress, misinterpret, or mistrust their own emotions and feelings. Many are unsure of their true feelings; many cannot distinguish one from another and can speak of feelings in only broad terms such as *sad, upset,* or *OK.*

Simplistic as it sounds, a written list of feeling words can help a client identify and express feelings. As the client struggles to identify and sort out personal feelings, he or she is encouraged to review the list as an aid in finding the words needed to describe feelings. Even a short list of 25 to 50 words can serve as a starting place and help the client distinguish one feeling from another—for example:

controlled	embarrassed	attached	abandoned
excited	courageous	worthless	serene
concerned	tender	secure	curious
manipulated	tough	lost	ashamed
hateful	sarcastic	protected	guilty
desperate	competitive	isolated	vulnerable
joyful	confident	relieved	apathetic
disloyal	fearful	detached	warm

While discussing feelings, the client should be helped to understand that feelings and emotions are a normal human experience. Because feelings are real and important, they should not be hidden or denied. Although some feelings are pleasant and some unpleasant, they are neither good or bad. How one chooses to behave in response to feelings may be appropriate or inappropriate, but the feelings themselves simply exist and are neither right nor wrong in a moral sense.

A feelings list can prove useful in work with individuals, families, and groups. If you believe the use of a feelings list would help your clients, the authors suggest that you prepare one consisting of words that will be meaningful to individuals served by your agency. A client's age, life experience, culture, and educational level need to be considered when compiling a list. (Also see Item 8.6 for additional information on emotion.)

SELECTED BIBLIOGRAPHY

Black, Claudia. *It Will Never Happen to Me.* Denver: MAC Publishing, 1981.

Mayer, Adele. *Incest: A Treatment Manual for Therapy with Victims, Spouses and Offenders.* Homes Beach, FL: Learning Publications, 1983.

Porter, Eugene. *Treating the Young Male Victim of Sexual Assault.* Syracuse, NY: Safer Society Press, 1986.

14.24 The Life Book

PURPOSE: To help a child in a foster care or adoption placement develop a sense of identity and understand his or her experiences with separation and placement.

DISCUSSION: The ***life book*** is both a therapeutic tool and a personalized record of a child's life experience. Backhaus (1984) explains that

> a Life Book is an individually made book covering the child's life from birth to present, written in the child's own words. It generally includes a narrative describing what has happened to the child, when, and why, as well as what the child's feelings are about what has happened. The book may also incorporate photos, drawings, report cards, awards and certificates, letters from previous foster or adoptive parents and birth parents, a birth certificate, a genogram, and anything else a particular child might want to include. It is current practice to assemble a Life Book for older children who are being adopted as part of their preparation. Life Books . . . can be invaluable for those being adopted, living in foster or residential care, or returning to birth parents. (p. 551)

The life book is especially useful in helping a child:

1. Develop a sense of continuity and identity.
2. Understand past separations and placements and reduce confusion and misconceptions about these and other disruptive experiences.
3. Avoid the unhealthy use of fantasy and denial in trying to cope with painful life experiences.
4. Remember significant people and childhood events.
5. Maintain in one place a record of important personal data (i.e., birth and medical information, pictures of family and significant others, school records, etc.).

The worker involves the child in the creation of the book and refers to it when discussing the child's life experience and his or her feelings about those experiences.

SELECTED BIBLIOGRAPHY

Backhaus, Kristiana. "Life Books: Tool for Working with Children in Placement." *Social Work* 29 (November–December 1984): 551–545.

Gillespie, Donna. *My Life's Book: A Handbook for Foster Parents.* King George, VA: American Foster Care Resouces, 1996.

14.25 Client Advocacy

PURPOSE: To secure services that the client needs and is entitled to but unable to obtain on his or her own.

DISCUSSION: When the social worker assumes the role of ***client advocate,*** he or she speaks, argues, bargains, and negotiates on behalf of an individual. This form of advocacy is also termed *case advocacy,* in contrast to what is known as *class advocacy* (see Item 14.50). An advocacy stance may be necessary when a client has been unable to obtain services to which he or she is entitled; when the client was subjected to discrimination or unfairness by a professional, agency, or business; and when the client is unable to respond effectively to these situations. Because advocacy is form of a confrontation and one cannot be sure how those to be confronted will respond, some risks are involved in choosing this tactic. Remember these guidelines:

1. Make sure your client wants you to become his or her advocate. Do not engage in advocacy unless you have an explicit agreement with your client and he or she understands both the potential benefits and risks. To the extent possible, involve your client in all decisions concerning the actions you will take.

2. Realize that your advocacy can damage your relationship or your agency's relationship with another agency or professional and that this damaged relationship may create problems in the future when you need their cooperation to serve other clients. Do not use advocacy until you have tried approaches with fewer risks or that are less likely to polarize the affected parties.

3. Your decision to assume the role of client advocate should arise out of a genuine desire to be of service to your client and never from a wish to punish another agency or a desire for self-aggrandizement.

4. Before you select this confrontational tactic, be sure you understand the facts of the matter. Do not base your decisions on hearsay or on a one-sided description of what happened and why. Realize that clients sometimes misunderstand or misinterpret the explanations given to them by agency representatives. Do not base your plan of advocacy on the assumption that you understand another agency's policies, procedures, or eligibility criteria. Get the facts before you decide how to proceed.

5. Once you decide that the tactic of advocacy is required, arrange for a meeting with the appropriate agency or program representative. Face-to-face meetings are almost always more effective than phone calls and letters. However, a letter outlining your client's situation and your concern may be needed prior to the face-to-face meeting. Respect an agency's chain of command (e.g., do not ask to speak with a supervisor until you have spoken to the line worker who was in contact with your client; do not ask to speak with the administrator until you have spoken with line worker's supervisor).

6. Before you speak with the agency representative, write down exactly what you intend to say and the questions you will ask. Begin your conversation with a courteous request for an explanation of why your client was denied service or treated in a certain way. Communicate your concerns in a factual and nonabrasive manner, but speak in a tone the conveys that you feel strongly about the matter. Keep a written record of who you talk to, their position and responses, and the time, date, and place of the communication.

7. If the information you gather indicates that the agency wanted to provide the service requested by your client but could not because of a technicality or an unreasonable requirement, ask for information on how the decision can be appealed and who else you and your client should speak to. Ask if administrators, board members, or a legislative committee should be informed of the difficulty faced by your client or perhaps consulted on how this matter can be resolved.

8. If the information you gather indicates that the agency or program did, in fact, treat your client in an unfair and inappropriate manner, explain that if the matter cannot be resolved and corrected, you will take your concern to those higher in the chain of command or make a formal complaint. Consider using a measured expression of anger to demonstrate your resolve.

9. If further action is required, you will need to secure information on how to file a complaint or initiate an appeal. In some cases, you will need legal advice before proceeding. As preparation for an appeal or formal complaint, you will need detailed documentation of what happened and what was attempted, step by step, to resolve the matter. You will need names, dates, and the content of all communications and copies of all letters sent and received.

SELECTED BIBLIOGRAPHY

Mickelson, James. "Advocacy." In *Encyclopedia of Social Work,* 19th ed., vol. 1, edited by Richard L. Edwards. Washington, DC: NASW Press, 1995, pp. 95–100.

Sunley, Robert. *Advocating Today: A Human Service Practitioner's Handbook.* New York: Family Service Association of America, 1983.

Weissman, Harold, Irwin Epstein, and Andrea Savage. *Agency-Based Social Work: Neglected Aspects of Clinical Practice.* Philadelphia: Temple University Press, 1983.

14.26 Empowerment

PURPOSE: To assist a client to develop a sense of control and power.

DISCUSSION: Many of the clients served by social workers have been "beaten down" by discrimination and oppression and by social and economic forces beyond their control. They may believe that they are powerless to change their life situations. In order to counter such feelings and perceptions, social workers need to emphasize empowerment in their work with clients. As used here, ***empowerment*** refers to various decisions and actions designed to help people understand the social, economic, and political context of their current situation; identify, increase, and exercise their personal and political power; and take action, individually or as a group, to improve their situation. In this definition, *power* refers to an individual's or a group's capacity to influence the behavior of others, change public opinion, and bring about change in the behavior of other people and organizations.

An empowerment strategy places an emphasis on helping a client secure access to and control over needed resources, on client involvement in decision making, and on helping the client acquire the knowledge and skills needed to function independently. This approach rests on the assumption that the individual in question already possesses or has the potential to learn necessary competencies and that the client's difficulty is created primarily by a social barrier or a lack of resources. The strategy of empowerment will not prove beneficial if this assumption is not valid in a given case.

In some circles, the term *empowerment* has become little more that a buzzword. Even in social work, there is some debate over whether empowerment is a new paradigm for practice or only a new word for well-established methods of working with people. Whether a new or old idea, a truly empowering approach requires that the social worker adhere to certain guidelines:

1. Recognize that people cannot begin to solve their problems or take control of their lives until they are given responsibility for defining the problems they face, for selecting the solution, and can gain access to the resources they deem important to that solution. In order to accurately define their problem and assess their situation, clients need access to available information relevant to their situation.

2. View your helping role as primarily that of a partner or a consultant to the client. View the client as the only true expert on his or her problems or situation. Thus, it is the client's definition of the problem and the client's thoughts on what should be done about it that are most relevant to the change process.

3. Help clients build self-confidence, take the personal risks necessary to break out of self-defeating and self-limiting patterns, and build a social support network. Encourage them to participate in groups so they do not feel alone and so they develop a group consciousness. The small group is an ideal environment for clients to learn and practice such skills as communication, critical thinking, problem solving, persuasion, assertiveness, negotiation, and mutual support. In direct work with these clients, make frequent use of active teaching techniques (e.g., coaching and role-play) that can help the client learn these important skills.

4. Uncover potential sources of power. Assist the client in making an inventory of his or her power sources such as knowledge derived from life experience, motivation, time, energy, knowledge of the community, understanding of particular problems, sense of humor, willingness to take risks, verbal ability, voting, writing letters to persons in authority, feelings of solidarity with others, membership in groups and organizations, and the like.

5. Help your clients understand the people, organizations, and systems with which they must interact in order to change their life situations. Provide or help them obtain information about how these people and systems make decisions and why they behave and function as they do.

6. Assist the client in making a planned and disciplined use of the power he or she does possess. Recognize that persons who finally discover that they have some power do not always use this power in an appropriate manner. Sometimes they are overly eager or aggressive and as a result they alienate others and create unnecessary opposition. While encouraging clients to use their power, help them understand that numerous realities will limit how others can respond. For example, an agency may not be able to respond completely to clients' requests because of time and budget limitations, rules, regulations, and the needs of others.

7. Recognize and build on client strengths. Search for the positive in the situation. Provide encouragement and a sense of hope. Make generous use of reframing (see Item 14.12) to help the client view mistreatment and injustice from a different angle. For example, help the client let go of anger by viewing the past as a painful but invaluable source of wisdom regarding what is really important in life and how and why people behave as they do. Help the client see that if one chooses to be taught rather than hurt, one has even more opportunities to grow as a person. Help your client recognize that even distress can be beneficial if it pushes a person to carefully reexamine his or her situation and take action to change those things that are causing pain and discomfort.

8. Help clients experience a sense of personal power and control by allowing and encouraging them to make decisions and follow through on those decisions. Be prepared to respect their choices and allow them to experience the consequences of those choices—both the positive and the negative.

9. Help your clients understand the factors and forces that contributied to their feelings of powerlessness. It should be noted, however, that individuals who seriously examine how they have been mistreated or held back may become engulfed by rage. Some get "stuck" at this point and become prisoners of their own anger. Help your clients express their feelings and then move beyond bitterness.

SELECTED BIBLIOGRAPHY

Dunst, Carl, Carl Trivette, and Angela Deal. *Enabling and Empowering Families.* Cambridge, MA: Brookline Books, 1988.

Gutierrez, Lorraine, and Enid Cox. *Empowerment in Social Work Practice: A Source Book.* Pacific Grove, CA.: Brooks/Cole, 1998.

Guterrez, Lorraine, and Paula Nuris, eds. *Education and Research for Empowerment Practice.* Seattle: University of Washington School of Social Work, Center for Policy and Practice Research, 1994.

Lee, Judith. *The Empowerment Approach to Social Work Practice.* New York: Columbia University Press, 1994.

14.27 Crisis Cards

PURPOSE: To help a client manage a recurring troublesome situation.

DISCUSSION: Crisis cards are a set of 3'' × 5'' cards on which the client has written various suggestions to himself or herself on how to cope with and manage a situation that could easily escalate out of control. For example, if the client is a father who is easily angered by his son's rebellious behavior, crisis cards might be used to help the father maintain self-control.

The suggestions written on the cards are ones identified by the client during discussions with the worker. Brainstorming may be used to identify the various options. They must be ones that make sense to the client and are likely to work, given the client's patterns and circumstances. For example, the father just mentioned might prepare the following seven cards:

Card 1: Remember that this will pass. Don't do anything foolish! Remember the times when I was a kid and also drove my parents nuts.

Card 2: Look at the family photo album and think of happier times.

Card 3: Read my Bible and pray.

Card 4: Call my friend Jim (555-6789) and ask him to listen to my frustration.

Card 5: Work out on my weight-lifting set.

Card 6: Cook one of my favorite meals.

Card 7: Walk to the store and back.

When the father finds himself getting angry and in danger of losing control, he refers to the cards and looks for a suggestion that might help him control his anger.

In addition to helping the client prepare a set of crisis cards, it is usually important to help the client work out a system for recognizing when he or she needs to use the cards. For example, the father could be helped to formulate a 10-point anger scale, ranging from 0 (no anger) to 10 (close to being violent). As the father learns to monitor his level of anger, he comes to recognize that at point 5 on the scale, he is to refer to the crisis cards.

The crisis cards technique can be adapted for use in work with whole families. For example, during a family meeting, the members might brainstorm various options on how they could better handle recurring conflicts or misunderstandings and then write the options on a set of crisis cards. A set of cards might also be used by someone learning to cope with a newly acquired disability or a difficult job-related task. Such cards and self-messages can also be used by someone working to maintain sobriety or trying to change a behavior pattern (e.g., keep to a diet, stick with a program of physical exercise, etc.).

SELECTED BIBLIOGRAPHY

Kinney, Jill, David Haapala, and Charlotte Booth. *Keeping Families Together: The Homebuilders Model.* New York: Aldine de Gruyter, 1991.

14.28 The Client in Crisis

PURPOSE: To assist the client in coping with a personal crisis.

DISCUSSION: The social worker will encounter many clients who are in a state of crisis. Although the word *crisis* is widely used, it has a specific meaning within the field of mental health. Essentially, a crisis consists of a perception and the reaction to that perception. When an individual is in ***crisis,*** he or she perceives a particular situation to be an intolerable and overwhelming difficulty and one with which he or she is unable to cope. Consequently, the individual reacts with great anxiety, panic, despair, and disorganization. A crisis is a sudden but temporary breakdown in a person's ordinary and usual capacity to cope with and manage one's life. Among the events that can precipitate a crisis are the death of a loved one, loss of a job, divorce, birth of a child with a severe disability, serious illness or accident, house fire, rape or mugging, or other traumatic event.

A crisis is a time of both danger and opportunity. It is dangerous because if the crisis is not resolved constructively, it can set in motion a downward spiral that leads to a level of functioning lower than that which existed prior to the crisis. On the other hand, a crisis can be an opportunity to learn new coping skills and make life changes that actually elevate one's usual level of functioning. A crisis is *time limited* and it is expected that, within a matter of weeks, the person will come to some level of adjustment and equilibrium. And, as suggested, that adjustment may be either positive or negative, depending, in part, on how others respond to the person during the crisis.

It is important to distinguish a personal crisis from a particular coping pattern that Kagan and Schlosberg (1989) term "perpetual crisis" or "crisis oriented." They explain that

> living in a crisis-oriented family is like riding a roller coaster 24 hours a day: terrifying, energizing and addicting. . . . Real, rather than perpetual crisis, puts us into acute grief. . . . For families in 'perpetual crisis' the grief process is blocked. . . . Crisis becomes a way of life. . . . Instead of becoming vulnerable and facing change, crisis-oriented families protect themselves from facing difficult issues. (pp. 2–3)

The following practice guidelines apply when working with a person in a real crisis but not with persons in "perpetual crisis":

1. Realize that this state of disorganization will diminish over time; with or without professional help, the crisis will typically be over within about six weeks. The purpose of crisis intervention is to help the client deal with the crisis in a positive way and prevent the development of more serious and long-standing problems.

2. Listen actively and offer emotional support. A person in crisis is in a heightened state of either anxiety or depression and also feels a sense of failure because he or she is unable to cope. The client is probably preoccupied with the precipitating event and will have difficulty focusing attention on anything else. Before the client can consider alternatives, make decisions, or plan ways for resolving problems, he or she will need much emotional support from the worker and significant others. This support may range from simply acknowledging the existence of the upsetting experience to offering strong verbal reassurance (e.g., "You did the right thing in leaving your house and coming to our shelter").

3. Involve others in the helping process. People in crisis are often most receptive to assistance provided by those whom they know and trust (e.g., family, friends, employer, minister, neighbors, etc.). Encourage the client to reach out to others, or, with his or her permission, contact these significant others and enlist their help on behalf of the client.

4. Allow the client to express emotion. Calmly allow the client to cry or express feelings of fear or anger while you continue to provide emotional support and acceptance. The client's strong emotions and intense feelings will diminish with time.

5. Communicate hope. A hopeful attitude is an essential element in responding to a person in crisis. If you communicate a belief in the client's ability to cope, he or she will be less fearful and will gradually regain self-confidence.

6. People in crisis are preoccupied with their pain and problems. They have tunnel vision and can think of little else. Consequently, they are not able to step back and objectively analyze their situation. You will need to ask questions and actively examine the details of their situation as a way of helping them think more clearly.

7. Use partialization. The person in crisis feels as if he or she is facing a giant and completely unmanageable problem. By breaking the problem down into several smaller ones, to be addressed one at a time, the client will feel more hopeful about regaining control.

8. Provide factual information. Often, a crisis arises because the person has misconceptions about his or her situation or because intense feelings have distorted his or her perception of reality (e.g., "I just know that I'm going to lose my job" or "This goes to prove that no company is going to hire someone in a wheelchair like me"). Provide factual information related to the person's concern (e.g., "No, I don't think it is because you are in a wheelchair that you weren't hired; there are laws against discrimination of that kind"). When appropriate, give honest feedback needed to correct misunderstandings (e.g., "Mr. Jones told me that you weren't hired because you were belligerent and sarcastic during the interview").

9. A person in crisis has difficulty making decisions and anticipating the consequences of his or her actions. Thus, you may need to provide highly specific directions as to what the person needs to do or what will probably happen if he or she takes a certain course of action. It is especially important to help the client anticipate the consequences of destructive behaviors (e.g., "If you lose control and again injure your child, she will be placed in a foster home").

10. Reinforce adaptive behavior. Help the individual identify what worked in the past; encourage the client to take similar actions to address his or her current problem. An important part of crisis intervention is to encourage clients to take action so they begin to regain a faith and trust in their own capabilities.

11. Consider using a behavioral contract (see Item 14.6) as a means of providing the client with structure and direction. This helps the client mobilize inner resources, and it also sends the message that you have confidence in his or her ability to take the steps needed to get through the crisis.

SELECTED BIBLIOGRAPHY

Gilliland, Burl, and Richard James. *Crisis Intervention Strategies,* 3rd ed. Pacific Grove, CA: Brooks/Cole, 1997.

Hoff, Lee Ann. *People in Crisis,* 4th ed. San Francisco: Jossey-Bass, 1995.

Kagan, Richard, and Shirley Schlosberg. *Families in Perpetual Crisis.* New York: W. W. Norton, 1989.

Roberts, Albert, ed. *Crisis Management and Brief Treatment.* Chicago: Nelson-Hall, 1996.

14.29 The Client Who Is a Child

PURPOSE: To adapt basic social work techniques and approaches to the special needs of the child under age 12.

DISCUSSION: Children are not miniature adults. Because many of the interviewing techniques that are effective with adults may not work with children, some new skills, such as the use of play, need to be added to the worker's repertoire. Several guidelines should be considered when working with a child:

Planning the Interview

1. Anticipate how the child's level of development will affect his or her capacity to understand and use language. How and what children think and feel are closely tied to their developmental stages. Realize, however, that there is much variation among the children in a particular age group.

2. Be clear about why you are meeting with the child and what you hope to accomplish. Plan several alternative methods to accomplish your goal. Anticipate what might go wrong (e.g., child will not talk, child cries, child will not leave parent, etc.) and consider how you might handle such situations.

3. Plan to use some form of play or activity to facilitate communication. Play is a normal activity for children; it is a child's natural means of communication. Prior to the interview, assemble play materials that may be needed. For young children, provide art materials (e.g., finger paints, clay, building blocks) as well as objects that can be used to portray family themes (e.g., dolls, puppets, doll house, toy animals). For older children, consider simple card or board games, puzzles, or electronic games. The skillful interviewer of children is someone who can be playful and think or feel like a child.

4. Conduct the interview in a room that is familiar and comfortable to the child. If that is not possible, consider an open space that affords some privacy (e.g., a public park or school playground).

Introducing Yourself and Getting Started

5. When first meeting a child, explain who you are and how you want to be addressed (e.g., "My name is Ron Hoffman. Please call me Ron. My job is to help children who are having problems at home"). If the child seems fearful or unwilling to talk, try doing something unexpected (e.g., "Brian, we are going to be doing a lot of talking and we may get thirsty. Should we get some juice now or should we wait until later?"). Place yourself at the child's level physically; sit or squat so you do not tower over the child. Initiate some friendly interaction by showing an interest in items the child is wearing or carrying or ask about the child's school or favorite games or TV shows. If the child refuses to interact, engage in a parallel activity and then gradually initiate conversation about the activity. For example, if the child does not talk but begins to play with a doll, pick up another doll and engage in similar play. This will often prompt some interaction and an opportunity for verbal exchange.

6. If the child is frightened, attempt to normalize the situation (e.g., "When I was your age, I was afraid to talk to new people"). It may be necessary to ally the child's fears that he or she is in trouble or that the interview is some kind of punishment. Many young children will relax and open up to a "dumb" adult. By playing the role of a bumbling adult and asking some ridiculous questions (e.g., "Are you married?" "Do you know how to fly an airplane?" "Do you own a candy store?"), you may get the child to respond. You might also fumble the spelling of the child's name so he or she has to correct you and thereby take control and feel more powerful.

7. If the child is at least 6 or 7 years of age, ask what he or she knows about the purpose of the interview. This will reveal what the child is expecting. Then explain why you want to speak with the child. Ask if he or she has talked to anyone else about the meeting and what others have said about the meeting or perhaps what instructions the child was given about what to say and do.

8. Do not disguise the interview as recreation; this may confuse the child about who you are and your role. Also be cognizant that little or no confidentiality can be provided to a child. Do not promise to keep secrets. If the child appears reluctant to talk for fear of retaliation by others, you may need to describe what you can do to keep him or her safe.

Gathering Information from a Child

9. If the child is below about age 6, much of the information you gather will be from your observations of the child's play and interactions with you and others. At this young age, a child will often act out his or her thoughts and feelings. However, in order to draw valid inferences from observations, it is important to observe the child in several different settings and at different times of the day. Conclusions should not be based on a single session.

10. Children between the ages of 3 and 6 are eager to please adults, quite suggestible, and easily influenced by an adult's leading questions. Children this age are very sensitive and reactive to an adult's nonverbal communication; they may modify their story to make it fit what they believe the adult wants to hear. It is important to be warm and accepting, or children may judge that you disapprove of what they are saying and cease talking. Young children are influenced more by the social context of the message (i.e., who said it and how, when, and where it was said) than by the literal meaning of the words.

11. Children under about age 6 will often project their own thoughts and feelings onto dolls or pictures. Thus, consider using dolls or pictures to set up a make-believe situation relevant to the topics you wish to explore and then ask the child to complete the story or describe what the dolls or characters in the picture are doing, thinking, and feeling. You may need to initiate the storytelling about the dolls or pictures, but once the child is attentive, you can ask the child to continue the story. The techniques of active listening (e.g., paraphrase, summarization, etc.) do not work with children below age 6 or 7.

Young children are easily distracted and tend to move quickly from topic to topic. Consequently, they may describe only once or with just a few words what they think or feel about an important topic and then they are ready to move on to something else. Asking them to stick with one topic is seldom successful; however, you may initiate a return to the original topic at a later time. Children often become noncommittal (e.g., not answering or shrugging) if pressured and when uncomfortable or unsure how to respond. Thus, it is important to facilitate the child's expression without being so directive that the child withdraws.

12. If the child is older than about 6 years, he or she will be better able to use words to express thoughts and feelings and answer questions—if the questions are simple and age appropriate. Children of this age frequently need assistance to fully describe a situation or event. For example, you may need to ask: What happened next? Then what did you do? Where did this happen? Who else was with you? However, because it is difficult for them to describe reasons behind their behavior, you should avoid "why" questions.

13. By age 9 or 10, children are able to describe others by describing patterns of behavior and using concepts to describe personality traits and attitudes. Because they can now think conceptually, they pay more attention to the words of a message. Also, they are able to detect phony or insincere messages and they become suspicious when they observe incongruency between a person's words and behavior.

Story completions, dolls, and drawing may still be necessary interviewing techniques for children between about ages 7 and 9, but many children older than 9 years will respond thoughtfully to an interviewer's questions if the interviewer is nonthreatening and unhurried. Children of this age group find it easier to talk about personal matters if they can do so while playing a simple card game or a board game like checkers that does not require a great deal of concentration. Puppet-to-puppet interaction can facilitate communication and talking on play telephones usually works well. Sentence completions are also useful (e.g., When at home, I am afraid that . . .). Many 7- to 10-year-olds respond well to humor, if it is not subtle.

Understanding How Children Think

14. Children between the ages of about 3 to 6 are subjective, concrete, and egocentric in their thinking. For example, they believe an event that makes them happy will have the same effect on all people. They report their feelings in a global manner and their thinking is characterized by an "all-or-nothing" pattern. For example, things are either good or bad; the child is unable to understand mixed feelings or ambivalence. The child may describe a person as mean and minutes later describe the same person as nice or fun. Such thinking in extremes and absolutes causes them to categorize both themselves and others as either good or bad, smart or dumb, and so on. Children of this age describe themselves and others in terms of external characteristics (e.g., age, hair color, grade in school, etc.); they do not mention personality traits except in global terms such as "she is happy" or "he is a bad person."

15. Beginning at about age 6, the child's thinking becomes more objective and logical. Gradually, the child acquires the ability to imagine himself or herself in the place of another person and to understand that everyone can be different in how they think, feel, and respond. However, even a 7-year-old may still believe that he or she is the total cause for how others, especially parents, feel and behave. It is not until about age 9 or 10 that children truly understand that they do not cause all of the behaviors and emotions they observe in others.

16. By about age 10, the child no longer thinks in absolutes, and views himself or herself as a separate person and a mixture of characteristics and abilities (e.g., someone who is skilled at some things but not others or good sometimes and bad at other times). At this age, he or she understands it is possible and normal to simultaneously feel opposing emotions (e.g., to be angry at someone you love). Also, the child now has the ability to reflect on his or her own thoughts and actions and can figure out how others will probably react in a particular situation or react to certain information. Thus, the child can now manipulate words and information in order to influence how others will behave.

Assessing Truthfulness of Child's Statements

17. Social workers who investigate reports of abuse and neglect and those who conduct child custody evaluations frequently find themselves in situations where they must form a judgment about whether a child is telling the truth. Children from 4 to 6 years old can and will tell a simple lie in order to avoid punishment (e.g., "I didn't break the cup"), but they do not have the cognitive abilities necessary to fabricate a complex story having several interrelated elements, actions, or actors. In trying to describe something that happened, they can often recall central actors or central events but not the connecting details, such as what happened before and after and how one action lead to another. They have what some call a "script memory." For example, they can remember events (e.g., a birthday party) and rituals (e.g., going to bed, mealtime, etc.) but do not accurately remember events that are not part of their usual routines. Children this age frequently exaggerate events or boast when describing their abilities and experiences; however, when asked, "Is that pretend or real?" or "Is that an 'I wish' story or is it true?" they generally can articulate the difference between what was true and what was an exaggeration.

18. Children between the ages of 7 and 11 value honesty and fairness and generally avoid telling a lie. It is rare for them to fabricate. However, they have the cognitive abilities necessary to add or selectively withhold information and will use deception as a means of avoiding punishment or getting what they want and they tend to embellish on the truth in order to tell an exciting story. Children aged 9, 10, or 11 are eager to please adults and inclined to say what they believe adults want to hear. They have good memories of central actors and events and good free recall (i.e., able to recall and describe without the aid of detailed questioning by an interviewer).

19. As a general rule, the younger the child, the less likely he or she is to fabricate a falsehood. However, it is important to remember that children—like adults—can and do misunderstand and misinterpret their experiences and will, at times, lie. In cases where a child self-reports sexual abuse, deliberate false reports are rare among children below age 12, and also quite rare among teenagers. Most efforts to study this matter conclude that about 5 percent of self-reports by children are erroneous and arise from misinterpretations of nonsexual behavior and psychological disturbance. However, the rate of false reports becomes higher when the child is the focus of custody or visitation disputes and is encouraged by one parent to accuse the other of some wrongdoing.

20. Sometimes a parent or parent figure will pressure a child to lie to a social worker. Certain behaviors indicate that a child is reciting a fabricated story in order to please or protect a parent—for example, inconsistency regarding the major elements of the story or extreme consistency regarding major events but with no supporting detail; flat affect (i.e., absence of anxiety, fear, guilt, shame, anger, etc.); use of adult phrases and terminology; the only emotion expressed is anger (i.e., suggests motive of revenge); and visual description only (i.e., child describes what was seen but is unable to describe smell, sounds, and touch associated with the situation described). If a parent has coached a child, the parent is usually threatened by the social worker's request for a private interview with the child.

21. Be cautious about interpreting the meaning of a child's play. Indeed, young children incorporate their thoughts, feelings, and recent experiences into their play. However, children also incorporate into their play various themes drawn from TV programs and books, from incidents described by their friends, and from events they have observed outside the home. Thus, it may be difficult to pinpoint the exact source of the themes that appear in a child's play.

22. Themes of violence are common in the stories told by normal, nonabused, young children. For example, among nonabused 3-year-olds, about 66 percent of girls and 90 percent of boys include acts of violence and destruction in the stories they tell to other children and adults. Thus, talk about violence is not, by itself, an indicator of physical abuse or exposure to domestic violence.

23. The social worker should not assume that a young child can accurately describe when an event happened. Young children do not use clocks or calendars to measure time. In fact, preschool children do not grasp the concept of time; young grade school–age children typically use events such as nap time, lunch time, Christmas, start of school, and other events as markers of time. Such markers, rather than clock times and dates, should be used to establish time frames.

Additional Suggestions

24. Realize that during an interview, you get only a sample of the child's behavior. The child may behave differently in other situations and with other people. The farther removed the child is from his or her usual social and family context, the more cautious you must be in drawing conclusions about the child's behavior. For example, the child who appears anxious or withdrawn during an office interview may simply be fearful of an unfamiliar environment. In-home interviews are important to an accurate assessment of a child's functioning.

25. Allow the child to set the pace of the interview, following his or her lead. Permit him or her to move around and explore the room. Children—especially young children—have short attention spans and are easily distracted. Excessive squirming and a lack of attention probably indicates that the child is tired and the interview should end.

26. The vocabulary you use should be appropriate to the age of the child. With a 12-year-old, you can use words and expressions similar to those used with adults. But with a 4-year-old child, your expressions must be simple and concrete.

27. Because young children are especially responsive to nonverbal communication, it is helpful to make frequent use of facial expressions, touch, voice tone, and gestures. However, do not kiss or caress the child; this makes most children uncomfortable, and it opens the door to a misinterpretation of your intentions and a possible accusation of sexual abuse. Touch can be especially confusing and threatening to a child who has been physically or sexually abused.

28. Answer a child's question honestly and directly (e.g., "I believe you will be in foster care until the school term ends"). Do not use euphemisms; do not beat around the bush. Avoid giving elaborate explanations. When providing important information, try to give it in phases and small doses.

29. When behavior-control rules are necessary during an interview, explain the rules, along with any consequences for breaking them (e.g., "You are not permitted to hit me; if you do hit me, I will put away the toys and today's meeting will end").

30. During an interview, give the child as much choice and control as possible. But be sure to offer choices among alternatives that you can accept. This point is illustrated in the following statements: *Misleading:* "Well, Ellen, what would you like to do? We can do whatever you like." *Correct:* "Ellen, today you can use the finger paints or the crayons. Which one do you want to use?"

31. Outings, treats, or gifts should be used judiciously. Although they are an extension of normal adult-child interaction and may be helpful in building a relationship, they are easily misinterpreted. Also, be careful that your gift of even a small toy is not viewed as competition with the child's parents.

32. Children are protective of their parents. A child will usually defend his or her parents, even abusive parents. Be objective and concrete in talking about the parent-child relationship and the parents' behavior (e.g., "Your dad does has a problem with alcohol. He gets drunk about once a week. He cannot stop drinking. That is why your parents are getting a divorce"). Do not criticize the parents.

33. A series of interviews should usually have structure and a routine, depending on each child's needs. For example, some children like interviews that have definite beginning and ending rituals. Others, however, may want relief from structure and need freedom to do more of what they feel like doing.

The Child in Out-of-Home Placement

34. Many of the children known professionally to social workers are in out-of-home placement (i.e., foster family care, group homes, institutional care, etc.). Realize that placement is always disruptive and emotionally traumatic to a child. Many children blame themselves for the family problems that led up to the placement and view placement as a punishment for some real or imagined wrongdoing.

35. Be sensitive to the pain of their separation and loss experiences. Relationship losses, especially a series of losses, have long-lasting, negative effects on a child. Thus, it is critically important to minimize the number of separations experienced by a child. If a child must be separated from someone to which he or she is emotionally attached, the move should be as gradual as possible, thus giving the child an opportunity to prepare and time to adjust. A ritual such as a going-away party helps the child make this transition by symbolically ending one relationship and beginning another. Without such a ritual, the child might feel as if he or she was given away or rejected; a transition ritual gives the child permission to let go of one relationship and begin a new one. After the physical separation, it is important that the child be able to return to his or her former home for occasional visits.

36. Remember that the child's biological parents are central to his or her identity. Do everything possible to maintain frequent contacts and visits between the child in placement and his or her parents, siblings, and other close relatives. In the long run, frequent visitation is helpful to the child, even if the visits are at times upsetting.

37. Some children make a fairly good adjustment to placement but most experience much inner turmoil. The child usually feels insecure and uncertain about why he or she is in placement. Thus, assume that the child has many questions about his or her past, present, and future; make it easy for him or her to ask these questions. If a child does not understand why he or she is separated from his or her parents and has little or no contact with the parents, the child will usually create an elaborate fantasy that explains the situation. Be factual and honest when describing the child's current situation and possible changes in the future. It is better for the child to struggle with an unpleasant reality than to adjust to a pleasant fantasy.

38. Because foster children experience so much change and because their lives are so unpredictable, you must be prepared to become a predictable figure in their lives. The foster child is especially sensitive to any hint of rejection. Contacts should occur on a regular basis. If you must miss an appointment, explain the reason directly to the child. If you may not be able to keep a promise, do not make it!

39. Children often feel shame and embarrassment about being in foster care, and consequently they fabricate a story to explain their situation. When the fabrication is discovered, the child acquires a reputation for being a spinner of tall tales or a liar. Thus, it is important to help these children develop an understandable and acceptable explanation of why they are in an out-of-home placement so they can more comfortably describe their living situation to teachers, friends, and others.

40. When speaking with foster parents, adoptive parents, or group care staff, be truthful about the child's behavior, situation, and history. Efforts to conceal the child's life experience in an attempt to protect the child or because you fear others will not understand almost always backfire.

SELECTED BIBLIOGRAPHY

Allen-Meares, Paula. *Social Work with Children and Adolescents.* White Plains, NY: Longman, 1995.

Garbarbino, James, and Frances Stott. *What Children Can Tell Us: Eliciting, Interpreting and Evaluating Information from Children.* San Francisco: Jossey-Bass, 1989.

Morris, Richard, and Thomas Kratochwill, eds. *The Practice of Child Therapy,* 3rd ed. Boston: Allyn and Bacon, 1998.

Ney, Tara, ed. *True and False Allegations of Child Sexual Abuse.* New York: Brunner/Mazel, 1994.

O'Connor, Kevin, and Charles Schaefer. *Handbook of Play Therapy,* vol. II. New York: Wiley, 1994.

Webb, Nancy. *Social Work Practice with Children.* New York: Guilford, 1996.

14.30 The Client Who Is an Adolescent

PURPOSE: To adapt basic social work techniques and approaches to the needs of the adolescent.

DISCUSSION: The developmental period between ages 12 and 18 is often a stormy one. Many parents experience serious conflicts with their adolescent children; most of these focus on issues of authority and control. Parents typically worry that their adolescent children will become involved with drugs and irresponsible sex or become injured by recklessness. Some parents become so upset and angered that they physically abuse their adolescent children or kick them out of the home.

The problems most likely to bring the adolescent to the attention of a social worker include family conflict, running away, violence, delinquency, pregnancy, drug abuse, threat of suicide, and the need for foster care or residential treatment. The following guidelines are useful for working with adolescents:

1. Adolescents are typically idealistic, painfully self-conscious, struggling with authority issues, fiercely attached to peers, preoccupied with bodily changes and their sexuality, seeking popularity and conformity within their peer group, and desperately trying to develop an identity apart from their family.

2. Adolescents are resilient and have great capacity to grow and change. An effective social work intervention can have a positive, lifelong impact. Because these are often lively, inquisitive, and questioning clients, work with adolescents can be stimulating and genuinely fun.

3. Adolescents have an intense need to be heard. However, you must listen for the underlying meaning rather than to the words used, because often the words themselves are offensive and shocking. Listen nonjudgmentally and encourage them to talk about life—as they experience it—about their needs, hopes, and dreams.

4. Adolescents need an environment that is predictable and provides structure and limits. However, adolescents will usually test the rules and limits put in place by an adult. Before you create a new rule, be sure it is really necessary, can be enforced, and is worth fighting over. Inform adolescents of rules and the consequences for violating a rule. Be fair and consistent in enforcing rules and imposing consequences.

5. Because of their high energy level, interaction with adolescents should allow for movement and activity. If possible, avoid office interviews; rather, try talking with adolescent clients while walking, shooting baskets, working out in a gym, or riding in a car. Movement makes it easier for adolescents to talk and express feelings.

6. Because the peer group is so important during adolescence, group approaches (e.g., group discussion, psychodrama, and group counseling) can be useful. Most adolescents are more accepting of a group-related intervention than a one-to-one interview. Adolescents in need of out-of-home placement usually do better in a group home setting than in foster family care. Behavioral contracting works fairly well with adolescents (see Item 14.6).

7. Keep parents informed and involved in your work with their child while providing the adolescent with as much confidentiality as is legally permissible. By helping parents recall and talk about their own adolescence, you can often increase their understanding and acceptance of their teenager.

8. Adolescents are sensitive to any hint of artificiality in others, even though they themselves may pretend to be someone they are not. Thus, it is important to be genuine. Do not try to talk and act like their peers. It is nearly impossible to keep up with the latest adolescent fads, music, and slang. Imitating adolescent talk is likely to make you appear phoney.

9. Be alert to the fact that when you work with adolescents, your own unresolved parent-child and authority issues often rise to the surface and you may project them onto your client.

10. Many adolescents are involuntary clients. Given the authority struggle common to this period, this is a very uncomfortable situation for adolescents. Silence is their usual means of resisting adult intrusion. Also, adolescents challenge adult authority by being rude, contradictory, and using abusive language.

11. Because adolescents' emotions are so intense and characterized by ambivalence, many adolescents find it difficult to verbalize how they are feeling, at least in ways that others can tolerate. Allow them to express private thoughts and feelings but do not push them toward such expressions since this will be perceived as control and invite further resistance.

12. Most adolescents are preoccupied with the here and now. Many have tunnel vision and seem unable to think beyond today or tomorrow. Gently encourage adolescents to examine their current decisions and actions in light of their hopes and dreams, opportunities, and goals. When their thinking is clearly unrealistic or dangerous, it is usually best to tell them so in a respectful but firm manner.

13. Many adolescents in the United States and Europe appear to be afflicted with a pervasive sense of hopelessness concerning their future. They complain that life is pointless since they have little chance of getting a good job and that violence and pollution is making life unbearable. Many feel as if their elders have robbed them of a future, and consequently they feel cheated, angry, and distrustful. Since they feel hopeless and bitter, they have little motivation and few interests other then getting through the day with as little discomfort as possible.

14. During adolescence, some individuals are attracted to and drawn into gang activity. Goldstein (1993) explains that

> youth join gangs and commit illegal activities therein to satisfy needs no different from those motivating all youths, gang or nongang. Adolescents of all types seek recognition from peers, status, clarification of their identity, pride, tangible resources, self-esteem, excitement, camaraderie. Such needs are age-appropriate, developmentally desirable, and to be encouraged, not thwarted. It is of course, the *means* by which such need satisfaction is sought that is at issue. Effective gang interventions will provide means for satisfying such needs in prosocial, growth-enhancing, and societally acceptable ways—and not ignore or deny their pressing reality. (pp. 477–488)

Youth gangs or street gangs have existed in major U.S. cities since the late nineteenth century. In the past, their illegal activity was mostly theft. In recent years, many youth gangs have adults as leaders, have grown more violent, and are often involved in serious criminal activity such as drug dealing and murder. Economic gain from drug dealing has become a driving force behind the expansion of gang activity. Consequently, it is increasingly difficult to distinguish between some youth gangs and organized crime.

SELECTED BIBLIOGRAPHY

Aldgate, Jane, Anthony Maluccio, and Christine Reeves. *Adolescents in Foster Families.* Chicago: Lyceum Books, 1989.

Carrell, Susan. *Group Exercises for Adolescents: A Manual for Therapists.* Newbury Park, CA: Sage, 1993.

Goldstein, Arnold. "Gang Interventions: Issues and Opportunities." In *The Gang Intervention Handbook*, edited by Arnold Goldstein and C. Ronald Huff. Champaign, IL: Research Press, 1993.

McWhirter, J. Jeffries, Benedict McWhirter, Anna McWhirter, and Ellen McWhirter. *At-Risk Youth: A Comprehensive Response.* Pacific Grove, CA: Brooks/Cole, 1998.

Sommers-Flannagan, John, and Rita Sommers-Flannagan. *Tough Kids, Cool Counseling.* Alexandria, VA: American Counseling Association, 1997.

14.31 The Client Who Is Elderly

PURPOSE: To adapt social work techniques and approaches to the special needs of the elderly.

DISCUSSION: By the year 2030, about 20 percent of the U.S. population will be age 65 or older. Social workers must give increasing attention to the needs of older people, especially those in their seventies, eighties, and nineties. The following guidelines will help the worker serving the elderly client:

1. Most elderly people strive to maintain their independence. As a person ages, he or she experiences many losses (e.g., death of loved ones, loss of health, etc.); becoming staunchly independent is a normal coping mechanism. Consequently, elderly clients may be resistant or ambivalent about receiving services they perceive as limiting their freedom. To the greatest extent possible, enable elderly clients to retain control, make choices, and maintain independence.

2. A good way to break the ice and get the relationship with an older person off to a good start is to show an interest in the furnishings in his or her room or home, such as family pictures, unique pieces of furniture, homemade items, and the like. When addressing the elderly client, use the titles *Mr., Mrs., Miss,* or *Ms.* until you receive permission to use a first name.

3. In the beginning, always focus on the client's most obvious and concrete needs, which are the ones he or she can most easily discuss. Like most other clients, the elderly person understands and can easily talk about needs like transportation, housing, medical care, and home maintenance, but will finds it more difficult to talk about personal matters and express feelings in the presence of someone he or she does not know very well.

4. Allow and even encourage the client to reminisce. Thinking and talking about the past is a normal activity for the elderly—it is not a sign of deteriorating mental abilities. Listen carefully to the reminiscence; it will reveal much about the client's values, feelings, and current concerns.

5. As individuals grow older and closer to death, they think more about their life's achievements and disappointments. Typically, their religious beliefs and spirituality take on added importance and many desire to communicate what they have learned from life. Look for opportunities that allow the elderly to teach what they have learned about life and living.

6. During their later years, older people typically become intensely aware of their unique relationship to children and grandchildren. It may be of great importance for them to stay in contact with offspring or reactivate relationships that have deteriorated. Some may want to reach out to estranged offspring and patch up differences or make amends for the harm they caused. Do everything possible to facilitate intergenerational family communication.

7. If the elderly client is much older than you, the two of you probably have different mores, values, and attitudes. For example, "taking charity" is difficult for many older people, and they usually find it harder than younger persons to accept counseling and psychotherapy. Many are concerned about the cost of services. Early in your contact, clarify any financial implications. Some older clients will simply reject services rather than inquire about the cost or reveal their inability to pay.

8. Most elderly people suffer from some degree of vision and hearing loss. Thus, it is important to speak clearly and repeat the message as often as necessary. Your nonverbal communication is especially important as a means of compensating for the client's auditory deficit. Also, the pace of an interview will usually be slower with an elderly person, and the client's lack of energy may limit the length of the interview. Be careful, however, not to "talk down" to the client.

9. For both physical and psychological reasons, an interview in the client's home is usually more comfortable than an office interview. Most will prefer an informal and friendly social worker over one who is more formal. Elderly clients may be especially bothered by unusual clothing or hairstyles worn by a worker.

10. Given the impact of racism, discrimination, and prejudice on people, be especially sensitive when interacting with elderly people who are members of racial or ethnic minorities. As a general rule, they will be a bit more suspicious and distrustful of agencies and more sensitive to anything that might appear demeaning and disrespectful. The values common to a particular ethnic group may make life either more or less difficult for the aging person. For example, the elderly of certain ethnic groups (e.g., Chicano, Chinese, and Native American) usually occupy a position of respect and influence within families, and the importance of hard work as a value within an ethnic group (e.g., Slavic-American) may cause the nonworking elderly person to feel particularly unworthy and unimportant.

11. Be alert to *indicators of elder abuse and neglect* (especially self-neglect), such as bruises, cuts, burns, or untreated injuries that are explained in a vague or defensive manner; improper clothing for the weather; wandering outside at odd hours or into dangerous areas; mail, newspapers, or other deliveries that are not picked up; unusual activity or no signs of movement from their home; unpleasant odors associated with hygiene or housekeeping; the person does not recognize you or does not know where he or she is or the day or time; the person has means to meet basic needs but is facing an eviction, utility shutoff, or has many unpaid bills; or the person is dependent on a stressed, chemically dependent or mentally ill caregiver and basic needs are not being met.

SELECTED BIBLIOGRAPHY

Burlingame, Virginia. *Gerocounseling: Counseling Elders and Their Families.* New York: Springer, 1995.

Dunkle, Ruth, and Theresa Norgard. "Aging Overview." In *Encyclopedia of Social Work,* 19th ed., vol. 1, edited by Richard L. Edwards. Washington, DC: NASW Press, 1995, pp. 142–153.

Toseland, Ronald. *Group Work with the Elderly.* New York: Springer, 1995.

14.32 The Woman Who Is Battered and Abused

PURPOSE: To understand domestic abuse and respond appropriately to a battered woman.

DISCUSSION: As used here, the term *battered woman* refers to an adult female who has been physically, sexually, and/or emotionally abused by a spouse or intimate partner. Unfortunately, this type of abuse is quite common and it results in many serious injuries and deaths. In the United States, a woman is more likely to be assaulted, injured, raped, or killed by a her male partner than by a stranger or any other type of assailant. The vast majority of the abusers are men and the abuse occurs most often within a heterosexual relationship. However, it may also occur within gay and lesbian relationships. (For ease of discussion, the authors shall refer to the offender or abuser as the male and the victim as female.)

The abuse can take several forms but all are intended to control the woman—for example:

- *Physical injury or threats of injury* (e.g., pushing, choking, punching, beating, hitting with objects, forcing sex, threatening to hurt her or the children)
- *Emotional abuse* (e.g., humiliating her, making her the object of demeaning jokes, blaming her, undermining her confidence, saying she is crazy, insisting that she deserves to be punished, denying her opportunity to make significant decisions)

- *Isolation* (e.g., controlling what she does, who she talks to, and where she goes, closely monitoring her activities)
- *Economic manipulation* (e.g., controlling her access to money, giving her an allowance, preventing her from getting or keeping a job, threatening to take all possessions and leave her with nothing)
- *Intimidation* (e.g., displaying weapons, abusing pets, destroying her property, threatening to commit suicide if she does not do what he wants)
- *Using the children* (e.g., threatening to take the children, threatening to report the woman for child abuse).

Typically, there is a cycle of abuse with three major phases: (1) tension building, (2) the explosion, and (3) the "honeymoon." In some cases, the cycle may be quite short, such as a matter of days; in other cases, it may take several months to cycle through these phases:

- *Phase 1—Tension building.* Tensions between the two people begin to rise. Some outbursts may occur but these are minimized and rationalized away by both parties. The woman typically tries to protect herself and maintain some control over the situation by being compliant and not showing anger.
- *Phase 2—Explosion.* The abuser finally explodes. Anger is expressed in extreme verbal abuse, physical violence, and/or rape.
- *Phase 3—Repairing the damage (Honeymoon).* The abuser expresses sorrow for what he has done. He fears that she will leave, and to keep her from leaving, he becomes very attentive, loving, and thoughtful. Since this loving behavior does not fit with his prior behavior, she becomes confused and may doubt her own perceptions and sanity. She probably wants to believe that the episode of abuse was atypical and out of character. She may conclude that she is the one responsible for the abuse and think: "If only I would have done things right, he would not have gotten angry." This period of good behavior by the abuser eventually runs its course and the violent behavior and the cycle begins again.

The men who abuse women typically have several of the following characteristics:

- Extreme and irrational jealousy and possessiveness toward the woman, often coupled with an unjustifiable belief that she is interested in other men
- Desire to control the woman and isolate her from friends and family by saying such things as "All we need is each other—no one else"
- Quick to anger and have an explosive temper
- Moods and behavior may fluctuate from being kind and gentle to being violent and oppressive
- Refuses to take responsibility for his own behavior; blames others, especially the woman, for whatever goes wrong in his life
- Often a history of having been abused as a child or a witness to frequent family violence

- Often a history of legal violations related to violence
- Either denies or rationalizes his outbursts and abusive behavior
- Usually feels remorse after a violent episode, promises that it will never happen again, and, for a time, becomes a very devoted and loving partner; however, this does not last and eventually he repeats the abusing and violent behavior

There are a number of reasons why battered women are often reluctant to leave the abusive relationship or return to it after only a brief separation:

- Fear of retribution and even more serious violence
- Lack of money and no suitable place to live
- Fear of losing her children, home, possessions, and economic security
- Feelings of self-doubt, low self-esteem, shame, or a distrust of other people
- Fear of not being believed or of being blamed for causing the abuse
- Religious beliefs and morals that emphasize maintaining a marriage
- Desire to preserve the family for benefit of the children
- Wanting to believe that the abuse will stop or a tendency to deny or minimize the seriousness of the abuse
- A tendency to equate love with dependency

An abusive situation should be considered especially dangerous if there is a pattern of frequent and/or severe violence, the abuser and/or the abused woman use drugs or alcohol, the woman or children have been threatened with death, the abuser has access to deadly weapons, either the abuser or victim has a psychiatric impairment, the abuser has a history of criminal activity, the abuse has taken the form of forced sexual acts, the abuser has threatened suicide, the abuser has tortured or killed animals as a display of his willingness to take extreme action, and the woman has made suicide threats or attempts.

Social workers and programs offering services to battered women must strive toward the following goals:

- Ensure that the woman and her children are safe and protected.
- Help the woman understand the nature and cycle of abuse and that she has options that can keep her and her children safe.
- Help her make decisions, formulate plans, and obtain the services she will need in order to ensure safety in the future.
- Help her and her children heal from the psychological effects of abuse and reestablish a sense of personal boundaries.

Those working directly with the abused women should keep the following guidelines in mind:

1. Do not immediately assume that the battered woman is in a heterosexual relationship; refer to the abuser as "partner" until you learn the gender of the offender.

2. Give immediate attention to helping the woman with her basic needs such as the need for safety, food, shelter, transportation, assistance in caring for the children, legal counsel, and so on.

3. Because a woman caught up in a abusive relationship is prone to intense self-doubt and self-blame, be sure to establish a warm, caring, and nonjudgmental relationship; listen attentively and respectfully to her story, her fears and confusion, and her reasons for wanting to maintain the relationship. She may want to remain in the relationship because she and\or her children truly love him and believe that he will change.

4. Focus on the woman's strengths, such as the decisions and behaviors that have kept her alive or that protected her children; help her to identify and name her survival skills as a way of counteracting her feelings of self-doubt and helplessness.

5. If she decides to remain with the abuser, assist the woman in developing an escape plan (safety plan) that she can immediately implement if she is again threatened. The plan should include her packing and then hiding from the abuser a bag that contains money, clothing, personal items, and copies of legal documents that she (and her children) would need to live apart from the abuser.

6. Anticipate that the woman's emotions and moods will fluctuate widely and that she will experience great ambivalence about ending the relationship; discourage her from speaking with the abuser when she is feeling especially insecure and confused. At such times she is vulnerable to his influence and is likely to return to him without really considering the danger.

7. If the woman's children have witnessed the abuse of their mother, anticipate that they, too, are feeling frightened and confused and are in need of counseling.

8. Do not assume that the woman has some underlying need or problem that causes her to remain in an abusive relationship. However, as a response to ongoing abuse, the woman may indeed develop problems such as alcohol or drug abuse, depression, anxiety and posttraumatic stress disorder.

9. Understand that the woman may have to leave and return to the abuser several times before she is finally convinced that the abuse will not end unless the abuser is motivated to make use of a program of therapy and training.

10. After leaving an abusive relationship, it may take from two to four years before the battered woman recovers emotionally and becomes significantly less fearful, anxious, and depressed. The same can be said for the children who have experienced the terror of seeing their mother beaten and threatened.

SELECTED BIBLIOGRAPHY

Cardarelli, Albert. *Violence between Intimate Partners*. Boston: Allyn and Bacon, 1997.

Gondolf, Edward. *Assessing Woman Battering in Mental Health Services*. Thousand Oaks, CA: Sage, 1997.

Walker, Lenore. *Abused Women and Survivor Therapy*. Washington DC: American Psychological Association, 1994.

14.33 The Adult Client with Cognitive Delay

PURPOSE: To adapt usual social work methods to the special needs of an adult with a cognitive delay (mental retardation).

DISCUSSION: The two key features of *mental retardation* are significantly subaverage general intelligence and significant limitations in adaptive behaviors such as communication, self-care, and academic skills. There are many forms of mental retardation and dozens of causes such as inborn errors in metabolism, chromosomal aberrations, ingestion of toxic chemicals, malnutrition, viral infections, and head trauma.

Roughly 3 percent of the U.S. population has some degree of mental retardation. Of those, about 80 percent have delays in the mild to moderate range and 20 percent are in the ranges termed severe and profound. Signs of cognitive delay are usually apparent early in childhood. Early diagnosis and early medical and educational intervention are of critical importance to minimize the effects of the condition (see Items 12.19 and 12.20).

Because of the stigma attached to the word *retardation,* the term *cognitive delay* is increasingly used by educators and parents as a substitute, especially when speaking about children. However, *mental retardation* is a diagnostic category in the *DSM-IV* and a term frequently used by physicians and health care professionals. The term *developmental disability* is a legal and programmatic category of mental disability. Although definitions may vary slightly from state to state, a ***developmental disability*** is often defined as a severe disability caused by physical or mental impairment that limits a person's development, appears before the age 18 (or 22), is likely to be lifelong, and affects the person's functioning in self-care, learning, self-direction, language, independent living, mobility, and/or economic self-sufficiency. The developmental disabilities are mental retardation, cerebral palsy, autism, severe dyslexia, and epilepsy. Of these, mental retardation is the one most frequently diagnosed.

Most adults with mental retardation hold jobs (albeit low-paying ones) and many marry and have children. Although society shows concern and empathy for children with cognitive delays, it tends to reject or stigmatize adults with this condition.

The following guidelines will aid the social worker serving an adult client with cognitive delay:

1. Individualize the client. Focus mostly on the client's abilities. Discard any stereotypes you may have concerning people with this condition. They have the same physical, emotional, social, sexual, and spiritual needs as everyone else. Because they experience much frustration, many develop emotional problems and unusual behavioral patterns.

2. Adjust your approach to the client's abilities (e.g., his or her intellectual level, language skills, etc.). To the extent possible, clients should participate in making de-

cisions that affect their own lives. This may be limited in the case of one who has a very severe disability, but other clients may be excellent sources of information about their own preferences, abilities, and limitations.

3. People with cognitive delay have limited verbal skills and difficulty with abstract thinking. Thus, be prepared to utilize alternatives to verbal communication and the ordinary helping skills. Behavioral techniques, special teaching methodologies, nonverbal group work techniques, role-playing, modeling, and the creative arts are examples. (This is not to say that verbal techniques cannot be effective with some clients.) Be sure to ask the client what approach he or she prefers and what works best.

4. Because the client's attention span may be short, the length of interviews will need to be adjusted accordingly; and because the client's memory may be limited, each contact and communication should be planned as a discrete event rather than as a continuation of previous conversations. When you give explanations, you may need to repeat them and use several concrete examples and illustrations. Your language must be clear, straightforward, and simple but never patronizing.

5. Because the client's life situation is so heavily affected by the people in the client's immediate environment (e.g., family members, group home manager, neighbors, employers, etc.), the social worker must be prepared to formulate interventions designed to change these people's level of understanding and the expectations they place on the client. The social work practice roles of client advocate, case manager, broker, and mediator are especially important in work with this client group.

6. In your interactions with your client, do nothing that might reinforce inappropriate behaviors. For example, hugging is not a conventional greeting among adults who do not know each other very well. Thus, initiate a handshake rather than allow yourself to be hugged by the client.

7. Address adults with cognitive delay as you would any other adult. For example, always use *Mr.* or *Miss,* unless you know each other so well that you are on a first-name basis. Avoid demeaning language, such as referring to an adult as a "kid."

8. Certain behavioral patterns and medical disorders are associated with some forms of mental retardation. This area of knowledge is of critical importance in assessment and case planning and in working as part of a team with other disciplines, such as psychology, physical therapy, occupational therapy, medicine, speech therapy, special education, and vocational rehabilitation.

9. The principles of normalization should guide the delivery of social services and the formulation of client habilitation plans. *Normalization* refers to the utilization of approaches and services that are as culturally normative as possible. The phrase *culturally normative* means typical or conventional. Normalization does not refer to being "normal" but rather to attempts to decrease deviance (i.e., differences that are socially created). Moreover, normalization does not imply that the person with a disability should be placed in situations that generate unusual frustration or impossible competition just because those situations are typical for the "average" person. However, it does call for actions that remove forms of overprotection and recognizes that learning and living one's life involves a degree of risk taking and possible failure.

10. It is in relation to clients with severe disabilities that a social worker is likely to encounter the legal procedures known as guardianship and conservatorship. In a ***guardianship*** arrangement, a court finds a person to be legally incompetent because of age or mental or physical incapacity, and therefore invests another person (the guardian) with the power to manage the incapacitated person's money and property and to make certain other decisions such as those related to health care. In a ***conservatorship,*** the court appoints another (the conservator) for the more limited purpose of managing the legally incompetent person's estate. Neither of these two procedures should be confused with ***power of attorney,*** which does not involve a court finding of legal incompetence but simply involves the use of a notarized document in which one legally competent person voluntarily gives to another the legal power to take certain actions such as selling a property, depositing or withdrawing funds from a bank, or paying bills.

SELECTED BIBLIOGRAPHY

Beirne-Smith, Mary, James Patton, and Richard Ittenbach. *Mental Retardation*, 4th ed. New York: Merrill, 1994.

Freedman, Ruth. "Developmental Disabilities: Direct Practice." In *Encyclopedia of Social Work*, 19th ed., vol. 1., edited by Richard Edwards. Washington, DC: NASW Press, 1995, pp. 721–729.

Hilton, Alan, and Ravic Ringlaben, eds. *Best and Promising Practices in Developmental Disabilities.* Austin, TX: Pro-Ed, 1997.

14.34 The Client with Brain Injury

PURPOSE: To consider the aftereffects of a brain injury in assessment and case planning.

DISCUSSION: A growing number of individuals in U.S. society suffer the effects of brain injury. Brain injury results in significant but often subtle alterations in memory, judgment, impulse control, perception, emotionality, speech control, and motor control. Such changes can have a profound effect on the person's capacity for social functioning, employability, and family relationships.

The most common causes of brain injury are blows to the head and strokes. The actual effects of an injury depend primarily on what parts of the brain are damaged and the type of damage. For example, the effects of stroke (cerebral vascular accident or CVA) can be quite circumscribed because a blocked blood vessel will cause damage to a very specific area of the brain. For this reason, once the location of stroke-caused damage is known, the aftereffects can be predicted with some accuracy. By contrast, the aftereffects of a traumatic brain injury, such as one acquired in an auto accident or a beating to the head, can be defuse and unpredictable because the tearing and shearing of tissue occurs in several areas of the brain.

Individuals with significant brain injury, especially if caused by trauma, will often develop a pattern of rigid thinking. Because they have difficulty detecting subtle differences among ideas and nuances in meaning and are frustrated by complexity and ambiguity, they tend to hold tightly to their understandings and interpretations. They are inclined to view an issue or position as either entirely right or entirely wrong and have difficulty accepting a middle ground and considering both the advantages and disadvantages of a proposal. This "black or white" type of thinking makes it difficult for them to make workable decisions and causes others to perceive them as rigid, abrasive, opinionated, and narrow-minded.

Stroke

Typically, the most visible sign of a stroke is a paralysis on one side of the body. Damage to the left side of the brain results in right-sided paralysis and problems with speech and language (termed *aphasia*). In addition, the person tends to be slow, hesitant, and disorganized when faced with an unfamiliar situation.

CVA damage to the right brain results in left side paralysis and causes difficulties in perception. The person tends to be impulsive, have poor judgment, and overlook his or her limitations. This individual can often describe and explain tasks that need to be done but is not able to do them. He or she has trouble both expressing emotions and perceiving the emotional signals of others.

Many of those who have had a stroke have what is termed *one-sided neglect*, meaning that they may have lost sections of their visual field or have lost sensory signals to parts of their bodies. For example, a man with a paralyzed arm may repeatedly allow it to dangle dangerously near the hot burner of a stove. Another illustrative example is the woman who looks at her own leg and then becomes upset because she concludes someone is laying in bed beside her. Persons with such perceptual problems can easily become confused while traveling or moving about.

Other problems commonly associated with a stroke include (1) the person becomes careless and neglectful of personal grooming and appearance; (2) loss of memory retention span (i.e., a decrease in the number of things that can be retained and attended to at one time); (3) decreased capacity for short-term memory, which makes new learning difficult; (4) difficulty in generalization (i.e., applying what was learned in one situation to another); (5) emotional lability (i.e., laughing or crying for no apparent reason); (6) sensory deprivation (i.e., loss in the ability to taste, hear, see, perceive touch, etc.); and (7) fatigue.

Traumatic Brain Injury

As indicated earlier, brain injury caused by a blow to the head tends to affect more areas of the brain than an injury caused by stroke. Trauma to the brain may result in paralysis or other physical symptoms such as seizures and a decrease in strength and coordination; however, it is common for the person to appear physically normal but experience a number of cognitive, behavioral, and emotional problems. Difficulties in memory, judgment, attention, perception, and impulse control can result in major problems in social interaction and job performance and can be especially troublesome if others assume these problems are caused by laziness or intellectual deficit rather than impaired brain functioning.

For the social work practitioner who may encounter a client who has had a stroke or a traumatic brain injury, several guidelines are important:

1. Be alert to the possibility of brain injury effects whenever presenting problems involve personality changes, impulsiveness, poor memory, and poor judgment. Inquire as to a history of a concussion, coma, stroke, skull fracture, or other injuries to the head caused by, for example, car accidents, sports injuries, or violence.

2. If there is reason to suspect the existence of a brain injury, consult with a rehabilitation specialist, neurologist, or neuropsychologist concerning the symptoms and determine if a referral for an in-depth evaluation is indicated. A medical doctor who specializes in physical rehabilitation and in treating the aftereffects of stroke and head injury is called a *physiatrist.* This medical specialty is known as physiatry (not to be confused with psychiatry).

3. Realize that rehabilitation programs can be successful in teaching patients how to compensate for some of the deficits caused by brain injury. Rehabilitation is most beneficial when started as soon as possible after the brain damage has occurred.

4. The family of a person who has had a stroke or acquired a head injury will need information, guidance, and support in learning to cope with the many changes they face in relating to a loved one who may seem like a "different person." Support groups exist in most communities.

5. Individuals with brain injury may fabricate an explanation or make up a story in order to cope with or hide their problems of poor memory and learning difficulties. They may hold tightly to false beliefs because the beliefs help them make sense out of the unorganized bits of information they possess and the confusion they experience. The family may be distressed and angry when the person with brain injury insists that an obviously false belief is true.

6. The family should be encouraged to review relevant legal documents, contracts, wills, financial agreements, and the like and to develop legal protection against impulsive decisions and poor judgments made by a family member who experiences the effects of a head injury.

7. National organizations such as the National Head Injury Foundation and the National Stroke Association provide information as well as support to the survivors of head injury and stroke and their families.

8. State departments of vocational rehabilitation may have special employment programs for persons with serious cognitive deficits caused by head injury. Such services may include job coaching and extended or supported employment programs. Cognitive deficits that preclude competitive employment may qualify a person for Social Security Disability Income benefits.

SELECTED BIBLIOGRAPHY

Goldberg, Stephen. *Clinical Neuroanatomy Made Ridiculously Simple.* Miami: Med Master Inc., 1990.

Miller, Laurence. *Psychotherapy of the Brain-Injured Patient.* New York: W. W. Norton, 1993.

Williams, J. M., and T. Kay, eds. *Head Injury: A Family Affair.* Baltimore, MD: Paul Brooks, 1991.

14.35 The Client with a Serious Mental Illness

PURPOSE: To adapt social work techniques and approaches to the special needs of a client with a serious mental illness.

DISCUSSION: There are three major categories of serious mental illness: schizophrenia, bipolar disorder, and major depression. All three are diseases of the brain caused primarily by biochemical and structural changes in the brain tissue. Each may be episodic and vary in intensity and the degree to which it impairs a person's functioning. Some of those who experience these illnesses may lose touch with reality (i.e., become psychotic), whereas others may only have trouble with memory, judgment, or feelings of low self-worth.

Schizophrenia is a baffling and debilitating illness. About 1.5 percent of the population is afflicted with this disturbance of the thinking processes. The usual age of onset is between 15 and 25 years old, when the frontal lobes of the brain are rapidly maturing. Symptoms frequently appear between the ages of 18 to 21 and are exacerbated by the stress of emancipation from the family. Many experts believe that a stressful environment, viral infections, and other physiological conditions may trigger the onset of this illness in those predisposed by heredity.

An individual with schizophrenia will exhibit several of the following symptoms:

- *Delusions* (e.g., has false beliefs that have no factual basis)
- *Hallucinations* (hearing voices is the most common hallucination; visual hallucination [seeing nonexistent things] is relatively rare but is more likely if the individual is also abusing illegal drugs or psychiatric medications; olfactory and tactile hallucinations are less common but possible)
- *Disordered thinking* (e.g., making loose or illogical connections between thoughts; shifting rapidly from one topic to another; reaching conclusions that are unrelated to facts or logic; making up words or using sounds or rhythms that have no meaning to others)

- *Blunted or inappropriate affect* (e.g., narrow range of emotional reactions; the emotions or feelings do not fit the situation; speaks in monotone)
- *Extreme withdrawal* (e.g., withdrawal from ordinary life experiences and social interaction; deterioration in work or school performance; apathy in regard to appearance and self-care)

About one-fourth of those who have a schizophrenic episode get well and never have another episode. Some have occasional relapses. Between 20 to 30 percent develop symptoms that are persistent throughout life.

The other two types of serious mental illness—major depression and bipolar disorder—are known as *mood disorders* or *affective disorders.* Individuals suffering from a ***major depression*** experience persistent feelings of sadness and melancholy. They often become tearful, irritable, or hostile for no apparent reason. Other symptoms common to depression include:

- Poor appetite and weight loss or increased appetite and weight gain
- Change in sleep pattern (sleeping too little or too much)
- Excessive fatigue; loss of energy
- Change in activity level (either increased or decreased)
- Loss of interest in being with others
- Loss of interest or pleasure in usual activities
- Decreased sexual drive
- Diminished ability to think, concentrate, or make decisions
- Anxiety and rumination over problems
- Feelings of worthlessness or excessive guilt that may reach delusional proportions
- Recurrent thoughts of death or self-harm; wishing to be dead or contemplating or attempting suicide

About 1 percent of the population suffer from ***bipolar disorder,*** which is characterized by swings between periods of depression and mania (a hyperactive state). Mania is often characterized by:

- An exaggerated or irritable mood
- Decreased need for sleep
- Inflated self-confidence and grandiose ideas
- Increased energy and activity
- Overoptimism, poor judgment, quick and impulsive decision making
- Unusually high levels of involvement in work, pleasurable activities, and sexuality
- Rapid and pressured speech and racing thoughts
- Distractibility

Most often, the depressive phase follows the manic phase. Sometimes, the two phases are separated by periods of near normal functioning. These episodes may come and go and last from several days to several months. Without treatment, there is usually an increase in the severity of the symptoms and the frequency of the episodes.

Some individuals experience the bipolar disorder with only the depressive or manic symptoms rather than both. These are termed *bipolar disorder, depressive type* and *bipolar disorder, manic type.* Often, a person's mental health history will predict how the bipolar disorder will manifest itself in the future. For example, a person who historically experiences depression in the autumn may continue to experience more severe symptoms during these months of the year. There is evidence that this disorder has a basis in heredity.

When working with a client with a serious mental illness, the social worker should follow several guidelines:

1. These illnesses, especially the mood disorders, can usually be treated effectively with proper medications. Thus, an individual with a serious mental illness should be under the care of a physician, preferably a psychiatrist, who can prescribe medications and monitor their effects. A combination of medication and other forms of mental health care, such as psychotherapy and supportive services, is the preferred treatment for most persons with a serious mental illness. (See Item 14.36 on psychotropic medication.)

2. Because depression gives rise to intense emotional pain and feelings of hopelessness, the risk of suicide must always be considered. (See Item 12.23 on suicide risk.) Of those with schizophrenia, about one in four attempts suicide and about one in ten dies of suicide. Thoughts of suicide or self-mutilation by someone suffering from schizophrenia place him or her at extremely high risk.

3. Delusions are a common symptom in schizophrenia. By definition, a *delusion* is a set of ideas and beliefs that remain fixed, even in the face of clear evidence to the contrary. Be very cautious about how you respond to a person's delusions. Remember that a delusion serves a purpose; it helps the individual cope with or make sense out of some mental or perceptual confusion. The person believes in the delusions because they feel right and provide an explanation. Listen carefully to the delusion and try to understand the assumptions on which it is built, but do not judge, criticize, or argue or use logic in an effort to eliminate this symptom. Do not challenge or confront the delusional thoughts, for that will probably destroy the relationship you have with the individual and cause him or her to feel angry and misunderstood. Also, confronting a delusion increases the risk that you will become part of the delusional system of thought and perhaps defined as an enemy or part of a plot or conspiracy.

4. A very small percentage of persons who become psychotic will experience *command hallucinations,* which are voices that tell these people to hurt themselves or others (e.g., a voice telling them to jump off a bridge or kill the mayor). These command hallucinations, although rare, are very dangerous. All threats to personal safety must be taken seriously. If this symptom cannot be controlled by medication, the individual should be hospitalized.

5. The individual with a persistent and serious mental illness is usually in need of services that will assist him or her with the everyday tasks of living. Such services include case management, counseling, case advocacy, budgeting, and assistance in securing income, a job, housing, transportation, medical care, and the like. The *clubhouse model*—which provides peer support, acceptance, meaningful work and activity, and other services—is especially helpful and important to persons with a persistent mental illness (see Chapter 6).

6. A family member's mental illness has a profound impact on others in the family. The social worker should address the concerns of the family by doing the following:

- Help family members grieve the loss of their loved one who, because of mental illness, may now seem like a stranger.
- Provide practical information about mental illness. Ask about their possible fear of physical assault and worry over irresponsible financial decisions by the family member who is mentally ill.
- Encourage family members to join a self-help or support group such as the National Alliance for the Mentally Ill.
- Remain accessible to the families, especially during family crises that can be precipitated by relapses.
- Help the parents and siblings recognize their own rights to a life apart from the anguish and worry they feel toward the family member who is mentally ill.
- Assist family members to secure services such as case management and respite care to relieve them of the daily responsibility of care giving and provide opportunities for rest and renewal.
- Inform family members of legal issues and rights related to securing and refusing treatment.

7. It should be noted that the treatment and management of a mental illness can be further complicated by the presence of another serious problem such as substance abuse, a personality disorder or a developmental disability. The term *dual diagnosis* is applied to such a situation. A *personality disorder* is a deeply ingrained, inflexible, lifelong, and maladaptive pattern of emotional responses and behaviors that are often harmful or distressful to others. However, individuals with a personality disorder seldom see anything unusual about their own behavior and typically blame others for whatever difficulties they encounter in life. Because they do not feel inner pain or anxiety, they do not usually seek treatment voluntarily. There are several types of personality disorders. They are not brain disorders and appear to develop in response to family and social influences.

SELECTED BIBLIOGRAPHY

American Psychiatric Association. *Diagnostic and Statistical Manual of Mental Disorders (DSM-IV)*, 4th ed., rev. Washington DC: American Psychiatric Association, 1994.

Austrian, Sonia. *Mental Disorders, Medications and Clinical Social Work.* New York: Columbia University Press, 1995.

Kaplan, Harold, and Benjamin Sadock. *Synopsis of Psychiatry*, 8th ed. Baltimore: Williams and Wilkins, 1998.

14.36 The Client on Psychotropic Medication

PURPOSE: To provide appropriate guidance to the client taking psychotropic medication.

DISCUSSION: The social worker will encounter many clients who take medication to control psychiatric symptoms. These medications fall into discrete groups, each of which alleviates a particular set of symptoms. The major groups are antipsychotic, antidepressant, antianxiety, antimanic, psychomotor stimulants, and sedative-hypnotics. Each medication has a chemical name, a generic or general name (e.g., Fluoxetine), and a registered trade or brand name (e.g., Prozac). Each has a specific target symptom, contraindications, potency, and potential side effects. The selection of a specific medication is based on the patient's medical history, physical exam, laboratory tests, use of other medications, use and abuse of alcohol or street drugs, and, of course, the disorder being treated. Physicians generally advise against taking psychotropic medications during pregnancy.

When an individual is hospitalized and/or experiencing disabling symptoms, he or she may be started on a quick-acting medication or given a fairly large dose. Most will not need to take the same dosage after leaving the hospital or after the severe symptoms subside, and a physician may want to reduce the dosage or switch to a medication that is slower acting but has other advantages. Usually, it is desirable for physicians to reduce the dosage to the minimum effective level but reductions are best done gradually—a process that may take weeks or months. Even when on a "maintenance dose," some people find that their symptoms worsen from time to time. This may be due to stress, biochemical changes, or some other factors.

Some patients are frightened when a doctor suggests that they take less medication because they fear a return of symptoms. On the other hand, some are reluctant take medication because they fear side effects or because it is perceived as a loss of control or a blow to their self-esteem.

Different types and groups of medications have different side effects. Among the side effects associated with certain psychotropic medications are dry mouth; weight gain; drowsiness; oversensitivity to the sun; menstrual cycle disturbance; spasms of eye, face, neck, and back muscles; blurred vision; shuffling gait; and tremors. Children and the elderly are particularly prone to experience side effects. A psychotropic medication may exacerbate nonpsychiatric medical problems such as hypertension, liver disease, epilepsy, and glaucoma. Despite these side effects, it must be remembered that symptom control is of critical importance to persons suffering from a major mental illness. There is a benefit-risk balance with all medications. In general, a physician will reduce the side effects by prescribing the lowest dosage that produces the desired effects, discontinuing a problematic medication and trying another, avoiding the simultaneous use of two medications that have a similar effect, and, whenever possible, treating only one symptom at a time.

When working with a client taking psychotropic medications, several guidelines should be kept in mind:

1. The decision to prescribe a medication is a complex medical judgment to be made only by a competent physician, preferably a psychiatrist. For ethical and legal reasons, a social worker must never give medication instructions outside the physician's directions.

2. Encourage your client to maintain regular contact with a physician so the effects of the drug can be monitored and dosage can be properly regulated. If you observe what appears to be unusual or unexpected side effects, but your client is unwilling to see a physician, get the name and dosage of the medication and consult with a physician. Also, inform the physician if your client is no longer taking a medication as prescribed.

3. Make sure your client and your client's family and friends understand the dangers of modifying the prescribed daily dosage and of exchanging medications with others. Also, alert your client to the dangers of using alcohol or street drugs while taking any medication. If your client takes more than one medication, an adverse drug interaction could occur. This happens when the two drugs mixed together have an effect very different from when each is taken alone. Side effects can also occur when the client mixes a psychotropic medication with nonprescription drugs such as a cold medicine. Some foods (e.g., aged cheese) may cause adverse reactions when eaten by a person on certain medications.

4. As in the case of other forms of medical treatment, an adult has a right to refuse psychotropic medications. Exceptions are when a court has declared that the individual is legally incompetent to make that decision and/or when his or her behavior constitutes an imminent threat to self or others. Because the decision to reject a needed medication can have tragic results when symptoms recur, you should do everything possible to inform the patient and his or her family and close friends of the possible consequences. In the final analysis, however, the decision of a legally competent adult must be respected.

SELECTED BIBLIOGRAPHY

Diamond, Ronald. *Instant Psychopharmacology*. New York: Guilford, 1999.

Gitlin, Michael. *The Psychotherapist's Guide to Psychopharmacology*, 2nd ed. New York: Free Press, 1996.

Gorman, Jack. *The Essential Guide to Psychiatric Drugs*. New York: St Martin's Press, 1997.

14.37 The Client Who Is Gay, Lesbian, or Bisexual

PURPOSE: To consider the special issues that may arise in the provision of services to persons who are gay, lesbian, or bisexual.

DISCUSSION: Regardless of their practice settings, social workers will encounter clients who are gay, lesbian, and bisexual. Although sexual orientation, per se, will seldom be the presenting problem, the fact that many of these clients experience rejection, oppression, and discrimination must be considered in the planning and provision of health and human services.

At one time, the word *gay* was applied to both men and women who were homosexual. In recent decades, *gay* has come to refer to male homosexuals. Women who are homosexual often refer to themselves as *lesbians*.

The term *homosexual* is used to describe an individual whose thoughts and feelings of sexual attraction are mostly for persons of the same sex. By contrast, the term *heterosexual* refers to an individual whose thoughts and feelings of sexual attraction are mostly for people of the opposite sex. The person termed a *bisexual* experiences an attraction to both males and females. Gays and lesbians often refer to the person who is heterosexual as being "straight."

Because a precise and universally agreed upon definition of homosexuality is lacking, studies on the number of people in the population who are gay or lesbian yield estimates of about 2 to 10 percent. The developmental processes that may give rise to homosexuality are not well understood; the same can be said about heterosexuality. Researchers are not able to clearly explain why some individuals are sexually attracted to the opposite sex, some to their own sex, and some to both sexes. However, there is growing evidence that one's fundamental sexual orientation may be rooted in biological processes and, for most people, firmly established by adolescence. Thus, it is misleading to speak of either homosexuality or heterosexuality as a sexual "preference" or "choice." One's sexual behavior may be a choice but one's sexual orientation is not.

In U.S. society and in many others, those who are gay, lesbian, or bisexual encounter disapproval, rejection, and misunderstanding. This can lead to discrimination against gays and lesbians in employment, housing, health care, social services, and other areas. The term *homophobia* refers to an irrational fear of homosexuality. In all too many cases, homophobia gives rise to hatred and violence directed against persons who are known to be or suspected of being gay or lesbian.

Fear of rejection, discrimination, and violence, as well as a desire to protect family and friends from criticism and embarrassment causes many who are gay or lesbian to hide or deny their sexual orientation. Needless to say, an unwillingness or an inability to openly acknowledge and be at peace with something so basic as one's sexual identity can be a source of emotional turmoil within one's self and tension within family and other relationships.

The following are some guidelines for working with clients who are gay or lesbian:

1. Carefully examine your own behavior, attitudes, belief system, and moral standards for signs of possible bias, prejudice, and discrimination toward people who are gay or lesbian. Give special attention to the following:

- Your beliefs on whether homosexuality is a pathological condition or a normal variation of human sexuality
- Your level of comfort in hearing descriptions of affection and sexual activity within same sex-relationships
- Your beliefs and values regarding the parenting of children by persons who are gay or lesbian

If you conclude that you cannot offer this client acceptance, understanding, and compassion, you have an ethical obligation to remove yourself from those activities and assignments that put you in contact with these clients.

2. Do not be afraid to acknowledge your own lack of information and understanding. Assume that there is a widespread ignorance of homosexuality among persons in the helping professionals, among clients who are straight, and even among many clients who are gay or lesbian. Work hard to learn about the perceptions, concerns, and experiences of people who are gay and lesbian. Become familiar with leaders and support groups within the gay and lesbian community and seek their consultation and guidance on how best to work with gay and lesbian clients. As in attempts to learn about any other minority group, it is appropriate to ask questions if they are asked in a respectful and nonjudgmental manner and if the questions are pertinent to the services being provided to the client.

3. Realize that it is not uncommon for persons who are gay or lesbian to have gone through many years of confusion and uncertainty before finally recognizing and accepting their sexual orientation. They may deny their sexual attractions. They may become sexually active with the opposite sex as a way of reassuring themselves and others that they are heterosexual. Such periods of inner confusion are especially difficult for the adolescent and may lead some to consider suicide.

4. Although many who are gay or lesbian are comfortable with and open about their sexual orientation, others are not. Recognize and appreciate the turmoil and stress that results when a gay or lesbian individual feels forced by society to hide his or her true self and live in fear of being shamed, rejected, or injured and in fear of embarrassing or offending one's family and loved ones. The client should be helped to express pain and anger and sense of injustice.

5. Because so many who are gay or lesbian have been hurt by prejudice and discrimination, clients who are gay or lesbian are likely to be cautious and fearful when seeking services from an agency or entering into a helping relationship. They may hide their sexual orientation until they are sure the social worker is free of prejudices. A social worker who is gay or lesbian and quite sure his or her client is gay or lesbian may elect to self-disclose in order to lessen the client's fear. The social worker who is straight may use some personal stories to reveal that he or she understands the insidious effect of stereotypes and prejudice and thereby demonstrate to the client a capacity for acceptance and understanding. One of the worst things to say is any version of "some of my best friends are gay."

6. When working with a gay or lesbian couple who are in a long-term relationship, expect that their relationship problems will be similar to those of heterosexual couples. For example, their disagreements and conflicts will probably center on matters such as money management, balancing home and work responsibilities, child care, an unsatisfactory sexual relationship, unfaithfulness, domestic abuse, and substance abuse. However, their relationship is more uncertain because it lacks the status and protection that comes with a legal marriage and matters such as securing health insurance for one's partner, arranging survivors benefits, child custody, hospital visitation rights, and adoption are especially complex and unpredictable.

7. As a group, gay men have been hard hit by *Acquired Immunodeficiency Syndrome* (*AIDS*), a deadly disease caused by a virus known as HIV. Many gay men have suffered the loss of friends or lovers to the disease, and others live in fear of contracting the disease. Men, women, and children can be infected by the virus. The symptoms of AIDS typically do not develop until several years after being infected. HIV is spread primarily by (1) having vaginal, anal, or oral sex with someone who is infected; and (2) by sharing needles for injecting drugs with someone who is infected. The virus can be passed from an infected mother to her baby during pregnancy or child birth and, in rare instances, through breast feeding. Prior to 1985, when a program to test all donated blood began, transfusions with HIV-contaminated blood also spread the disease.

SELECTED BIBLIOGRAPHY

Appleby, George, and Jeane Anastas. "Social Work Practice with Lesbians, Gay, and Bisexual People." In *Social Work: A Profession of Many Faces*, 8th ed., edited by Armando Morales and Bradford Sheafor. Boston: Allyn and Bacon, 1998, pp. 213–245.

Child Welfare League of America. *Issues in Gay and Lesbian Adoption*. Washington, DC: Child Welfare League of America, 1995.

Cornett, Carlton. "Clinical Social Work Practice with Gay Men." In *Theory and Practice in Clinical Social Work*, edited by Jerrold Brandell. New York: Free Press, 1997.

Goldstein, Eda. "Clinical Practice with Lesbians." In *Theory and Practice in Clinical Social Work*, edited by Jerrold Brandell. New York: Free Press, 1997.

Laird, Joan, and Robert-Jay Green, eds. *Lesbians and Gays in Couples and Families: A Handbook for Therapists*. Washington, DC: NASW Press, 1996.

Morales, Julio. "Gay Men: Parenting." In *Encyclopedia of Social Work*, 19th ed., vol. 2, edited by Richard Edwards. Washington, DC: NASW Press, 1995, pp. 1085–1095.

Shernoff, Michael. "Gay Men: Direct Practice." In *Encyclopedia of Social Work*, 19th ed., vol. 2, edited by Richard Edwards. Washington, DC: NASW Press, 1995, pp. 1075–1085.

Woodman, Natalie. "Lesbians: Direct Practice." In *Encyclopedia of Social Work*, 19th ed., vol. 2, edited by Richard Edwards. Washington, DC: NASW Press, 1995, pp. 1597–1604.

14.38 The Client with an Eating Disorder

PURPOSE: To understand the unique needs of clients with eating disorders (e.g., anorexia, bulimia, and obesity) and identify appropriate intervention techniques.

DISCUSSION: Increasingly, social workers are assisting clients with eating disorders. ***Eating disorder*** is an umbrella term that describes any of several problems linked to compulsive behaviors in a person's relationship to food. At one extreme is the person who self-starves; at the other extreme is the person who eats to excess and becomes obese. Clients with eating disorders typically experience a combination of physical and psychosocial problems. Although there is evidence of eating-disordered behaviors throughout recorded history, the social factors affecting these disorders have only been addressed in recent years. Due to inconsistent definitions of the various eating disorders, little is known about the incidence of these problems except that for anorexia and bulimia, approximately 90 percent of the victims are women and the problems are most acute in the teen and young adult age groups.

There are many examples of harmful behaviors related to food and nutrition. It is not uncommon, for example, for male athletes to intentionally overeat to gain weight (e.g., offensive linesmen in football) or lose weight (e.g., wrestlers seeking to reach weight division) in an effort to succeed in competition. Nor is it uncommon for older people to experience food-related problems when, for example, "cooking for one" seems like too much trouble or one is expected to adapt to the institutional food in a nursing home. Fad diets and misguided fasting that fail to produce a balanced nutritious diet can disturb body chemistry and contribute to a person's eating disorder. The three most prevalent forms of eating disorders, however, are anorexia nervosa, bulimia nervosa, and obesity.

Anorexia Nervosa

Anorexia nervosa is a condition characterized by intentionally maintaining one's body weight substantially below that expected of a healthy individual (i.e., 15 to 25 percent below recommended weight for a person of that age, height, and gender). This disorder is most commonly found in middle- and upper-class adolescents, with symptoms typically beginning between ages 12 and 18. An estimated 90 to 95 percent of the people with anorexia are female, with approximately 1 in every 200 adolescent girls experiencing this disorder (Cassell 1994, 11). The causes of anorexia are not known, but it is thought to be associated with high stress, pressure from one's cultural group, presence of an eating disorder among other members of the person's family, as well as the person's biological predisposition. The literature is mixed regarding whether events during childhood such as extreme diets or eating habits and physical or sexual abuse are associated with anorexia.

Some psychological indicators of anorexia are a distorted perception of one's own body size, weight, and shape; an intense fear of becoming obese; and high self-expectations or perfectionism. Some physical symptoms are excessively low weight, the absence of or irregularity in the menstrual cycle, dry skin, loss of hair, refusal to eat normal amounts of food, and anxiety about eating, with episodes of spontaneous or induced vomiting.

The recommended interventions when working with a person experiencing anorexia nervosa are first to assist the person to take steps to restore physical health and regain a normal weight and then to implement the necessary interventions to prevent the recurrence of this condition. When a person is literally starving, his or her physical condition must be addressed before the social and psychological factors. Treatment may involve a period of hospitalization and the use of medications. Various drugs may be used in treatment, but the results to date of studies of drug therapy show mixed results.

When intervening with the anorexic (and also the bulimic) person, it is important to be very direct about the person's behaviors and the consequences of those behaviors, as well as to gain the person's trust as a foundation for helping him or her reestablish a sense of self-worth. Specific psychosocial interventions may include individual and family therapy, ongoing supportive treatment of the individual, cognitive therapy, behavior modification techniques, and participation in self-help groups. Recovery from anorexia nervosa requires actions on many fronts, including a team of professionals, family, and other significant people in the client's lives. Eating a sufficient amount of nutritious food is difficult for the anorexic to accomplish without considerable reinforcement from others. It is thought that about one-half of the diagnosed and treated anorexics recover within two to five years. Yet, about 18 percent never recover and, for them, the possibility of death from suicide or conditions resulting from the person's depleted physical condition is quite high.

Bulimia Nervosa

Bulimia nervosa is characterized by a morbid fear of becoming fat. With this disorder, a person usually stays within 10 percent of normal body weight but experiences lack of control over eating behaviors. As opposed to the person with anorexia who avoids food when under stress, the bulimic deals with stress by turning toward food. Periodically (at least three times a month), the person with this disorder experiences a severe craving for food and he or she binges, followed by induced vomiting, use of laxatives, severe dieting, excessive exercise, or fasting as a means of preventing weight gain. The bulimic cycle can be understood as the fear of becoming overweight leading to self-starvation, with a periodic eating frenzy followed by guilt and efforts to void the weight produced by the food, thus reinforcing the fear of becoming fat—and the cycle continues.

The causes of bulimia are not known, but symptoms usually begin in adolescence or early adulthood. The typical bulimic is thought to be a successful White woman in her mid- to late-20s. Because of this stereotype, bulimia is considered a "woman's disease" and men tend to deny or hide the fact that they experience this disorder. Estimates of the number of young women experiencing bulimia are as high as 15 to 20 percent; however, young men, too, experience bulimia at the substantial rate of about 5 to 10 percent (Cassell 1994, 42). The binge and purge cycle can have disastrous effects and can cause fatigue, seizures, and muscle cramps, as well has having a long-term effect on the person's teeth and bone density.

It is often difficult to determine if a client might be experiencing bulimia because there are no obvious physical symptoms such as the loss of weight or emaciation found in persons with anorexia. However, some clues are periodic consumption of large amounts of food, usually eaten alone or secretly; preoccupation with food or one's weight; excessive exercise or fasting; trips to the bathroom following meals; diminished sexual interest (sometimes); and depression or self-loathing due to inability to control bingeing.

As compared to persons who are anorexic, bulimics are more likely to seek and accept treatment, but their strong need for perfection leads to frustration when there are no immediate cures. Some interventions that are helpful in working with people experiencing bulimia are focused on helping them become more accepting of failures to achieve perfectionism in their lives, improving nutrition, and the use of antidepressant medication to deal with links to depression if suspected. When social workers are involved in cases of bulimia, cognitive-behavioral therapy is most often used to assist in interrupting the pattern of eating restricted foods and bingeing, while also addressing the client's distorted view of foods and his or her body. The client is also helped to reveal the problem with family and other significant people in his or her life and seek their help in maintaining a balanced diet. Finally, group approaches have been successful in helping bulimics self-disclose to reduce guilt, learn to self-monitor their eating behaviors, gain nutrition information, discuss alternatives to the binge and purge cycle (e.g., relaxation techniques), and address cultural pressures they experience regarding body weight.

Obesity

Obesity is a condition that results when a person's caloric intake regularly exceeds his or her biological needs. The term *moderate obesity* applies when a person is 20 to 100 percent above the recommended weight for his or her age, gender, and height, whereas a person experiencing *morbid obesity* would exceed the 100 percent level. More than 20 percent of the U.S. population is moderately or morbidly obese, with the percentage of women slightly exceeding men experiencing this eating disorder. Obese people more frequently experience high blood pressure, diabetes, heart disease, complications of pregnancy, and early death than the general population.

The causes of obesity are not well understood, but psychological, biological, and social factors all are associated with obesity. Psychological factors include overeating as a compensation for boredom, unhappiness, depression, and painful life events. In addition, between 20 and 40 percent of obese people periodically engage in binge eating. Increasingly, research indicates an association between obesity and one's genetic makeup. Also, the eating patterns of a person's family and the cultural patterns regarding food selection and intake have an effect on both one's weight and the acceptance of being overweight.

Low-income people are prone to obesity because they tend to purchase inexpensive foods that are often high in fat content. Social workers are sometimes in a position to assist with nutrition education and offer guidance on identifying foods that can achieve a balanced diet at a reasonable cost. In family counseling and mental health services, social workers are also likely to provide services to obese people regarding social ostracism and the resultant poor self-image that results.

Treatment for obesity begins with a reduction of calorie intake, but is sustained when combined with exercise and various behavior modification techniques intended to change patterns of eating. The obese person who has low self-esteem or is socially isolated is best treated with individual therapy, whereas groups have proven most successful with children who are more influenced by peer group discussion. Drug intervention has not proven successful in most cases, and surgery designed to reduce food intake is recommended only for persons far above their recommended weight, under age 50, and at great health risk because of their obesity.

The goals of a social worker's interventions should include helping obese clients learn to self-monitor their food intake, create environmental conditions (e.g., family and friends) that have a positive influence on eating patterns, provide individual and group therapeutic services when warranted, facilitate involvement in appropriate exercise programs, and help the client connect to social groups where isolation can be diminished. Meaningful weight loss will be a long-term process, Without continuing support and encouragement for maintaining the activities that have resulted in weight reduction, there is a high probability that the weight will be regained.

SELECTED BIBLIOGRAPHY

Bray, George, Claude Bouchard, and W. P. T. James, eds. *Handbook of Obesity.* New York: Marcel Dekker, 1997.

Cassell, Dana K. *The Encyclopedia of Obesity and Eating Disorders.* New York: Facts on File, 1994.

Logan, Sayde L. "Eating Disorders and Other Compulsive Behaviors." In *Encyclopedia of Social Work,* 19th ed., edited by Richard Edwards. Washington, DC: NASW Press, 1995.

Shekter-Wolfson, Lorie F., D. Blake Woodside, and Jan Lackstrom. "Social Work Treatment of Anorexia and Bulimia: Guidelines for Practice." *Research on Social Work Practice* 7 (January 1997): 5–31.

Williamson, Donald A. *Assessment of Eating Disorders: Obesity, Anorexia, and Bulimia Nervosa.* New York: Pergamon, 1990.

14.39 The Client Experiencing Grief or Loss

PURPOSE: To understand the needs of clients experiencing grief or suffering from the loss of a loved one and to identify appropriate intervention techniques.

DISCUSSION: The experience of grief and the pain of losing a loved one is as old as humanity. Since social workers assist people in working through painful experiences that affect their social functioning, virtually every social worker will at some time deal with the effects on clients of the loss of someone or something they love. Grief can occur because of an immediate event in a client's life, knowledge of a loss that is likely to occur in the near future (anticipatory grief), or "anniversary reactions" to grief-causing events that retrigger emotions and cause the individual to regrieve the loss.

Grief is defined as experiencing intense emotional suffering in response to the loss of or separation from someone or something that is deeply loved. Clients may experience grief due to many factors such as the separation or divorce of one's parents, the placement of a child in foster care, a stillborn child, a planned or spontaneous abortion, voluntary relinquishment of parental rights, the decline of physical or mental functioning, retirement or the loss of a job, a terminal diagnosis, the death of someone to whom the client has close emotional ties, the loss or death of a pet, or even the loss or destruction of personal possessions in a robbery or disaster. Sometimes one loss triggers other losses. For example, the divorce of one's parents may change a family's financial circumstances so that a child not only loses a two-parent family but may also have to move to another neighborhood and change schools. These *secondary losses* are significant and may be sources of grief. Whatever the cause, the social worker should be alert to the manifestations of grief and various expressions of grieving, as well as being knowledgeable about successful intervention approaches.

Expressions of grief are affected by one's relationship to the lost person or object, age or developmental stage, cultural background, gender, the suddenness or type of death or loss, the person's coping patterns, and so on. In Western culture, for example, women grieve more openly than men, and religious beliefs and cultural rituals vary widely in regard to accepting death and bringing closure for the survivors.

The intense grief period typically diminishes in six months to a year, but the process of grieving often takes as long as three to five years (or even longer). Over time, most people are able to resolve the loss and reduce the extensive pain experienced without the assistance of professional helpers (i.e., through the support of family and friends). In fact, personal growth often occurs as a person successfully deals with grief, and the outcome can be viewed as positive. For example, people sometimes gain increased independence and self-confidence, find new areas of interest and talent, develop new and rewarding relationships, and so on.

Cook and Oltjenbruns (1998) identify the following as normal manifestations of grief:

Intrapsychic

- Shock
- Emotional numbness
- Sadness
- Fatigue
- Loss of energy/strength
- Change in appetite
- Headaches
- Health concerns (e.g., blurred vision, difficulty breathing, abdominal pain, constipation, urinary frequency, no menstrual cycle, etc.)

Behavioral

- Crying
- Withdrawal or overdependence on others
- Loss of interest in daily tasks
- Restlessness
- Hostile outbursts

Somatic

- Tightness in throat
- Shortness of breath
- Disturbed sleep patterns
- Anger
- Fear
- Depression
- Anxiety
- Apathy
- Hopelessness
- Helplessness
- Worthlessness
- Guilt
- Disorientation
- Inability to concentrate
- Hallucinations
- Preoccupation

Sometimes, however, the response is so intense that it is dysfunctional or the person's progress in dealing with grief stalls. In those situations, the social worker will need to use a more clinical approach.

Current knowledge about grieving emphasizes several tasks that must be completed, as opposed to the prior view that there are distinct phases that are experienced in sequence. The key tasks (Worden, 1991) are the following:

- Accepting the reality of the loss of the person or object
- Experiencing and resolving the emotions associated with the grief
- Readjusting to life without the deceased person or lost object
- Reinvesting emotional energy in other relationships or focusing energy in ways to retain or honor the memory of the lost person or object

These tasks are overlapping and the individual revisits each one many times before a satisfactory adjustment is achieved.

Basic *supportive counseling* is perhaps the most useful form of social work intervention. People should be encouraged to grieve, to identify the scope of the loss they have experienced, to talk about the events of the loss, and to gain information about the process of grieving. When clients are focused on accepting the reality of the loss, it is helpful to encourage talking about the experience (usually repeatedly) and to take concrete actions related to the loss such as planning the funeral, taking care of financial matters, and so on. As acceptance of the loss begins, a worker might then help the person recall positive experiences from before the loss occurred. This might be done through talking about photographs, visiting places of special significance, or encouraging the client to use art, stories, poems, or other forms of expression. In addition, it is important to assist people in moving forward with their lives through solving problems that may have arisen from the loss (e.g., insurance claims, managing day-to-day issues, etc.), developing new roles and relationships, and engaging in new activities.

When the normal grief reaction does not begin to be resolved over time, depending on the specific circumstances, *individual, couple,* or *family therapy* might prove useful. When using therapeutic approaches, a social worker might draw from almost any of the practice frameworks described in Chapter 6 (e.g., psychodynamic, person-centered, cognitive-behavioral, task-centered, exercise, relaxation techniques, or the several family intervention approaches). One specific approach used when dealing with grief is termed *regrief therapy.* It is utilized when the person has not been able to complete the tasks in the grief process. Using this approach, the social worker invites the client to bring to a session items that are symbolic of the lost person or object and the client is helped to revisit the relationship and find emotional release. Another specialized technique is *guided mourning,* a cognitive-behavioral approach in which the client is encouraged to recall the details of the painful loss experience and to find appropriate ways to say good-bye through ritual and journaling about one's emotional reactions.

Support groups are useful in assisting people to deal with grief, particularly when those in the group have experienced a similar form of loss. These groups can offer advice about day-to-day tasks such as handling finances or taking on new household tasks, giving emotional support by providing an safe place where the grieving person can talk about the loss, and sharing experiences as a way of helping others see that their emotions are normal and to anticipate grief symptoms that may emerge.

SELECTED BIBLIOGRAPHY

Cook, Alicia Skinner, and Kevin Ann Oltjenbruns. *Dying and Grieving: Lifespan and Family Perspectives,* 2nd ed. Fort Worth: Harcourt Brace, 1998.

McNeil, John S. "Bereavement and Loss." In *Encyclopedia of Social Work,* 19th ed., vol. 1, edited by Richard L. Edwards. Washington, DC: NASW Press, 1995, pp. 284–291.

Worden, J. W. *Grief Counseling and Grief Therapy: A Handbook for the Mental Health Practitioner.* New York: Springer, 1991.

SECTION B

TECHNIQUES AND GUIDELINES FOR INDIRECT PRACTICE

Due to the complexity and multiple layers of decision making in organizations and communities, facilitating change in these large systems is usually a time-consuming and labor-intensive process. The social worker engaged in these activities should recognize that these complex social organizations were built by people and can be changed by people, but the process of changing them is often difficult. Typically, large system change efforts must be sustained over a long period of time, although occasionally intensive work on a project during a somewhat limited time period is as effective. Successful outcomes depend on such factors as timing (Is the organization or community ready to consider alternative ways of operating?), knowledge of alternative programs (Are there viable solutions to the issues being addressed?), and the involvement of key people in the organization or community.

Intervention Activities. Like all social work practice, much of the activity by social workers to change human services organizations and communities is based on relationships. As compared to direct-service practice where the central relationship is with clients, these relationships are with administrators, board members, the media, elected officials, and others who may be in a position to make or influence decisions. Many of the actions of the social worker to interpret problems or promote changes in the functioning of the agencies or the community occur through personal conversations with decision makers and often are hardly perceptible. We sometimes neglect to consider these actions as intervention, yet they serve to promote change.

Some actions by social workers in organizations and communities are best described as maintenance or incremental change activities. Much of that work is geared toward facilitating teamwork, resolving disputes within an agency, generating ideas for new or innovative services, raising funds for programs, or developing grant applications. These forms of intervention are central to improving the services to clients or the future clients of human services agencies.

The more dramatic change activities are those that attempt to solve immediate and stressful problems. Those interventions include activities such as pressing for changes in agency mission or programs, organizing staff to address issues, chairing a committee or leading a problem-solving group, designing new programs, helping the media interpret social problems to the public, advocating for vulnerable groups, and lobbying key decision makers. Most of the techniques in the following section of this book are useful for the social worker engaging in this type of change activity.

Monitoring Activities. Similar to the direct services, the monitoring of indirect-service activities uses techniques that can be used either to inform actions while the change effort is in process (i.e., formative evaluation) or to sum up the results of an action after it is completed (i.e., summative evaluation). The tools for monitoring and evaluating practice are in Chapter 15.

14.40 Working with a Governing or Advisory Board

PURPOSE: To understand the responsibilities of governing and advisory boards in the operation of human services organizations.

DISCUSSION: Human services agencies operate at the will of the people. If they are public agencies, they are created and at least partially funded through the actions of elected officials. Some private agencies are business concerns operated for the profit of owners or stockholders, but most are incorporated as nonprofit organizations and exist because the people of a community recognize the need for the agency's services.

Maintaining linkage to the community is important to the agency's continued sanction and success. An agency must have community support to adequately fulfill its needs for resources (e.g., funding, volunteers, public image) and must also be responsive to the community's changing service needs. One means of sustaining community linkage is through effective utilization of an *advisory board,* if a public agency, and the appropriate functioning of its *governing board,* if a private, nonprofit agency.

In private or nonprofit social agencies, the ***governing board*** is the body that is sanctioned to manage the organization. Legally, the board is responsible for the total management of the organization and the members are personally liable for its financial security. However, board members cannot and should not be present on a day-to-day basis to manage the operation of the agency. That is the job of the executive director or chief administrator. When a governing board shares its authority with the executive director, who then engages other staff members to provide the services, it is important that the lines of authority are clearly drawn so that there is no confusion that interferes with the provision of client services. A governing board typically is responsible for the following activities:

1. *Policymaking.* The governing board is legally charged with formulating the goals, objectives, operating policies, and programs of the agency. It should periodically review and revise the agency bylaws to assure that the operation of the agency conforms to the established goals and procedures.

2. *Planning.* As a link between community interests and agency, the board should engage in long-range planning that helps the agency project community needs and evolve programs appropriate to its mission.

3. *Funding.* A governing board is legally responsible for procuring the funds needed to operate the organization, budgeting the use of those resources, establishing procedures for the allocation of those funds, and overseeing fiscal operation of the organization. The board, then, can be expected to engage in preparing and/or approving budgets and grant applications and in representing the agency in appeals for funds from foundations, public fund allocation committees, and other funding agencies such as the United Way.

4. *Staffing.* In discharging the authority to operate the agency, the board hires an administrator (i.e., executive director) to manage the day-to-day operation of the organization. Within the hiring guidelines and personnel procedures established by the board, the administrator assures that qualified staff provide the agency's services.

5. *Facilities.* The board is responsible for assuring that the organization has appropriate housing for the operation of the established programs. If a capital campaign is required to secure needed space for program activities, for example, the board should play a major role in this activity.

6. *Community interpretation.* The board is a critical liaison with the community. It not only interprets community needs to the agency but also helps the community learn about the agency's programs and services. The board typically serves in the capacity of planning the agency's public relations activities and lobbying for policy decisions made by other community groups that may affect the agency.

7. *Evaluation.* Ultimately, the governing board must be accountable for all aspects of agency operation. Therefore, it must assess the effectiveness of the services provided and periodically evaluate the efficiency of the agency's operations.

Particularly in private agencies, the composition of the board is important. It should be representative of the community but also bring expertise or resources that are needed. Some agencies, but not all, select members with the expectation that they will be major fund-raisers or donors (i.e., the principle of the 3Gs applies: get money, give money, or get off the board).

In a public agency, by contrast, the ***advisory board*** (also called an *advisory council* or *advisory committee*) has no legal authority or responsibility for the operation of the organization. It is established either because the public officials responsible for the operation of the organization desire citizen input and/or because public law requires an advisory body as a channel for citizen participation. As the name implies, it offers advice, but that advice may or may not be heeded by administrative staff—at times a point of confusion if board and staff alike are not clear about the differences between governance and advisory functions. Azarnoff and Seliger (1982, 124) identify the following as typical responsibilities of an advisory board:

1. *Recommend policies and practices to the body legally created to govern the organization.* Consultation from an advisory board serves to inform the decision-making process. While usually the advisory function is found in public agencies, it can also serve the private agency regarding specific issues or special programs or projects.

2. *Evaluate agency services and recommend improvements.* Where staff are oftentimes too close to the services to offer an objective view of service provision or when the credibility of the staff to accurately assess the agency's functioning is in question, advisory committees can perform this valuable function.

3. *Assist in determining the needs of consumers.* Advisory boards are in a good position to represent the interests of the agency's clientele or potential clientele. For this reason, among others, it is important that clients or people familiar with client needs serve on advisory committees.

4. *Publicize agency activities.* Like the governing board, the advisory committee can inform the public of the agency's programs and methods of service delivery.

The members of both governing and advisory boards volunteer their time and talents to the agency. The motivations of board members may vary from a desire to help others, to a desire to use their special knowledge to benefit the community, to seeking personal recognition and social status. It is important to understand these motivations and use this resource in a manner that both serves the agency and satisfies the board member's need.

SELECTED BIBLIOGRAPHY

Azarnoff, Roy S., and Jerome S. Seliger. *Delivering Human Services.* Englewood Cliffs, NJ: Prentice Hall, 1982.

Duca, Diane. *Nonprofit Boards: Roles, Responsibilities, and Performance.* New York: John Wiley & Sons, 1996.

Tropman, John. *Nonprofit Boards: What to Do and How to Do It.* Washington, DC: Child Welfare League of America, 1997.

14.41 Conducting Effective Staff Meetings

PURPOSE: To design and conduct efficient staff meetings that promote intraagency communication.

DISCUSSION: An important factor in the successful operation of a social agency is the quality of staff communication, making the staff meeting a critically important tool in agency management. Properly used, the staff meeting enhances communication and can prevent organizational problems caused by staff who act on inaccurate or incomplete information. Improperly used, staff meetings can be both costly for the agency and frustrating for the staff. A one-hour meeting involving a staff of eight, for example, is the equivalent of a day's salary for one person. The cost of the meeting should be justified by its benefits for achieving the agency's purpose, as compared to the staff providing service to clients during that time.

It is important to distinguish between a staff meeting and other types of meetings, such as case staffings and consultations and the meetings used for case assignments or by special committees and project teams. The distinction between staff meetings and team meetings can be made in terms of *purpose* (e.g., exchange of information regarding the agency versus practice techniques related to specific cases); *content* (e.g., discussion of policies, procedures, organizational maintenance, and professional practice issues versus a specific issue of practice activity regarding a case situation); *formality* (i.e., formal versus informal); *membership* (e.g., inclusive of practitioners and support staff versus involving only practitioners who are members of the team); and *size* (e.g., typically large and somewhat impersonal versus small, intensive, and personally disclosing interaction).

Staff meeting time should not be spent on routine or easily understood information that can be disseminated by other means such as memos or routing documents among the staff. Staff meeting time is best spent only on matters that require verbal clarification, feedback from staff, or a staff decision. It should be noted, however, that research by Barretta-Herman (1989) suggests that social agency staff tend to resist both written and electronic communications in favor of face-to-face contact.

Staff meetings should be held at the same time each week or month, have a set starting and ending time, and last not more than one hour. Attendance should be mandatory and the leader should prepare and circulate an agenda in advance of the meeting and take responsibility to keep the discussion moving. However, staff meetings are not solely a management responsibility. All staff should be expected to contribute agenda items, be prepared for discussion of those items, and assume responsibility for following through on items that require their attention. If an issue requires extensive discussion or if in-service training is the best way to deal with a problem, a separate meeting should be scheduled. In many settings, the preparation of minutes is useful to disseminate information and properly record staff decisions in order to keep upper levels of administration informed of the activities of this unit.

Barretta-Herman's (1990, 145) analysis of staff meetings in human services organizations identifies three elements of successful meetings.

1. They fulfill their objectives as defined jointly by management and practitioners.
2. They provide a forum for active discussion, creative problem solving, and participation of staff members.
3. The structure of the meeting ensures decisions made are followed through with action.

SELECTED BIBLIOGRAPHY

Barretta-Herman, Angeline. "The Effective Social Service Staff Meeting." In *Business Communication: New Zealand Perspectives,* edited by Frank Slegio. Auckland: Software Technology, 1990, pp. 136–147.

———. "Computer Utilization in the Social Services." *New Zealand Journal of Social Work 7* (Fall 1989).

Brody, Ralph. *Effectively Managing Human Service Organizations.* Newbury Park, CA: Sage, 1993.

14.42 Building Teamwork and Cooperation

PURPOSE: To encourage and develop interagency and interprofessional cooperation.

DISCUSSION: In many cases, no one professional and no one agency can provide all of the services needed by the client. Thus, if the client is to be served, several professionals must work as a team. Teamwork and cooperative behavior grow from a proper mix of values, attitudes, and interpersonal skills.

The following guidelines can encourage cooperation and teamwork:

1. In general, individuals and organizations cooperate with each other when it is of benefit to do so. Those benefits may be personal, professional, organizational, political, or financial. An increased frequency of interaction usually leads to increased cooperation if the parties have similar goals, beliefs, and values. Cooperation is fostered by emphasizing what the parties have in common and how they will benefit from working together.

2. Genuine teamwork and interagency cooperation does not occur by accident; they must be encouraged and nurtured. Statements of thanks, recognition, praise, and taking a personal interest in other team members help to reinforce cooperative behavior. Where appropriate, invite other members of the team to office parties and social gatherings as a way of building relationships and promoting goodwill. Do not engage in gossip or any other activity that might diminish respect for other professionals or agencies.

3. Teamwork and cooperation is built on a common purpose. That purpose is to serve the client and to accomplish what no one professional or single agency can achieve alone. Whenever necessary, help the team members or agency representatives revisit the question: What are we trying to achieve for our clients?

4. When functioning as part of a team, encourage the selection of a leader or chairperson who is nondefensive, supportive of others, and respected by the group. Strive to be proactive and willing to plan and prepare carefully for team meetings and assume a leadership role when appropriate.

5. Concern for client confidentiality is a reason commonly given for not working closely with other agencies and professionals. Sometimes this issue is more imagined than real. Clients can be asked to sign a release of information, thus removing this barrier. If professionals or agencies want to work together but are hesitant to do so because of confidentiality, they should ask their agency's legal counsel to recommend a workable procedure.

6. Be alert to the fact that many interagency conflicts center on questions of which agency has primary fiscal responsibility for providing a particular service. In other words, many disagreements boil down to the question of whose budget is to be used to pay the cost of services.

7. Understand your role and responsibility and those of the people with whom you are working. Make sure everyone knows what they can and cannot expect of each other. Consider developing interagency agreements that will clarify these relationships (see Items 13.13 and 13.14). Several forms of documents might be used to define interagency expectations such as contracts, letters of agreement, protocol statements, purchase of service agreements, and policy manuals.

8. Remember that even under the best circumstances, teamwork can be challenging. This is especially true when the team is attempting to make difficult, value-laden decisions. Members should be willing to address directly and openly the conflicts or hidden agendas that disrupt team efforts. Conflict that arises from thoughtful differences of opinion is healthy. However, conflict that stems from prejudice, displaced hostility, or thoughtless loyalty to actions of the past is disruptive and must be addressed. Attempts to suppress or avoid conflicts or significant differences of opinion by denial, capitulation, or domination often make the problem even worse. When it is necessary to express a difference of opinion, use I-statements (see Item 8.5) and other communication skills that convey your message in a clear, straightforward, and nonthreatening manner. Try to resolve interprofessional and interagency conflicts by focusing on shared values and goals and by using negotiating skills.

9. Realize that some of those with whom you must work may not be committed to teamwork. When this is evident, be firm but diplomatic in expressing the need for cooperation and for putting the good of the client before other considerations.

SELECTED BIBLIOGRAPHY

Garner, Howard G., and Fred P. Orelove. *Teamwork in Human Services: Models and Applications across the Life Span*. Boston: Butterworth-Heinemann, 1994.

Ginsberg, Leon, and Paul R. Keys, eds. *New Management in Human Services*, 2nd ed. Washington, DC: NASW Press, 1995.

14.43 Supervising Staff and Volunteers

PURPOSE: To use supervisory principles to enhance the performance of staff and volunteers.

DISCUSSION: The fundamental purpose of supervision is to ensure that the agency's services and programs are provided in an efficient and effective manner. The term *supervision* is rooted in a Latin word that means to "look over." However, modern supervisory practice places less emphasis on viewing the supervisor as an overseer or inspector and more emphasis on the supervisor being a leader, a teacher, and a master of the work to be done.

Within an agency's organizational structure, it is the supervisor and the function of ***administrative supervision*** that links the line worker to the agency's upper-level administrative and management personnel. As a midlevel administrator, the supervisor must attend to such tasks as recruiting, selecting, and orienting new staff; planning, delegating, and coordinating work activities; monitoring and evaluating worker performance; ensuring compliance to agency policy and procedure; serving as a channel of communication between line workers and the administration; protecting workers from organizational forces that would distract them from their primary responsibilities or interfere with their work; serving as an advocate for workers; and representing the agency in community affairs and interagency coordination.

The term ***supportive supervision*** refers to supervisory activities that address issues and concerns related to staff morale; work-related anxiety and worry; job satisfaction; commitment to the agency's mission and policies; worker self-confidence and self-esteem; and emotional well-being. This aspect of supervision is extremely important in human services agencies where high levels or stress and worker burnout are serious personnel problems.

Kadushin (1992, 135) explains that ***educational supervision*** "is concerned with teaching the worker what he [or she] needs to know in order to do [a] job and helping him [or her] to learn it. Virtually every job description of the supervisor's position includes a listing of this function: 'instruct workers in acceptable social work techniques'; 'develop competence through individual and group conferences'; 'train and instruct staff in job performance." The educational component relates to the transmission of knowledge, skills, attitudes, and values.

In a typical human services agency, supervision is provided to staff members or volunteers in one or more of the following ways:

- *Individual supervision.* Regularly scheduled, one-to-one meetings between the supervisor and supervisee
- *Group supervision.* Regularly scheduled meetings between the supervisor and a small group of supervisees
- *Ad hoc supervision.* Brief and unscheduled meetings requested by the supervisee to discuss a specific question or issue
- *Peer supervision.* Regularly scheduled meetings attended by a small group of supervisees in order to discuss their work and seek guidance and suggestions
- *Formal case presentations.* Regularly scheduled meetings at which one or more supervisees present an in-depth description of their work on a specific case or project and invite advice and guidance on how it could be improved

Individual supervision is an essential component of staff supervision. Every supervisee needs and deserves regularly scheduled private time with his or her supervisor. An atmosphere of privacy, fairness, and emotional safety must exist in the supervisor-supervisee relationship if a supervisee is to accurately describe and discuss job-related concerns and difficulties. Kaiser (1997, 7) reminds us that practitioners "must have a place to go where they can carefully and honestly examine their own behavior. That place, ideally, is the supervisory relationship."

Of central importance in supervision is the ongoing monitoring and evaluation of the supervisee's performance. This process of evaluation focuses on the supervisee's behaviors and actions as related to his or her roles, responsibilities, and work assignments.

Evaluations are of two types: formal and informal. An *informal evaluation* consists of the ongoing feedback and suggestions offered by the supervisor. This type of evaluation takes place on a weekly or even a daily basis. A *formal evaluation* is a detailed review and comparison of the supervisee's performance to the agency's written standards, performance criteria, and job expectations. It occurs once or twice a year, depending on the agency's personnel policies (see Item 15.8).

The results of the formal evaluation are placed in a written report. This report typically consists of the ratings assigned to the various items on an evaluation form and a few paragraphs that describe special strengths and abilities and/or special problems and deficiencies in performance. The report may also include a plan for correcting noted deficiencies prior to the next formal evaluation. Addressing the issues identified by the formal evaluation should become a part of the supervisor's and worker's or volunteer's ongoing supervisory agenda.

Following are guidelines for those providing supervision:

1. Understand that social workers who assume the role of supervisor have special ethical obligations. According to the *NASW Code of Ethics* (1996), social workers who provide supervision:

- Should have the necessary knowledge and skill to supervise . . . appropriately and should do so only within their areas of knowledge and competence.
- Are responsible for setting clear, appropriate, and culturally sensitive boundaries.
- Should not engage in any dual or multiple relationships with supervisee and in which there is a risk of exploitation of or potential harm to the supervisee.
- Should evaluate supervisee's performance in a manner that is fair and respectful. (NASW, 3.01 a–d)

2. Reward good performance. Because supervisors in human services agencies can seldom offer monetary rewards, they must be creative in utilizing other types of rewards such as recognition, offering desirable or stimulating work assignments, and special privileges.

3. Hold supervisees accountable for their performance. Never ignore sloppy or unprofessional performance or deliberate violations of policy and procedure. When it is necessary to correct or discipline a supervisee, this should be done immediately after the infraction is discovered and in private. Disciplinary actions must be fair, decisive, very clear, and based on facts. Such actions must communicate to the supervisee exactly what is expected in the future and the consequences if performance is not improved. Failure to do so can frustrate and demoralize other agency staff and consume an inordinate amount of a supervisor's time and energy.

4. Remember that example is the best teacher. The supervisor must constantly model the values, attitudes, and behavior he or she expects of supervisees.

5. Make work assignments that are clear and appropriate to the supervisee's level of knowledge, skill, and experience. The supervisee should be helped to learn job-related skills and obtain the training he or she needs to perform at a higher level (see Items 10.3, 11.13, and 14.51).

6. Adjust the frequency and intensity of the supervisory process to the supervisees' level of competency and experience and to the nature of their job responsibilities.

7. If dismissal of the employee is a possibility, the supervisor must understand and strictly adhere to the relevant procedures outlined in the agency's personnel manual. Such procedures should reflect state and federal law on employee-employer relations. These procedures typically require that the employee be given written warnings of possible termination, a written description of his or her unacceptable performance, and a reasonable opportunity to improve his or her performance prior to termination. When attempting to terminate the employment of an individual, the supervisor must operate on the assumption that the individual may file a lawsuit and that the dismissal will have to be explained and justified in court.

Some behaviors by the employee are so serious that they should result in an immediate move to terminate employment. These include:

- Clear and serious violations of the *NASW Code of Ethics* (e.g., sexual relations with a client, abuse of client, or sexual harassment of client or staff)
- Theft of agency money, equipment, or property
- Concealing, consuming, or selling drugs on agency premises
- Reckless or threatening actions that place clients or staff at risk of serious harm
- Deliberate withholding of information from a supervisor or agency personnel that they need to know in order to properly serve clients and maintain the integrity and reputation of the agency and its programs
- Deliberate falsification of agency records and reports
- Solicitation or acceptance of gifts or favors from clients in exchange for preferential treatment
- Clear and repeated insubordination

SUGGESTED BIBLIOGRAPHY

Kadushin, Alfred. *Supervision in Social Work.* New York: Columbia University Press, 1992.

Kaiser, Tamara. *Supervisory Relationship: Exploring the Human Element.* Boston: Brooks/Cole, 1997.

NASW Code of Ethics. Washington DC: NASW Press, 1997.

Shulman, Lawrence. *Interactional Supervision.* Washington DC: NASW Press, 1993.

14.44 Leading Small Group Meetings

PURPOSE: To schedule and conduct efficient and productive committee and group meetings.

DISCUSSION: Group decision making has become increasingly popular in the human services. Therefore, social workers spend considerable time participating in groups, agency staff meetings, interagency team meetings, and various agency and community committees. While group consideration of issues potentially leads to better decisions, group meetings, without proper planning and direction, can waste much valuable time and reduce the opportunity for making significant community or organizational change. As the leader of a small group, the social worker is responsible for making the meeting as productive and efficient as possible. The following principles and guidelines should be followed by the worker when he or she is in a leadership position:

1. *Prepare for the meeting by engaging in the following activities:*
   - Clearly identify the purpose of the meeting and never have a meeting unless there is a real need for one.
   - Decide who should participate.
   - Identify objectives for the meeting and anticipate what the participants will and should expect. You may want to involve them in the planning.

- Decide the best time and place for the meeting, and determine how participants will be notified of the purpose, agenda, time, and place of the meeting.
- Decide how much time will be required for the meeting and construct a realistic agenda. Plan to address high-priority items first.
- Decide what physical arrangements are necessary (e.g., room reservations, seating arrangements, audiovisual equipment, refreshments, etc.).
- Decide if a written report will be needed and, if so, who will prepare it and how it will be distributed.
- Decide if a follow-up meeting will be needed.

2. *Get the discussion off to a good start.*
   - Make sure that all members are introduced to each other. This might be done with formal introductions or over refreshments. Use name tags if members do not already know each other.
   - Explain the purpose of the discussion and its relevance to the participants.
   - Distribute materials needed for the discussion (e.g., fact sheets, outlines, case examples).
   - Create an atmosphere that helps the participants feel unthreatened and responsible for contributing to the discussion.

3. *Keep the discussion orderly, efficient, and productive.*
   - Make sure the goal is understood by all and that it is a goal that makes sense to the group. Keep the participants oriented toward that goal. For example, occasionally ask: Are we still on target for reaching our objectives?
   - Be alert to extended departures from the topic. If the group is drifting away from the topic, call this to everyone's attention. Ask if the digression means that there is disagreement on the goal or if it is an indication that the group is ready to move on to another topic.
   - If there is much repetition in the discussion, ask if the group has exhausted the subject at hand. If so, help them get started on a new topic.
   - Be the group's timekeeper. Keep the group informed of the time limits so high-priority topics will get the attention they deserve.
   - Bring the discussion to a conclusion, which might include:
     a. A summary of progress made by the group
     b. Comments about planning and preparation for another meeting
     c. Assignments for follow-up and implementation
     d. Commendations when appropriate
     e. Request an evaluation of the meeting in order to improve future ones

4. *Give all members an equal opportunity to participate.*
   - Explain in your opening remarks that the role of the group leader primarily will be that of coordinator to ensure that all members have an opportunity to be heard.
   - Address your comments and questions to the group as a whole, unless specific information is needed from a particular person.
   - Make sure that all members have a chance to participate. While no one should be forced to speak, neither should anyone be prevented from speaking.

- Scan the group every minute or two. Look for indications that a member wants to speak. If this is seen and the member has been quiet, bring that person into the discussion by asking if he or she would like to add something to the discussion.
- If the group contains members who dominate the discussion, try to control them for the benefit of the group. A number of techniques can be used; begin with a more subtle approach and become directive only if necessary. Some possible ways to deal with such members are:
  - **a.** When possible, seat the talkative members where they are more easily overlooked by other members.
  - **b.** When a question is asked of the group, meet the eyes of those members who have spoken infrequently and avoid eye contact with the dominant talkers.
  - **c.** When a frequent talker has made a point, cut in with something like: How do the rest of you feel about that idea?
  - **d.** Adopt a rule that each person can make but one statement per topic.
  - **e.** In private, ask the excessive talkers to help in getting the quiet members to speak more often.
  - **f.** Point out the problem and ask others to contribute more—for instance: "We have heard a lot from John and Mary, but what do the rest of you think about . . . ?"
- If asked by a member to express a personal opinion about a controversial issue, try to bounce the question back to the group, unless members already have expressed their opinions. Say, "Well, let's see how others feel about this first." If you must express a personal opinion, do so in a manner that will not inhibit others from speaking on the topic.
- Don't comment after each member has spoken; it is too easy to get into a "wheel" pattern of communication, with the leader becoming the hub of the wheel.
- React to what members say with acceptance and without judgment, showing only that a point is understood or that it needs clarification. If evaluation seems necessary, invite it from others with a question such as: Does that fit with your perception on the matter?
- Use nonverbal communication to promote discussion. Nods and gestures can be used to encourage participation, especially from the quiet members.

5. *Promote cooperation and harmony in a small group.*

- Be alert to the possibility of hidden agendas, and call them to the attention of the group. The group usually can solve a problem of conflicting purposes if it is brought into the open for discussion.
- Emphasize the importance of the mutual sharing of ideas and experiences and the need for clear communication.
- Use the word *we* often to stress the group's unity of purpose.
- Keep conflicts focused on facts and issues. Stop any personal attacks.
- Do not let the discussion become so serious that the members do not have some fun. Humor can reduce tension. Effective discussion is characterized by shifting between the serious and the playful.

6. *Use questioning techniques to maintain attention on a topic and stimulate analytical thinking.*
   - Use open-ended questions rather than closed-ended ones.
   - Questions should be understandable to all. Vague or obtuse questions frustrate the members.
   - Questions should be asked in a natural and conversational tone of voice.
   - Questions should usually be addressed to the group as a whole, rather than to a particular individual. This motivates everyone to think and respond.
   - Questions occasionally should be asked of persons who are not giving their attention to the discussion. This usually stimulates the individual and the whole group to redirect its attention to the topic.
   - Questions should be asked in a manner that indicates the leader's confidence in the person's ability to respond.
   - Questions should be selected to maintain the focus on the topic under discussion. Avoid questions that would cause the group to leave its task and go off on a tangent.

7. *Encourage critical thinking.*
   - Ask for more detail and specification. Dig for the rationale and assumptions behind an opinion or a belief. Help those offering opinions to furnish evidence for the positions they take.
   - See that the evidence offered for a position is tested and not accepted at face value.
   - Assign one or two members of the group to challenge ideas and play devil's advocate so that differences are aired openly.

SELECTED BIBLIOGRAPHY

Brilhart, John. *Effective Group Discussion*, 8th ed. Madison, WI: Brown and Benchmark, 1995.

Fatout, Marian, and Steven R. Rose. *Task Groups in the Social Services.* Newbury Park, CA: Sage, 1995.

Tropman, John E. *Making Meetings Work: Achieving High-Quality Group Decisions.* Newbury Park, CA: Sage, 1995.

14.45 The RISK Technique

PURPOSE: To facilitate committee or group members in expressing their fears or concerns about an issue or proposed action.

DISCUSSION: At times, committees (and especially staff committees) need to address fears and concerns related to some perceived risk or threat. For example, when new policies are adopted by a board, when new legislation is passed that affects a social program and/or the resources available, or when administrators establish a change in routine, it becomes important to identify and clarify the facts and issues in the situation and set aside rumors and fantasized outcomes. In these situations, the RISK technique can be useful.

To use this technique, the leader must take a nondefensive posture and communicate an interest in having the group members express all fears, issues, concerns, complaints, and anticipated problems. By maintaining this approach, the leader encourages members of the group to express their views and to listen and understand one anothers' fears.

For example, assuming that a proposed change in a social agency is that all workers would double the number of days they are on 24-hour call each month, the agency supervisor might elect to use the ***RISK technique*** by taking the following steps:

1. The leader schedules a meeting with all agency workers and presents a detailed description of the proposed change in the "on-call" section of the agency's personnel policy.

2. The leader explains that he or she will utilize the RISK technique to help workers identify all of their concerns about this proposed change.

3. The leader begins by asking workers to voice any and all fears, concerns, and worries they have in relation to the proposed change. These "risks" are written on newsprint for all to see, with the wording of the statement acceptable to the person raising the concern. Discussion of the items is not permitted at this time. (Note that up to this point, the RISK technique is similar to brainstorming, Item 14.49.)

4. The leader continues to encourage workers to voice additional concerns about the proposed change. It is important to allow adequate time for this session because the concerns that are most disturbing and threatening often will not surface until late in the session.

5. The initial session ends and the leader schedules a second meeting to occur in the next three to seven days. Meanwhile, all workers receive a written listing of the risk items identified during the meeting.

6. At the second meeting, the leader encourages workers to voice any additional risks they may have thought of since the initial meeting or to change the wording of any risk statements. The group is then asked to discuss and react to each risk item and decide if it is, indeed, a serious and substantive concern or issue. The risks considered to be minor or of little concern are dropped from the list. Those remaining are further discussed and clarified. At this point, the second meeting is ended with the understanding that the identified risks are viewed as those of the group as a whole, and not the person who first identified any risk.

7. The leader places the group's identified risks (i.e., the final list from the second meeting) on an agenda for a meeting between the workers and administrators.

SELECTED BIBLIOGRAPHY

Brilhart, John K., and Gloria J. Galanes. *Effective Group Discussion,* 8th ed. Madison, WI: Brown and Benchmark, 1995.

14.46 The Nominal Group Technique (NGT)

PURPOSE: To help consensus-oriented groups arrive at decisions.

DISCUSSION: Committees that depend on a consensus approach sometimes get stuck in reaching a decision. One technique that helps bring issues into the open and moves the group toward consensus is the ***Nominal Group Technique*** (***NGT***). It is particularly suited for groups of six to nine people; if used with a larger group, the committee should be divided into smaller groups. Depending on the scope and complexity of the matter being addressed, it might take from as little as an hour and a half to a much longer period to complete the process.

The main elements of the NGT process are the following:

1. The participants generate ideas in writing.
2. Round-robin feedback is given from group members with each idea recorded in a terse phrase on a flipchart.
3. Group discussion of each recorded idea is held for clarification and evaluation.
4. Individual voting establishes priorities among ideas with a group decision being mathematically derived through rank ordering or rating.

The following guidelines are suggested as the structure for a NGT session:

1. The chair acts as facilitator and does not vote.

2. The issue is stated on a flipchart.

3. The pros and cons are freely discussed for 10 minutes.

4. Each person is asked to spend 5 to 15 minutes working silently, writing down ideas or solutions on a piece of paper. The chair polls each committee member for one idea or solution.

5. Each idea or solution is listed on the chart and numbered. The chair then polls each member for a second idea or solution and repeats this process until the lists have been exhausted.

6. An additional 10 more minutes are allowed for clarification of the ideas or solutions presented—not for defense of the position.

7. All members vote on a secret ballot, ranking their top five choices 1, 2, 3, 4, 5. By adding the scores for each idea or solution, the lowest scores will reflect the most favored positions.

8. Have a full evaluation discussion of the several items at the top of the list. Encourage critical thinking, invite disagreement, and seek careful analysis of the items.

9. If a clear consensus is not reached, revote and then discuss the items again. This can be repeated until a synthesis of ideas is developed or there is clear support for one idea.

The NGT process encourages active involvement by all participants as they consider and write down their ideas. Too often, in a group process, a few members carry the discussion and others do not actively and creatively think about the issues from their own perspectives. The interactive presentation of the issues allows all committee members an opportunity to express themselves and respond to the ideas from both the verbal and less-verbal members.

SELECTED BIBLIOGRAPHY

Brilhart, John K., and Gloria J. Galanes. *Effective Group Discussion,* 8th ed. Madison, WI: Brown and Benchmark, 1995.

Toseland, Ronald W., and Robert F. Rivas. *An Introduction to Group Work Practice,* 2nd ed. Boston: Allyn and Bacon, 1995.

14.47 Chairing a Committee

PURPOSE: To effectively serve as chair of a committee and lead it to successful action.

DISCUSSION: The committee is a particular type of small group for which the social worker might assume a leadership function. As chairperson of a committee, the social worker should make use of the guidelines for working with small groups (see Item 14.44). In addition, chairing a committee requires the use of a formal task-oriented approach to groups that can be facilitated by the selective use of Items 14.45 and 14.46.

Essential knowledge for both the chairperson and committee members is familiarity with parliamentary procedures. For almost a century, *Robert's Rules of Order* (Robert 1990) has been the accepted procedures to be followed in formal committee proceedings. Table 14.1 provides a summary of these rules of order.

Above all else, a committee chair must believe in the worth and wisdom of group decision making. The decisions made by a small group, as compared to those made by a single individual, are more likely to be based on accurate and complete information and on a wider range of considerations; thus, the decisions are more likely to be the best ones possible. That is not to say that committees do not make bad decisions. They do. But a group is less likely to make a bad decision or a serious error in judgment than is an individual acting alone.

Tropman, Johnson, and Tropman (1992) remind us that the committee chair must be alert to the danger of *groupthink,* a situation of false agreement or false consensus that arises when a powerful committee member takes a strong stand on an issue and other members simply acquiesce rather than argue an opposing point of view. Soon after the meeting, the other members will usually complain and agree among themselves that the decision reached was a bad one. Needless to say, this conflict could have been avoided if the chair had made sure all points of view were expressed and debated and no one member or faction dominated the meeting.

People are usually willing to serve on a committee if they believe their time will be used efficiently and the committee's work will result in a real and positive change.

TABLE 14.1 Summary of Parliamentary Procedure

Guidelines/ Description	Type of Action	Purpose of Action	Interrupts Debate?	Requires Second?	Debatable?	Amendable?	Vote Required?
	PRIVILEGED MOTIONS						
■ #1–12 in order of priority	1. Fix time to adjourn	Establish plan to discontinue meeting	No	Yes	No	No	Majority
■ #1–4 supersede all other actions	2. Recess	Temporary break in meeting	No	Yes	Yes	Yes	Majority
	3. Question of privilege	Challenge rights of assembly or a member to take an action	Yes	No	No	No	None
	4. Point of order	Clarify or challenge process	Yes	No	No	No	None
	SUBSIDIARY MOTIONS						
■ #5–12 facilitate action on other motions	5. Table the motion	Delay action to a specified meeting	No	Yes	No	No	Majority
	6. Previous question	Close debate and vote immediately	No	Yes	No	No	2/3
	7. Limit debate	Set limits on future debate	No	Yes	No	Yes	2/3
	8. Postpone definitely	Temporarily delay action to a specified time	No	Yes	Yes	Yes	Majority
■ Each may be made while motion below is on the floor	9. Refer to committee	Delay until committee can review matter and report back	No	Yes	Yes	Yes	Majority
	10. Amend the amendment	One amendment to primary amendment is permitted at a time	No	Yes	Yes	Yes	Majority
	11. Primary amendment	Propose change in main motion	No	Yes	Yes	Yes	Majority
	12. Postpone indefinitely	Remove motion from consideration	No	Yes	Yes	No	Majority

Process Starts Here ➡	MAIN MOTION OR RESOLUTION						
■ Routes to opening main motion	■ New motion	Introduce action for first time	No	Yes	Yes	Yes	Majority
	■ Reconsider prior action	Reconsider previous vote	Yes	Yes	Yes	No	Majority
	■ Resume consideration	Take up motion previously tabled	No	Yes	Yes	No	Majority
	INCIDENTAL MOTIONS						
■ No order of precedence	■ Move to appeal	Challenge ruling of the chair	Yes	Yes	Yes	No	Majority
■ Arise from process of debate and may occur at any time	■ Move to suspend rules	Override existing procedures	No	Yes	No	No	2/3
■ Yeild only to privileged motions	■ Request point of order	Correct parlimentary process error	Yes	No	No	No	None
	■ Withdraw motion	Remove motion from consideration	Yes	No	No	No	None
	■ Division of question	Act on parts of motion or amendment	No	No	No	No	None
	■ Division of assembly	After voice vote, request vote count	Yes	No	No	No	None
	■ Request for information	Seek clarification	Yes	No	No	No	None

On the other hand, many people have reasons for disliking and avoiding committee work. Among their reasons are the following:

- There is a lack of clear purpose (e.g., members are not sure why they are meeting or what they are to accomplish).
- There is a lack of leadership and direction by the chairperson (e.g., the chair does not keep the group moving and focused; real issues are not addressed or difficult decisions are avoided).
- The chair and/or members do not take the assignment seriously (i.e., lack of motivation or interest in the work of the committee).
- The committee's work is disregarded by top management (e.g., a committee is asked to study an issue and make a recommendation but the recommendation is ignored; sometimes the committee discovers that there was never an intention to follow the committee's recommendation).
- Committee discussion is controlled or dominated by one individual or a clique.
- There is a lack of preparation for the meetings (e.g., no agenda, needed information is not made available, etc.).
- There is a lack of follow through (e.g., members or the chair promises to do something but fails to do so).
- The chair or members have a hidden agenda (e.g., some members have an ax to grind or will accept only one outcome, regardless of majority opinion).

One means of helping a committee avoid pitfalls that can lead to unproductive meetings is to engage the members in setting goals and operating procedures for the committee. Whether it is new or a committee that has continued over an extended period of time, it is useful for the chairperson or other members to periodically review and renegotiate the objectives and methods of operation so that all members can fully participate in the work. Dyer (1995) identifies several steps that should be followed in building a productive committee:

1. *Develop a realistic priority level.* It is important to give members a chance to discuss why they are serving on the committee, clarify the relative importance of this work in the context of their total responsibilities, and indicate the amount of time they are able to commit to this activity. Sharing these matters helps to establish the pace at which the committee can operate and allows the chair to identify persons who have the time and interest to carry major responsibilities.

2. *Share expectations.* Each person should be asked to identify his or her greatest concerns about working on this committee, how he or she sees it functioning, and what actions are necessary to ensure positive outcomes.

3. *Clarify goals.* The committee members should collectively discuss and write down a statement that represents the group's *core mission.* Subgoals can then be developed to reflect the intermediate or short-range objectives necessary to accomplish this mission. Each decision and action should be examined for its contribution to the mission or subgoals that have been established.

4. *Formulate operating guidelines.* The committee members should then establish procedures for their operation. Answers to the following questions will provide guidance for the chair and allow members to know how to proceed:

- How will we make decisions?
- What will be our basic method of working as a group?
- How do we make sure everyone gets a chance to discuss issues or raise concerns?
- How will we resolve differences?
- How will we ensure that we complete our work and meet deadlines?
- How will we change methods that are not producing results?

In addition, it should be recognized that the formality with which a committee operates often depends on its size, the existing relationships among the members, and the speed with which it needs to make decisions. The purpose of some committees is best served by a very open dialogue that explores topics in depth before action is taken. For others, the work is more task oriented, with subcommittees considering the issues and preparing reports of their deliberations on which the full committee will act.

SELECTED BIBLIOGRAPHY

Dyer, William G. *Team Building: Issues and Alternatives,* 3rd ed. Reading, MA: Addison-Wesley, 1995.

Robert, Henry M. *Robert's Rules of Order,* 9th ed. Glenview, IL: Scott Foresman, 1990.

Tropman, John E., Harold R. Johnson, and Elmer J. Tropman. *Committee Management in Human Services,* 2nd ed. Chicago: Nelson-Hall, 1992.

14.48 Problem Solving by a Large Group

PURPOSE: To help a large group of people arrive at a decision.

DISCUSSION: At times, it is necessary for a social worker to initiate problem-solving activity within a large group. The technique described here is intended to elicit ideas from all members and provide an opportunity for participation, even when as many as 30 or more people are involved.

The technique begins with the group leader explaining the purpose of the meeting—for example: "We need to come up with a method of collecting information from the agencies in town on trends in the number of homeless people applying for help." The following steps should then be followed:

1. *Each individual is asked to think privately about the problem and possible solutions.* Members are asked to make written notes on their thoughts.

2. *Dyads are formed.* Each person in the dyad is instructed to interview his or her partner and to try to understand that person's perspective on the problem and proposed solutions. The dyads work for 10 minutes.

3. *Quartets are formed.* For 15 minutes, each group of four people discusses the problem and possible solutions. Each quartet records the key points of its deliberation on a large piece of paper, which is hung on the wall for all to see.

4. *Each individual studies the papers for 10 minutes.*

5. *The whole group reassembles and shares their analysis of the problem and proposed solutions.* This final step sets the stage for the prioritizing of proposed solutions to be explored in more depth.

SELECTED BIBLIOGRAPHY

Brody, Ralph. *Effectively Managing Human Service Organizations.* Newbury Park, CA: Sage, 1993.

Kahn, Si. *Organizing: A Guide for Grassroots Leaders.* Washington, DC: NASW Press, 1991.

Rivira, Felix G., and John L. Erlich. *Community Organizing in a Diverse Society.* Boston: Allyn and Bacon, 1992.

14.49 Brainstorming

PURPOSE: To help a client identify several possible solutions to a problem.

DISCUSSION: Problem solving includes the important step of identifying all possible alternatives or solutions. Too often, some potential solutions are overlooked because they do not fit preconceived notions or expectations. Rigidity and following old habits of thought can limit creativity during the problem-solving process. The technique of ***brainstorming*** is designed to overcome this limitation. It can be applied to any problem for which there may be a range of solutions. The objective of brainstorming is to free persons temporarily from self-criticism and from the criticism of others in order to generate imaginative solutions to a specific problem. However, it should not be used until the problem has been clearly defined. Brainstorming is most often used in work with groups or committees, but many workers adapt its principles for use in one-on-one counseling sessions.

A brainstorming session begins with the identification and listing of a wide variety of possible solutions. Many may be unrealistic, but it is only after all alternatives have been identified that the participants are permitted to evaluate the proposed solutions in search of those that are feasible. A social worker setting up a brainstorming session will give the participants several instructions, such as:

1. Participants are encouraged to develop a large number of solutions. The goal is to generate a quantity of solutions—quality will be determined later.
2. Participants are encouraged to be freewheeling in their thinking. Even wild ideas are welcomed and accepted without judgment.
3. Participants are encouraged to combine and elaborate on the solutions that are offered.

4. Participants are not permitted to criticize or evaluate one another's proposed solutions.

During the brainstorming session, a recorder writes down all the ideas as fast as they come up. Do this on a blackboard or flipchart so the visual record stimulates additional ideas. The leader of the session should quickly stop any criticism of ideas, whether verbal or implied by tone of voice or nonverbal gesture. Also, the group leader needs to keep the participants focused on the problem under consideration.

Once all of the proposed solutions or ideas have been heard and recorded, the session moves to a second stage: the critical examination of each idea. De Bono (1992) suggests a useful technique for ensuring that six types of questioning and thinking are applied during the evaluation stage. Each of these six categories of thinking is called a "hat" and each hat has a color. Thus, for example, when the group is asked by the group leader to "put on your red hats," the group is being asked to evaluate the proposed solutions in terms of hunches, intuition, and gut feelings. If asked to put on the "black hat," the group is to view the solutions in a highly critical and skeptical manner.

The six thinking hats are as follows:

White hat (focus on objectivity and data): What information do we have? How reliable is this information? What additional information do we need?

Red hat (focus on hunches and intuition): What are our gut feelings about this proposed solution? Does it "feel" right? Let's trust our instincts!

Black hat (focus on caution and risk): What are the legal, policy, political, and funding problems we will encounter? This cannot be done and will not work because . . . .

Yellow hat (focus on optimism): It needs to be done, so let's try! Who cares if it has never been done before? Let's try something different! It will work if we really want it to work!

Green hat (focus on creativity and other combinations of ideas): Are there still other ways of thinking about this? Can we combine the best parts of several different proposals?

Blue hat (focus on the big picture and holistic thinking): How does this idea fit with other things we know about this issue? Are we missing something important? Let's summarize the conclusions we have reached and the decisions we have made so far. Is our way of discussing and approaching this issue working for us? Are we making progress toward a decision or solution?

A brainstorming session, plus the evaluation of each proposed solution (50 might be generated in a single session), could take several hours.

SELECTED BIBLIOGRAPHY

De Bono, Edward. *Serious Creativity.* New York: HarperCollins,1992.

Kottler, Jeffery. *Advanced Group Leadership.* Pacific Grove, CA: Brooks/Cole, 1994.

14.50 Class Advocacy

PURPOSE: To advance the cause of a group in order to establish a right or entitlement to a resource or opportunity.

DISCUSSION: The term ***class advocacy*** refers to actions on behalf of a whole group or class of people. This is in contrast to *client advocacy* (see Item 14.25), in which the advocacy is on behalf of a specific individual. Because class advocacy seeks change in law and public policy at either the local, state, or national level, it is essentially a political process aimed at influencing the decisions of elected officials and high-level administrators. It entails building coalitions with other groups and organizations that share concerns about a social issue. The social worker typically participates as a representative of an organization, rather than as an independent practitioner.

Since the goal is to bring about a change, resistance, opposition, and conflict should be expected. Those with power can and will use their power to resist change, creating some risk for the advocates. When a person sets out to alter the status quo, there is a good chance that he or she will ruffle some feathers, lose some friends, create some enemies, or get labeled as a troublemaker. Thus, not everyone is comfortable with this type of advocacy. Further, each organization must examine the pros and cons of taking on an advocacy role and decide whether having its representatives perform this role fits with the purpose of the organization.

For those who become engaged in class advocacy, the following guidelines may increase the chances of success:

1. Realize that advocacy can make a difference. You can bring about needed changes in laws, policies, and programs. Bringing about change is difficult—but not impossible.

2. Remember that you cannot do it alone. Individual social workers will need to join with others. A group has more power than an individual. Also, your organization needs to join with other organizations that share your concerns. Several organizations, working together, have more power than a single organization working alone.

3. Working with other organizations will mean that your own organization will have to share some resources, make some compromises, and perhaps do things differently than it prefers. In the long run, however, your organization will accomplish more as part of a coalition than it will by working alone.

4. Many improvements are needed in our human services systems. Since you cannot do everything that needs to be done, you must decide which concern has the highest priority. Choose your cause very carefully. If you or your organization take on several causes at one time, you may be spread too thin. It is better to make real gains in just one area than to make minimal gains or fail completely in several.

5. It is also important to choose a cause where success is possible. Be realistic! Do not waste your organization's time and energy on a lost cause. That will only result in frustration. As in other aspects of life, a successful experience generates hope and

a feeling that other successes are possible. If the members of an organization can see even small successes, they will be more willing to invest themselves in future advocacy efforts and be more motivated to work on other needed changes in the system.

6. Successful advocacy is built on a foundation of careful analysis and planning. It is important to define what you see as a problem and carefully study the problem—before you make a decision on what to do about it. Do not launch an effort to change something until you know exactly what has to be changed, why it has to be changed, and what will be involved in bringing about the change.

7. Before you take action, carefully assess what achieving your goal will require in the way of time, energy, money, and other resources. Do you have the resources? If not, it is best to scale down your goals or wait until later when you are better organized and more capable of reaching your goal.

8. Try to understand those who oppose you. There is always resistance to change. Analysis of the situation to be changed should include understanding why there is resistance. The advocate needs to know how opponents think and feel when asked to change. You need to be able to put yourself in your opponent's shoes (i.e., you must have empathy). People always have reasons for opposing change. You may not agree with their reasons, but you must understand them if you are to figure out a way to successfully overcome that resistance.

9. Successful advocacy requires self-discipline. It is important to think before you act. Class advocacy requires that you build coalitions and those coalitions are built on mutual trust and mutual self-interest. One of the most serious errors one can make in advocacy is to act impulsively. If that happens, the other organizations in the coalition may pull back or be reluctant to cooperate because they fear that your recklessness will cause damage to their organization or to the coalition. Also, if you act impulsively, those who oppose you can more easily discredit your organization.

10. Advocacy involves the use of power. You may not have as much power as you want, but do not overlook the power you do have. Essentially, ***power*** is the ability to make others behave the way you want them to behave. Think of power as a resource that can be used or "spent" for a particular purpose. There are different kinds of power. It is important to study your own organization and its membership in order to discover the type of power that you do possess.

Among the types of power social workers have is the power that comes from knowledge and expertise. For example, if you are advocating on behalf of children, you have detailed information about children and troubled families, and you know how the system works or does not work for the benefit of children and families. Information, if carefully assembled and presented, can have a powerful impact on legislators, agency administrators, and the public.

No doubt some members of your organization are highly respected in the community. They are held in high esteem by the public because of their past achievements. They have credibility that gives them a type of power. Individuals who are respected can have a significant influence on legislators and administrators. You need to encourage and help those respected individuals to become spokespersons for your organization.

Do not forget that personal commitment, time, and energy are also types of power. Much can be accomplished just by sticking with a task and seeing it through to the end. Organizational solidarity is also a type of power. If legislators and decision makers can see that members are solidly behind their organization, they will pay attention to what the organization's leaders have to say.

Within your organization are members who are natural leaders. Some may be charismatic and articulate. They can excite people and get them to work together on a cause. Charisma is a rare quality, but it is definitely a type of power. Identify those individuals in your organization and let them speak for your cause.

11. There are times when class advocacy must take the form of a lawsuit (Morales and Sheafor 1998). Many changes and reforms would never have happened without lawsuits and court decisions. For example, within the past 25 years, most of the reforms in the areas of mental health and mental retardation grew out of lawsuits. An organization committed to advocacy will, at times, need to encourage and support lawsuits that have potential for bringing about a needed change.

12. Most people in the United States depend on television and newspapers for information. If one wants the public to understand and support a cause, it is important to learn to work with the media (see Item 14.54). If there is someone associated with the organization who knows how to work in advertising and the use of media, make use of that person. If not, approach an advertising agency or perhaps a school of journalism and ask if it would be willing to help you get your message on TV or in the newspapers.

SELECTED BIBLIOGRAPHY

Homan, Mark S. *Rules of the Game: Lessons from the Field of Community Change.* Pacific Grove, CA: Brooks/Cole, 1999.

Morales, Armando T., and Bradford W. Sheafor. *Social Work: A Profession of Many Faces,* 8th ed. Boston: Allyn and Bacon, 1998.

Tropman, John E. *Successful Community Leadership: A Skills Guide for Volunteers and Professionals.* Washington, DC: NASW Press, 1997.

Walls, David. *The Activist's Almanac: The Concerned Citizen's Guide to Leading Advocacy Organizations in America.* New York: Simon and Schuster, 1995.

14.51 Teaching and Training

PURPOSE: To guide and assist others in the acquisition of information, knowledge, or skills.

DISCUSSION: Social workers do a lot of teaching. They frequently teach skills related to parenting, interpersonal communication, stress management, job seeking, independent living, and so on. Their teaching may be directed to clients, volunteers, colleagues, or concerned citizens. It may occur within the context of a one-to-one relationship, a workshop, or a formal classroom situation. In direct work with clients, the teaching activities usually resemble a tutorial or coaching relationship, but nevertheless is teaching. Several guidelines can help the social worker increase his or her effectiveness as a teacher:

1. The adage "It hasn't been taught until it has been learned" underscores the difference between teaching and learning. Teaching activities are planned and controlled by the teacher, but learning is not. Learning occurs within the learner and is tied to such factors as motivation, ability, and readiness. The teacher's job is to find a way of engaging and motivating the learner to examine and consider the materials to be taught.

2. That which we teach and learn falls into three broad categories: knowledge, beliefs and values, and skills. Of these three, *knowledge* is the easiest to teach because there is an agreed upon language to explain facts, concepts, and theories. This is not so when we focus on values and attitudes. In fact, *values and attitudes* cannot be taught directly, but they can be "caught" or learned from a teacher. If the teacher models or exhibits the desired beliefs, values, and attitudes, the learners may modify their own in order to imitate those of the teacher. *Skills,* too, are best learned through modeling and demonstration. They then can be performed and practiced in a real or simulated situation in order to master the behaviors or actions related to the skill.

3. It is said that the truly educated person is one who has learned how to learn. Unfortunately, no one is sure how to teach others to learn, because everyone seems to develop a unique approach to learning. What works for one person may not work for another. The uniqueness of how we learn relates to such factors as our sensory preferences (hearing, seeing, kinesthetic, etc.), our need for or resistance to structure and direction, our desire for either competition or cooperation, our tendency to move from the specific (parts) to the general (whole) or vice versa, our tendency to either break apart or build concepts, our need to read and write in order to learn, our preferences for either solitary or group learning, and so forth. An important first step in teaching, then, is to plan for differences in how people learn. An effective teacher must be prepared to use several different methods when teaching a single topic. Also, we need to help the learners identify and better understand how they learn and seek out learning opportunities appropriate to their individual styles.

4. Identify and teach essential terminology and concepts. Language is the foundation of learning because we use language to communicate ideas and experiences. The acquisition of specialized vocabulary is a fundamental step in the acquisition of new learning. For example, before someone can learn to do the work of the social worker, he or she must first master the terminology and basic concepts related to the profession's values, roles, principles, and practice theories. The teacher, however, should carefully plan the introduction of new concepts in order to avoid overloading the learner with too much new material at one time.

5. Help people learn by helping them develop skills and techniques that facilitate learning. These include reading, writing, verbal communication, listening, time management, problem solving, goal setting, decision making, and so on.

6. When planning a class or training session, begin with an analysis of learner characteristics (e.g., developmental stage, formal education, prior work experience, life experience, etc.) and the identification of the knowledge, values, and skills they are expecting (and expected) to learn. Then select or design the methods that are most likely to engage the learners and push and pull them toward the learning objectives.

7. Review and consider using existing curricula and teaching materials, but realize that such materials nearly always need to be modified and adapted. Materials and methods that worked well with one group of learners may not work for others.

8. To the extent possible, use teaching techniques that actively engage both the learner's mind and body (e.g., role-plays, simulation exercises, debates, and discussions). Reduce to a minimum the time spent in formal presentations. Lectures are among the least effective methods. As humans, we are thinking, feeling, and behaving beings. In order to teach, we must attend to and activate the learner's thinking, feelings, and behavior.

9. When teaching a skill, utilize the model known as "watch one, do one, teach one." First, have the learners observe someone performing the skill activity, then have them do it, and, finally, have them teach it to someone else. Another model is to understand the skill, use the skill, find new uses for the skill, and, finally, teach the skill to someone.

10. Place emphasis on helping the learner immediately use the information, knowledge, or skill being taught. In the human services there is only one reason for learning and that is to do something with whatever has been learned. Thus, encourage the learner to ask: Why am I interested in this topic? What can I do with it? How can I apply it? How will it help me answer some other question or solve a problem?

11. Critically evaluate your teaching. There are four levels on which we can assess our effectiveness as teachers:

- *Level 1.* We may simply ask the learners if they liked it. This is the most commonly used method of evaluating teaching. The problem is that one can enjoy a class or a workshop, but learn little or nothing. Moreover, learning is not always an enjoyable experience.
- *Level 2.* We can determine if the learners actually learned something new. Did they leave the session with knowledge or skills that they did not have when they began? To assess training at this second level, some type of presession and postsession testing is necessary.
- *Level 3.* Assuming that new learning occurred, we can then ask if the new knowledge and skills were used after the session. To assess training at this level, we need a follow-up system for monitoring the learner's behavior subsequent to the training session.
- *Level 4.* Finally, we can determine whether the learners' application of the new knowledge and skills had a positive impact on their lives or work. Unless what is learned has a real and a positive impact, the session was of little value no matter how enjoyable or how much was learned.

SELECTED BIBLIOGRAPHY

Bercher, Harvey J. *Staff Development in Human Service Organizations.* Englewood Cliffs, NJ: Prentice Hall, 1988.

George, Alan. *Train and Develop Your Staff: A Do-It-Yourself Guide for Managers.* Brookfield, VT: Gower, 1997.

14.52 Preparing a Budget

PURPOSE: To prepare an estimate of income and expenditures for a human services agency or a special project.

DISCUSSION: A budget is an important planning tool that lists an agency's anticipated income and its intended use during a designated period, usually one or two years. Typically, a budget will be revised several times during the period it is in use. For example, the *preliminary budget* will be used to estimate expenses and serve as the basis for planning to secure funding to carry out the programs included in that preliminary budget. That budget will be revised once various commitments have been made by the funding sources. This *operating budget,* when approved by a legislative body (in the case of a public agency) or by a board of directors (in the case of a private agency), becomes the authorization for the agency's executive director to spend the amounts listed for each budget category. However, in the course of the budget period, there may be a shortfall in one or more income categories, unanticipated costs in expenditure categories, or emergent reasons to shift funds for one category to another. In these situations, the budget revisions would need official approval from the agency's governing body.

Given the relative fluidity of demand for services, agencies must have the capacity to make changes in programming or staffing during budget periods. However, it is best to try to anticipate any substantial changes far enough in advance to include the necessary funds in the program budget. Advocacy efforts should be timed to coincide with the development phase of budgeting if at all possible.

As part of the process of building a budget, many questions should be asked and answered, such as:

- What agency goals and objectives are to be addressed during the budget period?
- How do any proposed programmatic changes affect the agency's income and expenses?
- What types and how many employees are needed to carry out the agency's programs? What salaries and benefits are needed to attract and retain them? What liability insurance is needed to protect the employees and the agency? What training will be required for staff and volunteers—and what is the cost of that training?

- What type of programs are needed to reach and serve the agency's consumers? How might changes in program activities affect budget items such as numbers of staff with various competencies, training expenses, travel, supplies and equipment, consultation, and so on?
- What central office space and outreach locations are needed? What is required to keep the space clean, well maintained, and protected? What will be the cost of rent, utilities, insurance, security, and so forth?
- What is required to develop and maintain community support for the agency such as printing and publications, postage, public relations materials, membership development activities, audits, and the like?
- What total income will be needed to carry out the anticipated programs during the budget period? What are the sources of this income (e.g., agency fund-raising efforts, United Way, government appropriations, fees for service, grants, contracts, bequests, etc.) and how reliable is each as a base of support?
- If the budget must be cut at some later time, what reductions could be made that will do the least damage to the agency's capacity to carry out its mission?

In a stable organization, the budget should be built on past experience with allowance for anticipated changes in income or expenditures or to accommodate new programming. In an era of declining support for human services, funding for new programs must come through curtailment of some programs or more efficient use of existing resources. Since most human services agencies are highly labor intensive, the personnel aspects of the budget become the most critical to consider if any substantial change is anticipated. In addition, the constant tug between efficiency (cost per unit of service) and effectiveness (ability to achieve service objectives) should be addressed as part of the budgeting process.

Three types of budgeting are commonly found in human services agencies: (1) line-item budgeting, (2) incremental budgeting, and (3) program or functional budgeting. Each yields different information about the cost of doing business.

Line-Item Budgeting

This type of budget is the most commonly used in social agencies. It requires that the various income and spending categories be identified and that the amount of money anticipated in each category be stated (see Figure 14.2). The accounting system of the agency is usually organized around these categories, making it possible to obtain a historical picture of the income and expenditures that will serve as the basis for projecting the future. Since a preliminary budget is a planning device, it must be prepared in advance of the year it will be in effect. In other words, next year's budget must be based on incomplete information about how well this year's budget estimated income and expenses. Thus, a preliminary line-item budget will reflect educated guesses about how each budget line will play out during the remainder of the current year and how it will change during the subsequent year.

The line-item budget must then be backed up by an audit report verifying the last year's actual income and expenditures and listing the amounts of any other assets, endowment, or building fund reserves that are excluded from the operating budget.

FIGURE 14.2 Sample Line-Item Budget

Categories	Last Actual Year	Year-to-Date	Current Budget	Proposed Budget
Income				
Beginning Balance	6,375	10,648	6,000	32
Contracts for Service	17,358	7,156	15,000	18,000
Contributions	5,392	938	5,000	5,000
Grants	5,000	2,500	5,000	–0–
Gifts and Bequests	14,321	7,106	10,000	10,000
Investment Income	4,987	2,386	5,000	5,000
Membership Dues	2,510	1,050	2,500	2,500
Program Service Fees	48,746	24,657	50,000	55,000
Sales	–0–	–0–	–0–	–0–
United Way Allocation	20,000	10,000	20,000	29,000
Total Income	124,689	66,443	118,500	124,532
Expense				
Salaries	67,518	35,447	70,894	74,439
Employee Benefits	4,756	2,557	5,114	5,265
Payroll Taxes	2,171	1,180	2,360	2,385
Consultation Fees	10,000	4,120	10,000	11,000
Professional Development	2,500	1,195	2,500	2,500
Total Personnel	86,945	44,499	90,868	95,589
Supplies and Equipment	8,938	6,053	9,000	9,500
Telephone	3,063	1,600	3,200	3,200
Printing and Photocopying	984	407	600	600
Occupancy	12,000	6,300	12,600	13,200
Travel	570	287	600	600
Membership Dues	1,000	1,000	1,000	1,000
Miscellaneous	541	295	600	600
Total Operating Expenses	27,096	15,942	27,600	28,700
Total Expenses	114,041	60,411	118,468	124,289
Ending Balance	10,648	6,020	32	243

Incremental Budgeting

Based on estimates of increases or decreases in revenue, a series of budget projections might be built on the basis of the current line-item budget. That is, using a "what if?" approach, a budget might be developed to reflect the impact of 5 and 10 percent budget reductions, no change in revenue, or 5 and 10 percent revenue increases. An incremental budget is particularly helpful in reflecting the impact of inflation and identifying the service implications of either increases and decreases. Such a budget is useful in assessing the cost of adjusting an organization's current program to provide new services. The availability of computer spreadsheet programs (see Item 9.4) has simplified the process of developing incremental budgets and thus examining the impact of various alternatives.

Program or Functional Budgeting

A final type of budget used by social agencies is the program or functional budget. Again, this is based on a line-item budget and adds the feature of attributing portions of the total cost in each income and expense category to the various components or functions of agency operation. This approach makes it possible to estimate income and expenditures related to any function of the agency, thus providing a picture of the cost-effectiveness of that function. Attributing the income or expenses to particular program areas calls for careful estimates (e.g., the amount of executive director's time devoted to fundraising) and an accurate identification of how income is generated (e.g., fees received for a particular service).

Preparing a program budget involves using the income and expense items from the "Proposed Budget" column (see Figure 14.2) of the line-item budget and projecting a distribution of those items according to both the operational support services (e.g., management, fund-raising, etc.) and each of the various service programs (e.g., adoption, foster care, family counseling, etc.) of the agency.

SELECTED BIBLIOGRAPHY

Feit, Marvin D., and Peter Kwok Chei Li. *Financial Management in Human Services.* New York: Haworth, 1998.

Kettner, Peter M., Robert M. Moroney, and Lawrence L. Martin. *Designing and Managing Programs: An Effectiveness-Based Approach.* Newbury Park, CA: Sage, 1990.

Weiner, Myron E. *Human Services Management: Analysis and Applications,* 2nd ed. Belmont, CA: Wadsworth, 1990.

14.53 The 5 Ps of Marketing Human Services

PURPOSE: To interest the public in participating in or supporting the work of a human services organization.

DISCUSSION: Increasingly, human services agencies draw on the marketing technology of modern business to attract needed resources. Most social workers are not accustomed to thinking about their agency's services as a product to be advertised, displayed, and sold. Doing so, however, helps workers better understand what actions are necessary to attract funding, the clients who need their services, competent board members and volunteers, and paraprofessional staff members such as foster parents.

Horejsi (1989) suggests that five concepts—the 5 Ps—should be considered when developing a human services marketing strategy. He also suggests that it helps to understand the dynamics of the marketing process if social workers think about all the factors that influence their own decisions when they consider buying an automobile or some other major item.

Product

Successful salespeople are enthusiastic about their product and they can explain its advantages, as compared to the other products, that might attract the potential customer's interest. Thus, social agency personnel must truly believe in the worth of their product (service). They must be able to explain its worth and advantages in simple language and, if possible, back up their beliefs with data drawn from independent evaluations.

If social workers and other agency personnel really believe in their services, their conviction will be communicated in their statements and nonverbal behavior. If, for some reason, the agency's "product" is not "selling" well (e.g., not attracting support or clients), it is time to figure out why and modify or improve the service so it becomes more attractive.

Potential Buyer (or Consumer)

In order to understand what attracts supporters and clients to a service program, it may be necessary to conduct some type of market survey. What are the characteristics of those who buy this product? What are its most attractive features? Who has used the service in the past? If other programs have stronger community support, why are they now more attractive than yours? The answers to such questions help an agency better understand its potential supporters and consumers and help target marketing efforts toward those groups most likely to respond.

For purposes of marketing, it is important to remember that there is no such thing as a general public. There are, however, subgroups of people who share common interests and values. It is important to determine which subgroups are most likely to be interested in a particular program. Demographic factors such as age, religion, ethnic background, income, and education may have a bearing on which subgroups can be attracted to which agency. An agency should not waste time and resources trying to attract those unlikely to ever develop interest in supporting or using its services.

For human services agencies there are several important subgroups or special publics that a marketing strategy might address, depending on what aspect of the agency or program is being promoted. Consider the following:

- *Agency family.* This includes the board, members of various committees, and the staff.
- *Volunteers.* People who have volunteered their time to assist an agency in providing services have a special commitment to that agency and are especially interested in its activities.
- *Clients, former clients, and their families.* Those who have benefited from the agency's efforts can become valuable advocates for an agency. One negative evaluation from this group can offset the public relations benefits from several satisfied clients.
- *Supporters.* Many agencies have a group of members or other interested supporters who provide various forms of assistance such as financial contributions, assistance with fund-raising efforts, and speakers' bureau participants.

- *Community influencers.* Each community has a few people who help shape public opinion (e.g., the media, people who speak out on issues, etc.) or make important decisions that affect human services (e.g., elected officials, directors of other agencies, United Way board members, etc.). They must be informed about the services of your agency.
- *Special-interest groups.* Associated groups that have a particular interest in your agency's work might include such professional bodies or organizations as NASW, the AMA, the local bar association, related human services agencies, or influential groups such as the League of Women Voters, NAACP, and so on.

Place

Once the attention of the target audience has been attracted, the agency needs a place or location where the services can be provided and an identity for the program established. In the human services field, this place of business is typically the social agency. Whether the targets of the marketing approach decide to contribute or use an agency's services will depend, in part, on their first impressions of the agency's building and offices, its personnel, and its program. First impressions are exceedingly powerful. Consumers will appreciate an appropriate atmosphere when entering the agency and expect respect, courtesy, and fairness in their treatment from clerical and professional staff.

Price

In the marketplace, price is measured in terms of dollars (i.e., how much a customer has to pay to get the wanted product). In the human services, price is more appropriately viewed as what an agency supporter or consumer must give up (i.e., pay) in order to support or utilize the services. If contributors or volunteers give their money and time, they are not able to give those dollars or hours to some other worthy cause. Thus, they want to know that their gifts are appreciated and will make a real difference in someone's life. Or perhaps they want to make sure their association with the agency will yield some personal benefit, such as interesting training, job-related experience, or a feeling of being useful.

It is important to be completely honest about price. For example, in an effort to recruit foster parents, a child welfare agency needs to be accurate in describing the "price" to be paid by the foster parent in terms of time, frustration, worry, and probably some out-of-pocket expenses. If one is not honest, the buyer will later feel cheated and become justifiably angry with the agency.

Promotion

Working with the media (see Item 14.54) is an effective way to reach a large number of people with a message about an agency. Stories in newspapers and on TV can make people aware of a particular agency and its needs, but they are not usually effective in bringing people to the decision that they will support it with their time or money. The same can be said for presentations and public appearances at service clubs, schools, public meetings, and so on; they help, but it takes something more to get a real commitment. When it comes to making that final decision of whether to support an agency, face-to-face interaction with agency personnel is of critical importance.

As in business, a satisfied customer is the best advertisement an agency can have; on the other hand, a dissatisfied customer can do a lot of damage to an agency's image and reputation. As a general rule, presentations by satisfied customers (e.g., long-time financial supporters, enthusiastic volunteers, clients pleased with agency services, etc.) are more persuasive than presentations by agency staff.

SELECTED BIBLIOGRAPHY

Andreason, Allan R. *Strategic Marketing for Nonprofit Organizations*, 4th ed. Englewood Cliffs, NJ: Prentice Hall, 1990.

Horejsi, Charles R. "Foster Home Recruitment: A Marketing Perspective." Missoula: Department of Social Work, University of Montana, 1989. (Unpublished document).

Lauffer, Armand, and E. Allen Brawley. "Should Marketing Techniques Replace Traditional Planning and Coordinating Methods in the Design and Development of Programs?" In *Controversial Issues in Communities and Organizations*, edited by Michael J. Austin and Jane Isaacs Lowe. Boston: Allyn and Bacon, 1994, pp. 236–250.

14.54 Dealing with the Media

PURPOSE: To inform the public and generate support for the services offered by an agency.

DISCUSSION: The public has a right to know about the social programs and agencies supported by taxes or voluntary contributions. All too often, the public hears only negative information about these services and the people who use them. Social workers have a responsibility to help the public fully understand the impact of human services on the quality of life for all persons. Social workers can make a valuable contribution to their agencies, clients, and community by developing the skills to work with the media in providing this information.

General Advice

Keep the following points in mind when working with the media:

- *Be proactive.* Rather that hoping the media will come to you for information or a story, reach out to them. Work at creating opportunities to describe your agency and program in a positive way. Remember that human-interest stories are especially attractive to reporters.
- *Have the authority to speak for the agency.* Make sure you are authorized to represent the agency and, if more than one person from the agency is authorized to deal with the media, make sure the efforts are coordinated. Also, be clear if at any time you are speaking for yourself rather than for the agency.
- *Establish personal relationships with the media.* If the reporters and photographers know and trust you and are aware that you are willing to help them, it can mean the difference between your agency or program just getting covered and getting good coverage. Keep the media informed of what is going on in your agency, be sure the information is accurate, and avoid professional jargon.

- *Be available.* Make it easy for the media to contact you by providing all reporters who cover your agency with your home and office telephone numbers and the name and numbers of someone else to call if you are not available.
- *Observe deadlines.* Know the deadlines of news shows and do not expect reporters to attend to your interests when they have deadlines to meet. If necessary, be willing to reschedule so they can give your story full attention.
- *Be fair.* When you release a story, make sure that all media organizations get your news release or a phone call as close to the same time as you can manage.
- *Be understanding.* If your story does not run, there may be good reasons. It could have been thrown out at the last minute for something of more urgent news value. It is all right to ask if there was something wrong with the story—something that could be corrected in future stories.
- *Make corrections when necessary.* Handle errors in stories carefully. Unless a serious error has been made, no comment is usually necessary. When a comment is in order, go to the reporter who made the error and handle the correction in private. Explain the error and indicate any damage that may have been caused. Control your emotions and focus only on the facts.
- *Say thanks.* Express your appreciation every time you submit material, whether it is used or not. At least once a year, thank your media professional's boss for the interest and investment in your program.

The Press Kit

A useful tool for establishing and maintaining relationships with either the print or electronic media is to prepare a press kit for distribution to editors and reporters. A press kit is simply a 9½" × 12" two-pocket folder that contains information that interprets the agency and suggests stories for the media. The folder should be colorful or in some way attract the attention of the reporter. A cover letter should be included that draws attention to the contents of the press kit.

Meltsner (no date, 4) suggests the following materials as the minimum for inclusion in a press kit:

- *Agency information.* This may be a brochure, annual report, or a brief description of the agency's goals, programs, and clientele.
- *Calling card.* A business card should contain the agency contact person's name, address, and telephone number. This should be displayed prominently, perhaps by stapling it to the pocket of the folder.
- *Campaign or public relations effort information.* If you have a particular goal for this public relations effort, such as raising funds for a specific program or recruiting volunteers to work with troubled children, explain this with a brochure about the project or a short information sheet.
- *At least one backgrounder.* A backgrounder is a sheet that familiarizes the reader with concepts, terms, and data that might be useful in preparing a story about the agency—for example: What is mental health? What kind of problems are addressed in family counseling? What is the legal definition of child abuse? What is a developmental disability?
- *A fact sheet or news release.* Depending on what you want the media to cover, you may include a fact sheet that contains basic information (who, what, where,

when, why, and how) that allows the reporter to create his or her own story. A news release is a one- to three-page story that can be printed as is or reduced or expanded into the reporter's own story. If possible, include a black-and-white photograph with a caption to help the reporter visualize the situation you are addressing.

- *A public service announcement.* Prepare a draft of a 30-second radio spot describing your project.
- *At least one reprint.* To suggest ideas for a story, include previously published articles about the agency or the project.

The Newspaper Release

When preparing a newspaper release, you will improve the chances of it being used if the format is familiar to the reporter and the information requires a minimum of editing. For example, a newspaper may want a news release typed double or triple spaced and with wide margins so it can be easily edited or transmitted electronically. Contact each newspaper for specific instructions regarding their preferences.

Write in a clear, simple, and logical style. Use short sentences and paragraphs. Remember that reporters are interested in the *who, what, where, when, and why* of a story. Begin with the most important information and place the less critical information and supplemental details at the end. Keep in mind that editors often shorten a story by cutting from the end. Remember, too, that editors like direct quotations and that by providing one or two glossy print photographs it is possible to add human interest to the story.

Be sure to clearly identify your agency's name, address, and phone number and provide the name of the person to be contacted for further information. The newspaper will need to know if the item is for "immediate release" or if it should be held for release on a specific date.

Radio and Television News

Information presented on a television or radio news broadcast can reach a large segment of the public. The human-interest flavor of stories originating from social agencies is especially amenable to the images of television. The social worker attempting to utilize these forms of media should know how to prepare materials for broadcast and be well prepared if being interviewed for radio or television.

If you are hoping for television coverage, schedule the event to be covered when a camera crew is likely to be most available—usually between 10:00 A.M. and 2:00 P.M. Avoid evenings and weekends.

If you expect to be interviewed or be a guest on a talk show, be clear about what you want to say and then rehearse. Have in mind some case examples, but be sure to disguise them in a way that will protect confidentiality. Radio and television news stories are almost always concise, making it necessary to limit your message to 30 to 60 seconds. Also, avoid using words or giving examples that would be offensive or misunderstood by the public.

If necessary, consider videotaping the event or story yourself. Television stations sometimes are willing to consider using a good-quality tape if it is brief and newsworthy.

SELECTED BIBLIOGRAPHY

Brawley, Edward A. "Mass Media." In *Encyclopedia of Social Work,* 19th ed., vol. 2, edited by Richard L. Edwards. Washington, DC: NASW Press, 1995, pp. 1675–1682.

———. *Human Services and the Media: Developing Partnerships for Change.* Longhorne, PA: Harwood Academic Press, 1995.

Fox, James Alan, and Jack Leaven. *How to Work with the Media.* Newbury Park, CA: Sage, 1993.

Meltsner, Susan. "Public Relations Tools for Human Service Providers: The Press Kit." (Unpublished materials, not dated).

14.55 Fund-Raising for a Human Services Agency

PURPOSE: To secure funds from the community to support a special project or the ongoing work of a social agency.

DISCUSSION: If a private, not-for-profit human services agency is to survive and develop its programs, it must have a secure and expanding funding base. In the final analysis, that depends on the willingness of numerous individuals to contribute their money to the agency rather than to another cause.

A key to agency survival is what some prefer to call *fund development.* This refers to the identification and nurturance of contributors who genuinely believe in the value of the agency and can be counted on to make a significant contribution, year after year.

Many local health and human services agencies are affiliated with large federated campaigns such as the United Way or the American Cancer Society. A small, independent agency must compete with these experienced and sophisticated fund-raising agencies for the interest, goodwill, and money of potential contributors.

For some agencies, a major fund-raising campaign is an occasional event in which funds to start a new program or build a facility are solicited. Inexperienced persons are seldom prepared for the demands and complexity of such a campaign. It takes time, energy, and know-how to successfully raise funds. It is estimated that it will take a minimum of three months to plan and raise funds from individuals and local businesses (e.g., through canvassing and direct mail); three to six months to raise funds from local foundations, service clubs, and unions); and at least six to eight months to raise funds from a national foundation, United Way, or financial institution (Community Resource Center, no date). Also, that investment of time and energy usually means that other responsibilities in the agency must be set aside in order to free time for fund-raising. Thus, it is important to assess the need and the chances of success before embarking on a fund-raising effort.

Guidelines for Fund-Raising

The following principles can assist the social workers in a fund-raising effort:

- Realize that even under the best of circumstances, raising money for human services agencies is a difficult and time-consuming activity.

- Fund-raising for the ongoing work of a social agency should employ methods that can be repeated each year.
- Perquisite to success in fund-raising is a sound marketing program that keeps the public well informed about the agency and its services (see Items 14.53 and 14.54).
- It is critical to plan ahead. Allow plenty of time (i.e., 12 to 18 months), remembering that the most difficult time to raise funds is when you urgently need them.
- Look for money at the local level first. Local people are the ones most likely to have a vested interest in seeing the program succeed.
- Fund-raising is a very personal activity. In reality, people give money to other people, not to an organization or cause. Build networks and get to know key people in the organizations you plan to solicit and have those individuals help you gain access to and establish credibility with others in that organization.
- It costs money to raise money. Make sure that the cost of fund-raising is built into the agency's budget.
- Get volunteers and the agency board of directors involved. They will have credibility in the community and their involvement increases their ownership of the program.
- It is important to research the priorities of potential funding sources and match their priorities with yours.
- Fund-raising involves asking people for their money. If you do not ask, you will not get it. (Some suggestions on how to ask are given later.)
- Get expert advice if you are unsure of how to proceed in a fund-raising campaign. You can damage future efforts if you attempt to carry out a poorly developed plan.

Elements of a Fund-Raising Campaign

Hundreds of decisions and actions make up a successful fund-raising campaign. Here are some of the major steps to follow:

1. *Formulate a goal.* After a careful examination of agency needs, establish a realistic goal as to how much money is to be raised and set a realistic time frame for reaching that goal.

2. *Consult those with expertise.* Draw together those who have worked on previous campaigns and determine what has and has not worked. Consider hiring a professional fund-raiser if your own prior efforts have not been successful, if you are unsure how to proceed, or if you need to raise more than $100,000.

3. *Develop a plan.* Select the strategy and methods most likely to be successful. Draw on the agency's former experience and use an approach that has worked in the past. Be cautious about attempting an approach with which you have no experience. When constructing your budget, factor in the amount of staff time needed and the cost of postage, supplies, public information materials, and travel.

4. *Select a chairperson.* This person should be a respected and trusted individual with good name recognition in the community. Most important, the chairperson

must be someone who has the energy and time required and is committed to achieving the campaign goal. Recruit the chairperson during the planning stage so he or she can shape the overall strategy. This individual must be capable of recruiting many other volunteers.

5. *Build an organizational structure.* A successful campaign requires an organizational structure that ensures rapid communication, coordination, and careful monitoring of campaign activities and volunteers. Because many of the contributions will come from those working on the campaign, the effort should embrace and involve a great many individuals, community groups, and organizations. Many campaigns use some type of pyramid structure made up of several team captains, each responsible for overseeing the work of several campaign workers. A campaign might also have several divisions or special units that seek contributions from certain segments of the community (e.g., labor unions and small businesses).

6. *Recruit and train the campaign workers.* Workers must be asked to help—people seldom volunteer for fund-raising. The campaign chair, board members, and friends of the agency must actively recruit as volunteers persons who have the contacts and influence necessary to secure contributions. Some of the individuals willing to help may not be comfortable asking for money. They can help with other important tasks such as preparing informational packets, office work, and bookkeeping.

7. *Prepare informational material.* Simply written brochures should explain the agency's program, what money is needed, and how it will be spent. This information may also need to be presented in the form of newspaper, television, and radio ads. Agency staff who best know the various programs the agency offers should play a key role in identifying appropriate content. Other materials—such as logos, letterhead, banners, slide shows, bumper stickers, press releases, speeches, and so on—are also needed. It is important that public relations experts provide guidance on the preparation of these items. Pursue contributions for these materials from wealthy individuals or very large corporations.

8. *Maintain proper records.* The campaign must maintain a complete and accurate record of contributions and expenses. Any hint of dishonesty, fraud, or incomplete bookkeeping will seriously damage the agency's ability to raise funds in the future.

9. *Provide recognition.* All those who contributed and all those who worked on the campaign should receive recognition and thanks. This creates a sense of pride and goodwill and increases the chances that these people and groups will assist in future campaigns.

10. *Evaluate the campaign.* After the campaign is complete, the agency board, campaign chairperson, and other key leaders should carefully evaluate what worked, what did not work, and how future campaigns could be improved. This evaluation should determine how much it cost (money, staff time, etc.) to raise the funds. If the campaign was not successful or if it was burdensome for the agency, outside consultation may be needed.

Asking for Money

Many of us are hesitant to ask others for money, but that is what fund-raising is all about. Following are several suggestions to help reduce this problem:

- Those who ask others for money must have already given their fair share. Those doing the asking must be able to say, "I have given $500; I am asking that you give at least $250."
- It is critically important that the right person ask another for money and that the request be made in the right way, for the right reason, and at the right time. This is a further reminder that people do not give money to agencies or even causes; people give primarily because a specific person (e.g., someone they know and trust) has asked them to give.
- Small amounts of money can be raised from an individual by mail and telephone campaigns. Big money is raised through face-to-face contact with the donor.
- Ask for a specific amount of money and be sure to ask for enough (e.g., "We need $1,000 to send five children to camp").
- Assess the person's capability of giving before you ask. In other words, do some background research and determine what an individual or company is capable of giving. Ask for that amount.
- Be persistent. Keep asking until you get what you want or receive a firm "no."
- If an individual cannot make a cash donation, ask if an in-kind donation might be possible (e.g., time, used equipment, expertise, etc.).

SELECTED BIBLIOGRAPHY

Community Resource Center. "Some Principles of Philanthropy." Denver: Community Resource Center. (Unpublished materials, not dated).

Edles, L. Peter. *Fundraising*. New York: McGraw-Hill, 1993.

Edwards, Richard L., Elizabeth A. S. Benefield, Jeffrey A. Edwards, and John A. Yankey. *Building a Strong Foundation: Fundraising for Nonprofits*. Washington, DC: NASW Press, 1996.

Grace, Kay. *Beyond Fundraising*. New York: John Wiley & Sons, 1997.

14.56 Developing Grant Applications

PURPOSE: To secure funding from a governmental agency or private foundation.

DISCUSSION: The resources available to a social agency are usually fully committed for operating existing programs. Any incremental increases in funds that might be obtained each year are often consumed by normal salary increases and inflation. The opportunity to demonstrate or test program innovations or conduct research on some aspect of the agency's program frequently cannot be done without the infusion of grant funds. A social worker who is knowledgeable about locating sources of grant funds and skilled at preparing applications for such funds is a valuable asset to his or her agency.

Before a social worker (or team of workers) can begin the grant-writing process, three prerequisites must be met. First, the idea or program innovation to be demonstrated or studied must be clearly identified and carefully thought out. Second, in addition to the persons developing the program or project, the agency's administrators and governing body must be committed to the idea. Finally, an assessment of the competence and capacity of both the individuals and the agency to carry out the activity must indicate that this work can be successfully completed. The worker should be prepared to invest considerable up-front time and effort into preparing a grant application, which frequently must be done in addition to ongoing work assignments. Yet, it is often the only way to improve services.

Sources of Grant Funding

A variety of funding sources might be considered. Sometimes a local or national business will underwrite a project that is of interest to them. A computer company, for example, might donate equipment to demonstrate the potential effectiveness of a computerized interagency referral network.

Also, a group of persons interested in a project might undertake a fund-raising effort (see Item 14.55) to help support this activity. However, the primary sources for a project are grants from government agencies or private foundations.

Government Grants. The largest amount of money is available through agencies of the federal government, although states may also allocate such funds. Most government grants relate to areas that the sponsoring agency has defined in relation to its purpose and priorities. The public is notified of available funding through a *Request for Proposals* (*RFP*). Grant applications are reviewed by a panel of experts and awarded on a competitive basis. Some discretionary funds may also be available to staff at government agencies to allow for innovative program ideas that are not currently among the agency's established priorities. It is helpful to discuss your ideas with persons in the regional and national offices of the government agencies who administer the funds in your area of interest (e.g., aging, child welfare, AIDS, etc.) before investing much time and energy in developing a proposal. These staff members can help you assess the fit between your proposal and the agency's interest and provide such facts as the typical size of grants the odds of success.

Two published sources of information are particularly useful regarding grant possibilities from the federal government. The *Catalog of Federal Domestic Assistance* is an essential sourcebook published each year with a supplement that updates after six months. It contains a comprehensive listing and description of federal programs. Programs are cross-referenced by function (e.g., housing, health, etc.), by subject (e.g., drug abuse, economic development, etc.), and by the federal agency in which the program is administered. The description of each program includes information such as uses and restrictions on the funds, eligibility requirements, and the application and award process. A second source is the *Federal Register.* It is published every government working day and contains notices, rules and regulations, guidelines, and proposed rules and regulations for every federal grant-giving agency. Both the *Catalog of Federal Domestic Assistance* and the *Federal Register* are usually available through public libraries, university libraries, or the research and grant administration office of most universities. Copies can be obtained from the Superintendent of Documents, Government Printing Office, Washington, DC 20402 or on the Internet.

Private Foundations. Another potential source of support for innovative program ideas is the private foundation. Small agencies and service demonstration projects are more likely to obtain support from these private sources than from government agencies. Most foundations develop specialized areas of interest, and some make resources available only for programs located in a specific geographic region. Perhaps the most helpful sources are directories developed by the Foundation Center that annually publishes *The Foundation Directory*. Part 1 of that directory includes those foundations that give away more than $200,000 per year and Part 2 contains those that give smaller amounts. The Foundation Center also periodically publishes a series of specialized directories of grant sources that are focused on areas such as children, youth, and families; aging; the economically disadvantaged; health; and women and girls. Another directory, *The Directory of Corporate and Foundation Givers*, provides background information about potential funding sources in the private sector. Once again, many local libraries and universities will have copies of these publications.

Computer Searches. Several databases are also available to aid in searching for funding sources—both governmental agencies and foundations. Searches by topic (key words), geographic region, funding agency, and academic discipline make it possible to narrow a vast amount of information to a small number of organizations or RFPs that are appropriate for the project. The Sponsored Programs Information Network (SPIN), for example, is an extensive on-line database of potential sources available in many research universities.

Guidelines for Developing a Proposal

The planning and preparation of a proposal is a labor-intensive process. Make sure you have the necessary time and motivation. A hastily written proposal, or the so-called all-purpose proposal, has little chance of success. If it is worth doing at all, it is worth doing well. Several guidelines are of critical importance:

1. *Do your homework.* Make a thorough study of the potential funding source (foundation or government agency) before deciding to submit a proposal. Pay special attention to official funding priorities, history of prior awards, eligibility, geographical limitation, type and size of grants available, funding cycle, process for selection, and so on. Secure the name, address, and phone number for the proper contact person.

2. *Make informal inquiries.* Save time for yourself and for the funding agency by informally inquiring about its possible interest in your ideas. However, assume that the recipient of your inquiry is busy, impatient, skeptical, not especially interested in your problems, and faced with many more requests than he or she can even read thoroughly, let alone fund. Be very businesslike in your approach. Be prepared to describe your proposal clearly and concisely in one or two pages or in five minutes on

the phone. If you think you will be making an application, obtain an application packet and all relevant instructions.

3. *Write the proposal.* Study the instructions in the RFP and follow them to the letter. Be prepared to answer each and every question. You should anticipate answering at least the following questions:

- What do you want to do, how much will it cost, and how much time will it take?
- How does the proposed project relate to the funding agency's area of interest and priorities?
- Are there other projects like the one you are proposing? How is yours similar or different?
- How do you plan to carry out the project? Does the proposed staff have the necessary training and experience? Why should you conduct this project, rather than someone else?
- Who stands to benefit from the proposed project? What impact will it have on your agency, clients, discipline, community, state, or nation? How will you measure, evaluate, and report the impact? Will the project be able to continue after the grant support has ended?

The written proposal must be very clear and well organized, with justification for the various expenditures described in detail. Often, the proposal cannot exceed a certain number of pages and a firm closing date is established. Sometimes the closing date is for a postmark, but usually the proposal must be in the hands of the granting agency by that date. If a team is writing a proposal, designate one person who will have final authority to edit the materials into a coherent document.

4. *Be a good salesperson for your project.* Your written proposal and/or oral presentations should reflect knowledge, enthusiasm, and commitment. If those selecting proposals to be funded become convinced that the people associated with the program are especially capable and responsible, they may work especially hard on finding a way to fund the proposal. Obtaining substantive letters of support from related agencies and key people in your community can help sell your proposal. Ask these people to address specific areas of the proposal (e.g., the need, the agency's history of sound management, the staff's ability to carry out the project, community support for the program, etc.).

5. *Be accountable.* If you receive the grant requested, be prepared to carry out the project according to your written plan and within the proposed budget. The acceptance of a grant carries with it the responsibility for managing the money properly, submitting regular progress reports, reporting project results, and giving appropriate credit to the funding source. Good stewardship of the grant funds is very important.

Proposal Contents. Throughout the proposal put a positive spin on the project and avoid the appearance of begging for support. Stress the quality of what you can do with grant support, as opposed to stressing why you have not done it before. Remember that your proposal is in competition for scarce grant resources and people usually will be giving points for each of the criteria set out in the RFP. Thus you should carefully follow the outline required by the funding source and explicitly address each of the criteria. In general, the following components will be expected:

1. *Cover page.* Include the project title, principal investigators, name of agency, dates for project activity, total budget request, and signatures of authorized agency personnel approving the application.

2. *Abstract.* Prepare a short statement of the objectives and procedures to be used, methods of evaluation, and plan for disseminating results.

3. *Statement of problem and objectives.* Indicate the rationale for this project and prepare a clear statement of the objectives in measurable terms.

4. *Methodology, procedures, and activities to be followed.* Describe the design and approach of the project, who will be served, and the administrative structure for the project. Lay out a clear plan of action with phases and dates for activity detailed. The use of Gantt and PERT charts (see Item 13.11) helps to make the process and timelines clear to reviewers.

5. *Evaluation methods.* Describe how the results or outcomes of the activity will be assessed.

6. *Dissemination of results.* Indicate how the results of the project will be disseminated so that others can benefit from the knowledge gained from this activity.

7. *Personnel and facilities.* Describe the staff required to carry out the project, include resumés of key personnel who will be assigned to this activity, and indicate how new staff will be selected. Also, describe any special equipment required, and indicate how the agency will make space available to accommodate project activities.

8. *Budget.* Provide a detailed budget of the anticipated costs of the project. Indicate what will be required from the funding source and what will be contributed by the agency or other sources. Many funding sources require that matching funds from local sources be identified as a requirement for funding. In some instances, a cash match is required, but in others, in-kind contributions (e.g., staff time or office space) are acceptable. A budget will usually include personnel costs (including fringe benefits), outside consultants or evaluators for the project, consumable materials (supplies, printing, postage, etc.), equipment, travel, and indirect costs. The latter relates to the real costs to an agency (space, heat, light, etc.) consumed by the project staff. Some federal agencies limit the indirect cost to 8 percent of the project expenses.

Reasons for Rejection. Finally, keep in mind the reasons that grant proposals are unsuccessful. Reviewers most commonly mark down proposals for the following reasons:

1. The proposal is either too trivial or beyond the ability and experience of the investigator or agency.

2. The need for the proposed project is not properly documented and/or the objectives are not clearly stated and relevant to the need.

3. The reviewer is not convinced that the proposed plan would achieve the desired results due to the competence of the staff, quality of the plan, or the support of the requesting agency.

4. There is not adequate commitment by the agency and/or community to continuing the service if the project proves successful and this grant is subsequently discontinued.

5. The proposal is not realistic in estimates of the funds, personnel, or equipment required to successfully carry out the project.

6. The evaluation procedure is inappropriate or unclear.

7. The proposal is poorly written.

8. The budget is not adequately developed, the required matching money is not evident, or the request is beyond the resources of the funding agency.

9. The proposal fails to follow the guidelines or meet the deadline for submitting a proposal.

SELECTED BIBLIOGRAPHY

Catalog of Domestic Assistance. Washington, DC: U.S. Government Printing Office, most recent edition.

The Directory of Corporate and Foundation Givers. Washington, DC: The Taft Group, most recent edition.

Federal Register. Washington, DC: U.S. Government Printing Office, published daily.

The Foundation Directory. New York: The Foundation Center, most recent edition.

Hall, Mary. *Getting Funded: A Complete Guide to Proposal Writing*, 3rd ed. Portland, OR: Portland State University, 1988.

Lauffer, Armand. *Grants, Etc.* Thousand Oaks, CA: Sage, 1997.

Locke, Lawrence F., Waneen Wyrick Spirduso, and Stephen J. Silverman. *Proposals That Work*, 3rd ed. Newbury Park, CA: Sage, 1993.

Ries, Joanne B., and Carl G. Leukefeld. *The Research Funding Guidebook: Getting It, Managing It, and Renewing It*. Newbury Park, CA: Sage, 1997.

14.57 Influencing Legislators and Other Decision Makers

PURPOSE: To influence the actions of legislators and other community decision makers regarding human services issues.

DISCUSSION: Decisions that are made at the local, state, and national levels by elected representatives and other public officials have substantial impact on the human services. Because social workers are in a unique position to observe how public social policy helps or hinders the most vulnerable members of society, their perspective needs to be communicated to public officials. "When social workers neglect to engage in the politics of social welfare policy, that is, in acts aimed at influencing policymakers' resource distribution decisions, the needs of social work clients and the profession itself are left out of the policy development process" (Domanski 1998, 156).

When planning an effort to influence a decision maker, the worker should keep several guidelines in mind. First, a social worker is more likely to influence a decision when he or she has an established relationship with the decision maker. Of course, when a social worker is new to a community or organization it will take time to build such relationships and, as new decision makers appear on the scene, it will also take time to cultivate a relationship with them. The worker should make a point to initiate such relationships before attempting to influence a particular decision if at all possible. Second, the decision maker is more likely to be influenced by the worker if the worker and his or her information can be trusted. The social worker should make a careful analysis of the issue and the people making the decision (see Items 12.29 and 12.30), never distort the facts or give information that cannot be substantiated, and be thoroughly prepared to discuss the matter. Finally, the worker should be selective about the issues presented to decision makers. Social workers are often asked to support many good causes, but too often these causes relate to issues about which the social worker is not thoroughly versed. One's credibility with decision makers can be diminished if too many issues are addressed or if the worker is not sufficiently prepared to speak to the matter knowledgeably.

When a social worker decides to attempt to influence a decision, it should be done in an assertive and planful way. In formulating their approach, they should remember that decision makers are most likely to be persuaded by persons they perceive as

- having intelligence, self-confidence, and competence.
- being similar to themselves in life experiences, values, and personal style.
- being powerful and able to deal out rewards or punishment.
- individuals with whom they can expect future interaction and from whom they seek social acceptance.

As a general rule, the decision makers most easily influenced are those who feel uncertain about the issue being discussed and those who have a strong need for approval from the persons attempting to persuade them.

Because social workers do not usually have the power or status necessary to directly persuade decision makers, they must often work through others who are in a better position to exercise influence. At other times, however, the worker should directly communicate with the decision maker through personal contact, in writing, or both.

Visiting with a Policymaker

Many legislators and other key decision makers spend their time in a somewhat restricted environment; they speak primarily with staff members, lobbyists, and colleagues. Hence, they often welcome the opportunity to hear the positions of people who have firsthand knowledge of issues they must decide. This communication might occur by attending a legislator's open forum or town meeting or by talking individually with the decision maker. Sometimes, when a decision maker is difficult to schedule, effective communication on a subject can occur with an aide or advisor to the decision maker.

The following guidelines can help to make visits with decision makers (or their advisors) effective:

- *Use time efficiently.* The decision maker's time is valuable. If you are to get that person's full attention and have a favorable climate for communicating your information, you must be efficient. When planning an individual meeting, schedule an appointment in advance and ask that a specific amount of time be reserved for the meeting. Be on time, even though you may have to wait for the legislator to complete other responsibilities before meeting with you. Also, get to the point quickly. Have your presentation planned so that you can pack a lot of information into a short time period. In both town meetings and individual meetings, an indirect approach to the topic may prohibit you from getting to the substantive issues.
- *Be positive.* Begin on a friendly note. Find a reason to praise the decision maker for some action taken in relation to prior contacts (if appropriate) and thank him or her for being willing to take time to hear your position on this matter.
- *Express your conviction.* Let the legislator know that, as a social worker, you are in a unique position to recognize the implications of this decision. While it would be counterproductive to be abrasive or overbearing, leave no doubt in the legislator's mind that you believe in what you are proposing. Back up your view with facts and examples. If the information is at all detailed, prepare a handout that can be distributed to the decision maker and others who may be present.
- *Be specific.* Be very sure that the person knows what you want him or her to do. Are you simply offering information? Do you want him or her to propose an amendment to a piece of legislation? Do you want him or her to vote in a particular way?
- *Follow up in writing.* Send or leave a statement that reflects your position and provides the facts that you presented. The purpose of this document is to supply material that will be placed in the legislator's file on the topic and to remind him or her of your position when it is time to take action. Be sure that your name, address, and telephone number are on the materials so you can be contacted to clarify points or provide information on related matters.

Writing a Policymaker

Although face-to-face contact is probably the most effective way to influence a legislator or other decision maker, many times that is not possible because of constraints of time, distance, resources, or the availability of the decision maker. Letters, telegrams, fax messages, e-mail, and telephone calls, when properly timed, can also be effective in influencing decisions. The addresses and telephone numbers of public officials will usually be listed periodically in newspapers or available at the local library. Locating other officials may require more research.

The following guidelines should be observed when writing to a decision maker:

- *Be accurate.* Be sure that you use the correct spelling of the person's name, the proper title, and the accurate address. Be sure that the decision maker has correct information about you in case he or she wants to respond to your communication.

- *Be brief and to the point.* Limit your communication to one page. Focus only on one issue or piece of legislation in each communication. If you are interested in several matters, send separate correspondence so each can be filed with materials about those matters.
- *Clearly identify the issue or bill that concerns you.* Provide identifying details (e.g., the bill's number, name, and dates) so there can be no misunderstanding of what you are writing about.
- *Write simply and clearly.* Remember that those who will read your material are very busy and may receive many pieces of correspondence each day. Make it easy for them to understand the points you wish to make. Clear and direct communication tells the reader you know what you are talking about.
- *Begin in a positive manner.* Address the legislator in a respectful manner and use titles appropriate to the office. If possible, praise or compliment the legislator for some previous action or statement and relate the preferred action on this matter to other positions he or she has supported.
- *Provide facts and figures that support your position.* Explain the impact of the decision and how many people will be affected. Short case examples are often effective in helping the reader understand how the issue affects individuals. If possible, describe how the action you support will save tax money in the future.
- *Clearly identify the action you desire.* Make sure the reader knows what you want to happen (e.g., vote for HR 254, oppose the filibuster of SB 1543, etc.).
- *Pay attention to timing.* Be sure to time communicating your opinion to just precede the debate on the topic. Typically, a legislator will make up his or her mind early in the hearing process and long before time for a final vote.
- *Follow up the action.* After the decision or vote is completed, write again, thanking the legislator for considering your viewpoint if he or she took the action you requested. If not, express regret about that action. Such follow-up reminds the person that you are truly concerned about the issue and will continue to observe his or her actions on this matter.

SELECTED BIBLIOGRAPHY

DeKieffer, Donald E. *The Citizen's Guide to Lobbying Congress.* Chicago: Chicago Review Press, 1997.

Domanski, Margaret Dietz. "Prototypes of Social Work Political Participation: An Empirical Model." *Social Work 43* (March 1998): 156–167.

Frantzich, Steven E. *Write Your Congressman: Constituent Communication and Representation.* New York: Praeger, 1986.

Moore, Elliott Davis. "Influencing Legislation for the Human Services." In *Skills for Effective Human Services Management,* edited by Richard L. Edwards and John A. Yankey. Silver Spring, MD: NASW Press, 1991.

Richan, Willard. *Lobbying for Social Change,* 2nd ed. New York: Haworth, 1996.

15 Evaluation and Termination

INTRODUCTION

Every helping relationship must end. Counseling must be concluded and groups or committees must eventually be disbanded. The change process ends with the termination of service and a final evaluation of the intervention. ***Termination*** is that important final phase in planned change when the worker guides concluding activities of the process in a manner that is sensitive to issues surrounding the ending of a relationship.

If a meaningful relationship has been formed between client and worker (a key to successful helping), it is not surprising that this ending phase is often experienced with mixed emotions. One common reaction is that the client and worker are pleased that the work together has been concluded. Consequently, the client will no longer need to invest time, resources, and emotional energy in the change process and the worker can move on to new responsibilities. A competing emotion is the sense of loss. Clients sometimes feel anger, rejection, sadness, and anxiousness when the relationship ends. Thus, the worker must provide an opportunity for the client to express his or her feelings and concerns and the worker must lay the groundwork for a resumption of service in the future should than be needed.

Occasionally, service will unexpectedly end at a time other than that originally planned or expected by the worker and client. The following circumstances may make an abrupt termination necessary:

- The client, for personal or financial reasons, decides to stop participating in the change activities.
- The worker accepts employment elsewhere.
- The helping process is blocked by a problem in the worker-client relationship necessitating transfer to another worker.
- The client requires specialized services that are best provided by another social worker, professional, or agency.

If the termination is prompted by the worker or agency, the worker should clearly explain what is happening and why. If the client simply stops participating, the worker should attempt to make a final contact to bring their relationship to an amicable closure.

Also, a final ***evaluation*** should occur at the conclusion of the change process. At this time, the degree of client change is measured and the social worker assesses the success the intervention. The growing impact of managed care on the practice of social work today (see Item 9.11), coupled with an already important obligation for accountability to clients, agencies, and the community, makes it imperative that social workers are skilled at evaluating their practice. As compared to the ongoing monitoring that occurs throughout the helping process, the final evaluation occurs during or after termination. In essence, the worker assesses the degree to which the intervention was effective in improving the client's functioning or situation. The social worker, the clients, the agency, and other sources of funding also need to know if the resources were used in an efficient manner. Ideally, an intervention is both effective and efficient (i.e., it is cost effective).

Two forms of evaluation are of primary concern to the social worker. ***Direct practice evaluation*** is the assessment of a worker's interventions and their impact on a specific client (e.g., an individual, family, or small group). This evaluation can serve two purposes. It can be *formative evaluation,* which is used to inform and guide the ongoing practice decisions and, as such, is a tool for monitoring the intervention and changing the planned intervention when necessary (see Chapter 14). Direct practice evaluation can also be used as a *summative evaluation,* in which one assesses the final outcome and identifies the factors that contributed to the relative success or failure of the intervention.

The second form, ***program evaluation,*** attempts to evaluate the effectiveness and efficiency of a program serving a large number of clients or perhaps even a whole community. Program evaluation, too, can be both formative and summative. It is formative if it is used for assessing a program and changing aspects of its functioning to better serve the agency's clients or community. It is summative when, for example, it is used to report the results of a demonstration program to a board of directors or a funding source.

A clear definition and description of the intervention goals is the important first item in all forms of evaluation. Unless the desired outcomes are specified in the early phases of the change process, the worker will not be able to measure its effect. Additionally, the worker must select the criteria by which to measure the variables (e.g., client behaviors, community knowledge) that are expected to change during the intervention. In research terms, the client's, agency's, or community's functioning is considered the *dependent variable* and the intervention used is the *independent variable.* In the evaluation of a family counseling program, for example, improvement of client functioning (dependent variable) may be viewed as an indicator of the success of services (independent variable).

When deciding what procedures to use to measure change in client functioning, the social worker should consider the following questions:

- *Validity.* Does the procedure measure what it is assumed or believed to measure?
- *Reliability.* Does the procedure yield similar results when the measurement is repeated under similar circumstances?

- *Ease of application.* Is the procedure sufficiently brief, easy to use, and understandable to the nonspecialist?
- *Sensitivity.* Is the measurement procedure able to detect relatively small levels of change and degrees of difference?
- *Nonreactivity.* Can the procedure detect differences without modifying or influencing the phenomena being measured?

When selecting measurement tools, the social worker should review the manuals that accompany the instrument for descriptions of how they are to be used. The worker should also examine the social work and psychology literature for information on their strengths and limitations (e.g., see Faul and Hudson's [1997] description of their Index of Drug Involvement), or through sources such as the *Mental Measurement Yearbook.* If this information is not available, the social worker should account for those limitations and make only tentative and cautious judgments based on this measurement.

The measurement techniques included in this chapter can be used for both monitoring practice (formative evaluation) and making a comprehensive or final assessment of the intervention activity (summative evaluation). Thus, these techniques could be placed in either Chapter 14 or Chapter 15 of this book. They are located in this chapter to give them more visibility to the reader.

SECTION A

TECHNIQUES AND GUIDELINES FOR DIRECT PRACTICE

The most important indicator of success in a direct practice intervention is the client's ability to sustain the gains achieved during the helping process without further assistance from the social worker. Ending the process with a sense of accomplishment, as well as information about what must be done in order to maintain that progress, is of vital importance.

Termination Activities. Although termination is recognized as a key element in planned change, it has been given surprisingly little attention in the social work literature. With the increased limits placed by managed care on the number of sessions a social worker can have with a client, this ending point increasingly is arbitrary and premature. However, termination should be discussed during intake and at appropriate times throughout the helping process, and concluded in a manner that leaves the client with positive feelings and improved capacity to sustain gains made during the period of service. Item 15.6 provides some guidelines for the worker closing a case and terminating a professional relationship.

Social workers should remember, too, that the *NASW Code of Ethics* (1996, Section 1.16) states that termination should be planned with the needs of the client as the primary consideration. If termination is necessary before the change process is completed, there should be an appropriate referral to other helping sources.

Evaluation Activities. The social worker is ethically obliged to be accountable for the quality of services provided. The 1996 *NASW Code of Ethics* recognizes that "social workers should monitor and evaluate (their) . . . practice interventions" (Section 5.02.a). Clearly, it is important to engage clients in the final review of the change process, encouraging them to judge the success and usefulness of the experience from their vantage point, and to secure their thoughts on the worker's performance. From this information, the worker (and sometimes his or her supervisor) can more accurately assess the worker's practice strengths and limitations and, where appropriate, seek consultation or training to enhance the quality of future practice.

In recent years, there has been a growing emphasis on the need for data-based or empirical evaluations. However, this development is not without controversy. Four themes characterize the arguments against empirical methodology. First, it is argued that it takes valuable time away from therapeutic interactions with clients to select or design scales, collect and analyze data, and then interpret the results. Second, because this form of evaluation is relatively new in programs of social work education, many senior practitioners and agency administrators lack the training needed to understand and utilize this approach to evaluation. Third, some opponents argue that social work intervention is primarily an act of human caring that cannot be broken into discrete components and measured in any meaningful way. Finally, some social science researchers who seek to identify clear cause and effect relationships argue that the methodological compromises inherent in attempts to evaluate practice seriously limit the value of the findings because (1) there can be so little control over extraneous variables, (2) research designs must be adjusted to fit unique client situations, (3) there are relatively few design options, and (4) it is difficult for the researcher, who also serves as the helper, to remain objective.

Proponents of empirical direct practice evaluation, including the authors of this book, believe that the benefits outweigh the limitations. In relation to the four themes discussed, these proponents argue that the criticisms are only partially true.

First, the measurement tools used in empirical evaluation typically focus on and gather information needed during the assessment, planning, and intervention phases of the helping process. One way or another, the worker needs to gather this information. Consequently, the use of tools for a more systematic measurement require very little additional time. In fact, when these data are used as formative evaluation, they can actually increase client involvement and motivation, and therefore help to focus and enhance practice.

Second, the workers who are unfamiliar with these techniques appear to be much more hesitant about using them than are their clients. Most people, for example, are accustomed to physicians measuring and recording changes in body temperature, blood pressure, and weight or even asking for judgments about degree of pain on a 1 to 10 scale, and so on. These routinely collected data are willingly provided by patients. Most social work clients would see little difference if they were asked, for example, to count the number of anger outbursts in a week, to rate their degree of anxiety, or to complete a scale that measures the level of marital conflict.

Relative to the third criticism of data-based direct practice evaluation, proponents argue that while social work includes artistic expression in the way the worker performs practice activities (see Chapter 3), the 160 specific techniques and guidelines described in this book alone are evidence that many practice activities can be broken out for purposes of description and evaluation.

Finally, the design and methods used in direct practice research do not pretend to yield findings that can be generalized to other populations. However, they provide useful evidence of a client's changing attitudes, behaviors, or beliefs and allow the social worker to examine the association between various interventions and these changes. Moreover, those who use these approaches recognize that these tools do not provide sufficient evidence to conclude that an intervention "caused" an observed change. One must be cautious not to overestimate the power of the data to depict practice outcomes.

It is important to consider empirical data as only one of several sources of evaluative information. To make the best judgment, it is helpful to apply the concept of *triangulation* (see Item 10.13). In such fields as surveying and archeology, a point is thought to be most accurately located if at least three sightings are in agreement. As applied to social work practice, triangulation would suggest that if the worker's observations and impressions, the client's or some independent party's assessment, and the empirical data are in relative agreement, one can be fairly confident about the accuracy of the conclusion.

A fundamental guideline for the social worker engaged in direct practice evaluation is that *the client or quality of practice must never be compromised in order to collect evaluative data.* Clients should be fully informed about how these data will be used and consent to participation in the evaluation process (see *NASW Code of Ethics*, 1996, Section 5.02.e).

A second guideline is that *practice decisions must precede the decisions on how to conduct the evaluation.* Once the desired outcome and overall intervention approach has been selected, the worker can specify researchable questions about the possible effects of the interventions—for example, "To what extent does Mrs. Garcia carry out the between-session tasks necessary to assure that her parental rights are not severed by the court?" "Is there a relationship between the initiation of family counseling and the Harris family's inclusion of the children in the process of family decision-making?" "Which intervention is most closely associated with changes in Mr. O'Neil's ability to be assertive: supportive counseling, assertiveness training, or a combination of both supportive counseling and assertiveness training?"

Once the questions are framed, the worker can select the most appropriate ways to measure change in the dependent variables (e.g., client actions, emotions, and behaviors). For example, frequency counts of such things as school attendance, acts of violent behavior, family arguments, episodes of crying, and so on, are one measure that can be used. For other factors, standardized measurement scales already exist (see Item 12.16) and for still others, the worker and client may need to develop their own individualized measurement scales (see Item 12.15). Next, the worker is ready to organize the data in order to assess what actually occurred and to interpret the results to the client. The items in Section A of this chapter reflect some of the most commonly used tools for organizing these evaluative data. Finally, the worker should compare these results with other viewpoints (i.e., triangulation) to arrive at his or her understanding of the change and either adjust interventions that are not working or include in the agency's records the final summative evaluation for use during a possible future interaction with that client.

SELECTED BIBLIOGRAPHY

Faul, Anna C., and Walter W. Hudson. "The Index of Drug Involvement: A Partial Validation." *Social Work 42* (November 1997): 565–572.

NASW Code of Ethics. Washington, DC: NASW, 1996.

The Mental Measurements Yearbook. Highland Park, NJ: Gryphon Press, see relevant issue.

15.1 Service Plan Outcome Checklist (SPOC)

PURPOSE: To record individual client progress on a menu of outcome goals and to accumulate the outcome scores for multiple clients in order to inform professional development plans.

DISCUSSION: The ***Service Plan Outcome Checklist*** (***SPOC***) is a recording and monitoring tool for collecting data on client progress in achieving identified goals. Unlike most other monitoring tools, the SPOC can be developed and used with multiple clients in a service unit.

A SPOC is relatively easy to construct. The central feature of a SPOC is a menu of outcome goals the unit typically helps its clients address. Although the format of the SPOC can be used in any agency, the list of outcomes included in the menu will be unique for each agency or service unit. Such a list can be derived from an analysis of client records, a review of the agency's mission and policies, and interviews with experienced workers. The menu of outcomes in Figure 15.1 was created for an outpatient mental health center with programs focused on providing counseling to persons from lower socioeconomic groups and to those who experience chronic mental illness.

The first step in using the SPOC is to ask the client during the initiation of service to review the list of desired outcomes from the service (left-hand column) and to place a check (✓) by all goals he or she would want to achieve and is willing to work toward. This selection might be done independently by the client or with the assistance of the worker. Workers often find that discussion of these items yields helpful information and provides a way to focus a first interview. If certain outcomes are mandated by a court, school, or other referring agency, these should be noted in the middle column—along with those selected by the client and worker. To assist with prioritizing services, the two or three most important service goals should also be identified.

The SPOC is similar to a service checklist (see Item 12.14) but additionally incorporates elements of an evaluation tool. If used with a client over an extended period, the rating of achievement could be conducted at interim points in the change

FIGURE 15.1 Service Plan Outcome Checklist: Metropolitan Mental Health Center

Elizabeth DeSantis	*Laura Logsdon*	2/27/99
Client/Family	Worker	Service Initiation Date

Instructions: Complete Steps 1–3 within two weeks of the initiation of service.

Step 1 In the far left column, select and (✓) all outcomes for intervention. If a desired outcome does not appear on the menu below, add items in the space provided at the end or back of the questionnaire.

Step 2 Review the items checked in Step 1 and circle the two or three that you consider the most important or of highest priority.

Step 3 Under the column "Person or Program That Defined Outcome/Date Intervention Began" indicate who (i.e., client, family member, worker, court, school) chose this outcome and when work on that specific outcome started.

At an interim point in the intervention and/or when services are terminated, complete Step 4 (i.e., the shaded area).

Step 4 Rate each checked item from "No Progress" to "Fully Achieved" by circling the number from 1 to 7 that best represents your judgment about progress made to date.

Place a (✓) by each desired outcome for this service. Then circle the two or three most important outcomes.	Person or program that defined outcome/date intervention began	Circle Rating (after services are provided) No Progress		About Half Achieved				Fully Achieved
____ 1. Reduce and manage anxiety	____	1	2	3	4	5	6	7
____ 2. Reduce and manage depression	____	1	2	3	4	5	6	7
✓ 3. Accept and respect self as a worthwhile person	ED 2/27/99	1	2	3	4	5	6	7
____ 4. Recognize and manage anger	____	1	2	3	4	5	6	7
____ 5. Establish/maintain control over addictions	____	1	2	3	4	5	6	7
✓ 6. Establish/maintain satisfactory relationship with spouse or partner	ED 2/27/99	1	2	3	4	5	6	7
____ 7. Establish/maintain positive relationship with children (or parents)	____	1	2	3	4	5	6	7

Place a (✓) by each desired outcome for this service. Then circle the two or three most important outcomes.	Person or program that defined outcome/date intervention began	Circle Rating (after services are provided) No Progress			About Half Achieved			Fully Achieved
____ 8. Cope effectively with grief/loss	____	1	2	3	4	5	6	7
____ 9. Meet basic needs (e.g., food, clothing, housing)	____	1	2	3	4	5	6	7
✓ 10. Establish/maintain good eating, sleeping, exercise habits	LL 3/7/99	1	2	3	4	5	6	7
____ 11. Establish/maintain positive support system	____	1	2	3	4	5	6	7
✓ 12. Learn to cope effectively with illness/ disability issues (circled)	ED 3/14/99	1	2	3	4	5	6	7
____ 13. Learn to handle abuse issues—present	____	1	2	3	4	5	6	7
____ 14. Learn to handle abuse issues—past	____	1	2	3	4	5	6	7
____ 15. Establish/maintain clear and nonabusive communication with children	____	1	2	3	4	5	6	7
____ 16. Establish/maintain clear and nonabusive communication with spouse/partner	____	1	2	3	4	5	6	7
____ 17. Establish/maintain behavior patterns free of criminal acts or association with deviant persons	____	1	2	3	4	5	6	7
✓ 18. Establish/maintain employment/ school attendance (circled)	Court 2/15/99	1	2	3	4	5	6	7
✓ 19. Establish/maintain a positive working relationship with the therapist	ED&LL 2/27/99	1	2	3	4	5	6	7
✓ 20. Add other outcomes desired if not on this list: *Improve communication with in-laws.*	ED 3/14/99	1	2	3	4	5	6	7

Source: Adapted from Jan Overmyer, Colorado State University.

process to assess the progress of the intervention effort. At a minimum, items identified for attention should be rated at the point of termination. A by-product of this final evaluation is that clients find it helpful to revisit their initial selection of outcome goals and consider what has actually been achieved.

When the SPOC is applied to all of a worker's clients, it yields information that can help a social worker identify those service categories in which clients do or do not achieve their goals. Figure 15.2, for example, illustrates the compilation of ratings for all of a social worker's terminating clients in a outpatient mental health center during a three-month period. This information can help a worker and his or her supervisor (or field instructor, if the worker is a student) identify areas where the worker performs well and point out other areas for which the worker should seek additional knowledge or training. For example, the data in Figure 15.2 suggest that this worker should learn more about helping clients cope with grief and loss.

FIGURE 15.2 Jan Overmyer's Service Plan Outcome Checklist Results (10/01/99 to 12/31/99)

Item #	Issue Selected	# and % Checked		# and % in Top 3		Achievement Rating 1	2	3	4	5	6	7	Mean
1	Manages anxiety	7	63.6%	2	18.2%	0	1	0	0	1	5	0	5.29
2	Manages depression	10	90.9	5	45.5	0	0	0	1	2	7	0	5.60
3	Respects self	8	72.7	6	54.5	0	1	0	0	2	5	0	5.25
4	Manages anger	9	81.8	4	36.4	0	1	0	1	3	4	0	5.00
5	Controls addictions	1	9.1	0	0.0	0	0	0	0	0	0	1	7.00
6	Relationship with partner	4	36.4	1	9.1	0	0	1	0	0	0	3	5.75
7	Relationship with child/parent	8	72.7	6	54.5	0	0	0	1	4	3	0	5.25
8	Cope with grief/loss issues	8	72.7	4	36.4	0	2	3	1	2	0	0	3.37
9	Basic needs met	4	36.4	1	9.1	0	0	0	1	1	1	1	5.50
10	Eating/sleeping/exercise	6	54.5	0	0.0	0	0	0	2	0	4	0	5.33
11	Positive support system	7	63.6	0	0.0	0	1	0	2	2	1	1	4.71
12	Cope with illness/disability	1	9.1	1	9.1	0	1	0	0	0	0	0	2.00
13	Present abuse issues	3	27.3	0	0.0	0	0	0	0	2	0	1	5.67
14	Past abuse issues	8	72.7	1	9.1	0	1	0	0	2	5	0	5.25
15	Positive communication/child	3	27.3	0	0.0	0	0	1	0	1	0	1	5.00
16	Positive communication/partner	3	27.3	0	0.0	0	0	0	1	1	0	1	5.33
17	Avoid criminal behavior/friends	2	18.2	0	0.0	0	0	0	0	0	0	2	7.00
18	Employment/school goals	9	81.8	2	18.2	0	1	0	0	1	4	3	5.78
19	Relationship with therapist	11	100.0	0	0.0	1	0	0	0	3	0	7	5.91
20	Additional outcomes	0	NA	0	NA				NA				NA
	Overall Achievement	*N* = 11 clients											5.27

Source: Adapted from Jan Overmyer, Colorado State University.

When a SPOC is used by all workers in a service unit, an administrator can identify the relative strengths and limitations of the staff. This information can be used to make more effective case assignments and to formulate plans for in-service training. Also, examination of the responses on the open-ended item can provide useful information about changing service demands and signal the need for new programs to address those items that are regularly added.

SELECTED BIBLIOGRAPHY

Fraser, Mark, Peter Pecora, and David Haapala. *Families in Crisis: Findings from the Family-Based Intensive Treatment Project,* vol. II. Salt Lake City: University of Utah Graduate School of Social Work, 1988.

Horejsi, Charles. *Assessment and Case Planning in Child Protection and Foster Care Services.* Englewood, CO: American Humane Association, 1996.

15.2 Client Self-Rating Scales

PURPOSE: To enable a client to visually track movement toward desired outcomes.

DISCUSSION: Clients find it helpful to receive feedback regarding the progress they are making. The social worker's verbal appraisal of progress is important, but when that is supplemented with a visual representation of change, the client's clarity about what is occurring is increased. A simple format for helping clients visualize change is a ***client self-rating scale.***

The first step in developing such a scale is to clearly state in positive terms each goal identified by the client and worker as a target for change. For example, "I want to increase the number of conflict-free interactions with my brother, John" or "My goal is to complete my homework assignments each night before 10:00 P.M." For each goal, the worker creates a chart. If some goals are interrelated, progress toward more than one goal might be recorded on the same chart. The chart is designed so that along the left axis scores from –10 to +10 are recorded. The most accurate way to determine the scores on this axis is to establish, in collaboration with the client, descriptors (or anchor points) reflecting the criteria for assigning scores (see Item 12.15). For example, –10 might reflect "I did not get any homework completed," –5 might be "at least two nights I completed all of my homework," a score of 0 could indicate that "homework was completed three nights that week," +5 might reflect "at least four times all homework was completed," and +10 could reflect "I always completed all of my homework." Along the bottom axis the dates of each session with the client are recorded as the process evolves (see Figure 15.3).

At each session the worker and client discuss the client's improvement (or deterioration) in moving toward each desired outcome. The client then arrives at a self-rating and the worker records the score on the chart. If the ratings related to more than one goal are included on a single chart, the scores can be recorded with different colors or by using solid, dotted, and dashed lines.

FIGURE 15.3 Client Self-Rating Scale

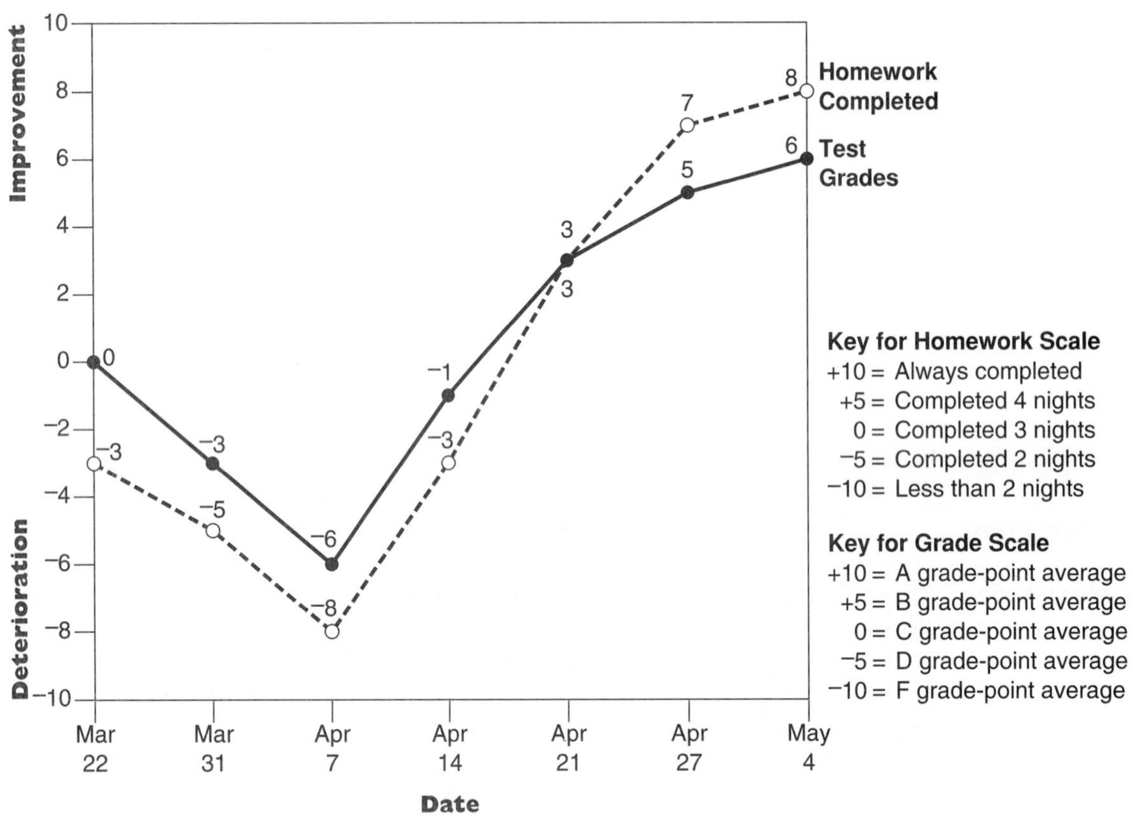

The trends reflected on the charts can be discussed with the client to identify factors that have influenced the scores. This visual representation of what has occurred helps clients identify and possibly decrease resistance and barriers to change as well as experience a sense of success.

SELECTED BIBLIOGRAPHY

Mattaini, Mark A. *More than a Thousand Words: Graphics for Clinical Practice.* Washington, DC: NASW Press, 1993.

Sutton, Carole. "Reviewing and Evaluating Therapeutic Progress." In *Client Assessment,* edited by Stephen Palmer and Gladeana McMahon. Thousand Oaks, CA: Sage, 1997.

15.3 Task Achievement Scaling (TAS)

PURPOSE: To determine the degree to which the client has completed agreed upon intervention tasks.

DISCUSSION: *Task Achievement Scaling* (*TAS*) is a tool that measures success in completing specified tasks. This evaluation procedure was developed for use in task-centered practice wherein work toward the client's goals and objectives is broken down into many small and separate tasks and then worked on sequentially. A ***task*** is an action or decision by the client or worker that is necessary in order to reach a desired outcome. A task is usually something that can be accomplished in a matter of days or, at most, in a few weeks. Usually, not more than three or four tasks are worked on at a time. Each session with the client begins with a review of the progress on tasks selected for attention during the previous session and ends with identifying tasks to be undertaken before the next session. Some tasks may be completed or judged to be no longer needed and dropped, some may be continued, and others added at each session.

The TAS is especially applicable as a means of evaluation when the service is relatively brief, when circumstances do not lend themselves to the establishment of a baseline measure, and when activities are concrete. For purposes of illustration, consider the client who has sought the social worker's guidance in obtaining a job. Many client tasks are involved, such as reading the help-wanted section of the newspaper, preparing and submitting a job application, rehearsing for a job interview, securing transportation to the job interview, obtaining suitable clothing for work, and so on. TAS allows the worker to measure progress on each task and compute an overall measure of the actual level of task achievement (e.g., not client motivation or good intentions) between sessions.

The format for a TAS is to define five points on an ordinal scale for each task. The following identifies the standard way of labeling and assigning a numerical value to the five scale points. Also, illustrative descriptors for each level of achievement developed by a social worker and a family working on the task of reaching agreement about a curfew with a teenage son are included here (adapted from Allison Campbell, Colorado State University):

(4) *Completely achieved* (e.g., a mutually acceptable contract regarding curfew signed by parents and son)

(3) *Substantially achieved* (e.g., a rough draft of a curfew contract drafted and discussed)

(2) *Partially achieved* (e.g., parents and son calmly discussed elements of a curfew contract)

(1) *Minimally achieved* (e.g., topic of a curfew contract discussed, but accompanied by arguing)

(0) *No progress* (e.g., no discussion of a curfew contract)

The process of defining the increments of success in task achievement is often helpful to clients, as it assists them in recognizing that what may appear to be overwhelming tasks can be accomplished in smaller incremental steps. Further, regularly measuring success in carrying out those tasks gives a clear indication of progress. However, successful helping often requires that several interrelated tasks are performed simultaneously. Task achievement scaling allows the worker to compute a global achievement score (i.e., the percent of achievement) for the combined tasks.

By summing the rating on each task and then dividing this amount by the highest sum possible, a percentage of success is determined. For example, if four tasks were targeted for accomplishment and all four tasks were "completely achieved," the highest sum possible would be 16 ($4 \times 4 = 16$). If, however, the actual scores in the four areas are 1, 2, 3, and 4, the summed score would be only 10. By dividing the actual score (10) by the highest possible score (16), the result would be 62.5 percent task achievement. In other words, the client achieved 62.5 percent of all that was agreed upon, planned, and translated into tasks.

Another use of the TAS is to track the percentage of tasks completed in a time-series format such as a "B design" using the single-subject format (see Item 15.5). Graphing the percent of task achievement from session to session can be informative to both clients and workers. Positive results can be reinforcing, whereas a downward trend can signal a decline in client interest or motivation. Using the time-series format also makes it possible to graphically compare the percent of task completion with some other variable to answer a practice question such as "Is the level of task achievement associated with the client's level of self-esteem?"

SELECTED BIBLIOGRAPHY

Alter, Catherine, and Wayne Evens. *Evaluating Your Practice: A Guide to Self-Assessment.* New York: Springer, 1990.

Reid, William, and Laura Epstein, eds. *Task Centered Practice.* New York: Columbia University Press, 1977.

15.4 Goal Attainment Scaling (GAS)

PURPOSE: To measure the degree to which a client has reached individualized goals.

DISCUSSION: *Goal Attainment Scaling* (*GAS*) is a procedure that provides an estimate of the degree of movement toward goals that accrues from an intervention with an individual or family. GAS has been successfully used in mental health, drug abuse programs, probation and parole, and other settings.

The application of GAS begins during the contracting and goal-setting phase of the change process. The basic format for a GAS (Kiresuk and Sherman 1968) is the same for all clients, although adjustments must be made to accommodate the number of goals selected. It consists of several five-point scales (usually two to four or five) that are individualized for the specific client to represent a set of possible outcomes—both positive and negative—related to the agreed upon goals. These may be individualized scales (see Item 12.15) or may reflect differing scores on a standardized assessment instrument (see Item 12.16). Here are the steps in the process of constructing a GAS:

1. *Identify two to five goals and develop a scale for each.* To establish a GAS scale, the worker and client begin by describing in a few words the client's condition or situation in relation to each identified goal before the intervention is begun. This description should be viewed as the second lowest point on the five-point scale and assigned a (0) value. The lowest point (–1) can then be described to reflect a step backward. Next, the best outcome that could reasonably be expected should be described and a value of +3 assigned. Then, two levels of improvement between the current situation and the best possible scenario can be described and assigned +1 and +2 values. In sum, a "–" score represents deterioration or regression, "0" represents no significant change, and the "+" scores identify three levels of improvement. Figure 15.4 reflects three scales developed for a married student being seen by a social worker in a college counseling center. The three goals the client hoped to achieve were an improved relationship with her spouse, increasing her interaction with other students, and gaining control of her frequent episodes of anger.

2. *Assign a weight to each goal area to indicate its importance in relation to other goals.* Since most people are accustomed to working in sets of 100, it is usually understandable to clients to divide 100 points between the two to five goals to reflect the degree of importance of each. If there were five goals and all were equal, each would have a weight of 20 (i.e., 100 divided by 5 = 20). However, if goal #1 was considered as important as the other four combined—and these four were considered equal—the weighting might be 50 for goal #1 and 12.5 for goals #2, #3, #4, and #5.

3. *Place a check (✓) in the cell that best describes the client's condition at the point intervention begins.* Usually this will be the "0" cell, but sometimes it might be one level higher or lower. This serves as the baseline for measuring change.

4. *When the service or intervention is terminated, place an X in the cell that best describes the client's condition at that time.* Although the GAS is intended to represent a before and after reading of the client's condition on each scale, in long-term service cases a reading is sometimes taken at intermediate times as a way of monitoring the change process.

5. *Determine the weighted change score for each goal.* Computing the change score for a scale involves subtracting the beginning score (✓) from the ending score (*X*) and multiplying by the weight. If the starting (✓) cell is "0," the highest possible score would be +3. However, in cases where the starting point is –1, there would be +4 higher points on the scale. That score is then multiplied by the weight for that outcome. In Figure 15.4, for example, the "Relationship Satisfaction" scale revealed change from 0 to +3. That score, then, was multiplied by the weight (50) to yield a weighted score of +150.

6. *Compute the percent of positive change score for each scale.* Determine the highest score a client might generate and divide that into the actual weighted score. For the "Anger Management" scale in Figure 15.4, there was one level of actual positive change, but two levels of improvement were possible. At a 25 weight, the highest possible score might have been 50 ($2 \times 25 = 50$). Thus, the actual change score (25) divided by the possible score (50) indicates 50 percent goal attainment.

7. *Compute an overall goal attainment score.* Find the sum of the possible positive scores for all of the goals and divide that score into the sum of the actual weighted scores to arrive at a percent of goal attainment. The shaded cell in Figure 15.4 (i.e., 58 percent) gives an indicator of the comprehensive goal attainment that accrued from this intervention.

FIGURE 15.4 Goal Attainment Scale Follow-Up Guide

Client: Amy Grant
Worker: Christine Stevens

(✓) = Beginning Level (✗) = Terminating Level	**Scale 1: Relationship Satisfaction**	**Scale 2: Peer Relations**	**Scale 3: Anger Management**	**TOTAL**
Scale Attainment Level	Weight = 50	Weight = 25	Weight = 25	Weight = 100
(–1) Most unfavorable treatment outcome thought likely	Index of Marital Satisfaction (IMS) score > 70	No contact with friends	Anger out of control 7 or more times per month	
(0) Less than expected treatment success	IMS Score 58–70 (✓)	Interacts less than once a month with friends (✓) (✗)	Anger out of control 5–6 times per month	
(+1) Expected level of treatment success	IMS Score 44–57	Interacts about once a month with friends	Anger out of control 3–4 times per month (✓)	
(+2) More than expected treatment success	IMS Score 30–43	Interacts about once a week with friends	Anger out of control 1–2 times per month (✗)	
(+3) Best anticipated treatment success	IMS Score < 30 (✗)	Interacts almost daily with friends	Anger never out of control	
Summary				
Weight	50	25	25	
Change Score	4	0	1	
Weighted Change Score	150	0	25	175
Possible Weighted Change	150	75	50	300
Percentage Achievement	100%	0%	50%	58%

Source: Adapted from Christine Stevens, Colorado State University.

If goal attainment scaling is used widely in an agency, data from the "Goal Attainment Scale Follow-Up Guide" can be utilized for program evaluation purposes. For example, data might be accumulated regarding the following:

- The types of goals chosen as targets for intervention, their frequency, and the percent of goal achievement on each
- The amount of progress made on particular goals by the clients served by a specific worker
- The relative success in goal achievement with particular groups of clients (e.g., age, ethnicity, gender, etc.)

SELECTED BIBLIOGRAPHY

Bloom, Martin, Joel Fischer, and John G. Orme. *Evaluating Practice: Guidelines for the Accountable Professional.* Boston: Allyn and Bacon, 1995.

Kiresuk, Thomas J., and Robert E. Sherman. "Goal Attainment Scaling: A General Method for Evaluating Comprehensive Community Mental Health Programs." *Community Mental Health Journal* 4 (1968): 445–453.

15.5 Single-Subject Designs (SSD)

PURPOSE: To evaluate changes in client actions, feelings, or attitudes over a specified period of time.

DISCUSSION: The most well-known methods for direct practice evaluation are single-subject research designs—also known as single-system, single-case, $N = 1$, subject replication, and time-series designs. As compared to more traditional forms of research that accumulate data from multiple respondents either before and after or with and without an intervention, ***single-subject designs*** (***SSD***) involve accumulating repeated measurements from a single subject (e.g., individual, couple, family, or group) over time. A SSD might also be used to examine a single intervention with multiple applications (e.g., multiple clients, multiple targets of change, or in multiple settings).

Two fundamental assumptions underpin SSD. First, it is assumed that if left unattended, the client's condition or problem will stay about the same or worsen. Second, it is also assumed that barring evidence to the contrary, one can cautiously conclude that if change occurs after the introduction of an intervention, the intervention is a dominant force in that change. Thus, by clearly specifying the client's behavior, attitude, or functioning *before* the intervention begins (i.e., a baseline measurement), any change that occurs during the period of intervention can be attributed to the intervention. Although it is not possible to conclude that the intervention *caused* an identified change, it can be said that there is (or is not) an *association* between the change and the intervention.

There is no uniform format for single-subject designs. In fact, one of the strengths of this methodology is its flexibility. Because the SSD monitors what occurs in practice, the design must be adaptable to changing practice situations. Unlike traditional social science research, therefore, it is appropriate to modify the design during the change process if a decision is made, for example, to alter the intervention plan or to take advantage of a temporary secession of service such as a vacation period to obtain another baseline. The following steps reflect a process for conducting a single-subject evaluation:

1. *Select a case situation in which it will be possible to take several measurements over time.* Because data that reveal trends in a client's actions or feelings provide the basis of this design, repeated measurements must be taken. These measurements might occur before the intervention is begun, during the intervention, and after the intervention is completed. The frequency of measurement will depend on the case situation and could be daily, weekly, monthly, and so on. The characteristic way of organizing SSD data is on a graph that depicts the independent variable (e.g., attitude, behavior, etc.) on the left axis (y-axis) and a timeline in days, weeks (or whatever) along the bottom (x-axis). Figure 15.5 depicts the typical format for graphing the basic components of a single-subject design.

2. *Select the target behaviors/attitudes/beliefs and determine how each is to be measured.* During the assessment and planning phases of the change process, the factors, conditions, or patterns targeted for change will have been identified and, in order to monitor change, a valid and relevant numerical measure must be selected. This may be a frequency count (how often something happens), a score on a standardized or individualized scale (see Items 12.15 and 12.16), or the scores generated from a Task Achievement Scale or a Goal Attainment Scale. The worker and client should establish a plan for taking the measurements under similar conditions (e.g., same location and time of day) so far as possible each time a measurement is made.

FIGURE 15.5 Components of a Single-Subject Design Graphing

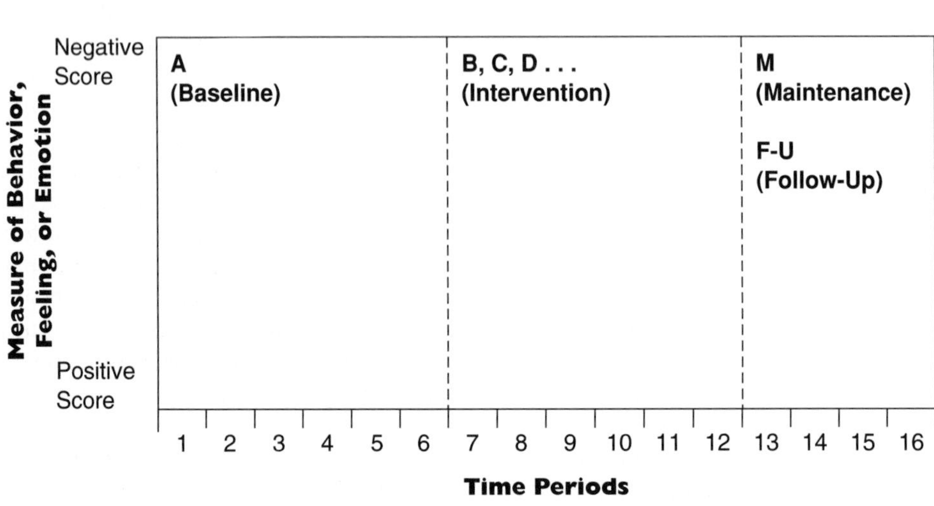

3. *Select a single-subject design and designate the phases of the process on the chart.* The different phases (e.g., baseline, intervention, and follow-up) of the process are identified across the top of the graph with dashed vertical lines separating each phase. *A* is used to represent a baseline period. The letters *B, C, D,* and so forth, identify distinctly different interventions. If multiple interventions are used simultaneously, a slash is placed between the letters representing those interventions (e.g., *B/C/D*). If there is a modification in the frequency or intensity of an intervention (e.g., shorter sessions or increased medication), those modifications can be noted with a superscript designation (e.g., B^1 B^2). *M* designates a period in which a minimum level of service is maintained before a case is closed (the maintenance phase) and *F-U* denotes a follow-up measurement after service has been terminated. Either include a descriptor (e.g., *B* = family therapy, *C* = supportive counseling) or provide a key for each phase of the process somewhere on the chart.

The variations of single-subject designs depend on the practice situation, the worker's creativity, and the questions the worker intends to answer. The most elementary SSD is the B design or a case study in which there are no baseline or follow-up data and the worker simply tracks what happens in regard to the independent variable(s) while the intervention is occurring. This *exploratory approach* allows the worker to observe what is happening during the intervention phase in order to adjust the practice approach, if necessary, or to inform future practice decisions.

A slightly more sophisticated form of SSD, a *descriptive study,* allows the worker and client to examine differences between a baseline period and the intervention phase (e.g., an AB design). This form of study might also allow the worker to identify changes in the client's functioning associated with different intervention strategies (e.g., an ABCD design). Figure 15.6 reports a study in which a school social worker concerned with a teenage boy's poor self-image collected baseline data (A phase) and, after counseling (B phase), failed to generate meaningful change in his scores on an Index of Self-Esteem, helped him find a place on the school's soccer team (B/C phase). Positive changes in the index scores helped the youth and worker recognize the importance of the youth's involvement with peers.

Discontinuing an intervention while continuing to measure the independent variable (ABA design) provides more substantial information regarding the association between the change and the intervention. If a behavior improves during the intervention phase and yet reverts to the original baseline level when the intervention is discontinued, one can conclude that the intervention indeed was related to the change. Even more verification of the influence of the intervention occurs by reinstituting the intervention (ABAB design). If the behavior again improves, one can be relatively confident that the intervention helped set the positive change in motion. An example of this use of SSD for an *explanatory study* can be found in Figure 15.7. In this study, the worker wanted to determine if the use of personal handwritten notes to a client who invested very little of herself in the change process would be associated with changes in the client's level of engagement. A seven-point scale measuring the client's level of engagement was developed and the ABAB format adopted. The results give a strong indication that the use of personal notes elevated this client's level of engagement.

Finally, a SSD might be selected to determine if an intervention has similar results with *multiple clients or change targets*. The SSD permits a worker to track more than one variable at a time to determine if the scores on the variables are correlated. For example, in the study reported in Figure 15.8, the social worker was providing therapy to the family of a teenager who was being released from a residential drug

FIGURE 15.6 Single-Subject (A B B/C) Design

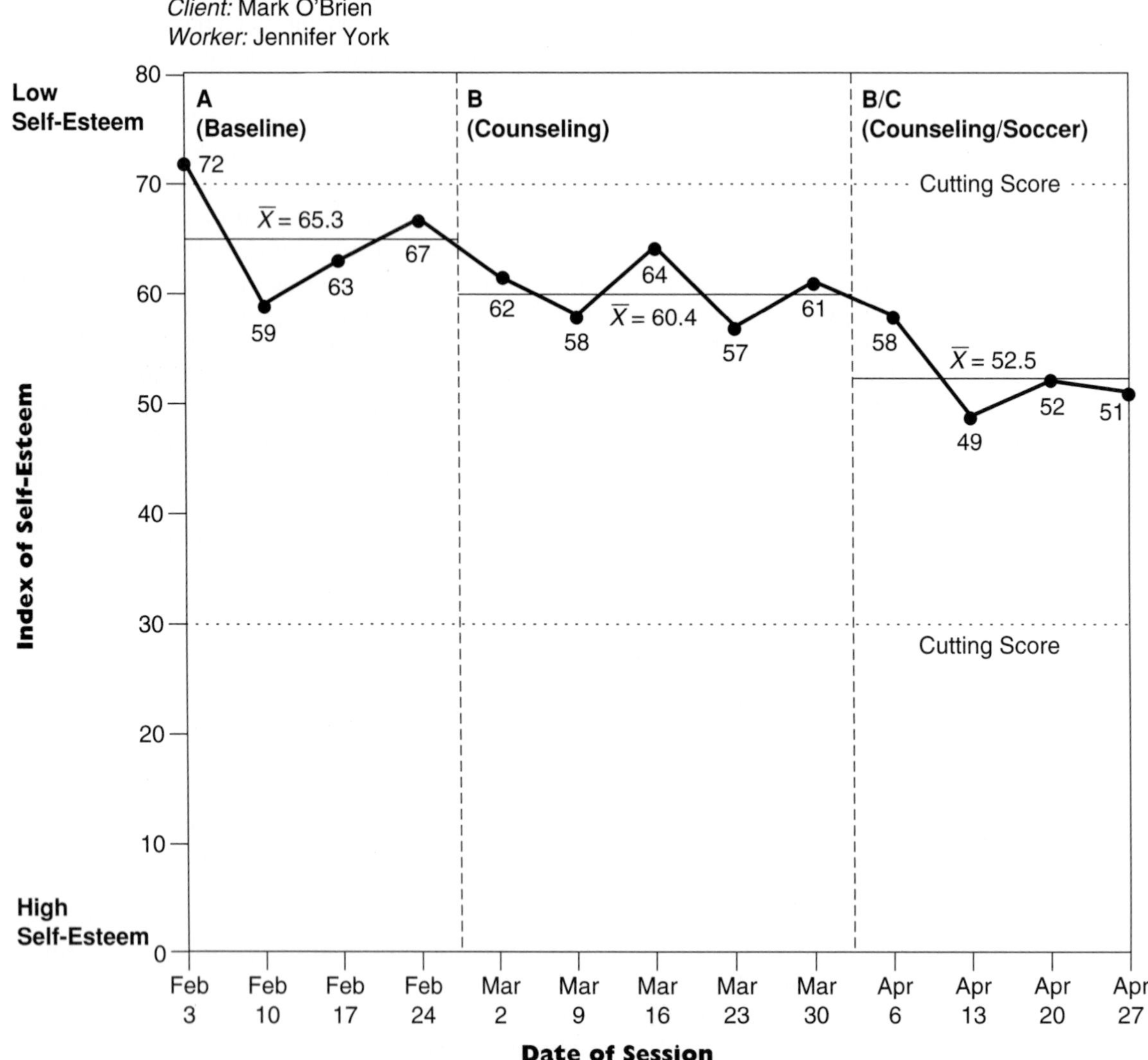

Source: Adapted from Jennifer York, Colorado State University.

and alcohol center. The practice assessment suggested that the parents were being dominated by the youth and had given up on efforts to provide discipline and structure. The worker was concerned that the reestablishment of the father's role in providing a more structured environment might be positive for the father but could alienate the youth and further strain family relations. By recording the father's and

FIGURE 15.7 Single-Subject (ABAB) Design

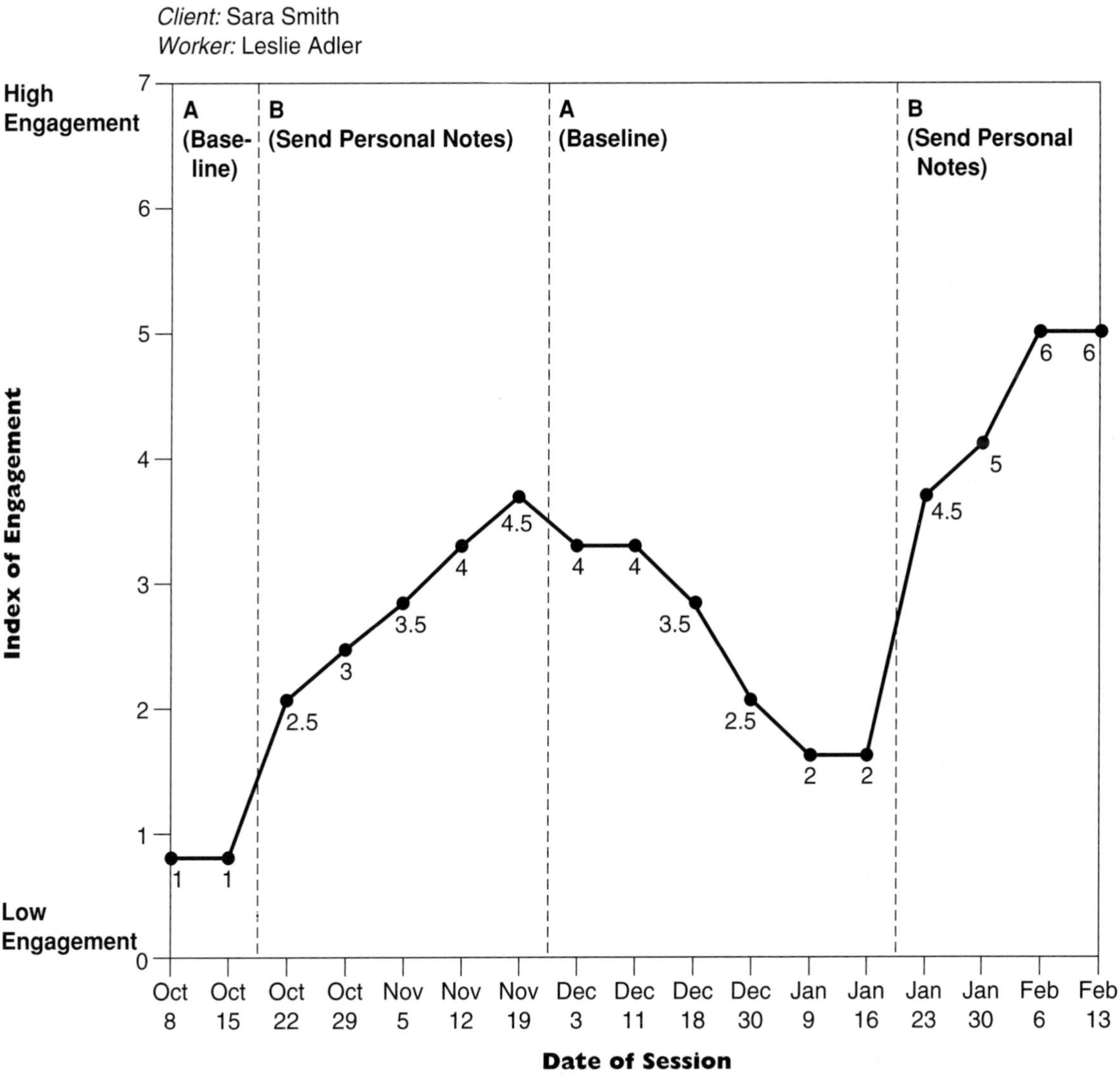

Source: Adapted from Leslie Adler, Colorado State University.

youth's scores from the Index of Family Relations, the worker was able to determine that during the beginning of the intervention, the youth felt that family relations were more strained, but once the parent roles were reestablished, he felt relationships had improved substantially.

FIGURE 15.8 Single-Subject (A B F-U) Design

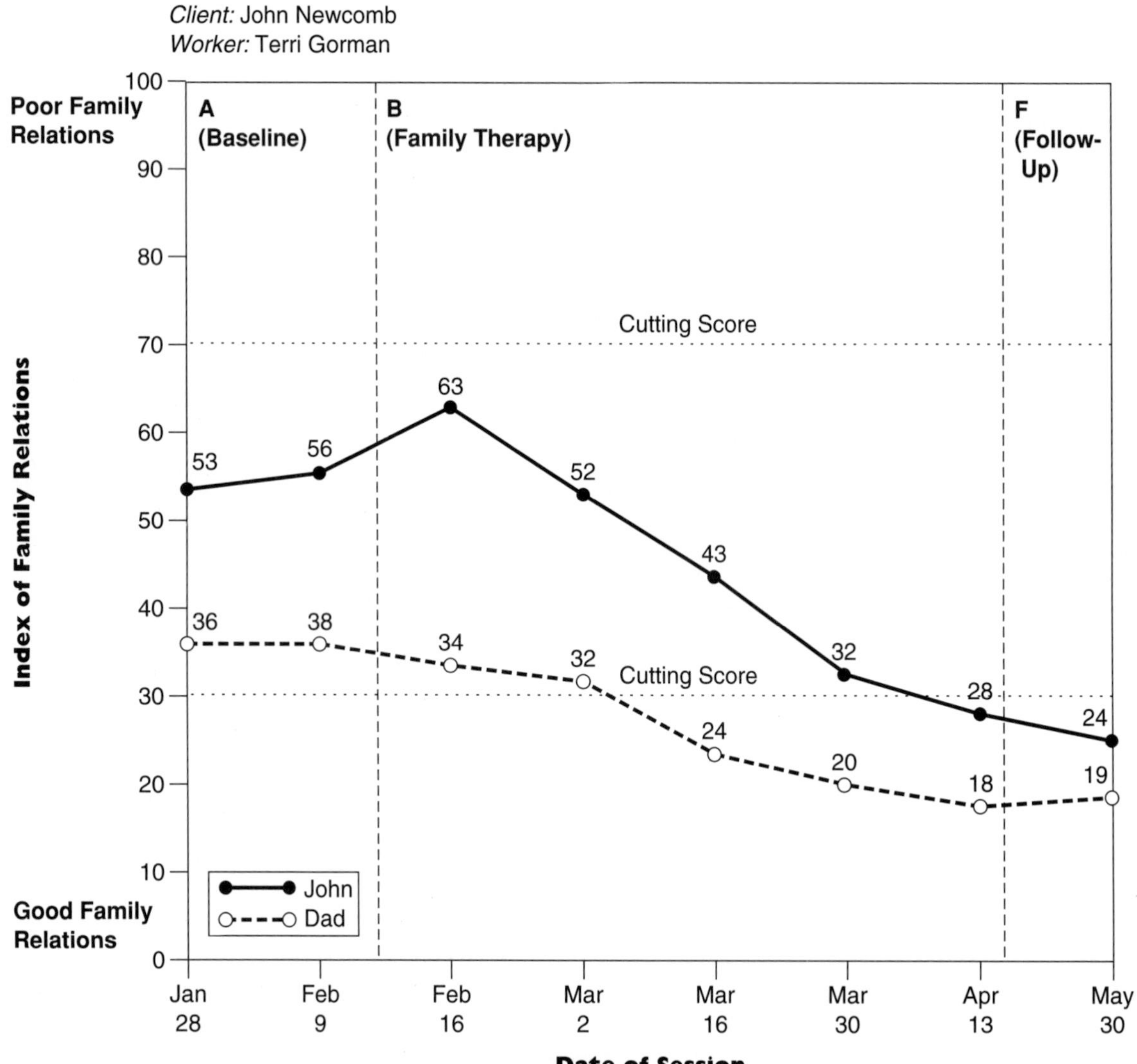

Source: Adapted from Terri Gorman, Colorado State University.

5. *Collect and record baseline, intervention, maintenance, and/or follow-up data on each factor.* When scores are obtained on each variable, the score should be plotted on the client's graph. Because the chart reflects the sequence of related scores through time, a *line chart* is the preferred format. The known data points should be connected with solid lines. If there are missing data at an interval when data regularly would have been collected, the two known points should be connected by a dashed line, which depicts an assumption that the missing data would have fallen along the line between the two known points.

Ideally, baseline measures should be repeatedly taken until a stable score on the variable is established. However, the realities of social work practice rarely permit many measurements. A minimum of three baseline measurements (before the intervention is begun) should be collected if at all possible. These measurements might be made during the assessment and planning phases of the change process (*current baseline* data) or might possibly be based on information already on record (*retrospective baseline* data), such as attendance records or previous scores on assessment instruments. It is also important to note on the y-axis if a high score represents a positive or negative outcome on each factor.

6. *Interpret the data and compare empirical evidence with other practice observations.* When data points have been entered on a graph, it is then possible to examine the data and make judgments about the success of the intervention. Several cautions should be considered when interpreting SSD data. First, if there is a sequence of interventions being evaluated, such as in an ABCD design, there could be a *carryover* effect in which the change made in one phase affects the next. Withdrawing all interventions (i.e., returning to a second baseline) can help to reveal if there has been a cumulative influence from the series of interventions. The *order of presentation* of various intervention strategies can also affect the impact of a specific intervention. This problem can be addressed in subsequent practice situations by changing the order of introducing the various intervention strategies. If one strategy appears most effective regardless of order, a worker can feel more confident about using that strategy in similar practice situations. Finally, SSDs often suffer from *incomplete and inaccurate data.* The realities of practice are that clients miss sessions, data collection instruments are not completed, clients sometimes provide incorrect information, and so on. These problems should not mitigate against conducting direct practice evaluation, but rather they argue for cautious interpretation of the results and reinforce the importance of triangulation.

Visual examination of the direction of change will often produce a clear picture of the client's situation. However, when data are erratic, it may be difficult to detect trends. When this happens, it is helpful to compute a *mean* or *median* score (see Item 10.13) to identify the most typical responses. For each phase of the process, then, horizontal lines represent the central tendency. In Figure 15.6, for example, the somewhat erratic scores masked a clear trend in this worker's effort to strengthen a youth's self-esteem. Therefore, mean scores (e.g., $\overline{X} = 65.3$) were computed for each phase to more clearly identify the pattern of change.

When a small number of measurements are taken, an extreme score may distort a mean. In these cases, a *trimmed mean* can more accurately reflect central tendency. It is computed by dropping both the highest and lowest 10 percent of responses and then computing the mean score. Other more sophisticated analyses of data can be conducted in which *trend lines* or *celeration lines* project the future direction of client performance on the factor being measured and, if there are sufficient data, it is possible to determine if a change is *statistically significant*. Rubin and Babbie (1997), for example, describe procedures for determining if the intervention phase scores are more than two standard deviations from the baseline scores (i.e., statistically significant at the .05 level). Also, statistical tables have been developed that identify levels of significance based on the proportion and frequency of observations. However, one should be cautious about using elaborate statistical manipulation, as it can imply more rigorous data collection than the SSD methodology permits. The effort devoted to determining statistical significance might be better spent on examining the *practical significance* of the information (i.e., the importance of the change).

SELECTED BIBLIOGRAPHY

Bloom, Martin, Joel Fischer, and John G. Orme. *Evaluating Practice: Guidelines for the Accountable Professional*. Boston: Allyn and Bacon, 1995.

Rubin, Allen, and Earl Babbie. *Research Methods for Social Workers*, 3rd ed. Pacific Grove, CA: Brooks/Cole, 1997.

Tripodi, Tony. *A Primer on Single-Subject Design for Clinical Social Workers*. Washington, DC: NASW Press, 1994.

15.6 Termination of Service

PURPOSE: To terminate the professional relationship between social worker and client in a timely and responsible manner.

DISCUSSION: Closing a case, or terminating services to a client, should be viewed as a planned component of the helping process. When deciding if termination is appropriate, the following factors should be considered:

- Have the intervention objectives been reached?
- Has an agreed upon time limit to service provision been reached?
- Is the problem or situation that brought the client to the agency sufficiently resolved so the client can now function at an acceptable level and not be at risk of being harmed by self or others?
- Has the worker and/or agency made a reasonable investment of time, energy, and skill without measurable results?
- Has the client and/or worker reached a point where one or both do not anticipate benefit from future contacts?
- Has the client become inappropriately dependent on the worker or agency?
- Would the client be more appropriately served by another agency or professional?

In some situations, a transfer of the client to another worker within the agency is necessary. This, too, is a type of termination. An intraagency transfer is necessary when one of the following occurs:

- The worker will no longer be available to serve the client (e.g., worker moving to another job, etc.).
- The client will be better served by another agency staff member.
- A conflict between the worker and client cannot be resolved and is interfering with service provision or client progress.
- For some reason, the worker simply does not like the client and cannot develop or demonstrate necessary empathy and warmth.
- There is a serious and insurmountable gap in mutual understanding and communication caused by difference in values, religious beliefs, language, or cultural background.

Ideally, termination is a mutual decision by worker and client that occurs when the service objectives have been reached. Many situations are far from ideal, however. All too often, the client decides to end the relationship before reaching the objectives, and sometimes circumstances dictate that the worker decide unilaterally to terminate. Examples of the latter include the following:

- The client is considered to be a physical danger to the worker or continually harasses the worker.
- The client files a lawsuit or an official complaint against the worker.
- The client violates, without good cause, a financial agreement regarding the payment of fees for service.

In the case of an intraagency transfer and in the case of a termination by the worker, the client should be notified in writing, and, if possible, during a face-to-face meeting. The reasons and circumstances surrounding the transfer or termination should be clearly documented in the case record.

The social worker has an obligation to make a termination or transfer as positive an experience as possible. Several guidelines can aid in this process:

1. The worker should do everything possible to keep termination from being abrupt or unexpected. Termination should be discussed during the planning and contracting phase of the helping process and the client should be reminded from the beginning that intervention is goal oriented and time limited. The client will be gradually prepared for termination if the intervention includes, as it should, an ongoing monitoring of progress (see Items 15.1 to 15.5).

2. In a case where an adult client wants to terminate but the social worker thinks he or she should continue, the worker should explain to the client the possible consequences of terminating. If the client still wishes to terminate, his or her decision should be respected. Usually, a child or adolescent client does not have the authority to decide the termination of services; in cases involving a minor, the minor's parent or guardian make the decision.

3. Special attention must be given to any termination prompted by an administrative decision to cut back on services provided, restrict case transfers within the agency, modify a client contract due to change in the worker's status with the agency, or the end of financial reimbursement from a third-party payer (e.g., an insurance company, Medicaid, etc.). When necessary, the worker is obliged to advocate on behalf of the client. Additional care must be observed if services were being provided under court order to be sure that all terms of the order have been met. When making decisions about termination, the worker should be guided by Section 1.16 of the *NASW Code of Ethics* (1996).

4. The social worker must anticipate how the termination might affect other people in the client's family and social network. In situations where a termination may place the client or others at risk of harm, it may be appropriate to notify others of the termination. This notification must, of course, be done in ways consistent with the law and ethics concerning confidentiality.

5. In some cases, termination can be difficult because of a social worker's own psychological needs. A worker with personal problems may want to be needed and appreciated so strongly that he or she maintains regular contact with a client even when there is no professional reason for doing so. This reflects a lack of self-awareness and is, of course, professionally irresponsible and unethical.

6. As termination approaches, it is desirable to gradually decrease the frequency of contact. If the client is quite dependent on the worker, this weaning process should be accompanied by efforts to connect the client with natural helpers and informal resources within his or her neighborhood or social network.

7. The feelings of loss and anger that often accompany the ending of any important relationship should be broached by the worker, even if not mentioned by the client. The scheduling of a follow-up interview or telephone contact several weeks after official termination may be reassuring to the client who fears separation. Also, the client should be informed that he or she can return to the agency if the need arises.

8. The ending of a meaningful professional relationship should utilize some type of ritual to mark this transition. Fortune (1995) notes that such markers include culturally appropriate good-byes such as hugging and shaking hands and, in the case of terminations within a support group or treatment group, they might involve the exchange of small gifts, potluck meals, and celebrations at which the participants recall highlights in the group's experience. Such ending rituals are especially important in work with children.

SELECTED BIBLIOGRAPHY

Fortune, Anne. "Termination in Direct Practice." In *Encyclopedia of Social Work*, 19th ed., vol 3, edited by Richard L. Edwards. Washington, DC: NASW Press, 1995, pp. 2398–2404.

National Association of Social Workers. *NASW Code of Ethics*. Washington, DC: NASW, 1996.

Zuckerman, Edward L. *The Paper Office: Forms, Guidelines, and Resources*, 2nd ed. New York: Guilford, 1997.

SECTION B

TECHNIQUES AND GUIDELINES FOR INDIRECT PRACTICE

When engaged in indirect practice activities, social workers must pay attention to issues that arise in the termination and evaluation phase of practice. When the work has resulted in meaningful experiences and relationships for the participants, bringing them to a close must be done carefully and thoroughly. Many of the guidelines for termination and evaluation identified in the introduction to Section A of this chapter also apply to indirect practice. There are, however, a few additional modifications.

Termination Activities. Organization and community change do not come easily. Although the effort to prevent problems can lead to dramatic savings in both human and financial costs (see Item 13.12), efforts to make agencies run more smoothly or to help communities address problems are not usually included in a social worker's job description. In order to engage in large system change, social workers typically invest or contribute their personal time or squeeze indirect service work into an already packed schedule. The conclusion of a successful organization or community change effort is therefore a time for celebration, or if unsuccessful, a time for critique and recognition of the significance of making the effort. Usually, such change effort is undertaken by a team of staff members or a special committee from the community. Pizza in a conference room, dinner out together, a gathering at someone's home, or some other symbolic recognition can be important concluding activities that terminate the process.

Evaluation Activities. A number of techniques are available for evaluating indirect practice. Some are used in conjunction with the evaluation of an agency's workers (see Items 15.7, 15.8, and 15.10). Other techniques that offer guidelines for a comprehensive program evaluation are described in Item 15.9, and, finally, Item 15.11 suggests some ways to assess the ongoing efficiency and effectiveness of the agency's operations.

15.7 Peer Review

PURPOSE: To evaluate the quality of a social worker's practice by comparing his or her activities against a set of principles and standards.

DISCUSSION: The process of ***peer review*** refers to a periodic examination of a social worker's performance by a fellow worker who understands the agency's clientele, policies, and procedures. Essentially, peer review is a form of quality control. Some settings, like hospitals, are required by accrediting organizations or regulatory agencies to establish peer review systems.

The first step in developing a peer review procedure is for the social workers to agree on a set of principles or criteria that reflect good practice in their particular setting. In order to keep the process relatively simple, the number of criteria should probably not exceed 10. Those participating also need to agree on the procedure for selecting cases to be reviewed. The random selection of cases from a worker's active case file is a common approach. Peer review sessions should be regularly scheduled (e.g., monthly); a single session should be limited to about one-half hour. A system of rotation ensures that each worker has a chance to conduct a peer review on all other workers in his or her unit or department. This can be a valuable learning opportunity. Results of the review should be recorded on a form. A recurring problem found in the performance of an individual worker may require remediation. And a recurring problem among all of the workers may signal a system problem and the need to examine existing policies and procedures.

Figure 15.9 presents an example of peer review for a five-worker unit form within a family agency. Many variations are possible.

SELECTED BIBLIOGRAPHY

Jackson, Josephine. "Clinical Social Work and Peer Review." *Social Work 32* (May–June 1987): 213–220.

Munson, Carlton. *Clinical Social Work Supervision*, 2nd ed. New York: Haworth, 1994.

Osman, Shelomo, and Sharon A. Shueman. "A Guide to the Peer Review Process for Clinical Social Workers." *Social Work 33* (July–August 1988): 345–348.

15.8 Worker Performance Evaluation

PURPOSE: To understand the purpose and procedures of performance evaluations in order to make such assessments productive for both workers and agencies.

DISCUSSION: ***Worker performance appraisal*** involves systematically assessing how well agency staff members are performing their jobs. Performance evaluations are designed to measure the extent to which the worker is achieving the requirements of his or position through regular informal evaluation. The regular appraisal of its employees is a fundamental part of the agency's obligation to be accountable to its clients, its community, and those who provide financial support. At the same time, such a comprehensive job performance review provides the social worker with an important opportunity for professional growth.

Matheson, Van Dyk, and Millar (1995, 1) suggest that, if properly conducted, the following positive outcomes can accrue from worker performance evaluations:

- Increase the person's motivation to perform effectively.
- Increase the self-esteem of the person being evaluated.
- Allow new insights for the person(s) doing the appraisal.

FIGURE 15.9 Sample Peer Review Policy and Review Form

Policy: Each social worker will participate in an ongoing cycle of peer review and consultation. The supervisor will be responsible for developing the peer review schedule. Each month, each social worker will have two cases reviewed by a peer and will also review two cases of another worker. The cases will be drawn at random from the worker's active caseload. The reviewer will complete the peer review form and submit it to the supervisor.

On a quarterly basis, the supervisor will analyze the peer review reports, identify common performance problems, and meet with staff to formulate a plan to address common performance problems.

Schedule

Reviewer	*November*	*December*	*January*	*February*
Greta	Mary	Larry	Ruth	Jim
Jim	Greta	Mary	Larry	Ruth
Ruth	Jim	Greta	Mary	Larry
Larry	Ruth	Jim	Greta	Mary
Mary	Larry	Ruth	Jim	Greta

Monthly Peer Review Form

Date __________ Social Worker ________________________ Reviewer ________________________

Case name and number ____

	Yes	*No*	*NA*
1. Client problem(s) clearly stated in record.	______	______	______
2. Client/family members involved in treatment planning.	______	______	______
3. Written treatment plan in record.	______	______	______
4. Intervention methods are appropriate for client's problems.	______	______	______
5. Frequency and duration of client contact is appropriate for problem.	______	______	______
6. Treatment planning, worker's action, and approach used reflect concern for permanency planning.	______	______	______
7. Appropriate and effective use made of community resources.	______	______	______
8. Progress toward goals is evident.	______	______	______
9. Case recording is clear, concise, and descriptive.	______	______	______
10. Required agency forms completed and included in record.	______	______	______

Other comments: ____

____

____

____

____

____

- Promote more clarification and better definition of the job of the person being evaluated.
- Facilitate valuable communication among the individuals taking part.
- Promote a better understanding among participants, of themselves, and of the kind of staff development activities that are of value.
- Clarify organizational goals and facilitate their acceptance.
- Allow the organization to engage in human resource planning, test validation, and development of training programs.

Certainly the outcome of a performance evaluation may have either positive or negative consequences for the worker. It may lead to decisions to promote, increase salary, or grant other rewards, or it may lead to a negative decision such as placing the worker on probation or the termination of employment. The later has the potential to entice a worker to compromise openness and self-disclosure and therefore limit the usefulness of this evaluation process for the worker's professional development. To minimize this possibility, an evaluation should be factual and objective to the degree possible. However, even a well-designed procedure requires judgment calls by the supervisor. Consequently, there will be times when the supervisor and the supervisee disagree on the conclusions.

In general, an evaluation can be considered relevant when the following criteria are met:

- It focuses on areas of performance or competency that are related to the supervisee's job and the agency's mission and goals.
- The evaluation criteria and standards, as well as the agency's preferred practices and outcomes, are clearly stated in writing and are made known to the supervisee at the beginning of the time period to be evaluated.
- The supervisee's work is compared to written performance standards and criteria that are realistic for the work assigned.
- The supervisee has been given ongoing feedback regarding his or her performance prior to the formal evaluation.
- The supervisor can cite and describe examples of performance that form the basis of the ratings.
- The evaluation process identifies and records differences in level of performance among supervisees.
- The evaluation takes into consideration the nature and complexity of the assignments given the supervisee.

Horejsi and Garthwait (1999, 206) warn supervisors of pitfalls that exist whenever one person attempts to evaluate or rate another's performance. These are:

- The *halo effect.* A supervisee is rated the same in all standards based on the observed performance in a few areas.
- The *attraction of the average.* Every supervisee is evaluated about the same or about average, regardless of real differences in their performances.

- The *leniency bias.* All supervisees are evaluated as outstanding or are assigned inflated ratings so as to avoid arguments or conflict or to avoid hurting their feelings.
- The *strictness bias.* All supervisees are evaluated and rated on the low side because the supervisor has unrealistically high expectations or holds the belief that low ratings will motivate them toward even higher levels of performance.

Following are the three elements critical to a useful and valid performance evaluation:

1. *People.* The supervisor or other person serving as evaluator must be competent. That person must know what constitutes good practice and be able to develop a trusting relationship with the worker. That trust must center on the desire to help the worker develop his or her potential as a social worker. The evaluator must be able to identify both worker competencies and deficiencies in performance and be able to articulate them in a way that builds on worker strengths in order to correct deficiencies. The evaluator must understand that new workers can be expected to have unevenness in their performances.

2. *Criteria.* The criteria on which the evaluation will be based must be made clear *before* the worker enters the time period to be covered by the evaluation. The lack of clear criteria can cause confusion and hard feelings. A typical direct-service worker's performance appraisal would focus on areas such as:
   - Capacity to establish and maintain appropriate relationships with clients (e.g., attitudes, values, and ethics as manifested in behavior toward clients; self-awareness and self-discipline; ability to manage especially difficult relationships)
   - Knowledge and skills in the helping process (e.g., engagement of clients, data collection and assessment, planning and intervention, interviewing and communication skills, documentation of work and recordkeeping)
   - Knowledge of and adherence to agency policies, procedures, and objectives
   - Use of supervision and learning opportunities
   - Management of workload and job stress
   - Intraagency relations (e.g., communication and teamwork with other staff members)
   - Interagency relations (e.g., creation and maintenance of working relationships with other agencies, programs, and resources)
   - Productivity (e.g., numbers of clients served, new programs started, fees generated)

3. *Process.* The examination of performance must focus on worker behavior, not on explanations or rationalizations for the behavior. The written aspect of the evaluation may take the form of a narrative statement, rating scales, or a combination. Once prepared, these written materials should be reviewed, discussed, revised, if necessary, and signed by both the worker and supervisor, with notation regarding any disagreements, and then placed in the worker's permanent record. The docu-

mentation of disagreements could help the worker defend against arbitrary personnel actions. From discussion of the evaluation materials, the worker and supervisor can establish goals, adjust assignments, and plan activities that will strengthen the worker's performance prior to the next evaluation.

SELECTED BIBLIOGRAPHY

Horejsi, Charles, and Cynthia Garthwait. *The Social Work Practicum.* Boston: Allyn and Bacon, 1999.

Matheson, Wayne, Cornelius Van Dyk, and Kenneth Millar. *Performance Evaluation in the Human Services.* New York: Haworth, 1995.

Rapp, Charles A., and John Poertner. *Social Administration: A Client-Centered Approach.* New York: Longman, 1992.

15.9 Program Evaluation

PURPOSE: To determine how well a social program is meeting its objectives.

DISCUSSION: A social program is a planned sequence of activities designed to achieve desired individual or social change. Hence, ***program evaluation*** refers to the systematic examination of a program to determine whether and/or how it is achieving its goals and objectives. When evaluating an agency program, four dimensions need to be examined: inputs, process, outputs, and outcomes.

As used here, the term *input* refers to the agency's clients as described at the point of intake. Input includes, for example, clients' presenting concerns, problems, and needs, as well as the particular circumstances or situations that brought them to the agency (e.g., court ordered, family crisis, etc.). An evaluation of intake factors might also include demographic characteristics of the clients such as age, gender, ethnicity, income level, and so on.

Process refers to all that happens to the clients once they begin receiving services. For example, the process dimension would include examination of the types and duration of services received and the characteristics and competence of those providing the services. It might also examine the philosophy of the practice frameworks selected to serve the clients.

The term *output* would describe client characteristics and circumstances at the time of case closure or when the clients end their formal relationship with the agency. For example, possible outputs for an agency providing foster family care might include the child being dismissed from the program at age 18, reunification with the biological family, or referral to another agency for specialized services.

An *outcome* refers to the clients' level of social functioning at the point of case closure. This dimension of a program evaluation focuses on the degree to which clients experience positive and significant changes when receiving services. Data accumulated from routine collection of direct practice evaluations (see Items 15.1 through 15.5) might be used for this program evaluation.

The following guidelines are useful for assuring that a program evaluation is productive:

1. *Identify the users of the evaluation data and report* (e.g., administrators, practitioners, program planners, legislators, fund-raisers, etc.). What do they really want and need from this evaluation? What type of information can they understand and use? Is it reasonable to believe that evaluation results will affect the continuation, modification, or termination of the program? Do not begin a program evaluation effort unless the results can make a real difference in terms of the program's operation and the services provided.

2. *Decide if an evaluation is feasible.* Do you have the necessary time, money, and skill available? Do you have access to experts in program evaluation? Are the data you need actually available? Are all key staff members committed to the idea of evaluation? Is the program stable enough to undergo scrutiny? Has the program been in operation long enough to make an evaluation worthwhile?

3. *State the goals and objectives of the program.* Are there clear statements of the program goals and objectives? You cannot evaluate a program until you know precisely what it is trying to accomplish.

4. *Describe the program's interventions that are to be evaluated.* Intervention activities must be logically connected to program goals and objectives and must focus on factors or forces over which it has control. Clearly describe the units of intervention or the services. For example, to describe when an intervention activity is happening, you might ask: When does it begin and end? Does the worker decide when an intervention has occurred or does the client or someone else? Can you distinguish an intervention from other client-staff interactions? Can you decide when a service has been used? (For example, if a client attended only two of five scheduled sessions of a parenting class, has he or she received parent training?)

5. *Select measurable indicators of change.* Once you are clear as to the specific attitudes, behaviors, or conditions your program is trying to change, and you are clear as to the interventions used to bring about those changes, you need to select indicators of change that can be detected and measured. Make sure these indicators are ones that can be reasonably attributed to your program's intervention. Also, decide if it is reasonable to believe that the desired effects of the intervention will occur within the time frame you are using. If you cannot wait to measure long-term benefits, you must choose indicators that reflect more immediate changes.

6. *Select appropriate and feasible data collection and measurement tools and/or instruments.* Developing a valid and reliable instrument is a complex, time-consuming, and expensive process, so try to use available instruments. Examine evaluations done on similar programs and use instruments that others have found useful.

7. *Plan how you will collect, tabulate, and analyze the data.* Do not collect more data than you can manage and use. Make sure the data you want are actually available. For example, if you plan to gather data from case files, are you sure all of them

contain the information you need? If your data are stored in the computer system, can you get them out? Can the information you seek be obtained without a release from the client? If your evaluation design involves contacting former service consumers, will you be able to locate them?

8. *Interpret the results of your evaluation.* The final product of your effort is to report the results. Caution should be used in making this interpretation. Factors other than the nature of the intervention may account for a program's success or failure. For example, low staff morale may produce poor outcomes despite a well-conceived program.

SELECTED BIBLIOGRAPHY

Chambers, Donald E., Kenneth R. Wedel, and Mary K. Rodwell. *Evaluating Social Programs.* Boston: Allyn and Bacon, 1992.

Kause, Daniel. *Effective Program Evaluation: An Introduction.* Chicago: Nelson-Hall, 1996.

Martin, Lawrence L., and Peter M. Kettner. *Measuring the Performance of Human Service Programs.* Thousand Oaks, CA: Sage, 1996.

Mika, Kristine L. *Program Outcome Evaluation: A Step-by-Step Handbook.* Milwaukee, WI: Families International, 1996.

Yates, Brian T. *Analyzing Costs, Procedures, Processes, and Outcomes in Human Services.* Thousand Oaks, CA: Sage, 1996.

15.10 Client Satisfaction Questionnaire (CSQ)

PURPOSE: To determine clients' satisfaction with the services received.

DISCUSSION: A *Client Satisfaction Questionnaire* (*CSQ*) is a method for soliciting client opinions about the services provided by a human services agency. A CSQ asks clients to rate important aspects of the helping process, such as the atmosphere of the agency, the success of the intervention, the competence of the staff, and so on. By placing the responses in rank order, it is possible to compute an average score from multiple clients to arrive at an indicator of client satisfaction regarding agency services. Typically, a questionnaire is administered at the point of termination or shortly thereafter, although some agencies administer a CSQ after three to five interviews and periodically thereafter if the client receives services for a longer period.

Figure 15.10 is an example of a typical CSQ. Although CSQs vary in length, they should be easy for a client to complete; therefore, they should not request too much detailed information. If more information is desired, administration of the CSQ might be coupled with an in-depth interview (by phone or face to face) on specific variables related to the client's satisfaction or dissatisfaction.

A limitation of the CSQ format is that it records only the client's perceptions of what happened as a result of the intervention. Certainly, reality may differ from that perception or the perception may change over time. Also, there is a tendency for satisfied clients to return a greater portion of the questionnaires (particularly if a

FIGURE 15.10 Sample Client Satisfaction Questionnaire

Evaluating Your Experience at ABC Agency

Thank you for taking a few minutes to evaluate the services you have received at our agency. Your answers to this brief questionnaire will help us improve our services. Feel free to offer additional comments in the space provided or on the back of this page.

Instructions: For each question below, check (✓) your answer.

A. How do you feel about the way you were treated by the receptionist?
 ___ (1) dissatisfied
 ___ (3) no feelings either way
 ___ (5) satisfied
 Comments:

B. How do you feel about the length of time you had to wait before our agency provided you with service?
 ___ (1) unhappy or dissatisfied
 ___ (3) no feelings either way
 ___ (5) pleased or satisfied
 Comments:

C. Did you accomplish what you expected to achieve when you came to this agency?
 ___ (5) yes, completely
 ___ (4) mostly accomplished
 ___ (3) some accomplishment
 ___ (2) no real progress
 ___ (1) worse off than before
 Comments:

D. Did you feel your situation/problem(s) changed when you became involved with this agency?
 ___ (1) things became much worse
 ___ (2) things somewhat worse
 ___ (3) no change
 ___ (4) things somewhat better
 ___ (5) things became much better
 Comments:

E. Which of the following statement comes closest to your feelings about the impact of this agency's services on your situation or problem?
 ___ (1) made things much worse
 ___ (2) made things somewhat worse
 ___ (3) no change
 ___ (4) made things somewhat better
 ___ (5) made things much better
 Comments:

F. How competent do you feel the social worker was to deal with your situation or problem?
 ___ (5) very competent
 ___ (4) moderately competent
 ___ (2) somewhat incompetent
 ___ (1) very incompetent
 Comments:

G. If a friend needed services from an agency like ours, would you recommend our agency?
 ___ (1) never
 ___ (2) probably not
 ___ (4) probably yes
 ___ (5) definitely yes
 Comments:

H. Overall, how do you feel about your experience with our agency?
 ___ (1) very dissatisfied
 ___ (2) dissatisfied
 ___ (4) satisfied
 ___ (5) very satisfied
 Comments:

It is helpful to know something about the person completing this questionnaire.

___ Male
___ Female

___ Client
___ Parent of agency client
___ Spouse of agency client

Client's age:
___ under 21
___ 21–50
___ 51–65
___ over 65

mailed questionnaire is the process selected) than those who are dissatisfied—skewing the data toward positive responses.

The process for implementing the use of a Client Satisfaction Questionnaire is the following:

1. *Decide what population of clients to sample.* The sample could be representative of agency clientele in general, of clients who have received a particular type of service, or of clients who make up a particular demographic group (e.g., clients over age 60). A basic knowledge of sampling methods is required in order to draw a representative sample. Criteria for CSQ distribution should be determined by the evaluator and relate to the purpose of the evaluation, statistical requirements, and administrative convenience.

2. *Design the questionnaire.* Keep it as simple and brief as possible and avoid professional jargon. The agency may want to gather certain client and demographic information in order to determine if satisfaction with or complaints about services are related to factors such as the client's ethnicity, age, socioeconomic status, and the like. However, asking for such information tends to weaken assurances of anonymity.

3. *Administer the questionnaire.* This step can often be carried out by clerical staff, volunteers, or social service aides; however, those administering the questionnaire must be trained in its use in order to increase reliability. The assurance of confidentiality to respondents is very important. A mailed CSQ can provide the client with anonymity but does presume that the client can read. If the target population consists of former clients, the questionnaire can be either mailed or administered by phone. If it includes clients who are still in regular contact with the agency, the questionnaire can usually be administered by a receptionist. The greatest amount of work in administering the questionnaire will probably be in following up on those clients who fail to return the questionnaire; these clients will have to be called or sent a letter to obtain a reasonable return rate. If the responses are to be anonymous, there will be problems in follow-up; therefore, a guarantee of confidentiality without the added assurance of anonymity may be preferable. Statistical techniques can determine whether there are significant differences between those who return the questionnaire immediately and those who require urging.

4. *Tabulate and analyze the questionnaire data.* Manual tabulation may be possible for short questionnaires. Computer processing is desirable for long questionnaires and when a large number must be tabulated.

SELECTED BIBLIOGRAPHY

Berlin, Sharon B., and Jeanne C. Marsh. *Informing Practice Decisions.* New York: Macmillan, 1993.

Hagedorn, Homer, Kenneth Beck, Stephen Neubert, and Stanley Werlin. *A Working Manual of Simple Program Evaluation Techniques for Community Mental Health Centers.* Washington, DC: Government Printing Office, 1976, DHEW Pub. No. (ADM) 79–404.

Royse, David. *Program Evaluation: An Introduction.* Chicago: Nelson-Hall, 1992.

15.11 Agency Evaluation

PURPOSE: To identify data that should be collected to assess the ongoing performance of a social agency.

DISCUSSION: Social agencies are expected to demonstrate that they are efficient and effective in the provision of services. Agency boards, legislative bodies, and other funding sources regularly demand that agencies review their functioning and report the results of that evaluation. Individual workers, too, are often interested in performance indicators that might stimulate organizational changes necessary to improve the quality of services provided. Thus, it is useful for social workers to be familiar with some of the indicators typically used in agency performance reviews.

Evaluation must be preceded by a clear statement of goals. Often, the first task in agency evaluation is for the governing board or other policymakers to explicate the current goals and objectives for the organization. It is only with this information that appropriate performance indicators can be selected and methods of data collection identified. Chambers, Wedel, and Rodwell (1992, 119) describe this early phase as making an *evaluability assessment*—that is, determining if there is sufficient clarity to initiate a viable appraisal process.

An agency's evaluation should address the degree to which its programs respond to community need, the quality of services offered, the satisfaction of clients, efficiency in use of resources, and so on. The following are some of the areas that should be considered in specifying an agency's goals:

- *Responsiveness.* Does the agency and its programs respond to public and community needs and identified concerns?
- *Relevance.* Do sponsors, constituents, and consumers find the programs appropriate to the needs they seek to address and do they consider them supportive of community values?
- *Availability.* Are the amount and type of services provided sufficient to meet the needs of the community?
- *Accessibility.* Is the location, cost, and times services are offered appropriate for the clientele of the agency? Are there other potential constituent groups who do not receive services due to accessibility issues?
- *Quality.* Do the services meet expected standards of quality as judged by client satisfaction and expert opinion?
- *Awareness.* Is the general population, as well as other human services providers, sufficiently aware of the services offered to assure that persons who need the services know how to obtain them?
- *Productivity.* Does the program efficiently use its resources to accomplish the agency's goals?

With clarity about the questions to be answered when collecting data, it is then possible to select a set of *performance indicators* that will help to measure the agency's level of success and, when appropriate, lead to changes for improving its functioning. Selecting appropriate indicators and finding accurate data regarding them is a complex task. For example, one such study regarding public welfare agencies, the Human Services Indicator Project, identified 500 possible indicators. These were screened to 75 data sets that "represented significant organizational performance areas, were factors over which managers had some control, and included areas where the data were likely to be easily available" (Neves, Wolf, and Benton 1986, 135). The following sampling of indicators illustrates a few essential areas to include in measures of agency success:

- *Personnel-related factors.* Rate of turnover, absenteeism, staff vacancies, number of hours contributed by volunteers, frequency of in-service training, and so forth
- *The intake process.* Data on the number and sources of referrals, number of telephone contacts, number of people on the waiting list, average length of time between first contact and initiation of service, and so on
- *Service-related factors.* Number of new cases opened each month, average length of service per case, number of clients served, number and type of cases referred elsewhere, number of former clients returning for service, average cost per client, client satisfaction with services, and so on
- *Staff productivity.* Size and type of caseload per worker, number of counseling sessions provided each day, number of hours spent per case, amount of inter- and intraagency contacts per month, number of miles of work-related travel each week, and the like
- *Cost of providing services.* Average cost of staff time per case, number of clients paying a fee for service, average travel cost per case, average time spent in case recording, estimated value of volunteer hours per week, and so on

These data, once collected, must be carefully analyzed. Data collected over time will allow for the examination of trends within the agency and adjustments to improve the efficiency and effectiveness of the agency. Also, the data can be compared to data from similar agencies, making it possible to gain a relative picture of the agency's functioning.

SELECTED BIBLIOGRAPHY

Chambers, Donald E., Kenneth R. Wedel, and Mary K. Rodwell. *Evaluating Social Programs.* Boston: Allyn and Bacon, 1992.

Harrison, Michael I. *Diagnosing Organizations: Methods, Models, and Processes.* Beverly Hills: Sage, 1987.

Neves, Carole M. P., James F. Wolf, and Bill B. Benton. "The Uses of Management Indicators in Monitoring and Performance of Human Service Agencies." In *Performance and Credibility: Developing Excellence in Public and Nonprofit Organizations,* edited by Joseph S. Whorley, Mark A. Abramson, and Christopher Bellavita. Lexington, MA: Lexington Books, 1986.

Using the Cross-Reference Guide

Location of Selected Techniques and Guidelines Related to Client System Served

The chapters in Part III of *Techniques and Guidelines for Social Work Practice* were organized around the basic skills required of a social worker, the tasks that must be performed to manage one's workload, and the activities related to the worker's own personal and professional development. In Part IV, the various techniques were placed in five chapters that reflect the phases of the planned change process (i.e., progressing from intake and engagement to evaluation and termination). Some of these techniques and guidelines are unique to a particular activity or client system being served, whereas others are appropriate for use with several client groups. To facilitate ready access to the most appropriate technique a social worker might consider when working with a specific client group at a given phase of the change process, the following cross-referencing guide has been included in this edition.

A Cross-Referencing of Selected Techniques and Guidelines to Client Systems and Special Situations

Chapter	The Individual as Client	The Family as Client	People Having Special Needs or Requiring Unique Responses
8 Basic Communication and Helping Skills	All of Chapter 8	All of Chapter 8	All of Chapter 8
9 Workload and Caseload Management	9.4 9.10 9.7 9.11 9.8 9.9	9.4 9.10 9.7 9.11 9.8 9.9	9.4
10 Personal and Professional Development	10.8 10.9 10.10 10.11	10.8 10.9 10.10 10.11	
11 Intake and Engagement	All of Chapter 11, Section A	11.1 11.5 11.2 11.3 11.4	11.2 11.8 11.5 11.9 11.6 11.10 11.7
12 Data Collection and Assessment	12.1 12.7 12.15 12.21 12.2 12.8 12.16 12.22 12.3 12.9 12.17 12.23 12.4 12.10 12.18 12.24 12.5 12.13 12.19 12.25 12.6 12.14 12.20	12.2 12.15 12.3 12.16 12.7 12.11 12.12 12.14	12.19 12.20 12.21 12.24 12.25 12.26
13 Planning and Contracting	13.1 13.5 13.2 13.6 13.3 13.7 13.4	13.1 13.7 13.3 13.4 13.6	13.7
14 Intervention and Monitoring	All of Chapter 14, Section A	14.10 14.13 14.14	14.28 14.32 14.36 14.29 14.33 14.37 14.30 14.34 14.39 14.31 14.35
15 Evaluation and Termination	15.1 15.5 15.2 15.6 15.3 15.4	15.1 15.5 15.2 15.6 15.3 15.4	

Therapeutic and Self-Help Groups	Committees and Task-Oriented Groups	Agency Administration and Operation	Organizations and Communities	Professional/ Career Enhancement
All of Chapter 8	All of Chapter 8	All of Chapter 8	All of Chapter 8	
9.4		All of Chapter 9		
10.9 10.11 10.12	10.9 10.11 10.12	10.1 10.9 10.3 10.12 10.6 10.13 10.8 10.14	10.6 10.12 10.13 10.14	All of Chapter 10
11.6 11.7 11.9 11.10	11.4	11.3 11.4	11.11 11.12 11.13 11.14	
	12.28	12.26 12.27 12.28	12.26 12.27 12.30	
13.8	13.13	13.9 13.14 13.10 13.11 13.13	13.9 13.13 13.10 13.14 13.11 13.12	
14.20 14.21 14.22	14.40 14.44 14.41 14.45 14.42 14.47 14.43	14.40 14.47 14.53 14.41 14.49 14.54 14.42 14.51 14.55 14.43 14.52 14.56	14.48 14.54 14.50 14.56 14.51 14.57 14.53	
	15.7	15.7 15.11 15.8 15.9 15.10	15.10 15.11	15.7

AUTHOR INDEX

SUBJECT INDEX